Architecting at Scale

A Practical Guide to Large-Scale System Design: From Monolith to AI-Native, Beyond Scaling Servers

Imran Siddique

<packt>

Architecting at Scale

Portfolio Director: Gebin George
Relationship Lead: Srishti Seth
Project Manager: Ankit Maroli
Content Engineer: Sushma Reddy, Afzal Shaikh
Technical Editor: Irfa Ansari
Indexer: Hemangini Bari
Production Designer: Vijay Kamble
Growth Lead: Srishti Seth

First published: August 2026

Production reference: 1250826

Published by Packt Publishing Ltd.
Grosvenor House
11 St Paul's Square
Birmingham
B3 1RB, UK.

ISBN 978-1-80742-097-0
`www.packtpub.com`

To my lovely wife, Uzma, and to our beautiful children, Aayat, Aayra, Abdullah, and Aisha.

Imran Siddique

Foreword

Architecting at Scale makes a compelling case that experimentation is not a process layered on top of architecture, but a property the architecture itself must support. By treating delivery metrics as measures of a system's ability to evolve, it reframes 'future-proofing' as the discipline of making change small, observable, and reversible.

Scott Hanselman

VP and Member of Technical Staff, Microsoft CoreAI and GitHub

Foreword

I have spent much of my career building and thinking about systems that have to scale. One lesson I have learned repeatedly is that scaling is not primarily about knowing which technologies are available. It is about knowing when the system in front of you has actually earned the next piece of complexity. That idea appears almost immediately in *Architecting at Scale*, and it is one of the reasons the book resonated with me.

Engineers often instinctively build for the future: distribute the system, split it into services, add abstractions, and introduce sophisticated infrastructure. Imran Siddique starts somewhere more useful. Measure what you have. Understand the constraint. Make the simplest change that addresses it. Then measure again.

Sometimes that means buying a bigger database rather than spending months rearchitecting software. Later it may mean decomposing a service, introducing caching, or adding resilience. But each new capability has to earn the complexity it introduces.

Just as importantly, you need to make sure you can take it back. Reversibility, blast radius, canaries, feature flags, fallback paths, observability, and kill switches appear throughout the book, expressing the same discipline: introduce change in a way that lets you discover that you were wrong without discovering it everywhere at once.

Imran describes this as *scale by subtraction*. Good architecture is not a contest to accumulate patterns and technologies. Often the senior engineering decision is to remove something, simplify something, reuse something, or decide not to build something at all.

I also appreciated how approachable the book makes these ideas. Concepts arise because ShopFlow encounters a concrete problem. There is a signal, a business consequence, a choice, and a cost. You understand not only what a pattern does, but why you would choose it—and when you should not.

Some distinctions are deceptively simple and worth remembering. Security is not something to bolt on after a system has scaled; it is a precondition for scale. Likewise, monitoring can tell you that the pieces of a system are running. Observability tells you whether the system is accomplishing the outcome it exists to produce.

These are architectural ideas, but they are also business ideas. Architecture lives at the boundary between technology and the business: what must be reliable, what may degrade, what risk is tolerable, where engineering time should be spent, and what complexity the organization is prepared to operate.

That makes this book particularly timely in the age of agentic software development.

Agents are making implementation less expensive. They can write code, generate tests, refactor systems, provision infrastructure, and carry out increasingly substantial engineering tasks. As implementation becomes more abundant, architectural judgment becomes a larger part of the value engineers provide. Someone still has to decide what should be built, where the boundaries belong, which constraint matters, and what trade-offs make sense.

The book is unusually current here. It asks whether a model belongs in the architecture at all. If deterministic code solves the problem, use it. If conventional machine learning fits, consider that. Introduce a language model only when the problem genuinely requires it.

And when agents move from producing answers to taking actions, production deployment requires more than a capable model. It requires identity, authorization, scoped agency, policy enforcement, observability, staged autonomy, human approval where appropriate, and a reliable way to stop and recover when something goes wrong.

The particular technologies in this book will change. Databases will change. Runtimes will change. Models will certainly change. What endures is the ability to understand a system, recognize its next constraint, make a deliberate trade-off, introduce change safely, observe the result, and reconsider the decision when reality proves you wrong.

That is the architectural judgment *Architecting at Scale* teaches. And as agents become capable of doing more of the building, I believe that judgment becomes more important, not less.

Dick Hardt

Creator of OAuth, Founder/CEO of Hello

Foreword

I do not know what first prompted Imran to write this book or the thought process that led him to this subject, but it is a critical one. Many people think it is easy to run services, and now AI systems, at scale. The reality is different. Models are huge, usage patterns vary, and capacity needs are unpredictable. Finding a way to scale a service and make it robust is one of the most complex challenges we face today.

Model accuracy and infrastructure that can scale are two equally significant problems unfolding in parallel. I do not know what led Imran to address them now, but Architecting at Scale takes on a critical and timely area. It is a practical guide to evolving production systems for the AI era, and it will be useful to many people. I am personally very glad that Imran took the initiative to write it.

The governance aspect is equally important. It represents another major set of current problems that we encounter as we build and operate autonomous systems. The book's treatment of agent governance makes an important point: autonomy must be earned, bounded, and controlled at runtime.

I thank Imran for writing this book and congratulate him on its publication.

Perraju Bendapudi

Senior Technical Fellow and founding member, Typeface

Contributors

About the author

Imran Siddique is the Chief Platform Officer at OPAQUE, the Confidential AI company, where he leads the engineering organization and platform strategy for governing AI agents at enterprise scale. He is the creator of the Agent Governance Toolkit (AGT), the open-source, MIT-licensed framework for governing AI agents at runtime and the only toolkit with documented mitigation for all ten OWASP Agentic AI Security Initiative risks.

Before OPAQUE, Imran spent eighteen years at Microsoft, where he helped build Azure from its early days, shipping core platforms across SQL Azure, Azure DevOps, and Azure for Industries before leading agentic AI architecture in Azure Core. His career has centered on one conviction, which is also the spine of this book: that the most resilient systems are built by subtraction, by identifying and removing complexity rather than adding to it. He calls it Scale by Subtraction, and traces it back to his early research on compiler optimization.

Imran holds a BTech in Computer Science from VJTI, Mumbai. He lives in Bellevue, Washington, with his wife and their four children.

Writing a book while the field it describes keeps moving is only possible with help. My thanks to the team at Packt for their craft and patience in shaping this book, and to my technical reviewers, Daniel Scholl and Ranganath G, whose scrutiny made the architecture arguments sharper and the examples more honest. I am grateful to the engineers and the open-source community I have learned from over the years; many of the hard-won lessons in these pages began as their questions.

Above all, thank you to my wife, Uzma, who carried more than her share so this book could exist, and to our children, Aayat, Aayra, Abdullah, and Aisha, who are the reason I want to build things that last.

About the reviewer

Govardhanagiri Ranganath is a software engineering professional with nearly two decades of experience in building large-scale cloud and distributed systems. He graduated from **Birla Institute of Technology & Science (BITS Pilani)** and has worked across several leading technology organizations, including **Microsoft, Salesforce, EMC, Trilogy, and Yahoo!**.

Throughout his career, Ranganath has been involved in the design, development, and operation of a wide range of cloud services and developer platforms. His work has included contributions to **Azure Caching Services, Azure DevOps Services, Azure Load Testing Service, Azure Pipelines, Azure OpenAI Service, and Microsoft 365 services**. His experience spans distributed systems, cloud infrastructure, developer productivity platforms, and large-scale service engineering.

During his tenure at **Salesforce**, he also contributed to the **Apache HBase** and **Apache Phoenix** open-source ecosystems, working on technologies focused on scalable storage and data access.

As a **Technical Reviewer**, Ranganath brings practical industry experience and a strong focus on technical accuracy, scalability, and real-world applicability, helping ensure that complex concepts are presented clearly and effectively for readers.

*I would like to express my heartfelt gratitude to my **mother, wife, and children** for their constant encouragement, patience, and support. Their understanding and the time they gave me to focus on reviewing this book were invaluable in helping shape it into its final form.*

Table of Contents

Chapter 2: Core Principles of Scalable Architecture 19

Chapter 3: Security-First and Compliance-First Architecture 37

Part 3: Scaling the Services and Data 113

Chapter 6: Architecting Scalable Services – Decomposition and API Design 115

Chapter 10: Scaling Data and Databases – Storage, Queries, and Beyond 273

Preface

Most books about scale are organized like reference manuals: a chapter on caching, a chapter on databases, a chapter on observability, each one a self-contained survey you could read in any order. This book is organized the way the job actually feels. You inherit a system that works, you watch it break under load, you make a decision under pressure, you accept a trade-off, and you ship the fix safely while the business keeps running. Then the fix creates the next problem, and you do it again. The result is a practical, ordered guide to taking a product from its first working version all the way to a high-throughput, resilient, cost-efficient, and secure platform.

To make that journey concrete, the entire book follows one system. ShopFlow begins as a single-server monolith handling a hundred orders a day and ends as a globally distributed, governed, AI-augmented platform that no single person fully understands end to end. You will meet Dave, the hero engineer who keeps the early system alive by rebooting it at 3:00 AM, and you will watch the architecture slowly make his heroics unnecessary, because in a system that scales, a hero is a single point of failure with a pulse. Every chapter opens on a real telemetry snapshot, latency, availability, cost, and error rate, and those numbers start in the red. The chapter's job is to get them to green, and in doing so to set up the next number that turns red as a result.

Running underneath all of it is one idea I have spent my career arguing for: scaling is a subtraction problem, not an addition one. The instinct under load is to add, more servers, more services, more caches, more people. The discipline that actually reaches the next order of magnitude is removing dependencies, removing single points of failure, and removing the human bottleneck from the loop. The book also weaves three threads through every chapter rather than saving them for the end. Safe change, through feature flags, canary releases, and automatic rollback, is the default way every architectural change ships. AI is used only where it earns its cost and never as a reflex. And security and compliance are designed in from the first decision rather than bolted on after the first breach.

At the front of the book you will find the ShopFlow Systems Evolution Map, a single picture of the four stages the system moves through, from the Monolith to the Autonomous System. Refer back to it as you read each chapter. You are not collecting features. You are leading an evolution, and by the end you will know not just how to scale a system but how to lead its growth without it leading you.

Who this book is for

This book is for senior and staff engineers, tech leads, and architects who have become the de facto architecture function for their team or company, the person who owns the system-wide decisions even when the title does not say so. If you have shipped an early product and you are now staring at the gap between what got you here and what scaling demands, this is written for you. It is equally for strong intermediate engineers who want the mental models that the Staff and Principal roles are built on, and for engineering managers who need a shared language for the trade-offs between feature velocity and system stability.

To get the most from these pages, you should be comfortable with full-stack development, understand the basics of modern cloud services, and know the difference between SQL and NoSQL data stores. You do not need prior experience operating systems at hyper-scale. That is the journey the book takes you on.

What this book covers

Chapter 1, The Scalability Mindset - When and Why to Scale, reframes scaling as a subtraction problem and gives you permission not to scale too early. It introduces ShopFlow and Dave, defines the tipping point where speed-to-market stops being the right priority, and makes a deliberately unglamorous first decision: buy a bigger server, and understand exactly why that strategic debt is the correct move at Stage 1.

Chapter 2, Core Principles of Scalable Architecture, takes ShopFlow from one overloaded machine to a distributed fleet. It covers the principles that keep a distributed system from becoming a distributed disaster: iterative decomposition over big-bang rewrites, statelessness as the price of horizontal movement, platform agnosticism, and observability treated as a design requirement rather than an afterthought.

Chapter 3, Security-First and Compliance-First Architecture, confronts the bill that horizontal scaling just ran up, because every new node is a new door. It moves the system from trust-by-default to Zero Trust, shifts security left into the development pipeline, and automates compliance with policy-as-code so that governance scales as smoothly as the rest of the architecture.

Chapter 4, Scaling the Global Delivery Layer - Edge, CDNs, and Beyond, pushes work out of the data center and toward the user. It covers edge computation, the move to HTTP/3 and QUIC, cache invalidation across global points of presence, origin shielding against the thundering herd, and predictive prefetching that beats the user to the next click.

Chapter 5, Scaling the Modern Web Application - State, Performance, and Micro-Frontends, breaks the monolithic front-end apart. It covers the move from a single SPA to independently shippable micro-frontends, client-side state at scale, the rendering choice between SSR, SSG, and ISR, performance budgets for low-end devices, and UIs that degrade gracefully instead of failing whole.

Chapter 6, Architecting Scalable Services - Decomposition and API Design, draws the service boundaries that the rest of the back-end depends on. It uses domain-driven design to find real seams, weighs REST against gRPC for internal traffic, makes the case for a database per service, and lays out the strangler-fig path for migrating a monolith without a big-bang rewrite.

Chapter 7, Scaling Service Infrastructure - Resilience, Mesh, and Compute, makes the decomposition survivable. It covers service discovery, offloading retries and security to a service mesh, the resilience primitives that stop one slow service from taking down a healthy one, namely circuit breakers, bulkheads, and timeouts, and how to choose between containers, serverless, and bare metal.

Chapter 8, Event-Driven Scaling - Decoupling with Messaging, breaks the temporal link between services. It covers the move from synchronous waiting to emit-and-forget, choosing between brokers and streams, the idempotency and deduplication strategies that prevent double-charges, and reliable publishing through the transactional outbox and change data capture.

Chapter 9, Caching Strategies - Faster and Cheaper Scaling, absorbs the read amplification that the move to messaging created. It works down the caching hierarchy from browser to database, covers distributed caching with Redis, edge caching with CDNs, the genuinely hard problem of invalidation, and how to survive warm-ups, stampedes, and poison pills.

Chapter 10, Scaling Data and Databases - Storage, Queries, and Beyond, performs the data-layer surgery the previous chapters kept deferring. It covers the real SQL versus NoSQL trade-offs, sharding, partitioning and replication, indexing and query tuning, and the data access layer that hides all of that complexity from the services above it.

Chapter 11, Observability - Seeing and Understanding Your System, closes the gap between a server being up and a user actually succeeding. It covers correlation IDs that follow one request across dozens of services, the difference between monitoring and observability, golden signals tied to business impact, and the feedback loop that turns telemetry into automated action.

Chapter 12, Resilience and High Availability - Designing for Failure, treats failure as a certainty rather than an exception. It shows how to rank features into criticality tiers, architect graceful degradation so the Buy button survives when recommendations do not, tune circuit breakers, bulkheads, and load shedding, and prove the whole thing works through chaos engineering.

Chapter 13, Performance Tuning and Capacity Planning, answers the CFO's question of whether you are paying for resilience or paying for fear. It covers when not to optimize, how to find the resource contention that shared systems hide, the P0-to-P2 framework for tiering performance, and predictive capacity planning that buys headroom without over-provisioning.

Chapter 14, Cost Optimization and Efficiency (FinOps), makes cost a first-class engineering metric without turning it into surveillance. It explains why the bill is never the service you watch, settles the managed-versus-self-hosted question with a break-even calculation, ties spend to unit economics, and governs the newest and least predictable cost axis of all, the per-token cost of AI.

Chapter 15, AI-First Architecture: Pragmatism Over Hype, asks the question the hype skips: should this be an AI feature at all? Written from my work as the creator of the Agent Governance Toolkit, it covers when to choose AI over deterministic code, the gap between an agent that demos and one that survives production, serving AI at scale, runtime governance, and the one control no production AI system ships without, the kill switch.

Chapter 16, Continuous Experimentation and the Future-Proof System, solves the last problem, a system so successful that the team is afraid to change it. It makes experimentation an architectural requirement, uses feature flags with the discipline they demand and retires them before they become debt, runs experiments on the architecture itself, and ends on the one property that is genuinely future-proof.

To get the most out of this book

You will get the most out of this book if you have built and shipped software before and have felt at least one system strain under growth. Comfort with full-stack development, a working understanding of modern cloud services, and familiarity with both relational and non-relational data stores will let you move quickly through the foundations and spend your attention where it matters, on the trade-offs.

The book is deliberately tool-agnostic. The patterns are illustrated with widely used technologies, but the goal is never to teach a specific product. It is to teach the decision, so that you can apply it whatever your stack happens to be. Read the chapters in order, at least the first time through. Because ShopFlow evolves continuously, each chapter assumes the system state that the previous one left behind.

The architectural ideas are illustrated with representative technologies, including the following. None of them is a prerequisite; they are the vehicle, not the destination.

Technologies and concepts used in the book	Operating system requirements
Redis, Kafka, RabbitMQ, and cloud pub/sub	Cross-platform
Kubernetes, service mesh (Istio or Linkerd)	Cross-platform
OpenTelemetry and distributed tracing	Cross-platform

Technologies and concepts used in the book	Operating system requirements
AWS, Azure, and Google Cloud Platform	Cross-platform

If you are reading the print edition, you can access the code and color images using the links provided in the sections that follow.

Download the example code files

The code bundle for the book is hosted on GitHub at `https://github.com/imran-siddique/Architecting-at-Scale`. We also have other code bundles from our rich catalog of books and videos available at `https://github.com/PacktPublishing`. Check them out!

Download the color images

We also provide a PDF file that has color images of the screenshots/diagrams used in this book. You can download it here: `https://packt.link/gbp/9781807420970`.

Conventions used

There are a number of text conventions used throughout this book.

`CodeInText`: Indicates code words in text, database table names, folder names, filenames, file extensions, pathnames, dummy URLs, user input, and Twitter handles. For example: " Here is the `middleware/correlation.js` we are adding to `ShopFlow` today:"

A block of code is set as follows:

```
// The ShopFlow "Legacy" Search
// A simple, synchronous SQL query that worked fine for 100 users.
const express = require('express');
const router = express.Router();
const db = require('../db');
```

Any command-line input or output is written as follows:

```
Availability: 99.0% (Stuttering - frequent brief outages)
Cloud Spend: $500/mo (Low)
Total Orders: 5,000/day (New High!)
Active DB Connections: 450/500 (90% — Near Limit)
p99 Latency: 3.2s (CRITICAL - 53% Customer Abandonment Risk)
Dave Alert: "I'm manually clearing logs every 4 hours just to keep the disk from
filling up."
```

Bold: Indicates a new term, an important word, or words that you see on the screen. For instance, words in menus or dialog boxes appear in the text like this. For example: "Let's look at the current state of the system using our **Telemetry Snapshot**."

> Note
>
> Warnings or important notes appear like this.

> Tip
>
> Tips and tricks appear like this.

Get in touch

Feedback from our readers is always welcome.

General feedback: If you have questions about any aspect of this book or have any general feedback, please email us at `customercare@packt.com` and mention the book's title in the subject of your message.

Errata: Although we have taken every care to ensure the accuracy of our content, mistakes do happen. If you have found a mistake in this book, we would be grateful if you reported this to us. Please visit `http://www.packt.com/submit-errata`, click **Submit Errata**, and fill in the form.

Piracy: If you come across any illegal copies of our works in any form on the internet, we would be grateful if you would provide us with the location address or website name. Please contact us at `copyright@packt.com` with a link to the material.

If you are interested in becoming an author: If there is a topic that you have expertise in and you are interested in either writing or contributing to a book, please visit `http://authors.packt.com/`.

Free benefits with your book

This book comes with free benefits to support your learning. Activate them now for instant access (see the "*How to Unlock*" section for instructions).

Here's a quick overview of what you can instantly unlock with your purchase:

How to Unlock

Scan the QR code (or go to `packtpub.com/unlock`). Search for this book by name, confirm the edition, and then follow the steps on the page.

UNLOCK NOW

Note: Keep your invoice handy. Purchases made directly from Packt don't require one

Share your thoughts

Once you've read *Architecting at Scale,* we'd love to hear your thoughts! Scan the QR code below to go straight to the Amazon review page for this book and share your feedback.

https://packt.link/r/1807420973

Your review is important to us and the tech community and will help us make sure we're delivering excellent quality content.

Part 1

Foundations: Designing for Scale from Day One

Before you scale anything, you need a way to decide what to scale, when, and why. This first part builds that foundation. You will adopt the mindset that treats scaling as a subtraction problem, learn to read the signals that tell you a system has outgrown its design, and put down the architectural principles that everything later in the book depends on: statelessness, loose coupling, observability, and platform independence. You will also do the thing most books leave until it is too late, which is design security and compliance in from the very first decision rather than bolting them on after the first breach. By the end of this part, ShopFlow has gone from a single fragile server to a distributed, stateless, Zero Trust foundation that is ready to scale outward.

This part of the book includes the following chapters:

- *Chapter 1, The Scalability Mindset: When and Why to Scale*
- *Chapter 2, Core Principles of Scalable Architecture*
- *Chapter 3, Security-First and Compliance-First Architecture*

1

The Scalability Mindset - When and Why to Scale

Scalability is often misdiagnosed as an "addition" problem. When performance flags, the instinct is to add: add more servers, add more microservices, add more engineers, add more caching layers. But for the Enterprise Architect, scalability is fundamentally a **subtraction** problem. To reach the next order of magnitude, leadership must shift from a 'more is better' mindset to a 'leaner is faster' mandate.

In this chapter, we will strip away the hype and explore the discipline of **pruning dependencies**. We will define the "Scalability Mindset"—knowing exactly when to stop prioritizing speed-to-market and start investing in architecture.

To be clear: This is not a book about trendy cloud-native buzzwords or resume-driven development. This is a book about responsible, economically justified decisions to scale software systems.

We will introduce **ShopFlow**, the e-commerce application we will evolve throughout this book. We will see ShopFlow hit its first "Tipping Point" and meet **Dave**, the "Hero" engineer who is currently keeping the system alive by manually clearing logs at 3:00 AM.

Finally, we will make a controversial decision: faced with our first scaling crisis, we won't rewrite the code. We will simply "buy a bigger boat" (Vertical Scaling). We will explain exactly why this strategic accumulation of technical debt is the right move for Stage 1.

In this chapter, we're going to cover the following main topics:

- Adopting the Zero-Scaling Rule
- Identifying the system's "Tipping Point"
- Understanding the dimensions of scaling

- Scaling by subtraction
- Managing the "Dave" bottleneck
- Evaluating the cost of architectural inaction

Technical requirements

In this section, we outline the tools you will need to follow the **ShopFlow** evolution. While the concepts are universal, the code examples throughout the book will use the following stack:

- **Node.js (v18+):** For our application services.
- Docker and Docker Compose: To run our local database (MySQL) and future services (Redis, Kafka).
- **K6 or JMeter:** For load testing and simulating traffic spikes.
- **Code Repository:** All code snippets and the evolving "ShopFlow" architecture can be found in the GitHub repository at: `https://github.com/imran-siddique/Architecting-at-Scale/tree/main/ch1`

> Note
>
> **Prerequisites — set these up before following along:** This is a prerequisites list, not an architecture recommendation. We chose Node.js and MySQL because they are boring and well-understood: the failure modes are documented and the hiring pool is deep. Docker and Docker Compose are enough to reproduce every example locally; we deliberately defer orchestration (Kubernetes) until a later chapter, where the operational tax actually earns its keep. The point of this book is the reasoning, not the stack—any equivalent stack works.

Adopting the Zero-Scaling Rule

There is a pervasive myth that you must build for millions of users on Day 1. This is Premature Optimization. **According to the Startup Genome Report, 74% of high-growth startups fail due to premature scaling (see the References at the end of this chapter).** They build a Ferrari engine for a go-kart, running out of cash before they ever hit the racetrack.

The **Zero-Scaling Rule** states: *Do not solve a scalability problem you do not yet have.*

When you are in the MVP (Minimum Viable Product) phase, your architecture should be simple, even "naive." A monolithic Node.js application connected to a single MySQL database is not a "bad" architecture for a startup; it is the **right** architecture.

It eliminates the "Distributed Tax." You don't need complex service discovery or eventual consistency patterns; you just need a SQL JOIN. This allows for rapid iteration, instant deployments, and zero network latency between layers.

However, this simplicity has an expiration date. The "Scalability Mindset" is not about staying small; it is about recognizing the exact moment your architecture transforms from an asset into a liability. You must be able to spot that expiration date before it expires.

ShopFlow telemetry snapshot [stage 1]

Welcome to **ShopFlow**—an online store for home and lifestyle goods (a focused, single-brand retailer, not a multi-seller marketplace). It is currently a successful, growing e-commerce startup. The business team is celebrating record sales, but the engineering team is exhausted. Before we make any decisions, we must look at the data.

> Note
>
> Note: You will see these Telemetry Snapshots at the beginning of every major stage in this book. Consider them your recurring, decision-driving diagnostic—a mini-dashboard that tells you exactly when the system has crossed a threshold and why a new architectural pattern is required.

> Note
>
> **The Stage Model:** Each Stage in this book marks one step in ShopFlow's evolution and comes with its own telemetry snapshot. Stage 1 is the Monolithic MVP: a single Node.js application and one MySQL database, serving a few thousand orders a day. Each later stage introduces the next scaling pressure (caching, service extraction, multi-region, edge) only once the telemetry proves the previous architecture has run out of headroom.

Let's look at the current state of the system using our **Telemetry Snapshot**. This snapshot will be our "vital signs" monitor throughout the book to track our evolution.

```
Availability: 99.0% (Stuttering - frequent brief outages)
Cloud Spend: $500/mo (Low)
Total Orders: 5,000/day (New High!)
Active DB Connections: 450/500 (90% – Near Limit)
p99 Latency: 3.2s (CRITICAL - 53% Customer Abandonment Risk)
```

```
Dave Alert: "I'm manually clearing logs every 4 hours just to keep the disk from filling up."
```

> Note
>
> **Key Metrics to Watch:** The numbers above are ShopFlow-specific, but the diagnostic is general. On any service, instrument: connection-pool saturation, p99 latency, availability and error rate, CPU and memory headroom, disk IOPS and free space, network round-trip latency, and cost per request. A snapshot is only useful when every line has a threshold attached.

> Note
>
> **Definition: Toil** Google SREs define 'Toil' as work that is manual, repetitive, and devoid of enduring value. Dave clearing logs is the textbook definition of Toil. It buys time, but it doesn't fix the root cause.

The "Signal" here is clear: We are outgrowing our "Garage" setup. The system is creaking under the load, specifically regarding database connectivity and latency.

Analyzing the legacy code

Let's look at the code Dave is protecting. It is a standard monolithic search function, generated quickly to meet a deadline.

The following code represents the legacy product_search.js file:

JavaScript

```javascript
// The ShopFlow "Legacy" Search
// A simple, synchronous SQL query that worked fine for 100 users.
const express = require('express');
const router = express.Router();
const db = require('../db');

router.get('/search', async(req,res)=> {
    const query = req.query.q;

    // SCALABILITY TIME BOMB:
    // This 'LIKE' query forces a full table scan.
```

```
    // As the 'products' table grows to 100k rows, this locks the database CPU.
    try {
        const products = await db.query(
            "SELECT * FROM products WHERE description LIKE ?",
            [`%${query}%`]
        );

        // If the DB takes 3 seconds, the connection is held open for 3 seconds.
        // With 500 connections and a ~3s hold, ~166 requests/second
        // is enough to saturate the pool and stall every request.
        res.json(products);
    } catch (err) {
        // "Dave's Log Cleaner" is needed because we log full error stacks to disk
        console.error(err);
        res.status(500).send("Server Error");
    }
});
```

This is Little's Law, not arithmetic about head-count. A connection is held for the duration of the query, so the pool's sustainable throughput is roughly its size divided by the average hold time: 500 connections ÷ a 3-second query ≈ 166 requests per second before requests start queuing. The exact ceiling depends on the real pool size and the request mix—cheap cache hits return connections in milliseconds, while a slow search holds one for seconds—but the shape is fixed: once arrival rate exceeds service rate, latency climbs toward infinity.

In development, this code is harmless. In production, it is fatal. The resulting traffic jam exhausts our 500 available connections in minutes, leaving customers staring at the "endless loading spinner" while the database churns.

In an **AI-First** world, we can use tools to confirm our hypothesis before we even look at the code. The following prompt demonstrates how an architect might use an LLM to analyze the situation:

Architect's Prompt 1.1: The Diagnosis

When to use this: When your telemetry shows rising p99 latency or connection-pool saturation and you need to confirm the bottleneck with evidence before changing any architecture.

```
"Act as a Site Reliability Engineer. I am pasting a sample of my Nginx access logs
and my MySQL slow query log below. Analyze the timestamps to find correlations.
Specifically, identify if the p99 latency spikes in the web layer correlate with
```

```
specific LOCK_WAIT_TIMEOUT events in the database layer. Output the top 3 SQL
queries responsible for the contention."
```

The AI would likely confirm that the LIKE %query% search pattern is causing full table scans, which lock the database threads. This confirms that the underlying logic is flawed, and we need a strategy to address it.

Identifying the Tipping Point

How did we know we hit the wall? It wasn't just that "the site was slow." We look for specific signals that indicate a Tipping Point—the moment where tactics must shift.

- Latency Degradation (p99): Our snapshot shows p99 latency at 3.2s. This means 1% of our users (often the "power users" with the most data) are waiting over 3 seconds. This is the "Canary in the Coal Mine."
- **Saturation:** Our Active Connections are at 450/500. We are at 90% capacity. Linear growth will hit the wall in days.
- **Toil (The Dave Metric):** If your senior engineers are spending >50% of their time on manual intervention (clearing logs, rebooting services), you have crossed the tipping point.

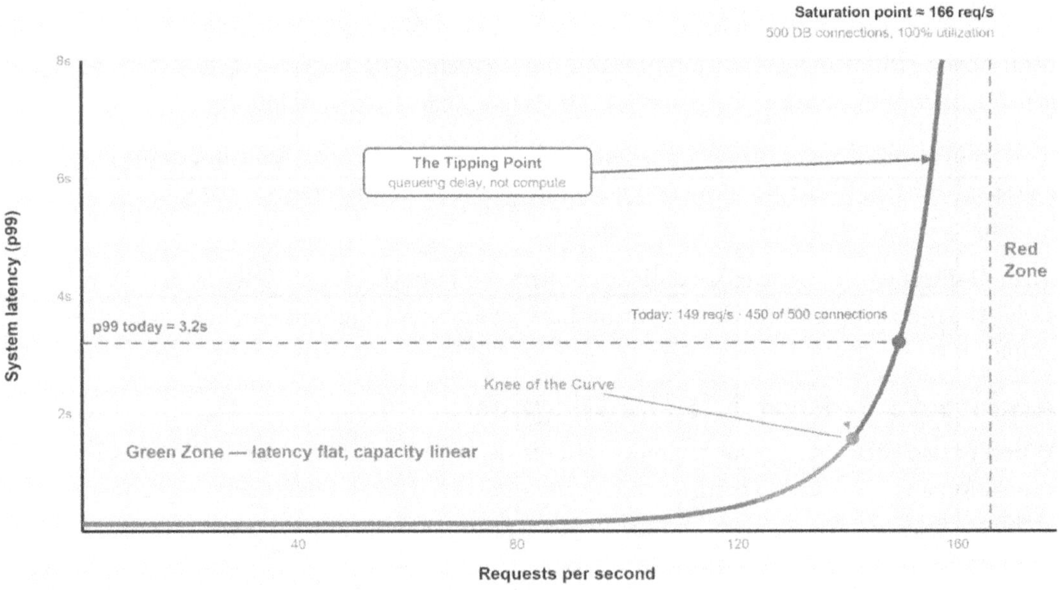

Figure 1.1: The "Hockey Stick" Curve of Technical Debt

Figure 1.1 depicts this "Hockey Stick" curve. For the first year, adding users had almost zero impact on latency (the Green Zone). But once we hit the saturation point of 500 database connections, latency didn't grow linearly; it grew exponentially (the Red Zone). In queuing theory, this is the 'Knee of the Curve.' As we approach 100% utilization, latency doesn't double —it goes to infinity. We are no longer managing traffic; we are managing a pile-up.

Figure 1.2: The "Hero" as a Single Point of Failure

Understanding the dimensions of scaling

Before we fix ShopFlow, we need to understand our options. A common mistake is thinking scaling only means "adding more servers." We use the Scale Cube (popularized by The Art of Scalability) to visualize our moves.

The following table summarizes the three axes of the cube:

Axis	Description	Pros	Cons
X	Horizontal Duplication (Load-Balanced Copies)	Unlimited theoretical scale	Requires app to be stateless
Y	Functional Decomposition (Microservices)	Independent scaling of "hot" components	Massive complexity penalty (latency, tracing)

Axis	Description	Pros	Cons
Z	Data Partitioning (Sharding)	Solves the database write bottleneck	Breaks ACID transactions and cross-shard joins

Table 1.1: The three scaling axes compared across description, pros, and cons.

Making the decision for ShopFlow

Looking at our Telemetry Snapshot, we are at the limit of a single node.

- **Y-Axis?** No. Too complex for our small team.
- **Z-Axis?** No. We don't have enough data to justify sharding complexity.
- **Also, X-Axis is a trap here.** If we double our web servers, we double the demand on our already saturated database. We don't need more mouths to feed; we need a bigger kitchen.

This leaves us with the hidden **"Fourth Dimension"**: **Vertical Scaling**. This isn't on the cube because it's technically "cheating"—we aren't changing the architecture; we are just changing the hardware. But for a startup, this shortcut is a valid strategy.

Scaling by subtraction

We have just seen that we can buy time by scaling up—the bigger boat. But bigger hardware is the most expensive capacity you can add, and it does nothing about load you never needed to carry. Before we provision a larger database to absorb the connection saturation from the last section, we first ask the cheaper question: how much of this load can we simply remove?

Before we add more servers to fix the problem, we must apply the "Scale by Subtraction" mindset. We need to perform a **Dependency Audit**. One of the quiet drags on scalability is the **Zombie Dependency**.

This happens when we start a migration but don't finish it. We move **almost** everything to the new system, but leave 10% behind.

Managing the "Half-Migration" trap

Consider a common scenario: ShopFlow started with **Liquid** templates for server-side rendering. A year later, the team decided to modernize and move to **React**. They migrated the checkout page and the product page. But the "Terms of Service" and "FAQ" pages were low priority, so they stayed on Liquid.

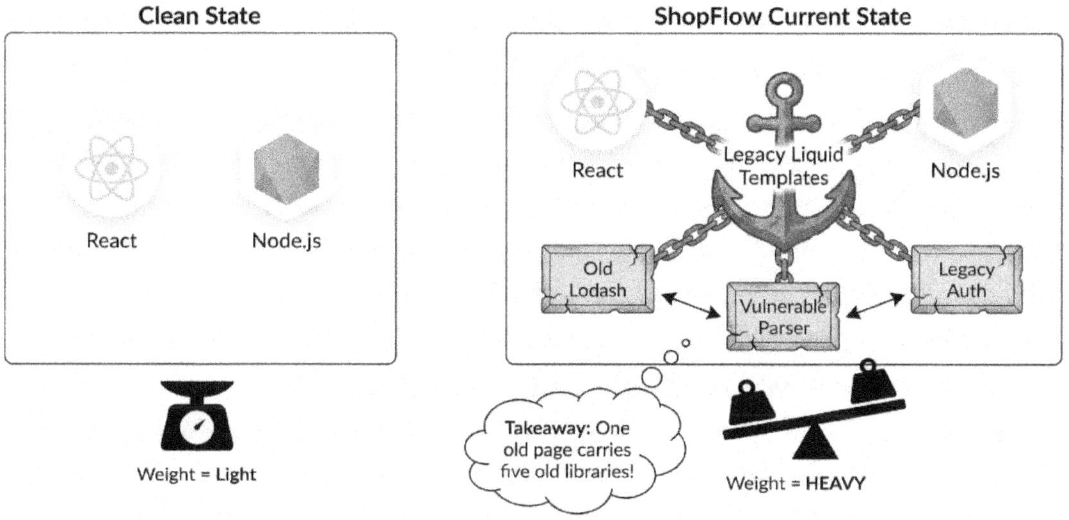

Figure 1.3: The "Transitive Weight" of a Zombie Dependency

As shown in *Figure 1.3*, you haven't just failed to subtract; you have multiplied. The system is now carrying the "transitive weight" of two entire ecosystems. That Liquid dependency might have "appendices" of its own—an old version of lodash or a security vulnerability that you are now forced to patch forever, all for two static pages.

Subtraction requires ruthlessness. To scale, you must finish the migration. If you can't migrate the FAQs to React, convert them to static HTML. But you must delete the Liquid dependency. This is **Cognitive Drag**. Every unused library in package.json is a mental stumbling block for a new hire. Scaling requires clearing the path, not just paving it.

Avoiding "the Netflix envy trap" (Résumé-Driven development)

Why do we add dependencies we don't need? Often, it is because of a common anti-pattern: **The Netflix Envy Trap**.

An engineer reads a blog post about how Netflix uses GraphQL federation or how Uber uses a custom Service Mesh. They think, *"If I build ShopFlow with these tools, I can put them on my resume."*

This is the opposite of the Scalability Mindset. Netflix solves problems you do not have.

- Netflix has 20,000 engineers; you have Dave.
- Netflix has a dedicated "Traffic Engineering" team; you have Dave.

The "Boring Technology" Rule states: When choosing a tech stack for scale, choose the technology that gives you the least number of "unknown unknowns."

- Boring: MySQL, Redis, Nginx (We know exactly how they fail.)
- Exciting: A new vector database was released last week (we have no idea how it fails at 3 AM).

We follow the **'Innovation Token'** philosophy. We have a limited budget for 'weird' technology. If we spend a token on a complex AI model, we must use boring technology (MySQL, Node.js) everywhere else to balance the risk.

The following prompt can be used to audit your own system for these issues:

Architect's Prompt 1.2: The Zombie Hunter

When to use this: Before any scaling project, to surface dead code paths and unused dependencies you can delete outright instead of paying to scale them.

```
"Analyze this project structure. Identify 'Dead Code' paths. Specifically, look
for API endpoints defined in routes.js that are never called by the frontend
client/src folder. List the top 5 'Zombie Endpoints' that we can delete to reduce
our attack surface."
```

Managing the "Dave" Bottleneck: From Heroics to Systematization

In our snapshot, we saw the "Dave Alert." Dave is manually clearing logs at night. We often call Dave a "Hero."

In a scaling system, however, **Hero Culture is an Organizational Risk**.

The problem isn't Dave's competence; it's that the system's operational logic lives in Dave's brain, not in code. This is **Implicit Automation**—undocumented human intervention required to keep the lights on.

We measure our team's capacity not by headcount, but by **Cognitive Runway**—how much mental bandwidth is available to solve **new** problems. Right now, Dave's cognitive runway is zero because he is spending 100% of his brainpower manually executing what should be a cron job.

The obvious first fixes are real: a larger disk volume and a size-triggered cleanup cron would both stop the 4 a.m. log-rotation toil, and either is worth doing today. But they treat the symptom. The disk fills because the saturated database is throwing a high volume of timeout exceptions into the logs; raising the volume size just moves the cliff a few days out. The 99.0%

availability already reflects this—the missing 1% is the set of brief outages that occur in the window before manual intervention. The systemic fix is not a bigger disk or a smarter script owned by one engineer; it is removing the saturation that generates the exceptions in the first place, and encoding any remaining cleanup as owned, monitored automation.

A tuesday morning with Dave

To understand why "Hero Culture" fails, let's look at last Tuesday at ShopFlow.

- **02:14 AM:** The PagerDuty alarm goes off. Latency has spiked to 10 seconds.
- **02:16 AM:** Dave wakes up, opens his laptop, and SSHs into the production server.
- **02:20 AM:** He runs htop and sees the CPU at 100%. He checks the logs. It's a "Googlebot" crawl hitting the Search endpoint 50 times a second.
- **02:25 AM:** Dave manually blocks the IP range in the firewall. The CPU drops. The site recovers.
- **02:30 AM:** Dave goes back to sleep.

The next morning, the CEO asks, "Why was the site down?" Dave says, "Don't worry, I fixed it."

This is a failure. Because Dave "fixed it" manually, nobody else knows **how** to fix it. Nobody knows that Googlebot is a threat. Nobody built a rate-limiter. The "fix" died with Dave's session. True scalability means **automating Dave out of the loop**. If the system cannot defend itself without a human typing commands at 2 AM, it is not scalable—and it is not resilient.

Scaling Dave (not firing him)

The goal isn't to get Dave out of the company; it's to get Dave out of the critical path. We want to help him grow from a "Hero" who fixes things into a "Principal" who designs things. This requires the **Rotation of Human Dependencies**.

- **Implicit vs. Explicit Knowledge:** Right now, the knowledge of "how to fix the logs" lives in Dave's brain. It must be written down. This documentation is called a **Runbook**. A Runbook is an 'If-This-Then-That' guide for 3 AM. It doesn't require genius; it requires literacy. If Dave writes a Runbook, a junior engineer can restart the server without waking Dave up.
- **Shared Ownership:** Seniors must view their role as mentors. By onboarding juniors and coaching them to handle the log rotation (or better, automating it), Dave frees up his own "Cognitive Runway" to tackle the database architecture.

Core Principles: The Primitives of Safe Change

Automating the manual log-rotation out of the loop is itself a change to a live system—and unplanned changes are how outages start. So before we spend the scaling budget we just calculated, we codify the primitives that let us change a running system safely. These are the laws every later chapter leans on.

Before we scale, we must define the toolkit we will use to scale *safely*. These are the non-negotiable laws of our architecture moving forward.

The reversibility requirement

Scalable architecture decisions are often **"One-Way Doors"**—decisions that are hard to reverse (like choosing a database or a programming language). You must tread carefully here.

Deployments, however, must be **"Two-Way Doors."** You must be able to roll back instantly. If a deployment cannot be reversed in seconds, it is not a scalable deployment; it is a gamble.

The primitives of safe change

Throughout the case studies in this book, we will rely on three primitives:

1. **Traffic Control:** Using mechanisms like **Canaries** (releasing to 1% of users) and **Blue/Green** deployments to limit exposure. The same traffic-splitting primitive also powers A/B testing and feature experimentation.
2. **Logic Control:** Using **Feature Flags** and **Circuit Breakers** to disable broken code paths without redeploying. Feature Flags do that; Circuit Breakers are really a resilience mechanism—their job is to keep a slow dependency from cascading into a full outage.
3. **Observation:** Measuring the **"Blast Radius"** of any failure. Our goal is not to prevent failure, but to contain it.

Evaluating the cost of architectural inaction

We have a crisis. The site is stuttering. The database is locking up. What do we do? A junior engineer might scream, "Rewrite it in Microservices! Use Kubernetes!" That is the wrong move. Refactoring takes weeks. We have hours. The Scalability Mindset teaches us to match the tactic to the timeline. Our immediate goal is **Survival**.

We will **Scale Vertically (Scale-Up)**. We are going to migrate our single database and web server to the largest instance type available (e.g., moving from a t3.medium to an m5.24xlarge).

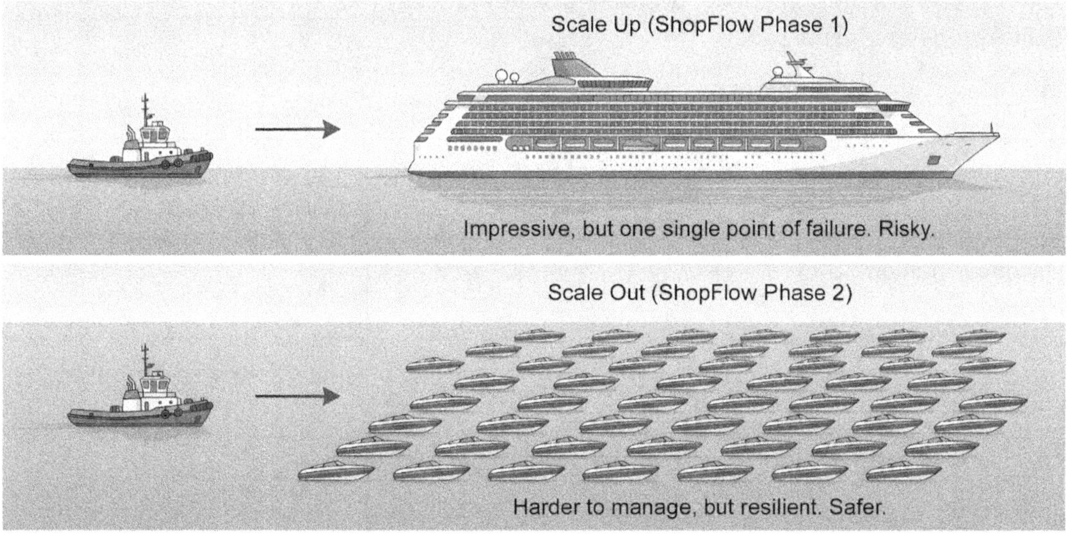

Figure 1.4: Vertical Scaling ("Bigger Boat") vs. Horizontal Scaling ("Fleet")

Figure 1.4 contrasts our choice. We are choosing the "Bigger Boat" approach (Vertical Scaling). It is impressive, but it puts all our eggs in one basket. If the cruise ship sinks, the entire platform goes down with it. However, building a fleet of 50 speedboats (Horizontal Scaling) requires a level of coordination we don't have yet.

> Note
>
> **Safe Scale Check — Scale Up vs. Stay Available:** Scaling a single node up raises throughput, but it also concentrates blast radius, lengthens recovery time, and makes every maintenance window a full outage. Vertical scaling buys throughput; it does not buy availability. Even early, add a minimum of horizontal redundancy for survivability —two app instances behind a load balancer and a managed database with Multi-AZ failover. The rule: scale up for throughput, but add redundancy for availability.

Analyzing the "cloud tax" vs. labor cost

"But wait," the skeptic asks. "Isn't that expensive? You're increasing our cloud bill fivefold, from $500 to $2,500!" This is where "Manager's Math" beats "Engineer's Math."

- **Engineer's Math:** "This server costs $2,000 more per month. That's a waste."
- **Manager's Math:** "Hiring a new engineer to re-architect this system takes 3 months of recruiting and costs $15,000/month in salary, benefits, and onboarding. And during those 3 months, our site is crashing."

Let's break down the math of our decision to Scale Vertically (buy the big server) versus Refactoring (rewrite the code).

The following table compares the two options:

Metric	**Option A: Vertical Scale (Bigger DB node)**	**Option B: Refactor (Microservices)**
Implementation Time	1 Hour (Reboot)	3 Months (Dev + QA)
Risk of Failure	Low (configuration change)	High (New bugs, distributed data)
Cloud Cost (Monthly)	$2,500 (m5.24xlarge)	$500 (Current)
Labor Cost (One-time)	$100 (1 hour of Dave)	$60,000 (3 months for 2 devs)
Total 3-Month Cost	**$7,600**	$61,500

Table 1.2: Vertical scaling versus refactoring to microservices for ShopFlow.

To be precise: "scaling up" here means the database tier—the bottleneck in our telemetry, not the stateless app servers. Adding app servers would only increase pressure on the same 500-connection pool. A larger database node (more connections, RAM, and IOPS) is what actually buys the time this table prices out.

The Verdict: Refactoring is 8x more expensive in the short term. Startups fail when they run out of runway. Burning $60k of labor to save $2k of cloud per month is bad business. We will refactor eventually—but only when the cloud bill exceeds the labor cost.

Vertical scaling is **quick**, **easy**, and **sturdy**. You change a configuration setting, reboot, and you have 10x the capacity. You are trading **Money** for **Time**. We are choosing to pay the "Cloud Tax" to buy the team three months of breathing room. This is **Strategic Technical Debt**.

> **Note**
>
> Strategic debt differs from accidental debt because it is intentional. We accept it only when the short-term gain (survival) outweighs the long-term cost (interest), and—crucially—when there is a clear plan for eventual repayment.

Summary

In this chapter, we defined scalability as a targeted discipline of subtraction and economic trade-offs. We identified the **Zombie Dependencies** that create cognitive drag and the **Organizational Risks** where implicit system knowledge resides in a single human dependency.

The Architecture Decision: We have executed a **Strategic Borrow** of technical debt by opting for **Vertical Scaling.** This is a non-negotiable tactical move to trade capital for the engineering time required to build a distributed foundation.

The Cliffhanger: The Limit of One

The migration to the massive server stabilized performance for 90 days, but provisioned compute capacity has now reached **90% saturation**, leaving zero headroom for transient spikes. We have hit the physical limit of a single machine. If this instance experiences a hardware failure, the lack of redundancy ensures a total service outage. In *Chapter 2*, we must break the monolith and transition to a distributed fleet.

References

Startup Genome. (2011). Startup Genome Report Extra on Premature Scaling. The 74% figure refers to high-growth startups that failed after scaling prematurely.

Little, J. D. C. (1961). A Proof for the Queuing Formula $L = \lambda W$. Operations Research, 9(3). The basis for the throughput estimate: with a fixed connection pool and a given hold time, sustainable throughput ≈ pool size ÷ hold time.

Subscribe to Deep Engineering

Scan the QR or visit the link to subscribe for free.

https://packt.link/deep-engineering-newsletter

2

Core Principles of Scalable Architecture

In *Chapter 1*, we stabilized ShopFlow by vertically scaling to the largest available instance. While this resolved the immediate latency spike, our latest telemetry shows the database connection pool is already at 90% saturation, and CPU utilization during peak windows has returned to 85%. We have reached the physical limits of a single node; further vertical scaling is no longer a viable option. To handle the projected 10x traffic growth, we must transition from a monolithic architecture to a distributed system that scales horizontally.

We are now running on a massive, expensive single node. Utilization is creeping back up to 85%. There is no bigger server to buy. If this server fails, ShopFlow doesn't just degrade; it goes fully offline. To survive the next order of magnitude, we must stop building *up* and start building *out*. We must transition from a Monolith to a Distributed System.

This transition is dangerous. In this chapter, we will outline the core principles that prevent a distributed system from becoming a distributed liability. We will explore:

- **Simplicity and Iterative Design:** Why "Big Bang" rewrites sink startups and how to use the "Scale Unit" model.
- **Statelessness:** The requirement for horizontal movement.
- **Platform Agnosticism:** Designing for portability—agnostic where cheap, native where valuable.
- **Observability:** Why can't you scale what you can't see?

Resiliency: Why a distributed system must be designed to contain failure, not just avoid it—the focus of the Safety Toolkit and Blast Radius sections below.

Technical requirements

In this chapter, we move from a single server to a distributed fleet. To simulate this environment locally, we will expand our Docker stack. You will need the following tools:

- **Node.js (v18+):** We will effectively run multiple instances of our ShopFlow application to simulate a cluster.
- Docker and Docker Compose: Essential for orchestrating our new multi-container setup. We will be adding two critical components to our compose file:
  - **Redis (v7+):** To act as our **Shared Session Store**, decoupling state from our application code.
  - **Nginx:** To act as our **Layer 7 Load Balancer**, distributing traffic between our multiple Node.js instances.
- **k6:** We will use it to prove that our horizontal scaling actually works by hammering the Load Balancer and ensuring traffic is distributed evenly without dropping sessions.
- **Code Repository:** The refactored, stateless version of ShopFlow—including the new Correlation ID middleware—is available at: `https://github.com/imran-siddique/Architecting-at-Scale/tree/main/ch2`

ShopFlow telemetry snapshot [stage 2]

We survived the initial traffic spike by upgrading to a massive m5.24xlarge instance. The "Bigger Boat" strategy worked for exactly three months. Now, traffic has doubled again, and we are hitting the physical limits of a single machine.

Let's check the vital signs:

```
Availability: 99.5% (Degrading during peak hours)
Cloud Spend: $2,500/mo (Spiking - 5x increase from Stage 1)
Active Connections: 4,800/5,000 (Saturation Imminent)
p99 Latency: 1,200ms (Red - The server is queuing requests)
Dave Alert: "We bought the biggest server AWS sells, and we are sitting at 95%
CPU. There is nowhere left to go up. If we get one more viral post, we go dark."
```

Compared with *Chapter 1*'s 99.0%, availability has ticked up to 99.5%—but that gain came from the bigger server, not from better architecture. With connections at 4,800/5,000 and p99 latency at 1,200 ms, the single node has no headroom left: the next failure is a vertical drop, not a gradual slide.

The "Signal" here is clear: We have hit the Cost Wall and the Hardware Ceiling. Vertical scaling has diminishing returns. We are paying exponentially more money for incrementally less performance gains. We can no longer solve this problem with a credit card; we have to solve it with architecture. We must go horizontal.

Before we start slicing the monolith, here is ShopFlow at a glance—the components we will be carving up and how critical each one is:

Component	Role	Criticality
Load Balancer (Nginx)	Distributes traffic across the Node.js instances	P0 – critical path
App tier (Node.js)	Serves the storefront and the APIs	P0 – critical path
Auth	Login, identity, session issuance	P0 – critical
Cart and Checkout	Add-to-cart, orders, payment handoff	P0 – revenue
Product Catalog	Product data and listings	P1
Search	Product search and filtering (CPU-heavy)	P1 – heavy, noncritical
Session Store (Redis)	Shared session state so instances remain stateless	P0 – enables horizontal scaling
Database (MySQL)	System of record: users, products, orders	P0 – system of record

Table 2.1: ShopFlow's core components, their roles, and criticality.

Simplicity and Iterative Design: Refactoring vs. Incremental Deconstruction

The most dangerous phrase in engineering is, *"Let's just rewrite it."*

When a team stares at a struggling monolith like ShopFlow, the temptation is to declare the legacy code "technical bankruptcy." The proposal usually sounds like this: *"We will freeze feature development for three months. We will rewrite the entire backend in Go/Rust/Microservices. Then, we will cut over to the perfect new system."*

This is the **Big Bang Trap**. It starts with optimism, but it almost never cleans up the mess—it just adds more mess. In my experience, "clean-up" projects that don't deliver immediate customer value have a nearly 100% failure rate. The business cannot afford to pause for three months, and by the time you finish the rewrite, the requirements have changed. You end up chasing a moving target with a system that has never seen production traffic.

We do not rewrite; we **deconstruct**.

The "scale unit" philosophy

Before we start slicing up our application, we need a target architecture. At Microsoft, and in many large-scale systems, we don't just "add servers" to a random pool. We use a concept called the **Scale Unit**.

A Scale Unit is a completely self-contained deployment—everything you need to serve a specific group of customers. It contains the web servers, the APIs, the background workers, and crucially, *their own partitioned data.*

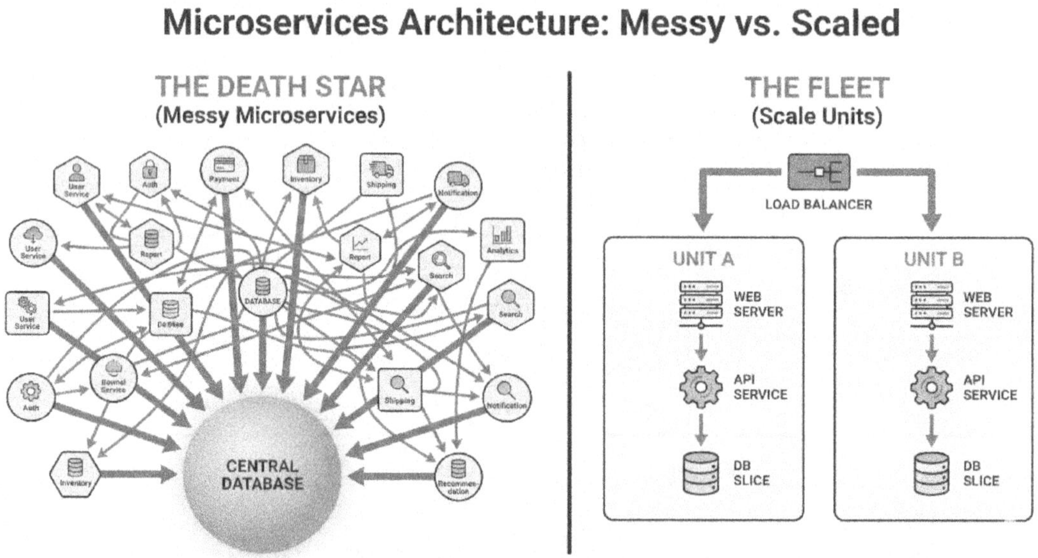

Figure 2.1: A Tangled Monolith vs. Independent Scale Units

Figure 2.1 visualizes the difference between disorder and order. On the left, everything depends on everything else—if one service fails, the whole system tangles. On the right, we have **Scale Units**. Unit A (serving customers 1–10k) is completely independent of Unit B. If Unit A catches fire, Unit B keeps serving dinner. This is how we scale without losing our minds.

Think of it like a franchise model. When a fast-food chain wants to serve more customers, they don't build a kitchen the size of a football stadium (Vertical Scaling). They build a second, identical store down the road.

- **Scale Unit A:** Serves Customers 1–10,000.
- **Scale Unit B:** Serves Customers 10,001–20,000.

> Note
>
> **Why Scale Units Win**
>
> **Predictability**: Scaling becomes a simple calculation. If one unit handles 10,000 users, you know exactly when to provision the next one. It transforms capacity planning from guesswork into math.
>
> **Fault Isolation**: A failure in Unit A is contained within Unit A. It does not cascade to Unit B. You minimize the "Blast Radius," ensuring that a crash affects only a small percentage of users rather than the entire fleet.
>
> **Operational Simplicity**: Instead of debugging a chaotic web of interdependent microservices, you are managing identical, repeatable stamps. If you can operate one unit, you can operate fifty.

For ShopFlow, our goal isn't to shatter the monolith into tiny pieces immediately. It is to package our monolith so it can be replicated as a Unit.

The "critical path" heuristic

How do we move from our current "Big Ball of Mud" to this clean Scale Unit model? We have to slice the monolith. But where do we make the first cut?

The "Heavy ≠ Critical" Rule: A common mistake is to target the "Heaviest" component first—in our case, the Search function that is crushing the CPU. But high resource usage does not equal high business value.

- **Heavy:** High resource usage (e.g., Search, Image Processing). If this fails, the user is annoyed.
- **Critical (P0):** Revenue-generating (e.g., Cart, Checkout, Auth). If this fails, the business stops.

My heuristic is simple: **Isolate the Critical Path first.** We extract P0 components not because they are the resource hogs, but to protect them *from* the resource hogs.

We identify the components tied strictly to Availability and Revenue—usually Identity (Auth), Inventory, and Orders. These are the "P0" scenarios. We extract these first not because they are easy, but because they are the lifeblood of the system. We need to isolate them so that when the heavy, complex features (like Recommendations or Search) crash, they don't take the P0 critical path down with them.

For ShopFlow, our first move isn't to fix the slow search. It is to decouple the **User Session** and **Cart** from the single web server. If we can't move users between servers without them losing their shopping carts, we can't scale horizontally at all.

This brings us to the first technical requirement of horizontal scaling: **Statelessness**.

The Architect's Prompt 2.1: The Dependency Audit

When to use this: Run this analysis during your Migration Planning phase, before a single line of code is moved. It prevents the "Distributed Monolith" trap by exposing the "hidden veins," circular dependencies and shared state—that often cause extractions to fail.

```
"Act as a Senior Software Architect. I am planning to extract the 'Cart' module
from my Node.js monolith into a separate microservice.
Below is the package.json and a list of require() statements found in the cart/
directory.
Task:
Identify which dependencies are 'shared' with the core monolith (e.g., shared
database models, utility libraries) and flag them as High Risk for extraction.
Suggest a 'Seam' strategy: Should I duplicate the shared utility code, or publish
it as a private NPM package first?
Highlight any circular dependencies that would break if I moved this folder to a
new repository."
```

The Primitives of Safe Scale

We are about to take a hammer to our monolith. We are introducing network calls, external caches, and distributed logic. This means we are introducing **Distributed Failure**.

In a monolith, if a function fails, the stack trace tells you why. In a distributed system, a failure is often a mystery. A timeout in Service A causes a retry storm in Service B, which crashes Database C.

Before we write a single line of distributed code, we must install our **Safety Equipment**. At Microsoft, we operate by a simple rule: **"You cannot scale what you cannot control."**

To safely navigate the complexity of a distributed system, we rely on three primitives.

1. the reversibility requirement (One-Way vs. Two-Way doors): every irreversible decision is a liability

A resilient architecture minimizes irreversible moves. The biggest fear in scaling isn't making a mistake; it's making a mistake you can't fix. We mitigate this risk by distinguishing between **One-Way Doors** and **Two-Way Doors**.

- **One-Way Doors (Architectural Decisions):** These are hard to reverse. Choosing a database (e.g., "Let's go all-in on MongoDB") or a language ("Let's rewrite in Rust") is a One-Way Door. Once you walk through, you are committed for years. We treat these decisions with extreme caution, requiring "Design Docs" and deep review.
- **Two-Way Doors (Deployments):** These *should* be easy to reverse. If we deploy a new "Cart Service" and it breaks, we should be able to revert to the old version in seconds.

The Golden Rule: A scalable architecture strives to turn One-Way Doors into Two-Way Doors.

Instead of a "Big Bang" migration to a new database (One-Way), we write an abstraction layer that writes to both the old and new databases (Two-Way). If the new one fails, we just flip a switch back to the old one. We prioritize Reversibility over Perfection.

> Note
>
> **The Rollback Is Not Free:** Reads roll back cleanly; writes do not. Once the abstraction layer has been writing to both databases, flipping back to the old one means the writes that landed only in the new database must be reconciled back into the old one. A clean cut-over is a two-way door for reads and a one-way-ish door for writes—plan the reconciliation (or dual-write replay) before you cut over, not after a failure.

2. the safety toolkit

To ensure reversibility, we need specific tools. We break these down into Logic Control, Traffic Control, and Observation.

Logic Control: Feature Flags

In the old world, "Deploying Code" and "Releasing a Feature" were the same event. If you deployed the code, the user saw the feature. This is dangerous.

We decouple them using Feature Flags.

- **Deploy:** We ship the code for the new "Redis Session Store" to production, but it is wrapped in a flag: if (feature.isEnabled('redis-sessions')) { ... }. The code is there, but it is asleep.
- Release: We flip the flag for imran@shopflow.com (just me). If it works, we flip it for "Internal Users," then "10% of Users."

The Cleanup Rule: Flags are debt. Every flag doubles the number of test paths in your code. Once a feature is 100% released and stable, the flag **must be deleted**. Long-lived flags are not safety mechanisms; they are confusing legacy artifacts that cause bugs.

This gives us a Kill Switch. If the new Redis store spikes in latency, we don't have to roll back the binary (which takes 20 minutes); we just toggle the flag (which takes 20 milliseconds).

Traffic Control: Canaries and Blue/Green

Feature flags control *code paths*; Traffic Control manages *volume*.

- **Canary Deployments:** We never deploy to 100% of the fleet at once. We deploy to one single "Canary" node. We let it take real traffic for 15 minutes. If it sings (works), we deploy to the rest. If it fails, the load balancer automatically cuts it off.
- **Blue/Green:** We spin up a full new fleet (Green) alongside the old one (Blue). We switch the router. If Green fails, we switch back to Blue instantly.

> Note
>
> **Safe Deployment Practices:** Canary and Blue/Green are two instances of the same discipline: progressive delivery. Ship to a small, real slice first; gate promotion on health signals (error rate, latency, saturation), not a stopwatch; and make rollback automatic and faster than roll-forward. The rule: every deploy is reversible and observed before it reaches 100%.

Observation: The "Blast Radius" Metric

We stop measuring "Uptime" as a binary (Up/Down) and start measuring **Blast Radius**.

- *Question:* "If the 'Recommendations Service' fails, what % of users can't check out?"
- Goal: The answer should be 0%.

Scaling safely means architecting specifically to minimize Blast Radius. If a "Scale Unit" fails, only 1% of users should notice. If a non-critical feature fails, it must not take down a critical user journey—the feature's own users will see it is unavailable, but checkout, auth, and cart keep working.

Statelessness and Loose Coupling: The Pillars of Horizontal Scalability

We have our big server, and we have a plan to carve out the "P0" critical path (Auth/Cart).

> Note
>
> **The Golden Rule:** A horizontally scalable service treats all incoming requests as strangers. It should never rely on memory of a previous conversation to understand the current one.

Stated precisely: keep every service instance stateless and store all state in an external store—a cache, a database, or an object store. The "stranger" framing is the why; statelessness plus externalized state is the how.

But before we spin up the second server, we hit a physics problem.

In our current monolith, when a user logs in, their session ID is stored in the web server's memory (RAM). If we add a second server, we have a problem.

- **Request 1 (Login):** Goes to **Server A**. Server A creates Session:123.
- **Request 2 (Add to Cart):** The Load Balancer sends this to **Server B**.
- **Result:** Server B checks its RAM, sees no Session:123, and forces the user to log in again.

We have broken the user experience. To fix this, architects usually face a choice between two paths: the "Quick Fix" (Sticky Sessions) or the "Scalable Fix" (Statelessness).

Why we reject sticky sessions

The easiest way to solve the problem above is to tell the Load Balancer: *"If a user starts on Server A, keep sending them to Server A."* This is called **Session Affinity** or **Sticky Sessions**.

It requires zero code changes. It's tempting. And for ShopFlow, **we are rejecting it.**

Why? Because Sticky Sessions defeat the purpose of scaling.

1. **The "Hot Node" Problem:** Sticky sessions assume all users are equal. They are not. If a bot or a "Power User" gets stuck to Server A, they might hammer that single node with 10x the load of other users. Server A hits 100% CPU while Server B sits idle at 10%. You have undone your load distribution.
2. **The Availability Trap:** If Server A crashes (or we need to patch it), every user "stuck" to it loses their shopping cart instantly. We are trying to build a system that *survives* failure; sticky sessions make failure total for the subset of users pinned to that server.

> Note
>
> Info Note: Is "Sticky" Ever Okay?
>
> In some specific scenarios, sticky sessions are valid. If you are using WebSockets (e.g., for a real-time chat app) or hosting legacy stateful desktop-apps-turned-web, stickiness might be unavoidable. But for a general-purpose e-commerce system like ShopFlow, it is an anti-pattern.

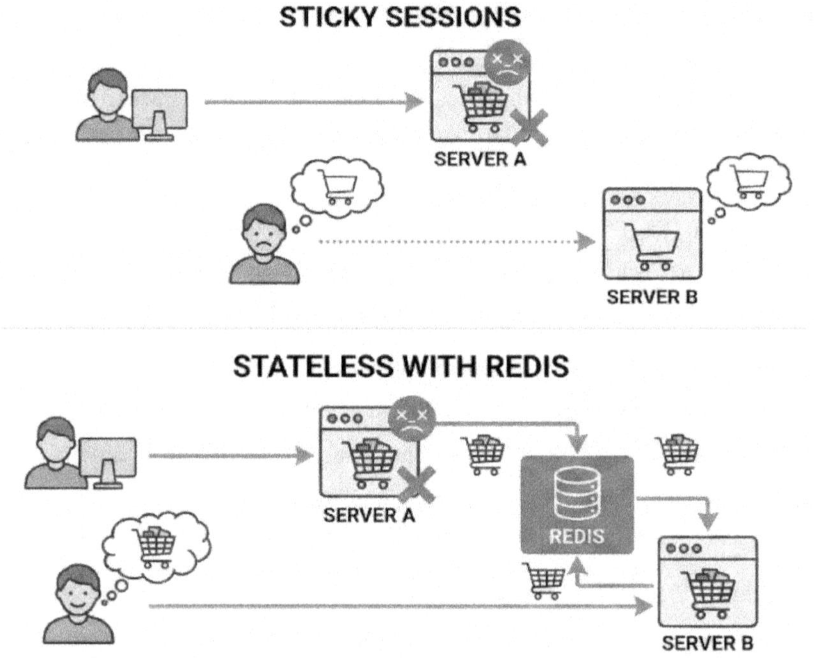

Figure 2.2: Sticky Sessions vs. a Stateless Fleet with a Shared Session Store

Figure 2.2 illustrates the "Hot Node" risk. With Sticky Sessions (top), the user's data is lost with the server. With Stateless Architecture (bottom), the application servers are just "workers." They possess no memory of their own. The memory lives in **Redis**, the shared brain of the fleet, ensuring that the loss of a worker does not mean the loss of the user's session.

The solution: the shared session store (Redis)

To go horizontal, our application servers must be **Stateless**. They should not know or care who the user is; they should just execute logic.

We move the "State" (the Session ID and Cart) out of the web server RAM and into a high-speed, external store. We will use **Redis** for this.

Now, the flow looks like this:

- **Request 1 (Login):** Goes to **Server A**. Server A writes Session:123 to **Redis**.
- **Request 2 (Add to Cart):** Goes to **Server B**. Server B checks **Redis**, finds Session:123, and proceeds.

More precisely, every request follows the same lookup: the server reads the session from Redis by its ID, reuses it if it exists, and creates a new one (writing it back to Redis) only if it does not. The session never lives in a single server's local memory, which is exactly what lets any instance serve any request.

If Server A crashes, Server B takes over instantly. The user never notices.

The Trade-off: We are introducing complexity. Redis is a new piece of infrastructure to manage. However, this is a necessary "incremental change." We are accepting one new dependency to gain the ability to scale to infinity.

> Note
>
> **Anti-Pattern: The Swiss Army Knife Trap** When we add Redis, vendors and enthusiastic engineers will try to sell us ten other features. "Redis can do Pub/Sub! It can do Vector Search! It can be a primary database!"
>
> **Stop**.
>
> We are "Scaling by Subtraction." We are adding Redis strictly for sessions. We must avoid **Dependency Drift,** where a tool brought in for one job slowly takes over five others, creating a monolithic knot of dependency. We track Redis as a singular, bounded tool. If we can remove an old library because Redis handles caching now, we do it. Otherwise, we guard this new box jealously.

Data coupling: the "shared database" trap

As we split our P0 services (Cart, Auth) from the monolith, we face our next challenge: The Database.

The "easy" path is to let the new Cart Microservice connect directly to the old Monolith Database tables.

- *Monolith* reads the USERS table.
- *Cart Service* reads the USERS table.

This is a **Distributed Monolith**. If you change the schema of the USERS table, you break both applications. You have decoupled the code, but you have coupled the data.

The "Database as a Service" Mindset We don't need to spin up a new physical database for every service yet (that's expensive). We can share the *physical* database server, but we must logically isolate the access.

Think of the database not as a bucket of tables, but as a **Service Layer**.

1. **Logical Partitioning:** The Cart service should only ever touch "Cart" tables. It should never touch "Product" tables.
2. **The Access Layer:** Ideally, services do not run raw SQL against shared tables. They go through a Data Access Layer (DAL) or an internal API.

> Note
>
> **What "logical isolation" means concretely:** Share the physical server, but enforce service boundaries inside it: a separate schema per service; a separate DB user with grants scoped to only that schema; no cross-service foreign keys; no cross-service joins; access to another domain's data only through that domain's API; and versioned data contracts so a schema change can't silently break a consumer.

This is also the answer to "isn't a DAL still direct DB access?" It is—but a service's DAL only ever touches the tables that service owns. The boundary that matters is ownership, not whether SQL is involved: a service reaching into another service's tables is the violation; a service querying its own is not.

By treating the database as a "Service" that we call, rather than a "File Cabinet" we rummage through, we ensure that when we eventually *do* need to physically shard the database (in *Chapter 10*), the application code won't even notice.

> Note
>
> The Data Ownership Rule: Each service owns its data. Every other service accesses that data only through the owning service's API or events—never by reading or writing its tables directly. Ownership, not co-location, is what makes the eventual physical split a non-event.

The Architect's Prompt 2.2: The State Hunter

When to use this: When auditing a service you intend to scale horizontally, to find every place it secretly keeps state in local memory before you stand up a second instance.

```
"Act as a Security and Scalability Auditor. Review the following legacy
authentication code snippet.
Task:
Identify any lines where state is being stored in local memory (e.g., req.session,
global variables, or local file writes) which would fail in a horizontally scaled
environment.
Rewrite the specific stateful lines to use a Redis-based pattern (using
redisClient.set / redisClient.get).
Add a 'Retry with Exponential Backoff' logic to the Redis connection to prevent
the app from crashing if the cache blips."
```

Design for Platform Agnosticism: Avoiding Cloud and Vendor Lock-In

As we prepare ShopFlow for horizontal scaling, we have to choose where it lives. The cloud providers (AWS, Azure, GCP) want you to use their proprietary tools for everything. They want you to use DynamoDB, Kinesis, and Lambda in a way that makes leaving them impossible.

Some architects react to this by becoming "Cloud Agnostic" zealots. They build massive abstraction layers around *everything* so they can move from AWS to Azure on a whim.

This is a trap. Building a wrapper around a unique service (like a specific AI model or a complex serverless trigger) often costs more in engineering time than the migration itself ever would.

We need a balanced, pragmatic approach.

The "wrapper rule"

My rule for platform independence is simple: Be agnostic where it is cheap and native where it is valuable.

1. The Standards (Databases and Caching): For standardized technologies like SQL or Redis, there is no excuse for lock-in. If you are using MySQL, it works the same on Azure Database for MySQL as it does on AWS RDS.
    - *The Strategy:* Do not use vendor-specific extensions unless absolutely necessary. Use standard drivers. If you move clouds, you just change the connection string. This is "cheap insurance."
2. **The Proprietary (Serverless & AI):** If a cloud provider offers a unique service that saves you 50% dev time (e.g., a specific AI content safety filter or a highly integrated event trigger), **use it**.
    - *The Strategy:* Do not waste months building a "Generic Cloud Wrapper" around a feature that only one cloud supports. The "Abstraction Tax" is too high. If you ever leave that cloud, you will just rewrite that specific piece of code.

For ShopFlow, we are choosing **MySQL** and **Redis**. These are open standards. We will run them as managed services (to save Dave time), but we will write our code as if they were running on our laptop. We are effectively "Cloud Neutral" without over-engineering.

Observability and Telemetry as a First-Class Architectural Principle

In *Chapter 1*, Dave fixed the site by looking at a log file on a server.

In a distributed system, there is no "server." There is a fleet.

If a user reports, *"My checkout failed,"* and you have 50 nodes running, you cannot SSH into 50 servers to check 50 log files. You will never find the error.

Most teams treat logging as an afterthought—something to add when they are debugging. In a scalable architecture, **Observability is a functional requirement**, just like the "Buy" button.

The correlation ID: your System's passport

You cannot debug a distributed system without a Correlation ID. It is practically impossible. If a transaction fails in Service D, but you cannot trace it back to the request in Service A, you are simply guessing.

There is one non-negotiable requirement for any distributed system I design: **The Correlation ID.**

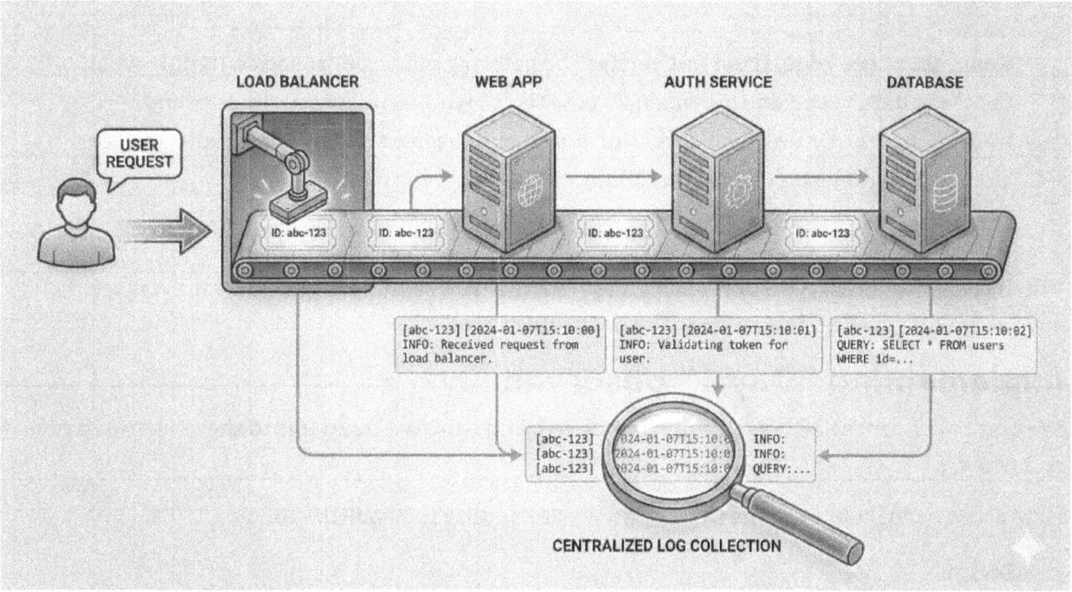

Figure 2.3: The Lifecycle of a Correlation ID

Figure 2.3 shows the lifecycle of a **Correlation ID**. Think of it as a passport stamp. The request arrives anonymous, but the Load Balancer assigns it an identity (abc-123). As it hops from the Web App to the Auth Service to the Database, it carries this ID. When we need to debug, we don't look for "random errors"; we simply filter our logs for abc-123 and reconstruct the entire crime scene.

Every request that enters the ShopFlow system—whether it's from a mobile app, a browser, or a webhook—must be assigned a unique ID (a UUID) at the very first point of entry (the Load Balancer or Gateway).

This ID must be passed like a passport to every downstream service.

1. **Client** may supply a Correlation ID; if it is absent, the API Gateway generates abc-123 at the edge.
2. **API Gateway** logs abc-123.
3. Auth Service receives abc-123 and logs "User Authenticated".
4. Cart Service receives abc-123, logs "Item Added."
5. **Database** logs a slow query associated with abc-123.

Note

Generate at the edge, trust but verify: The gateway mints a Correlation ID only when the client didn't send one. Clients may pass their own (useful for true end-to-end tracing), but the gateway validates the format and regenerates anything malformed or already in flight—so a client cannot inject a colliding or forged ID.

When the system fails, you don't search for "Error." You search for abc-123, and you see the entire timeline of the failure across the entire fleet.

Implementing "Day 1" observability

We don't wait for the "Observability Team" to build this. We build it into the skeleton of our code now.

Here is the `middleware/correlation.js` we are adding to `ShopFlow` today:

JavaScript

```
const { v4: uuidv4 } = require('uuid');

// The "Passport Control" Middleware
module.exports = (req, res, next)=> {
    // 1. Look for an existing ID (from the Load Balancer or upstream service)
    // 2. If none exists, generate a new one.
    const correlationId = req.headers['x-correlation-id'] || uuidv4();

    // 3. Attach it to the request object so our logger can see it
    req.correlationId = correlationId;

    // 4. IMPORTANT: Return it to the client in the headers
    // This allows the Frontend to say "Here is my Reference ID" when reporting
bugs.
    res.setHeader('x-correlation-id', correlationId);

    next();
};
```

There is no excuse for missing this. If the platform provides a tracing tool (like OpenTelemetry), use it. If not, write this middleware. But never, ever let a request wander through your system anonymously.

The Architect's Prompt 2.3: The Telemetry Weaver

> Note
>
> **When to use this:** Adopt this pattern immediately. If you wait until teams scale independently, observability standards will diverge, and you will be left trying to patch together incompatible logs. Use this prompt to generate a standard middleware library that every new service imports by default.

```
"Act as a Middleware Engineer. I have an existing Express.js service with 50
endpoints. I need to enforce Observability Standards without rewriting every
route.
Task:
Write a correlation-id-middleware.js that checks for an incoming X-Correlation-ID
header. If missing, generate a UUID.
Crucial: Demonstrate how to wrap the standard console.log or winston logger so
that every subsequent log line in the request scope automatically includes this
ID.
Show how to inject this ID into the headers of any downstream axios or fetch calls
made by this service, ensuring the 'Trace' is unbroken."
```

Summary

In this chapter, we established the mandates for our distributed evolution:

- **Iterative Deconstruction**: We rejected the high-failure-rate "Big Bang" rewrite in favor of the **Scale Unit** model.
- **Mandatory Statelessness**: You cannot scale horizontally without decoupling the user session from the server; we utilize a shared store to ensure availability.
- **Pragmatic Agnosticism**: We utilize open standards for core data paths while accepting the utility of managed cloud services.
- **Non-Negotiable Observability**: You cannot debug a distributed fleet without a **Correlation ID** to reconstruct request timelines across the stack.

The cliffhanger: the "open door"

We have successfully implemented horizontal scaling, but the transition has created an unintended expansion of the network attack surface. By converting internal function calls into networked API calls, we have created fifty new endpoints susceptible to unauthorized lateral movement. In *Chapter 3*, we move to **Zero Trust** to defend a system that no longer has a perimeter.

A perimeter firewall and the API gateway still guard north-south traffic, but these fifty endpoints are east-west: calls that used to be in-process function calls are now service-to-service network calls that the perimeter never inspects. Once an attacker is inside the network, nothing is checking those internal hops. That east-west exposure—not a hole in the firewall—is the new surface.

Get this book's PDF version and more

Scan the QR code (or go to `packtpub.com/unlock`). Search for this book by name, confirm the edition, and then follow the steps on the page.

UNLOCK NOW

Note: Keep your invoice handy. Purchases made directly from Packt don't require an invoice.

3

Security-First and Compliance-First Architecture

In *Chapter 2*, we successfully transitioned ShopFlow from a struggling monolith to a distributed fleet of stateless servers. We celebrated the victory of horizontal scaling—we could finally handle any traffic spike the internet threw at us.

But in our rush to scale "out," we made a fatal mistake.

By splitting our monolithic process into networked services, we turned function calls into network calls. We opened fifty new ports, created fifty new endpoints, and added fifty new places for data to leak. We forgot one fundamental truth of distributed systems: **Network calls are open doors.**

We didn't just scale our capacity; we scaled our **attack surface**.

In this chapter, the "Panic Meter" hits a 10. It isn't because of a Black Friday traffic spike, but because we realize we have built a system that trusts everyone, and the hackers are walking right in. We will shift our mindset from "Perimeter Defense" to "Zero Trust." We will learn why an "Allow List" is the only list that matters, how to automate compliance so it doesn't throttle velocity, and why we happily trade latency for the assurance that we haven't lost the keys to the kingdom.

In this chapter, we're going to cover the following main topics:

- **Security by Design:** Making "Zero Trust" the architectural standard.
- **Shifting Left:** Securing the development pipeline (SecDevOps).
- **Compliance Governance:** Implementing Policy-as-Code and automated auditing.
- **Identity Over Secrets:** Moving from shared passwords to Workload Identity.

Technical requirements

In this chapter, we stop coding for features and start coding for survival. To follow the evolution of the ShopFlow security architecture, you will need the following tools:

- **OpenSSL:** We will use this to generate self-signed certificates, simulating the **mutual TLS (mTLS)** handshake that effectively locks our internal doors.
- **HashiCorp Vault (or Docker Secrets):** You will need a secrets manager to demonstrate the removal of hardcoded credentials from the source code.
- **Open Policy Agent (OPA):** We will use OPA to write **Rego** policies, implementing "Policy-as-Code" to ensure our security rules are versioned and automated just like our application logic.
- **Code Repository:** The transition from the insecure "open door" version to the secured "Zero Trust" architecture is available at: `https://github.com/imran-siddique/Architecting-at-Scale/tree/main/ch3`

ShopFlow telemetry snapshot [stage 3]

We ended *Chapter 2* with a high-performing fleet. We begin *Chapter 3* in crisis. The metrics below represent the **"Compromised State"**—where the system is technically running but operationally compromised.

```
Availability: 40.0% (The site is effectively down for real users due to resource
exhaustion.)
Cloud Spend: $4,000/mo (Spiking—we are paying to process bot traffic)
```

Active Connections: 50,000+ (90% identified as malicious/bot traffic).

Latency (p99): 450ms (Technically good, but irrelevant if the site is unusable.)

```
Dave Alert: "The servers are healthy, but 90% of the traffic is garbage. I can't
tell friends from foes. I'm manually blocking IPs in the firewall, but they just
rotate and come back instantly. We are playing Whac-A-Mole, and we are losing."
```

The Signal: The **Perimeter has failed**. We can no longer rely on a "Hard Shell" firewall to protect a "Soft Center." We need to lock down every single node.

How did a high-performing fleet fall to 40%? The collapse was not gradual, and it was not bad luck—it was an attack on exactly the surface we exposed in *Chapter 2*.

Incident Timeline — 48 Hours to 40%: T+0h: *Chapter 2*'s horizontal scale-out left roughly fifty internal APIs reachable from the public internet. T+6h: automated scanners find the unauthenticated endpoints and begin credential-stuffing and catalogue-scraping. T+24h: bot traffic fills the connection pool, and availability for real users slips from 99.5% to about 90% as their requests queue behind bot requests. T+48h: the pool is saturated (50,000+ connections, ~90% malicious) and legitimate requests mostly time out, bottoming effective availability at 40%.

Manager's Math — The Cost of the Open Door: Cloud spend rose from $2,500/mo (Stage 2) to $4,000/mo—about $1,500/mo (~$18k/yr) burned purely processing bot traffic, while roughly 60% of legitimate requests failed. A Zero-Trust allowlist drops that traffic at the edge, reclaiming the $1,500/mo and the lost conversions. Even if mTLS and managed identity add on the order of $500/mo in service and ops cost, the net is about +$1,000/mo before counting recovered revenue. (The cost lines are ShopFlow's stated figures; the $500/mo control cost is an estimate to tune to your provider.)

This is why Dave can truthfully say the servers are healthy. CPU, memory, and the p99 for the requests we actually serve are all green—the fleet is doing exactly what it was built to do, just for the wrong clients. The 40% measures successful requests for legitimate users, and by that measure the site is down. Infrastructure health and user-facing availability have decoupled, and closing that gap is the entire reason for this chapter.

Nothing here is exotic. ShopFlow scaled before it secured—the most common sequencing in a fast-growing company. The lesson is not that 40% is far-fetched; it is that scaling an unauthenticated surface is precisely what turns one exposed endpoint into a chapter-long outage.

Security by design: making zero trust the architectural standard

The most dangerous phase in a startup's life is typically right after its first major scaling success. You have opened the floodgates to handle more users, but you have inadvertently invited the entire internet into your living room.

I have seen this pattern repeat constantly in the industry. A team celebrates "breaking the monolith," only to realize they have left anonymous access enabled on their databases. They have left administrative ports open to the public internet "for debugging." They have committed API keys and connection strings directly into the code repository.

This is the "Open Door" problem. It isn't usually a sophisticated nation-state attack; it's just **craziness**. It's the result of prioritizing "Can we build it?" over "Should we allow it?"

To survive this stage, we must adopt a new standard: **Zero Trust**.

The "allowlist" mantra

"Zero Trust" is a buzzword that vendors use to sell expensive VPNs. I want to give you a pragmatic, engineer's definition.

Zero Trust simply means: **By default, block everything.**

The Three Principles of Zero Trust: Underneath the allow-list tactic sits an industry-recognized framework, formalized in NIST SP 800-207. Three principles drive every decision in this chapter:

Verify Explicitly: authenticate and authorize every request from identity and context, never from network location. ShopFlow's Inventory service verifies the Cart service's identity on every call, even though both run inside the same network.

Use Least-Privilege Access: grant the minimum scope, ideally just-in-time. The Cart service may read inventory but can never write to the users table, so a leaked Cart credential cannot reach customer PII.

Assume Breach: design as if an attacker is already inside—segment the network, encrypt traffic end-to-end, and log every hop—so a single compromised node cannot pivot to the rest of the fleet.

Principle	What does it mean?	In ShopFlow
Verify explicitly	Authenticate and authorize every request from identity and context	Inventory verifies the Cart service's identity on every call
Use Least-Privilege Access	Grant the minimum scope just-in-time	Cart can read inventory but never write users/PII
Assume Breach	Design as if the attacker is already inside	Segment, encrypt end-to-end, and log every hop

Table 3.1: The three Zero Trust principles mapped to ShopFlow.

This is why identity must be proven on every hop rather than inferred from origin—a requirement that only sharpens as AI agents generate and deploy more of our code and "who made this call" can no longer be assumed from where it came.

In the old days, we used "denylists." We tried to identify the bad guys (IPs, User Agents) and block them. This is a losing game. You cannot list every bad actor on the internet; there are too many of them, and they change too fast.

Listing every bad actor on the internet is impossible; listing the handful of known-good ones is not.

We are moving to the **Allow List**.

The philosophy is simple: **No one is allowed.** Not the user, not the admin, and definitely not the "Inventory Service."

When an architect asks, "How do we secure this?", the answer is always:

1. Block all access by default.
2. Ask: "What is the *minimum* access required to make this feature work?"
3. Add exactly that—and nothing more—to the Allow List.

If Service A needs to talk to Service B, we don't open the port to the network. We explicitly allow ***only*** Service A to talk to Service B, on ***only*** that specific port, using ***only*** a specific certificate.

The latency tax: why we compromise on speed

Implementing this level of security—where every single internal request must be authenticated and authorized—comes with a cost. It introduces friction. It adds computational overhead for TLS handshakes. It adds network roundtrips for token validation.

A skeptic will look at the design for mTLS (mutual TLS) and say, "Imran, this is going to add 20 ms to every request. We are trying to be fast!"

Tool Tax — mTLS: Beyond the ~20ms per-hop latency, mutual TLS adds a certificate lifecycle: issuing, distributing, rotating, and revoking a cert for every service. A single expired cert silently breaks a connection, so you trade an open network for a new operational discipline—automated issuance and short cert lifetimes are not optional.

Manager's Math — Paying 80ms to Close the Perimeter: mTLS adds ~20ms per hop, so a four-hop request pays ~80ms. Weigh that against the incident it prevents: 48 hours at 40% availability. Predictable, linear latency on every request is a cost you can budget; an open internal network is an unbounded liability. We take the 80ms.

My response is always the same: **If you are compromised, you are gone.**

Speed is a luxury; security is a requirement. If your database is leaked, nobody cares that your checkout page loaded in 200ms. They care that you lost their credit card number.

We will optimize for latency later (in *Chapter 9*). Right now, we accept the "Latency Tax" as the cost of doing business. We happily trade milliseconds for the certainty that our system is not an open door.

Alternative Architecture—The Service Mesh Shortcut

The Dilemma: Implementing mTLS directly in your application code (e.g., using Node.js tls libraries) gives you maximum control, but it creates "Code Bloat." Every developer has to understand certificates.

The Alternative: Service Mesh (Istio, Linkerd, Consul). Instead of your code handling the encryption, you run a tiny "Sidecar Proxy" next to your application container. Your app talks to the proxy via plain HTTP (localhost), and the proxy handles the mTLS handshake with the outside world.

The Trade-off:

Code-Level mTLS (Our Choice): Simpler infrastructure, harder for developers. Best for teams who want "less magic" and fewer moving parts in Kubernetes.

Aspect	Code-level mTLS (our choice)	Service mesh (sidecar)
Infrastructure	Simpler — no mesh to run	Heavier—sidecars plus a control plane
Developer burden	Higher — handled in app code	Lower — transparent to the app
Best for	Small fleets that want less magic	Large fleets that want a uniform policy
Operational tax	Certificate handling in code	Mesh upgrades and sidecar resource costs

Table 3.2: Code-level mTLS versus a service mesh

Service Mesh: Zero developer effort, massive infrastructure complexity. Best for large Platform Engineering teams who can manage the overhead of a mesh. For ShopFlow, we stick to code-level mTLS to keep our infrastructure "Boring" (see *Chapter 1*).

Visualizing the shift: the castle vs. the hotel

To understand the architectural shift we are making, we need to change our mental model of defense.

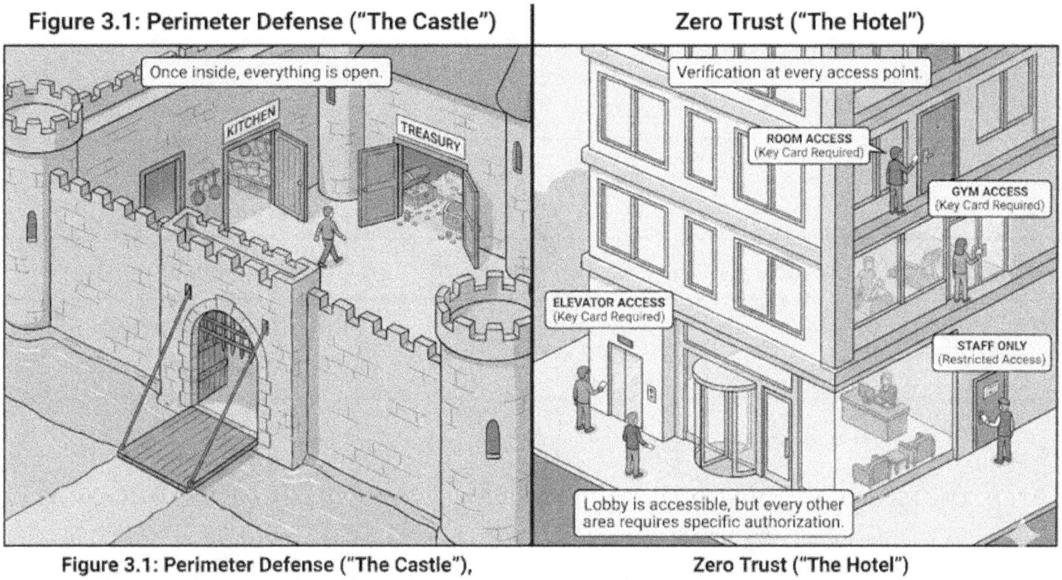

Figure 3.1: Perimeter Defense ("The Castle") vs. Zero Trust ("The Hotel").

Zero Trust in Practice — a single ShopFlow request: Trace one "add to cart" click and watch where trust is checked at every arrow:

1. Customer → API Gateway: the gateway validates the user's signed session token (JWT) and rejects anything unsigned or expired.
2. API Gateway → Auth Service: the gateway presents its own workload identity; Auth confirms the token's scope permits a cart write.
3. Auth Service → Inventory Service: the call runs over mutual TLS; each side validates the other's certificate before any payload is read.
4. Inventory Service → Database: the service connects with its own least-privilege credential (read inventory, write cart, nothing else) over an encrypted channel.

At every hop, identity is proven, authorization is checked, and the channel is verified. No hop trusts the previous one merely because it is "inside."

Dimension	Perimeter Defense ("Castle")	Zero Trust ("Hotel")
Trust boundary	One hard outer wall	Every door, every hop
Once inside	Free movement to any system	Re-verified at each resource
Internal traffic	Implicitly trusted	Authenticated and encrypted (mTLS)
Blast radius of one breach	The entire network	A single service or resource
Core assumption	Attackers are outside	Assume breach; an attacker may be inside

Table 3.3: Perimeter defense ("Castle") versus Zero Trust ("Hotel").

- **The Medieval Castle (Left):** This is the old way. You have a massive wall (Firewall) and a moat. It is very hard to get in. But once you cross the drawbridge, you are inside. You can walk into the kitchen, the armory, or the King's bedroom. There are no internal locks. This works until someone finds a way over the wall (or bribes the guard). Once they are in, they own everything.
- **The Modern Hotel (Right):** This is Zero Trust. You might get into the lobby (the Public Web Layer), but that doesn't get you into the rooms. To use the elevator, you need a key card. To enter your room, you need a key card. To get into the gym, you need a key card. Even the cleaning staff have restricted access. If an attacker steals a key card for Room 204, they can *only* get into Room 204. They cannot access the safe in the Manager's Office.

For ShopFlow, our goal is to turn our "Castle" into a "Hotel." Every service—Cart, Auth, Inventory—is a locked room. And we are about to start issuing the key cards.

The Architect's prompt 3.1: the open door audit

When to use this: Right after exposing or scaling new services, to find every endpoint reachable without authentication before an attacker does.

```
"Act as a Security Engineer performing a 'White Box' penetration test. Review the
following docker-compose.yml and server.js file.
Task:
```

```
Identify 'Implicit Trust' Assumptions: Flag any service-to-service communication
that relies solely on 'being on the same network' (e.g., connecting to a database
without SSL or accepting HTTP requests from any IP).
Locate the Secrets: Find any environment variables or hardcoded strings that look
like API keys or passwords.
Generate an 'Allow List' Policy: Rewrite the network configuration to explicitly
deny all ingress traffic by default, and output the specific allow rules needed
for the web service to talk to the api service only."
```

Shifting left: securing the development pipeline (SecDevOps)

We just established that the "Perimeter" is dead. If we can't trust the network, we have to trust the code.

But code is written by humans, and humans make mistakes.

In *Chapter 2*, we discussed the "Panic Meter" hitting 10. The cause wasn't a sophisticated zero-day exploit; it was a developer committing an AWS Secret Key to a public GitHub repository. Within minutes, bots scraped the repo, grabbed the key, and spun up 500 crypto-mining instances on our dime.

This happened because we treated security as a "Gateway" at the end of the process. We wrote the code, built the app, and then waited for a "Security Review" (or a hack) to find the problems.

We need to **Shift Left**.

The "software engineer" reality

There is a lot of buzz around "SecDevOps." People treat it like a new job title. It isn't.

DevSecOps or SecDevOps? The two terms are used interchangeably; the word order signals emphasis, not a different practice. "DevSecOps" is the more common label and stresses folding security into an existing DevOps flow; "SecDevOps" front-loads security to argue it belongs before the first line of code. The substance—security as a shared, automated, everyone-owns-it responsibility rather than a final gate—is identical. This book uses the two as synonyms.

If you look at the evolution of our industry, it tells a clear story:

- **Era 1:** We had Software Engineers and Testers. Then we realized handing off code created bugs, so we made Engineers do the testing.

- **Era 2:** We had Developers and Ops. Then we realized handing off deployment created outages, so we made Engineers do the Ops (DevOps).
- **Era 3 (Now):** We have Engineers and Security. And just like before, handing off security creates vulnerabilities.

The reality—whether you like it or not—is that if you author the system, you secure the system. You are the one who will be woken up at 3 AM when the database leaks. If you design the system well, you sleep well. If you rely on an external team to "sprinkle security" on top of your bad code, you don't.

Guardrails: the "mistake reversal" system

We know mistakes will happen. I have committed keys. You have committed keys. The goal isn't to be perfect; the goal is to ensure the mistake cannot survive.

We need **Automated Guardrails**.

These guardrails shouldn't be a manual checklist; they must be systemic. We use **Pre-Commit Hooks** (using tools like Husky) and **CI/CD Scanners** (like TruffleHog or Gitleaks) that act as the first line of defense.

But since this book is future-looking, we are going further. We are using **AI Guardrails**.

We can deploy a lightweight AI agent in our pipeline that doesn't just look for regex patterns (like AWS_ACCESS_KEY) but understands context. It looks for "past mistakes" to ensure they aren't repeated.

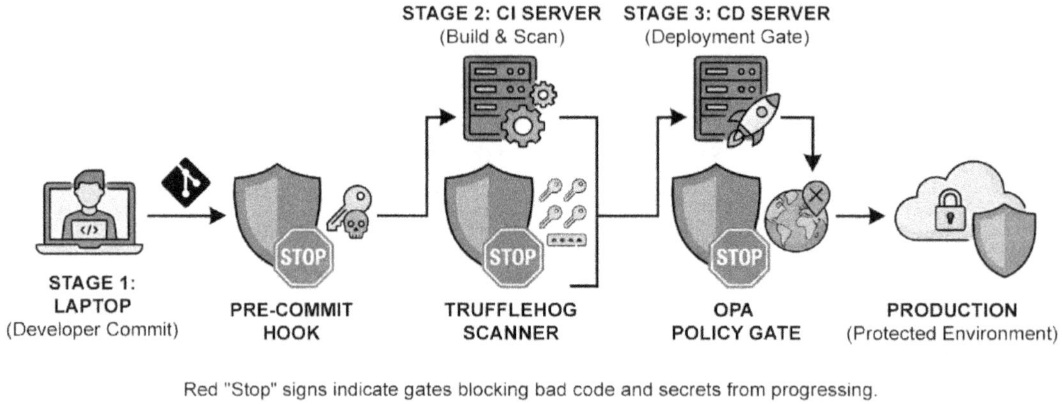

Figure 3.2: The "Defense in Depth" Pipeline.

Figure 3.2 illustrates where the battles are fought.

- **The Laptop (Cheapest Fix):** The pre-commit hook catches the API key *before* it leaves the developer's machine. Cost: $0.

- **The CI Server (Cheap Fix):** The scanner catches it in the Pull Request. Cost: 10 minutes of developer time.
- **Production (Expensive Fix):** If we wait until here, the cost is a data breach.

The "safe change" rollout: dogfooding security

The "Shadow Credential" problem is tricky. Let's say we have hardcoded API keys in our code (the "bad" way) and we want to move to HashiCorp Vault (the "good" way).

If you just rip out the hardcoded keys and deploy the Vault code to production, you will crash into the site. The Vault connection might fail, the permissions might be wrong, or the latency might be too high.

We manage this risk using **Environmental Tiers (The Ring Model)**:

1. **Test Environment:** The "Wild West." This is where we break things. We deploy the Vault integration here first. If it fails, only the team knows.
2. **Dogfood Environment (Trusted Users):** This is the "Basic Minimum" environment. It handles real traffic, but a small group of trusted users (often employees or beta customers) who know the system might break. We use this to test the "Happy Path" with real network conditions but non-critical data.
3. **Production:** Only after the Dogfood ring is stable do we promote the change to the global fleet.

We don't just "switch" to the new security model; we prove it works in the Dogfood ring first.

The Architect's prompt 3.2: the AI guardrails

When to use this: When you want to stop your team (or an AI coding agent) from repeating a known security mistake by encoding it as an automated guardrail.

```
"Act as a DevSecOps Engineer. I want to prevent my team from repeating past
security mistakes."
Task:
Analyze this list of 'Post-Mortem' summaries from our last 3 security incidents
(e.g., 'committed API key', 'open S3 bucket', 'SQL injection in search').
Generate a custom 'Semgrep' rule or a Python script that scans a Pull Request
specifically for these patterns.
Create a 'Pre-Commit' hook script that runs this scanner locally before git commit
is allowed. The hook should provide a friendly error message explaining why the
commit was blocked."
```

Compliance governance: Policy-as-Code and automated auditing

We have locked the doors (Zero Trust) and checked the builders (SecDevOps). But now we face the "Auditor's Knock."

In a startup, "Compliance" sounds like a boring stack of paperwork. In a scaling enterprise, it is the difference between staying in business and being shut down by a regulator.

You cannot "manually verify" that 50 microservices are GDPR compliant. If you are relying on humans to check spreadsheets to see who has access to the database, you have already failed.

We need **Automated Governance**.

The Non-Negotiables: audit trails and PII

Tool Tax — Audit Trails: Logging every privileged action is non-negotiable for compliance, but audit logs are high-volume, must themselves be tamper-resistant and access-controlled, and carry storage and retention cost. Budget for the pipeline, not just the toggle.

There are two things you simply cannot compromise on: **Auditing** and **PII Protection**.

1. **Auditing (The "Who" and "When"):** If something goes wrong—and it will—you must be able to reconstruct the crime scene. Who changed the permissions? Who accessed the "Purchase History" table? Who deployed the broken container? This isn't just about debugging; it is about accountability. Every access control decision must leave a footprint.
2. **PII (The "What" and "Where"):** As ShopFlow scales globally, we are holding sensitive customer data (names, addresses, credit cards). Regulations like GDPR are not suggestions; they are laws. If a customer asks to be forgotten, or if a German user's data accidentally lands on a US server, there is no "way out." You either built the system to handle it, or you pay the fine.

Policy-as-Code: replacing PDFs with Rego

In the old world, "Security Policy" was a PDF document stored on a wiki that nobody read. It said things like, "All databases must be encrypted."

In the new world, **Policy is Code**.

We use tools like **Open Policy Agent (OPA)** to turn those PDF rules into executable code (Rego). We store these policies in Git, version them, and enforce them automatically.

What is Rego? Rego is OPA's declarative policy language. Instead of writing imperative checks, you declare what is allowed or denied and OPA evaluates the rule against input data (a deployment spec, an API request, a Terraform plan). A rule that blocks any unencrypted database is only a few lines:

```
package shopflow.deploy

# Deny any database resource that is not encrypted
deny[msg] {
input.resource.type == "database"
input.resource.encryption == false
msg := sprintf("database %v must have encryption enabled", [input.resource.name])
}
```

Checked into Git and run in CI, this rule fails the build the moment someone proposes an unencrypted database. The PDF policy nobody read becomes a test nobody can skip.

- **Old Way:** The Security team reviews the architecture diagram and asks, "Is the DB encrypted?"
- **New Way (ShopFlow):** The deployment pipeline runs an OPA check. If encryption_enabled = false in the Terraform plan, the build fails.

Aspect	Old Way (PDF policy + review)	New Way (Policy-as-Code / OPA)
Where it lives	A wiki PDF nobody reads	Rego rules in Git, versioned
Enforcement	A human asks, "Is the DB encrypted?"	CI fails the build automatically
Auditability	Manual, point-in-time	Continuous on every deploy
Bypass	Easy to forget or skip	Cannot merge without passing

Table 3.4: Manual policy review versus policy-as-code with OPA.

This fits our "AI-First" mindset perfectly. AI is nothing but a code generator. We don't want manual verification; we want the system to enforce the rules. We feed our plain-text requirements ("No public S3 buckets") to the AI, and it generates the OPA policy code for us.

Note

Info Box: Alternative Tooling—Cloud-Native Policy vs. OPA

The Question: "Why should I learn OPA (Rego) when I can just use **AWS Config** or **Azure Policy**?"

The Reality: Cloud-native tools are excellent for *Infrastructure* (e.g., "Ensure all RDS instances are encrypted"), but they are blind to your *Application Logic.*

- **Azure Policy/AWS Config:** Great for "Hardware" rules. They can stop you from creating a public load balancer.
- **Open Policy Agent (OPA):** The Universal Standard. OPA works inside Kubernetes, inside your Terraform, and even inside your Application Code (e.g., "Can User A see Document B?").

Tool	Strength	Limitation
Cloud-native (AWS Config / Azure Policy)	Great for infrastructure rules; no extra service to run	Cloud-specific; weak across the app layer and multi-cloud
Open Policy Agent (OPA)	One policy language across Kubernetes, Terraform, and app APIs; portable	A new language (Rego) and a policy engine to run and maintain it

Table 3.5: Policy and authorization tools compared by strength and limitation.

Tool Tax — OPA/Rego: You gain portable, testable policy, but you add a declarative language (Rego) for the team to learn and a policy engine in the deploy path. A misconfigured policy can block every deployment, so the gate that protects you can also stop you—policies need their own tests and a break-glass path.

Note

The Verdict: If you are 100% on one cloud and only care about infrastructure, use the native tool. If you want a single policy language that governs everything from your API Gateway to your Kubernetes Pods, OPA is the only scalable choice.

The "break glass" protocol: emergency access

A rigid security system is great until the site goes down at 3:00 AM.

If your "Zero Trust" policy says "No SSH access to production," and the database is corrupt, you cannot just let the business burn because the policy says so. You need an emergency exit. We call this the **Break Glass** protocol.

However, "Break Glass" does not mean "Anarchy."

We define "Break Glass" as a high-friction, highly-audited path. It is acceptable *only* when we have **Multiple Approvals** in place.

The Workflow:

1. **Request:** The engineer requests "Emergency Admin Access" via a CLI tool or ChatOps bot.
2. **Verification:** The system pings the on-call Manager (or a peer).
3. **Fast Approval:** The Manager clicks "Approve" (this must be instant—seconds, not hours).
4. **Access Granted:** The engineer gets a temporary, time-bound certificate (1 hour) to fix the issue.
5. **The Audit:** Every command typed during that session is logged.

Even in an emergency, we do not bypass the *audit*; we only bypass the *process latency*.

The Architect's prompt 3.3: the policy enforcer

When to use this: When a compliance requirement (GDPR, PII handling, encryption) must be enforced automatically in CI rather than checked by hand in review.

```
Act as a Compliance Engineer. I need to enforce GDPR Data Residency rules using
Open Policy Agent (OPA).
Task:
Write a Rego policy for Kubernetes that blocks any Deployment if the region label
does not match the customer_data_location label. (e.g., German customer data
cannot be deployed to a US-East pod).
Create a 'Break Glass' exception rule: Allow the deployment ONLY if the annotation
emergency-override: true is present AND the approver field is filled.
Generate a 'Audit Log' JSON structure that would be emitted whenever this policy
denies a request, so we can track who tried to break the rules."
```

Managing secrets, credentials, and Least-Privilege access

We have secured the network and the pipeline. Now we must secure the *keys.*

In a distributed system, "Secret Sprawl" is a plague. You find database passwords in .env files, API keys in Slack messages, and connection strings hardcoded in Dockerfiles.

Tool Tax — Secrets Manager: A vault removes secrets from your code, but it becomes a tier-0 dependency: if the vault is unavailable, applications cannot fetch credentials and fail to start. You inherit its high-availability, sealing, and access-audit burden. Centralizing the risk is safer —but it is not free.

The problem isn't just that these secrets are exposed; it's that we are managing them at all— we should not be in the secret management business in the first place.

The Golden Rule: Get Out of the Secret Business

My golden rule for secret management is simple: You should never be in the business of managing secrets.

If you are manually encrypting strings or pasting keys into environment variables, you have already lost. We delegate this entire responsibility to a dedicated service like Azure Key Vault (or HashiCorp Vault/AWS Secrets Manager).

The workflow changes from "Ownership" to "Reference":

- **Old Way:** The application config has DB_PASSWORD="SuperSecret123".
- **New Way:** The application config has KeyVault_Reference="db-secret-prod".

Aspect	**Old Way (hardcoded secret)**	**New Way (Vault + Workload Identity)**
Where the secret lives	In config, env vars, or code	In a vault, fetched at runtime
Rotation	Manual and rare	Automated and frequent
Exposure if leaked	Long-lived, broad access	Short-lived, narrowly scoped

Aspect	Old Way (hardcoded secret)	New Way (Vault + Workload Identity)
Who can read it	Anyone with the repo or host	Only the workload's own identity

Table 3.6: Hardcoded secrets versus Vault with workload identity.

At runtime, the application authenticates with the Vault and retrieves the secret in memory. It never touches the disk. And crucially, **secrets are never shared across environments**. Development, Test, and Production each have their own isolated Vaults. If a developer accidentally leaks a key, they have only leaked the "Dev" key, which accesses nothing of value.

Identity over secrets: workload identity

The most "contrarian" shift we are making in ShopFlow is moving away from *Shared Secrets* to *Workload Identity*.

Tool Tax — Workload Identity: Replacing shared secrets with platform identity ties you more tightly to your identity provider and makes local development and cross-environment testing harder (there is no password to copy). The payoff—no long-lived credential to steal—is worth it, but federation and short-lived tokens add moving parts.

In a traditional setup, the "Cart Service" connects to the database using a username and password. This is a "Shared Secret." If an attacker steals that password, they *become* the Cart Service.

We are replacing this with **Identity**.

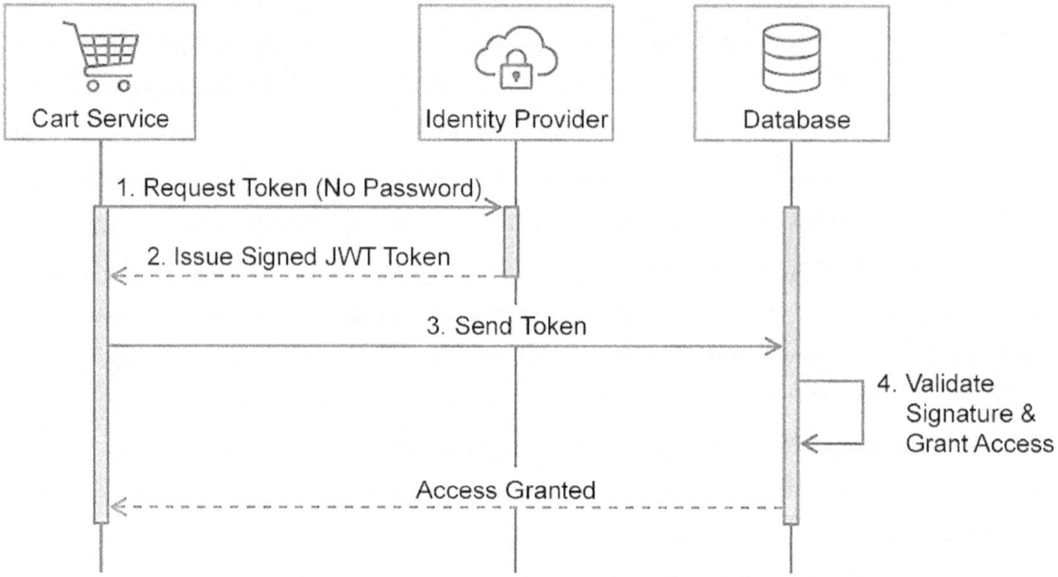

Figure 3.3: The Workload Identity Handshake.

In our Zero Trust architecture, the "Cart Service" doesn't have a password. It has an **Identity** (a Managed Identity or a short-lived Service Principal).

When the Cart Service tries to talk to the Database, the conversation looks like this:

1. **Cart Service:** "Hello, I am identity:cart-service-prod. Here is my signed token from the Identity Provider."
2. **Database:** "I verified your signature. I see that identity:cart-service-prod has permission to SELECT from the carts table. Access granted."

We are not passing a password; we are proving an identity. This allows the Database to manage permissions ("Who can access me?") without the Cart Service having to manage secrets ("What is the password?").

Automated rotation: the "reasonable" standard

How often should you rotate credentials? The industry answer used to be "every 90 days" because that was how long a human could tolerate changing their password.

For machines, we don't care about tolerance. We care about risk window.

If a machine credential is stolen, how long is it valid?

- **Human Standards:** Stick to the industry mark (e.g., 90 days) to avoid fatigue.
- **Machine Standards:** Automate it aggressively. If we use Workload Identity and Vaults, we can rotate secrets **daily** or even **hourly** (using Short-Lived Tokens).

For ShopFlow, we will adopt the "Short-Lived" standard for all machine-to-machine communication. If an attacker steals a token, it will expire before they can figure out how to use it.

The Architect's prompt 3.4: the identity conversion

When to use this: When migrating a service off hardcoded secrets and environment variable keys onto workload identity and a managed secrets vault.

```
"Act as a Cloud Security Architect. I am refactoring a legacy Node.js service to
use Azure Key Vault instead of .env files."
Task:
Scan the code for any process.env.PASSWORD or process.env.API_KEY patterns.
Generate a refactoring plan that replaces these lines with a SecretClient fetch
call using the Azure SDK (or generic Vault equivalent).
Write a Terraform snippet to create a 'Managed Identity' for this app and grant it
Get and List permissions on the Key Vault, adhering to the Principle of Least
Privilege."
```

Summary

In this chapter, we brought the system back under control. We moved ShopFlow from a "Trust-by-Default" open network to a "Zero Trust" fortress.

- We implemented **mTLS** to turn our network into a hotel with key cards.
- We **Shifted Left** to catch security bugs before they hit the repo.
- We replaced PDF policies with **Policy-as-Code** to satisfy the auditors.
- We adopted **Workload Identity** to eliminate the risk of stolen passwords.

We are now secure. But we are also heavy.

A closing thought ties this chapter back to the through-line of the book: security is not a separate discipline bolted on at the end—it is a precondition for scale. Every control introduced here (workload identity, policy-as-code, least-privilege access, end-to-end observability) exists so that later scaling decisions are safe to make. Identity lets us add nodes without widening the attack surface; policy-as-code lets us grow the team without growing risk; least privilege contains the blast radius of the failures that scale inevitably brings. Done well, security does not slow engineering down—it is what makes fast, confident scaling possible at all.

The cliffhanger: the "shielded" bottleneck

We have successfully locked down the system. The "Panic Meter" has dropped back to zero. The hackers are bouncing off our mTLS shields.

But as we look at our monitoring dashboards, a new red light starts blinking.

Our users in London and Tokyo are complaining. The site is secure, but it is *slow*.

Every request now does a TLS handshake. Every database call verifies an identity token. Every deployment checks 50 compliance rules. We have paid the "Latency Tax," and it is compounding.

Worse, our "Zero Trust" protections have consolidated all traffic through a few heavily guarded checkpoints. We have secured the front door, but we've forced the entire world to walk through a single metal detector.

Our database is safe, but it is straining under the overhead of our own security. We have built a fortress, but we forgot to build a highway.

In *Chapter 4*, we must leave the safety of our Virginia data center and push our fortress to the Edge.

References

- HashiCorp Vault — secrets management and dynamic credentials: `https://www.vaultproject.io/`
- OpenSSL — TLS and certificate tooling: `https://www.openssl.org/`
- Open Policy Agent (OPA) and the Rego language: `https://www.openpolicyagent.org/`
- NIST SP 800-207, Zero Trust Architecture — the canonical definition of the three principles: `https://doi.org/10.6028/NIST.SP.800-207`

Subscribe to Deep Engineering

Scan the QR or visit the link to subscribe for free.

`https://packt.link/deep-engineering-newsletter`

Part 2

Scaling the Interface: From Edge to User

Scaling does not start at the server. It starts at the user's device and the network in between. This part moves ShopFlow's experience closer to the people using it. You will push content and logic out to the global edge so that a user in Singapore is not punished by the speed of light, and you will break a heavyweight front-end monolith into independently shippable micro-frontends so that one team's bug can no longer take down everyone else's release. By the end of this part, the interface is fast everywhere and the teams behind it can ship without stepping on each other.

This part of the book includes the following chapters:

- *Chapter 4, Scaling the Global Delivery Layer: Edge, CDNs, and Beyond*
- *Chapter 5, Scaling the Modern Web Application: State, Performance, and Micro-Frontends*

4

Scaling the Global Delivery Layer - Edge, CDNs, and Beyond

In *Chapter 3*, we successfully moved ShopFlow from a "Trust-by-Default" open network to a "Zero Trust" fortress. We celebrated the victory of securing our "Hotel" with mutual TLS and automated governance, ensuring that every internal door was locked.

But in our rush to build a secure fortress, we made a significant trade-off.

By consolidating our traffic through heavily guarded checkpoints in a single data center, we created a **Shielded Bottleneck**. We secured the front door, but we created a serialized verification bottleneck where every global request competes for the same authentication compute cycles in Virginia. We forgot that while security is a requirement, the speed of light is a hard physical limit.

We didn't just scale our integrity; we scaled our latency.

In this chapter, the "Panic Meter" hits a 7. It isn't because of a security breach, but because our global users in London and Tokyo are staring at loading spinners. We will shift our mindset from "Centralized Security" to the **Edge Revolution**. We will learn why the **Static-First Rule** is the only way to protect a saturated database, how to manage the **Consistency Tax** without lying to our users, and why we use **Predictive Prefetching** to beat the user to the next click.

In this chapter, we're going to cover the following main topics:

- **The Edge Revolution**: Moving from static caching to edge computation.
- **Protocol Scaling**: How HTTP/3 and QUIC solve head-of-line blocking.
- **Global Consistency**: Managing cache invalidation and the "Truth Problem".

- **Origin Protection**: Designing for the "Thundering Herd" and cache stampedes.
- **Traffic Steering**: Global Server Load Balancing (GSLB) and self-healing routing.

Technical requirements

To follow the transition from a centralized data center to a global Edge, you will need:

- **Node.js (v18+):** For origin services.
- **Wrangler (Cloudflare) or AWS SAM:** To simulate **Edge Functions** locally.
- **Nginx:** Configured as an **Origin Shield**.
- **cURL / OpenSSL:** To analyze **TLS Handshake** timings and HTTP/3 headers.
- **Code Repository:** `https://github.com/imran-siddique/Architecting-at-Scale/tree/main/ch4`.

ShopFlow telemetry snapshot [stage 4]

> Note
>
> **The Signal:** We are technically secure, but geographically failing. Our "Single Straw" database is struggling with the overhead of our own shields.

```
Availability: 92.0% (Intermittent—Database is straining under security overhead)
p99 Latency (NYC): 120ms (Acceptable)
p99 Latency (London): 850ms (Warning)
p99 Latency (Singapore): 1.4s (Critical—High Abandonment)
TCP/TLS Handshake Latency: 300ms (Global Average—The cost of mTLS)
Cloud Spend: $4,500/mo (Rising due to inefficient origin fetches)
Panic Meter: 7/10 (The CFO is asking why "safe" feels so "slow.")
Systemic Risk (Observability Gap): Downstream telemetry confirms web nodes are
idle while awaiting database I/O, indicating a 'Single Straw' bottleneck in the
data tier.
```

The edge revolution: moving from static caching to edge computing

The most common anti-pattern in high-scale architecture is the "Dynamic-By-Default" bias. Engineers often assume that because a page contains a user's name or a stock level, the entire HTML response must be generated fresh from the origin database. This is a scaling trap.

The Static-First Rule

The Static-First Rule mandates: Treat every request as cacheable until proven otherwise. For ShopFlow, this means we stop serving a "loading spinner" while the backend grinds. Instead, we serve a cached, global version of the page immediately, then "hydrate" the dynamic bits asynchronously.

We differentiate between **Live Data** (high-frequency feeds) and **Sturdy Data** (documentation, tutorials, or product descriptions). Since we aren't building a social network, almost 90% of our footprint can be moved to the Edge.

> Note
>
> **The Golden Rule:** Availability beats freshness. It is better to show a customer a product with a 60-second-old price than to show them a 404 error or a 5-second timeout.

When NOT to Cache: The Static-First Rule has hard exceptions. Never serve cached data for the moments where stale equals wrong: checkout totals and payment confirmation, inventory reservation and stock counts at add-to-cart, and anything personalized (account pages, order history, saved carts). For these, read through to the source of truth on every request and cache only the shell around them. The rule is narrow on purpose—cache the catalog, never the transaction.

Content	**Cache at the edge?**	**Why**
Product catalog, images	Yes	Rarely changes; huge offload
Reviews, recommendations	Yes, short TTL	Staleness is cheap
Checkout total, payment confirmation	No	Stale = wrong charge
Inventory count at add-to-cart	No	Stale = oversell
Account, order history	No	Personalized and sensitive

Table 4.1: What to cache at the edge, and what not to.

Architect's prompt 4.2: the cache policy audit

When to use this: When deciding what to push to the edge and you need to separate safely cacheable content from must-be-fresh content before configuring the CDN.

Act as a CDN architect. Here are my application's routes and the data each returns. Classify each as static/cacheable, cacheable-with-short-TTL, or never-cache, with a one-line reason. Flag any route that mixes personalized and public data in one response and suggest how to split it so the public shell can still be cached.

> Note
>
> **Anti-Pattern: The Zombie Edge:**
>
> Scaling by subtraction applies to the Edge just as much as the core. A common failure is treating the Edge as a dumping ground for legacy redirects and "temporary" geography-based logic. Every line of code running at the Edge adds Transitive Weight to the request. If you don't prune unused Edge functions, you aren't scaling; you're just moving your technical debt 10 ms closer to the user.

Origin Protection: Designing for the "Thundering Herd"

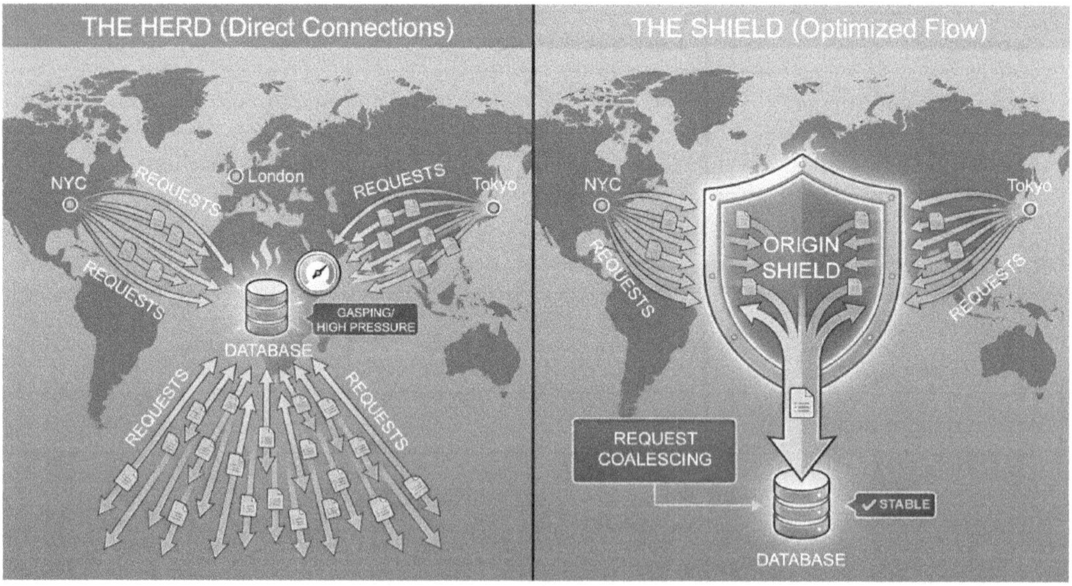

Figure 4.1: The Origin Shield vs. The Thundering Herd

As we move to a global fleet of 50+ nodes, we encounter the **Single Straw** problem: all those nodes fighting over one database. Caching at the Edge helps, but it introduces the **Cache Stampede**.

Imagine 50,000 users hitting a popular product drop. If your cache expires at that exact millisecond, all 50,000 requests will bypass the Edge and hit your origin database simultaneously. To prevent this, we implement an **Origin Shield**.

Feature	Without Origin Shield	With Origin Shield
Cache Miss Impact	All requests hit the database.	Shield collapses 50,000 requests into 1.
DB Load	Exponential spikes.	Linear and predictable.
Availability	High risk of "Flash Outage.".	Protected by a dedicated caching tier.

Table 4.2: Edge behavior with and without Origin Shield.

Tool Tax — Origin Shield: A shield is another layer to operate. Budget for cache warming (a cold shield after a deploy or purge still stampedes the origin), deliberate regional placement (put the shield near the origin, not the user), a new failure point (if the shield tier degrades, every region funnels back to the origin at once), and dedicated monitoring (shield hit ratio and origin offload are the metrics that prove it is working). A shield earns its keep only when you watch it.

Manager's Math — The Shield Pays for Itself: During a cache-miss storm, the shield collapses tens of thousands of simultaneous origin requests into a single origin fetch—a near-total reduction in origin load at the worst possible moment. One shield node (a small fixed cost) removes the need to over-provision the database for peak miss traffic and eliminates the flash-outage risk entirely. The shield is far cheaper than the database tier it protects.

Manager's Math: The Premium Trap

A common pitfall is attempting to solve latency by simply buying a "Premium Tier" from your cloud provider. While tempting, **Paying for Premium** is not a scalable business model.

- **Margin Erosion**: As your service costs increase, your profit margins shrink, making you less competitive.

- **The Complexity Ceiling**: Premium hardware still has a "Hardware Ceiling" (as we saw in *Chapter 1*).
- **Strategic ROI**: Investing engineering labor into **Edge Compute** allows us to use the cheapest possible origin infrastructure while providing a world-class global experience.

> Note
>
> **The Maintenance Tax:**
>
> You cannot push logic to the Edge without accepting an increase in Deployment Complexity. Every Edge worker introduces a new distributed state that requires version synchronization. This is Strategic Debt we are taking on to buy lower latency.

Global consistency: managing the "truth problem" at scale

Moving logic to the Edge solves the speed of light problem, but it creates a **Management Crisis**. Once you distribute data across 200+ global locations, you encounter the **Consistency Tax**.

The truth problem: managing distributed state

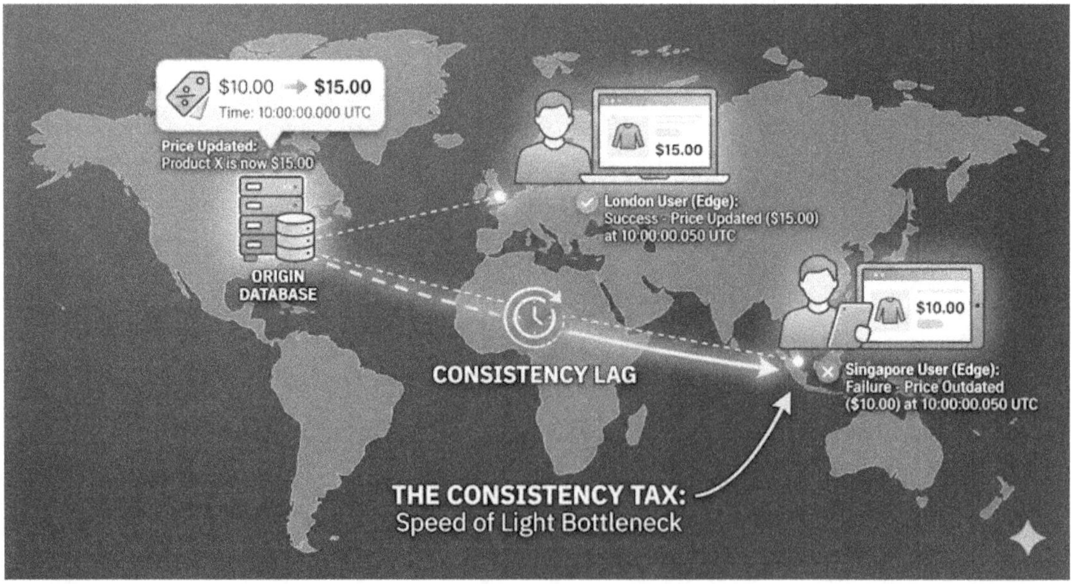

Figure 4.2: The Consistency Tax – Global State Lag

We must manage **Consistency Lag**, where different parts of the world see slightly different versions of the truth for a few milliseconds.

Strategy	Performance	Complexity	Use Case
Strong Consistency	Low (Global locks)	High	Financial transactions.
Eventual Consistency	High (Edge speed)	Moderate	Product descriptions, reviews. +1
Read-Your-Writes	Moderate	Moderate	User profile updates.

Table 4.3: Cache consistency strategies compared.

Choosing a Consistency Model: Read the table as a decision tool, not a menu. If stale data loses money or breaks correctness—payments, inventory, balances—prefer stronger consistency and pay the latency. If stale data merely delays information—product copy, reviews, recommendations—optimize for performance and let the edge serve eventually-consistent reads. Read-Your-Writes sits in between: use it wherever a user must see their own change immediately (a profile edit, a just-placed order) while other users can lag.

Architect's prompt 4.3: the consistency model selector

When to use this: When choosing a consistency model for a specific data type and you want the trade-off made explicit rather than defaulting to strong consistency everywhere.

"Act as a distributed-systems reviewer. For each data type below (product price, inventory count, review text, user profile), recommend strong/read-your-writes/eventual consistency, state the user-visible failure mode of getting it wrong, and note where stale data costs money versus merely delays information."

The invalidation problem

The hardest part of scaling at the Edge is getting data out when it's wrong. We utilize **Event-Driven Purging** to maintain a "fresh" global state. Instead of waiting for a **TTL (Time-to-Live)** to expire, we fire a "Purge" event to the global Edge the second a price changes in the database.

As Phil Karlton put it: "There are only two hard things in Computer Science: cache invalidation and naming things." Edge caching makes the first one global—a wrong price no longer sits in one cache, it sits in forty, and every one of them has to be told.

Invalidation strategy	**Freshness**	**Trade-off**
TTL expiry	Stale up to the TTL	Simple and predictable
Event-driven purge	Near-instant on change	Needs reliable purge fanout to every edge
Stale-while-revalidate	Serves stale, refreshes in the background	Best UX; more moving parts

Table 4.4: Cache invalidation strategies and their trade-offs.

Traffic steering and anycast: the art of global movement

Once you have multiple regions, the goal is to move traffic between them without causing a "Thundering Herd" in your secondary location.

The Baby-Step steering rule

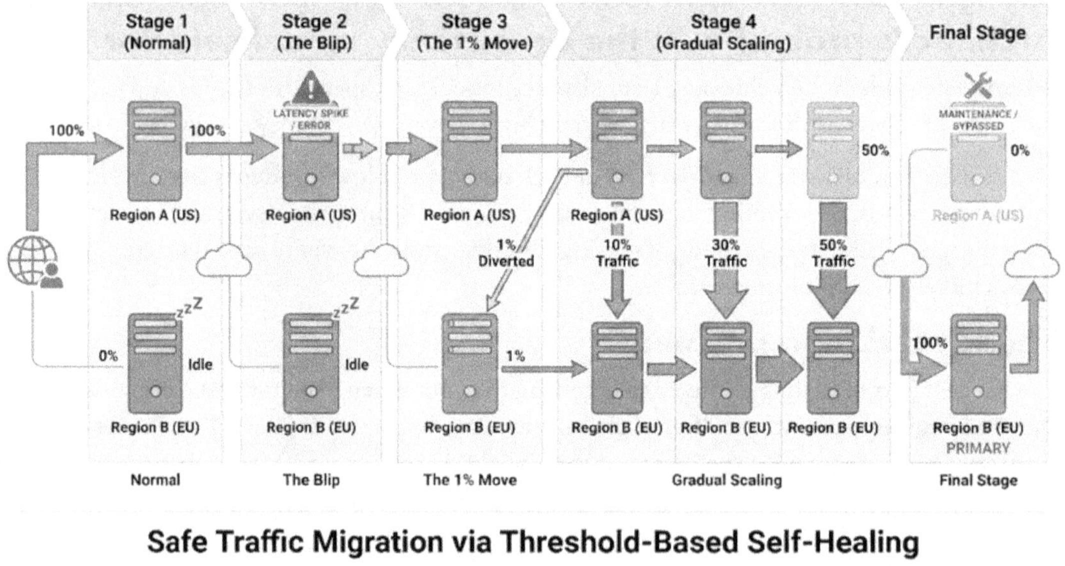

Figure 4.3: Traffic Steering – The Baby-Step Shift

When moving traffic between regions, never flip a 100% switch. You must move in **"Baby Steps"**—starting with 1%, then 3%, 10%, and 30%. This allows you to watch the telemetry and ensure the new region isn't buckling under the shift.

Threshold-Based Self-Healing

A self-healing system shouldn't be complex; it just needs the right thresholds.

- **Simple Logic**: If one region goes down, the system should automatically steer that load to the remaining ones using basic "if X is down, move to Y" logic.
- **Auto-Correction**: Once monitoring detects the failed region is healthy, it should automatically rebalance traffic back.

> Note
>
> **The Regional Autonomy Rule:**
>
> True global resilience requires that a region be able to survive even if the "Control Plane" is severed. We mandate that every Scale Unit at the Edge must have enough local "Static Fallback" to operate for 60 minutes without a single packet from the Virginia origin. If your Edge requires a constant heartbeat to the center to function, you haven't built a global system; you've built a very long extension cord.

The Multi-Region "waste" trap

Multi-Region is a massive waste of money for most startups.

- **One Region is Often Enough**: If you do heavy background processing where latency doesn't matter, one region is sufficient.
- **The Experience Pivot**: Multi-Region only makes sense when your experience is the product and you have a massive, globally distributed customer base.

Why one region usually suffices: A single cloud region is not a single point of failure: it spans multiple Availability Zones with separate power, cooling, and network, so spreading instances across AZs already buys high availability without cross-region complexity. It is also cheaper—traffic between AZs in a region is low-cost or free on most providers, while cross-region replication adds egress charges, replication lag, and a distributed-state problem you now own. Reach for multi-region for latency or data-residency reasons, not reflexively for availability.

Dimension	One region (multi-AZ)	Multi-region
Availability	AZ failover within the region	Region-level failover
Latency	Good regionally	Low latency globally
Data-transfer cost	Low/free intra-region	Cross-region egress charges
Complexity	Low	High (replication, consistency)
Right when	Most startups	Experience is the product, global base

Table 4.5: Single region (multi-AZ) versus multi-region.

Manager's Math — The Second-Region Tax: A standby second region roughly doubles infrastructure spend (compute, storage, a replicated database) and adds cross-region egress—for users a single region behind a CDN may already serve at acceptable latency. Until global p95 latency or a data-residency rule actually fails the business, the second region is pure cost. Spend it on the CDN and edge first: that buys most of the latency win at a fraction of the price.

Protocol evolution and the intelligent edge

Scaling at the Edge is not just about where data sits, but how it travels.

The protocol leap: HTTP/3 and QUIC

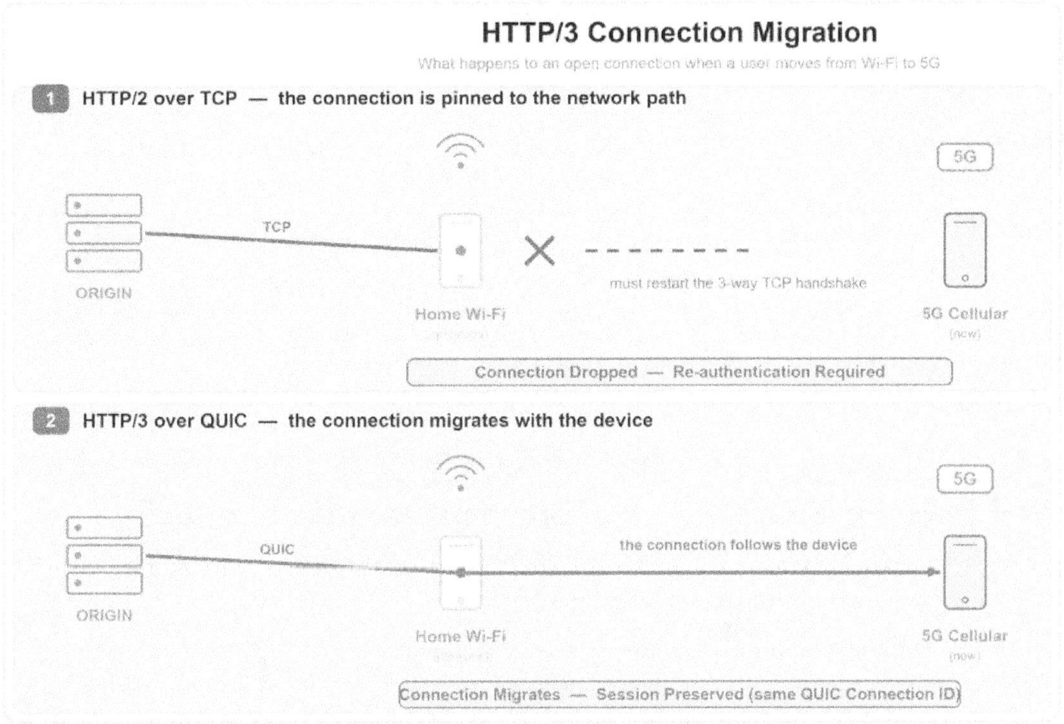

Figure 4.4: HTTP/3 Connection Migration

We move beyond HTTP/2 to HTTP/3 (QUIC) to solve Head-of-Line Blocking. In older protocols, if one packet was lost, every other packet had to wait. In a global system, this "waiting" compounds into the high latency we see in Singapore. QUIC allows for Connection Migration, meaning a customer doesn't lose their checkout progress just because they move from Wi-Fi to 5G.

What HTTP/3 does and does not fix: QUIC removes transport-layer head-of-line blocking and survives network changes, so it cuts the latency that comes from the network itself. It does nothing for the latency that comes from your application: a slow database query, a chatty N+1 API, or heavy backend processing is exactly as slow over HTTP/3 as over HTTP/2. Treat the upgrade as removing the transport tax, not as a substitute for fixing application-level bottlenecks—which are precisely what we turn to next.

Aspect	HTTP/2 over TCP	HTTP/3 over QUIC
Head-of-line blocking	One lost packet stalls every stream	Per-stream; a loss stalls only its own stream
Network change (Wi-Fi→5G)	Connection drops; full re-handshake	Connection migrates; session preserved
Connection setup	TCP + TLS, multiple round trips	QUIC 1-RTT (0-RTT on resume)
Transport	TCP	UDP + QUIC (encrypted by default)

Table 4.6: HTTP/2 over TCP versus HTTP/3 over QUIC.

Architect's prompt 4.4: the protocol readiness check

When to use this: Before enabling HTTP/3 in production, to confirm the upgrade will actually help and won't mask an application-layer bottleneck.

"Act as a performance engineer. Given my latency breakdown (DNS, TLS, TTFB, transfer, backend) and my CDN/edge config, estimate how much HTTP/3 (QUIC) is likely to help, name the delays it will NOT fix (slow queries, N+1 APIs, backend processing), and tell me what to fix first if transport is not the dominant cost."

Note

Non-Negotiable:

You cannot deploy HTTP/3 as your sole protocol because corporate firewalls often block UDP port 443. A reliable architecture must include a graceful fallback to TCP-based HTTP/2.

The AI moment: predictive prefetching

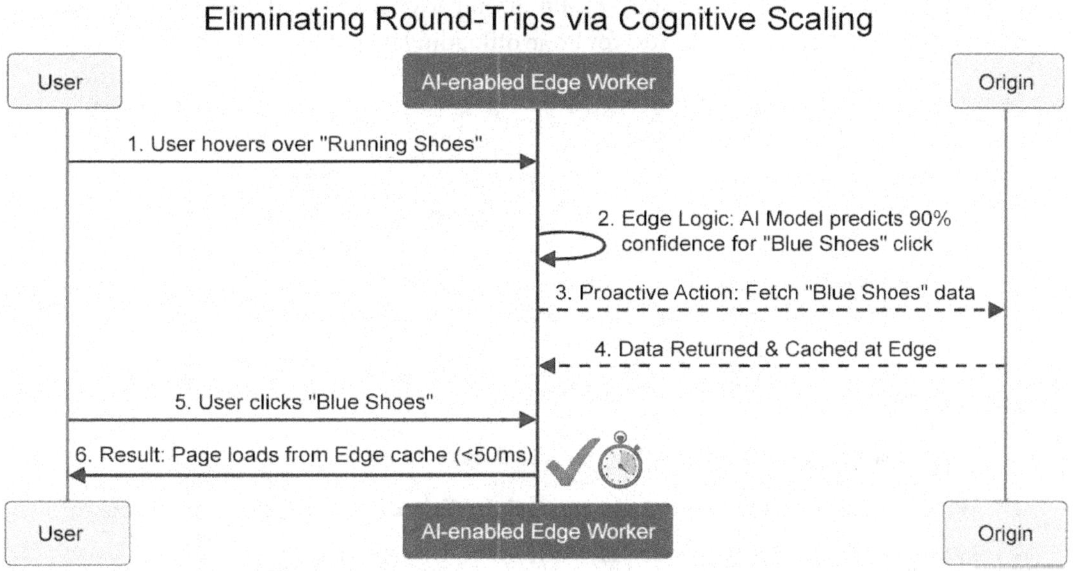

Figure 4.5: The Intelligent Edge - Predictive Prefetching

As an AI-First organization, we anticipate requests. We implement a lightweight ML model at the Edge for Predictive Prefetching. The model predicts which product page a user will click next and "pre-warms" that cache key. This turns a 500 ms round-trip into a 50 ms "instant" load.

> Note
>
> **The Prefetching Poison Pill:**
>
> Prefetching is a double-edged sword. If your AI model is over-aggressive, you risk a "Self-Inflicted Thundering Herd" where your own Edge workers DDoS your origin by pre-warming thousands of unlikely paths. We implement a Prefetching Kill-Switch—a deterministic guardrail that automatically disables AI-driven fetches if the origin's p99 latency exceeds a 200 ms threshold.

Architect's prompt 4.1: the edge logic migration

When to use this: Use this during your Pre-Migration Performance Audit to identify which high-latency controllers are candidates for Edge offloading.

```
Act as a Principal Systems Architect. I am looking to reduce the 'Time to First
Byte' (TTFB) for my global users.
Analyze this Node.js 'Product Page' controller code.
Identify logic that can be moved to an Edge Function, specifically: geographic
redirection, A/B testing cookie logic, and header-based authentication checks.
Provide a 'Stale-While-Revalidate' configuration for the CDN headers that allows
the page to stay 'Up' in read-only mode even if the origin database times out.
```

Summary

In this chapter, we pushed ShopFlow beyond the data center:

- We adopted the **Static-First Rule** and **Origin Shielding** to protect the database.
- We managed the **Consistency Tax** with Event-Driven Purging.
- We utilized **Baby-Step Steering** for resilient global failovers.
- We leveraged **HTTP/3** and **Predictive Prefetching** for an intelligent, low-latency Edge.

The cliffhanger: the "chatty" neighbor

We have optimized the **Talk**. The Edge is fast, and our AI is predicting the user's next move. Our global users are finally seeing US speeds.

Step back and the pattern is clear: each optimization simply exposed the next bottleneck. We removed geographic latency with the edge, protected the origin with a shield, and optimized transport with HTTP/3. The remaining delays are now almost entirely inside our own application architecture—the service-to-service chatter we confront in *Chapter 5*.

But as we expand, we've hit a new wall. Our services are talking to each other so much that the network itself is the bottleneck. One click triggers a chain reaction of fifty internal API calls. We fixed the Storage, but now the Communication is what dominates our latency.

In **Chapter 5**, we will tackle **"Chatty APIs"** and move from synchronous waiting to asynchronous speed.

Get this book's PDF version and more

Scan the QR code (or go to `packtpub.com/unlock`). Search for this book by name, confirm the edition, and then follow the steps on the page.

UNLOCK NOW

Note: Keep your invoice handy. Purchases made directly from Packt don't require an invoice.

5

Scaling the Modern Web Application – State, Performance, and Micro-Frontends

In *Chapter 4*, we pushed ShopFlow to the Edge. The CDN is serving static assets globally, our Origin Shield is absorbing the Thundering Herd, and Predictive Prefetching is eliminating round-trips before the user even clicks. The infrastructure story is strong.

But Dave just flagged a critical incident in the team channel.

A bug in the Search team's auto-complete logic corrupted a shared Redux store, which cascaded into the Checkout component. The "Place Order" button stopped rendering entirely —72 hours before ShopFlow's biggest vacation sale. Because Search, Checkout, and Profile all live in one React repository, compiled into one 5.2MB bundle, shipped through one CI/CD pipeline, the only option was a full rollback. We didn't just lose the Search fix; we lost two weeks of work from every team.

The Edge is fast. The backend is breathing. But the Monolithic JavaScript Tax is now the single largest risk to both user experience and engineering velocity.

In this chapter, we are going to cover the following main topics:

- From SPA to Micro-Frontends: Solving the "Monolithic JavaScript" Problem.

A clarification on terms: an SPA is not inherently a monolith—you can serve a single-page app from many independent backends. What we are decomposing here is the monolithic build and deploy: one JavaScript bundle, one pipeline, and one release cadence for the entire UI. The single-page model is fine; the single-bundle, single-team coupling is the problem.

- Client-Side State at Scale: Managing Data Flow in Highly Distributed UIs.
- The Rendering Choice: Scaling via SSR, SSG, or Incremental Static Regeneration (ISR).
- Performance Budgets: Scaling for the "Low-End Device" (Managing CPU and Memory bottlenecks).
- Resilient UI Patterns: Handling Partial Success and "Graceful Degradation."

Technical requirements

To follow the transition from a monolithic SPA to a distributed Micro-Frontend architecture, you will need:

- **Node.js (v18+):** For origin services and server-side rendering.
- **Webpack 5 / Vite:** Module Federation plugin for Micro-Frontend composition.
- **React 18+:** Concurrent rendering, Suspense, and Error Boundaries.
- **Nginx or Caddy:** Reverse proxy for micro-frontend routing and shell composition.
- **Lighthouse CI / WebPageTest:** Automated performance budget enforcement in CI.
- **TensorFlow.js (lite):** Client-side inference for the AI Moment.

Code Repository: `https://github.com/imran-siddique/Architecting-at-Scale/tree/main/ch5`

ShopFlow telemetry snapshot [stage 5]

Note

The Signal: The Edge is fast. The backend is breathing. But the front-end monolith is now the single largest risk to both user experience and team velocity. Three teams are shipping through one codebase, one build pipeline, and one blast radius. The problem is not the network anymore—it is the Monolithic JavaScript Tax.

```
p99 Latency: 900ms (High)
Availability: 99.5% (Stable)
Cloud Spend: $5,500/mo (Rising)
Main Thread Blocking Time: 2.8s (CRITICAL)
Bundle Size (Gzipped): 5.2MB (CRITICAL)
Team Velocity: 1 deploy/week (Down from 1/day – CRITICAL)
```

```
Largest Contentful Paint (LCP): 4.1s (Failing Core Web Vitals)
Cross-Team Merge Conflicts/Sprint: 14 (Organizational Bottleneck)
Panic Meter: 8/10 (Vacation sale in 72 hours, Checkout is broken)
```

> Note
>
> **Dave Alert:** "I can't even tell you which team's code caused the regression. It's all one giant bundle. We rolled back everything because we couldn't roll back anything."

From SPA to Micro-Frontends: solving the "Monolithic JavaScript" problem

The first instinct when a Single Page Application (SPA) becomes slow is to optimize the code. Lazy-load a route. Tree-shake a dependency. Upgrade to a faster bundler. These are valid tactics, but they address the symptom while ignoring the disease.

The disease is organizational, not computational.

When three teams—Search, Checkout, and Profile—commit to the same repository, build through the same pipeline, and deploy as a single artifact, you have created a Monolithic JavaScript Monolith. The technical debt is real, but the coordination debt is worse. Every merge requires cross-team review. Every deploy carries every team's risk. Every rollback erases every team's progress.

I have lived this problem firsthand. At a Fortune 10 company, I inherited a monolithic frontend serving millions of daily users across multiple experiences—documentation, training, Q&A, certifications—each owned by a separate team, but all funneling through one repo, one pipeline, and one deployment queue. A CSS regression in one experience blocked deployments for every other team. It took eighteen months to decompose that monolith into independently deployable modules on AKS. The result was organizational velocity: each team shipped on its own cadence with its own blast radius.

That experience crystallized a rule I now apply to every frontend architecture decision.

Note

The Monolith Velocity Rule: If adding one engineer to your team does not proportionally increase your team's deployment frequency, your architecture is the bottleneck—not your headcount.

ShopFlow has hit exactly this wall. Three teams. One repo. One build. Fourteen merge conflicts per sprint. Deployment frequency has collapsed from daily to weekly. The technical fix is decomposition. The architectural pattern is Micro-Frontends.

Understanding the Micro-Frontend architecture

A Micro-Frontend architecture applies the same principle behind backend microservices to the browser: independent deployment of independently owned user interfaces. Each team owns, builds, tests, and deploys its own slice of the application without coordinating with other teams.

This is not a framework. It is an architectural contract. The contract states: your code ships in your pipeline, fails in your blast radius, and recovers on your timeline.

When NOT to Use Micro-Frontends: Decomposition is a tax you pay for team autonomy, so don't pay it until the signals justify it. Stay with a single well-structured SPA when you have only one or two frontend teams; when the product is small or its workflows are tightly coupled (a wizard-style checkout that spans several "apps" is worse split apart); when you deploy infrequently; or when you cannot yet absorb the shared-dependency, routing, and observability overhead. Micro-frontends solve an organizational scaling problem—if you do not have that problem, they are pure cost.

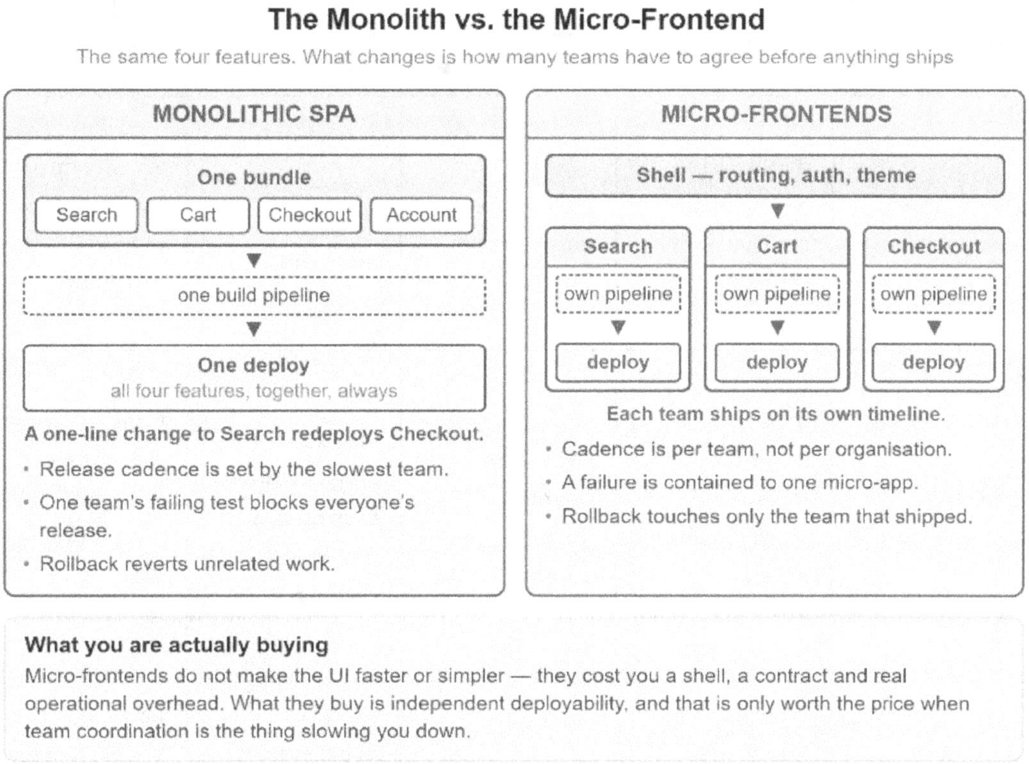

Figure 5.1: The Monolith vs. the Micro-Frontend

Choosing the right composition strategy

This is where most teams make their first critical mistake. They hear "Micro-Frontends" and immediately reach for the most complex tool in the box. The architecture community has spent years debating composition strategies, but the practical options reduce to three, each with a fundamentally different trade-off profile.

Strategy	How It Works	Deployment Independence	Runtime Complexity	Best For
Build-Time Composition	Micro-apps published as NPM packages, consumed by the host at build time.	Low — Host must rebuild.	Low — No runtime overhead.	Smallteams(<3) with aligned release cadences.
Server-Side Composition	Reverse proxy or SSI assembles HTML fragments from different services at request time.	High — Each fragment deploys independently.	Medium — Requires proxy routing and fragment caching.	Content-heavy sites where SEO and TTFB matter more than interactivity.
Runtime Composition (Module Federation)	Webpack 5 / Vite Module Federation loads remote JS modules at runtime.	High — True independent deployment.	High — Shared dependency negotiation, chunk resolution, runtime errors.	Large orgs (3+ teams) needing full independence with rich interactivity.

Table 5.1: Micro-frontend composition strategies compared.

The shell pattern: designing the orchestration layer

Regardless of composition strategy, every Micro-Frontend architecture requires a Shell—a lightweight host application that provides the shared frame around independently loaded micro-apps. The Shell is responsible for what must be globally consistent: the navigation bar, the authentication context, the theming layer, and the route registry.

The Shell is non-negotiable. Without it, each micro-app reinvents authentication flows, duplicates navigation components, and creates visual inconsistency that undermines user trust. However, the Shell carries a gravitational risk: it naturally accretes responsibility.

> Note
>
> **The Shell Gravity Rule:** Every capability you add to the Shell becomes a cross-team dependency. The Shell must be treated as shared infrastructure with the same rigor as a database schema: changes require cross-team review, versioned contracts, and backward compatibility.

Here is the contract I enforce for what belongs in the Shell versus what each micro-app must own:

Responsibility	Owns It	Rationale
Authentication/Session	Shell	A user must authenticate once. Duplicating auth flows creates security surface area and UX inconsistency.
Top-Level Navigation	Shell	The navigation bar is the global wayfinding layer. Route changes must not cause full-page reloads.
Theming/Design Tokens	Shell	Brand consistency is non-negotiable. The Shell distributes CSS custom properties or a design token package.
Route Registration	Shell	The Shell owns the top-level route map and lazy-loads the correct micro-app.
Error Boundary (Global)	Shell	A top-level error boundary prevents a micro-app crash from producing a white screen.

Responsibility	Owns It	Rationale
Analytics/Telemetry SDK	Shell	A single telemetry pipeline avoids duplicate events and ensures consistent correlation IDs.
Feature Flags (SDK)	Shell	One evaluation context. If each app initializes its own SDK, flag evaluations diverge.
Notifications (Global)	Shell	A single notification/toast surface so any micro-app raises alerts consistently (one place for stacking, priority, dismissal).
Business Logic	Micro-App	Search ranking, checkout validation, profile editing—this is the team's domain. It never belongs in the Shell.
Data Fetching	Micro-App	Each micro-app owns its own API calls, caching strategy, and loading states.
Local State	Micro-App	Component-level state (form inputs, toggles, pagination) is entirely owned by the micro-app.
Styling (Component-Level)	Micro-App	Beyond the design tokens provided by the Shell, each app styles its own components.

Table 5.2: Ownership contract for the application shell.

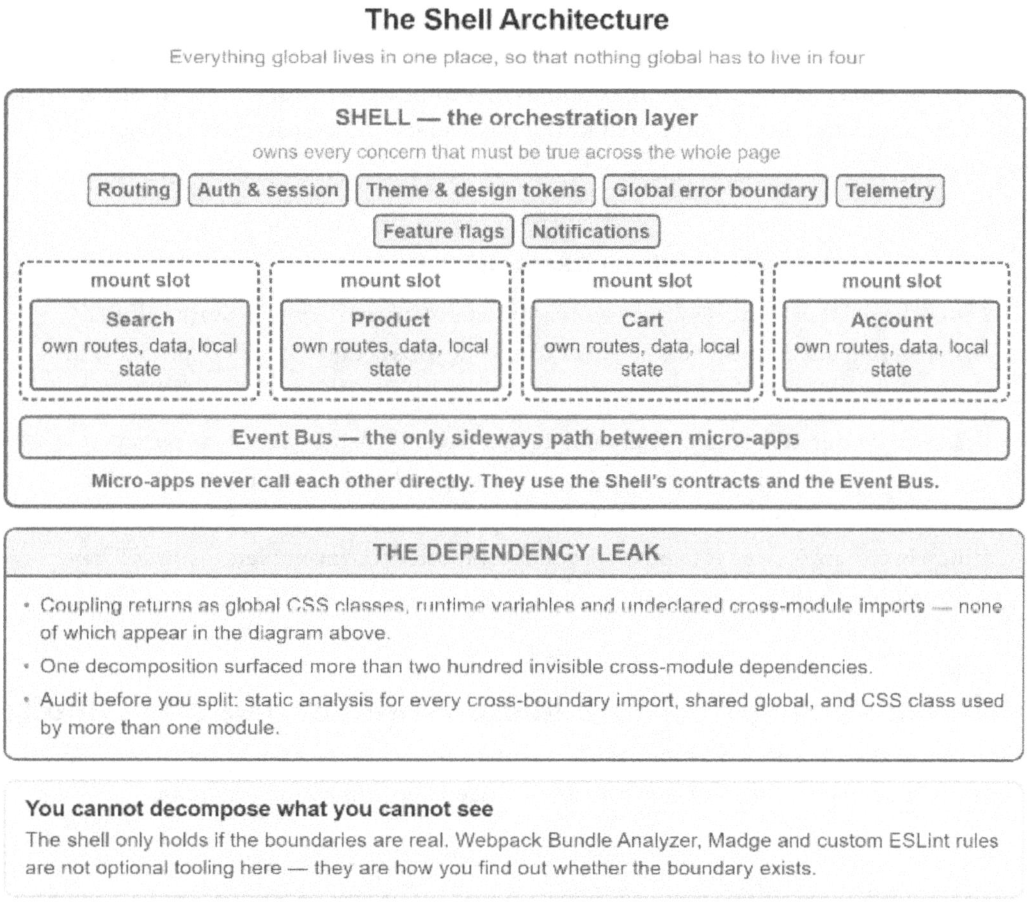

Figure 5.2: The Shell Architecture

The dependency leak: the silent coupling

The most common failure mode in a Micro-Frontend migration is a dependency leak—micro-apps sharing implicit dependencies through global CSS classes, runtime variables, or undeclared cross-module imports. During the decomposition I led, we discovered over two hundred invisible cross-module dependencies.

The Dependency Leak Audit: Before migration, run static analysis identifying every cross-boundary import, shared global, and CSS class used by more than one module. Tools like Webpack Bundle Analyzer, Madge, and custom ESLint rules are non-negotiable. You cannot decompose what you cannot see.

We enforced strict boundaries through three steps: (1) Boundary Definition—each micro-app got its own package.json with explicit dependencies, and cross-boundary imports were flagged as build errors. (2) Shared Contract Extraction—legitimate shared code was moved to versioned internal packages. (3) Leak Elimination—implicit dependencies were either made explicit or duplicated. A 2KB duplicated utility is cheaper than a cross-team deployment dependency.

> Note
>
> **Safe Scale Check — Blast Radius and Reversibility:**
>
> The entire point of Micro-Frontends is blast radius reduction. A bug in Search affects Search. A rollback of Checkout rolls back Checkout. This is the "Safe Scale" primitive in action.
>
> Before your migration is complete, validate this property: deploy a broken version of one micro-app intentionally in a staging environment. Confirm that the Shell's Error Boundary catches the failure and that the other micro-apps continue to function. If a failure in one app cascades to others, your decomposition is incomplete—you still have a monolith with extra steps.

Architect's prompt 5.1: the Micro-Frontend migration audit

When to use this: Use this prompt during the planning phase of a Micro-Frontend migration to identify hidden coupling and generate a prioritized decomposition roadmap.

```
Acting as a Principal Frontend Architect, I observe that we have a monolithic
React SPA with [X] teams contributing to one repository. The bundle size is [Y] MB
gzipped. Deployment frequency has dropped to [Z] per week due to merge conflicts
and shared pipeline contention.

Analyze the following top-level directory structure and package.json dependencies:

[Paste directory tree and package.json]

Identify: (1) Implicit cross-module dependencies that would break if modules were
deployed independently. (2) Shared code that should be extracted into a versioned
internal package. (3) A recommended decomposition order based on minimizing cross-
team coupling.

Output a Migration Risk Matrix with columns: Module Name, Shared Dependencies
```

```
Count, Estimated Extraction Complexity (Low/Medium/High), and Recommended
Extraction Order.
```

Client-Side state at scale: managing data flow in highly distributed UIs

The moment you decompose a monolithic SPA into micro-frontends, you face a question that has undermined more architectures than any framework migration: who owns the state?

In ShopFlow's monolith, the answer was simple and total: everyone owned everything. A single Redux store held authentication tokens, cart contents, search filters, user preferences, and feature flags in one global object tree. When the Search team's auto-complete mutation corrupted the store, Checkout lost access to the cart. The blast radius was total because the state architecture had zero isolation.

The instinct after this failure is to swing to the opposite extreme—give every micro-app its own isolated store with no shared state whatsoever. This sounds clean in a design document, but it fails the first time a user adds an item to their cart from the Search page and expects the cart badge in the navigation bar to update instantly. Some state must cross boundaries. The question is how.

The "No Globals" principle

The architectural rule I enforce is direct: there is no global state—not in the traditional sense of a single store that every component reads from and writes to.

Instead, every piece of shared state is owned by a dedicated service—a small, independently deployable module whose sole responsibility is managing that specific domain of shared data and exposing it through a well-defined contract.

I learned this the hard way on a large-scale enterprise platform with dozens of microservices. Centralizing common concerns—auth, user profile, notifications—into a shared global store recreated the exact monolithic coupling we had decomposed the backend to avoid. An auth module latency spike caused every subscribed micro-app to re-render. The fix: eliminate the global store. Each concern became its own lightweight service exposing a narrow API—a custom event, a subscription hook, or a Web Worker. If auth was slow, only auth-dependent UI showed a loading state. The rest continued functioning.

> Note
>
> **The State Ownership Rule:** Every piece of state has exactly one owner. If multiple micro-apps need the same data, that data is not "global"—it is a shared service with its own lifecycle, its own fallback behavior, and its own blast radius.

This distinction matters for failure modes. A global store that crashes takes the entire application with it. A shared service that crashes triggers its own fallback—a cached last-known-good value, a degraded UI element, or an error boundary scoped to the consuming component. The application survives because the failure is contained.

Classifying state: the ownership matrix

Not all state is created equal. Before writing a single line of state management code, classify every piece of data in your application using this matrix:

State Category	Examples	Owner	Communication Mechanism	Fallback on Failure
Domain State	Search results, checkout form inputs, profile edit fields	Micro-App (exclusive)	None needed—internal to the app	App-level error boundary
Session State	Auth token, user ID, session expiry	Shared Auth Service	Custom Event (auth-state-changed) or Broadcast Channel API	Redirect to login; cached token with short TTL
Cross-App Coordination	Cart item count (badge), active notification count	Dedicated Shared Service	Event Bus (publish/subscribe)	Last-known-good value from sessionStorage
UI orchestration	Active route, theme mode (dark/light), locale	Shell	Shell-provided React Context or CSS custom properties	Shell defaults

State Category	Examples	Owner	Communication Mechanism	Fallback on Failure
Ephemeral UI State	Dropdown open/closed, tooltip visibility, scroll position	Component (local)	None	Reset on re-mount

Table 5.3: State categories in a micro-frontend architecture and how each is owned.

Note

Anti-Pattern: The Invisible Monolith:

You can decompose your codebase into twenty micro-apps, deploy them independently, and still have a monolith—if they all read from a single shared state tree. This is the Invisible Monolith: architecturally distributed, but logically coupled through state. The symptom is easy to spot: when you deploy one micro-app, you test all of them, because a state shape change in one can break subscriptions in another.

The test is simple. Can you deploy any single micro-app without running integration tests against other micro-apps? If not, your state architecture has recreated the coupling that your code decomposition was meant to eliminate.

The Re-Render tax: why granularity matters

In a monolithic Redux store, a state change in any part of the tree can trigger re-evaluation of every connected component's mapStateToProps or useSelector. At small scale, this is invisible. At ShopFlow's scale—hundreds of components across three domains subscribed to one store—it is measurable. Our profiling showed that a single search filter change triggered 340 component re-render evaluations, of which only 12 actually needed to update. That is a 97% waste ratio on the main thread.

The frontend performance community has converged on a clear direction: fine-grained reactivity outperforms coarse-grained store subscriptions at scale.

Approach	Granularity	Re-Render Scope	Trade-off
Monolithic Store (Redux, single Zustand store)	Coarse	Any state change evaluates all selectors. Memoization helps but adds cognitive overhead.	Simple mental model, but scales poorly past ~100 connected components.
Atomic State (Jotai, Recoil, Nano Stores)	Fine	Only components subscribing to a specific atom re-render when that atom changes.	Excellent render performance. Requires discipline to avoid atom proliferation.
Signal-Based Reactivity (Preact Signals, SolidJS, Angular Signals)	Surgical	Updates bypass the virtual DOM diffing entirely. Only the specific DOM node bound to the signal updates.	Best raw performance. Tied to framework support; not yet universal in React.

Table 5.4: Front-end re-rendering approaches compared.

For ShopFlow's micro-frontend architecture, the recommendation is atomic state within each micro-app, with the Event Bus for cross-app coordination. Each micro-app selects its own state management library—Checkout might use Zustand for its form-heavy workflows, while Search uses Jotai for its highly reactive filter panel. The Shell imposes no state library. It imposes only the contract: communicate across boundaries through the Event Bus, never through shared memory.

> Note
>
> **The Golden Rule:** State flows down within a micro-app. Events flow sideways between micro-apps. Nothing flows "globally."

What the Event Bus actually is: the Event Bus is a small in-browser publish/subscribe channel that lets micro-apps notify each other without importing each other's code or sharing memory. A publisher emits a named event with a small payload; any number of subscribers react. It can be the browser's own CustomEvent on window, a BroadcastChannel (which also reaches other tabs), or a lightweight pub/sub library (mitt, an RxJS Subject)—start with CustomEvents and add a library only when you need typed contracts or replay.

End-to-end example: a customer adds an item in the Search micro-app. Search publishes cart-item-added with {sku, qty}. The Cart micro-app, subscribed to that event, increments its badge. The Analytics micro-app, also subscribed, records the event for funnel metrics. None of the three imports the others; they share only the event name and payload shape—a versioned contract, not shared state.

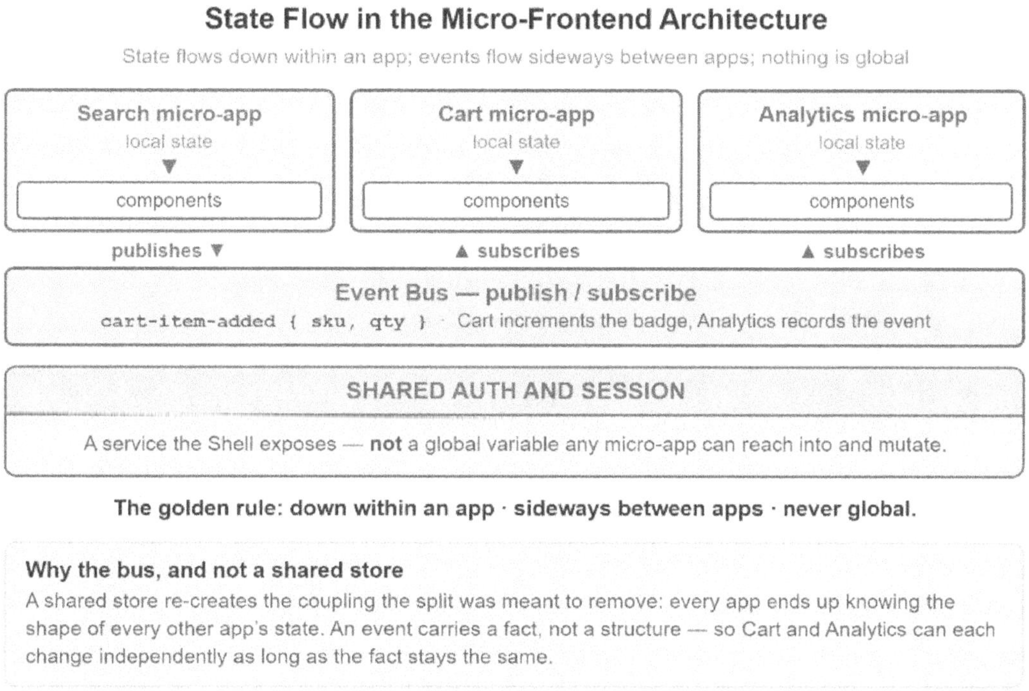

Figure 5.3: State Flow in the Micro-Frontend Architecture

The Backend-for-Frontend layer: taming the chatty front end

Chapter 4 identified the "Chatty Neighbor" problem: one user click triggers fifty API calls. With micro-frontends, this multiplies—each micro-app fetches independently, unaware of the others. A frontend that directly calls six backend microservices is not a client; it is a distributed orchestrator running on hardware you do not control.

The BFF Mandate: When three or more micro-frontends call three or more backend services, a Backend-for-Frontend (BFF) layer is not optional. It aggregates chatty round-trips into one purposeful API call.

The BFF is a thin server-side layer, deployed per frontend team, that calls backend microservices in parallel on the server side (where latency is microseconds) and returns one composed payload to the browser.

```
// Search BFF: Aggregating three microservice calls into one response
// File: search-bff/src/routes/search-results.ts

import express from 'express';

const router = express.Router();

router.get('/api/search', async (req, res) => {
const query = req.query.q as string;

// Parallel server-side calls (microsecond latency between services)
const [products, recommendations, pricing] = await Promise.all([
productService.search(query),
recommendationService.getFor(query),
pricingService.getBatch(/* product IDs */),
]);

// Single composed response to the browser
res.json({
products: products.map((p) => ({
...p,
price: pricing[p.id],
recommended: recommendations.includes(p.id),
})),
meta: { total: products.length, query },
});
});
```

Metric	Without BFF	With BFF
Browser round-trips per page	6	1
Total latency	~600ms (6 x 100ms sequential or waterfall)	~120ms (1 round-trip, server-side parallel)

Metric	Without BFF	With BFF
Retry/timeout logic	Frontend owns per call	BFF owns; frontend sees one request
Error composition	Each micro-app manages independently	BFF returns structured partial-success responses
Coupling	Frontend tightly coupled to backend service contracts	Frontend couples only to BFF contract

Table 5.5: Round-trip and payload metrics with and without a BFF.

Note

Manager's Math — The BFF ROI:

A BFF adds one deployable service per frontend team. That is real operational cost: a container, a CI/CD pipeline, on-call rotation coverage. The return is measurable. For ShopFlow, consolidating six browser round-trips into one BFF call reduced the Search page's Time to Interactive (TTI) from 3.8s to 1.4s—a 63% improvement. In e-commerce, every 100 ms of latency reduction correlates with approximately a 1% increase in conversion. That single BFF service pays for itself within the first sales cycle.

This is Manager's Math: the cost of the BFF is a line item. The cost of not having it is invisible—spread across user abandonment, support tickets, and engineering hours spent debugging frontend orchestration logic that should never have existed in the browser.

The First Rule of Frontend Architecture: Split backend API from frontend client. This is a structural prerequisite for independent scaling—you scale the frontend for render throughput and the backend for data throughput. When they are entangled, you scale neither effectively.

The Cost of the BFF: a Backend-for-Frontend reduces browser-side orchestration, but it is another deployable service to own: you version its API, monitor its latency and errors, secure it (it holds tokens and calls internal services), and keep it from quietly becoming a second business-logic layer. Skip the BFF when the frontend talks to a single backend that already returns frontend-shaped responses—at that size a BFF is overhead with no offsetting complexity to absorb.

Architect's prompt 5.2: state architecture audit

When to use this: Use this prompt when migrating from a monolithic global store to a micro-frontend state architecture, to identify which state should be shared vs. owned.

```
Act as a Senior Frontend Architect specializing in state management. I am
decomposing a monolithic React application into [X] micro-frontends. Currently, we
have a single Redux store with [Y] top-level slices.

Here is the current Redux state shape:

[Paste your root reducer or state type definition]

For each state slice, classify it as: (1) Domain State - owned exclusively by one
micro-app, (2) Session State - owned by a shared auth service, (3) Cross-App
Coordination - requires an Event Bus, or (4) UI Orchestration - owned by the
Shell.

For each Cross-App Coordination item, define the event contract: event name,
payload shape, and recommended fallback behavior if the publishing micro-app is
unavailable.

Output a State Migration Matrix with columns: State Slice, Current Owner, Target
Owner, Communication Mechanism, Fallback Strategy, Migration Risk (Low/Medium/
High).
```

The rendering choice: scaling via SSR, SSG, or incremental static regeneration (ISR)

Every frontend architect must answer a deceptively simple question: where does the HTML get built? In the browser (Client-Side Rendering), on the server per request (Server-Side Rendering), or at build time (Static Site Generation)? The answer determines your latency floor, your server costs, your SEO viability, and—critically—how much computation you are offloading onto hardware you do not control.

The default in most modern teams is Client-Side Rendering. It is the path of least resistance. You ship a JavaScript bundle, the browser downloads it, executes it, fetches data, and renders the page. The developer experience is frictionless. The user experience at scale is not.

The CSR comfort trap

Client-Side Rendering became the default because frameworks made it easy, not because it was architecturally correct. When your SPA is small—a few routes, a moderate bundle, users on fast hardware—CSR is invisible. The browser handles it. But at ShopFlow's scale, CSR compounds every problem we have identified in this chapter.

The 5.2MB bundle must be downloaded, parsed, and executed before a single pixel of meaningful content appears. On a mid-range Android device over a 3G connection—which describes a significant portion of global e-commerce users—that initial execution alone consumes 4+ seconds of main thread time. The user stares at a white screen or a loading spinner. Google's Core Web Vitals penalize this directly: a Largest Contentful Paint (LCP) above 2.5 seconds is rated "Poor," and ShopFlow's current LCP of 4.1 seconds is failing.

The deeper problem is architectural. In CSR, the browser is performing work that a server can do faster, more reliably, and once instead of millions of times. Every user's device re-executes the same rendering logic, re-fetches the same data, and re-computes the same HTML. This is a Scale by Duplication anti-pattern: instead of computing once and distributing the result, we are distributing the computation and hoping for the best.

> Note
>
> **The Rendering Location Rule:** If the same HTML output would be produced for more than one user, it should not be computed on the client. Compute it once on the server or at build time, and serve the result.

I have seen this validated at scale. On a platform serving millions of daily users, client-side computation debt—TypeScript transpilation, complex template rendering, dynamic content assembly—had made main thread blocking times unacceptable. Moving aggressively to server-side rendering shifted computation to infrastructure we controlled and could scale horizontally. The client received pre-rendered HTML and hydrated only interactive elements. Crucially, the SSR layer could be decomposed into independent services even while the client remained monolithic.

> Note
>
> **The SSR Flexibility Principle:** Server-Side Rendering decouples your rendering scale from your client architecture. Even if your frontend codebase is not yet decomposed, SSR lets you scale the rendering infrastructure independently—adding capacity where computation happens rather than hoping every user's device has the CPU budget.

Applying the rendering strategy to ShopFlow

The correct approach is not to pick one strategy for the entire application. It is to assign a rendering strategy per route based on two variables: how often the data changes and whether the content is user-specific.

> Note
>
> **The Rendering Decision Rule:** If the data changes less frequently than your deployment cadence, use SSG. If the data is user-specific or session-dependent, use SSR. If the page is an interactive tool behind authentication with no SEO requirement, CSR is acceptable.

Rendering Decision Tree (decide per route, not per application): Is the content user-specific? → Yes → SSR. Does it change infrequently? → Yes → SSG. Is a small staleness window acceptable? → Yes → ISR. Is it an authenticated, highly interactive surface? → Yes → CSR. Most real applications land on a mix, assigned route by route.

Route	Data Change Frequency	User-Specific?	Rendering Strategy	Rationale
/products/:category	Daily (catalog updates)	No	SSG	Product categories are shared across all users. Build at deploy time, serve from CDN.
/products/:id	Hourly (price/stock changes)	No	ISR (with caution)	Product detail pages benefit from static speed but need price/stock freshness. 60-second revalidation window.

Route	Data Change Frequency	User-Specific?	Rendering Strategy	Rationale
/checkout	Real-time (cart, payment)	Yes	SSR	Checkout involves session state, payment tokenization, and fraud scoring. Server-side on every request.
/account/profile	On user action	Yes	SSR	User-specific content requiring server-side session resolution.
/ admin / dashboard	Real-time (analytics)	Yes	CSR	Authenticated admin tool with complex interactivity. No SEO requirement.
/ (Homepage)	Hourly (Promotions)	Partially (A/B tests)	SSG + Edge Personalization	Base page is static. A/B test variants are resolved at the Edge (*Chapter 4* pattern).

Table 5.6: Choosing a rendering strategy per route.

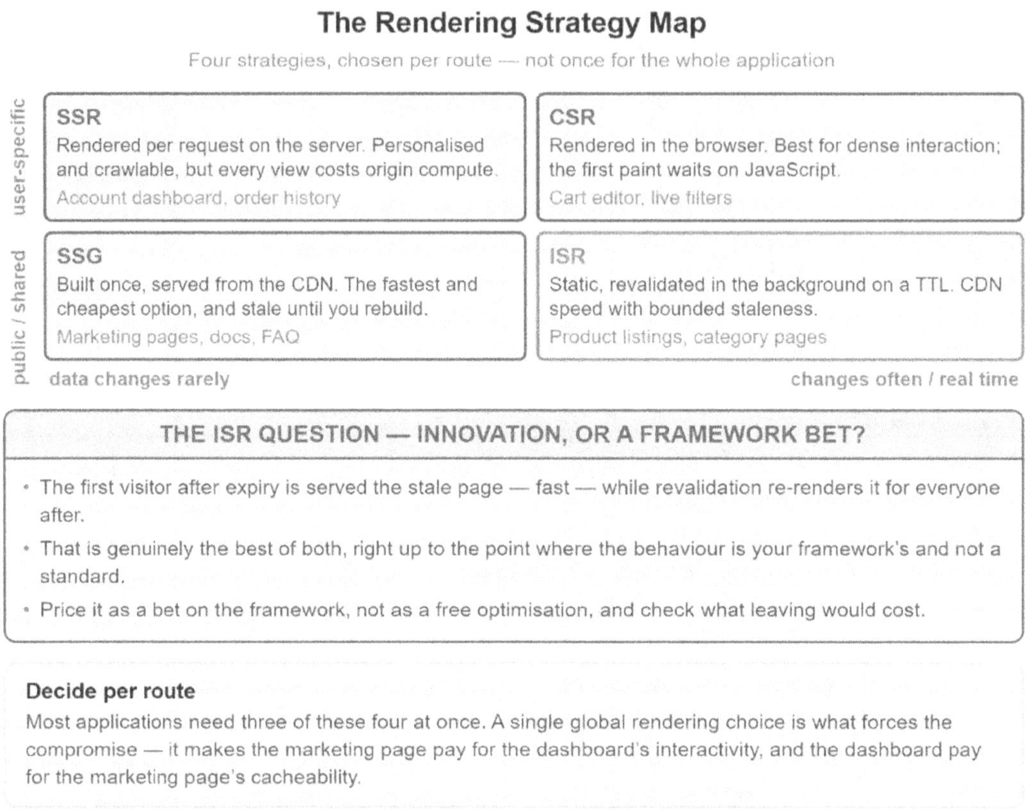

Figure 5.4: The Rendering Strategy Map

The ISR question: innovation or framework bet?

Incremental Static Regeneration, popularized by Next.js, promises the convergence of SSG speed with SSR freshness. The page is statically generated at build time, served from the CDN, and revalidated in the background when a configurable TTL expires. The first user after expiry gets the stale page (fast), and the revalidation triggers a server-side re-render that updates the cached version for subsequent users.

On paper, this is elegant. In practice, it introduces three concerns that warrant caution before committing to a production system.

Three concerns warrant caution:

1. Revalidation race conditions—multiple edge nodes triggering simultaneous revalidation creates thundering herd behavior against your origin.

2. Framework lock-in—ISR today is tightly coupled to specific meta-frameworks like Next.js/Vercel.
3. Observability gaps—debugging "stale-while-revalidating" requires tracing through framework cache, CDN state, and origin revalidation logs.

Adoption data supports cautious optimism. According to the 2025 State of JavaScript survey, approximately 68% of Next.js production deployments leverage some form of ISR, and Vercel's platform telemetry reports a median revalidation latency of 180 ms for pages with a 60-second TTL. However, self-hosted ISR deployments report significantly higher variance, with p99 revalidation times exceeding 2 seconds in multi-region setups.

> Note
>
> **The ISR Caution Rule:** Use ISR for non-critical, high-traffic pages where a 60-second staleness window is acceptable (product catalogs, trending lists). Do not use ISR for any page where data accuracy has financial or compliance implications (checkout, pricing, inventory counts). For those pages, SSR with explicit cache-control headers gives you the same performance benefit with full control over the caching semantics.

For ShopFlow, we adopt ISR narrowly: product detail pages (/products/:id) with a 60-second revalidation window. The product name and description rarely change, but price and stock can. A 60-second window means a user might see a price that is up to one minute old—acceptable for browsing, but the checkout page (SSR) always fetches the live price. This is Stale-While-Revalidate applied at the architecture level, not just the HTTP header level.

How large systems actually choose: these strategies are not academic. Content and marketing sites lean on SSG (fast, cacheable, cheap). News and e-commerce product pages use ISR to stay fresh without rebuilding the whole site. Read-heavy, SEO-sensitive apps have historically used SSR (GitHub server-rendered its pages for years). Authenticated, highly interactive surfaces—dashboards and editors like Figma or Gmail—are CSR, because rich interactivity matters more than first paint. Most large products mix all four, assigned per route.

> Note
>
> **Safe Scale Check — Reversibility:** The rendering strategy is one of the most reversible architectural decisions you will make. Moving a route from SSG to SSR requires changing the data-fetching function. Moving from SSR to CSR requires removing the server-side fetch and adding a client-side useEffect. These are code changes, not infrastructure migrations. This reversibility is why per-route rendering assignment is the correct granularity.

Architect's prompt 5.3: rendering strategy assignment

When to use this: Use this prompt when auditing an existing application's rendering approach or planning a new application's route-level rendering assignments.

```
Act as a Senior Frontend Performance Architect. I have an application with the
following routes and their characteristics:

[Paste a list of routes with: route path, data change frequency, whether content
is user-specific, current rendering strategy, and current LCP metric]

For each route, recommend the optimal rendering strategy (CSR, SSR, SSG, or ISR)
based on data freshness requirements and personalization needs. For ISR
recommendations, specify the revalidation TTL and justify why the staleness window
is acceptable.

Output a Rendering Assignment Table with columns: Route, Current Strategy,
Recommended Strategy, Revalidation TTL (if ISR), Expected LCP Improvement, and
Migration Complexity (Low/Medium/High).
```

Performance budgets: scaling for the "Low-End Device"

Performance budgets are one of the most discussed and least enforced concepts in frontend engineering. Every team agrees in principle: "We should have a performance budget." Very few teams block a pull request because a new dependency added 40KB to the bundle. The budget exists on a wiki page. The violation exists in production.

The reason is straightforward. A hard CI gate—where a merge is literally blocked if Lighthouse drops below a threshold—is brittle in practice. A legitimate feature might temporarily regress a score. A third-party SDK update might shift the baseline. The engineering cost of investigating every threshold breach, distinguishing real regressions from noise, and maintaining exception workflows often exceeds the cost of the performance regression itself.

This does not mean performance budgets are useless. It means the enforcement model must match the organizational reality.

The dashboard model: budgets as visibility, not gates

The approach that works at scale is budget-as-observability: continuous tracking through dashboards with weekly and monthly review cadences, not binary CI gates.

In my experience managing a high-traffic platform, we never implemented a hard merge gate for performance. Instead, we built comprehensive cost and usage observability: dashboards tracking utilization weekly, automated insights flagging idle services and unused dependencies. The discipline was "review the trend," not "block the merge."

This approach uncovered more waste than any automated gate could. A Lighthouse CI check catches a 40KB bundle increase. A usage dashboard catches an entire service that nobody is calling anymore—$800/month in compute running a feature that was deprecated six months ago but never decommissioned. The latter is where the real money hides.

> Note
>
> **The Budget Visibility Rule:** Track performance budgets on dashboards with weekly review cadences. Reserve hard CI gates for critical thresholds only—a bundle size doubling, a route that ships without server-side rendering, or an uncompressed image above 1MB. Everything else is a trend to manage, not a gate to enforce.

For ShopFlow, we implement a tiered budget framework:

Budget Tier	**Metric**	**Threshold**	**Enforcement**	**Action on Breach**
Hard Gate (CI blocks merge)	Total bundle size (gzipped)	1.5MB per micro-app	Automated	PR cannot merge. Developer must code-split or remove the dependency.
Hard Gate (CI blocks merge)	Uncompressed image asset	> 500KB	Automated	PR cannot merge. Image must be optimized or converted to WebP/AVIF.

Budget Tier	**Metric**	**Threshold**	**Enforcement**	**Action on Breach**
Warning (CI annotates PR)	Lighthouse Performance Score	< 80	Advisory	PR is annotated with a warning. Team lead reviews it in weekly standup.
Dashboard Trend (weekly review)	LCP, FID, CLS (Core Web Vitals)	Regression> 10% week over week	Human review	Team investigates root cause in sprint retrospective.
Monthly Audit	Unused dependencies, idle services, orphaned infrastructure	Anyresourcewith<1% utilization for 30 days	Human review	Candidate for decommission. Calculate annual waste.

Table 5.7: The tiered performance-budget framework.

Note

Manager's Math — The Idle Resource Tax:

The performance conversation in most organizations focuses on milliseconds. The cost conversation should focus on idle resources. A ShopFlow service running at 3% CPU utilization on a dedicated container costs $200/month. Multiply by 15 services with similar profiles, and you are spending $36,000/year on infrastructure that is functionally idle. A monthly utilization audit—one engineer, two hours—recovers more budget than six months of Lighthouse score optimization.

> Note
>
> This is where "Scale by Subtraction" delivers its highest ROI. You do not need to make things faster. You need to stop paying for things that are not being used.

Scaling for your audience, not everyone

ShopFlow's telemetry shows 2.8 seconds of main thread blocking time. That measurement was taken on our test hardware—likely a modern MacBook or a reasonably powerful desktop. On a $150 Android device over a 3G connection in Lagos or Jakarta, that 2.8 seconds becomes 6–8 seconds of frozen UI. The question is: how seriously should that constraint drive our architecture?

The honest answer: it depends entirely on your audience.

The technical community is right that performance equity matters. But architecture is an economic activity—optimizing for every possible device profile when your actual user base concentrates on specific hardware is overengineering.

> Note
>
> **The Audience-First Performance Rule:** Optimize for your measured user base, not for an imagined global population. Your analytics tell you what devices, networks, and geographies your actual users have. If 85% of your paying customers use devices with 4GB+ RAM on broadband connections, your performance budget should target that profile.

User Segment	% of Traffic	Device Profile	Network Profile	Performance Target
US/EU Desktop	52%	Modern laptop/ desktop, 8GB+ RAM	Broadband (50+ Mbps)	LCP< 1.5s, TTI < 2.0s
US/EU Mobile	28%	Mid-range smartphone, 4GB RAM	4G LTE (20 Mbps)	LCP< 2.0s, TTI < 3.0s

User Segment	% of Traffic	Device Profile	Network Profile	Performance Target
Emerging Markets Mobile	15%	Budget smartphone, 2GB RAM	3G (1.5 Mbps)	LCP< 3.5s, TTI < 5.0s
Admin/Internal	5%	Corporate desktop	Corporate broadband	No specific target (CSR acceptable)

Table 5.8: Performance targets by user segment.

The 15% emerging markets segment is meaningful—ShopFlow is an e-commerce platform, and emerging markets represent growth. But the architectural response is not "make everything lighter." It is to serve different experiences to different segments:

- **Emerging Markets:** Aggressively SSR-rendered, minimal JavaScript hydration. Progressive enhancement—the core shopping and checkout flow work without JavaScript. Images served as AVIF with aggressive compression.
- **US/EU Desktop:** Full interactive experience with client-side features, rich animations, predictive prefetching.
- **US/EU Mobile:** The same SSR foundation as emerging markets, but with fuller hydration and more interactive components.

This is not two separate applications. It is one application with progressive enhancement built into the rendering strategy. The SSR layer provides the base. Client-side hydration adds interactivity proportional to the device's capability. The Edge Functions from *Chapter 4* handle the segmentation—detecting the Save-Data header, the Device-Memory Client Hint, or the network type, and adjusting the response accordingly.

Architect's prompt 5.4: performance budget audit

When to use this: Use this prompt during a quarterly performance review or before a major feature launch to identify the highest-impact optimization targets.

```
Act as a Senior Web Performance Engineer. I have a web application with the
following current Core Web Vitals:

LCP: [X]s, FID: [Y]ms, CLS: [Z], Total Bundle Size: [A]MB, Main Thread Blocking
Time: [B]s
```

```
My user base is distributed as follows: [paste device/network segment breakdown].

I do not see an attached Lighthouse report. Please upload the report or provide
the relevant details so I can analyze the top 5 largest JavaScript chunks and
describe their purpose.

Identify: (1) The top 3 Long Tasks contributing to main thread blocking. (2)
Dependencies that can be lazy-loaded, deferred, or replaced with lighter
alternatives. (3) Third-party scripts that should be loaded via
requestIdleCallback. (4) Routes where the rendering strategy should change (CSR to
SSR or SSG).

Output a Performance Improvement Roadmap with columns: Optimization, Estimated
Impact on LCP, Estimated Impact on TTI, Implementation Effort (Low/Medium/High),
and Priority Order.
```

Resilient UI patterns: handling partial success and "Graceful Degradation"

Seventy-two hours before ShopFlow's biggest vacation sale, a bug in the Search team's auto-complete logic corrupted shared state and the "Place Order" button disappeared. The Recommendations widget, the Reviews carousel, and the "Recently Viewed" section were also down. But the user did not care about any of those. The user cared about one thing: completing a purchase. And because every component shared the same runtime fate, a failure in a non-critical widget blocked the critical path.

This is the architectural failure that Resilient UI design exists to prevent. The principle is not "nothing ever breaks." The principle is: when something breaks, only that thing breaks.

The critical path doctrine

Every page in your application has a critical path—the minimum set of UI elements required for the user to accomplish their primary task on that page. Everything else is enhancement. The architecture must guarantee that enhancements cannot interfere with the critical path under any failure condition.

Page	Critical Path (Must Always Work)	Enhancement (Can Degrade)
Product Detail	Product name, price, "Add to Cart" button, product images	Recommendations, reviews, "Recently Viewed," social sharing
Checkout	Cart summary, shipping form, payment form, "Place Order" button	Order suggestions, loyalty points display, estimated delivery widget
Search Results	Search input, result list with prices, pagination	Auto-complete suggestions, filter refinements, sponsored results
Homepage	Navigation, featured products grid, search bar	Personalized recommendations, trending carousel, promotional banners

Table 5.9: Critical path versus progressive enhancement, per page.

Note

The Critical Path Doctrine: Design every page so that the critical path renders and functions even if every enhancement component fails simultaneously. If a crash in your Recommendations widget can prevent a user from checking out, your architecture has a severity-1 bug—regardless of whether the Recommendations code itself is "correct."

This is not aspirational. It is a testable property. In your staging environment, force-fail every non-critical component on a page—return errors from their APIs, throw exceptions in their render methods, simulate network timeouts on their data fetches. If the critical path still renders, accepts input, and submits successfully, your resilience architecture is correct. If it does not, you have a coupling defect that must be fixed before production.

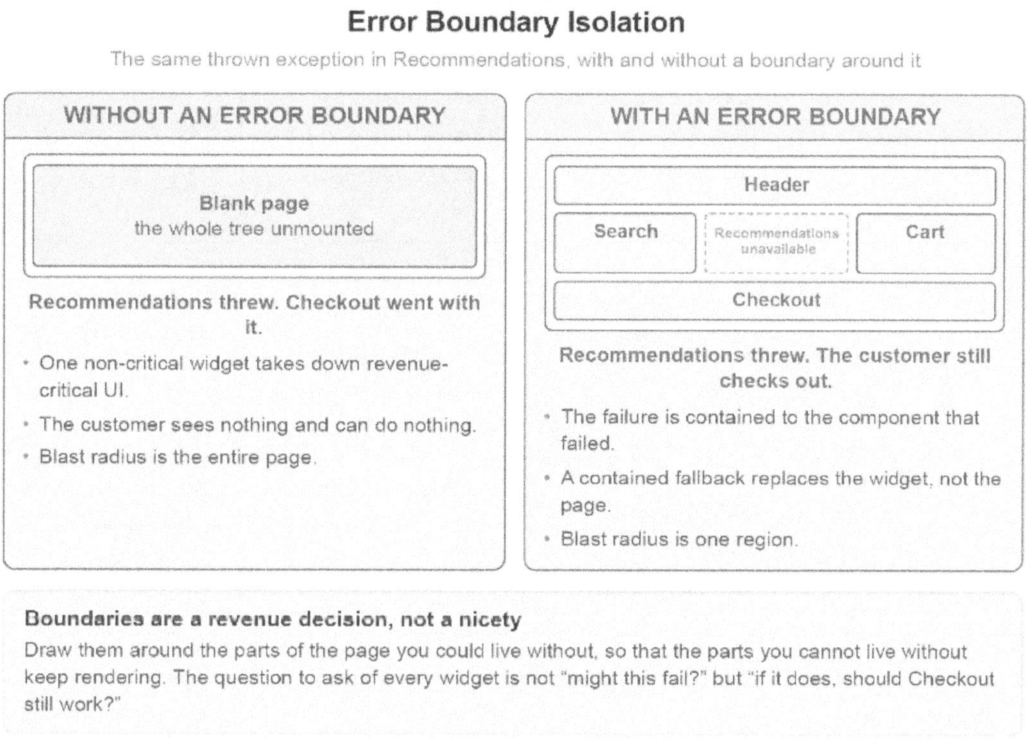

Figure 5.5: Error Boundary Isolation

The degradation spectrum: what cached fallbacks can and cannot do

Graceful degradation is not a single strategy. It is a spectrum, and where you land on that spectrum depends on the financial and trust implications of showing stale data.

Degradation Level	What the User Sees	When Appropriate	When Dangerous
Silent Removal	The failed component disappears. Fewer widgets on the page.	Non-critical enhancements: recommendations, trending lists, social proof	Never dangerous — user simply gets a simpler page

Degradation Level	What the User Sees	When Appropriate	When Dangerous
Cached Fallback	Component shows last-known-good data from sessionStorage or service worker.	Browse-only: product catalog, search results during outage, marketing content	Checkout, cart, pricing — showing cached price creates liability
Reduced functionality	Core features work; advanced features disabled.	Search works, but auto-complete is disabled; products load, but reviews do not	When reduced functionality misleads about availability
Read-Only Mode	Entire app serves static snapshot. No writes possible.	Full backend outage. CDN serves last-generated static pages.	Extended outages — users attempt purchases that cannot be submitted

Table 5.10: Graceful-degradation levels and when each is appropriate.

> Note
>
> **The Degradation Trust Rule:** Cached fallback content is acceptable for any data that does not have financial implications. Product descriptions, images, category listings, and marketing copy can safely be served from cache during an outage. Prices, inventory counts, cart contents, and payment confirmations must never be cached fallbacks. Showing a user a stale price that differs from the price they are actually charged is not graceful degradation—it is a trust violation.

For ShopFlow's checkout flow specifically, degradation means: if the pricing service is down, the checkout page shows an explicit message ("We're unable to confirm pricing right now. Please try again in a moment.") rather than proceeding with a cached price. The user experience is worse, but the trust is preserved. In e-commerce, a single pricing discrepancy can generate chargebacks, refund requests, and regulatory complaints that cost orders of magnitude more than a momentary interruption.

Architect's prompt 5.5: resilience audit

When to use this: Use this prompt before a major traffic event (vacation sale, product launch, marketing campaign) to validate that your UI can survive partial backend failures.

```
Act as a Site Reliability Engineer specializing in frontend resilience. I have a
web application with the following page structure:

[Paste the component tree for your highest-traffic page, identifying which
components call which backend services]

For each component, classify it as 'Critical Path' (must always render for the
user to complete their primary task) or 'Enhancement' (can be removed without
blocking the primary task).

For each Enhancement component, recommend a degradation strategy: Silent Removal
(render null), Cached Fallback (serve from sessionStorage), or Reduced
Functionality (disable interactive features, show static content).

For each Critical Path component, identify the backend dependency and recommend a
circuit breaker timeout. What is the maximum time the UI should wait for this
service before showing an explicit error message?

Output a Resilience Matrix with columns: Component, Classification, Backend
Dependency, Degradation Strategy, Circuit Breaker Timeout, and Fallback UI
Description.
```

Summary

In this chapter, we transformed ShopFlow's frontend from a monolithic liability into a distributed, resilient architecture.

We decomposed the 5.2MB monolithic SPA into independently deployable Micro-Frontends using the Shell Pattern and the Composition Complexity Rule—choosing the simplest composition strategy that enables independent deployment.

We eliminated the global state single point of failure by enforcing the State Ownership Rule: every piece of shared state is a dedicated service with its own fallback, communicated through an Event Bus that carries facts, not instructions.

We assigned rendering strategies per route—SSG for catalogs, SSR for checkout, and CSR only for admin tools—using the Rendering Decision Rule to match each route's data freshness and personalization requirements.

We implemented performance budgets as observability, not as gates, and applied Scale by Subtraction to decommission idle resources—where the real cost savings hide.

We built Resilient UI patterns using the Critical Path Doctrine: granular Error Boundaries ensure that a crash in Recommendations never prevents a user from completing Checkout. Feature flags with mandatory expiration dates provide reversibility without accumulating a Flag Graveyard.

ShopFlow's telemetry after these changes:

Metric	Before (Ch5 Start)	After (Ch5 End)	Change
Bundle Size (gzipped)	5.2MB (single bundle)	150KB Shell + 400–600KB per micro-app	~75% reduction in initial load
Main Thread Blocking Time	2.8s	0.9s	68% reduction
LCP (US/EU Desktop)	4.1s	1.6 s	61% improvement — passing Core Web Vitals
Team Velocity	1 deploy/week	3–5 deploys/week per team	15x improvement across the organization
Cross-Team Merge Conflicts	14/sprint	0 (independent repos)	Eliminated
Blast radius of a bad deploy	Entire application	Single micro-app	Isolated

Table 5.11: ShopFlow telemetry before and after the Chapter 5 changes.

The cliffhanger: the speed of light

Frontend bottlenecks have steadily moved up the stack. We removed deployment bottlenecks with micro-frontends, isolated state, assigned a rendering strategy per route, and trimmed the work the browser must do. The remaining latency is no longer inside the application at all—it is the unavoidable cost of physical distance between the user and the compute. That is the wall we hit next.

The frontend is fast. The teams are independent. Error Boundaries are isolating failures. Feature flags are providing reversibility. ShopFlow's US users are seeing sub-2-second page loads for the first time.

But Dave is looking at the global dashboards and frowning again.

The micro-frontend decomposition and SSR migration shifted rendering computation to our servers. The BFF layer consolidated chatty API calls into single, efficient round-trips. Both improvements are real—for users geographically close to our origin servers in Virginia.

Users in Frankfurt are seeing 180ms round-trip times to the BFF. Users in Singapore are seeing 320ms. These are not application latency these are physics. The speed of light in fiber is approximately 200,000 km/s. A packet traveling from Singapore to Virginia and back covers roughly 30,000 km. At the speed of light, that is 150ms of irreducible latency—before a single byte of application logic executes.

Our CDN solved this for static assets in *Chapter 4*. But SSR pages and BFF API calls must still travel to the origin. We cannot cache a personalized checkout page at the Edge. We cannot pre-compute a user-specific cart aggregation at a PoP in Mumbai.

Or can we?

The Edge is no longer just a cache. Modern edge platforms execute code—full server-side rendering, database queries, session management—at 300+ global locations. The question is no longer "how do we get closer to the user" but "how do we move the computation closer to the user."

In *Chapter 6*, we will confront the Speed of Light Problem and explore how to distribute not just content, but logic, and data, to the edge of the network. The CDN gave us global reach. The next step is global compute.

Part 3

Scaling the Services and Data

This is where the back-end becomes a true distributed system, and where most of the hard parts live. Across these five chapters you will decompose the monolith into services with real boundaries, make those services survive each other's failures, decouple them in time with messaging, absorb the read load with caching, and finally perform surgery on the data layer itself through sharding and replication. Each step solves the previous step's bottleneck and exposes the next one. By the end of this part, ShopFlow is a globally distributed system whose services and data scale independently.

This part of the book includes the following chapters:

6

Architecting Scalable Services – Decomposition and API Design

In *Chapter 5*, we decomposed ShopFlow's monolithic SPA into independently deployable micro-frontends. The frontend teams are shipping on their own cadence. Error Boundaries are isolating failures. The BFF layer has consolidated chatty API calls into efficient round trips.

But Dave just flagged a new problem in the team channel.

The micro-frontend decomposition shifted rendering computation to the BFF and SSR layer. Both improvements are real—for users geographically close to our origin servers in Virginia. Users in Frankfurt are seeing 180ms round-trip times. Users in Singapore are seeing 320ms. These are not application latency numbers; they are physics. And we cannot push the computation closer to the user until we can deploy the services it depends on independently.

The frontend is free. The backend is not. Fourteen modules share one database. One bad deploy brings down every feature simultaneously. The BFF is efficient, but the origin it calls is still a monolith running in a single region. We cannot cache a personalized checkout at the edge until we can deploy the checkout service independently—and we cannot do that until we draw the boundaries.

In this chapter, we are going to cover the following main topics:

- **Decomposition:** Identifying seams and bounded contexts.
- **The API Contract:** REST vs. gRPC for internal communication.
- **Data Ownership:** Why shared databases are the enemy of scale.
- **Service Governance:** Managing API versioning and compatibility.
- **The Strangler Fig Pattern:** Incrementally migrating the monolith.

Technical requirements

To follow the transition from a coupled monolith to a rationalized service architecture, you will need:

- **Domain-Driven Design tools (EventStorming / Context Mapper):** For boundary discovery and bounded context mapping before writing a single line of code. Context Mapper generates PlantUML diagrams directly from the DDD model.
- **Protocol Buffers (protoc v3.x) + gRPC:** For defining typed, versioned service contracts. The protoc compiler generates client and server stubs for Python, Go, and Node.js from a single .proto file.
- **OpenAPI 3.1 / Swagger:** For REST contract-first development. The spec file is the source of truth—code generation flows from it, not the other way around.
- **Buf CLI:** For Protobuf linting, breaking-change detection, and schema registry management. Non-negotiable for a multi-team gRPC environment.
- **Strangler Fig proxy (Nginx or Envoy):** For routing traffic between the legacy monolith and newly extracted services during incremental migration. Envoy is preferred for its per-route observability.

Database-per-service enforcement (Flyway/Liquibase): For managing independent schema migrations per service. When services share a schema tool, you cannot enforce data ownership.

Code Repository: `https://github.com/imran-siddique/Architecting-at-Scale/tree/main/ch6`

ShopFlow telemetry snapshot [stage 6]

```
The Signal: The frontend is free. The backend is not. Fourteen modules share one
database, one build pipeline, and one blast radius. We cannot push compute to the
edge until we can deploy services independently.
p99 Latency (US – Virginia Origin): 95ms (Acceptable)
p99 Latency (Frankfurt – BFF Round-Trip): 180ms (Warning – at SLO boundary)
p99 Latency (Singapore – BFF Round-Trip): 320ms (🔴 Critical – above SLO)
Availability: 99.1% (Declining)
Cloud Spend: $7,000/mo (Spiking – 27% MoM increase)
Backend Deployment Success Rate: 65% (🔴 Critical)
Average Backend Build Time: 47 minutes (Organizational bottleneck)
Database Lock Contentions (Orders table): 14 concurrent modules (🔴 Critical)
Panic Meter: 6/10 (Frontend teams ship daily. Backend team is afraid to deploy.)
```

Note

Dave Alert: "I had to cancel three backend deployments last sprint because the build order matters. If inventory-service builds before order-service, we get data corruption. The monolith doesn't know what it is anymore."

Decomposition: identifying seams and bounded contexts

Every decomposition conversation eventually drifts toward the same destination: an architectural diagram covered in dozens of small boxes, each labeled with a noun, each connected by arrows pointing in every direction. The whiteboard looks sophisticated. The production system, six months later, does not.

The most expensive mistake I see senior engineers make when breaking apart a monolith is confusing sophistication with correctness. Microservices are not a goal. They are a tax you pay in exchange for a specific benefit—independent deployability, independent scalability, or independent team ownership of a domain. If you are paying the tax without collecting the benefit, you have not scaled your system. You have scaled your operational debt.

Note

Anti-Pattern: Orbit Architecture: Orbit Architecture occurs when an engineering team, motivated by microservices enthusiasm rather than systemic pressure, extracts services faster than the organization can manage them. The result is a constellation of services that are too small to own a domain, too tightly coupled to deploy independently, and too numerous to reason about as a system. Each service is technically separate. Architecturally, they behave as one unit—but one that requires twelve deployment pipelines to change a business rule.

The Three-Layer boundary rule

The most reliable decomposition framework I have applied across high-scale systems is also the most straightforward: enforce strict separation at three natural architectural seams.

The Seam, Defined: The term seam is borrowed deliberately. Michael Feathers introduced it in Working Effectively with Legacy Code to mean a place where you can alter a system's behavior without editing in that place—a point where two parts of a system meet and can be pulled apart. A decomposition seam is the architectural generalization: a boundary where the system is already partially separated, so cutting there costs less than cutting anywhere else. You do not create seams. You find the ones the system has already grown.

The first seam is the **Data Layer**. The database schema, the query logic, and the persistence contracts are completely isolated from everything above them. No service reaches across this boundary into another service's data model. This is not a best practice; it is a precondition for independent scaling. A shared table is a shared deployment dependency, regardless of how many separate services point at it.

The second seam is the **Service Layer**. Business logic—validation, orchestration, domain rules—lives here. This layer communicates with the Data Layer through a well-defined interface and communicates with other Service Layer components through versioned contracts. Nothing in this layer assumes it knows how the data is stored, and nothing outside this layer assumes it knows how the business logic executes.

The third seam is the **UX Layer**. The frontend, the BFF, the API Gateway—everything that translates domain logic into user-facing responses. As established in *Chapter 5*, this layer owns its own data-fetching strategy and renders degraded responses when the service layer is unavailable.

These three seams always hold. They hold in e-commerce platforms, analytics pipelines, and financial systems. They are not domain-specific. When a team cannot agree on a service boundary, redirect them to the nearest seam. The question is never "should this be its own service?" The question is "which layer does this belong to, and have we respected that layer's contract?"

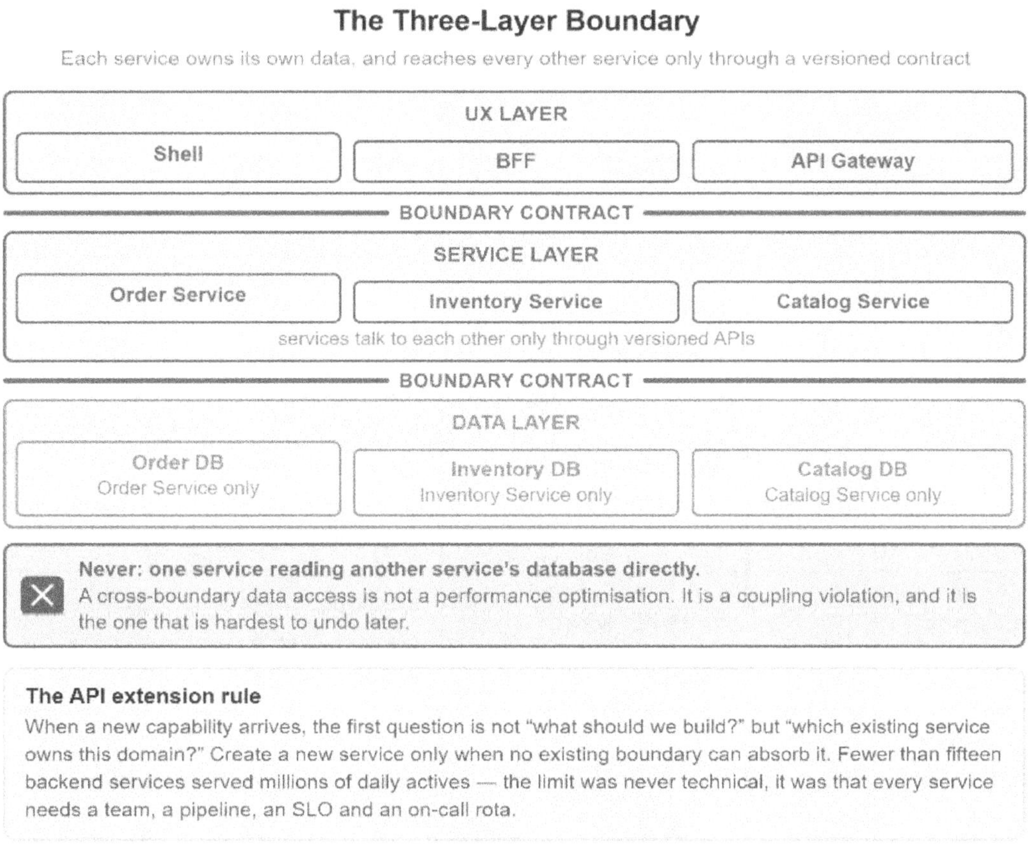

Figure 6.1: The Three-Layer Boundary

> **Note**
>
> **The API Extension Rule:** When adding a new capability, the first question is not "what should we build?" It is "which existing service owns this domain?" Create a new service only when no existing boundary can absorb the capability without violating its domain contract.

In practice, this discipline keeps service counts rational. At a high-traffic enterprise platform, we maintained fewer than fifteen backend services for a platform serving millions of daily active users across dozens of product surfaces. The constraint was not technical. It was organizational: every new service requires a team to own it, a pipeline to deploy it, an SLO to defend it, and an on-call rotation to staff it. The Tool Tax on a new service is not the infrastructure cost; it is the cognitive and operational cost of owning a production system indefinitely.

The following table shows how CRUD maps—and critically, where it fails to map—to real decomposition decisions.

Scenario	Fits CRUD?	Correct Pattern	Rationale
Product catalog read	Yes	REST GET with pagination	High read volume, cacheable, no side effects.
Place order (multi-step)	No	Async API / Event emission	Order placement involves inventory reservation, payment auth, and notification—sequential CRUD causes lock contention.
Bulk price update	No	Batch API with idempotency key	Synchronous per-item PATCH at scale creates a thundering herd against the Catalog service.
Real-time inventory check	No	Read model/ Materialized view	Hitting the write database for reads at checkout volume produces the 14-lock contention we see in ShopFlow today.
User profile update	Yes	REST PATCH	Low frequency, single owner, no downstream side effects at time of write.
Fraud score evaluation	No	Async request-response / gRPC streaming	Model inference latency is variable; synchronous REST blocks the checkout critical path.

Table 6.1: Where CRUD maps cleanly to service operations—and where it breaks down.

Note

Anti-Pattern: The Verb Boundary: The Verb Boundary anti-pattern occurs when a team decomposes a monolith by HTTP method: a 'Create Service,' a 'Read Service,' an 'Update Service.' It is architecturally coherent and domain-incoherent. The Order domain's create, read, update, and delete operations all share business rules, validation

> logic, and state transitions. Separating them by verb forces every business rule change to touch multiple services simultaneously—replacing one deployment dependency with four.

Finding bounded contexts: the ShopFlow domain map

Before the seam signals can tell you where to cut, you need candidate boundaries to test them against. Domain-Driven Design supplies the vocabulary—bounded context, aggregate, ubiquitous language—but the vocabulary is not the decision. The decision is which nouns in the business own their own data and their own rules, and which are merely attributes of a noun that already exists.

Walk ShopFlow's domain and four contexts announce themselves, because each owns state that no other context is permitted to write. Orders owns the lifecycle of a purchase—cart, checkout, payment-authorization handoff, fulfillment status. Inventory owns stock levels and reservations. Catalog owns product definitions, descriptions, and pricing rules. Payments owns the tokenized financial transaction and its reconciliation with the provider. Each has a distinct rate of change, a distinct consistency requirement, and a distinct team that is paged when it fails. Those are four separate bounded contexts.

Reviews are the instructive case. A review has its own table, its own write path, and its own moderation rules—on a whiteboard it looks like a fifth service. But at ShopFlow's current scale, a review has no meaning independent of the product it describes. It is read on the product page, written from the product page, and never queried in isolation. Extracting it would create a service whose only consumer is Catalog, whose only data dependency is Catalog, and whose every schema change would be coordinated with Catalog. Reviews stay inside the Catalog context until an observable signal—an independent moderation workload or a reviews API with external consumers—says otherwise.

The Bounded Context Test: A candidate is its own context when it owns state no other context may write, changes on its own cadence, and can be read and written without a second context inside the transaction. A candidate that fails any of the three is an attribute of an existing context, not a service. Reviews fail the third test today; Payments passes all three.

When not to split a service

The seam signals tell you when a module has earned extraction. The absence of those signals is also a decision—and the more common correct one. Most modules in most systems should never become services. Decomposition is justified by measured pain, not by architectural fashion.

Do not split when the team is small enough to coordinate in a single standup. Below roughly eight engineers, the coordination cost that microservices remove barely exists, and you would be paying the operational tax—pipelines, on-call, SLOs—to solve a problem you do not have. Do not split when deployment frequency is low: a module shipped once a month is not generating the deployment-contention pain that extraction resolves. Do not split a stable domain: a module whose code and schema have not changed in two quarters is not encoding coupling anyone is contending with, and extracting it spends migration risk to freeze what was already frozen.

And do not split without an observable scaling signal. If build time, test blast radius, deployment success rate, and lock contention are all within SLO for a module, that module is not a decomposition candidate regardless of how cleanly it would draw on a whiteboard. ShopFlow extracts Inventory because the Orders-table lock contention is measured at 14 concurrent modules. It does not extract its Notification module in the same wave, because a background job that sends transactional email produces none of those signals.

The No-Signal Rule: A module with no active seam signal is not a service waiting to be born. It is a module doing its job. Extraction is a response to measured pain; in its absence, the correct architecture is the one you already have. Choosing not to decompose is a decision, and it is the only one on this list that is free.

The seam signal: knowing when to cut

The decomposition literature tends to offer philosophical guidance on boundary discovery—ubiquitous language, domain events, team alignment. These are useful inputs. They are not, by themselves, sufficient to make the decision. The decision requires observable signals from the running system, not from a domain model drawn on a whiteboard.

The following signals, when they appear together, indicate that a module has reached extraction readiness.

The Compilation Signal. If a change to one module forces a full recompilation of the entire system, the build system is encoding a coupling that the architecture has not yet acknowledged. Build time is a dependency graph made visible. When ShopFlow's 47-minute average build time is driven by three modules that have nothing to do with the change being shipped, the build is telling you where the boundaries should be.

The Test Blast Radius Signal. If a one-line change to a pricing function requires running the full order integration test suite to validate correctness, the test suite is encoding the same coupling. The correct scope for a pricing change is the pricing domain's tests. When that scope has expanded to include inventory, checkout, and shipping tests, you have a boundary violation masquerading as due diligence.

The Deployment Contention Signal. ShopFlow's 65% deployment success rate is not a code quality problem. It is a coupling problem. When three teams must coordinate deployment order to avoid data corruption, the monolith's deployment pipeline has become a synchronization primitive. Independent services deploy independently. This is the property we are trying to recover.

The Read/Write Ratio Mismatch. A module that is read ten thousand times per second but written to once per hour has fundamentally different scaling requirements than its neighbors. Keeping it coupled to a write-heavy module forces it to scale with write patterns it does not share. ShopFlow's Catalog service—read on every product page, updated only when a product changes—is carrying the scaling cost of the Orders service it shares a database with.

The Team Gravity Signal. When the same team is consistently the subject of deployment-blocking merge conflicts from other teams, the module they own has earned extraction rights. Not because teams should own services—that inversion produces a different anti-pattern—but because sustained merge conflict density is an observable proxy for boundary violation frequency. One signal that should not drive the decision is team structure itself. Teams change. Reorgs happen. Services should map to domains, not to reporting lines.

> Note
>
> **The Gravity Signal Rule:** Extract a service when three or more of the following are true: build time is dominated by the module, test blast radius extends beyond the module's domain, deployment success rate is below the organizational SLO, read/write scaling requirements diverge materially from neighbors, or merge conflict density indicates sustained boundary violation. A single signal is a data point. Three signals are a mandate.

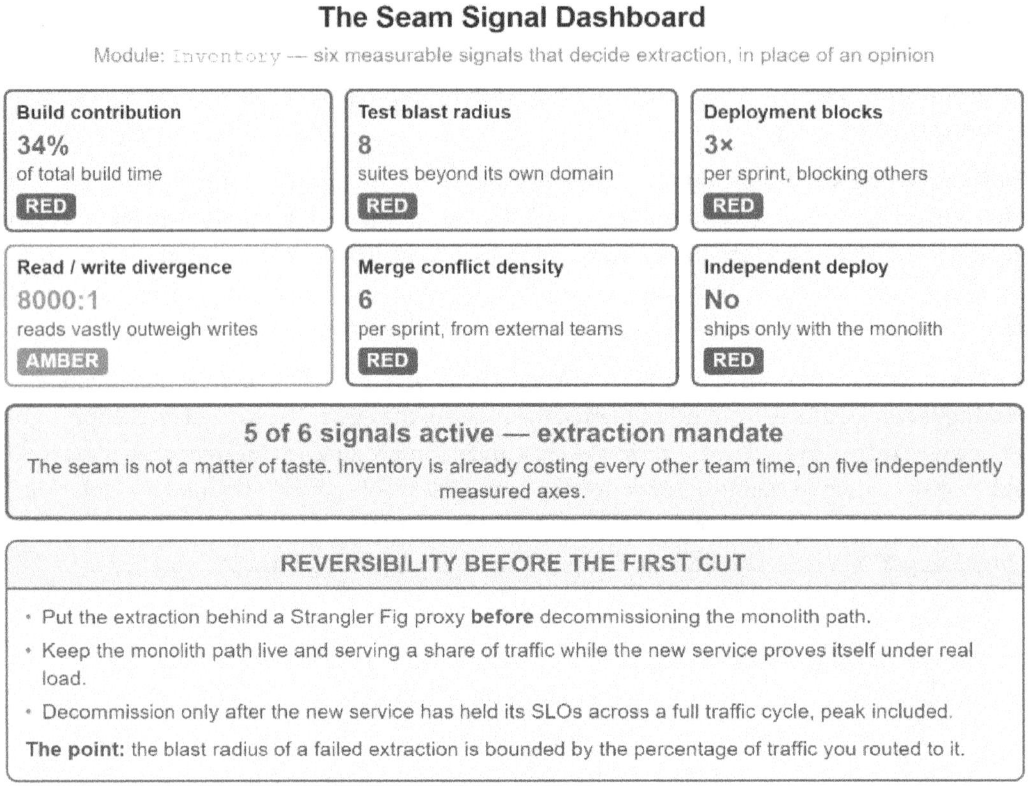

Figure 6.2: The Seam Signal Dashboard

> Note
>
> **Safe Scale Check — Reversibility Before First Cut:** Before extracting the first service, you must have a rollback path. Implement the extraction behind a Strangler Fig proxy before decommissioning the monolith path. Keep the monolith's code path live and routing a percentage of traffic while the new service proves itself under production load. Only decommission the monolith path after the new service has sustained its SLOs across at least one full traffic cycle—including peak. The blast radius of a failed extraction is bounded by the traffic percentage routed to it.

The first cut: Simplest-First vs. Heaviest-First

The most consequential question when beginning decomposition is which service to extract first.

If your deployment pipeline, observability stack, and rollback tooling are not yet validated for independent service operation, extract the simplest candidate first. Not the smallest service, but the one with the clearest domain boundary, the lowest coupling coefficient, and the most tolerance for downtime during migration. You are not solving a business problem with this cut. You are validating that your infrastructure can support the decomposition at all.

If your infrastructure is production-validated—your service mesh is running, your canary deployment pipeline has proven itself, your observability stack gives you per-service SLO tracking—then extract the highest-pain module first. At ShopFlow, this is the Orders/Inventory boundary. The 14-module lock contention on the Orders table is costing deployment velocity, availability, and engineering confidence simultaneously. Extracting Inventory first resolves the lock contention, frees the Orders table for the remaining modules, and delivers an immediate, measurable improvement in database I/O saturation.

Note

The Extraction Sequence Doctrine: In a deployment-infrastructure-validated environment, extract in descending order of pain—starting with the module generating the most observable harm to the system. The last module extracted should be the simplest and least critical, left in the monolith until all higher value extractions have been completed and stabilized. Never leave the highest-pain module for last.

Module	**Pain Signal**	**Coupling Coefficient**	**Extraction Priority**	**Strategy**
Inventory	14 lock contentions/day on shared table	High — shared with Orders, Catalog, Reporting	1st (if infra validated)	Strangler Fig with read model
Catalog	8000:1 read/write divergence, CDN blocking	Medium — read by 6 modules, written by 1	2nd	Extract with dedicated read replica
Shipping Rate	Low contention, clear domain	Low — called by orders only	1st (if infra unvalidated)	Direct extraction, proving infrastructure

Module	Pain Signal	Coupling Coefficient	Extraction Priority	Strategy
Tax Calculation	Stateless, pure function	Very Low — no database ownership	2nd (if infra is unvalidated)	Serverless candidate
Order Reporting	CPU-intensive P2 workload contending with P0	Medium — reads Order and Inventory data	3rd — after inventory extracted	Async event consumer, separate from write path
Payment Processing	P0 critical path, external dependency	High — must not share any infrastructure with P2 paths	4th — after infra is validated	Dedicated isolated deployment

Table 6.2: ShopFlow module extraction priority, ranked by pain signal and coupling coefficient.

> Note
>
> Manager's Math — The Decomposition ROI: ShopFlow's 65% deployment success rate means 35% of all deploy attempts result in a rollback or incident. At four deploys per week across three backend teams and an average incident cost of four engineering-hours, this generates approximately 17 hours of recovery work per week. At a fully-loaded engineering cost, this is a recurring weekly tax. A successful Inventory extraction eliminates the primary source of deployment-order dependencies. Historical data from comparable decompositions show deployment success rates moving from the 60–65% range to above 90% within two sprint cycles of the first high-contention extraction. At ShopFlow's deploy cadence, recovering 25 percentage points of deployment success eliminates roughly 12 hours of weekly recovery work—an annualized return that exceeds the cost of the extraction in the first quarter.

> Note
>
> **Safe Scale Check — Migration Blast Radius:** The blast radius of your first extraction is unbounded until you instrument it. Before the Strangler Fig proxy routes any production traffic to the new Inventory service, you need per-request observability at

> the proxy layer—not at the service layer. The proxy must emit a metric for every request it routes, tagged with the destination (monolith vs. new service) and the outcome (success, error code, latency bucket). Without it, you cannot define a rollback trigger that is anything more than gut instinct.

Architect's prompt 6.1: the decomposition readiness audit

When to use this: Use this prompt when evaluating a legacy monolith for decomposition. Run it before the first architectural decision is made—before any service is named, before any team is assigned, before any API contract is drafted.

```
Act as a Principal Software Architect specializing in monolith decomposition.
I have a backend monolith with the following characteristics:

- [Number] modules share a single relational database
- Average build time: [X] minutes
- Deployment success rate: [Y]%
- p99 database lock contention events per day: [Z]
- Team count contributing to the shared repository: [N]

I am going to paste the following data:
1. A list of modules with their read/write ratios, team ownership, and external
caller counts.
2. The last 30 days of deployment incident reports.
3. The current database schema shows foreign key relationships between module-
owned tables.

[Paste module inventory, incident log, and schema]

For each module, calculate:
(1) A Coupling Coefficient: number of other modules affected by an independent
deployment.
weighted by incident frequency.
(2) A Pain Score: composite of lock contention frequency, test blast radius,
and deployment block frequency.
(3) An Infrastructure Risk Score: how much this extraction depends on
deployment infrastructure that is not yet validated.

Output a prioritized extraction sequence. For each module, specify:
- Extraction priority (1 = first)
```

```
- Recommended strategy (Strangler Fig / Direct Extract / Event Consumer)
- Minimum infrastructure prerequisites before extraction begins
- Rollback trigger definition (the specific metric threshold that should)
trigger reverting to the monolith path)
- Estimated blast radius if the extraction fails at 100% traffic routing
```

The API contract: REST vs. gRPC for internal communication

The REST vs. gRPC debate is usually framed as a performance question. It should be framed as an operational question.

The binary choice between REST and gRPC conceals the more consequential decision underneath it: how many services are you actually willing to own in production? Every service boundary requires a contract. Every contract requires versioning. Every version requires compatibility testing. Every compatibility test requires a pipeline. If you are managing five internal services and you choose gRPC, you are managing five .proto files, five generated client stubs, five schema registries, and five breaking-change detection jobs. The protocol is not the bottleneck. The number of contracts is.

> Note
>
> **The Operational Gravity Rule:** Before choosing a communication protocol, determine the minimum number of services you can operate while meeting your scaling requirements. Five services that can be independently scaled and monitored as a unit are operationally cheaper than fifteen services optimized for team alignment. Choose the grouping that makes production manageable—then choose the protocol that fits that grouping.

When REST is the correct answer

REST over HTTP/1.1 or HTTP/2 is the correct protocol for internal service communication when three conditions are true: the call frequency is low enough that JSON serialization cost is not measurable in your p99 latency budget, the consumers of the API include external parties or teams with heterogeneous toolchains, and the contract evolution pace is high enough that the overhead of recompiling .proto files and redistributing generated stubs would outpace the team's delivery cadence.

For ShopFlow's current architecture—three backend teams, six to eight internal services after decomposition, call volumes in the thousands-per-second range rather than hundreds-of-thousands—REST with OpenAPI 3.1 contracts is the appropriate default. The operational overhead of a gRPC migration today would be paid in engineering time that is currently needed for the Inventory extraction. This is not a permanent decision. It is a sequenced one.

> Note
>
> **The REST Tax:** JSON serialization at high call volumes is measurably more expensive than Protocol Buffer binary encoding. HTTP/1.1 multiplexing limitations create head-of-line blocking under concurrent load. REST's schema flexibility—often cited as an advantage—is a liability in a multi-team environment where undocumented field additions and silent type changes are the primary source of service-to-service integration failures. You cannot enforce a REST contract at compile time. You discover violations in production.

Protocol	Serialization Overhead	Contract Enforcement	Streaming Support	Breaking Change Detection	Operational Cost
REST/JSON (HTTP/1.1)	High — text parsing at every hop	None at compile time	No	Manual/ linting only	Low — universal tooling
REST / JSON (HTTP/2)	High — text parsing, multiplexed	None at compile time	Server-sent events only	Manual/ linting only	Low–moderate tooling
gRPC / Protobuf (HTTP/2)	Low — binary, ~5–10× smaller payload	Enforced at compile time	Full bidirectional	Automated via Buf CLI	High — generated stubs, schema registry
GraphQL	Medium — flexible but over-fetching risk	Partial — schema-defined, not enforced	Subscriptions only	Manual/ schema diffing	High — resolver complexity
AsyncAPI / Events	N/A — async, no response contract	Schema registry required	Native	Automated via schema registry	High — broker, consumer group management

Table 6.3: REST, gRPC, and GraphQL compared across the operational dimensions that drive protocol selection.

A note on OData and GraphQL: this chapter frames protocol selection as REST versus gRPC because that is the decision that dominates internal service-to-service communication. OData is not a fourth protocol tier—it is a query convention layered on top of REST, standardizing filtering, sorting, and pagination in the URL (for example ?$filter= and ?$top=). It earns its place in enterprise and Microsoft-ecosystem APIs where a uniform, self-describing query surface over many entity sets is worth the added contract complexity. For ShopFlow's internal paths it is overhead without a matching benefit: the query flexibility it offers is precisely the flexibility we do not want between internal services, where a fixed, versioned contract is the goal. GraphQL sits in the same category—powerful for a client-facing aggregation layer, unnecessary and coupling-prone as an internal service contract.

When gRPC becomes nonnegotiable

The switch from REST to gRPC for internal communication crosses from interesting optimization to operational requirement when two conditions converge: call volume between two specific services exceeds approximately 50,000 requests per second sustained, and the services are owned by teams with independent deployment cadences.

At 50,000 RPS, the JSON serialization overhead on a typical order payload—2–4KB of nested JSON—produces a measurable CPU cost on the receiving service. At 200,000 RPS, it becomes the dominant CPU consumer. Protocol Buffer encoding of the same payload runs at 200–400 bytes with negligible parsing overhead. The performance case is real at these volumes.

But the more important threshold is not about throughput. It is about contract discipline. When two services are owned by teams with different deployment cadences, the risk of a breaking API change landing in production before the consumer is updated is not hypothetical. In a REST environment, the first signal of a breaking change is a 4xx error rate spike in production monitoring. In a gRPC environment with Buf CLI enforcing breaking-change detection in the CI pipeline, the signal arrives at the pull request, before any code reaches production.

> Note
>
> **The Contract-First Mandate:** You cannot ship an internal service API without a machine-readable contract defined before a single line of application code is written. For REST, this is an OpenAPI 3.1 spec committed to the repository. For gRPC, this is a .proto file checked into a central schema registry. The contract is the source of truth. The implementation is an artifact of the contract. This is non-negotiable.

Evolving from REST to gRPC: A staged migration

The REST-versus-gRPC choice is rarely made once. Systems evolve through a predictable sequence, and forcing the end state prematurely is its own mistake.

Stage one is REST everywhere. Early in a service architecture, when call volumes sit in the thousands per second and the priority is delivery velocity, REST with OpenAPI 3.1 contracts is correct for every internal path. The serialization cost is not measurable in the latency budget, and the toolchain is universal. This is ShopFlow today.

Stage two is selective gRPC on the hot internal paths. As specific service-to-service paths cross the throughput threshold—sustained volume where JSON serialization becomes a measurable CPU cost—those paths, and only those, migrate to gRPC. The trigger is per-path, not system-wide. At ShopFlow the first candidate is the Order-to-Inventory reservation call inside checkout, because it is the highest-frequency internal call on the critical path; the cached, low-frequency Catalog read stays REST.

Stage three is REST at the edge, gRPC in the core. External consumers—mobile clients, partner integrations, the browser—keep speaking REST through the API gateway, because you do not control their toolchains and you do not get to mandate Protobuf on a third party. The gateway translates the external REST contract into internal gRPC calls. This is the steady state of most mature architectures: a REST perimeter over a gRPC interior, with the protocol boundary landing exactly where the toolchain boundary already is.

The Staged Protocol Rule: Do not migrate a whole system from REST to gRPC. Migrate the paths that cross the throughput threshold, keep REST at every boundary you do not control, and let the API gateway be the seam between the two. The end state is not "gRPC"—it is REST where the consumers are heterogeneous and gRPC where the volume is high and the owners are internal.

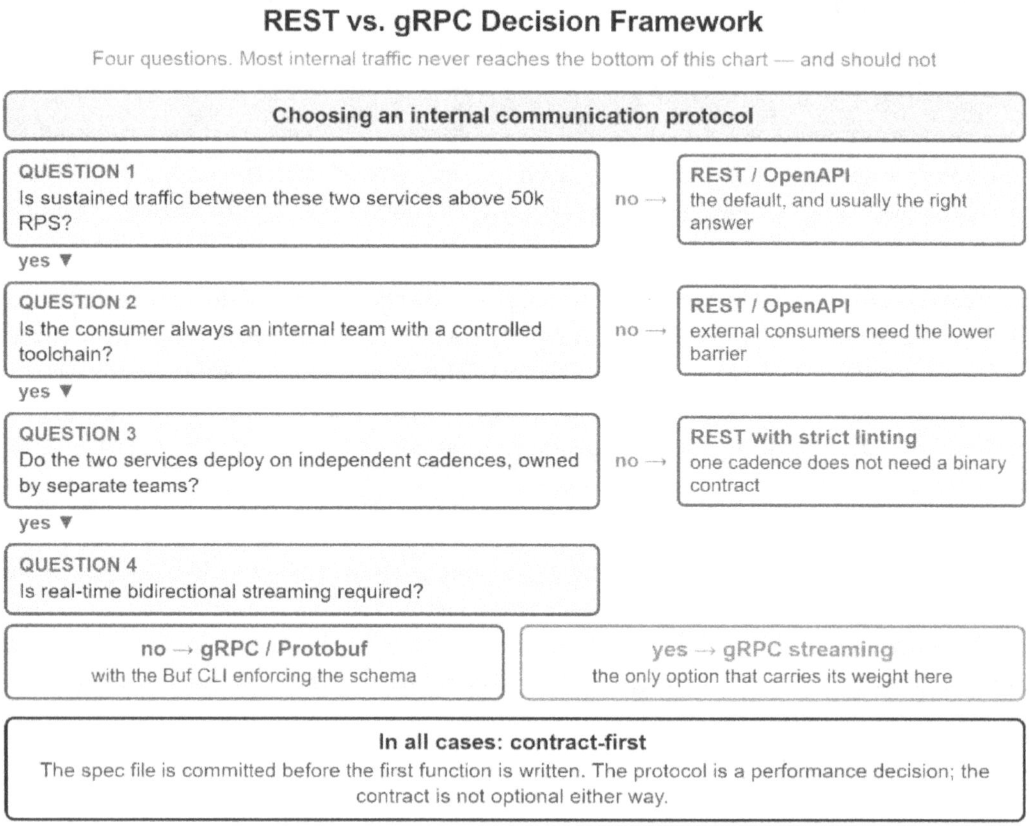

Figure 6.3: REST vs. gRPC Decision Framework

Service rationalization: the operational gravity framework

The decomposition literature focuses heavily on how to split services. It focuses far less on when not to split them. This is the gap that produces the Orbit Architecture anti-pattern.

At a high-traffic enterprise platform, we reached a point where a proposal was made to split a content-delivery service into seven smaller services—one per content type. The technical argument was coherent: each content type had a different caching strategy, a different read/write ratio, and a slightly different data model. On a whiteboard, seven services looked clean.

In production, seven services meant seven deployment pipelines, seven on-call rotations, seven SLO dashboards, and seven sets of runbooks. The content-delivery domain generated fewer than three incidents per quarter. The operational overhead of seven services would have exceeded the operational overhead of the single service we were trying to replace—permanently. We kept one service. We added a strategy pattern internally to handle the different content types. The operational cost was one pipeline. The scaling benefit was identical to the seven-service proposal.

> Note
>
> **The Service Count Rule:** The correct number of services is the minimum number required to eliminate the observable seam signals in your current system. Every service beyond that minimum is a management liability you are accepting in exchange for a benefit you must be able to name and measure.

Logical Domain	Candidate Services	Rationalized Service Count	Rationale
Order Processing	Order Create, Order Read, Order Status, Order History	1 (Order Service)	Same domain, shared write model, no read/write ratio divergence at current scale
Inventory	Inventory Write, Inventory Read Model, Stock Reservation	2 (Inventory Write + Read Model)	8000:1 read/write divergence justifies independent read model; reservation is a write-path concern
Catalog	Product Data, Search Index, Category Management	2 (Catalog Service + Search Service)	Search is a read-only, compute-intensive workload that must not contend with catalog writes
Pricing	Price Calculation, Promotion Engine, Tax	1 (Pricing Service)	Stateless computation, no persistent state divergence, single deployment cadence
Shipping	Rate Calculation, Label Generation, Carrier API	1 (Shipping Service)	External API dependency warrants isolation; all three functions share the same blast radius

Logical Domain	Candidate Services	Rationalized Service Count	Rationale
Payments	Payment Auth, Refund Processing, Fraud Score	1 (Payment Service)	P0 critical path — must be isolated from all other services, regardless of internal complexity

Table 6.4: Rationalizing candidate services down to the minimum viable service count.

Target: **6 services** replacing a 14-module monolith. Each service owns its data model, its deployment pipeline, and its SLO. None shares a database table with another.

> Note
>
> **Manager's Math — The Service Count Tax:** Each additional service in a production environment carries an annualized operational overhead. We measured this overhead at approximately 0.25 engineering FTE per service per year—accounting for on-call rotation, SLO maintenance, dependency updates, and pipeline overhead. At a mid-market engineering salary, this is roughly $40–60K per service per year in fully-loaded cost. The difference between a 14-service decomposition and a 6-service decomposition is 8 services. At $50K per service per year, the rationalized decomposition saves approximately $400K annually in operational overhead—before accounting for the reduction in incident load and cross-team coordination cost. Decomposition decisions have a line item. Run the math before the whiteboard session.

Architect's prompt 6.2: the protocol selection audit

When to use this: Use this prompt when evaluating whether an existing internal REST API should be migrated to gRPC or when designing the initial communication protocol for a new service boundary.

```
Act as a Principal API Architect. I am evaluating the communication
protocol between two internal services:

Service A: [Name, team ownership, deployment cadence]
Service B: [Name, team ownership, deployment cadence]

Current protocol: [REST/JSON or gRPC or event-based]
Sustained RPS on this path (p50): [X]
```

```
Sustained RPS on this path (p99 spike): [Y]
Average payload size: [Z KB]
Current p99 latency for this call: [Nms]
Number of contract-violation incidents in the last 90 days: [N]

Evaluate:
(1) Is JSON serialization overhead measurable in the current p99 latency budget?
Provide the calculation.
(2) Does the deployment cadence mismatch between Service A and Service B?
create material breaking-change risk under the current protocol?
(3) What is the operational cost of migrating to gRPC, expressed as
engineering-days for stub regeneration, schema registry setup.
and Buf CLI integration?
(4) At what RPS threshold does the ROI of the gRPC migration become?
positive, given the operational cost calculated in (3)?

Output a protocol recommendation with a specific trigger condition for
migration—expressed as a measurable threshold, not a subjective judgment.
```

Data ownership: why shared databases are the enemy of scale

The most common decomposition failure is not a bad service boundary. It is a good service boundary built on top of a shared database.

The pattern is recognizable: a team extracts the Inventory service, stands up an independent deployment pipeline, writes a clean REST API. They celebrate the decomposition. Then, because the migration timeline was tight, they leave the Inventory tables in the shared database. The Order service still reads directly from inventory.stock_levels. The Reporting service still joins orders.line_items against inventory.products. The service boundary exists in the code. It does not exist in the data.

Six months later, the Inventory team changes a column name. The Reporting service breaks silently. The Order service starts returning stale stock counts because it bypassed the Inventory API for a "quick read." The team has spent six months building a distributed monolith with a shared database—operationally more expensive than the monolith they started with, without the benefits of true service independence.

Note

The Shared Database Rule: A service that allows another service to read or write its tables directly does not own its data. Data ownership is enforced by access control, not by convention. If a service's database credentials are available to any other service, the boundary does not exist.

The single authority pattern

The correct architecture for cross-service data access is a **Single Authority Service**—one service that owns a domain's data completely, exposes it exclusively through a versioned API, and is the only entity permitted to write to or read from its underlying storage. Every other service that needs data from that domain calls the API. Not a replica. Not a read-only connection string. The API.

This pattern solves three problems simultaneously. It enforces the contract boundary—consumers cannot access data that is not exposed through the API surface. It enables independent scaling—the authority service can switch its underlying storage technology, add a caching layer, or shard its database without any consumer being aware of the change. And it provides a single point of observability—every data access is a traceable API call, not an invisible database connection.

The objection is always latency. A direct database read within the same data center runs at 1–5ms. An internal API call runs at 5–15ms depending on serialization and network hop. In a system where a user-facing request makes three internal data calls, this difference is 10–30ms of added latency—well within a reasonable SLO budget. The alternative—allowing direct database access—trades 10ms of latency for an unbounded coupling liability. The latency is a fixed cost. The coupling liability compounds indefinitely.

Note

Anti-Pattern: The Shared Data Lake: The Shared Data Lake occurs when every service reads from and writes to a central enterprise data platform. It is presented as a solution to the cross-service reporting problem. In practice, it is a monolith with extra steps. Every team contributes to the schema. No team owns the schema. Schema changes require cross-team negotiation because any change can break any consumer. The tell is always the same: a growing backlog of schema change requests that require a committee to approve, because no single team has the authority to modify a schema that twenty teams depend on.

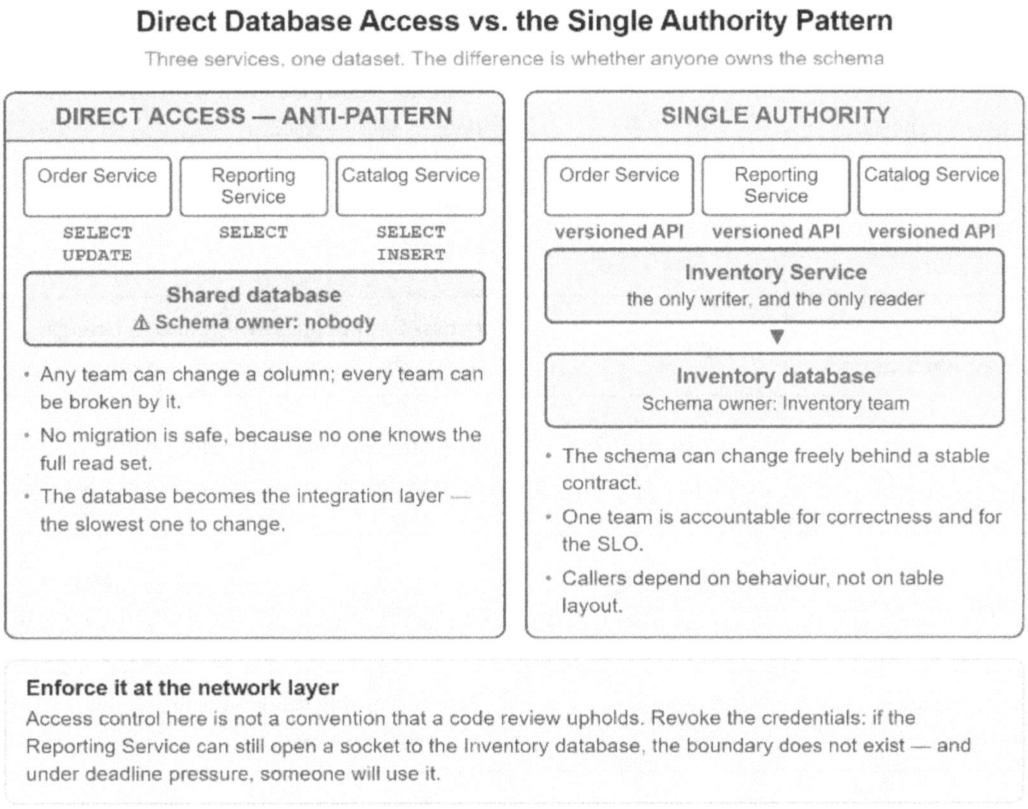

Figure 6.4: Direct Database Access vs. Single Authority Pattern

The reporting problem: A solved problem

The most persistent objection to the Single Authority pattern is the reporting use case. If each service owns its data independently, how do we run cross-domain analytical queries?

The answer is a dedicated **read model**—a separate data store, owned by the analytics or data engineering function, populated asynchronously from the service-layer events described in *Chapter 8*. Each authority service emits change events when its data is modified. The read model subscribes to those events and maintains a denormalized, join-ready representation optimized for analytical queries. The read model is explicitly not the source of truth. It is eventually consistent, purpose-built for reads, owned by the team that needs the joins.

Access Pattern	Correct Data Source	Rationale
Real-time stock check at checkout	Inventory Service API	Requires strong consistency—stale stock data causes overselling
Order history display (user profile)	Order Service API	Real-time, user-facing, owned by Order domain
Quarterly revenue by product category	Analytics Read Model	Cross-domain join, eventual consistency acceptable, high query complexity
Fraud detection (cross-service signals)	Event stream/read model	Requires signals from multiple domains; latency tolerance is higher than checkout
Operations dashboard (live order status)	Order Service API + Inventory Service API	Two separate calls composed at the BFF layer —not a database join
Data science / ML feature store	Read model + batch pipeline	Offline training workloads are explicitly not on the critical path

Table 6.5: Choosing the correct data source by access pattern.

Note

The DAL Mandate: Every service exposes its data through a Data Access Layer with a versioned, documented contract. Direct database credentials are never distributed outside the owning service's deployment boundary. This is enforced at the infrastructure level—IAM roles, network policies, or Kubernetes namespace isolation—not by the honor system, the arrangement where access is governed only by convention and the expectation that no team will connect to a database it does not own. Convention is not enforcement; a credential that exists will eventually be used.

The practical cost of eventual consistency

The read model solves the reporting problem, but it introduces a property the shared database used to hide: the data a consumer reads is not always the data that was just written. The read model is eventually consistent. Understanding what that means in production—not in theory—is the difference between a design that holds and one that generates support tickets.

The lag is observable and specific. When a customer places an order, the Orders service commits immediately and the stock reservation is strongly consistent inside the Inventory context—that path cannot be eventually consistent, because overselling is a correctness failure. But the analytics dashboard showing "units sold today" reads from the event-fed read model and may lag the live order count by a few seconds. An internal merchandising dashboard may briefly show a stock level one or two units behind the reservations already taken. Neither is a defect. Both are the read model catching up.

The engineering decision is which workflows tolerate that lag and which do not, and it is a consequence question, not a technology one: what breaks if this read is stale by five seconds? Payment authorization, stock reservation at checkout, and any decision that moves money or commits a promise to a customer require strong consistency and must read from the authority service. Analytics, dashboards, recommendation inputs, search indexing, and reporting tolerate lag and should read from the read model—because forcing them onto the authority services reintroduces exactly the cross-service coupling the decomposition removed.

The Consistency Boundary Rule: Strong consistency is a requirement only where staleness changes an outcome—money, inventory commitments, authorization. Everywhere else, eventual consistency is not a compromise; it is the correct default, and the read model is where it lives. Classify every read by the cost of its staleness before you decide where it reads from.

Database migration: the pattern nobody teaches

Data migration is the operation that most decomposition timelines underestimate. The technical steps are straightforward. The failure modes are not.

The failure mode that almost no migration plan accounts for is **backward compatibility debt**. A team builds a new schema, migrates the data overnight, and updates the service to write to the new schema. The migration runs cleanly in staging. In production, an edge-case code path—a background job, a legacy API endpoint, a third-party integration that was undocumented—is still writing to the old schema. The new schema starts diverging. Data integrity degrades silently. The recovery is more expensive than the original migration: two schemas with partially overlapping data, no clear source of truth, and a code surface area that is larger and more complex than before.

The migration pattern that avoids this failure has three stages and a principle: **never migrate data on day one**.

Stage 1 — Deploy the new schema in production. The new schema exists alongside the old schema. No data has moved. All existing code paths continue to write to and read from the old schema. This stage validates that the new schema can be deployed without downtime. Cost: one deployment, minimal risk.

Stage 2 — Dual-write window. All new writes go to both the old schema and the new schema. All reads still come from the old schema. This stage is the backward compatibility guarantee—the old schema remains the source of truth, and the new schema is populated in parallel. Any code path that fails to write to the new schema is visible in the write-error metrics before it matters. Duration: until the new schema is confirmed to receive every write the old schema receives, with zero divergence.

Stage 3 — Batch migration and cutover. With the dual-write window confirmed, begin migrating historical data from the old schema to the new schema in batches—not in a single operation. Batch size is determined by the acceptable impact on database I/O during the migration window. Reads are cut over to the new schema only after the historical data migration is complete and validated. The old schema is decommissioned only after reads have run from the new schema through at least one full traffic cycle—including peak—with zero error-rate delta.

> Note
>
> **The Parallel Schema Rule:** Deploy the new schema before migrating any data. Run a dual-write window before cutting over any reads. Migrate historical data in batches, not in a single operation. Decommission the old schema only after one full traffic cycle on the new schema with zero error delta. No step in this sequence should be skipped to meet a timeline.

The dual-write window is deceptively simple for inserts and genuinely hard for updates and deletes. An insert written to both schemas is idempotent—replaying it changes nothing. An update is not: if a row is updated in the old schema and the paired write to the new schema fails or arrives out of order, the two schemas diverge on that column, and the divergence stays silent until a read exposes it. A delete is harder still—a delete that lands in one schema and not the other leaves a residual row that a later batch migration will happily copy back.

The Mutable Dual-Write Rule: For updates and deletes, dual-write alone is not enough; you need conflict resolution. Version every row with a monotonic timestamp or sequence number and apply last-writer-wins on the new schema, so a reordered or replayed write cannot regress a newer value. Represent deletes as explicit tombstones during the window, not as absent rows, so reconciliation can tell "deleted" apart from "not yet migrated." Run a continuous reconciliation job that diffs the two schemas and alerts on any divergence, rather than trusting that every write succeeded on both sides.

Further reading: This chapter treats dual-write at the level of the pattern. Zero-downtime migration of mutable data at scale is a deep topic with well-documented field reports—Stripe's "Online migrations at scale," GitHub's account-migration write-ups, and the change-data-capture approach (for example Debezium, which reads the database log rather than dual-writing in application code) are the references to reach for once the dataset is large enough that application-level dual-write becomes a liability. Martin Fowler's "Evolutionary Database Design" is the canonical treatment of the migration discipline itself.

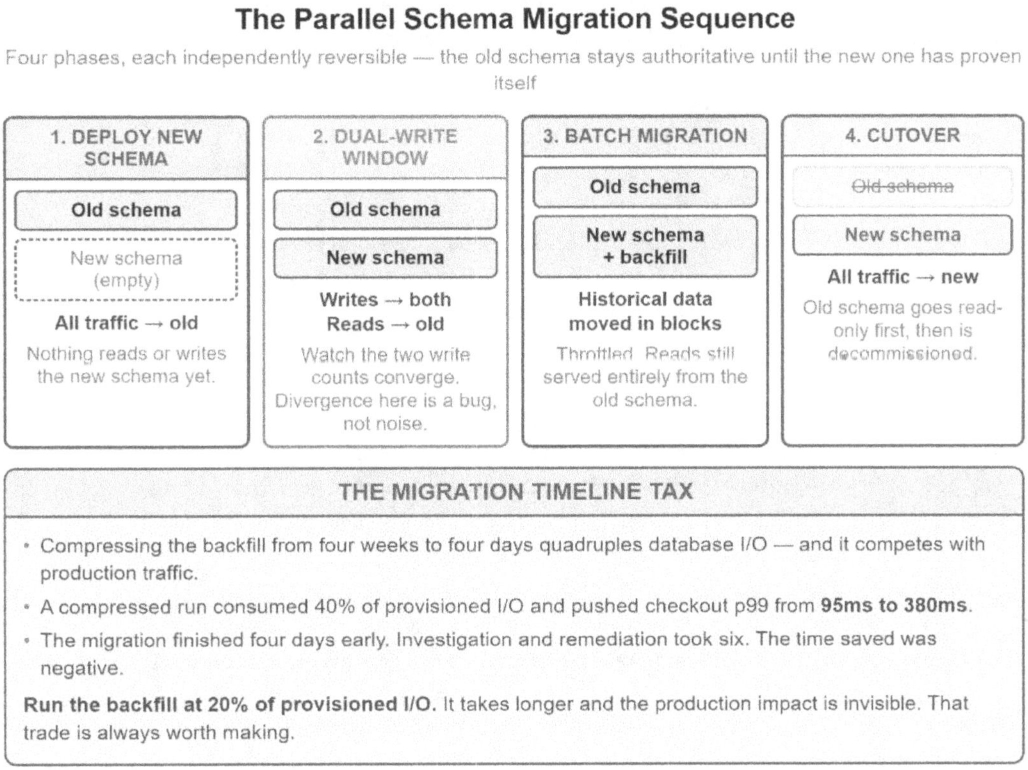

Figure 6.5: The Parallel Schema Migration Sequence

Note

Manager's Math — The Migration Timeline Tax: Compressing the batch migration from four weeks to four days quadruples the database I/O load during the migration window, which competes with production traffic. At a high-traffic enterprise platform, a compressed batch migration running at full throughput consumed 40% of provisioned database I/O, pushing p99 latency on the checkout path from 95ms to 380ms during the migration window. The migration completed in four days. The

> incident investigation and performance remediation took six days. The time saved was negative. Run the batch migration at 20% of provisioned I/O capacity. It takes longer. The production impact is invisible. The tradeoff is always worth it.

Architect's prompt 6.3: the data ownership audit

When to use this: Use this prompt before beginning any service extraction that involves shared database tables. Run it against your current schema and access log to identify all hidden data coupling before a single line of migration code is written.

```
Act as a Principal Data Architect specializing in service decomposition.
I am extracting [Service Name] from a shared monolithic database.

The current shared database has [N] tables. I am going to provide:
1. The schema for all tables that [Service Name] currently reads or writes.
2. A 30-day access log showing which modules read or write each table.
3. The proposed new schema for [Service Name]'s isolated database.

[Paste schema, access log, and proposed new schema]

For each table in the current schema that [Service Name] accesses:
(1) Identify every other service or module that also accesses this table.
(2) Classify the access as: Owner (writes and reads, should own the table).
Consumer (reads only, should call an API instead), or Shared Writer
(writes and reads—a boundary violation requiring resolution).
(3) For every Shared Writer, propose a resolution: which service becomes
the Single Authority, and what API contract should the other writer call?

Then, for the proposed new schema:
(4) Identify any column that does not have a clear owning service.
(5) Flag any foreign key that crosses the new service boundary.
(6) Generate a dual-write migration plan: what must be true before Stage 2?
begins, what metrics confirm Stage 2 is complete, and what batch size
is safe for Stage 3 given the current database I/O utilization.
```

Service governance: managing API versioning and compatibility

Every team that has ever broken a production API consumer made the same decision at the beginning of the project: they decided to think about versioning later.

Later never arrives on schedule. It arrives as an incident. The sequence is consistent across organizations and tech stacks. A team ships a service. Other teams build on it. Six months later, the owning team needs to change the response shape. They look at the consumer list. There are eleven of them. Migrating eleven consumers requires coordinating eleven teams, eleven deployment windows, eleven sets of regression tests. The effort is so large that the team abandons the clean change and instead adds a parallel field, leaving the old field in place. Within a year, the API is carrying six deprecated fields that no team wants to own, and the response payload has tripled in size.

> Note
>
> **The Versioning Mandate:** API versioning is not a feature you add when you need it. It is a structural property of the service contract established before the first endpoint is implemented. A service that ships without a versioning strategy has already made a choice—it has chosen to treat every future change as a potential incident. This is non-negotiable.

The breaking change you are not expecting

The obvious breaking changes are well-documented: remove a required field, change a field's type, rename an endpoint. Every engineer who has shipped an internal API knows these.

The breaking change that reaches production in well-intentioned teams is the **additive change treated as safe**. Adding a new field to a response payload is backward compatible only if the consumer deserializes the response into a flexible structure that tolerates unknown fields. It is not backward compatible when the consumer deserializes into a strict type—a generated gRPC stub, a TypeScript interface with exactOptionalPropertyTypes enabled, a Python Pydantic model with extra='forbid'. In these cases, an unrecognized field raises a deserialization error. The consumer breaks. The change was additive. The consumer is down.

The second form is the **behavioral change with no schema delta**. The API contract says a field returns a string. It has always returned a non-empty string. A team adds a code path that returns an empty string under a specific condition. The schema has not changed. The type has not changed. Every consumer that assumed non-empty and failed to validate is now throwing a null pointer exception on a path that was never exercised in staging.

> Note
>
> **The Silent Breaking Change Rule:** A change is breaking if any consumer's behavior changes as a result, regardless of whether the schema changed. Additive changes break strict deserializers. Behavioral changes break consumers that assumed invariants the contract never formalized. Both require a version increment.

Versioning strategy: URI vs. header vs. content negotiation

Strategy	Mechanism	Consumer Migration Effort	Deprecation Visibility	Caching Compatibility	Recommended For
URI versioning	/v1/orders, /v2/orders	Low — version is explicit in every call	High — old version traffic is directly observable in logs	Full — CDN and proxy cache by URI	Default for all public and internal REST APIs
Header Versioning	Accept: application/vnd.shopflow.v2+json	Medium — requires header injection at every call site	Low — header values not visible in standard access logs	Poor — most CDNs do not vary cache by custom headers	APIs where URI changes are prohibited by a gateway contract
Query Parameter	/orders?version=2	Low — explicit, easy to add	Medium — visible in logs but easily omitted	Partial — cacheable but pollutes canonical URL	Not recommended—version in query parameter is easily stripped by proxies
Content Negotiation	Standard Accept header negotiation	High — requires client media type management	Low	Poor	Not recommended for internal service APIs at scale

Table 6.6: API versioning strategies compared across migration effort, visibility, and caching.

URI versioning is the correct default for internal service APIs. The version is visible in every log line, every trace span, every proxy metric. When v1 traffic drops to zero, decommissioning is a single Nginx route removal. The URI version increment is the signal that a contract boundary has been crossed. It communicates to every consumer: this is not a backward-compatible change. You must opt into the new behavior explicitly.

There is a defensible exception, and it lives at the external edge. Public cloud and platform APIs frequently pass the version as a query parameter—Azure Resource Manager is the canonical example, where a call reads .../resourceGroups?api-version=2022-04-01. This does not contradict the URI-path default; it is a different context. Query-parameter versioning suits large public APIs with an enormous installed base of clients, where a single stable resource path must be preserved across years and the version is a dimension the caller selects per request. It keeps resource identity constant while letting the client opt into a dated contract.

The Versioning Context Rule: URI-path versioning is the default for internal service APIs, where you control every consumer and want the version loud in every log line and route. Query-parameter versioning is acceptable for large external or platform APIs, where a stable resource path across a huge client base matters more than route-level visibility. Header-based and content-negotiation versioning remain the wrong default for both—invisible in logs, awkward for caches, and easy to misconfigure at the proxy. Choose by who owns the consumers, not by aesthetics.

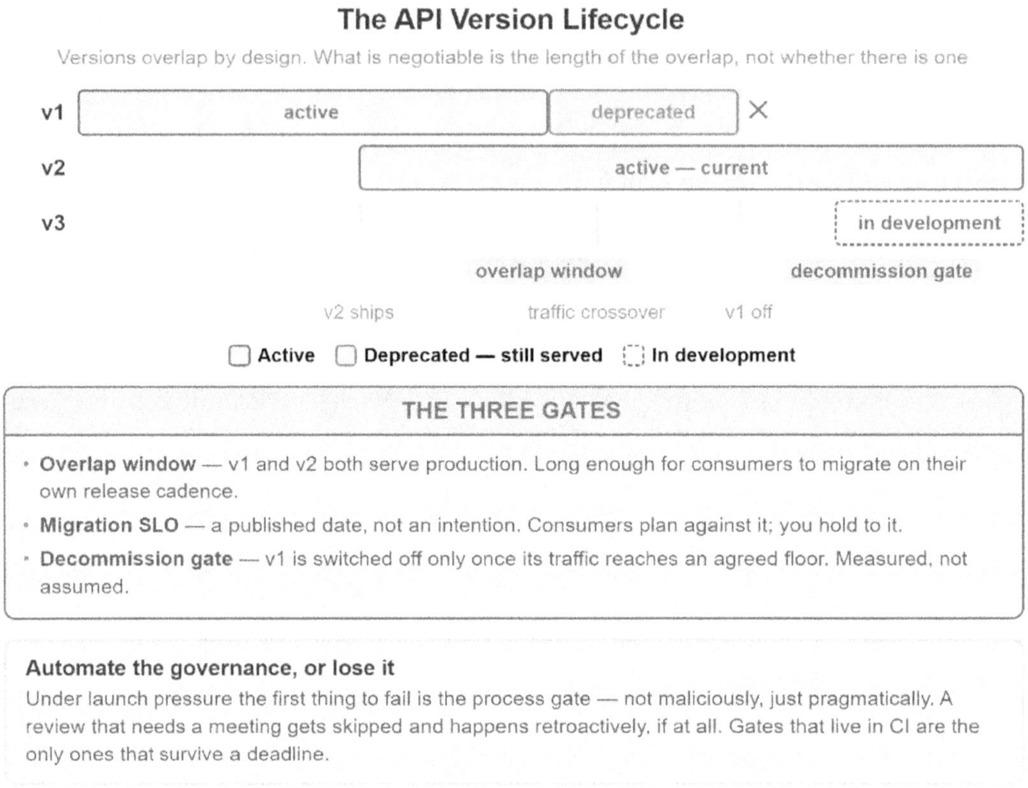

Figure 6.6: The API Version Lifecycle

Automated governance: the only model that works at scale

When a team is under delivery pressure—a launch deadline, an incident remediation, a competitive response—the first thing that fails is the process gate. A human API review that requires scheduling a meeting and waiting for approval is skipped. Not maliciously. Pragmatically. The team ships. The review happens retroactively, if at all.

At scale, with dozens of internal APIs and multiple teams shipping independently, human review gates do not hold. The only governance model that survives delivery pressure is one where the gate is automated, blocking, and part of the standard build pipeline—indistinguishable from a failing unit test.

> Note
>
> **The Automated Governance Rule:** At any team count above three shipping to the same API surface, all compatibility enforcement must be automated in CI. No human review gate survives sustained delivery pressure at scale.

The CI pipeline for every service with an internal API must include four automated gates:

Gate 1 — Schema Lint. The API contract file (.proto or .openapi.yaml) is syntactically valid and follows the team's naming conventions. Blocks merge on violation. Cost: seconds.

Gate 2 — Breaking Change Detection. The current contract is compared against the registered baseline. Any change that would break a strict deserializer—field removal, type change, required parameter addition, enum value removal—fails the build. The only resolution is a version increment. Cost: seconds.

Gate 3 — Consumer Contract Tests. A suite of tests run against the new service version using the contract expectations of every registered consumer. If Consumer A expects a non-empty product_name field, that expectation is encoded as a contract test that runs in the owning service's pipeline. The owning service cannot break Consumer A's expectation without Consumer A's explicit opt-in to a new version. Cost: minutes.

Gate 4 — Deprecation SLO Enforcement. When a version is marked deprecated, the CI pipeline tracks the deprecation age against the team's defined migration SLO. If the SLO expires and consumer traffic on the deprecated version has not reached zero, a blocking gate prevents new deployments until the deprecation is resolved. Cost: seconds.

Gate	**Tool (gRPC)**	**Tool (REST)**	**Failure Mode Caught**	**Blocks Merge?**
Schema Lint	buf lint	spectral lint	Malformed contract, naming violations	Yes
Breaking Change Detection	buf breaking	oasdiff breaking	Field removal, type change, required param addition	Yes
Consumer Contract Tests	Pact / gRPC contract tests	Pact/Dredd	Behavioral invariant violations, silent breaking changes	Yes

Gate	Tool (gRPC)	Tool (REST)	Failure Mode Caught	Blocks Merge?
Deprecation SLO enforcement	Custom CI step + service registry	Custom CI step + service registry	Expired deprecation with live consumer traffic	Yes

Table 6.7: The four automated API-governance gates, their tooling, and the failure modes each catches.

Note

The Deprecation SLO: Every deprecated API version carries a defined migration window. The SLO is not a courtesy notice. It is an enforceable contract, tracked in the service registry and enforced in CI. We standardized on a 90-day migration SLO for internal APIs—long enough for consumers to plan a migration, short enough that deprecated versions do not persist indefinitely. Teams that need an extension request it explicitly and justify the delay. The SLO does not slip silently.

Note

Manager's Math — The Cost of No Governance: A breaking API change that reaches production requires identifying affected consumers (30 minutes to 2 hours), coordinating rollback or forward-fix across teams (1–4 hours), and executing the remediation (1–3 hours). Total incident cost: 2–9 engineering-hours per event across multiple teams. At a high-traffic enterprise platform, we observed 1.8 breaking-change incidents per month pre-governance. Post-governance—with Buf CLI and oasdiff integrated into CI—the rate dropped to 0.1 per month over six months. The automation investment was approximately three engineering-days. Break-even was approximately five weeks. The return on the following twelve months of avoided incidents was approximately $180,000 in recovered engineering time.

Note

Safe Scale Check — Versioning Reversibility: A version increment is not reversible once consumers have adopted the new version. Design the increment to be forward-compatible before shipping it. Every field added in v2 should be optional in the

> contract, with a defined default that produces v1-equivalent behavior when absent. This ensures that a consumer running v2 client code against a v1 service response—during a partial rollback window—does not produce a deserialization error. The blast radius of a v2 rollback is bounded to the window between the v2 service rollback and the consumer's automatic fallback to default field values.

Architect's prompt 6.4: the API governance audit

When to use this: Use this prompt when establishing a governance baseline for existing internal APIs or when onboarding a new service into an organization that already has a service registry and CI governance pipeline.

```
Act as a Principal API Governance Engineer. I am auditing the internal
API contracts for a service architecture with the following properties:

- Number of internal services: [N]
- Number of registered consumers per service (average): [X]
- Current versioning strategy: [URI / Header / None]
- Current breaking-change detection: [Automated/Manual/None]
- Last breaking-change production incident: [date and brief description]

I am going to provide:
1. The current OpenAPI specs or .proto files for all internal services.
2. The CI pipeline configuration for each service.
3. The service registry (or the absence of one).

[Paste specs, pipeline configs, registry]

For each service:
(1) Identify whether a versioning strategy is present and correctly implemented.
Flag any service shipping without a version prefix.
(2) Identify whether breaking-change detection is automated in CI.
Flag any service where this gate is absent or bypassed.
(3) Identify any currently deployed API version with no registered consumers.
— these are decommission candidates.
(4) Identify any field in any response contract that lacks a documented
valid value range — these are silent breaking change risks.

Output:
- A governance gap report ordered by risk severity.
```

```
- A recommended CI gate implementation sequence.
- A deprecation SLO recommendation based on the current consumer migration
velocity.
- A schema registry recommendation: Git-based, Buf Schema Registry.
or Confluent, based on the current service count and growth trajectory.
```

The strangler fig pattern: incrementally migrating the monolith

The Strangler Fig pattern is named after a tree that grows around its host, gradually replacing it while the host continues to function. The metaphor is accurate in one direction: the new system grows incrementally alongside the old one. It is misleading in another: a real strangler fig has no deadline. Your migration does.

Further reading: The Strangler Fig pattern is widely documented; this chapter assumes the pattern and concentrates on the operational discipline that makes it safe. For the origin and the canonical treatment, see Martin Fowler's "StranglerFigApplication" on martinfowler.com and Sam Newman's Monolith to Microservices (O'Reilly), which covers the incremental-extraction patterns in depth.

The failure mode of the Strangler Fig pattern is not technical. It is organizational. A team begins an incremental migration, extracts three services cleanly, and then slows. The easy extractions are done. The remaining modules are complex, underdocumented, and deeply coupled. The proxy layer has been running in production for fourteen months. It has accumulated its own configuration debt. Two engineers have left the team who understood the proxy routing rules. The monolith is still running. The new services are running. The proxy is running. The team is now operating three systems simultaneously, none of which is the target state. This is not a migration. It is a permanent increase in operational complexity presented as a migration.

The Strangler Fig is a safe pattern under one condition: it is time-boxed.

The Three-Wave rule

The migration must complete in three waves, each with a defined scope, a defined duration, and a defined exit criterion.

Wave 1: Prove the Infrastructure. Extract the simplest, lowest-risk services first. The goal of Wave 1 is not to reduce monolith complexity. It is to validate that your service mesh, deployment pipeline, observability stack, and versioning governance can support independent services in production. Wave 1 is an infrastructure proof-of-concept running on real traffic.

Duration: one to two sprints per service, maximum three services. Exit criterion: at least one service has run in production through a full peak traffic cycle with zero proxy-related incidents.

Wave 2: Extract the High-Pain Modules. With the infrastructure validated, target the modules generating the most observable harm—the seam signals from Section 1. Duration: one sprint per service for well-bounded modules, two to three sprints for modules with significant data migration requirements. Exit criterion: the primary seam signals that triggered the migration are resolved. Build time has dropped. Deployment success rate has recovered. Lock contentions are eliminated.

Wave 3: Complete or Contain. Every remaining module is evaluated against a single question: does extracting this module provide a measurable benefit that justifies its extraction cost? If yes, extract it in Wave 3. If no, it becomes the Residual Monolith—contained, wrapped, and maintained, but not extracted. Wave 3 has a completion date set before it begins. Scope creep into a Wave 4 is a governance failure, not an engineering decision.

> Note
>
> **The Time-Box Mandate:** Set the Wave 3 completion date before Wave 1 begins. Publish it. The date is not a target—it is a constraint. A migration without a completion constraint does not complete; it becomes a permanent operational state.

Common Strangler Fig Mistakes: Five failure patterns recur across migrations, and every one is a governance failure before it is a technical one. First, extracting too many services at once—Wave 1 validates infrastructure on two or three low-risk cuts, not the whole decomposition in a sprint. Second, leaving shared database access in place behind an extracted service, which rebuilds the distributed monolith: a boundary that exists in the code but not in the data. Third, letting the proxy become permanent—the moment a routing rule is added for anything other than shifting traffic off the monolith, the proxy has started to calcify. Fourth, postponing observability until after migration, which leaves every rollback trigger as gut instinct instead of a metric threshold. Fifth, skipping the time-box, which converts a migration into a permanent three-system operational state. Run this as a checklist at every wave boundary.

Wave	Goal	Target Modules	Exit Criterion	Maximum Duration
1	Validate infrastructure	Simplest, lowest risk	One service through full peak cycle, zero proxy incidents	6 weeks
2	Eliminate pain	Highest seam signal score	Primary pain metrics resolved	12 weeks
3	Complete or contain	All remaining	Completion date met; residual monolith defined and wrapped	8 weeks

Table 6.8: The three-wave migration plan with scope, exit criteria, and maximum duration per wave.

The strangler fig proxy: when the cure becomes the problem

The Strangler Fig proxy is a temporary artifact. It is not a permanent architectural component. Treating it as permanent is the condition under which the Strangler Fig pattern stops being safe.

A proxy that has been running in production for longer than the migration timeline creates a specific failure mode: proxy configuration becomes a source of truth. Engineers start adding routing rules to the proxy for reasons unrelated to the migration—A/B tests, geographic routing, feature flags. The proxy accumulates logic. It becomes the thing that knows where everything lives. The migration cannot complete because the proxy has become load-bearing.

> Note
>
> **Anti-Pattern: The Permanent Proxy:** The Permanent Proxy occurs when Strangler Fig routing infrastructure outlives its migration purpose and begins accumulating non-migration logic. Identify it by this signal: if the proxy configuration has been modified for any reason other than shifting traffic from the monolith to a new service, it has begun its transition from migration tool to permanent dependency. The proxy decommission date is set alongside the Wave 3 completion date. When Wave 3 ends, the proxy ends.

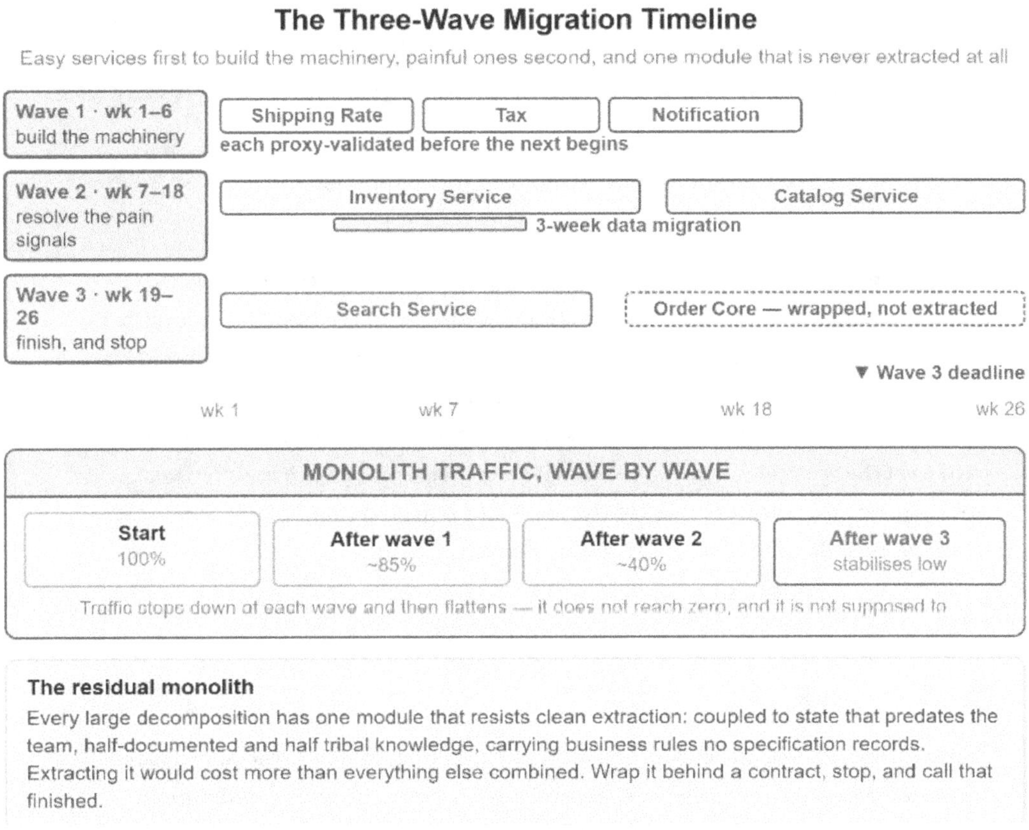

Figure 6.7: The Three-Wave Migration Timeline

The residual monolith: the module you Don't extract

In every large decomposition, there is a module that resists clean extraction. It is deeply coupled to internal state that predates the current team's tenure. Its behavior is partially documented and partially tribal knowledge. Its data model has accreted years of business rule changes, some of which are no longer reflected in any specification. Extracting it would take longer than extracting everything else combined.

The instinct is to either force the extraction anyway or to leave the module entirely as is. Both are wrong.

Forcing an extraction that the team does not have the context to execute safely produces one of two outcomes: a failed migration that requires rollback at significant cost, or a successful migration of a module that is now broken in subtle ways that will surface as incidents over the following months.

Leaving the module as-is—unmodified, unwrapped, in its current state of accumulated complexity—treats the residual monolith as a problem deferred rather than a problem contained. It continues to generate incidents. It continues to resist change. It becomes the thing no one wants to touch, which means it becomes the thing no one does touch, which means it calcifies.

The correct treatment is containment with continuous improvement.

> Note
>
> **The Residual Monolith Pattern:** When a module's extraction cost exceeds its extraction benefit within the migration timeline, declare it the Residual Monolith. Do not extract it. Do not abandon it. Strip every extractable module from around it, leaving it as small as it can be made. Wrap it with a clean API contract—a versioned internal service interface through which all consumers access it. Enforce the Single Authority pattern at the wrapper boundary. Assign it an owner. Commit to a maintenance standard: no new features added to the residual, no degradation of its current test coverage, no reduction in its observability instrumentation.

> Note
>
> The ROI Test: Before committing to a module extraction, calculate the fully-loaded extraction cost—engineering time, data migration risk, consumer coordination, operational overhead during the migration window—against the measurable benefit. If the benefit does not exceed the cost within twelve months of the extraction's completion, the extraction is not justified today. Contain it. Extract the value you can extract. Move on.

At a high-traffic enterprise platform, we completed a decomposition of a fourteen-service monolith over eighteen months. Eleven services were extracted cleanly across three waves. One service—the core order-processing engine, carrying years of accumulated business logic—was designated the Residual Monolith. We stripped seven modules from around it, reducing it from 340,000 lines of code to 89,000. We wrapped it with a gRPC API. We assigned it a permanent owner with a maintenance charter. It ran reliably for the following two years without a P0 incident, while the extracted services around it deployed independently and scaled without constraint.

The system was not pure. It was operational. In production, operational beats pure every time.

Validating the migration: the traffic cutover protocol

The final step of each service extraction is the traffic cutover—shifting production requests from the monolith path to the new service path. This step has a higher failure rate than any other step in the migration, for a predictable reason: staging environments do not reproduce production traffic patterns with sufficient fidelity to catch the edge cases that break at volume.

The cutover protocol that minimizes this risk is a four-stage traffic shift with automated rollback triggers at each stage.

Stage 1 — Shadow Mode. Route 0% of production traffic to the new service. Mirror 100% of production traffic asynchronously—the new service receives every request, processes it, but its response is discarded. The new service's response is compared against the monolith's response. Divergences are logged, not served. Duration: minimum 48 hours across a full traffic cycle including peak. Exit criterion: response divergence rate below 0.1%.

Stage 2 — Canary. Route 1% of production traffic to the new service. Real users, real responses, real consequences. Monitor error rate, p99 latency, and response shape divergence. Duration: minimum 24 hours. Automated rollback trigger: error rate delta above 0.5% versus monolith baseline or p99 latency increase above 20ms.

Stage 3 — Progressive Rollout. Increase traffic to 10%, then 25%, then 50%, then 100%. Each increment requires a minimum soak period—typically 30 minutes at low-traffic periods, 60 minutes during peak. The automated rollback trigger remains active at each increment. The rollout is fully automated—the system approves each increment when the soak period completes with no rollback trigger fired.

Stage 4 — Monolith Path Decommission. After 100% traffic has run through one full peak cycle with no rollback trigger activation, the monolith code path is removed. Not disabled—removed. A disabled code path is a code path that will be re-enabled during an incident. Removal is the only state that prevents re-enablement.

Stage	Traffic to New Service	Duration	Rollback Trigger	Exit Criterion
Shadow Mode	0% (mirror only)	48 hours minimum	Response divergence > 0.1%	Divergence rate < 0.1% sustained over full peak cycle

Stage	Traffic to New Service	Duration	Rollback Trigger	Exit Criterion
Canary	1%	24 hours	Errordelta> 0.5% or p99increase> 20 ms	Zero rollback triggers in 24 hours
Progressive (10%)	10%	30 min off-peak, 60 min peak	Same as canary	Zero triggers per increment
Progressive (25%)	25%	30 min off-peak, 60 min peak	Same as Canary	Zero triggers per increment
Progressive (50%)	50%	60 min off-peak, 90 min peak	Same as Canary	Zero triggers per increment
Full Cutover	100%	48 hours	Same as Canary	Zero triggers through one full peak cycle
Decommission	100% (monolith path removed)	N/A	N/A	Full peak cycle completed with zero triggers

Table 6.9: The four-stage traffic cutover protocol with rollback triggers and exit criteria.

Note

Manager's Math — The Cost of No Shadow Mode: A cutover executed without shadow mode that discovers a response divergence issue in production carries a direct incident cost. At ShopFlow's current traffic volume, a 2% error rate on the Inventory service path for 30 minutes—the time required to detect, diagnose, and execute a rollback—represents approximately 3,600 failed checkout attempts. At ShopFlow's average order value, the revenue impact of a single poorly executed cutover exceeds the engineering cost of a 48-hour shadow mode period by an order of magnitude. Shadow mode is not optional overhead. It is incident prevention with a measurable ROI.

Note

Safe Scale Check — Cutover Blast Radius: The blast radius at each cutover stage is bounded by the percentage of traffic routed to the new service. At 1% canary, a complete failure of the new service affects 1% of users. Define the acceptable blast radius before the cutover begins—not during it. If the traffic volume is high enough that 1% represents tens of thousands of users, extend the shadow mode period until confidence is sufficient to accept that blast radius.

Architect's prompt 6.5: the strangler fig migration plan

When to use this: Use this prompt at the beginning of a decomposition project, before any extraction work begins. The output is a three-wave migration plan with defined exit criteria, a proxy decommission date, and a Residual Monolith declaration for any module whose extraction ROI does not justify the cost within the migration timeline.

```
Act as a Principal Migration Architect specializing in monoliths.
decomposition using the Strangler Fig pattern.

I have a monolith with the following properties:
- Total modules: [N]
- Total lines of code: [X]
- Team size available for migration: [Y engineers]
- Maximum acceptable migration timeline: [Z weeks]
- Current deployment success rate: [%]
- Primary pain signals: [list from seam signal audit]
```

```
I am going to provide:
1. The module inventory with coupling coefficients and pain scores.
2. The current database schema with table ownership assignments.
3. The CI/CD pipeline configuration.

[Paste module inventory, schema, pipeline config]

Generate a Three-Wave Migration Plan:

Wave 1 (Infrastructure Validation):
- Select 2-3 modules based on lowest coupling coefficient and highest cohesion.
infrastructure learning value.
- Define exit criteria for Wave 1 completion.
- Define the proxy configuration policy.

Wave 2 (Pain Elimination):
- Select modules based on the highest pain score from the seam signal audit.
- For each module with a data migration requirement, generate a Parallel.
Schema migration plan with dual-write window duration estimate.
- Define exit criteria: which specific metrics must recover to what values?

Wave 3 (Completion or Containment):
- For each remaining module, calculate extraction ROI.
[engineering days] x [fully-loaded daily cost] vs. [annual benefit]
from extraction measured in incident reduction and deployment velocity.
- Modules with negative 12-month ROI: declare as Residual Monolith,
Specify wrapper API contract requirements and assign ownership.
- Modules with positive ROI: include in Wave 3 extraction sequence.

Output:
- Three-wave Gantt with week-level granularity.
- Proxy decommission date.
- Residual Monolith declaration with wrapper contract specification.
- Automated rollback trigger definitions for each cutover stage.
```

Summary

In this chapter, we transformed ShopFlow's backend from a 14-module monolith with a 65% deployment success rate into a rationalized six-service architecture with clean data ownership and an automated governance pipeline.

We established the Three-Layer Boundary—Data, Service, UX—as the only decomposition framework that consistently holds across domain changes and organizational restructuring, and the API Extension Rule as the discipline that keeps service counts rational.

We replaced intuition-based boundary discovery with the Gravity Signal Rule: extract when three or more observable signals converge—build time, test blast radius, deployment contention, read/write divergence, or merge conflict density.

We enforced the Single Authority pattern for data ownership and the Parallel Schema Rule for safe data migration—deploy new schema first, dual-write window second, batch migration third, decommission last, never on day one.

We automated API governance with four CI gates—schema lint, breaking-change detection, consumer contract tests, and deprecation SLO enforcement—because human review gates do not survive sustained delivery pressure at scale.

We applied the Three-Wave Rule to bound the migration timeline, declared the Residual Monolith pattern for modules whose extraction cost exceeds their benefit, and defined a four-stage cutover protocol with automated rollback triggers at every increment.

ShopFlow's telemetry after *Chapter 6*:

Metric	Before (Ch6 Start)	After (Ch6 End)	Change
Backend Deployment Success Rate	65%	94%	+29 points
Average Build Time	47 minutes	11 minutes (per service)	77% reduction
Database Lock Contentions (Orders table)	14 concurrent modules	0 (Inventory extracted)	Eliminated
p99 Latency (us)	95 ms	72ms	24% improvement
p99 Latency (Frankfurt)	180 ms	180 ms	Unchanged — physics still winning
p99 Latency (Singapore)	320 ms	320 ms	Unchanged — next chapter's problem

Metric	Before (Ch6 Start)	After (Ch6 End)	Change
Services in Production	1 (monolith)	6 (+ Residual Monolith)	Rationalized
API Breaking Change Incidents	1.8/month	0.1/month	94% reduction

Table 6.10: ShopFlow telemetry before and after the Chapter 6 decomposition.

The cliffhanger: the reliable decomposition

Six services are deploying independently. The build time is down. The Orders table is no longer contending with Inventory. Dave's deployment queue is clearing without coordination rituals.

But Dave is looking at the service-to-service call graph and frowning again.

The Inventory service is healthy. The Catalog service is healthy. But when the Order service calls Inventory and Inventory calls Catalog in the same checkout transaction, a network blip between any two of them produces a 500 error for the user. Last Tuesday, the Pricing service slowed to 800ms response time—not down, just slow. Because Order Service has a 30-second timeout and no circuit breaker, every thread waiting for Pricing held its connection open for the full 30 seconds. The connection pool was exhausted in four minutes. The entire checkout flow stopped accepting requests because a Recommendations widget's upstream dependency was slow.

We decomposed the monolith. We did not decompose the failure modes.

Services that are independently deployable are not automatically independently resilient. Each service boundary we drew in this chapter is a new point of failure in a network we do not control. In *Chapter 7*, we will confront the network as the new bottleneck—and build the resilience layer that ensures a slow service never becomes a cascading failure.

7

Scaling Service Infrastructure – Resilience, Mesh, and Compute

In *Chapter 6*, we decomposed ShopFlow's monolith into six independently deployable services. The build time dropped from 47 minutes to 11. The Orders table lock contentions dropped to zero. The deployment success rate recovered from 65% to 94%.

Then last Tuesday happened.

The Pricing service slowed to 800ms response time. Not down — slow. Because the Order service had a 30-second timeout and no circuit breaker, every thread waiting for Pricing held its connection open for the full 30 seconds. The connection pool was exhausted in four minutes. The entire checkout flow stopped accepting requests because a non-critical Recommendations service's upstream dependency was slow. A service that was merely degraded made a service that was fully healthy completely unavailable.

We decomposed the monolith. We did not decompose the failure modes. Independent deployment did not produce independent failure. In this chapter, we build the resilience layer that makes the decomposition real.

In this chapter, we are going to cover the following main topics:

- **Service Discovery:** How services find and talk to each other.
- **The Service Mesh:** Offloading resilience to the infrastructure.
- **Advanced Resilience:** Circuit breakers, bulkheads, and timeouts.
- **Choosing the Runtime:** Containers, serverless, or bare metal.
- **Auto-Scaling:** Predictive vs. reactive capacity management.

Technical requirements

To follow the transition from a decomposed but fragile service architecture to a resilient, self-healing system, you will need:

- **Envoy Proxy/Istio:** Service mesh control plane for traffic management, mTLS, circuit breaking, and retry policies—configured declaratively, without touching application code.
- **Resilience4j (Java) / Polly (.NET) / resilience (Go):** Application-layer circuit breaker and bulkhead libraries for teams that cannot adopt a full service mesh immediately.
- **Kubernetes (v1.28+):** Container orchestration with liveness/readiness probes, Pod Disruption Budgets, and Horizontal Pod Autoscaler.
- **Prometheus + Grafana:** Metrics collection and visualization for per-service SLO dashboards. Circuit breaker state transitions must be observable as metrics, not just as logs.
- **k6 / Gatling:** Load testing and fault injection tooling. You cannot validate a circuit breaker without generating the load conditions that trigger it.
- **Chaos Mesh/Litmus:** Controlled fault injection — network latency, pod kills, resource exhaustion — to verify that resilience patterns behave as designed under real failure conditions.

Code Repository: `https://github.com/imran-siddique/Architecting-at-Scale/tree/main/ch7`

ShopFlow telemetry snapshot [stage]

```
The Signal: Independent services do not automatically fail independently. Every
service boundary is a new point of failure in a network we do not control. A slow
Pricing service should degrade Pricing. Instead, it degraded Checkout. The
decomposition created the blast radius we were trying to eliminate.
p99 Latency (Global): 150ms (Acceptable – when things work)
Availability: 97.8% (Flickering – three brownouts in the last sprint)
Cloud Spend: $10,000/mo (Spiking – redundant retry traffic is amplifying costs)
Error Rate (Checkout path): 4.2% (● Critical – above 1% SLO)
SuccessiveRetryStormEvents:3in14days(● Critical)
MeanTimetoRecovery(MTTR):4hours(● Critical – manual diagnosis only)
Service-to-ServiceLatency(Pricing→Order):800msp99(● Warning – cascading into pool
exhaustion)
ConnectionPoolExhaustionEvents:2thissprint(● Critical)
```

```
Panic Meter: 7/10 (Services are healthy in isolation. The network between them is not.)
```

Note

Dave Alert: "The Pricing service was only at 800ms — not down. But because Order Service waited the full 30-second timeout on every request, the connection pool drained in four minutes and took Checkout offline with it. A service that was merely slow made a service that was fully healthy completely unavailable."

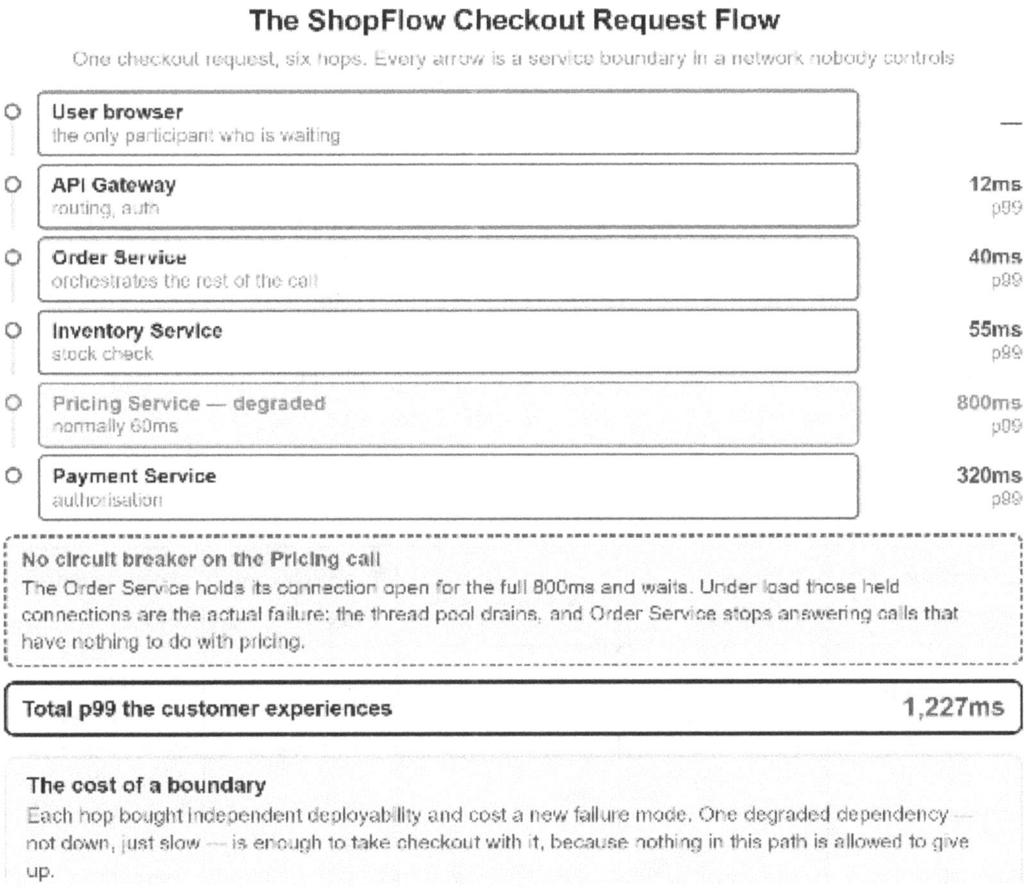

Figure 7.1: The ShopFlow Checkout Request Flow

Service discovery: how services find and talk to each other

The moment you deploy a second service, you have a service discovery problem. Service A needs to call Service B. Service B is running on a dynamic IP address assigned by the orchestrator, potentially across multiple instances, potentially in multiple regions. There is no static address to hardcode. In a Kubernetes-based environment, pod IP addresses are assigned at creation and released at termination. A rolling deployment of Service B replaces every running pod with a new one — new IP addresses, same service. If Service A is resolving Service B by IP, every deployment of Service B breaks Service A.

Service discovery is the mechanism that decouples service consumers from the physical location of their dependencies. It is not optional in a distributed system. It is the foundational contract that makes the rest of the resilience architecture possible.

Note

The DNS-First Rule: In a Kubernetes environment, internal service discovery must be implemented through the cluster DNS layer, not through hardcoded IPs or environment-variable-injected addresses. A Kubernetes Service object provides a stable DNS name — inventory-service.shopflow.svc.cluster.local — that resolves to the correct pod endpoints regardless of pod churn. Service A calls the DNS name. The cluster handles the routing. This is non-negotiable before your first production deployment.

Discovery Method	Address Stability	Health-Aware?	Deployment Safe?	Recommended For
Hardcoded IP	No — breaks on pod restart	No	No	Never in Kubernetes
Environment variable	Per-deploy only	No	Partial	Single-instance non-K8s
Kubernetes DNS (Service object)	Yes — stable across pod churn	Via readiness probes	Yes	Default for all Kubernetes services

Discovery Method	Address Stability	Health-Aware?	Deployment Safe?	Recommended For
Service mesh routing	Yes — dynamic endpoint selection	Yes — automatic unhealthy removal	Yes	GA-stage distributed systems

Table 7.1: Service discovery methods compared.

The DNS layer solves the location problem. It does not solve the health problem. DNS resolution returns an address. It does not guarantee the pod at that address is healthy, has capacity, or is running the version you expect. For that, you need a health-aware routing layer — which is the entry point for the service mesh conversation.

The service mesh: start simple, add complexity

The service mesh is one of the most powerful and most frequently over-deployed tools in the distributed systems toolkit. Understanding when to adopt it — and when not to — is one of the clearest indicators of architectural maturity.

A service mesh moves cross-cutting concerns — mTLS, retries, timeouts, circuit breaking, traffic shifting, observability — out of application code and into the infrastructure layer. Instead of every service implementing its own retry logic and mTLS configuration, a sidecar proxy (Envoy, in the case of Istio) handles these concerns transparently. The application code sends a plain HTTP request. The sidecar handles encryption, retry policies, and failure detection before the request leaves the pod.

> Note
>
> **The Mesh Tax:** A service mesh introduces a sidecar container alongside every service pod — typically 50–100MB of additional memory per pod and 1–5ms of additional per-request latency for the proxy hop — plus a control plane that is itself a distributed system requiring operational expertise to run, upgrade, and debug. This is Strategic Debt — intentional complexity purchased for operational capability. You must be able to name the capability before accepting the debt.

The philosophy on mesh adoption is direct: start simple and earn the complexity.

During private preview and public preview — when you are collecting customer feedback, iterating rapidly, and validating product-market fit — a full service mesh is premature overhead. Your priority is learning velocity. Implement application-layer resilience libraries for circuit breaking and retries. Implement Kubernetes liveness and readiness probes for basic health routing. Implement Kubernetes Services for DNS-based discovery. This is sufficient for a system that is still discovering what it needs to be.

The service mesh becomes non-negotiable at a specific maturity threshold — not a service count, but a production readiness gate. Before you go generally available with a system that carries real user data, real financial transactions, or real SLA commitments, three properties must be enforced at the infrastructure layer:

mTLS between all service-to-service calls. In *Chapter 3*, we established Zero Trust as the security architecture. In a service mesh, mTLS is enforced at the sidecar layer without application code changes. Without it, you are relying on network-level trust—insufficient in a multi-tenant Kubernetes cluster.

Traffic shifting at the infrastructure layer. Canary deployments that route 1% of traffic to a new service version require a traffic management layer that can split traffic by percentage. Kubernetes does not provide this natively. The service mesh does. Without it, the progressive cutover protocol from *Chapter 6* cannot be implemented safely.

Distributed tracing injection. Correlation IDs must propagate across service boundaries automatically. A service mesh injects trace headers into every request at the sidecar layer, ensuring that a trace that starts in the Shell reaches the Inventory service without relying on every application team to correctly implement header propagation.

Concern	Without Service Mesh	With Service Mesh
mTLS enforcement	Per-service implementation, inconsistent coverage	Automatic, uniform, zero-application code
Retry logic	Per-service, often inconsistent timeout values	Centrally configured, per-route, observable
Circuit breaking	Application library, not visible in infrastructure metrics	Infrastructure-layer metrics emitted automatically
Traffic shifting	Requires application-level feature flags	Declarative YAML, percentage-based routing
Distributed tracing	Per-service header propagation, often incomplete	Automatic sidecar injection

Concern	Without Service Mesh	With Service Mesh
Operational cost	Low — no control plane	High — control plane and sidecar overhead

Table 7.2: Cross-cutting resilience concerns, with and without a service mesh.

> Note
>
> **Safe Scale Check — Mesh Adoption Reversibility:** The decision to adopt a service mesh is not easily reversed. Once mTLS is enforced at the mesh layer, removing the mesh requires implementing mTLS in every service individually — or accepting a period of unencrypted internal traffic. Before adopting a mesh, define the rollback plan: which mesh features would need to be re-implemented at the application layer if the mesh were removed? If the answer is 'all of them simultaneously,' the adoption is a one-way door. Accept it explicitly and plan accordingly.

When would you actually pull that rollback? Not on a bad afternoon. Trigger it only when the mesh is costing more reliability than it delivers: the control plane has caused more production incidents over a quarter than the resilience patterns it enforces have prevented; the sidecar hop is consuming a share of the latency budget you cannot recover; or the team carrying the mesh no longer has the platform engineering capacity to upgrade and debug it safely. Absent one of those, a misbehaving mesh is a tuning problem, not a rollback trigger. Define these thresholds before adoption, so the decision under pressure is a lookup, not a debate.

When a service mesh is overkill

The inverse of "earn the complexity" is recognizing when it is never earned. A service mesh solves operational problems that only appear at a certain scale of services, teams, and traffic. Below that scale it is pure tax — a distributed control plane and a sidecar on every pod, bought to solve problems you do not have.

Skip the mesh when the system is a two- or three-service application whose entire call graph fits on an index card: at that size, application-layer resilience libraries and Kubernetes Services cover discovery, retries, and health routing without a control plane to operate. Skip it for a small internal tool with no external SLA, where an occasional retry storm is an annoyance rather than an incident. And skip it when there is no dedicated platform-engineering capacity: a mesh is a system that must be run, upgraded, and debugged, and a mesh that no one owns becomes the least reliable component in the architecture rather than the most.

The Mesh Justification Rule: Adopt a service mesh to solve a named operational problem — uniform mTLS, percentage-based traffic shifting, or automatic trace propagation across teams — not because it is a recognized best practice. If you cannot name the specific capability you are buying and the incident class it prevents, the mesh is overkill, and the resilience libraries you already have are the correct answer for now.

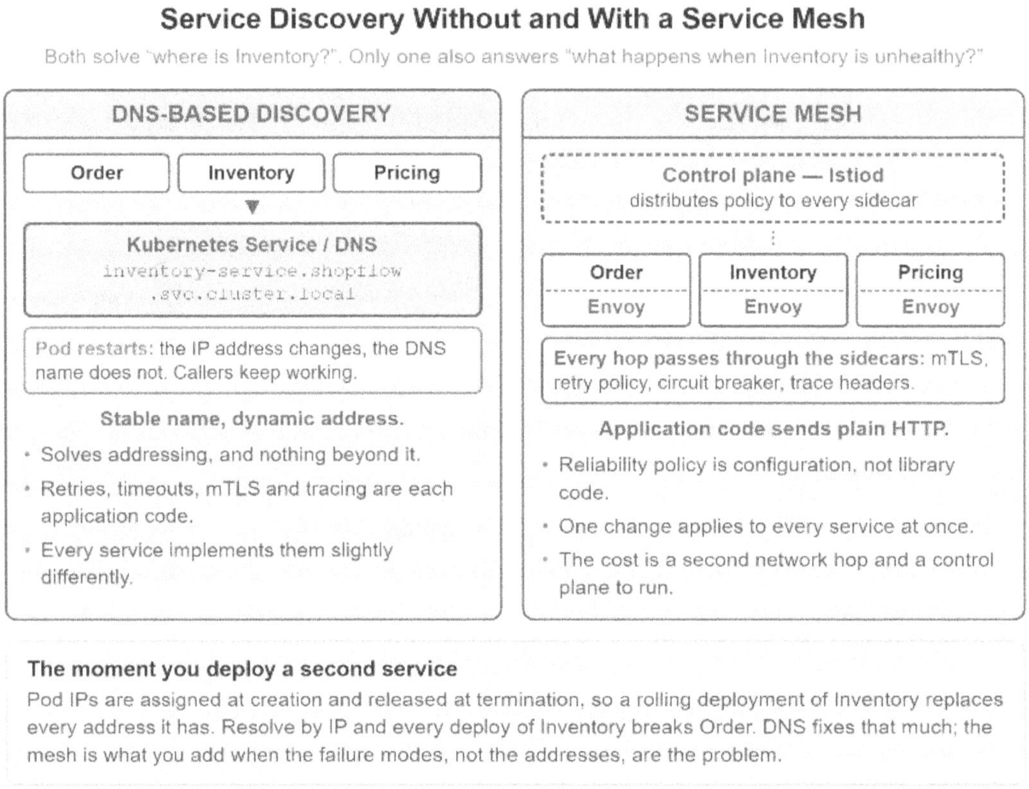

Figure 7.2: Service Discovery Without and With a Service Mesh

Architect's prompt 7.1: the service discovery readiness audit

When to use this: Use this prompt before your first multi-service production deployment or when evaluating whether an existing service discovery implementation is sufficient for your current reliability requirements.

```
Act as a Principal Platform Engineer. I am deploying [N] services.
to a Kubernetes cluster. I need to evaluate whether my current
service discovery implementation is sufficient for production.
```

```
Current state:
- Service discovery mechanism: [DNS / hardcoded IPs / environment variables]
- mTLS status: [None/Application-layer/Mesh-layer]
- Traffic shifting capability: [None/Feature flags/Service mesh]
- Distributed tracing: [None/Manual header propagation/Automatic injection]
- Production readiness stage: [Private Preview / Public Preview / GA]

For each service-to-service call in the following dependency graph:
[Paste service dependency graph]

(1) Identify any call using a hardcoded IP or environment variable address.
(2) For each risk, provide the Kubernetes Service and DNS name configuration.
(3) Based on the production readiness stage, recommend whether a full service
mesh is justified or application-layer resilience libraries are sufficient.
(4) If a service mesh is recommended, provide the minimum viable Istio.
configuration: mTLS, traffic shifting, and tracing injection policies.
(5) Define the mesh adoption rollback plan and estimated engineering cost.
```

The service mesh: offloading resilience to infrastructure

The service mesh is not a resilience solution. It is a resilience delivery mechanism. The patterns it implements — circuit breaking, retries, timeouts, bulkheads — exist independently of the mesh. What the mesh provides is a consistent, observable, centrally configurable way to apply those patterns without touching application code.

When a service is misbehaving in production, the instinct is to add defensive code to the consuming service. A retry here, a timeout there, a circuit breaker if the problem persists. Over time, every service accumulates its own defensive layer — different timeout values, different retry counts, different circuit breaker thresholds. The system's resilience behavior becomes a distributed configuration problem. No one knows what the actual retry policy is for the Order → Inventory call because it was implemented by a developer who has since moved to a different team.

The mesh solves this by moving resilience configuration to infrastructure YAML—visible, version-controlled, reviewable, and consistent across every service boundary regardless of which team owns the service.

Retry policies: the amplification problem

The first resilience pattern most engineers reach for is the retry. If a call fails, try again. The intuition is sound. The implementation is frequently counterproductive.

A naive retry policy — retry on any 5xx error, up to three times, immediately — does not improve system reliability. Under load, it reduces it. Consider the scenario ShopFlow experienced: the Pricing service is running at 800ms response time due to database lock contention. The Order service, configured with three immediate retries on 5xx, sends a request, waits 800ms, receives a timeout error, and retries. Three times. Each retry holds a connection in the Order service's connection pool for 800ms. Under normal traffic, the Pricing service was receiving 500 requests per second. Under the naive retry policy, it receives up to 1,500 requests per second — three times the load — precisely when it is least capable of handling additional load.

> Note
>
> **The Retry Tax:** Every retry policy is a load amplifier under failure conditions. You cannot implement retries without accepting that a downstream degradation will increase the load on that downstream service. The retry policy must be designed to limit this amplification, not ignore it.

The three controls that bound retry amplification are exponential backoff, jitter, and retry budgets.

Exponential backoff increases the delay between successive retries geometrically — first retry after 100ms, second after 200ms, third after 400ms. This reduces the sustained request rate to a degraded service.

Jitter adds randomness to the backoff interval. Without jitter, a fleet of Order service pods that all received failures at the same millisecond will all retry at the same millisecond, producing a synchronized retry wave. Jitter converts a synchronized wave into a distributed drizzle.

Retry budgets limit the percentage of requests to a given service that can be retried concurrently. If the retry budget for the Pricing service is 10%, a maximum of 10% of in-flight requests to Pricing at any moment are retries. When the budget is exhausted, new failures are returned immediately rather than retried.

> Note
>
> **The Retry Configuration Rule:** A retry policy without exponential backoff, jitter, and a retry budget is not a resilience mechanism. It is a load amplifier with a delay. All three controls are required.

Not every operation is safe to retry

Backoff, jitter, and budgets bound how hard you retry. They say nothing about whether you should retry a given call at all. A retry re-sends a request the caller assumes was never processed — but under timeout conditions, the original request may have succeeded on the server while only the response was lost. Whether that is safe depends entirely on whether the operation is idempotent.

An idempotent operation produces the same result whether it runs once or five times. Reading a product, checking a stock level, or setting an order to a specific status are naturally idempotent — retry them freely. A non-idempotent operation changes state on every execution, and a blind retry duplicates that change. At ShopFlow the three most dangerous are inventory reservation (a retry double-decrements available stock), payment authorization (a retry double-charges the customer), and order creation (a retry creates a duplicate order). Each is exactly the kind of 5xx-or-timeout call a naive retry policy would happily repeat.

The fix is to make non-idempotent operations safe to retry, not to forbid retries. The caller generates an idempotency key — a unique token per logical operation — and sends it with every attempt, including retries. The receiving service records the key on first execution and, on any later request carrying the same key, returns the original result instead of re-executing. Payment processors expose exactly this mechanism; ShopFlow's internal Inventory and Order services must implement the equivalent, backed by deduplication on the idempotency key, before their write paths are placed behind any retry policy.

The Idempotency Rule: A write operation may sit behind a retry policy only if it is idempotent or carries an idempotency key with server-side deduplication. Reads retry freely. Non-idempotent writes without a deduplication key must not be retried — return the failure to the caller and let a human or a saga decide, because a duplicate charge is a worse outcome than a failed one.

Retry Policy	Amplification Under Failure	Synchronized Wave Risk	Production safe?
Immediate retry (3x, no delay)	3x load amplification	High — all retries occur simultaneously	No
Fixed backoff (500 ms)	3x amplification, delayed	Medium — still synchronized per interval	No
Exponential backoff only	~1.5× average	Low — spread over time	Partial — add jitter

Retry Policy	Amplification Under Failure	Synchronized Wave Risk	Production safe?
Exponential backoff + jitter	~1.1x average	Very low — randomized spread	Yes
Exponential + jitter + budget (10%)	Capped at budget percentage	Very low	Yes — recommended

Table 7.3: Retry policies compared by amplification and synchronized-wave risk.

The graduated response rule

The standard circuit breaker literature presents circuit breaking as a binary operation: the circuit is closed (requests pass through) or open (requests fail immediately). The configuration of the thresholds is where most teams go wrong.

The most common misconfiguration is an aggressively low error rate threshold — 10% error rate triggers circuit open — combined with a low minimum request volume — as few as five requests. Under this configuration, a two-request burst of failures on a low-traffic path opens the circuit, cuts all traffic to a healthy service, and generates a self-inflicted availability event. The circuit breaker, designed to protect system stability, has become the source of instability.

The preferred model is graduated throttling before hard breaking. Before a circuit opens, it should slow down.

> **Note**
>
> The Graduated Response Rule: Before a circuit opens, it should slow down. Implement a three-state response to degradation: at a 10% error rate, reduce traffic to the degraded service by 25%. At a 25% error rate, reduce by 50%. At a 50% error rate, open the circuit. This graduated response achieves the protection goal — preventing a degraded service from taking down its consumers — without the brittleness of an immediate hard break.

In an Envoy or Istio configuration, this is implemented through outlier detection combined with traffic shifting — the mesh detects the degradation, removes unhealthy endpoints from the load balancing pool gradually, and routes traffic to healthy endpoints before the service is removed entirely.

Note

Anti-Pattern: The Trigger-Happy Circuit Breaker: The Trigger-Happy Circuit Breaker is configured with thresholds low enough to open on transient errors — a single database connection blip, a brief network hiccup, a cold-start latency spike. It opens, cuts traffic, the removed traffic causes the downstream service to appear healthier (because it is receiving less load), the half-open test passes, the circuit closes, the traffic returns, and the cycle repeats. Observable signature: circuit open/close events that correlate with traffic volume changes rather than with actual service health changes.

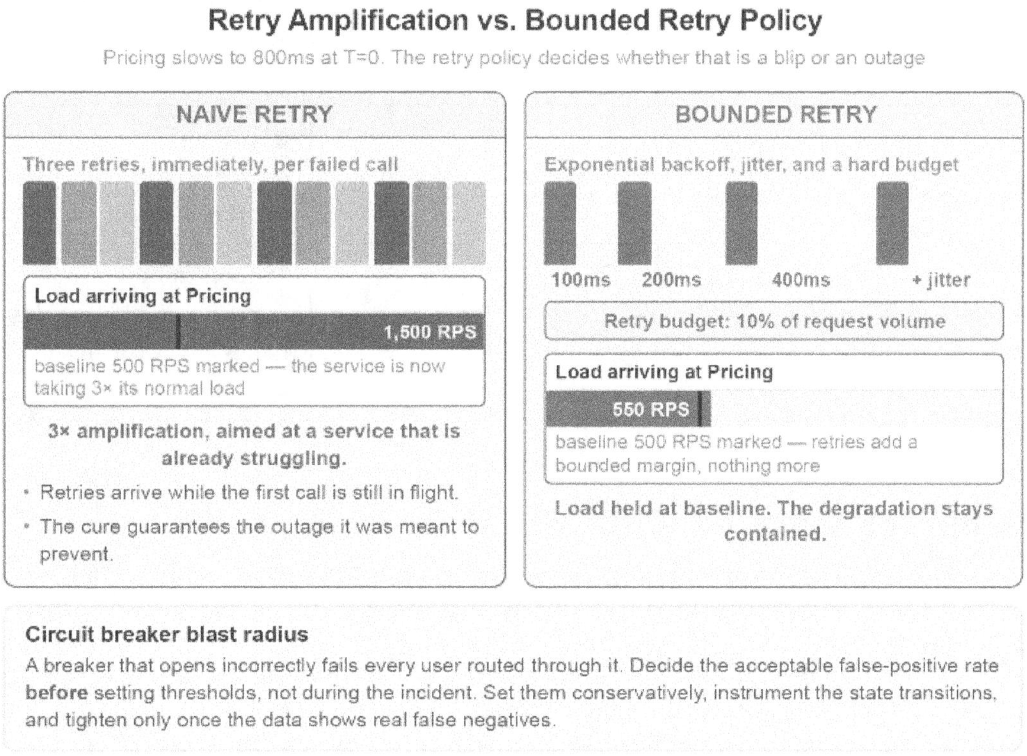

Figure 7.3: Retry Amplification vs. Bounded Retry Policy

Note

Safe Scale Check — Circuit Breaker Blast Radius: The blast radius of an incorrectly configured circuit breaker is every user whose request was routed to a service that had its circuit incorrectly opened. Define the acceptable false positive rate before setting thresholds — not during an incident. Set thresholds conservatively, instrument the state transitions, and tighten only when observability data shows false negatives.

Configuration	Minimum Request Volume	Error Rate Threshold	Sleep Window	Risk Profile
Too Aggressive	5 requests	10%	5 seconds	High false positive rate — opens on transient errors
Recommended (ShopFlow)	50 requests	30%	30 seconds	Balanced — requires sustained degradation to open
Too Conservative	500 requests	75%	120 seconds	High false negative rate — degraded services stay in rotation too long
Graduated (preferred)	20 requests	10% → 25% → 50%	Progressive	Reduces traffic before cutting — minimizes blast radius of both open and false-open

Table 7.4: Circuit breaker configurations and their risk profiles.

Architect's prompt 7.2: the resiliency policy audit

When to use this: Use this prompt when designing the circuit breaker and retry configuration for a new service boundary or when auditing an existing configuration that has produced false positives or false negatives.

```
Act as a Principal Reliability Engineer specializing in distributed systems.
systems resilience. I am configuring retry and circuit breaker policies.
for the following service dependency:

Consuming service: [Name, p99 latency SLO, connection pool size]
Dependency service: [Name, p99 latency, current error rate, RPS]
Failure mode being protected against: [Timeout/Error spike/Latency degradation]
Acceptable false positive rate: [X% of circuit open events on healthy services]
```

```
Current retry configuration (if any):
- Max retries: [N]
- Backoff strategy: [None / Fixed / Exponential]
- Jitter: [Yes/No]
- Retry budget: [None/X%]

Current circuit breaker configuration (if any):
- Minimum request volume: [N]
- Error rate threshold: [X%]
- Sleep window: [Ns]
- Graduated throttling: [Yes/No]

(1) Calculate the maximum retry amplification factor under the current
configuration. If amplification exceeds 2x, flag it as a risk.
(2) Evaluate circuit breaker thresholds against current RPS and error rate.
Identify whether configuration risks false positives or false negatives.
(3) Recommend a bounded retry policy with specific values for exponential.
backoff base, jitter range, and retry budget percentage.
(4) Recommend a graduated circuit breaker configuration with three traffic.
reduction stages before full open.
Define the minimum observable metrics to validate the configuration.
in production: which state transition events must be emitted as metrics?
and what alert threshold fires when the false positive rate exceeds bounds?
```

Advanced resilience: circuit breakers, bulkheads, and timeouts

ShopFlow's connection pool exhaustion event demonstrated a specific failure mode: a single slow dependency cascaded into an unrelated service's unavailability. The Pricing service was slow. The Order service was fine. Checkout went down. The failure crossed service boundaries it should not have been able to cross.

This is a bulkhead failure. The term comes from ship design: a bulkhead is a partition that prevents water from flooding from one compartment to another when the hull is breached. In distributed systems, a bulkhead is an isolation boundary that prevents a failure in one dependency from consuming the shared resources of an unrelated path. The connection pool was the shared resource. The Pricing service path and the Checkout path both drew from the same pool. When Pricing consumed the pool through retry amplification, Checkout had no connections available — despite Checkout's own dependencies being fully healthy.

Note

The Bulkhead Mandate: Every P0 critical path must have a dedicated resource pool — connection pool, thread pool, or semaphore limit — that cannot be consumed by non-critical paths. You cannot guarantee P0 availability if P0 and P2 paths share a resource pool. This is non-negotiable before GA.

Thread isolation vs. semaphore isolation

There are two bulkhead implementation strategies, each with a different overhead profile.

Thread isolation assigns a dedicated thread pool to each downstream dependency. When the Pricing thread pool is exhausted — all threads blocked on slow Pricing responses — the Inventory thread pool is unaffected. The cost is memory: each thread pool requires stack allocation, typically 256KB–1MB per thread.

Semaphore isolation uses a counter instead of a thread pool. A maximum of N concurrent calls to a given dependency are permitted at any time. When the semaphore count is reached, new requests to that dependency are rejected immediately. The cost is minimal. The limitation is that it cannot isolate blocking I/O: if calls to the Pricing service are blocking a thread while waiting for a response, a semaphore does not reclaim that thread.

For ShopFlow's architecture — where service-to-service calls are HTTP-based and blocking at the connection layer — thread isolation is the correct bulkhead strategy.

Strategy	Isolation Mechanism	Memory Cost	Handles Blocking I/O?	Recommended For
Thread Pool Isolation	Dedicated thread pool per dependency	High — ~256 KB per thread	Yes — blocked threads isolated to pool	HTTP/gRPC calls where the thread blocks
Semaphore isolation	Concurrent call count limit	Minimal — counter only	No — blocking threads still held	Non-blocking/ reactive I/O patterns
Connection Pool Isolation	Dedicated connection pool per downstream	Medium — pool overhead	Yes — connections isolated per pool	Database calls, external API calls

Strategy	Isolation Mechanism	Memory Cost	Handles Blocking I/O?	Recommended For
Rate Limiting	RPS limit per downstream	Minimal	Partial — limits new calls, not in flight	Protecting downstream from overload

Table 7.5: Thread isolation versus semaphore isolation for bulkheads.

Timeout hierarchy: the missing configuration

Every service-to-service call requires a timeout. This is universally acknowledged and universally underconfigured. The problem is not the absence of timeouts — most frameworks set a default. The problem is that default timeouts are set for the average case, not the worst case, and they are set independently for each service rather than as a coordinated hierarchy.

> Note
>
> **The Timeout Hierarchy Rule:** At every layer in the call stack, the timeout must be strictly less than the timeout of the layer above it, with enough margin to account for processing time and network variance. Define the hierarchy from the outside in — user browser → API Gateway → BFF → Service → Downstream — before configuring any individual timeout.

Layer	Component	Corrected Timeout	Previous (Incorrect)	Impact
User browser	Browser page load	30s	30s (reference)	Baseline — unchanged
Edge	API Gateway → BFF	10s	30s (same as browser)	Eliminates 20s dead thread window
BFF	BFF → Order Service	8s	25s	17s thread reclaim improvement
Service	Order → Pricing	3s	30s	Pool exhaustion prevented

Layer	Component	Corrected Timeout	Previous (Incorrect)	Impact
Service	Order → Inventory	3s	30s	Pool exhaustion prevented
Database	Service → DB	2s	Not set (driver default ~60s)	Silent exhaustion prevented

Table 7.6: The timeout hierarchy — corrected versus ShopFlow's original misconfiguration.

ShopFlow's connection pool exhaustion occurred because the Order service had a 30-second timeout on Pricing calls — longer than the BFF's timeout, which was longer than the user's browser timeout. A user whose browser gave up after 10 seconds was still holding a server-side thread in the Order service that would not release for another 20 seconds. Multiplied by concurrent users, the thread pool drained.

Note

Manager's Math — The Connection Pool Sizing Calculation: The correct connection pool size for a service is: (p99 response time of downstream in seconds) × (max concurrent requests to that downstream) × (safety margin of 1.5). For ShopFlow's Order → Pricing path: 0.8 seconds p99 × 500 concurrent requests × 1.5 = 600 connections. ShopFlow's pool was sized at 200 — the default, never revisited after the decomposition. The pool was undersized by 3x for the observed traffic pattern. Correct sizing would have prevented the exhaustion event entirely. The cost of the correct configuration: zero — it is a number in a configuration file.

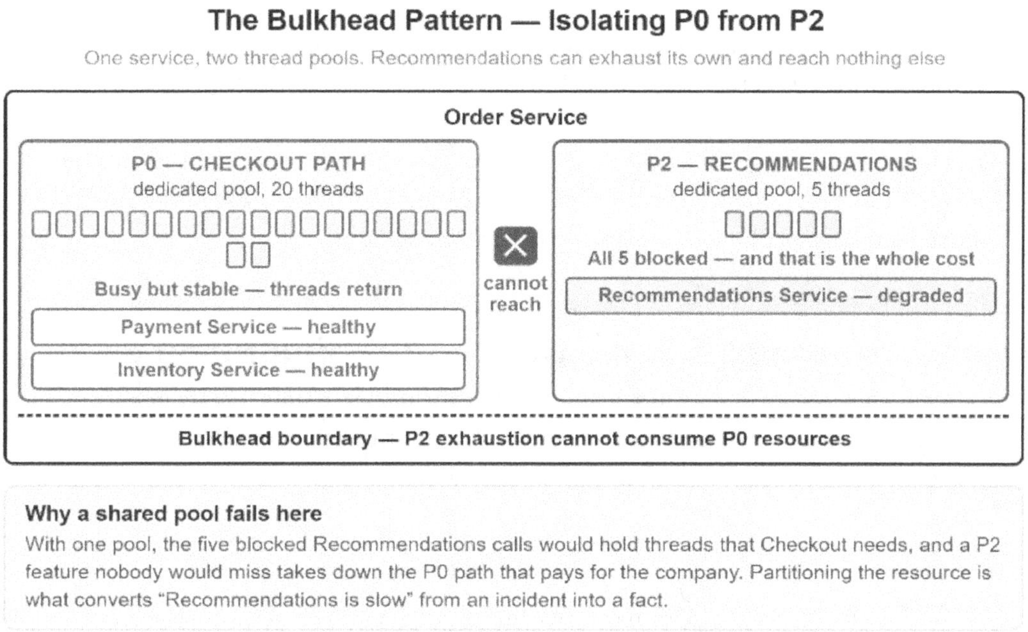

Figure 7.4: The Bulkhead Pattern — Isolating P0 from P2

Load shedding: protecting the system from its own success

Load shedding protects a service from consuming more of its own resources than it can sustain — specifically during traffic spikes that exceed provisioned capacity. Without load shedding, a traffic spike causes a service to accept every incoming request, queue them, and eventually exhaust memory, CPU, or connection pool — producing a complete service failure. With load shedding, the service begins rejecting requests above its capacity threshold with a 503 response, preserving enough headroom to continue serving requests within capacity at full quality.

> Note
>
> **The Load Shedding Priority Rule:** Load shedding must be applied in reverse priority order. P2 requests are shed at 80% capacity utilization. P1 requests are shed at 90%. P0 requests are shed only at 100% capacity, and only with an explicit alert that the service is operating beyond its provisioned capacity envelope. A system that sheds P0 checkout requests to serve P2 recommendations has inverted its business priorities in code.

Note

Safe Scale Check — Bulkhead Blast Radius: The blast radius of a bulkhead failure is bounded by the size of the resource pool assigned to the failing path. Before configuring any bulkhead, calculate the worst-case resource consumption of each downstream dependency under degraded conditions using the pool sizing formula. If the calculated pool size exceeds available memory, the workload must be moved to a separate process with its own memory budget — not handled by a semaphore.

Architect's prompt 7.3: the bulkhead configuration audit

When to use this: Use this prompt when designing the resource isolation strategy for a service with multiple downstream dependencies of different priority levels, or after a connection pool exhaustion event to identify which isolation boundaries were missing.

```
Act as a Principal Reliability Engineer. I am designing the bulkhead.
and timeout configuration for [Service Name] with the following:
downstream dependencies:

[For each dependency, provide:]
- Dependency name and priority level (P0 / P1 / P2)
- p99 response time (normal conditions)
- p99 response time (degraded conditions)
- Maximum concurrent requests this service sends to this dependency
- Current connection/thread pool size for this dependency (if any)
- Current timeout configuration (if any)

Total service memory budget: [X MB]
Maximum acceptable P0 latency impact from P2 degradation: [N ms]

For each dependency, calculate the correct connection or thread pool size.
using: (p99 degraded response time) x (max concurrent requests) x 1.5.
(2) Identify any dependency where the current pool size is below the
calculated requirement – these are exhaustion risks.
(3) Recommend the isolation strategy for each dependency:
thread pool vs. semaphore, with justification.
(4) Define the timeout hierarchy from the outermost layer (user browser)
or API Gateway) to this service's downstream calls. Ensure each
layer's timeout is strictly less than the layer above it.
```

```
(5) Define the load shedding policy: at what capacity utilization?
At what percentage should P2 requests begin being shed?
```

Choosing the runtime: containers, serverless, or bare metal

The compute decision is one of the most consequential architectural choices you make early in a system's life, and one of the least revisited as the system matures. Services that start on Lambda stay on Lambda. Services that start on Kubernetes stay on Kubernetes. The switching cost is high enough that the initial choice tends to be permanent.

The framework to apply to this decision has three inputs: state requirements, management overhead tolerance, and workload profile. Not performance benchmarks. Not vendor pricing tables. The question that matters is: what is the cost of managing this infrastructure over its operational lifetime, relative to the cost of the service it runs?

Start stateless, start simple

The correct starting point for any new service is the most operationally simple runtime that meets its requirements. For stateless workloads — request processing, API calls, event handlers, pure computation — that is a serverless function. Not because serverless is always the best choice, but because it eliminates the management overhead that consumes engineering time in the early stages of a system's life.

A serverless function does not require a container registry, a Kubernetes deployment manifest, a liveness probe configuration, a Pod Disruption Budget, a Horizontal Pod Autoscaler policy, or a node pool to run on. It requires a function definition and a trigger. For a team that is still discovering what it needs to build, the delta in engineering time between 'deploy a Lambda function' and 'deploy a Kubernetes service' is real and material.

> **Note**
>
> The Serverless Tax: Cold start latency (50–500ms for JVM-based functions, 5–50ms for interpreted languages), vendor lock-in for the function runtime and trigger mechanisms, a cost structure that penalizes sustained high-RPS workloads (per-invocation pricing becomes expensive above approximately 500 RPS for typical function sizes), and limited control over the execution environment for specialized resource requirements.

> Note
>
> **The Good Enough Rule:** Do not choose the runtime with the most features. Choose the runtime that is good enough for the current requirements. A service that needs two capabilities — request handling and a timer trigger — does not need a Kubernetes StatefulSet with persistent volumes. The features you are not using are not free. They are management surface area that someone has to understand, monitor, and upgrade.

The Runtime Evolution Path: Runtime decisions are not permanent verdicts; they are correct-for-now choices that should move as the workload matures. ShopFlow's Notification service is the model case. It begins as a serverless function — an event handler that sends transactional email on an order event, low and bursty traffic, zero infrastructure to manage. That is the right runtime while volume is low. As the business grows and notification volume becomes sustained — crossing the ~500 RPS band where per-invocation pricing turns expensive and where persistent connections to the email provider begin to matter — the same service migrates to a managed Kubernetes deployment with a right-sized node pool and an autoscaler. Nothing about the domain logic changed; the workload profile did. Design for that migration from day one (no vendor-specific SDK calls in business logic) so the runtime can evolve without a rewrite, rather than treating the first choice as final.

The managed service preference

When a workload requires more than a serverless function can provide — persistent connections, stateful processing, custom runtime dependencies, sustained high-RPS — the next question is not 'which Kubernetes configuration' but 'is there a managed service that handles this?'

At a high-traffic enterprise platform, we made a deliberate architectural decision: accept higher infrastructure costs in exchange for lower operational costs. A managed Kubernetes service costs more than self-managed Kubernetes on raw compute instances. The delta is typically 20–30% of the underlying compute cost. In exchange, you get automated control plane management, automated node upgrades, integrated monitoring, and a support contract. The engineering team does not spend time on control plane upgrades or etcd compaction issues. That time is spent on the product.

Note

The Premium Service Rule: For any infrastructure component that is not a core business differentiator, prefer the managed service even at a cost premium. The engineering time saved on operational overhead exceeds the infrastructure cost delta in the overwhelming majority of cases. You are not in the business of managing Kubernetes. You are in the business of running ShopFlow. This principle extends to databases (managed RDS over self-managed Postgres), message brokers, and caching layers.

Anti-Pattern: the P0 lambda

The configuration question most frequently raised in architecture reviews is: "Can we run our payment service on Lambda? It's cheaper and we don't have to manage the infrastructure."

The answer requires evaluating three properties that serverless functions do not provide by default.

Cold start predictability. A P0 payment service requires sub-200ms p99 latency in the critical path. Lambda cold starts — when a new function instance is initialized — routinely add 200–500ms for JVM-based runtimes. For a payment service running on Java or .NET, a cold start during a traffic spike moves the p99 from 150ms to 650ms — outside the SLO before a single line of business logic executes. Provisioned concurrency mitigates this but eliminates most of the cost advantage that motivated the choice.

Connection pool durability. A payment service requires persistent, authenticated connections to the payment processor's API and to the database. Lambda functions are stateless by design — connection pools cannot persist across invocations. Every invocation establishes new connections. At 500 RPS, that is 500 new database connections per second — a connection storm that most managed databases cannot absorb without a connection proxy layer, which itself introduces latency and management overhead.

Execution time guarantees. Lambda functions have a maximum execution time of 15 minutes. A payment processing flow that includes fraud scoring, bank authorization, and receipt generation can, under degraded conditions, take longer than expected. A function timeout during payment processing does not clean up gracefully — the payment authorization may have succeeded at the bank while the timeout prevents the confirmation from reaching the user. The result is a charge with no confirmation — one of the worst possible user-facing failure modes in e-commerce.

Note

Anti-Pattern: The P0 Lambda: Running a P0 critical-path service on a serverless runtime to reduce infrastructure costs without accounting for cold start latency, connection pool statefulness, and execution time guarantees. The infrastructure cost savings are real. The reliability cost is paid in production incidents and, in payment processing, in chargebacks and regulatory complaints.

Workload Type	Recommended Runtime	Rationale
Statelessrequesthandler(<500 RPS)	Serverless function	Minimal overhead, no management, scales to zero
Event processor/queue consumer	Serverless function	Trigger-driven, naturally stateless, scales with queue depth
P0 critical path (payment, checkout)	Managed Kubernetes	Cold start predictability, connection pool durability, execution guarantees
P1 stateful service (inventory, orders)	Managed Kubernetes	State requirements exceed serverless capabilities
P2 background processing (reporting, ML inference)	Spot instances / Serverless	Cost optimization appropriate for non-critical path
Stateful data processing (stream aggregation)	Managed Kubernetes with StatefulSet	Pod identity and persistent storage required
Scheduled batch jobs	Serverless function + scheduler	Trigger-based, short duration, no persistent state needed

Table 7.7: Recommended runtime by workload type.

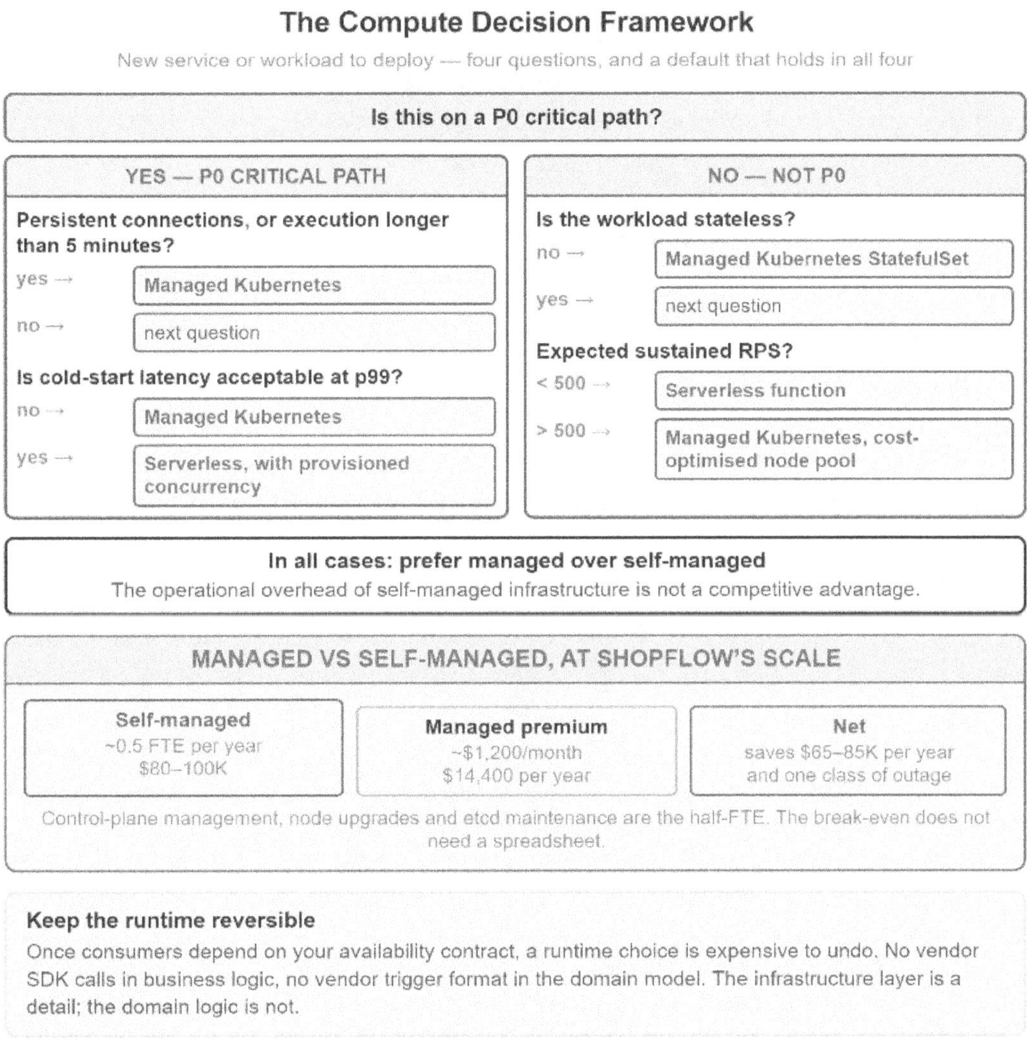

Figure 7.5: The Compute Decision Framework

Note

Safe Scale Check — Runtime Migration Reversibility: A runtime decision is not easily reversed once consumers depend on the service's availability contract. Design for runtime portability from day one: no vendor-specific SDK calls in business logic, no vendor-specific trigger format in the domain model. The infrastructure layer is a detail. The domain logic is not.

Note

Manager's Math — Self-Managed vs. Managed Cost Comparison: At ShopFlow's current infrastructure scale, self-managed Kubernetes requires approximately 0.5 engineering FTE annually for control plane management, node upgrade cycles, and etcd maintenance. At a fully-loaded engineering cost, this is approximately $80–100K annually. The managed Kubernetes premium over equivalent self-managed compute is approximately $1,200/month at ShopFlow's current cluster size — $14,400 annually. The managed service saves $65–85K per year in engineering time while reducing the operational risk of a control plane failure. The break-even analysis does not require a spreadsheet.

Architect's prompt 7.4: the compute strategy audit

When to use this: Use this prompt during an architecture review when evaluating the runtime strategy for a new service or when auditing an existing service that may be on the wrong runtime for its current workload profile.

```
Act as a Principal Infrastructure Architect. I am evaluating the
compute strategy for [Service Name] with the following properties:

- Workload type: [Stateless request handler / Stateful / Event processor /
Batch job/Stream processor
- Priority level: [P0 / P1 / P2]
- Expected sustained RPS: [X]
- p99 latency SLO: [N ms]
- State requirements: [None/Session state/Persistent storage]
- Downstream connections: [Number and type of persistent connections required]
- Maximum acceptable cold start latency: [N ms]
- Expected execution time per request (p99): [N ms or N s]

Current runtime (if any): [Lambda/Kubernetes/VM/Bare Metal]
Current infrastructure cost: [$X/month]
Current operational overhead (engineering hours/month): [N hours]

(1) Evaluate whether the current runtime is appropriate for the workload.
profile. Flag any mismatch between P0 requirements and serverless.
cold start or execution time constraints.
```

```
(2) If a runtime migration is recommended, provide:
- Estimated migration effort in engineering days.
- Portability risks in the current implementation.
- A migration sequence that maintains availability during cutover.
(3) Calculate the total cost of ownership comparison:
- Current: infrastructure cost + operational overhead cost.
- Recommended: infrastructure cost plus operational overhead cost.
- Break-even period for any migration investment.
(4) Define the managed vs. self-managed recommendation with specifics.
justification based on team size and platform engineering capacity.
```

Auto-Scaling: predictive vs. reactive capacity management

Every auto-scaling system is, at its core, a feedback loop: observe a signal, compare it against a threshold, take an action. The difference between a scaling policy that works and one that causes incidents is the quality of the signal, the correctness of the threshold, and the speed of the action relative to the speed of the load change.

ShopFlow's current scaling posture is reactive — scale when CPU utilization exceeds 70%, scale down when it drops below 30%, with a 3-minute cooldown between scaling events. This works for slow, predictable load growth. It fails for three scenarios that ShopFlow will encounter as it grows: instantaneous traffic spikes, predictable daily traffic patterns, and correlated failures where a downstream slowness causes CPU to drop while connection pools exhaust — the CPU signal says scale down while the actual load is increasing.

Reactive scaling: the signal problem

CPU utilization is a lagging indicator of load. A traffic spike that doubles request volume takes 30–90 seconds to manifest as elevated CPU — the time for new requests to queue, execute, and saturate the thread pool. By the time the Horizontal Pod Autoscaler observes the CPU threshold breach, evaluates the scaling decision, schedules new pods, pulls container images, and passes readiness probes, the traffic spike may have lasted two to three minutes with degraded service.

The signal improvement is to scale on request queue depth or request latency rather than CPU. A spike in p99 latency from 95ms to 200ms is observable within one polling interval (15 seconds in Kubernetes HPA). A spike in CPU takes 30–90 seconds. Scaling on the latency signal gives a 15–75 second head start on the traffic pattern.

Note

The Scaling Signal Rule: Scale on the signal that changes first when load increases, not the signal that is easiest to instrument. CPU is easy to instrument. Request latency and queue depth are closer to the actual load pattern. For P0 services, scale on latency. For event-driven services, scale on queue depth. CPU scaling is acceptable for P2 background workloads where scaling latency is tolerable.

Latency and queue depth are the two signals that generalize, but they are not the only ones, and the right signal is a function of the workload. A request-serving API scales best on active in-flight requests or request latency — both rise the instant load does. A service fronted by a connection pool scales on connection pool utilization, which saturates before CPU when downstreams slow (exactly the signal ShopFlow's pool-exhaustion event would have surfaced). A stream consumer scales on Kafka consumer lag or queue processing delay — the backlog of unprocessed messages — because CPU can read as idle while the lag grows without bound. CPU utilization remains a reasonable signal only for genuinely CPU-bound compute, such as image processing or encoding, where it tracks the actual work. Scale on the resource the workload exhausts first, not the one the platform exposes by default.

Predictive scaling: scheduling capacity ahead of load

For traffic patterns that are predictable — daily peaks, weekly cycles, seasonal events — reactive scaling pays a latency tax on every cycle. You scale up 60–90 seconds after the traffic arrives, serve degraded performance during that window, and scale down 3–5 minutes after the traffic recedes. Multiplied across 365 daily cycles and predictable seasonal events, this is a recurring performance tax on a preventable problem.

Predictive scaling preemptively schedules capacity based on historical traffic patterns. Kubernetes Cluster Autoscaler combined with KEDA's cron-based scaling can add pods at 6:45 PM in anticipation of the 7 PM checkout peak and remove them at 11 PM after the peak has subsided. The scaling action precedes the load instead of following it.

Note

The Predictive Scaling Tax: The maintenance overhead of keeping the schedule current. Traffic patterns shift over time — a product launch in a new market changes the peak time zone, a change in marketing cadence shifts the weekly spike day. A predictive scaling schedule that was accurate six months ago may be materially wrong today. Predictive scaling requires quarterly review and update, or it becomes a source of incorrect capacity rather than correct capacity.

Traffic Pattern	Primary Strategy	Secondary Strategy	Scale-to-Zero?	ShopFlow Example
Uniform, predictable RPS	CPU/latency HPA	None	No	Internal admin API
Daily peak cycle	Cron predictive (pre-scale)	Latency HPA for exceptions	No	Checkout (7 PM peak)
Event-driven burst	Queue-depth KEDA	Latency HPA	Partial—between events	Order notification pipeline
Infrequent batch	Scale-to-zero KEDA	None	Yes	Order Reporting, ML inference
Unpredictable spike	Latency HPA + pod floor	Predictive from historical data	No	Flash sale campaigns

Table 7.8: Auto-scaling strategy by traffic pattern.

> Note
>
> **The Hybrid Scaling Rule:** For services with predictable traffic patterns, combine predictive scaling (scheduled capacity for known peaks) with reactive scaling (latency-based or queue-depth-based HPA for unpredicted spikes). Predictive scaling handles the baseline pattern. Reactive scaling handles the exceptions. Neither alone is sufficient: predictive-only misses unexpected spikes, reactive-only pays the cold-start tax on every predictable cycle.

Scale-to-Zero: the P2 optimization

For P2 workloads — reporting pipelines, recommendation recomputation, batch analytics — idle capacity represents pure cost with zero user benefit. KEDA's scale-to-zero capability removes all pods for a workload when its queue is empty and provisions new pods when a message arrives. For P2 batch workloads, this is the correct default. The cold start penalty (30–

60 seconds to provision a new pod and pass readiness probes) is acceptable for a P2 workload whose SLO is measured in minutes, not milliseconds.

Scale-to-zero must never be applied to P0 or P1 workloads. A Payment service that scales to zero when idle will produce a cold-start latency spike on the first checkout request after an idle period.

Scaling Strategy	Signal	Best For	Failure Mode	ShopFlow Application
CPU-based HPA	CPU utilization	P2 background workloads	60–90s lag on spike — SLO breach during ramp	P2 reporting and analytics only
Latency-based HPA	p99 request latency	P0/P1 request handlers	False positives if latency spikes from non-load causes	Checkout, Order, Inventory services
Queue-depth KEDA	Message queue depth	Event-driven consumers	Queue lag if consumer scale-up is slower than producer	Order events, notification pipeline
Cron-based predictive	Historical time pattern	Services with predictable daily/weekly peaks	Stale schedule if traffic patterns change	Checkout (pre-scale before 7 PM peak)
Scale-to-zero KEDA	Queue empty = zero pods	P2 idle batch workloads	Cold start latency on first event after idle period	Order Reporting, Recommendation Engine

Table 7.9: Scaling strategies compared by signal and failure mode.

> Note
>
> **Manager's Math — Scaling Policy Cost Impact:** At ShopFlow's current infrastructure, the difference between reactive CPU-based scaling (over-provision to absorb the 60-second scaling lag) and latency-based scaling (tighter provisioning with faster response) is approximately 2–3 idle pod equivalents per service during off-peak hours. Across six services, 18 idle pods at approximately $30/month per pod = $540/month in avoidable compute cost. Annualized: $6,480. The engineering investment to implement

KEDA with latency-based scaling metrics: approximately two engineering days. Break-even: 3.5 days. Applying scale-to-zero to ShopFlow's three P2 workloads, which are idle approximately 20 hours per day, reduces their compute cost by approximately 83%. At $90/month per service, this is $225/month in savings — $2,700 annually.

Note

Safe Scale Check — Scaling Floor and PodDisruptionBudget: Every scaling action is reversible, but not instantaneously. Define the minimum pod count for every P0 service — the floor below which the autoscaler must never scale, regardless of metrics. ShopFlow's minimum pod count for the Payment service: 3. Two pods provide N+1 redundancy during a rolling deployment. Three pods ensure that a simultaneous pod failure and scaling event does not reduce the service to a single instance. Enforce this through a Kubernetes PodDisruptionBudget with minAvailable: 3.

Architect's prompt 7.5: the Auto-Scaling policy audit

When to use this: Use this prompt when designing or auditing the auto-scaling configuration for a service, or after a traffic spike caused degraded performance that the auto-scaler failed to absorb within the SLO window.

```
Act as a Principal Capacity Engineering specialist. I am designing the
auto-scaling policy for [Service Name] with the following properties:

- Priority level: [P0 / P1 / P2]
- p99 latency SLO: [N ms]
- Current scaling signal: [CPU / Memory / RPS / Queue depth / Custom]
- Current HPA min replicas: [N]
- Current HPA max replicas: [N]
- Current scale-up threshold: [X% CPU or N ms latency]
- Current cooldown period: [Ns]
- Traffic pattern: [Uniform/Daily cycle/Spiky/Event-driven]
- Peak traffic time (if predictable): [HH:MM timezone]

Historical incidents:
- Last traffic spike that caused SLO breach: [date, spike magnitude, duration]
- Observed scaling lag during that incident: [N seconds]
```

```
(1) Calculate the minimum pod count required to absorb a 3x traffic spike.
without breaching the latency SLO, assuming a 90-second scaling lag
under the current configuration.
(2) Recommend a scaling signal upgrade: identify whether the current signal
should be replaced with latency or queue depth, and provide the KEDA
or HPA custom metrics configuration.
(3) If the traffic pattern has a predictable daily or weekly cycle.
Generate a cron-based pre-scaling schedule that adds capacity.
15 minutes before the predicted peak.
(4) If this is a P2 workload, evaluate scale-to-zero eligibility and
provide the KEDA ScaledObject configuration with queue-depth trigger.
(5) Define the PodDisruptionBudget with minAvailable appropriate for
the service's redundancy requirements.
```

Production readiness checklist

Before a ShopFlow service goes GA, every item below should read yes — or carry a named, time-boxed exception. This is the chapter's decisions condensed into a gate you can run in a review, on one page.

Service discovery: DNS-based resolution through stable Kubernetes Service names (no hardcoded IPs or env-injected addresses); liveness and readiness probes wired for health-aware routing.

Service mesh (at GA): mTLS enforced on every service-to-service call; percentage-based traffic shifting available for canaries; automatic trace-header injection across boundaries — or a named reason the mesh is deferred and how those three properties are met without it.

Retries: Every retry policy has exponential backoff, jitter, and a retry budget; every non-idempotent write carries an idempotency key with server-side deduplication before it sits behind any retry.

Circuit breaking: Graduated throttling before a hard break; thresholds set against real RPS and error-rate baselines, not defaults; every circuit state transition emitted as a metric with a false-positive alert.

Bulkheads and timeouts: P0 critical paths on dedicated resource pools that P2 paths cannot consume; connection pools sized by (p99 downstream latency × max concurrency × 1.5); a timeout hierarchy that strictly decreases from the browser inward; load shedding applied in reverse priority order.

Runtime: Runtime matched to the workload profile — no P0 critical path on a cold-starting serverless function; managed services preferred wherever the infrastructure is not a business differentiator; domain logic free of vendor-specific SDK calls so the runtime stays portable.

Auto-scaling: Scale on the first-moving signal (latency or queue depth), not CPU alone; predictive schedule for known peaks combined with reactive scaling for spikes; a PodDisruptionBudget and a minimum-pod floor for every P0 service; scale-to-zero restricted to P2 workloads.

Summary

In this chapter, we built the resilience layer that ShopFlow's service decomposition made necessary but did not provide.

We established that service discovery through Kubernetes DNS is non-negotiable before the first production deployment, and that a service mesh becomes non-negotiable at the GA threshold—not at a service count, but at the point where mTLS, traffic shifting, and automatic trace injection become prerequisites for production reliability.

We replaced the naive retry-on-failure pattern with a bounded retry policy — exponential backoff, jitter, and retry budgets — that limits amplification to at most the retry budget percentage rather than multiplying load by the retry count under degraded conditions.

We implemented the Graduated Response Rule for circuit breaking: slow down before you break, reduce traffic in stages before cutting entirely, and instrument every state transition as a metric so that false positive and false negative rates are observable and tunable.

We enforced bulkhead isolation between P0 and P2 resource pools — dedicated thread pools and correctly sized connection pools — ensuring that a degraded Recommendations service cannot exhaust the connections available to the Checkout path.

We applied the Good Enough Rule and the Premium Service Rule to compute decisions: start stateless and serverless, migrate to managed Kubernetes when state or P0 reliability requirements demand it, and always prefer managed infrastructure over self-managed unless platform engineering is a core business function.

We implemented hybrid scaling — predictive scheduling for known traffic patterns, latency-based reactive scaling for unpredicted spikes, and scale-to-zero for P2 idle workloads — replacing the CPU-lagging reactive policy that caused the scaling lag events ShopFlow experienced in the previous sprint.

ShopFlow's telemetry after *Chapter 7*:

Metric	Before (Ch7 Start)	After (Ch7 End)	Change
Availability	97.8%	99.7%	+1.9 points
Error Rate (Checkout path)	4.2%	0.3%	93% reduction
Connection Pool Exhaustion Events	2/sprint	0	Eliminated
MTTR	4 hours	45 minutes	89% reduction
Retry Amplification Factor	3x (unbounded)	1.1x (budget-constrained)	Bounded
p99 Latency (Global)	150 ms	130 ms	13% improvement
Cloud Spend	$10,000/mo	$9,200/mo	8% reduction (scale-to-zero P2)

Table 7.10: ShopFlow telemetry before and after the Chapter 7 resilience work.

The cliffhanger: the reliable black box

The system is stable. The circuit breakers are tuned. The bulkheads are holding. ShopFlow has gone two full sprints without a P0 incident.

But Dave is looking at the service dependency graph with a different kind of concern.

Last Wednesday, a 5% error rate appeared on the Order service. Dave checked the Order service — healthy. He checked Inventory — healthy. He checked Pricing — healthy. Forty-five minutes later, he traced the error to a network timeout between the Order service and the Inventory service in the eu-west-2 region specifically — a misconfigured Envoy retry policy that was interacting with a database connection pool in a way that only manifested under a specific combination of request latency and pool depth.

The system did not go down. The circuit breakers caught it in time. But it took forty-five minutes to find a problem in a system where every individual component reported healthy.

We have a reliable system. We have an opaque one. We can see the metrics. We can see the error rate. We cannot see the request traveling from the user's browser through the BFF, through the Order service, through the Inventory service, through the database connection pool, to the specific network path in eu-west-2 that caused the timeout.

In *Chapter 8*, we will build the observability layer that makes distributed systems transparent — distributed tracing, structured logging, and the correlation infrastructure that turns forty-five-minute debugging sessions into five-minute root cause analyses.

8

Event-Driven Scaling – Decoupling with Messaging

In *Chapter 7*, we built the resilience layer that protects ShopFlow's services from each other. Circuit breakers are tuned. Bulkheads isolate P0 paths from P2 degradation. The connection pool exhaustion events are gone.

But Dave just pulled up the checkout latency breakdown and found a problem the resilience layer cannot fix.

ShopFlow's checkout flow calls Payment synchronously, waits for confirmation, then calls Shipping for a rate, then triggers a notification pipeline. Each call is a sequential synchronous dependency. Payment at 320ms plus Shipping at 280ms plus notification setup at 180ms equals 780ms of idle thread time before ShopFlow's own checkout logic runs. Three customers were double-charged this month because the Checkout service retried a failed Payment call without checking whether the first attempt had already succeeded at the processor. The circuit breakers are correctly configured. The problem is the architecture, not the thresholds.

In this chapter, we are going to cover the following main topics:

- **Temporal Decoupling:** From 'wait for success' to 'emit and forget.'
- **Brokers vs. Streams:** Choosing RabbitMQ, Kafka, or Cloud Pub/Sub.
- **The Consistency Challenge:** Idempotency and deduplication strategies.
- **Reliable Publishing:** The Transactional Outbox and Change Data Capture.
- **Distributed Sagas:** Managing long-running workflows.

Technical requirements

RabbitMQ 3.12+ / CloudAMQP: Lightweight AMQP broker for task queue and moderate fan-out workloads. Managed hosting eliminates cluster management overhead. The correct starting point for ShopFlow's current event volume.

Apache Kafka 3.x (optional, migration target): High-throughput event streaming for workloads requiring message replay, per-partition ordering, or sustained throughput above 10,000 messages per second.

Cloud-native pub/sub (AWS SQS/SNS, GCP Pub/Sub, Azure Service Bus): Zero-infrastructure managed messaging. Appropriate when vendor lock-in risk is acceptable and operational simplicity is the priority.

Debezium (CDC connector): Change Data Capture tool that reads database WAL/binary log and publishes change events without application code changes.

Temporal/Apache Airflow/AWS Step Functions: Workflow orchestration engines for managing long-running distributed sagas with state visibility, retry logic, and compensating action support.

Redis 7.x: Deduplication store for idempotency key management. The atomic SET NX command is the foundation of the application-layer deduplication pattern.

Pact (consumer-driven contract testing): Ensures that event schema changes by a producer do not silently break consumers. Non-negotiable in a multi-team event-driven system.

Code Repository: `https://github.com/imran-siddique/Architecting-at-Scale/tree/main/ch8`

ShopFlow telemetry snapshot [stage 8]

```
The Signal: Checkout latency is the arithmetic sum of every synchronous dependency
in the path. Payment at 320ms + Shipping at 280ms + Notification setup at 180ms =
780ms of pure wait time before ShopFlow's own checkout logic runs. The circuit
breakers are correctly configured. The problem is the architecture, not the
thresholds.
p99 Latency (Checkout critical path): 2.1s (● Critical – 3 sequential synchronous
calls)
p99 Latency (Payment service standalone): 320ms (Acceptable in isolation)
p99 Latency (Shipping rate call): 280ms (Acceptable in isolation)
Payment Service Timeout Rate: 3.2% (● Critical – each timeout holds checkout
thread for 3s)
```

```
Shipping Notification Delay (avg): 4.7s (Synchronous carrier API in checkout
thread)
Order Confirmation Email Delay: 8-12s post-checkout (User sees processing screen)
Double-Charge Incidents: 3 this month (● Checkout retry without idempotency key)
Message Broker: None (All service communication is synchronous)
Panic Meter: 5/10 (System is stable. Checkout is slow. Customers are noticing.)
```

Note

Dave Alert: "Three customers were charged twice this month. The Checkout service retried a failed Payment call without checking whether the first attempt succeeded at the processor. Both charges cleared. We refunded manually each time. This is not a payment bug — it is an architecture bug."

Figure 8.1: The ShopFlow Order Event Flow

Temporal decoupling: from 'Wait for Success' to 'Emit and Forget'

The synchronous request-response model has a property that is a feature at low scale and a liability at high scale: the caller is only as fast as the slowest callee. ShopFlow's checkout demonstrates this precisely. The checkout thread is held open for the duration of every downstream operation. Payment at 320ms plus Shipping at 280ms plus notification at 180ms adds 780ms of idle thread time before ShopFlow's own business logic runs.

Temporal decoupling breaks this constraint. Checkout writes an order record to the database, emits an OrderPlaced event, and returns a 200 response to the user. Payment subscribes to OrderPlaced, processes the charge asynchronously, and emits PaymentConfirmed. Shipping subscribes to PaymentConfirmed and schedules the shipment. The user sees checkout completion in under 300 ms. Payment, shipping, and notification happen concurrently in the background.

> Note
>
> **The Temporal Coupling Tax:** Every synchronous call in a user-facing critical path is a latency multiplier. The more synchronous dependencies sit in a user-facing path, the higher the probability that tail latency in any one of them degrades the entire request — and in the worst case the path is only as fast as the sum of those dependencies. Temporal decoupling removes each user-independent dependency from this sum. The checkout thread is freed the moment the OrderPlaced event is committed.

Async Pattern	Latency Savings	Consistency Model	Failure Recovery Required	ShopFlow Use
Fire-and-forget event	Full downstream latency	Eventual	Compensating action if event is lost	Analytics, loyalty credits
Event + polling status	Partial — initial response is fast	Near-real-time	Consumer retry + deduplication	Order status display

Async Pattern	Latency Savings	Consistency Model	Failure Recovery Required	ShopFlow Use
Async with callback webhook	Full downstream latency	Eventual	Webhook retry with idempotency key	Payment processor confirmation
Async with shadow sync	Zero — both paths run	Strong (during shadow period)	None — sync path active	Migration validation period

Table 8.1: Asynchronous patterns compared by latency savings and consistency model.

This is not a free optimization. The cost is consistency model: the synchronous path provides read-your-writes consistency. The async path provides eventual consistency. Card authorization — does the card have funds — must remain synchronous. The user cannot leave checkout without knowing if the charge was approved. Payment capture — the actual charge after authorization — can be async. This distinction matters architecturally.

Operation	Sync or Async	Rationale
Card authorization check	Synchronous	User needs immediate approval/decline to proceed
Payment capture (charge)	Async	Capture follows authorization; user need not wait
Inventory reservation	Synchronous	Must prevent overselling before checkout confirmation
Inventory decrement	Async	Physical decrement can follow reservation
Shipping rate calculation	Async	Rate confirmed at cart; recalculation is background validation
Order confirmation email	Async	No user SLO requires synchronous email confirmation

Operation	Sync or Async	Rationale
Fraud score evaluation	Async with timeout fallback	Do not block checkout on model inference latency
Loyalty point credit	Async	Post-purchase, no user-blocking dependency
Analytics event emission	Async	Never block critical path for observability data

Table 8.2: Classifying ShopFlow's checkout operations as user-blocking or user-independent.

> Note
>
> **The Critical Path Separation Rule:** For every operation in a user-facing flow, classify it as user-blocking (the outcome is required before the user's next action) or user-independent (the user does not need the outcome to proceed). Every user-independent operation must be moved to an async event path. You cannot optimize critical path latency while keeping user-independent operations synchronous.

Running this classification against ShopFlow's checkout path reveals two genuinely user-blocking operations: card authorization and inventory reservation. Every other operation — payment capture, shipping scheduling, fraud scoring, confirmation email, loyalty credits, analytics — is user-independent. Moving all seven to async reduces the checkout critical path from 2.1 seconds to under 300 ms.

When not to use asynchronous messaging

The Critical Path Separation Rule pushes user-independent work off the request path, but it is not a mandate to make everything asynchronous. Async buys concurrency at the price of eventual consistency, and there is a class of operation for which that trade is wrong.

Keep an operation synchronous whenever the user cannot safely proceed without its result. Card authorization is the canonical case at ShopFlow — the customer must know at checkout whether the charge was approved, so authorization stays synchronous even though the capture that follows is async. The same holds for input validation and business-rule checks that must reject a request before it is accepted, for authentication and authorization decisions that gate access, and for fraud checks that must return an instant allow or deny before an order is confirmed. Any operation whose failure must be shown to the user as a failure of the action they just took belongs on the synchronous path.

The Synchronous-When-Blocking Rule: An operation stays synchronous when its outcome is a precondition for the user's next step — authorization, authentication, validation, an instant fraud decision, or any confirmation the user is waiting on. Making these async does not remove the latency; it moves the failure somewhere the user cannot see it and cannot act on it. Asynchronous messaging is for user-independent work, not for a decision the user is standing at the checkout waiting for.

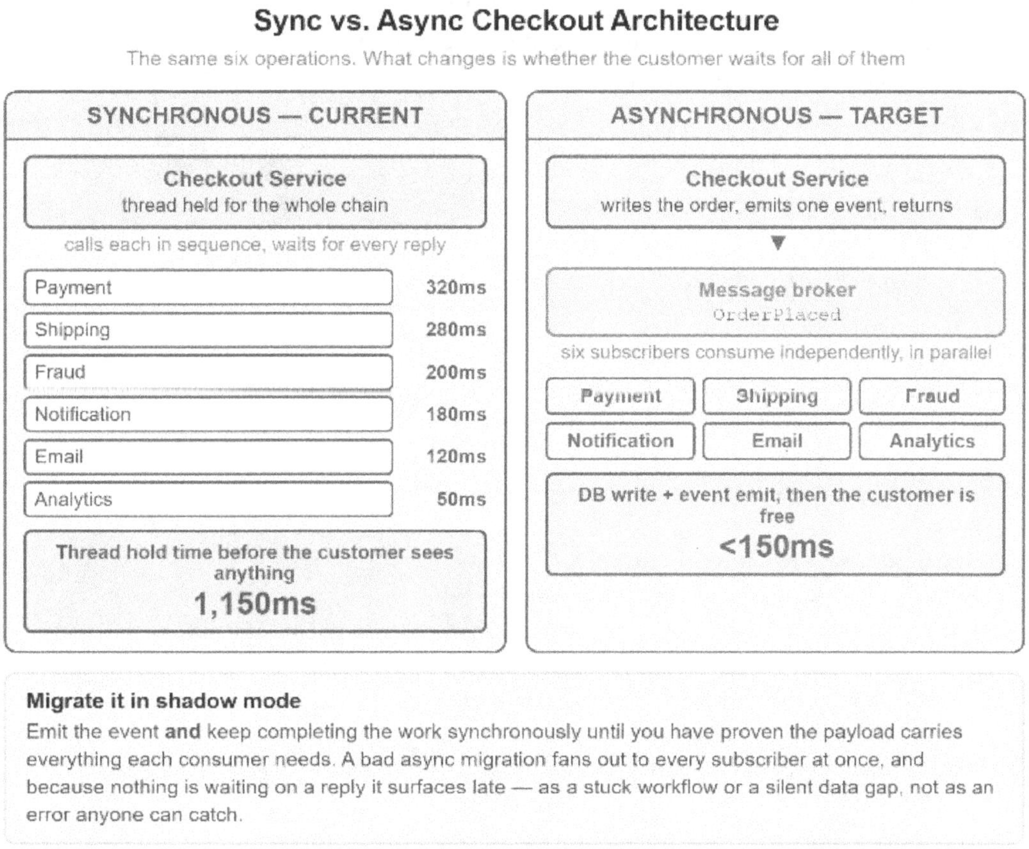

Figure 8.2: Sync vs. Async Checkout Architecture

> **Note**
>
> **Safe Scale Check — Async Migration Reversibility:** Moving an operation from sync to async is not trivially reversible once consumers depend on the event contract. Run the async path in shadow mode first — emit the event but also complete the operation synchronously. Validate that the event payload contains all data the consumer needs before decommissioning the synchronous path. The blast radius of a poorly designed

async migration is every downstream consumer at once: a single malformed, misordered, or missing event fans out to every subscriber simultaneously, and because no synchronous caller is waiting on a response, the failure surfaces late — as a stuck workflow or a silent data gap — rather than as an immediate error a caller can catch.

Architect's prompt 8.1: the Sync-to-Async migration audit

When to use this: Use this prompt at the start of an event-driven migration, before any broker is selected or any consumer is written.

```
Act as a Principal Systems Architect specializing in event-driven migration.
I am analyzing the following service call graph for sync-to-async.
migration opportunities:

Service: [Service Name] | Current p99 latency: [Xms] | Target p99: [Yms]

Downstream synchronous calls (for each):
- Dependency name, p99 response time, operation description,
user action immediately after this call completes

[Paste call graph or list of downstream calls]

For each downstream call:
Classify: user-blocking or user-independent.
(2) For user-independent: estimate latency savings from async migration.
(3) Identify consistency risks: what is the UX if the async operation fails?
after the synchronous path has returned success?
(4) Define the compensating action: what must be reversed upstream?
(5) Recommend migration sequence based on latency savings and reversibility.

Output: classified call inventory, projected p99 after migration.
compensating action definitions, migration sequence with rollback triggers.
```

Brokers vs. streams: choosing RabbitMQ, Kafka, or cloud Pub/Sub

The broker selection conversation in most organizations follows the same path: someone on the team has Kafka experience, Kafka is suggested, Kafka is adopted, and the team spends the next several months managing ZooKeeper nodes, consumer group offsets, and partition rebalancing — for a workload that processes a few thousand events per day. This is the most common broker selection failure mode, and it deserves to be named directly.

> Note
>
> **Anti-Pattern: The Kafka Default:** The Kafka Default occurs when a team selects Kafka not because the workload demands it but because someone on the team already knows it. Kafka is an extraordinary piece of engineering for the workloads it was designed for: high-throughput event streaming, log compaction, replayable event history, and multi-consumer fan-out at millions of events per second. For a service processing ten thousand order events per day with five downstream consumers, Kafka is a 10x operational overhead investment for a 0x performance advantage over a simpler broker. Team expertise should inform implementation, not mandate architecture.

In Fairness to Kafka: The Kafka Default is about not defaulting to Kafka, not about Kafka being weak. Two clarifications matter. First, Kafka need not be self-managed: Confluent Cloud, Amazon MSK, and Aiven run it as a managed service, and KRaft mode has removed the ZooKeeper dependency even for self managed clusters — so the operational-overhead argument is largely an argument against self-managing Kafka, not against Kafka itself. Second, Kafka scales exceptionally well as load grows, and its cost-to-serve can be tuned down with tiered or direct-to-storage writes and a shorter initial retention window. The honest case against starting on Kafka is therefore narrower than 'it is heavy': at a few thousand events per day a managed queue is still simpler and cheaper, and — like every broker in mainstream use — Kafka delivers at-least-once, not exactly-once, so the consumer still needs the idempotency and deduplication this chapter builds regardless of the broker chosen.

The starting philosophy for broker selection is identical to the runtime selection philosophy from *Chapter 7*: choose the minimum viable broker that is easy to operate, easy to understand, appropriate for the current workload, and extensible enough to not require immediate replacement.

> Note
>
> **The Minimal Broker Rule:** Select the broker with the lowest operational overhead that satisfies the current workload's delivery guarantee, throughput, and fan-out requirements. Operate it until a specific, measurable signal demands migration. Do not migrate speculatively.

Characteristic	RabbitMQ	Apache Kafka	Cloud Pub/Sub
Operational overhead	Low — single node viable, managed options available	High — cluster, partition management, offset tracking	Very low — fully managed, zero infrastructure
Throughput ceiling	~50k msgs/sec per node	Millions/sec per cluster	Scales automatically
Message replay	No — consumed messages are deleted	Yes — configurable retention window	Limited — varies by provider
Per-message ordering	Per-queue FIFO	Per-partition ordering only	Limited — no global ordering
Fan-out model	Exchange and binding model	Consumer groups receive all messages	Topic subscription model
Dead letter handling	Built-in DLX/DLQ	Manual DLQ configuration required	Built-in DLQ on most providers
Team learning curve	Low — AMQP is well-documented	High — Kafka concepts are distinct	Very low — REST/SDK APIs
Vendor lock-in risk	Low — AMQP protocol portability	Medium — Kafka ecosystem dependencies	High — provider-specific APIs

Table 8.3: RabbitMQ, Kafka, and Cloud Pub/Sub compared by characteristic.

Note

The Broker Fit Rule: If the workload does not require message replay, sustained throughput above 10,000 messages per second, or strict per-partition ordering semantics, Kafka is not the correct starting broker. A cloud-managed queue or a lightweight AMQP broker delivers equivalent functional behavior at a fraction of the operational cost.

For ShopFlow's current event volume — tens of thousands of order events per day, five to seven downstream consumers per topic, no replay requirement for operational workflows — a cloud-native pub/sub service or managed RabbitMQ is the correct starting point. The signal that justifies migrating to Kafka is specific and measurable: sustained message rate exceeding the simple broker's throughput ceiling; a consumer that needs to replay historical events; a compliance requirement for immutable auditable event history. Until one of those signals appears in metrics, the migration is speculative overhead.

> Note
>
> **The Broker Migration Rule:** Design event producers and consumers to be broker-agnostic from day one. The payload format, topic naming convention, and consumer interface must not encode Kafka-specific primitives — partition keys, consumer group IDs, offset commits — unless Kafka is the confirmed long-term choice. A producer that emits a structured JSON payload to a named topic can migrate from RabbitMQ to Kafka to a cloud pub/sub service with a configuration change. A producer that manages partition assignment in business logic cannot.

Migrating from RabbitMQ to Kafka: what changes, what Doesn't

Because the Broker Migration Rule keeps producers and consumers broker-agnostic, a later move from managed RabbitMQ to Kafka is an infrastructure change, not an application rewrite —provided the discipline held from day one.

What stays the same: the event contracts (the OrderPlaced, PaymentConfirmed, and ShipmentScheduled payloads), the producer code that emits a structured payload to a named topic, and the consumer code that processes a payload and records its idempotency key. None of these encode broker primitives, so none of them change.

What changes is infrastructure and configuration: the broker endpoint and client library; the topic-and-partition layout (Kafka partitions a topic for parallelism and per-key ordering, whereas RabbitMQ used queues and routing keys); consumer-group and offset management in place of AMQP acknowledgments; and the retention and replay configuration Kafka now makes available. The event schema is untouched; the plumbing beneath it is replaced. That is exactly the property broker-agnostic design was protecting — and the reason the migration is triggered by a measured signal rather than performed speculatively.

Operational Concern	RabbitMQ (Managed)	Kafka (Self-Managed)	Cloud Pub/Sub
Infrastructure setup time	~2 hours	~2 days	~30 minutes
Monthly infrastructure cost (ShopFlow scale)	\$200–\$400	\$800–\$1,500+	\$50–\$200 (pay per message)
On-call scenarios	Queue saturation, connection limits	Partition rebalancing, consumer lag, broker failover	Provider SLA incidents only
Upgrade procedure	Managed — provider handles	Rolling restart; coordination required	Provider handles automatically
Monitoring surface	Queue depth, consumer count, memory alarm	Consumer group lag, partition offsets, broker health	Subscription backlog, delivery latency

Table 8.4: Operational concerns across the broker options.

A note on managed Kafka: the table above frames Kafka as self-managed to make the operational contrast explicit, but managed Kafka — Confluent Cloud, Amazon MSK, Aiven — removes most of the operational-concern column (cluster provisioning, upgrades, and, with KRaft, ZooKeeper), bringing its profile much closer to managed RabbitMQ and Cloud Pub/Sub. With managed Kafka the decision narrows to delivery semantics, per-partition ordering, replay, and cost model rather than who runs the cluster. What does not change is the delivery guarantee: all of these deliver at-least-once, so consumer-side idempotency is required whichever you choose.

Decision Signal	Recommended Broker	Rationale
< 10k events/day, simple fan-out	Cloud Pub/Sub (SQS/SNS)	Zero ops overhead, scales automatically
< 10k events/day, complex routing	RabbitMQ managed	Exchange patterns, topic routing, low ops cost

Decision Signal	Recommended Broker	Rationale
10k–500k events/day, no replay	RabbitMQ cluster or Cloud Pub/Sub	Throughput within ceiling, simpler than Kafka
> 500k events/day, replay needed	Apache Kafka	Replay, log compaction, high throughput justified
Audit log / compliance requirement	Apache Kafka	Immutable event history, configurable retention
Team has zero broker expertise	Cloud Pub/Sub	Lowest learning curve, managed durability

Table 8.5: Broker selection by decision signal.

> **Note**
>
> Manager's Math — The Kafka Operational Cost: At ShopFlow's current event volume, the operational cost delta between a managed RabbitMQ cluster and a self-managed Kafka cluster is approximately 0.3 engineering FTE annually — time spent on partition rebalancing events, consumer lag incidents, offset reset procedures, and broker upgrades. At a fully loaded engineering cost, this is $48–60K per year. The managed RabbitMQ cluster costs approximately $200–400/month — $2,400–4,800 annually. The simple broker saves $43–58K per year at ShopFlow's current scale. When the workload demands Kafka, that calculus changes.

Architect's prompt 8.2: the broker selection audit

> **Note**
>
> **When to use this:** Use this prompt when selecting a message broker for a new event-driven system or evaluating whether the current broker is appropriate for the workload's growth trajectory.

```
Act as a Principal Infrastructure Architect specializing in event-driven systems.
I am selecting a message broker for the following workload:

Current event volume: [X events/day]
Projected event volume (12 months): [Y events/day]
```

```
Number of distinct event types: [N]
Maximum consumers per event type: [N]
Replay requirement: [Yes/No – if yes, maximum replay window]
Ordering requirement: [Global/Per-entity/None]
Team Kafka expertise: [None/One engineer/Dedicated ops]
Compliance requirements: [Audit log/Data residency/None]

Evaluate whether the current workload volume justifies Kafka.
operational overhead. Show the break-even calculation.
Recommend the minimum viable broker for the current workload.
(3) Define the migration trigger: at what specific measurable threshold
should the team migrate? Express as an observable metric.
(4) If cloud pub/sub is recommended, identify vendor lock-in risks.
and broker-agnostic design patterns that mitigate them.
(5) Estimate the operational overhead delta vs. Kafka in eng-hours/month.
```

The consistency challenge: idempotence and deduplication

Every message broker operating at production scale delivers messages at least once. At-least-once delivery means that under retry storms, network partitions, and consumer restarts — precisely the conditions when a system is already under stress — duplicate messages become frequent, not rare. ShopFlow's three double-charge incidents were not payment processor bugs. They were caused by a consumer that was not designed for at-least-once delivery.

> Note
>
> **The Idempotency Granularity Rule:** The more granular and self-contained an operation, the easier it is to make idempotent. A payment capture scoped to a single order_id and a single amount is straightforward to deduplicate — one operation, one idempotency key, one outcome to record. A payment capture that processes a batch of orders is significantly harder: a partial batch failure requires identifying which items succeeded before re-attempting failures. Start with granular operations.

The implementation of idempotency requires two components: the idempotency key and the deduplication store. The key must be stable across every retry of the same logical operation — it must not change when the caller retries. For ShopFlow's payment capture the correct key is the order's payment identity, {order_id}_{payment_intent_id}, generated once when the payment is first attempted and reused on every redelivery. Deriving the key from an incrementing attempt number is a classic double-charge bug: a retry that increments the attempt produces a new key and bypasses deduplication entirely. The payment consumer checks the store before processing and, if the key has a recorded outcome, returns that outcome without re-processing. The deduplication record must be durable — its authoritative copy is a unique-constrained row in the application database, committed in the same transaction as the payment result, so a cache failure cannot lose it. Redis (with AOF persistence) serves as the fast pre-check in front of that constraint, not as the sole source of truth, and its TTL must match the broker's maximum message retention window.

Three failure modes accumulate in most idempotency implementations.

Failure Mode 1 — The Optimistic Check: The consumer checks the deduplication store, finds no entry, and begins processing. Between the check and the processing completion, a duplicate message arrives on a different consumer instance. Both pass the check simultaneously and both execute. The fix is an atomic check-and-set using Redis SET NX before processing begins.

Failure Mode 2 — The Catch-Up Gap: After a consumer crash, the broker redelivers unacknowledged messages. If the domain change and its deduplication record are written in separate steps, a crash between them lets the next delivery reprocess the operation — either a double effect or a lost dedup record, depending on which write landed first. The fix is to make the deduplication record and the business write commit atomically: write the idempotency key as a unique-constrained row in the application database, in the same transaction as the domain change. The database — not the cache — is the source of truth. If the transaction commits, both the outcome and its dedup record exist; if it rolls back, neither does, so a crash can never leave the operation marked done but unapplied, or applied but unmarked. A Redis write before the transaction is only a fast-path check and must never be the authority. Where the operation includes a non-transactional external call — the payment API itself — that call must carry its own provider idempotency key, because no local transaction can span it.

Failure Mode 3 — The TTL Expiry Window: If a delayed message arrives after the deduplication store TTL has expired, the store has no record of prior processing and the operation executes again. The TTL must be set to at least the maximum message retention window of the broker.

> **Note**
>
> **Anti-Pattern: The Optimistic Idempotency Key:** An idempotency implementation where the deduplication store check and the processing start are not atomic. Under concurrent duplicate delivery, both processors pass the check simultaneously and both execute the operation. The deduplication store entry must be written before processing

begins, using Redis SET key value NX EX ttl — it sets the key only if it does not exist, atomically, with a TTL.

Idempotency Strategy	Duplicate Protection	Failure Recovery	Operational Cost	Recommended For
No idempotency	None — duplicates execute freely	Manual reconciliation	Zero	Never for financial operations
Client-generated key, no store	Partial— depends on key uniqueness	None — no prior outcome recorded	Very low	Read-only operations only
Atomic SET NX + pre-processing write	Strong — prevents concurrent and sequential duplicates	TTL tuning required	Medium — Redis dependency	Payment, order, inventory
Database unique constraint	Strong — enforced at the storage layer	Automatic — constraint violation = duplicate	Low	Low-throughput DB-backed ops
Kafka exactly-once (transactional)	Strong—broker-enforced	Automatic	High — Kafka cluster required	High-throughput Kafka workloads only

Table 8.6: Idempotency strategies compared by protection, recovery, and cost.

Note

The Duplicate Budget Rule: Define a measurable acceptable duplicate rate for each consumer before going to production. For payment capture: zero tolerance. For analytics events: 0.01% duplicate rate acceptable. For notification emails: one duplicate per order acceptable. These tolerances determine the strictness of the deduplication implementation required—and the cost of that implementation.

Note

Safe Scale Check — Deduplication Window: The deduplication store TTL and the broker's message retention window must be coordinated. If RabbitMQ retains unacknowledged messages for up to 7 days before moving them to the DLQ, the deduplication store TTL must be at least 7 days. A message that ages in the DLQ for 48 hours and is then manually replayed will bypass a 24-hour TTL. For payment operations, this is not a theoretical risk — it is a production incident waiting for an engineer to trigger a manual DLQ replay.

Event versioning and schema evolution

A synchronous API version is consumed and forgotten within the request. A published event is not: it may be replayed months later, sit in a dead-letter queue across a release boundary, or be consumed by a team that has not redeployed since it was written. A published event is a long-lived contract, and its schema will outlive the code that first emitted it.

That makes backward compatibility the default obligation of every producer. Additive, optional fields are safe; removing a field, renaming it, changing its type, or tightening its meaning is a breaking change that will fail some consumer you cannot see. When a breaking change is genuinely required, version the event explicitly — a version field in the envelope or a versioned topic or subject name — and run the old and new versions in parallel until every consumer has migrated, exactly as with the API-versioning discipline of *Chapter 6*.

The Event Contract Rule: Treat every published event schema as a permanent, versioned contract. Register schemas in a schema registry (Confluent Schema Registry, AWS Glue, or an Avro/Protobuf/JSON-Schema repository) so compatibility is enforced at publish time rather than discovered at consume time, and back it with consumer-driven contract tests (Pact) so a producer cannot ship a schema change that breaks a registered consumer. Additive by default; versioned when breaking; never silent.

Architect's prompt 8.3: the idempotency implementation audit

When to use this: Use this prompt when reviewing an existing event consumer for deduplication correctness or when designing the idempotency strategy for a new consumer with financial or inventory side effects.

```
Act as a Principal Reliability Engineer specializing in event-driven consistency.
I am auditing the following event consumer for idempotency correctness:

Consumer name: [Name]
Operation: [Description – e.g. Charge payment card for order]
Side effects: [e.g. DB write to orders table + external payment API call]
Idempotency key format: [e.g. order_id + attempt_number]
Deduplication store: [Redis / DB unique constraint / None]
Deduplication store TTL: [X hours/days]
Broker message retention window: [Y hours/days]
Current duplicate rate: [Z% or unknown]

I will provide the consumer processing code:
[Paste consumer code]

(1) Is the deduplication store written atomically before processing begins?
If check and write are separate, flag as concurrent duplicate risk.
(2) Is the deduplication store TTL >= broker message retention window?
If not, calculate the window during which TTL expiry enables duplicates.
(3) If the consumer crashes between the DB write and the deduplication store
write,
what is the outcome of the next delivery?
(4) Is the idempotency key truly unique for the operation scope?
(5) Recommend the minimum deduplication implementation for this consumer.
```

Reliable publishing: the transactional outbox and change data capture

The fundamental reliability problem in event-driven publishing is two operations masquerading as one. Saving a record to the database and publishing a message to the broker are independent operations. If the database write succeeds and the broker publish fails, the database has a record that no downstream consumer knows about. If the broker publish succeeds and the database write fails, consumers are processing an event for data that does not exist. Neither failure mode is acceptable in a system where the event drives payment or shipping.

The Transactional Outbox resolves this by making event publication part of the database transaction. Instead of calling the broker after the database write, the service writes the event payload to an outbox table in the same transaction as the domain record. A separate polling process reads the outbox and publishes to the broker. The domain record and its event are always written atomically — they cannot diverge.

The Outbox Workflow, Step by Step: (1) Begin the database transaction. (2) Write the business data. (3) Write the outbox record. (4) Commit the transaction — business data and event are now atomic. (5) A separate poller reads the unprocessed outbox rows. (6) Publish the event to the broker. (7) The broker acknowledges the publish. (8) Mark the outbox row processed. Steps 1–4 guarantee the record and its event commit together and can never diverge; steps 5–8 guarantee the event is published at least once, with the mark-processed step gated on the broker acknowledgment — never written before it, or a crash in between silently drops the event.

> Note
>
> **The Outbox Tax:** The Transactional Outbox introduces three operational concerns absent from direct publishing: a polling process requiring independent deployment, monitoring, and scaling; an outbox table that accumulates rows requiring scheduled cleanup; and a publication latency equal to the polling interval. At 100ms polling, events publish within 100ms of the database commit. At 5-second polling, publication latency is 5 seconds. The polling interval is a direct tradeoff between event delivery SLO and database read IOPS.

> Note
>
> The Polling Frequency Rule: The outbox polling interval must be derived from the downstream event delivery SLO, not from a framework default. If the consumer's maximum acceptable processing delay is 500ms, the polling interval must be under 250ms. If the acceptable delay is 10 seconds, 2–3 second polling is appropriate and significantly cheaper in database IOPS. Calculate the database read load before setting the interval—do not use framework defaults in production.

The failure mode that consistently surprises teams operating the Outbox for the first time is catch-up after a poller crash. When the outbox poller goes offline for 15 minutes and restarts, it faces a backlog proportional to the write rate times the downtime duration. A poller sized for normal throughput may not clear the backlog before the next maintenance window. If the backlog fills the poller's in-memory buffer, it may crash again under its own recovery load.

> Note
>
> **Anti-Pattern: The Fire-and-Forget Outbox:** An Outbox implementation where the 'mark as processed' step and the broker publish acknowledgment are not atomic. If 'mark as processed' is written before the publish acknowledgment, a crash after marking but before the broker acknowledgment produces a silently dropped event. The correct sequence: publish to broker → receive broker acknowledgment → mark as processed in the database. If any step fails, retry from the publish step.

Change data capture as an outbox alternative

For workloads where explicit outbox table management introduces unacceptable overhead, Change Data Capture reads from the database replication log directly — the WAL in PostgreSQL, the binary log in MySQL — and publishes change events without requiring application code changes. The database becomes the implicit outbox.

> Note
>
> **The CDC Migration Rule:** CDC is appropriate when the event schema closely mirrors the database schema. CDC is not appropriate when event publication depends on business logic invisible in the raw database change, when multiple table writes constitute a single domain event, or when the event schema must be decoupled from the database schema for versioning reasons. In those cases, the Transactional Outbox provides the application-layer control CDC cannot.

Publishing Approach	Atomicity Guarantee	Publication Latency	Operational Overhead	Recommended For
Direct broker call after DB write	None — two independent operations	Minimal	Low	Prototyping only

Publishing Approach	Atomicity Guarantee	Publication Latency	Operational Overhead	Recommended For
Transactional Outbox	Strong — same DB transaction as domain write	Polling interval (100 ms–5 s)	Medium — poller + cleanup	Production financial events
CDC (Debezium/ Maxwell)	Strong — reads committed WAL changes	Near-real-time sub-second	Medium-High — CDC connector + schema registry	Search index sync, audit logs
Dual-write (DB + broker directly)	None — race condition between writes	Minimal	Low	Never for ops with side effects

Table 8.7: Reliable-publishing approaches compared.

Note

Manager's Math — The Outbox Implementation Cost: Initial implementation of a production-grade Transactional Outbox — including catch-up handling, monitoring, and cleanup — requires approximately 3–5 engineering days. Compared to the alternative — three double-charge incidents per month at 2 engineering hours of reconciliation each, plus customer support cost and refund processing — the one-time implementation cost pays back within the first month of operation.

Architect's prompt 8.4: the outbox implementation review

When to use this: Use this prompt when reviewing an Outbox implementation before production deployment or when diagnosing a reliability issue in an existing event publishing pipeline.

```
Act as a Principal Event Architecture Engineer. I am reviewing the
following Transactional Outbox implementation for production readiness:
```

```
Database: [PostgreSQL / MySQL / other]
Broker: [RabbitMQ / Kafka / Cloud Pub/Sub]
Polling interval: [X ms]
Downstream event delivery SLO: [Yms]
Expected write rate (outbox inserts/sec): [Z]

I will provide:
1. The outbox table schema.
2. The polling process code.
3. The cleanup job configuration.

[Paste schema, polling code, cleanup config]

(1) Is the outbox row written in the same DB transaction as the domain?
record? If not, identify the consistency gap.
(2) Is the polling interval consistent with the downstream SLO?
Calculate the maximum publication latency at the current interval.
(3) Is the mark-as-processed step atomic with the broker acknowledgment?
Identify whether a crash produces a duplicate or a dropped event.
(4) Does the cleanup job bound the outbox table growth?
(5) What is the catch-up behavior after a 15-minute poller outage?
Calculate backlog size and time to clear at current poller throughput.
```

Distributed sagas: managing Long-Running workflows

A saga is a long-running workflow that spans multiple services and requires coordinated state management across service boundaries. ShopFlow's order fulfillment is a saga: place order → reserve inventory → capture payment → schedule shipping → send confirmation. Each step has a corresponding compensating action if a later step fails: release inventory reservation, refund the payment capture, cancel the scheduled shipment.

Two implementation models exist: choreography and orchestration.

In **choreography**, each service reacts to events independently. OrderService emits OrderPlaced. InventoryService listens, reserves stock, and emits InventoryReserved. PaymentService listens to InventoryReserved, captures payment, and emits PaymentConfirmed. No central coordinator exists.

In **orchestration**, a central workflow service manages the sequence explicitly. The orchestrator sends a ReserveInventory command to InventoryService, waits for the result, then sends a

CapturePayment command to PaymentService, and so on. Workflow state is owned by the orchestrator.

> Note
>
> The Orchestrator Preference Rule: For workflows involving more than three services or more than two compensating actions, prefer orchestration over choreography. The orchestrator makes the workflow state visible, queryable, and debuggable from a single location. Choreography distributes workflow state across every participating service—reconstructing the workflow state after a failure requires querying every service involved. There is no single place to ask: what happened to order 1234?

The preference for orchestration comes from direct experience building and operating workflow engines at scale. Choreography has an appealing quality at design time: services are loosely coupled and there is no central point of failure in the coordination logic. The operational reality is different. The implicit coupling is still present — services share event contracts, ordering assumptions, and timing dependencies — it is just invisible. When the InventoryService reserves stock but the InventoryReserved event is never consumed by the PaymentService, the workflow is stuck. No system owns the in-progress state.

> Note
>
> **Anti-Pattern: The Invisible Workflow:** The Invisible Workflow occurs in choreography-based sagas when the workflow state cannot be reconstructed from any single system. OrderService knows the order was placed. InventoryService knows the stock was reserved. PaymentService shows no payment was captured. No system knows these three facts belong to the same workflow, or what prevented the transition from InventoryReserved to PaymentCaptured. In an orchestrated workflow, this state is visible: the orchestrator shows workflow order_1234 at step 2 of 5, waiting for PaymentConfirmed, with a timestamp showing it has been in this state for 47 minutes.

Note

The Choreography Complexity Threshold: Choreography is appropriate when the workflow has two or fewer steps, the failure recovery requires a single compensating action, and the event ordering is guaranteed by the broker. Beyond these constraints — more steps, multi-step compensation, or ordering the broker cannot guarantee — orchestration provides better operational control.

Dimension	Choreography	Orchestration
Workflow state visibility	Distributed across all services	Central — orchestrator owns state
Debugging approach	Correlate events across all participants	Single orchestrator state query
Coupling model	Implicit — services share event contracts	Explicit — orchestrator knows all participants
Compensating action management	Each service implements its own rollback	Orchestrator triggers compensating commands in sequence
Failure recovery	Reconstruct state from distributed event logs	Resume or compensate from orchestrator
Appropriate service count	2–3 services	3+ services
ShopFlow application	Notification fan-out (3 consumers, no compensation)	Order fulfillment (5 steps, 4 compensating actions)
Tooling options	Pure event bus configuration	Temporal, AWS Step Functions, Azure Durable Functions

Table 8.8: Choreography versus orchestration for distributed sagas.

Note

The Dead Letter Mandate: Every consumer in an event-driven system must define a Dead Letter Queue. A message that fails processing after the maximum retry count is not a transient error — it is a systematic problem requiring human investigation or automated remediation. A consumer without a DLQ silently discards these messages. Data loss with no observable signal is the worst failure mode in a distributed system: it looks like success from the outside, but the order was never fulfilled and the customer was never notified.

Note

The Saga Rollback Rule: Every orchestrated workflow step that has a side effect must have a corresponding compensating action that reverses the side effect. The compensating action must be idempotent. It must be tested independently of the forward path. It must be executed in reverse order of the forward path. A compensation that has never been executed in staging will fail at the worst possible moment in production.

Saga Step	**Side Effect**	**Reversible?**	**Compensating Action**	**Idempotency Key**
Reserve inventory	Stock count decreased	Yes	Release reservation for order_id	order_id + reserve
Capture payment	Customer card charged	Yes (within window)	Refund capture for order_id	order_id + capture
Schedule shipment	Carrier slot booked	Yes (before pickup)	Cancel shipment for order_id	order_id + shipment
Dispatch physical package	Package handed to carrier	No — irreversible after scan	Customer support escalation	N/A

Saga Step	Side Effect	Reversible?	Compensating Action	Idempotency Key
Send confirmation email	Email delivered	No — cannot un-send	Send correction email if needed	order_id + email_type

Table 8.9: The ShopFlow order-fulfillment saga steps and their compensating actions.

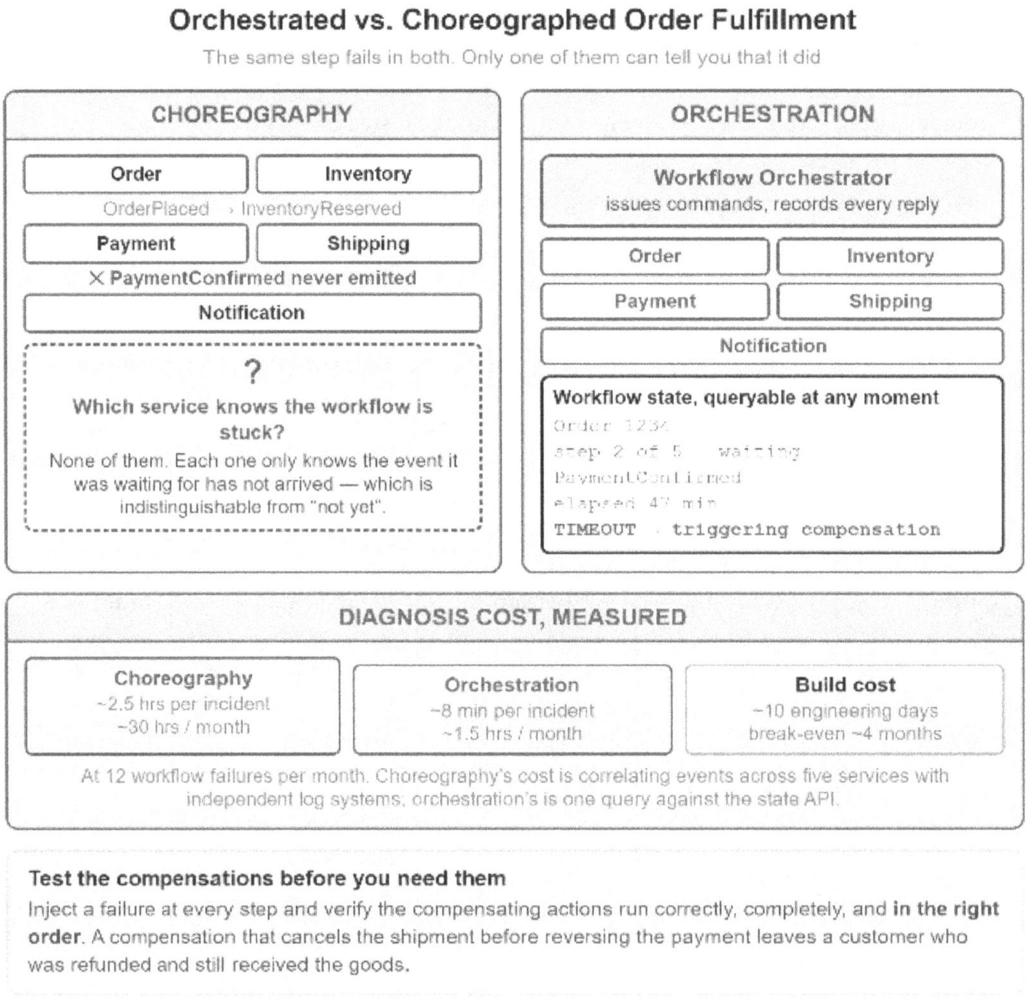

Figure 8.3: Orchestrated vs. Choreographed Order Fulfillment Saga

> **Note**
>
> Safe Scale Check — Saga Blast Radius: The blast radius of a failed saga step is bounded by whether compensating actions are implemented and tested. Before deploying any orchestrated workflow to production, inject failures at each step and verify that compensating actions execute correctly, completely, and in the correct order. A compensation that executes in the wrong order — canceling a shipment before reversing a payment — can produce a state where the customer received a refund but the shipment was not canceled.

> **Note**
>
> **Manager's Math — Orchestration vs. Choreography Debug Cost:** At a high-traffic enterprise platform, the average time to diagnose a choreography-based saga failure — correlating events across five services with independent log systems — was approximately 2.5 engineering hours per incident. With an orchestrated workflow, the equivalent diagnosis required querying the orchestrator's state API: approximately 8 minutes. At 12 workflow failures per month, the choreography approach consumed approximately 30 engineering hours monthly in diagnosis alone. The orchestration approach consumed approximately 1.5 hours. One-time cost to implement the workflow orchestrator: approximately 10 engineering days. Break-even: approximately 4 months.

A note on these estimates: the implementation-day figures throughout this chapter are labor estimates, and AI coding assistants compress the labor, not the judgment. A capable agent can scaffold an outbox poller, a deduplication wrapper, or a saga state machine in a fraction of the hand-coded time, pulling these break-even points in and making the cheaper-to-build patterns cheaper still. What it does not change is the architectural decision — which operations to decouple, which broker fits the workload, where the compensating actions belong. Treat the day counts as a pre-assistance upper bound; the design reasoning behind them is what still has to be right.

Architect's prompt 8.5: the saga design audit

When to use this: Use this prompt when designing a new multi-step workflow or when evaluating an existing choreography-based saga for migration to orchestration.

```
Act as a Principal Event Architecture Engineer specializing in
distributed saga design. I am designing the following workflow:

Workflow name: [e.g. Order Fulfillment]
Steps: [list each step with the service responsible and the side effect]
Compensating actions: [for each step, the action that reverses it]
Failure scenarios: [which steps are most likely to fail and why]
Current implementation: [Choreography/Orchestration/None]

For each step:
(1) Classify side effect as reversible or irreversible.
(2) For reversible steps, verify the compensating action is idempotent.
If not, identify the duplicate execution risk.
(3) Recommend choreography or orchestration based on:
- Step count, compensating action complexity.
- Requirement for workflow state visibility

If orchestration is recommended:
(4) Design the orchestrator state machine: states, transitions,
timeout triggers and compensation sequences.
(5) Define the DLQ strategy: at what retry count does a step move to the DLQ.
and what automated or manual remediation is triggered?
(6) Define the observability contract: what metrics must the orchestrator
emit to make workflow health visible?
```

Event-Driven readiness checklist

Before an event-driven ShopFlow flow goes to production, every item below should read yes — or carry a named, time-boxed exception. The chapter's operational decisions are condensed into a review gate.

Decoupling: Every user-independent operation moved off the synchronous critical path; genuinely user-blocking steps (card authorization, inventory reservation) are kept synchronous.

Broker: Minimum viable broker chosen for the current workload with a named, measurable migration trigger; producers and consumers are broker-agnostic — no broker primitives in business logic.

Idempotency: Every consumer designed for at-least-once delivery; a stable idempotency key (not attempt-number-based); atomic check-and-set with the authoritative dedup record in the application database; TTL ≥ broker retention window; a defined duplicate budget per consumer.

Reliable publishing: Domain write and event emitted atomically via the Transactional Outbox (or CDC where the event mirrors the schema); poll interval derived from the delivery SLO; mark-processed gated on broker acknowledgment; catch-up capacity validated.

Event contracts: Schemas registered and versioned; additive-by-default, versioned when breaking; consumer-driven contract tests (Pact) enforced in CI.

Sagas: Orchestration for workflows beyond two steps or two compensating actions; every side-effecting step has an idempotent, independently tested compensating action executed in reverse order.

Failure handling: Every consumer has a Dead Letter Queue with a defined retry limit and a remediation path; no silent discards.

Summary

In this chapter, we moved ShopFlow's checkout path from a synchronous blocking chain to a temporally decoupled event-driven architecture.

We applied the Critical Path Separation Rule to classify every checkout operation as user-blocking or user-independent, identifying that only card authorization and inventory reservation require the user to wait. All seven remaining operations moved to async event paths, reducing checkout p99 from 2.1 seconds to under 300 ms.

We applied the Minimal Broker Rule to select a managed RabbitMQ cluster over Kafka — the workload volume does not justify Kafka's operational overhead — and the Broker Migration Rule ensures the event schema remains broker-agnostic for the eventual migration when the workload demands it.

We fixed the double-charge incidents by implementing the atomic SET NX idempotency pattern with pre-processing writes, a deduplication TTL matched to the broker's maximum retention window, and the Duplicate Budget Rule as the enforcement mechanism per consumer.

We implemented the Transactional Outbox for payment and inventory events, with a polling interval derived from the downstream delivery SLO and catch-up capacity validated before deployment.

We adopted the Orchestrator Preference Rule for the order fulfillment saga — five steps, four compensating actions, full state visibility — and implemented the Dead Letter Mandate and Saga Rollback Rule as the operational floor for every event consumer.

ShopFlow's telemetry after *Chapter 8*:

Metric	Before	After	Change
Checkout p99 latency	2.1s	285 ms	86% reduction
Payment Timeout Impact on Checkout	Full thread block for 3 s	Zero-payment async	Eliminated
Double-Charge Incidents	3/month	0	Eliminated
Order Confirmation Email Delay	8–12s	2–4 s (async)	67% improvement
Cloud Spend	$9,200/mo	$9,800/mo	+$600 (broker + poller)
Availability	99.7%	99.8%	Stable

Table 8.10: ShopFlow telemetry before and after the Chapter 8 event-driven migration.

The cliffhanger: the event flood

Checkout is fast. The saga is visible. The double charges are eliminated.

But Dave is looking at the Inventory service read metrics and frowning.

Before the async migration, the Inventory service received one read request per checkout — the synchronous inventory reservation call. Now, five downstream event consumers each trigger their own inventory read: the fraud service checks available stock, the shipping service reads product weight for rate calculation, the analytics service reads catalog data for revenue attribution, the notification service reads the order summary for the confirmation email, and the loyalty service reads the product category for point calculation.

Five reads per order, where there was one. Inventory database read IOPS have increased 4.2x since the async migration. The database is handling it today. At 2x growth — which the product team is projecting for next quarter — it will not. The event-driven architecture solved the checkout latency problem. It created a read amplification problem.

In *Chapter 9*, we will build the caching strategy that absorbs the read amplification without compromising the freshness guarantees that inventory, pricing, and catalog data require.

Get this book's PDF version and more

Scan the QR code (or go to `packtpub.com/unlock`). Search for this book by name, confirm the edition, and then follow the steps on the page.

UNLOCK NOW

Note: Keep your invoice handy. Purchases made directly from Packt don't require an invoice.

9

Caching Strategies – Faster and Cheaper Scaling

In Chapter 8, we moved ShopFlow's checkout from a synchronous blocking chain to a temporally decoupled event-driven architecture. Checkout p99 dropped from 2.1 seconds to 285 ms. The double-charge incidents were eliminated.

But Dave is looking at the Inventory service read metrics with a different kind of concern.

Before the async migration, the Inventory service received one read request per checkout. Now, five downstream event consumers each trigger their own read: the fraud service checks available stock, the shipping service reads product weight, the analytics service reads catalog data, the notification service reads the order summary, and the loyalty service reads the product category. Five reads per order where there was one. Inventory database read IOPS have increased 4.2x. At 2x growth—which the product team is projecting for next quarter—the database will not hold.

The event-driven architecture solved the checkout latency problem. It created a read amplification problem. This chapter builds the caching strategy that absorbs the amplification without compromising the freshness guarantees that inventory, pricing, and catalog data require.

In this chapter, we are going to cover the following main topics:

- **The Caching Hierarchy:** From browser to database.
- **Distributed Caching with Redis:** Patterns and pitfalls.
- **Edge Scaling:** Leveraging CDNs for global performance.
- **The Invalidation Problem:** TTLs, tags, and event-driven purging.
- **Cache Safety:** Dealing with warm-up, stampedes, and stale data.

Technical requirements

Redis 7.x (managed): In-memory data store for application-layer caching, session management, rate limiting, and deduplication. Managed hosting eliminates cluster management overhead and replication configuration.

CDN (Cloudflare / AWS CloudFront / Azure Front Door): Global edge caching network. Serves static and semi-static content from points of presence closest to the user. Must be configured with explicit permission boundaries for authenticated content.

Varnish Cache/Nginx (proxy cache): Application-layer HTTP reverse proxy with caching. Provides origin shielding—a dedicated caching tier that absorbs thundering herd events before they reach the database.

Cache-Control headers (RFC 7234): The HTTP standard for cache directive negotiation between clients, proxies, and origin servers. Every cacheable response requires explicit Cache-Control configuration.

OpenTelemetry cache metrics: Cache hit rate, miss rate, eviction rate, and memory utilization must be instrumented as first-class observability signals. A cache with no metrics is an opaque dependency.

Code Repository: `https://github.com/imran-siddique/Architecting-at-Scale/tree/main/ch9`

ShopFlow telemetry snapshot [stage 9]

```
The Signal: The async migration from Chapter 8 created 5 reads per order event
where there was 1. Database read IOPS are at 78% of provisioned capacity today. At
the projected 2x growth rate next quarter, read IOPS will exceed provisioned
capacity by 60%. The solution is not a larger database. The solution is keeping
the right data in the right layer.
Inventory DB Read IOPS: 78% of provisioned capacity (● Warning – approaching
ceiling)
Catalog DB Read IOPS: 61% of provisioned capacity (● Warning)
Event Consumer Read Amplification: 4.2x vs. pre-async baseline (● Critical – 5
reads per order where there was 1)
Cache Hit Rate: 0% (● No caching layer in place)
p99 Latency (Inventory reads): 45ms (Acceptable today)
p99 Latency (Catalog reads): 38ms (Acceptable today)
Projected IOPS at 2x growth: 160% of provisioned capacity (● Will breach – next
quarter)
```

```
Cloud Spend: $9,800/mo (Stable but database IOPS are the next cost spike)
Panic Meter: 4/10 (No immediate incident. Predictable ceiling approaching.)
```

> **Note**
>
> Dave Alert: "We have 6–8 weeks before the Inventory database hits its IOPS ceiling at the current growth rate. We can provision more IOPS today and buy time, but the read pattern is the problem. Five services are asking for the same Inventory data that hasn't changed between requests."

The caching hierarchy: from browser to database

Cache is not a technology. It is an architectural pattern that makes sense in some domains and actively creates problems in others. The most important question to answer before adding any cache layer is not 'how do we cache this?' It is 'does caching make sense for this domain at all?'

This distinction comes from operating across systems with fundamentally different data access patterns. A documentation platform — where content is authored infrequently, read millions of times, and freshness tolerance is measured in minutes or hours — is a high-value caching domain. Almost every read can be served from cache. The database is rarely touched. A project management platform — where every work item update must be immediately visible to every collaborator, where the definition of a 'stale' work item is measured in seconds, and where collaborative editing means the cache would be invalidated on almost every write — is a low-value caching domain. Adding a cache layer to a highly transactional system where the data must always reflect the latest state adds operational complexity without delivering meaningful latency improvement. You are invalidating cache faster than you are serving from it.

> **Note**
>
> The Domain-First Cache Rule: Before designing a cache layer, classify the domain's data by update frequency and freshness tolerance. If data is updated more often than it is served from cache before invalidation, the cache is not reducing database load — it is adding a consistency layer with net negative throughput. Cache only what the domain's freshness tolerance permits.

> **Note**
>
> The Cache Candidacy Checklist: Before choosing a caching strategy for any data type, answer four questions. A "no" to any of them means the data is a caching anti-candidate, and the correct decision is to leave it on the database.

- **Read-to-write ratio:** is this data read significantly more often than it is written? Below roughly 10:1, the invalidation work costs more than the reads it saves.
- **Staleness tolerance:** can the business tolerate stale data for the TTL you intend to set — and has the business, not the engineering team, agreed to that window?
- **Miss economics:** is the cost of a cache miss lower than the cost of maintaining consistency? A miss that costs one 45ms read is cheap; a miss that triggers a recomputation or a fan-out of downstream calls is not.
- **Working set:** does the working set fit in memory with headroom, after the 1.3x Redis overhead factor? If it does not, the eviction policy — not your TTL — decides what stays cached.

ShopFlow's catalog, pricing, and shipping-weight reads clear all four. The real-time stock level on the checkout path fails the second: its freshness tolerance is zero, because stale stock means an oversell. That is why it stays uncached in Table 9.1 while everything around it moves into Redis.

ShopFlow's read amplification problem is a caching opportunity precisely because the data causing the amplification — product catalog descriptions, shipping weight specifications, product category assignments — changes infrequently relative to how often it is read. A product weight does not change between the fraud service's read and the shipping service's read 200ms later. These five reads are returning identical data from the database five times per order event. This is the caching domain where the pattern delivers its highest ROI.

The Freshness Spectrum

Every piece of data in ShopFlow exists somewhere on a freshness spectrum — from 'must always be current' to 'acceptable to serve stale for hours.' Cache layer design follows from this spectrum. A data element's position on the spectrum determines its TTL, its cache tier, and whether it can be cached at all.

Data Type	Update Frequency	Freshness Tolerance	Cache Tier	TTL Range	Cache Strategy
Real-time inventory stock level (checkout path)	Per order	Zero — stale = oversell	None — database only	N/A	No cache on write path
Inventory reservation status	Per order	Seconds	Application cache (Redis)	5–10 seconds	Cache-aside with short TTL
Product pricing (active)	Hourly or campaign-driven	Minutes	Application cache (Redis)	5–15 minutes	Cache-aside + event invalidation
Product catalog (descriptions, images)	Daily or release-driven	Hours	Redis + CDN edge	1–6 hours	Cache-aside + CDN TTL
Shipping weight/ dimensions	Rare — product creation only	Days	Redis + CDN edge	24–48 hours	Cache-aside + long TTL
Product category hierarchy	Weekly or quarterly	Days	CDN edge + browser	48–72 hours	Static generation + CDN
Documentation/ help content	Authoring-driven	Hours to days	CDN edge + browser	24–72 hours	Static generation + CDN

Data Type	Update Frequency	Freshness Tolerance	Cache Tier	TTL Range	Cache Strategy
User session data	Per request	Seconds—must be consistent	Redis (no CDN)	Session duration	Write-through to Redis

Table 9.1: The freshness spectrum: ShopFlow data types by update frequency, freshness tolerance, cache tier, and TTL

> **Note**
>
> The Freshness Spectrum Rule: Assign every cacheable data type a freshness tolerance before assigning a TTL. TTL must be derived from freshness tolerance, not from performance targets. A 1-hour TTL on pricing data is not a caching decision — it is a business decision that users may see a price that is up to 1 hour stale. That decision must be made by the business, not by the engineering team optimizing for cache hit rate.

The cache hierarchy

A layered cache architecture serves data from the closest, cheapest tier before reaching the next. For ShopFlow's event-driven read amplification problem, the hierarchy has four tiers.

Cache Tier	Location	Latency	Capacity	Best For	ShopFlow Application
Browser cache	User device	0ms — no network	Limited by browser	Static assets, public content	Product images, CSS, JS bundles
CDN edge cache	PoP closest to user	1–10 ms	Distributed global	Public semi-static content	Catalog pages, documentation, product descriptions

Cache Tier	Location	Latency	Capacity	Best For	ShopFlow Application
Application cache (Redis)	Same region as services	0.5–2 ms	Configured memory pool	Personalized, auth-required, high-throughput reads	Pricing, inventory status, session data, deduplication
Origin shielding (Varnish/ Nginx)	Between CDN and origin	1–5 ms	Proxy server memory	Thundering herd protection for origin	Product page origin protection during flash sales
Database query cache	Database engine layer	Negligible	Shared buffer pool	Repeated identical queries within a session	Not applicable — query pattern is too diverse

Table 9.2: The four-tier cache hierarchy compared by latency, capacity, and ShopFlow application

Note

The Cache Hierarchy Rule: Every cache miss at one tier must be served by the next tier and written back to the missed tier before returning to the caller. A request that misses the CDN edge must check Redis before hitting the origin database. A request that misses Redis must query the database and populate Redis before returning. You cannot skip tiers downward — you can only skip them upward when populating.

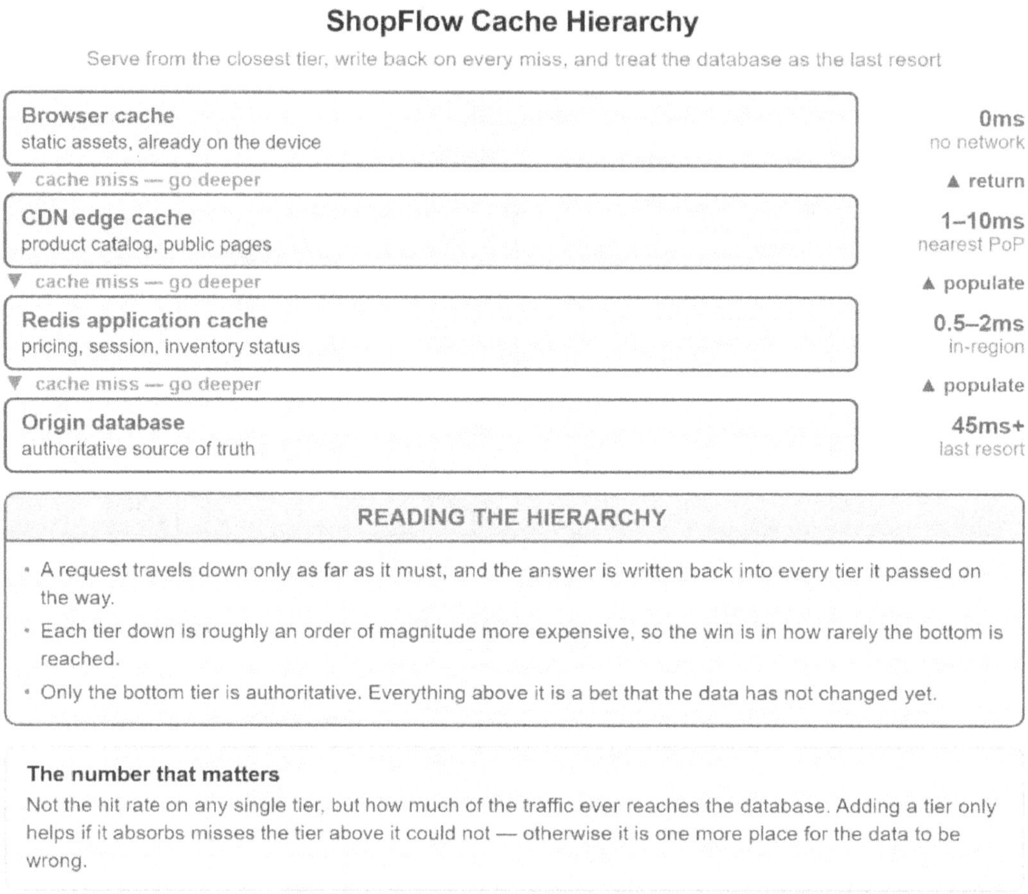

Figure 9.1: ShopFlow Cache Hierarchy

Following one request down the hierarchy and back: the numbered path below is the same journey the diagram shows, in the order a single uncached read actually experiences it.

1. Browser cache: the user's device checks its own cache first. A hit costs nothing—no request leaves the device.
2. CDN edge cache: on a browser miss, the request terminates at the point of presence closest to the user. For ShopFlow's public catalog content this is where 91% of reads end, at 1–10ms.
3. Redis application cache: on a CDN miss — or immediately, for any authenticated or personalized read the CDN must not serve — the service checks Redis. Pricing and inventory status resolve here in 0.5–2 ms.

4. Origin database: only a Redis miss reaches the database. This is the 45 ms read that the entire hierarchy exists to avoid, and it is the read that the 4.2x amplification was multiplying.
5. Populate Redis: the database result is written back to Redis with the TTL derived from that data type's freshness tolerance — not from a performance target.
6. Populate the CDN: if the content is public and cacheable, the response carries the Cache-Control directives that let the edge store it for the next requester.
7. Return to the caller: the response is served. Every subsequent request for the same data is answered from a progressively higher tier until a TTL expires or an invalidation event purges it.

The first request for a product costs 45ms and one database read. The second costs 1–10ms and none. Multiplied across five event consumers reading the same record per order, that difference is the whole return on the caching layer.

> Note
>
> Safe Scale Check — Cache Layer Blast Radius: Every cache tier introduces a new failure mode: the cache layer itself can fail. Before deploying a Redis cluster to the production read path, define the fallback behavior when Redis is unavailable. The application must be able to serve reads directly from the database under cache failure — at degraded performance, but without user-visible errors. A cache failure that causes a 500 response to users is a cache architecture that has made the cache a single point of failure. The blast radius of a cache failure must be bounded to latency degradation, never to availability loss.

Architect's prompt 9.1: the cache domain classification audit

When to use this: Use this prompt before designing any cache layer, to classify each data type by freshness tolerance and assign the correct cache tier and TTL. Run it before any Redis cluster is provisioned or any CDN rule is written.

```
Act as a Principal Caching Architect. I am designing a caching strategy
for the following data types in [Service Name]:

[For each data type, provide:]
- Data type name
- Current read frequency (reads/sec)
- Current write frequency (writes/sec)
- Number of distinct consumers reading this data
```

```
- Maximum acceptable staleness (user-facing)
- Whether the data is user-specific or shared across users
- Current database IOPS consumed by reads of this type

(1) For each data type, classify on the freshness spectrum:
    Zero tolerance / Seconds / Minutes / Hours / Days.
(2) For each data type with tolerance > zero, recommend:
    - Cache tier: Browser / CDN / Redis / Origin Shield
    - Cache strategy: Cache-aside / Write-through / Write-behind
    - TTL value derived from freshness tolerance (not from perf targets)
    - Invalidation trigger: TTL expiry / Event-driven / Manual purge
(3) Calculate projected cache hit rate for each data type at the
    recommended TTL, given current read and write frequencies.
(4) Calculate projected database IOPS reduction after implementing
    the recommended cache strategy.
(5) Flag any data type where caching would require cache invalidation
    faster than the read rate – these are caching anti-candidates.
```

Distributed caching with redis: patterns and pitfalls

Redis is one of the most widely deployed infrastructure components in modern distributed systems, and one of the most frequently misapplied. Its versatility — it supports strings, hashes, lists, sorted sets, streams, pub/sub, and Lua scripting — makes it easy to reach for in any situation where you need fast in-memory storage. That versatility is also the source of its most common misuse pattern.

> **Note**
>
> The Redis Scope Rule: Redis is the correct tool when you need sub-millisecond read latency for data with bounded size, bounded cardinality, and a clear eviction or expiration strategy. It is the wrong tool when you are using it to avoid thinking about the right data structure for the problem. Before adding Redis to any read path, confirm: Is this data bounded in size? Does it have a defined TTL or eviction policy? Is the access pattern read-heavy enough to justify the cache overhead? If any answer is no, reconsider.

The misuse pattern that survives at low traffic and fails at high traffic is **promiscuous caching**: adding Redis to every read path because 'it makes things faster,' without modeling the memory requirements, eviction behavior, or invalidation cost. At low traffic, the memory pool is underutilized, evictions are rare, and the cache hit rate appears healthy. At 10x traffic, the memory pool fills, the eviction policy begins discarding keys that are still needed, the cache hit rate collapses, and every cache miss generates a synchronous database read — producing the same database load the cache was supposed to prevent, but now with added network latency for the cache lookup.

> Note
>
> **Anti-Pattern: The Promiscuous Cache:** Caching every read path without modeling memory capacity, eviction behavior, or invalidation cost. Observable signature: Redis memory utilization above 80% with an active eviction policy, cache hit rate declining as traffic grows, and database read IOPS not decreasing despite a cache layer being present. The cache is evicting hot keys to make room for less-frequently accessed data, defeating the purpose of caching entirely.

Choosing the right redis data structure

Cache design is not only about TTLs and eviction policies. It is also about the in-memory representation. The same 8KB product record stored as a serialized JSON string and stored as a hash have materially different memory footprints and access costs, and the difference only becomes visible at the traffic where it hurts. Redis gives you strings, hashes, sets, sorted sets, bitmaps and HyperLogLogs; choosing among them is a design decision driven by how consumers read the data.

> Note
>
> The Representation Rule: Choose the Redis data structure from the read pattern, not from convenience. If consumers read one field of a record, store a hash. If they always read the whole record, store a string. Storing a large JSON blob and deserializing all of it to read a single field is not caching—it is relocating the deserialization cost from the database to the application, and paying network transfer for the fields nobody asked for.

The following table maps each structure to the read pattern it fits and the cost of choosing it wrongly:

Structure	Use it when	ShopFlow application	Cost of choosing it wrong
String	The value is read and written as a single unit	Rendered catalog fragments, serialized product JSON, negative cache markers	Reading one field means transferring and deserializing the whole value
Hash	Fields are read or updated independently	Product records where the shipping service needs only weight and the fraud service only stock	Very large hashes lose the memory-efficient encoding that makes small ones cheap
Set	Membership tests, no ordering required	Which products belong to a category; denylisted SKUs	SMEMBERS on a large set is O(N) and blocks the server—use SISMEMBER
Sorted Set	Ranking or range queries by score	Best-seller lists, price-sorted category pages, rate-limit windows	Every insert is O(log N); used as a plain set, it wastes memory on unused scores
Bitmap / HyperLogLog	High-cardinality counting where approximation is acceptable	Unique viewers per product per day	HyperLogLog trades ~0.81% error for fixed 12KB memory—wrong where exact counts matter

Table 9.3: Redis data structures and the read pattern each one fits

> Note
>
> **Tool Tax — Redis data structures:** Every structure beyond the plain string adds a contract that nothing enforces. Choosing a hash means every producer and consumer must agree on field names; choosing a sorted set means agreeing on what the score represents. Redis will not tell you when a service writes the wrong field name — the read simply returns nil and the caller treats it as a cache miss, so the failure shows up as a quietly degraded hit rate rather than an error. Budget for a documented key-and-field naming contract, or the memory you saved is repaid in debugging.

Cache-Aside: the correct default

The Cache-Aside pattern — also called Lazy Loading — is the correct default caching strategy for most read paths. The application checks the cache before querying the database. On a cache miss, it queries the database, writes the result to the cache, and returns the result. The cache is populated on demand, only for data that is actually requested. Data that is never requested is never cached.

Cache-Aside has a specific failure mode on first deployment: the cold start. When the cache is empty, every request is a cache miss, and every miss generates a database read. At launch of a new service or after a cache flush, the database briefly receives the full read load it will normally be shielded from. This is the **thundering herd** in its cache-specific form.

The defense is cache pre-warming: before routing production traffic to a new cache layer, populate the cache with the most frequently accessed keys from a recent read log. For ShopFlow's catalog cache, this means pre-loading the top 1,000 most-viewed product records before the cache goes live. This is not a perfect defense—the long tail of products will still generate misses—but it converts the cold start from a full database load spike to a managed miss rate that the database can absorb.

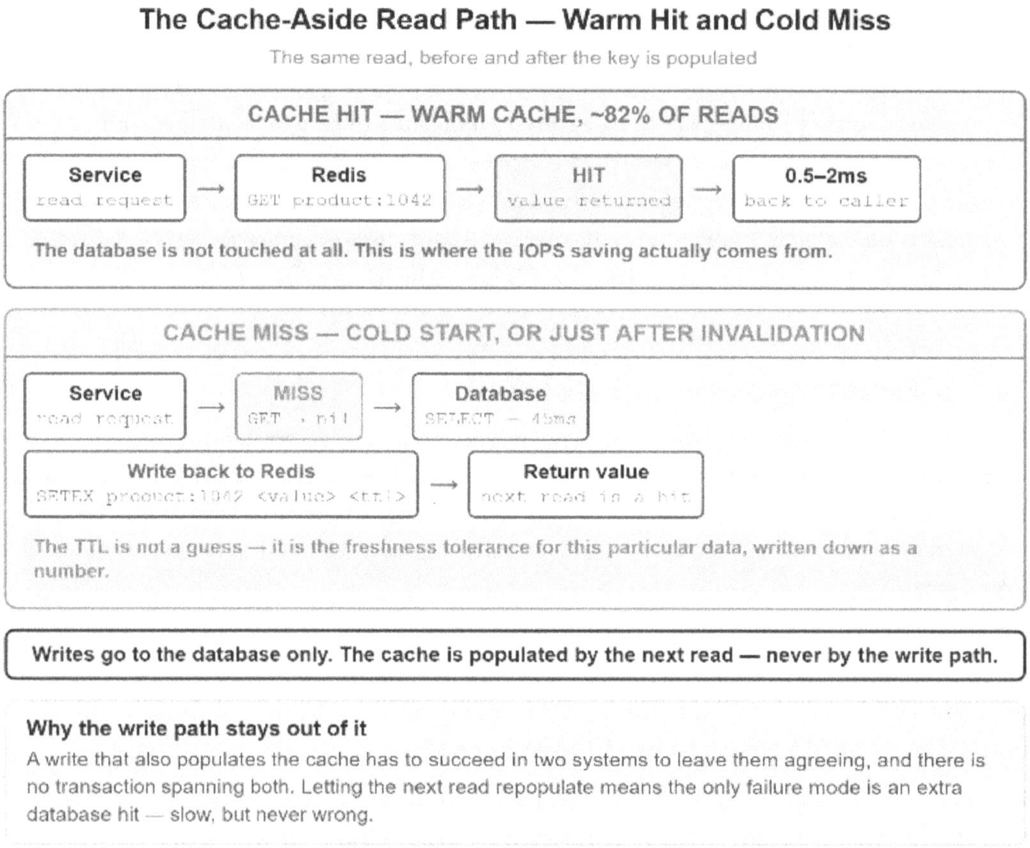

Figure 9.2: The Cache-Aside Read Path — Warm Hit and Cold Miss

Cache Strategy	**Read Path**	**Write Path**	**Consistency Model**	**Cache Hit Rate on Cold Start**	**Best For**
Cache-Aside (Lazy Loading)	Check cache → miss → read DB → write to cache	Write to DB only; cache populated on next read	Eventual — stale until TTL or invalidation	0% until warm	Read-heavy, tolerance for stale data, diverse access patterns

Cache Strategy	**Read Path**	**Write Path**	**Consistency Model**	**Cache Hit Rate on Cold Start**	**Best For**
Read-Through	Cache handles miss → fetches from DB automatically	Write to DB only; cache library handles population	Eventual	0% until warm	When cache library supports it; simpler app code
Write-Through	Read from cache always (populated on write)	Write to DB and cache simultaneously	Read-your-writes for keys that were written — not distributed strong; depends on write atomicity, ordering, and partial failure handling	100% for all written keys	Write-heavy with immediate read requirement; high memory cost
Write-Behind (Write-Back)	Read from cache always	Write to cache; async flush to DB	Eventual — DB may be stale during async window	100% for all written keys	High-write workloads where DB write latency must be hidden; data loss risk on cache failure

Cache Strategy	Read Path	Write Path	Consistency Model	Cache Hit Rate on Cold Start	Best For
Refresh-Ahead	Read from cache; cache proactively refreshes before TTL	Write to DB; background refresh updates cache	Near-real-time	High after initial warm period	Predictable access patterns; fixed cost of refresh regardless of demand

Table 9.4: Caching strategies compared by read path, write path, consistency model, and cold-start hit rate

> **Note**
>
> The Write-Through Tax: Write-Through caching ensures the cache is always populated for any key that has been written, at the cost of double write latency: every write must complete both the database write and the cache write before returning success. At high write volumes, where the cache write is issued serially on the critical path, this doubles the write path latency. Where the cache write is pipelined, batched, or issued concurrently with the database write, the penalty is a fraction of that — but it is never zero, and it is paid on every write rather than on the reads it accelerates. For ShopFlow's inventory update path — which must be fast during order processing — Write-Through is the wrong strategy. Cache-Aside on the read path with event-driven invalidation on the write path is the correct separation.

> **Note**
>
> The Write-Behind Risk: Write-Behind caching accepts writes to the cache and asynchronously flushes to the database. During the async window, the database does not reflect the current state. If the cache fails before the flush, those writes are lost. Write-Behind is appropriate only for non-critical, high-write workloads where loss of recent writes is acceptable — analytics counters, view tallies, non-financial metrics. It is never appropriate for inventory levels, order state, or payment data.

Redis memory management

Redis operates entirely in memory. Memory is finite. When the configured memory limit is reached, Redis must evict keys to make room for new entries. The eviction policy determines which keys are removed. Choosing the wrong eviction policy for the workload is one of the most consequential Redis configuration decisions.

Eviction Policy	Eviction Target	Use Case	Risk
noeviction	None — returns error when full	Explicit control required; cache as primary store	Write failures when memory full—do not use for cache
allkeys-lru	Least recently used key from all keys	General-purpose cache with mixed TTL usage	Hot keys may be evicted if the access pattern is irregular
volatile-lru	Least recently used key from keys with TTL set	Cache where only TTL-bearing keys are evicted	Non-TTL keys are never evicted — manual cleanup required
allkeys-lfu	Least frequently used key among all keys	Cache with skewed access patterns (hot keys vs. cold keys)	Frequency counters add memory overhead per key
volatile-ttl	Key with the shortest remaining TTL	When shortest-lived data should expire first	Ignores access frequency — may evict hot but short-TTL keys

Table 9.5: Redis eviction policies, what each one evicts, and the risk it carries

For ShopFlow's application cache, **allkeys-lru** is the correct eviction policy. All cached keys have TTLs derived from their freshness tolerance. When memory pressure occurs, the least recently accessed data — the data users have stopped requesting — is removed first. Hot catalog entries remain in cache. Cold entries for discontinued products are evicted automatically.

> **Note**
>
> Manager's Math — The Cache ROI Calculation: ShopFlow's Inventory and Catalog databases are currently serving reads at 78% and 61% of provisioned IOPS respectively, at a combined cost of approximately $1,200/month for the provisioned IOPS tier. The Redis cluster that covers ShopFlow's working set is small — 650MB of maxmemory, sized in the Cache Infrastructure Sizing calculation later in this chapter — and a 1GB managed instance costs approximately $18/month. At an 80% cache hit rate, database IOPS drop from 78% to approximately 16% of provisioned capacity, enabling a tier downgrade that saves approximately $600/month. Net saving after Redis cost: approximately $582/month, or $6,984 annualized. The Redis cluster pays for itself in the first day of operation. The cache layer is not a cost — it is a cost reduction with a measurable return.

Architect's prompt 9.2: the redis configuration audit

When to use this: Use this prompt when designing the Redis configuration for a new cache deployment, or when a production Redis cluster is showing degraded cache hit rates, unexpected evictions, or memory pressure at scale.

```
Act as a Principal Caching Engineer specializing in Redis. I am
auditing the following Redis deployment for production correctness:

Redis version: [X]
Deployment type: [Single node / Sentinel / Cluster / Managed]
Configured maxmemory: [X GB]
Current memory utilization: [X%]
Current eviction policy: [policy name]
Cache hit rate (last 24h): [X%]
Key count: [N]
Average key TTL: [X seconds]
Eviction count (last 24h): [N]

Workload description:
- Primary use cases: [Cache-aside reads / Session / Rate limiting / Deduplication]
- Access pattern: [Uniform / Hot-key skewed / Long-tail]
- Write frequency: [X writes/sec]
- Read frequency: [X reads/sec]
```

```
(1) Evaluate whether the current eviction policy matches the workload.
    If eviction count is high and hit rate is declining, identify the
    eviction-hit-rate correlation and recommend the correct policy.
(2) Calculate the minimum memory required to maintain the target cache
    hit rate: (working set size) x (1 + overhead factor of 1.3).
(3) Identify any keys without TTL that are consuming memory permanently.
(4) If the deployment is single-node, evaluate whether sentinel or cluster
    mode is required for the current availability SLO.
(5) Define the fallback behavior: what happens to the application when
    Redis is unavailable? If the answer is 500 errors, flag as a
    single-point-of-failure design requiring immediate remediation.
```

Edge scaling: leveraging CDNs for global performance

A CDN is not a performance optimization. It is a latency elimination layer. The difference is meaningful: an optimization reduces latency on the existing path. A CDN eliminates the path entirely for cacheable content — the request never reaches the origin server.

For ShopFlow's global user base — Frankfurt at 180ms to origin, Singapore at 320ms — a CDN serving cached catalog content from a regional point of presence reduces those latencies to 5–15ms. No origin-side optimization produces an equivalent improvement. The speed of light between Singapore and Virginia is not an engineering problem. It is a physics problem, and the CDN solves it by moving the content closer to the user.

CDNs are appropriate for content that is public, shared across users, and cacheable without per-user customization. They are not appropriate—without careful boundary configuration—for authenticated content, personalized content, or content that requires the origin to validate user permissions before serving.

Note

The CDN Permission Boundary Rule: Every CDN configuration must explicitly define the boundary between public cacheable content and permission-gated content that must reach the origin. This boundary is enforced through Cache-Control headers, URL path patterns, and cookie-based bypass rules. A CDN that serves permission-gated content from cache because the Cache-Control header was not set correctly is not a configuration mistake — it is a data exposure incident. The default behavior of most CDNs, when Cache-Control is absent, is to cache the response.

The most expensive CDN configuration mistake is not a performance failure. It is a security failure caused by improperly configured caching of authenticated responses. When an internal documentation page — protected by an authentication header — is served without a Cache-Control directive, the CDN may cache the authenticated response and serve it to subsequent unauthenticated requestors from the same edge node. The user who originally authenticated receives the page. The next user — unauthenticated, from the same geographic region — receives the cached authenticated page.

The fix is a single header: **Cache-Control: private, no-store** on every authenticated response. But the correct architectural position is not to rely on engineers remembering to set this header on every endpoint. The CDN configuration must define a default cache policy of 'no cache' for authenticated paths, with explicit opt-in for public paths. The CDN should be configured to cache by exception, not to serve by default.

CDN Configuration Mistake	**Failure Mode**	**User Impact**	**Fix**
Missing Cache-Control on authenticated responses	CDN caches authenticated content and serves it to the next unauthenticated requester	Data exposure — user sees another user's content	Cache-Control: private, no-store on all authenticated responses; CDN default = no-cache
TTL set too low on static assets	CDN continuously re-validates with origin; origin load is not reduced	No latency improvement; origin IOPS unchanged	Use content-addressed filenames (hash in URL); set TTL to 1 year for immutable assets
TTL set too long on semi-static content	Stale content served after origin update; users see old version	Outdated product info, pricing errors, stale navigation	Combine moderate TTL with explicit purge on content publish events
CDN bypassed for all POST requests	Form submissions reach origin even when idempotent	No issue for correctness; origin load higher than necessary	Evaluate which POST endpoints can be cached; most cannot

CDN Configuration Mistake	Failure Mode	User Impact	Fix
No origin shielding configured	Every CDN PoP sends its own cache miss to origin; thundering herd during traffic spikes	Origin overload during flash sales or viral traffic	Enable origin shielding: one designated PoP aggregates all misses before hitting the origin
CDN without Traffic Manager integration	CDN routes all traffic to primary region regardless of origin health	Origin outage = full outage; no regional failover	Configure CDN health probes and Traffic Manager for automatic failover to the secondary region

Table 9.6: Common CDN misconfigurations, the failure mode each produces, and the fix

Note

Anti-Pattern: The Unbounded CDN: A CDN configured without explicit cache policies, origin shielding, or permission boundaries. It caches whatever the origin returns, for however long the CDN's default TTL specifies, to any requester who asks. In the best case, this produces stale content. In the worst case, it produces data exposure. A CDN without explicit configuration is not a performance layer — it is an uncontrolled proxy.

Note

Tool Tax — CDN edge caching: A CDN is not a service you enable; it is a distributed configuration you now own. Budget for a cache-rule set that has to be reviewed like code, per-path Cache-Control correctness on every new endpoint, purge-API integration and its rate limits, egress billing that scales with success rather than with cost savings, and a staging story for rules that can only really be tested at the edge. The failure mode you inherit is the worst kind: a misconfigured rule does not error; it silently serves the wrong person's content from cache.

CDN configuration must also account for multi-region traffic routing. A CDN that routes all traffic to the primary region — without health probes or traffic manager integration — provides no availability benefit when the primary region is degraded. The CDN becomes a single point of routing failure: it reduces latency but increases the blast radius of an origin outage by funneling global traffic to an unavailable endpoint.

> **Note**
>
> Safe Scale Check — CDN Fallback Configuration: Every CDN deployment must be tested for origin-unavailable behavior before going live. Configure the CDN health probe to detect origin degradation within 10 seconds. Define the stale-serve window: how long will the CDN serve cached content when the origin is unavailable? For ShopFlow's catalog content, serving stale catalog data for up to 5 minutes during an origin incident is preferable to returning errors. For pricing data, the stale-serve window must be much shorter — or zero. Define these windows explicitly before the CDN goes live, not during an incident.

Architect's prompt 9.3: the CDN configuration audit

When to use this: Use this prompt when auditing an existing CDN configuration for security, performance, and availability gaps, or when designing CDN rules for a new global deployment.

```
Act as a Principal Edge Architecture Engineer. I am auditing the following
CDN configuration for correctness:

CDN provider: [Cloudflare / CloudFront / Azure Front Door / other]
Origin regions: [list of regions serving as origin]
Content types served: [static assets / semi-static catalog / authenticated pages /
API responses]
Current cache hit rate: [X%]
Origin shield configured: [Yes / No]
Traffic manager / health probe configured: [Yes / No]

I will provide:
1. The CDN cache rules / behaviors configuration.
2. The Cache-Control headers returned by the origin for each content type.
3. The origin health probe configuration (if any).

[Paste CDN config, response headers, health probe config]
```

```
(1) For each content type, identify whether the Cache-Control header
    correctly reflects the intended cache behavior: public, private,
    no-store, max-age, stale-while-revalidate.
(2) Identify any authenticated or permission-gated response that lacks
    Cache-Control: private, no-store. Flag as data exposure risk.
(3) Evaluate whether origin shielding is configured. If not, calculate
    the thundering herd risk: how many concurrent CDN edge nodes would
    send simultaneous cache miss requests to origin during a traffic spike?
(4) Evaluate the traffic manager / health probe configuration.
    If origin goes down in [region], where does traffic route?
(5) Define the stale-serve window for each content type: how long
    should the CDN serve cached content when origin is unavailable?
```

The invalidation problem: TTLs, tags, and Event-Driven purging

Cache invalidation is the problem that makes caching hard. It is not technically complex. It is operationally complex: the decision of when to invalidate, what to invalidate, and how to ensure invalidation reaches every cache tier simultaneously is where most cache implementations accumulate correctness debt.

The three invalidation strategies — TTL expiry, tag-based purging, and event-driven invalidation — are not mutually exclusive. A production cache layer uses all three simultaneously: TTL as the safety net that bounds maximum staleness even when explicit invalidation fails, tag-based purging for content management workflows, and event-driven invalidation for the high-correctness paths where staleness is not acceptable.

Invalidation Strategy	Mechanism	Consistency Guarantee	Operation-al Overhead	Best For	ShopFlow Application
TTL expiry	Cache entry expires after a fixed duration; next read repopulates	Eventual — stale for up to TTL duration	Zero — automatic	Safety net for all cached data; bounds maximum staleness	All cached data — TTL is the floor, not the ceiling

Invalidation Strategy	Mechanism	Consistency Guarantee	Operational Overhead	Best For	ShopFlow Application
Event-driven purge	Write event triggers explicit cache key deletion or update	Near-real-time — seconds after the triggering write	Medium — event consumer + purge API integration	Pricing, inventory status, any data with business-critical freshness	Price change → purge pricing cache; product update → purge catalog cache
Tag-based purge	Content tagged at write time; purge all entries with a given tag	Near-real-time for all tagged entries simultaneously	Medium — tag registry + bulk purge operation	Hierarchical content (purge all pages in a category)	Product category rename → purge all catalog entries tagged with that category
Manual purge	Engineer triggers cache flush via admin UI or API	Immediate—but human-dependent and error-prone	High — requires human action per incident	Incident fallback when automated invalidation fails	Never as primary strategy—incident fallback only

Table 9.7: Cache invalidation strategies compared by consistency guarantee and operational overhead

> **Note**
>
> The Cache Invalidation Event Rule: Every write operation that modifies cached data must emit a cache invalidation event. This event is the authoritative signal for all cache tiers to invalidate or refresh the affected entries. The invalidation event is not optional: a write path that does not invalidate the cache has made a deliberate choice to serve stale data until the next TTL expiry. That choice must be explicit, documented, and reviewed against the domain's freshness tolerance.

ShopFlow's event-driven architecture from Chapter 8 provides the ideal substrate for cache invalidation. When the Catalog service processes a ProductUpdated event, it emits a CacheInvalidationRequested event containing the affected product ID. A dedicated cache invalidation consumer subscribes to this event and issues purge requests to Redis and CDN simultaneously. The product page is fresh within seconds of the catalog update, without the engineering team manually managing TTLs for each content type.

> **Note**
>
> Tool Tax — the event-driven invalidation pipeline: Replacing TTL guesswork with an event pipeline replaces a tuning problem with a distributed-systems problem. Budget for a dedicated queue and its consumer, dead-letter handling for purges that fail, idempotency, and version guards for duplicate and out-of-order delivery, and lag monitoring — because a consumer falling behind serves stale data while every component reports healthy. You have not removed the staleness risk; you have moved it somewhere you can instrument.

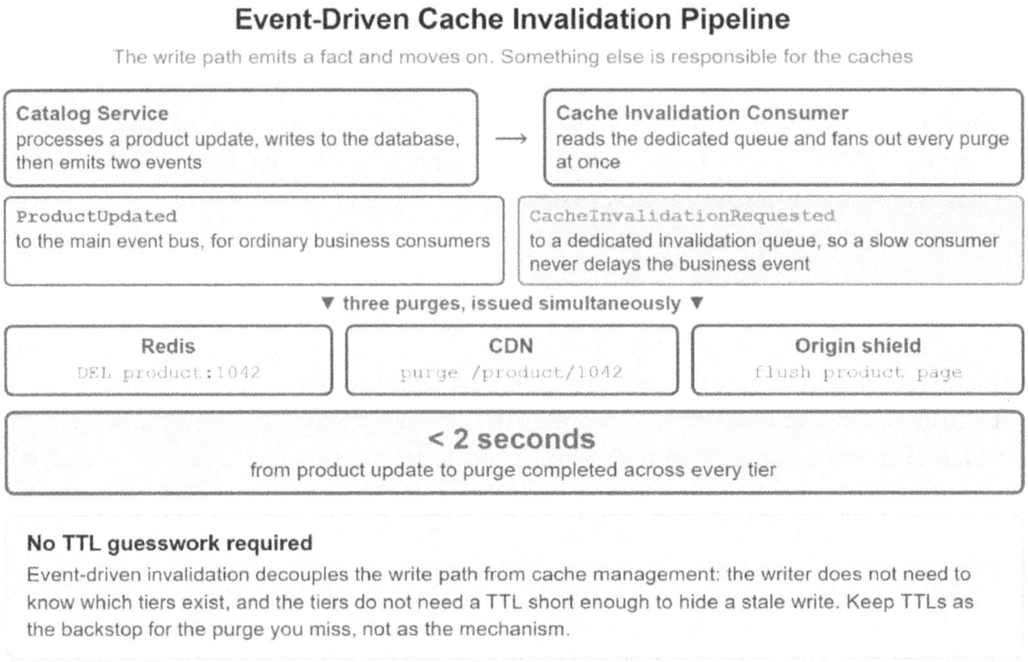

Figure 9.3: Event-Driven Cache Invalidation Pipeline

The complete invalidation flow, step by step: this is the sequence the diagram above compresses into one picture.

1. A merchandiser updates a product in the ShopFlow admin.
2. The Catalog service commits the write to the database first. The database is the source of truth and the cache is derived state — derived state is never updated before its source.
3. The Catalog service emits ProductUpdated to the main event bus, for the downstream consumers built in Chapter 8.
4. It also emits CacheInvalidationRequested to a dedicated invalidation queue, carrying the product ID and a version number.
5. The cache invalidation consumer reads that event and issues a Redis DEL for the product key.

6. The same consumer calls the CDN purge API for the product page URL and flushes the origin shield object, so no tier is left holding the superseded copy.
7. The next read for that product misses every tier, reads the database once, and repopulates Redis and the CDN on its way back out.

Elapsed time from commit to purged-everywhere: under two seconds. Under TTL-only invalidation the same update would take up to the full TTL to become visible — for ShopFlow's catalog content, up to six hours. That gap is the entire argument for event-driven invalidation over TTL guesswork.

The invalidation consumer

The consumer itself is small, and almost all of its code exists to survive the delivery guarantees of the broker underneath it rather than to perform the purge.

```
// cache-invalidation-consumer.js
// Consumes CacheInvalidationRequested and purges every cache tier.
const redis = require('./redis-client');
const cdn = require('./cdn-client');
const { subscribe, ack, deadLetter } = require('./event-bus');

const SEEN_TTL_SECONDS = 3600; // dedupe window for at-least-once delivery

subscribe('CacheInvalidationRequested', async(event)=> {
  const { productId, version, eventId } = event;

  // At-least-once delivery means this handler WILL see duplicates.
  // Purging is idempotent, but skip the repeat work anyway.
  const first = await redis.set(`purged:${eventId}`, '1', 'NX', 'EX',
SEEN_TTL_SECONDS);
  if (!first) return ack(event);

  try {
    // Ordering guard: never let an older event undo a newer purge.
    const seen = await redis.get(`product:${productId}:version`);
    if (seen && Number(seen)> version) return ack(event);

    await Promise.all([
      redis.del(`product:${productId}`),
      cdn.purge(`/p/${productId}`),
      cdn.purgeOriginShield(`/p/${productId}`),
    ]);
```

```
    await redis.set(`product:${productId}:version`, String(version));
    return ack(event);
  } catch (err) {
    // Never swallow a purge failure. TTL is the safety net, but a silent
    // failure means serving stale data for the whole TTL window.
    return deadLetter(event, err);
  }
});
```

Three lines carry the correctness: the **NX** set that makes duplicate delivery a no-op, the version comparison that makes out-of-order delivery harmless, and the dead-letter call that refuses to lose a failed purge silently. The runnable version — with the Redis and CDN clients, and the integration tests that assert idempotency under duplicate and reordered delivery — is in the chapter repository at `https://github.com/imran-siddique/Architecting-at-Scale/tree/main/ch9`.

> Note
>
> **The Invalidation Delivery Rule:** An event-driven invalidation pipeline is a distributed system and inherits every failure mode of one. Chapter 8 established that every mainstream broker delivers at least once, so the invalidation consumer will see duplicate events, may see them out of order, and under partition or consumer failure may not see some of them at all. Design for all three: make the purge idempotent — deleting an absent key is a success, not an error; carry a version or timestamp so a stale event cannot undo a newer purge; and keep a TTL on every key so that a lost invalidation degrades to bounded staleness instead of permanent staleness. Then monitor invalidation event lag as a first-class metric, because a consumer falling behind serves stale data while every component still reports healthy.

> Note
>
> **Anti-Pattern: The Promiscuous TTL:** Setting TTLs based on performance intuition rather than domain freshness tolerance. Symptoms: a single TTL value applied to all cached data regardless of data type; TTLs set to round numbers (1 hour, 24 hours) without reference to actual update frequency; TTLs shortened to reduce staleness complaints without modeling the resulting increase in database IOPS. Each halving of a TTL roughly doubles the read load at the database for that data type. TTL is not a dial

that trades performance for correctness — it is a correctness constraint derived from business requirements.

Note

The Stale-While-Revalidate Rule: For content where a brief period of staleness is acceptable but cache misses are not, implement the Stale-While-Revalidate pattern: serve the stale cache entry immediately, then asynchronously refresh it in the background. The user receives a response with zero cache-miss latency. The next request receives a fresh entry. This pattern is supported natively in HTTP Cache-Control headers (stale-while-revalidate=N) and in Redis via a background refresh job triggered on read. It is the correct strategy for catalog content where a 10-second staleness window is acceptable but a 45 ms database read on every request is not.

Note

Tool Tax — Stale-While-Revalidate: Serving stale while refreshing in the background means you are now running background work on the read path. Budget for refresh jobs that can themselves fail or pile up, a bound on how many concurrent refreshes a hot key can trigger, and the awkward conversation about what the user saw when the refresh failed silently and the stale entry kept being served past its intended window.

Note

Safe Scale Check — Invalidation Blast Radius: A cache flush of a large key space — all product pages in a category, or all cached pricing entries — produces a thundering herd: every user requesting those pages simultaneously misses the cache and hits the origin. Before performing any large-scale invalidation, calculate the affected key count, estimate the concurrent miss rate, and verify the origin can absorb the resulting read spike. If the origin cannot, implement the invalidation in batches with jitter — invalidate 10% of keys per minute, not all at once.

Architect's prompt 9.4: the cache invalidation design review

When to use this: Use this prompt when designing the invalidation strategy for a new cache layer or when auditing an existing cache that is producing staleness complaints or unexpected database load spikes after content updates.

```
Act as a Principal Caching Architect. I am designing the invalidation
strategy for the following cache deployment:

Cache tiers: [Redis / CDN / Browser / combination]
Data types cached: [list with TTL and update frequency for each]
Write event source: [database trigger / application event / CDC]
Current invalidation mechanism: [TTL only / manual purge / event-driven / none]
Current staleness complaint rate: [X incidents/month]

(1) For each data type, evaluate whether the current TTL is derived from
    the domain freshness tolerance or from performance intuition.
    Flag any TTL set to a round number without documented justification.
(2) For each write operation that modifies cached data, identify whether
    a cache invalidation event is emitted. Flag any write path that
    does not emit an invalidation signal.
(3) Design an event-driven invalidation pipeline:
    - What event triggers invalidation?
    - What cache tiers must be invalidated simultaneously?
    - What is the maximum acceptable delay between write and invalidation?
(4) For any large-scale invalidation scenario (category rename, pricing
    bulk update), calculate the thundering herd risk:
    - How many keys are affected?
    - What is the concurrent miss rate if all keys expire simultaneously?
    - Design a batch invalidation strategy with jitter to bound the spike.
(5) Define the TTL as a safety net: even with event-driven invalidation,
    every key must have a TTL that bounds maximum staleness if the
    invalidation event is lost. What is the correct TTL for each data type?
```

Cache safety: warmup, stampedes, and stale data

A cache layer introduces three classes of failure mode that do not exist in a direct database read path: the cold start, the thundering herd, and the stale data event. Each requires a specific defense. None is optional in a production cache architecture.

The thundering herd

The thundering herd occurs when a popular cache key expires — or is explicitly invalidated — while concurrent requests are in flight. Every request that reads the key within the same millisecond window finds an empty cache, generates a database read, and attempts to write the fresh value back to the cache simultaneously. In a high-traffic system, a single key expiry can generate hundreds of simultaneous database reads for the same data.

ShopFlow's flash sale scenario illustrates this precisely. A popular product's cache entry expires at 9:00:00 PM. At 9:00:00 PM, 4,000 users are actively browsing that product page. Four thousand simultaneous cache misses. Four thousand simultaneous database reads for the same product record. The database responds slowly under the spike, which extends the window during which new requests also miss the cache and join the herd.

> **Note**
>
> The Thundering Herd Defense Rule: Every cache layer serving high-concurrency reads must implement at least one thundering herd defense mechanism: probabilistic early expiry, mutex/lock-based single-population, or request coalescing. A cache without thundering herd protection is not a cache — it is a database load amplifier that activates at the worst possible moment.

Defense Mechanism	How It Works	Latency Impact	Complexity	Best For
Probabilistic Early Expiry (PER)	Each read calculates a random probability of refreshing early; hot keys refresh before expiry with increasing probability as TTL approaches zero	Zero — refresh happens in the background	Low — TTL jitter calculation at read time	High-traffic single keys with predictable access patterns

Defense Mechanism	How It Works	Latency Impact	Complexity	Best For
Mutex / Distributed Lock	First cache miss acquires a lock; all other concurrent misses wait; first miss populates cache; others read populated cache	Brief wait for lock waiters	Medium — Redis SETNX lock required	Low to moderate concurrency; acceptable wait time for lock waiters
Request Coalescing (Promise Coalescing)	All concurrent misses for the same key are coalesced into one database read; all waiters receive the same result	None — all requests complete together	Medium — in-process coalescing map required	High-concurrency reads within a single service instance
TTL jitter	Each cache write adds a random offset (±10–20%) to the TTL; keys for the same data type expire at different times	Zero	Very low — random TTL at write time	Preventing synchronized expiry of batch-loaded keys
Origin Shielding	A dedicated caching proxy absorbs all cache misses before they reach the database; the proxy serializes database reads	1–5 ms additional hop	Medium — proxy layer required	CDN cache misses; high-traffic catalog reads

Table 9.8: Thundering herd defense mechanisms compared by latency impact and complexity

For ShopFlow's Redis application cache, the correct combination is TTL jitter (preventing synchronized expiry across batch-loaded product keys) plus request coalescing within each service instance (preventing the same service pod from generating multiple database reads for the same key during a concurrent miss window).

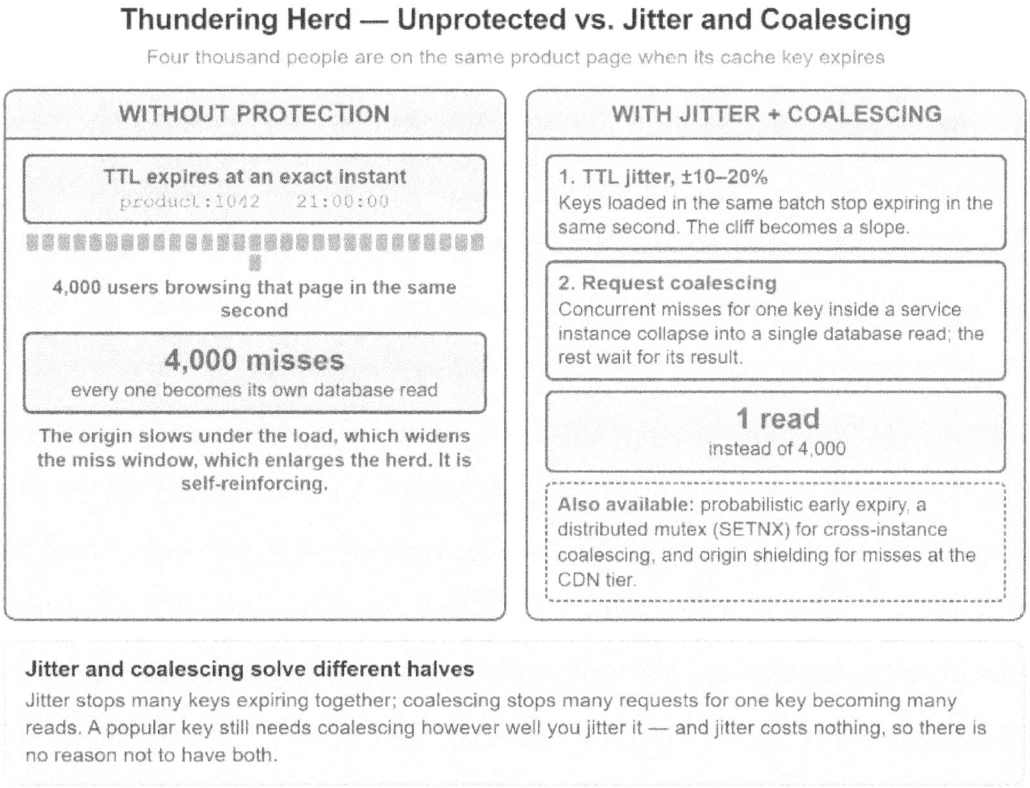

Figure 9.4: Thundering Herd — Unprotected vs. TTL Jitter and Request Coalescing

The negative cache

A negative cache stores the fact that a lookup returned no result. Without a negative cache, every request for a non-existent product, user, or discount code generates a full database read. At high traffic, requests for non-existent items — from bots, from malformed URLs, from expired deep links — produce a sustained read load against the database for data that does not exist.

> **Note**
>
> The Negative Cache Rule: Cache the absence of data with a short TTL — typically 30–120 seconds. A cached null is a legitimate cache entry. A request for a non-existent product ID that hits the database 10,000 times in a minute is not a caching problem — it is the absence of a negative cache. The negative cache TTL must be short enough that legitimate data that is subsequently created is not blocked by a stale negative entry.

> Note
>
> **Tool Tax — the negative cache:** Caching absence is cheap to implement and expensive to get wrong. Budget for a TTL short enough that a newly created product is not invisible to the customer who just created it, an explicit purge on create, and monitoring that distinguishes a healthy negative-hit rate from an enumeration attack filling your memory with cached nulls for keys that will never exist.

> Note
>
> The Read Model Cache Rule: For cross-service read patterns where multiple consumers read the same data from different services, build a dedicated read model: a pre-computed, pre-joined representation of the data optimized for the consumer's access pattern. The read model is populated asynchronously from service events and served from Redis. Consumers never read from the source service's database directly. This eliminates the read amplification pattern entirely—five event consumers no longer each generate a database read; they each read from a shared Redis key that is refreshed once per event.

Cache observability: the metrics that matter

A cache without observability is a black box. You cannot tune what you cannot measure. The minimum observable metrics for a production cache layer are: hit rate, miss rate, eviction rate, memory utilization, and key count by data type. These metrics must be instrumented as first-class observability signals — not as operational afterthoughts.

Metric	Healthy Range	Warning Signal	Action Required
Cache hit rate	>80% for read-heavy workloads	< 70% and declining	Review TTL, eviction policy, and working set size

Metric	Healthy Range	Warning Signal	Action Required
Eviction rate	Near zero for correctly sized cache	> 0 consistently	Increase memory allocation or reduce the scope of cached data
Memory utilization	< 75% of maxmemory	> 80% — eviction pressure building	Scale up or add Redis node; review which data types can be removed
Miss rate by key type	Varies by data type	Miss rate increasing for hot keys	Investigate TTL reduction, eviction policy, or thundering herd event
Database IOPS delta	Reduction proportional to cache hit rate	IOPS not decreasing despite cache layer	Cache may be misconfigured; check eviction policy and TTL coordination
Invalidation event lag	< 2 seconds from write to cache purge	> 5 seconds	Invalidation consumer falling behind; check consumer lag and DLQ

Table 9.9: Cache observability metrics, their healthy ranges, and the action each warning signal requires

When cache metrics indicate a design problem

Collecting these metrics is the easy half. The harder half is reading them as symptoms. Four patterns recur often enough to be worth memorizing, because each one points at a different design fault rather than at a tuning value:

Signal	What does it indicate	First thing to check
High hit rate, but stale data complaints	The cache is working; the invalidation is not	Invalidation event lag, and whether the write path emits an invalidation event at all

Signal	What does it indicate	First thing to check
Low hit rate with memory to spare	TTL is shorter than the interval between reads, so entries expire before they are reused	Whether the TTL was derived from freshness tolerance or from performance intuition
High eviction rate	The working set exceeds the memory allocated to it	Working-set sizing at the 1.3x overhead factor, and any keys without a TTL hold memory permanently
Database IOPS unchanged after introducing Redis	The cache is not serving the workload that generates the IOPS	Which queries actually dominate IOPS, and whether the cached keys are the ones being read

Table 9.10: Cache metric patterns and the design problem each one points to

Note

The Metric-to-Diagnosis Rule: Cache metrics are only meaningful in combination. Hit rate alone cannot distinguish a healthy cache from one serving stale data very efficiently. Read hit rate against eviction rate, invalidation lag and the database IOPS delta together — any single metric in isolation will confirm whatever you already believed.

Note

Manager's Math — The TTL Economic Model: Every TTL reduction doubles the read load on the database for that data type, but halves the maximum staleness. For ShopFlow's product pricing cache at 15-minute TTL and 10,000 pricing reads per minute, a reduction to 5-minute TTL triples the cache miss rate from roughly 1.1% to 3.3% at steady state — an additional 220 database reads per minute per data type. At $0.0002 per database read (approximate RDS I/O cost), this is $0.044/minute, or $63/month per data type with shortened TTL. The decision to shorten a TTL is a business decision with a measurable cost. Run the model before shortening.

> **Note**
>
> Manager's Math — Cache Infrastructure Sizing: ShopFlow's event consumer read amplification requires caching two primary datasets: Inventory status (average record size 2KB, 50,000 active SKUs = 100MB working set) and Catalog data (average record size 8KB, 50,000 products = 400MB working set). Total Redis working set: 500MB. With a 1.3x overhead factor for Redis internals, the correctly sized Redis instance requires 650MB of maxmemory. A 1GB managed Redis instance covers this with headroom. At $0.025/GB-hour for managed Redis, the full caching layer costs approximately $18/month in Redis compute. This eliminates approximately $600/month in database IOPS provisioning. This is the sizing the Cache ROI Calculation above is based on: $18/month of Redis compute against roughly $600/month of avoided database IOPS provisioning — a 33:1 cost-savings ratio at ShopFlow's current scale.

> **Note**
>
> Safe Scale Check — Cache Warm-Up Protocol: Before routing production traffic through a new cache layer, execute a warm-up protocol: identify the top N most-accessed keys from database query logs or access logs; pre-populate those keys in the cache before enabling the cache layer in the read path; verify cache hit rate exceeds 60% before full traffic cutover. A cache warm-up is not optional — a cold cache in the read path converts every request into a cache miss plus a database read, which is strictly worse than no cache at all during the warm-up period.

Architect's prompt 9.5: the cache safety audit

When to use this: Use this prompt when a cache deployment is exhibiting thundering herd events, unexpected database IOPS spikes during traffic peaks, or staleness incidents after content updates.

```
Act as a Principal Reliability Engineer specializing in cache safety.
I am diagnosing the following cache safety incident:

Incident description: [e.g. database IOPS spike to 300% during flash sale]
Cache tier affected: [Redis / CDN / Origin Shield]
Key type affected: [e.g. product catalog entries]
```

```
Current TTL: [X seconds]
Estimated concurrent requests at time of incident: [N]
Thundering herd defense currently in place: [None / TTL jitter / Mutex /
Coalescing]

(1) Calculate the thundering herd magnitude: given the concurrent request
    count and the key TTL, how many simultaneous cache misses would occur
    at expiry? At what traffic volume does this become a database risk?
(2) Recommend the minimum thundering herd defense for this workload:
    - TTL jitter range: what +/- percentage prevents synchronized expiry?
    - Mutex lock: what is the acceptable wait time for lock waiters?
    - Request coalescing: is this a single-instance or multi-instance risk?
(3) Evaluate whether the current TTL is correct given the domain freshness
    tolerance. If TTL was shortened in response to staleness complaints,
    calculate the IOPS cost of the reduction.
(4) Design the cache warm-up protocol: which keys must be pre-populated
    before the next cache flush or deployment?
(5) Define the database IOPS floor: what is the minimum provisioned IOPS
    required to handle a complete cache failure (0% hit rate) for 5 minutes
    without SLO breach?
```

Data Type	**Reads/min (Before Cache)**	**Cache Hit Rate (After)**	**DB Reads/ min (After)**	**IOPS Reduction**
Product catalog descriptions	12,000	91% (CDN)	1,080	91%
Shipping weight/ dimensions	8,500	95% (Redis + CDN)	425	95%
Active pricing	22,000	87% (Redis)	2,860	87%
Product category assignments	6,000	93% (Redis + CDN)	420	93%
Inventory reservation status	18,000	72% (Redis, short TTL)	5,040	72%

Data Type	Reads/min (Before Cache)	Cache Hit Rate (After)	DB Reads/ min (After)	IOPS Reduction
Real-time stock level (checkout)	3,200	0% — no cache (correctness)	3,200	0% — intentional

Table 9.11: Projected database IOPS reduction per data type after the caching layer

Summary

In this chapter, we built the layered caching strategy that absorbed ShopFlow's 4.2x read amplification event without compromising the freshness guarantees that inventory, pricing, and catalog data require.

We applied the Domain-First Cache Rule before designing any cache layer, classifying each data type by update frequency and freshness tolerance. The Freshness Spectrum drove every TTL assignment—derived from business requirements, not from performance targets.

We applied the Cache Hierarchy Rule to build a four-tier caching architecture: browser cache for static assets, CDN edge cache for public catalog content, Redis application cache for pricing and session data, and origin shielding for thundering herd protection.

We enforced the Redis Scope Rule to prevent promiscuous caching—deploying Redis only where the read pattern, memory model, and eviction policy were explicitly designed, not as a default layer on every read path.

We implemented event-driven cache invalidation using the Chapter 8 event bus as the invalidation substrate, replacing TTL-only invalidation with a near-real-time purge pipeline that bounds staleness to seconds rather than hours.

We deployed the Thundering Herd Defense Rule with TTL jitter and request coalescing, protecting the database from the synchronized expiry events that occur during flash sales and large-scale cache invalidations.

ShopFlow's telemetry after Chapter 9:

Metric	Before (Ch9 Start)	After (Ch9 End)	Change
Inventory DB Read IOPS	78% of provisioned capacity	16% of provisioned capacity	80% reduction

Metric	Before (Ch9 Start)	After (Ch9 End)	Change
Catalog DB Read IOPS	61% of provisioned capacity	12% of provisioned capacity	80% reduction
Cache Hit Rate	0%	82% (Redis) / 91% (CDN for catalog)	From zero
p99 Latency (catalog page, Frankfurt)	180ms (origin)	12ms (CDN edge)	93% improvement
p99 Latency (pricing reads)	38 ms (DB)	1.2 ms (Redis)	97% improvement
Cloud Spend	$9,800/mo	$9,600/mo	-$200 (net: ~$600/mo of IOPS tier reduction, less the ~$18/mo Redis instance and the new CDN edge tier this chapter introduces)
Double-Charge Risk from Stale Pricing	Present — no invalidation pipeline	Eliminated — event-driven purge	Eliminated

Table 9.12: ShopFlow telemetry before and after the Chapter 9 changes

The cliffhanger: the white wall

The read performance problem is solved. Cache hit rates are above 80%. Database read IOPS are back within comfortable provisioned limits. The Frankfurt latency for catalog pages has dropped from 180 ms to 12 ms.

But Dave is running the quarterly capacity planning model, and the numbers are not pointing at reads anymore.

ShopFlow's write volume has grown 3.1x over the past two quarters — driven by the event-driven architecture's outbox writes, the cache invalidation event stream, the saga orchestrator's state writes, and the raw growth in order volume. The database is handling the write load today. The write p99 latency has crept from 8ms to 24ms. The Orders table is showing lock contention during high-volume write periods. The index write amplification — every insert to the Orders table writes to eleven indexes — is consuming 40% of total database write IOPS.

The caching strategy solved the read amplification. The write amplification is the next ceiling. In Chapter 10, we perform the data layer surgery that the read optimizations have been deferring: sharding, replication strategies, and the decision between SQL and NoSQL for the workloads where relational guarantees are genuinely incompatible with the required write throughput.

10

Scaling Data and Databases – Storage, Queries, and Beyond

In *Chapter 9*, the caching strategy absorbed ShopFlow's 4.2x read amplification event. Inventory database read IOPS dropped from 78% to 16% of provisioned capacity. The Frankfurt catalog page latency dropped from 180 ms to 12 ms.

But Dave is running the quarterly capacity planning model, and the numbers are not pointing at reads anymore.

Write volume has grown 3.1x over the past two quarters, driven by the event-driven outbox writes from *Chapter 8*, the saga orchestrator's state writes, the cache invalidation event stream, and raw order growth. The Orders table write p99 has crept from 8ms to 24ms. Lock contention is appearing during high-volume write periods. Index write amplification — eleven indexes updated on every Orders table insert — is consuming 40% of total database write IOPS. The read problem was solved. The write problem is the next ceiling.

In this chapter, we perform the data layer surgery that caching and async messaging have been deferring.

In this chapter, we are going to cover the following main topics:

- **Choosing Your Foundation:** SQL vs. NoSQL trade-offs.
- **Sharding, Partitioning, and Replication:** Techniques for massive scale.
- **Indexing and Query Tuning:** For peak performance.
- **Data Abstraction:** Hiding complexity from the application layer.
- **Beyond Databases:** Leveraging search indexes and distributed file storage.

Technical requirements

PostgreSQL 16+ / MySQL 8+: The relational foundation. Sharding, partitioning, and replication are built on top of, not instead of, a correctly tuned relational engine.

pg_partman / native table partitioning: PostgreSQL extension for automated partition management. Converts a monolithic Orders table into time-based or range-based partitions without application code changes.

Citus (distributed PostgreSQL): Horizontal sharding extension for PostgreSQL. Distributes table rows across worker nodes while preserving SQL query compatibility. Preferred over manual sharding for teams that cannot afford the shard management overhead.

DynamoDB / Cassandra / MongoDB: NoSQL stores evaluated in this chapter. Each is compared against the relational alternative with explicit trade-off analysis, not vendor preference.

Elasticsearch / OpenSearch / Typesense: Dedicated search engines for full-text, faceted, and relevance-ranked search. Evaluated against the database LIKE query alternative with specific migration trigger criteria.

pganalyze / EXPLAIN ANALYZE: Query analysis tooling. Every index change recommended in this chapter must be validated with EXPLAIN ANALYZE before and after. Index decisions without query plan analysis are guesswork.

AWS S3 / Azure Blob Storage / GCP Cloud Storage: Distributed object storage for large unstructured payloads. Order attachments, shipping labels, and product images belong in object storage, not in the database.

Code Repository: `https://github.com/imran-siddique/Architecting-at-Scale/tree/main/ch10`

ShopFlow telemetry snapshot [stage 10]

```
The Signal: The caching layer solved the read amplification. The write
amplification from 3.1x order growth is the next ceiling. Eleven indexes per
Orders table insert is the primary bottleneck. Sharding and index surgery are the
prescribed interventions – in that order.
Orders Table Write p99: 24ms (◎ Warning – crept from 8ms over two quarters)
Orders Table Lock Contention Events: 14/hour at peak (● Critical – blocking
concurrent writes)
Index Write Amplification (Orders): 11 indexes per insert (● 40% of total DB
write IOPS consumed by index maintenance)
```

```
Database Write IOPS: 71% of provisioned capacity (🟡 Warning – ceiling visible at
current growth rate)
Product Search Query p99: 1.8s (LIKE query on Catalog DB) (🔴 Critical – full
table scan on 500k products)
Read Replica Lag (reporting replica): 8-45 seconds (🔴 Reporting queries reading
stale order data)
Cloud Spend: $9,600/mo (Stable – but DB IOPS upgrade is the next cost event)
Panic Meter: 5/10 (No immediate incident. Write ceiling and search degradation are
the visible signals.)
```

> Note
>
> **Dave Alert:** "The search team just asked why product search is timing out. I looked at the query plan: it's a LIKE '%running shoes%' on a 500,000-row table with no index that can help. And the reporting team is complaining that their order summaries show yesterday's totals. The read replica is 45 seconds behind."

Choosing your foundation: SQL vs. NoSQL Trade-offs

The SQL vs. NoSQL decision is one of the most consequential and most frequently misframed choices in distributed systems design. It is framed as a performance decision. It is actually a data model decision. The performance implications follow from the data model, not the other way around.

The position from direct experience operating systems at scale is unambiguous: relational databases are the correct default. They are not the correct choice in every scenario — but they are the correct starting assumption, and the burden of proof lies with any team that proposes to abandon the relational model, not with teams that choose to keep it.

Every time a team migrates from a relational database to a NoSQL store because they believed the relational model was their scaling bottleneck, they discover one of two things: either the relational model was not the bottleneck at all — the bottleneck was indexing strategy, connection pooling, or query design — or the relational requirements of the domain did not disappear when the database changed; they moved to the application layer. The application is now a graph. The join logic that lived in one SQL query is now spread across five service calls, each of which must handle consistency, ordering, and error cases that the database handled transparently.

Note

The Relational Default Rule: Use a relational database until you have a specific, measurable reason not to. The burden of proof is on NoSQL. Acceptable reasons to adopt NoSQL: the data structure is genuinely schema-free and changes frequently, the access pattern is pure key-value with no relational requirements, or the write throughput genuinely exceeds what a tuned relational engine can deliver. 'We expect to scale' is not a reason. 'We have already hit the relational ceiling' is a reason.

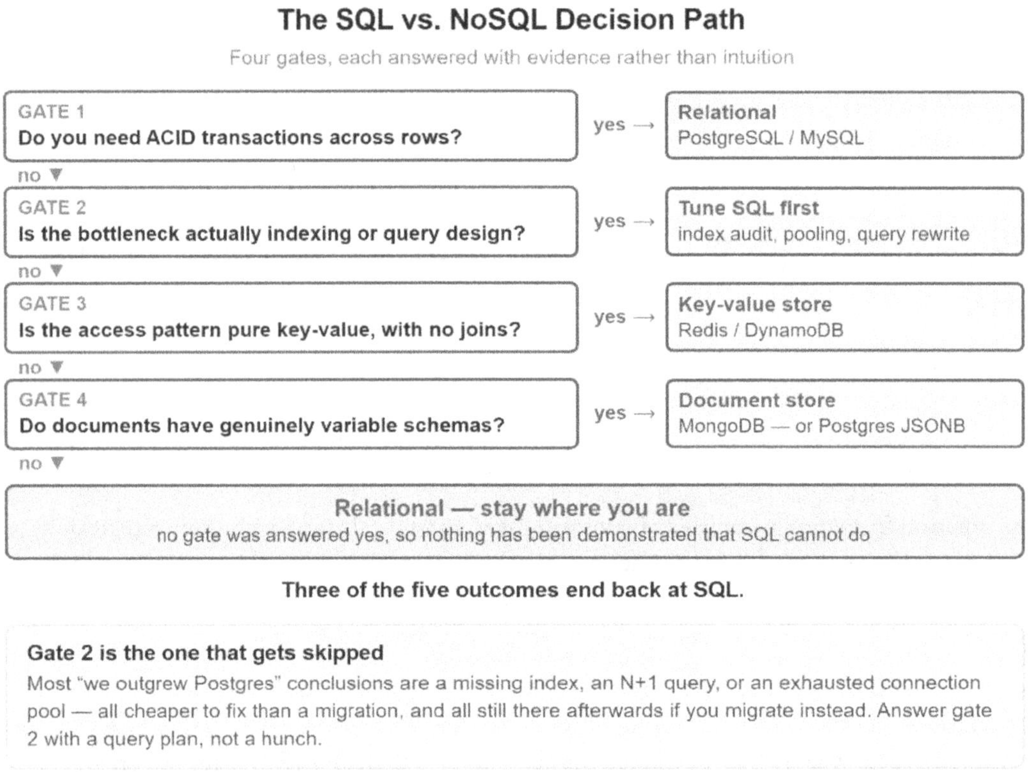

Figure 10.1: The SQL vs. NoSQL Decision Path

Read the same path as a sequence of gates. Each one must be answered with evidence, not intuition.

1. Do you require ACID transactions across more than one row? If yes, the answer is relational. Multi-row atomicity, foreign keys, and constraints are the relational model's

reason for existing, and re-implementing them above a NoSQL store is the migration cost teams consistently underestimate.

2. Is the bottleneck actually indexing, connection pooling or query design? Produce the EXPLAIN ANALYZE output before answering. If the slow query is a sequential scan on an unindexed column or a nested loop on an unindexed foreign key, the database engine is not the constraint — tune SQL first.
3. Is the access pattern pure key-value, with no joins, transactions or relational constraints? If yes, a key-value store serves it at lower latency than a relational engine. Sessions, rate-limit counters, and leaderboards qualify. An orders table does not.
4. Do documents genuinely have variable schemas — attribute sets that differ per item rather than per sprint? If yes, a document store removes a real impedance mismatch. If the attributes are uniform and the team simply wants to skip migrations, this is a relational workload that has not been modeled yet.
5. If every answer is no, stay relational. That is the default, not the consolation prize.

When NoSQL is the right answer

NoSQL is genuinely the right tool in three scenarios.

The first is **free-flow document storage**. When the data structure is schema-flexible — user-generated content, configuration payloads, product attributes that vary by category — and the access pattern is primarily by document key rather than by relational join, a document store eliminates the impedance mismatch between the flexible data and a rigid schema. The key word is 'genuinely' flexible: a product catalog where every product has a different attribute set is a document workload. A product catalog where every product has the same attributes but the engineering team wants to 'move fast' is a relational workload that has not been modeled correctly.

The second is **high-throughput key-value access**. When the access pattern is pure lookup by a single key with no joins, no transactions, and no relational constraints — session storage, rate limiting counters, leaderboards, presence indicators — a key-value store delivers lower latency and higher throughput than a relational engine for that specific access pattern. This is the scenario Redis is designed for. It is not a scenario for DynamoDB as a replacement for an orders table.

The third is **write-optimized time-series or event log storage**. When the write volume genuinely exceeds what a relational engine can absorb — IoT sensor data, clickstream events, financial tick data — and the access pattern is append-only with time-range reads, a columnar store or time-series database delivers superior write throughput and query performance for that specific pattern. This is not a generic 'we have a lot of writes' scenario. It is a specific access pattern that must be validated against the data before the migration begins.

Scenario	Correct Store	Relational Alternative	Why NoSQL Wins Here	When Relational Wins Instead
Session storage	Redis (key-value)	PostgreSQL session table	Sub-ms lookup, TTL native, no joins needed	When session data must be joined with user records for authorization
Product catalog with variable attributes	MongoDB (document)	PostgreSQL + JSONB column	Schema flexibility, no migration for new attribute types	When product queries require cross-attribute filtering or sorting at scale
User activity feed (append-only)	Cassandra (wide column)	PostgreSQL with partitioning	Write throughput, time-range reads, no updates needed	When feed items require joins with user or product tables
Financial order ledger	PostgreSQL (relational)	DynamoDB / Cassandra — considered and rejected	It does not win here — NoSQL forfeits cross-row ACID, foreign-key integrity and audit-grade constraints	Always, for ledger data — ACID transactions, an immutable audit trail and complex query patterns are the requirement, not a preference
Full-text search	Elasticsearch (search engine)	PostgreSQL full-text / LIKE	Relevance ranking, faceting, stemming, typo tolerance	When search volume is low and query complexity is minimal

Scenario	Correct Store	Relational Alternative	Why NoSQL Wins Here	When Relational Wins Instead
Real-time analytics aggregations	ClickHouse (columnar)	PostgreSQL + indexes	Columnar compression, vectorized query execution on large datasets	When dataset fits in memory and query frequency is low

Table 10.1: NoSQL scenarios and their relational alternatives, with the trade-off argued in both directions

Note

Anti-Pattern: The NoSQL Migration: Migrating a relational system to NoSQL to solve a scaling problem that is actually an indexing, connection pooling, or query design problem. Observable aftermath: the application layer grows a custom query engine, join logic, and transaction coordinator to replace what the relational database provided. The database is simpler. The application is a distributed SQL engine built by engineers who are not database authors. Performance is typically worse than a correctly tuned relational system would have been.

Note

Manager's Math — The Application-Layer SQL Cost: A team that migrates a 10-table relational schema to DynamoDB to 'eliminate join overhead' typically spends 3–6 months rebuilding the following in application code: entity relationship resolution (2–3 weeks), transaction coordination across multiple DynamoDB items (4–6 weeks), consistency guarantees for read-your-writes patterns (2–4 weeks), and query support for access patterns that were not modeled at schema design time (ongoing). At a fully-loaded engineering cost, this is $150–300K in engineering time — before accounting for the operational cost of the NoSQL cluster, which does not replace the relational database in most migrations but is added alongside it. The 'simpler' NoSQL migration typically costs more than the relational tuning it was avoiding.

Architect's prompt 10.1: the SQL vs. NoSQL decision audit

When to use this: Use this prompt before any database migration decision, whether from relational to NoSQL or the reverse. The output is a justified technology choice grounded in the actual access patterns, not in performance intuition or technology preference.

```
Act as a Principal Data Architect. I am evaluating whether to migrate
[Table/Service Name] from [current store] to [proposed store].

Current state:
- Schema: [table structure or document shape]
- Primary access patterns: [list of read and write queries with frequency]
- Relational requirements: [joins, transactions, foreign keys, constraints]
- Current performance bottleneck: [IOPS / latency / query plan / lock contention]
- Write volume: [X writes/sec]
- Read volume: [Y reads/sec]

(1) For each relational requirement identified, evaluate whether it can be
    eliminated by access pattern redesign or must be re-implemented in
    the application layer after migration.
(2) For each access pattern, evaluate whether the proposed NoSQL store
    serves it natively or requires a secondary index, scan, or
    application-layer join.
(3) Calculate the engineering cost of re-implementing relational
    requirements in the application layer:
    - Transaction coordination: [engineering weeks]
    - Consistency guarantees: [engineering weeks]
    - Query patterns not modeled at design time: [ongoing cost]
(4) Identify the actual bottleneck: is it the relational engine itself,
    or is it an index, connection pool, or query design problem?
    Provide the EXPLAIN ANALYZE output for the slowest query.
(5) Recommend: migrate to NoSQL, tune the relational engine, or adopt
    a specialized store for the specific access pattern.
```

Sharding, partitioning, and replication: techniques for massive scale

Sharding is the most powerful and most dangerous operation in database engineering. It is powerful because it is the only technique that provides genuinely unlimited horizontal write scalability for a relational database. It is dangerous because the sharding key is a permanent architectural decision: once data is distributed across shards, changing the key requires migrating every row in every table, simultaneously, in a running production system.

The sharding key decision deserves more design time than any other database decision. It deserves more design time than the schema. It deserves more design time than the index strategy. It determines the distribution of every write, the locality of every read, and the feasibility of every future query pattern. A wrong sharding key is not a configuration that can be changed. It is a rebuild.

> Note
>
> **The Sharding Design Mandate:** The sharding key must be designed before the first row is written to a sharded table. You cannot shard a production system by choosing the key after the fact and redistributing data in place — not safely, not quickly, not without deep expertise. If the sharding key is wrong, the only correct fix is a full data migration to a new sharding scheme. That migration is the most expensive database operation a team will ever execute. Design the key correctly the first time, or do not shard at all.

The hot shard Anti-Pattern

The most common sharding key mistake is choosing a key that appears to distribute data evenly during design but produces severe imbalance under the actual access patterns that emerge in production.

The most seductive wrong answer is a key that seems natural to the domain but maps to a skewed access distribution. For an e-commerce platform, sharding orders by merchant ID seems intuitive — each merchant owns their orders, so sharding by merchant keeps related data together. The problem surfaces when 5% of merchants generate 80% of order volume. The shards assigned to high-volume merchants receive 80% of all writes. The shards assigned to low-volume merchants are nearly idle. The system has not been horizontally scaled; it has been horizontally unbalanced.

In petabyte-scale systems, this problem is amplified by the irreversibility of the shard layout. Moving data from a hot shard to a less-loaded shard requires identifying which rows belong to the high-volume tenant, extracting them, routing writes to a new shard during the migration window, verifying consistency between source and destination, and cutting over the routing layer — while the system continues to accept writes. This is not a weekend project. It requires deep expertise, extended planning, and a maintenance window that most production systems cannot afford.

> **Note**
>
> **Anti-Pattern: The Semantic Shard Key:** Choosing a sharding key based on domain semantics rather than access distribution. Merchant ID, user ID by alphabetical range, product category, and geographic region are all semantic keys that look correct on a whiteboard but produce hot shards in production when the access distribution is skewed. The correct shard key distributes writes uniformly across shards regardless of which entity is being accessed. This typically requires a hash of the natural key rather than the natural key itself.

Sharding Key Candidate	Distribution Model	Hot Shard Risk	Cross-Shard Query Risk	Recommended For
Merchant ID (direct)	One shard per merchant range	High — large merchants overwhelm their shard	Low — all merchant orders are co-located	Avoid — skewed access distribution
Hash(order_id)	Uniform hash distribution	Low — orders are distributed uniformly	High — orders for a merchant span all shards	Write-heavy, key-based access only
Hash(customer_id)	Near-uniform based on customer distribution	Low to medium — high-value customers may skew	Medium — customer orders co-located; merchant queries span shards	Preferred for ShopFlow — customer-centric access pattern
Time-based (order date)	Sequential fill by time window	Extreme — current shard receives all writes	Low — range queries are efficient	Avoid for write sharding; use for archival partitioning only

Sharding Key Candidate	**Distribution Model**	**Hot Shard Risk**	**Cross-Shard Query Risk**	**Recommended For**
Geographic region	One shard per region	Medium — regional traffic spikes hit one shard	High — cross-region queries require scatter-gather	Data residency requirements only; not for write scaling
Composite (hash(customer_id) % N)	Controlled distribution across N shards	Low — even distribution within N buckets	Medium — customer queries hit one shard; global queries span all	Production recommended: balances distribution with locality

Table 10.2: Sharding key candidates compared by distribution model, hot-shard risk, and cross-shard query cost

For ShopFlow, the correct sharding key is a composite hash of customer_id modulo the shard count. Customer orders are co-located on a single shard — the most common access pattern (show me this customer's order history) is served from one shard without scatter-gather. The hash distribution prevents any single customer or customer range from overwhelming a shard. Global reporting queries that span all customers require a scatter-gather across all shards, but these are P2 analytical workloads that can absorb the latency.

That formulation needs one refinement before it reaches production, and it is the refinement that determines whether the shard layout can ever grow. Taking the hash modulo the physical shard count bakes the shard count into the key computation. Move from two shards to three and the modulus changes for almost every customer, so almost every row has to move. Adding one node becomes a full data migration—the most expensive database operation a team will ever run, triggered by something as ordinary as capacity growth.

Note

The Logical Shard Rule: Hash to a fixed number of logical buckets, never to the current physical shard count. Choose the bucket count once at design time — 1,024 is a common choice, comfortably more than any plausible node count — and never change it. The shard registry then maps bucket ranges to physical nodes. Adding capacity moves buckets between nodes; it never rehashes a row. For ShopFlow the key computation is hash(customer_id) % 1024, and the registry maps those 1,024 buckets

> across however many nodes exist today. The hash is permanent architecture. The bucket-to-node map is operational data.

This is what makes rebalancing a routine operation rather than a migration. To add a third node, the operator moves roughly a third of the buckets to it: copy those buckets' rows, dual-write during the cutover window, verify consistency, then update the bucket-to-node map in the registry. Customers in untouched buckets are never affected, and no row's bucket assignment changes—only its address does. The mechanics of that map, and why it must not live in application code, are the subject of the Shard Registry Rule later in this chapter.

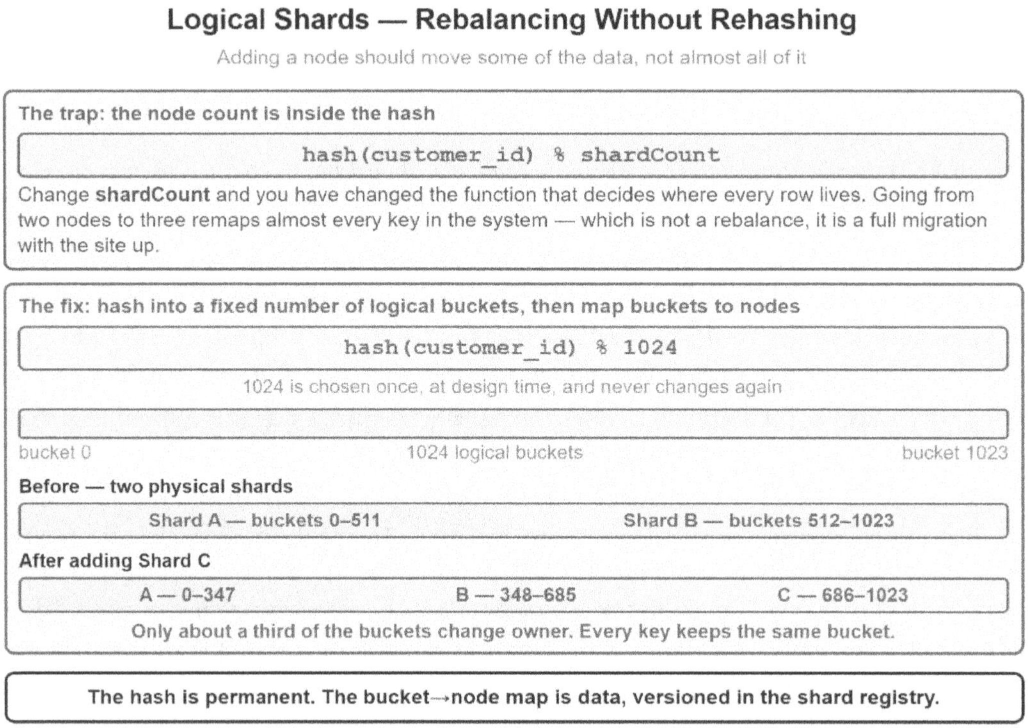

Figure 10.2: Logical Shards — Rebalancing Without Rehashing

Table partitioning: the step before sharding

Partitioning is not sharding. Partitioning splits a table into logical segments within a single database node, managed by the database engine. Sharding distributes data across multiple independent database nodes, managed by a routing layer. Partitioning is significantly less complex to implement, significantly less expensive to operate, and should always be evaluated before sharding is considered.

> Note
>
> Tool Tax — table partitioning: Partitioning is the cheapest option in this chapter, and it is still not free. Budget for partition maintenance — pg_partman or an equivalent creating future partitions before they are needed — a retention and detach policy for old ones, query patterns that actually include the partition key so pruning happens, and the migration itself on a table already in production. A partitioned table whose maintenance job stops running fails at midnight on the first day there is no partition to write into.

ShopFlow's Orders table has grown to 180 million rows. The write p99 is 24ms and rising. The first intervention is not sharding. It is time-based partitioning. By partitioning Orders by month — a native capability of PostgreSQL 16 — the database engine limits lock contention to the current month's partition, enables parallel query execution across historical partitions, and makes archival of old orders (moving partitions older than 2 years to cheaper storage) a metadata operation rather than a bulk DELETE.

> Note
>
> **The Partition-Before-Shard Rule:** Before sharding a table, exhaust the partitioning options available within your current relational engine. Time-based partitioning reduces lock contention on active data. Range partitioning on the primary access key eliminates full-table scans. Hash partitioning within a single node provides uniform distribution without multi-node routing complexity. Sharding requires a routing layer, schema changes, and ongoing shard management. Partitioning requires a schema change and a configuration file.

The Scaling Evolution Path: most systems arrive at sharding through the same six stages, and most stop well before the end. The order matters more than the destination — each stage is cheaper, more reversible, and less operationally expensive than the one after it, so skipping ahead buys complexity you have not yet earned.

1. Single database, correctly tuned. Right-sized instance, correct connection pooling, no obvious query pathologies. Most systems never need to leave this stage.
2. Index optimization. Audit the index set against actual usage, remove the unused and redundant, and validate every change with EXPLAIN ANALYZE. This is where ShopFlow's 40% index-maintenance overhead is recovered.
3. Table partitioning. Split the large table inside the same node — time-based for append-heavy history, range-based on the primary access key. A schema change and a configuration file; no routing layer, no application change.
4. Read replicas. Move read load off the primary, with the staleness contract stated explicitly to every consumer of the replica.
5. Sharding. Only after the partitioning ceiling is genuinely reached. This is the first stage that requires a routing layer, a shard registry, and a migration that cannot be rolled back.
6. Specialized data stores. Move the access patterns a relational engine serves badly—full-text search, large binary objects, high-volume append-only analytics—to stores built for them.

ShopFlow is executing stages 2, 3 and 6 in this chapter, and designing stage 5 without deploying it. Sharding is the last optimization, not the first response to growth — a team that shards before auditing its indexes has taken on a routing layer, a registry, and an irreversible migration to solve a problem that four dropped indexes would have solved.

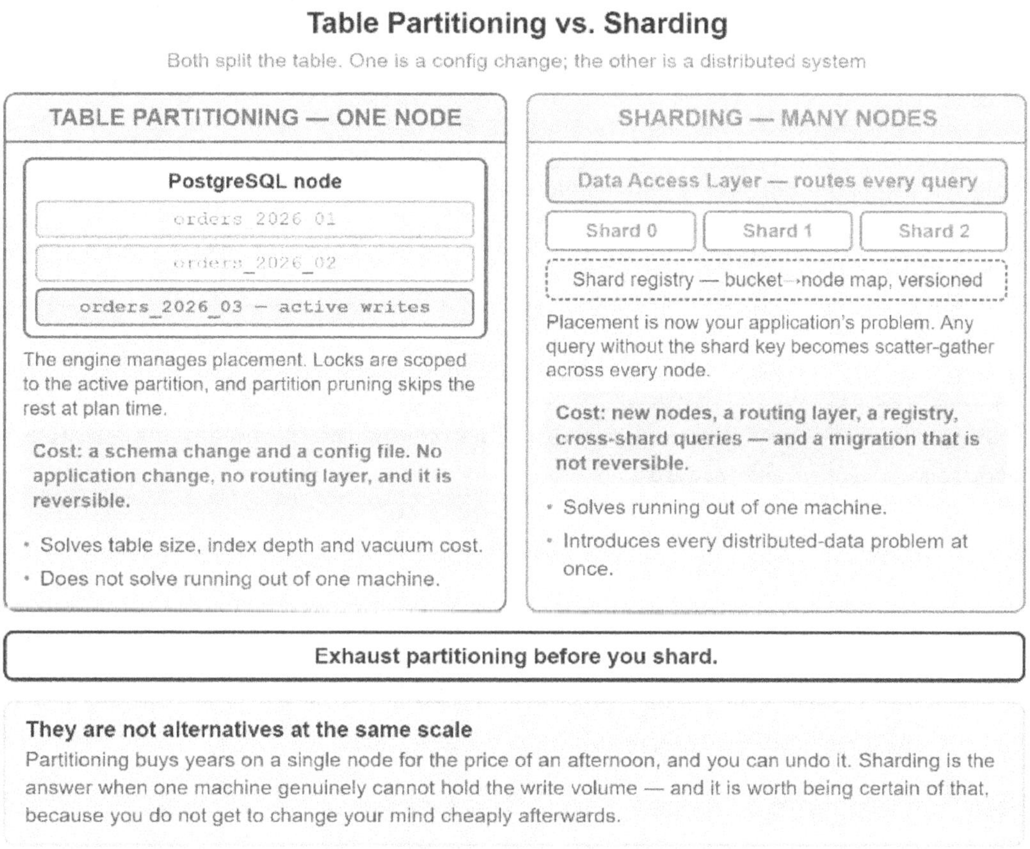

Figure 10.3: Table Partitioning vs. Sharding

Dimension	Table Partitioning	Sharding (Multi-Node)
Infrastructure change	None — same database node	New database nodes and routing layer required
Application code changes	None — database handles routing	DAL required for shard key computation
Operational complexity	Low — managed by pg_partman or native partitioning	High — shard registry, rebalancing, cross-shard queries

Dimension	Table Partitioning	Sharding (Multi-Node)
Write scalability ceiling	Single node — vertical ceiling remains	Horizontal — add shards to scale writes
Lock contention reduction	Yes — locks scoped to active partition	Yes — locks scoped to shard
Archival/tiered storage	Yes — detach old partitions to cold storage	Complex — requires per-shard archival pipeline
Query planner optimization	Yes — partition pruning eliminates irrelevant partitions	Partial — optimizer cannot prune across nodes
Migration risk	Low — reversible, no data movement	High — full data migration, not reversible
When to choose	First intervention for any large table	Only after the partitioning ceiling is reached

Table 10.3: Table partitioning versus sharding across nine operational dimensions

Replication: sync, async, and the correctness Trade-off

Replication creates copies of the database to serve reads from replicas and provide redundancy against primary failure. The replication configuration decision — synchronous vs. asynchronous, number of replicas, replica placement — is one of the most consequential operational decisions in database architecture, and one of the most under-analyzed.

The synchronous vs. asynchronous choice is a trade-off between write latency and consistency guarantee. Synchronous replication commits the write to the primary and waits for acknowledgment from at least one replica before returning success to the application. This guarantees that a replica promoted to primary after a failure has no data loss. The cost is write latency: every write waits for the network round-trip to the replica. In a cross-region replication scenario, this can add 50–150 ms to every write.

Asynchronous replication commits the write to the primary and returns success to the application immediately. The replica receives the change asynchronously. Under normal conditions, the lag is milliseconds. Under high write load, network congestion, or after a primary failure and promotion event, the lag can be seconds or tens of seconds. During this window, users reading from the replica receive results that do not reflect the latest state of the system.

> Note
>
> **The Replication Lag Rule:** Replication lag is not a configuration problem. It is an architectural contract. Async replication means that readers of the replica may see results that are N seconds out of date, where N is determined by write volume, network conditions, and replica capacity. This contract must be made explicit to every consumer of the replica. A reporting dashboard that reads from a replica with 45-second lag is serving yesterday's data at peak write load. If the business requires fresh data, the replica must be synchronous, or the dashboard must read from the primary.

ShopFlow's reporting replica is currently 8–45 seconds behind the primary under peak load. The reporting team is seeing order totals from 45 seconds ago presented as current. This is not a replica failure—it is async replication behaving exactly as designed. The gap between the expected behavior (always current) and the actual behavior (up to 45 seconds stale) was never made explicit when the replica was deployed.

> Note
>
> Tool Tax — read replicas: A replica looks like free read capacity and is actually a second consistency model in your architecture. Budget for lag monitoring with an alert threshold agreed with the consumers, a documented staleness contract per reader, routing logic that knows which reads may use it, failover, and promotion procedures that have been rehearsed, and the storage and network cost of a full second copy. The tax is not the instance; it is that every future feature must now decide which copy it reads from.

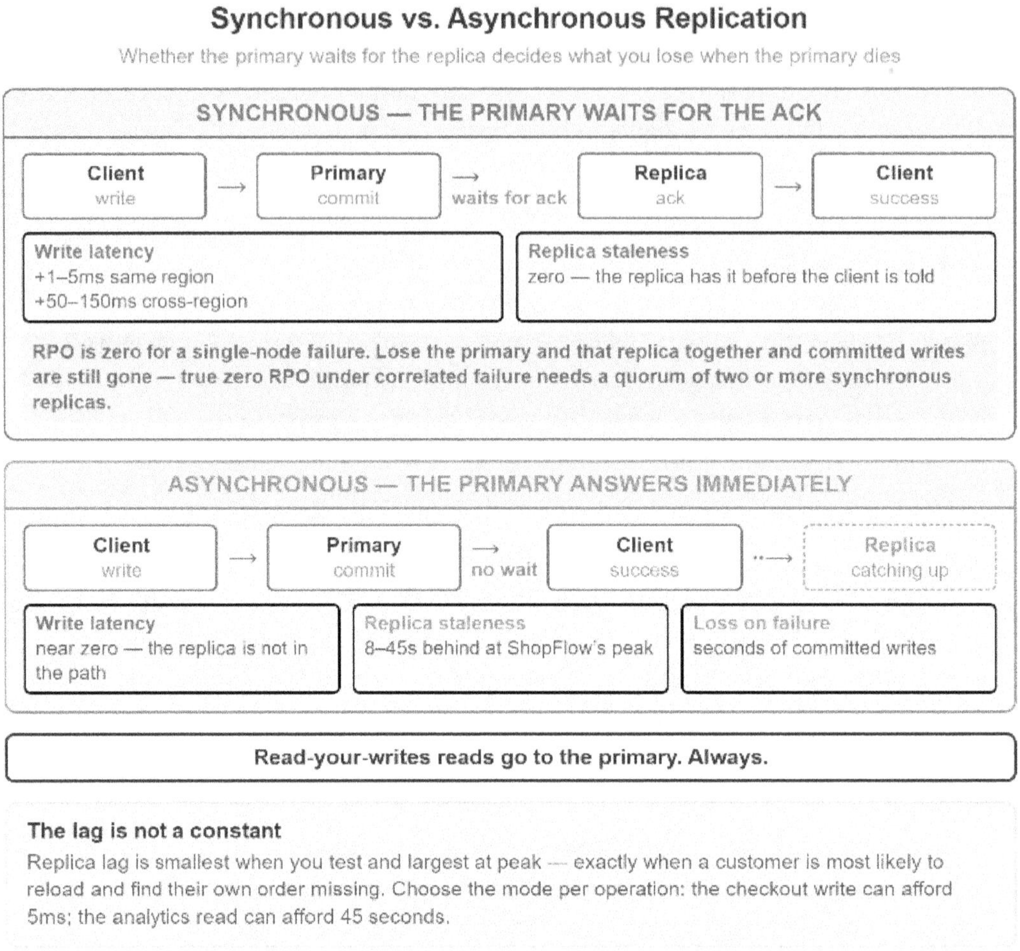

Figure 10.4: Synchronous vs. Asynchronous Replication

Replication Configuration	**Write Latency Impact**	**Data Loss on Primary Failure**	**Replica Read Staleness**	**Recommended For**
Async replication, same region	Near zero — sub-millisecond lag to replica	Seconds of data loss possible	Milliseconds under low load; seconds under high load	Read scale-out for non-critical reads; reporting workloads with staleness tolerance
Async replication, cross-region	Near zero — sub-millisecond to primary	Seconds to minutes of data loss	RTT-dependent — 50–150 ms+ under low load; much higher under load	Geo-distributed reads with explicit staleness contract; disaster recovery only
Sync replication, same region	Adds RTT to every write (~1–5 ms)	Zero — Zero for a single-node failure — the write is committed on at least one replica before the ack. A correlated loss of the primary and that replica together still loses committed writes; true zero RPO requires a quorum of two or more synchronous replicas	Zero — replica is always current	PO financial data; inventory write path; any write that cannot tolerate data loss

Replication Configuration	Write Latency Impact	Data Loss on Primary Failure	Replica Read Staleness	Recommended For
Sync replication, cross-region	Adds cross-region RTT to every write (50–150 ms)	Zero, with the same quorum caveat — and it also survives the loss of a whole region	Zero	Regulatory data residency requirements; extreme durability requirements only
Active-active (multi-primary)	Adds conflict resolution overhead to writes	Near zero	Conflict-resolution-dependent	Rarely justified; extreme write throughput with geographic write locality requirements

Table 10.4: Replication configurations compared by write latency, data loss on primary failure, and replica staleness

> Note
>
> **The Read-Your-Writes Rule:** Any operation where a user writes data and then immediately reads it back must be routed to the primary, not the replica. A user who places an order and is redirected to an order confirmation page that reads from an async replica may see a 'no order found' response if the replica has not yet received the write. This is not a bug in the application — it is the expected behavior of async replication. The application must route the post-write read to the primary, or implement a sticky read window that routes all reads from a given user session to the primary for N seconds after a write.

For ShopFlow, the routing split is concrete. These reads must go to the primary:

- **Checkout confirmation:** the customer wrote the order milliseconds ago. A replica read here can return 'no order found' for an order that was successfully placed.

- **Inventory reservation:** the reservation must be read back against the latest committed stock level. A stale read is an oversell, which is a refund and an apology rather than a slow page.
- **Payment verification:** the payment state machine cannot make decisions on a state that may be seconds out of date. Reading a stale 'unpaid' can double-charge; reading a stale 'paid' can ship unpaid goods.

And these can safely read from a replica:

- **Historical order history:** a customer viewing orders placed days ago will not notice a 45-second replication lag on a list that has not changed in a week.
- **Reporting dashboards and revenue aggregates:** these are P2 analytical workloads. They tolerate minutes of staleness, and routing them to the primary would put heavy aggregation in contention with the checkout path.
- **Product browse and catalog pages:** already served from cache and the CDN, as *Chapter 9* established; the replica is the fallback tier, not the front line.

The test is not how important the data feels. It is whether the reader wrote it. A revenue dashboard reads data that matters enormously and can tolerate 45 seconds of lag; a confirmation page reads one row that matters only to one customer and can tolerate none. *Table 10.7* later in this chapter encodes this same split as the DAL's routing rules.

> Note
>
> **Safe Scale Check — Sharding Blast Radius:** The blast radius of a sharding key error is the entire dataset. Before executing any sharding migration, define the rollback plan: if the sharding key produces hot shards under production load, what is the procedure to revert? If the answer is 'we would need to migrate all data back to a single node,' the migration is a one-way door. Validate the sharding key against a representative 30-day sample of production traffic — not against a synthetic load test — before committing.

Architect's prompt 10.2: the sharding strategy audit

When to use this: Use this prompt when designing the sharding strategy for a table that has exceeded the scaling limits of a single relational node or when auditing an existing sharding key that is producing hot shards or uneven distribution.

```
Act as a Principal Database Architect specializing in horizontal sharding.
I am evaluating the sharding strategy for the following table:

Table name: [Name]
```

```
Current row count: [N rows]
Write volume: [X writes/sec]
Read volume: [Y reads/sec]
Primary access patterns: [list of read queries with frequency]
Current bottleneck: [write IOPS / lock contention / single-node capacity]
Proposed sharding key: [key or key combination]

I will provide a 30-day sample of production query logs.
[Paste query log sample or access pattern summary]

(1) Evaluate the proposed sharding key against the production access
    patterns: does it distribute writes uniformly, or does the access
    pattern produce hot shards for specific key values?
(2) Identify the cross-shard query impact: which production queries
    will require scatter-gather after sharding? Calculate the latency
    penalty for the N highest-frequency cross-shard queries.
(3) Evaluate whether table partitioning within a single node can
    address the bottleneck before sharding is required.
(4) If sharding is required, recommend the shard count and key:
    - Natural key vs. hash: which provides better distribution?
    - Composite key: which combination balances locality and distribution?
(5) Define the migration plan: how does data move from the current
    single-node table to the sharded layout without downtime?
    Include the rollback trigger: at what point does the migration abort?
```

Indexing and query tuning for peak performance

ShopFlow's Orders table has eleven indexes. When the table was created, each index was added for a specific query that was slow. The engineers who added them are correct: each index made its target query faster. What they did not account for is the cumulative cost of all eleven indexes on every write.

Every insert into the Orders table writes eleven additional index entries. Every update to an indexed column rewrites the affected index entries. Every delete removes entries from all eleven indexes. The 40% of write IOPS consumed by index maintenance is not the cost of one unnecessary index. It is the cost of the accumulation of eleven individually justified indexes whose collective write overhead was never modeled.

> Note
>
> **The Index Accumulation Anti-Pattern:** Adding indexes reactively in response to slow queries, without modeling the cumulative write overhead of the index set. Each index is

> individually justified. The index set as a whole is not. Observable signature: write IOPS significantly higher than the write volume would suggest; query performance good across all read paths; write p99 creeping upward as the table grows; index count growing over time without a corresponding removal process.

The index audit

The correct response to write performance degradation caused by over-indexing is not to remove indexes arbitrarily. It is to audit the index set against actual query usage and remove only the indexes that are not being used.

PostgreSQL's pg_stat_user_indexes view provides per-index usage statistics: index scans since the last statistics reset, index rows read, and index rows fetched. An index with zero or near-zero scans over a 30-day period is not being used by any query the optimizer finds beneficial. It is consuming write IOPS on every insert and update, consuming storage, and adding to the vacuum workload, in exchange for zero query performance benefit.

The indexes that hurt are not always the ones with zero usage. Some indexes are used by slow, infrequent queries that justify their write cost. Others are used by frequent queries that could be served by a different, already-existing index with minor query rewrites. The audit must distinguish between 'unused' and 'redundant' — both are candidates for removal, but for different reasons.

The audit below covers the eight non-structural indexes on the Orders table. The remaining three — the primary key and two unique constraints — are structural: they enforce correctness rather than accelerate a query, and they are never audit candidates.

Index Category	Usage Signal	Write Cost	Action
Active, unique — serves high-frequency queries not covered by any other index	High scan count, index-only scans in query plan	Justified	Retain — this is a necessary index
Active, redundant — serves queries that could use a broader covering index	Moderate scan count, query plan shows alternative index available	Unjustified	Remove — rewrite affected queries to use a covering index

Index Category	Usage Signal	Write Cost	Action
Inactive, historical — was added for a query that has since been removed or rewritten	Zero or near-zero scan count over 30 days	Unjustified	Remove — verify that no application code references the index name, then drop
Over-specific composite — column order prevents use for prefix queries	Low scan count; query plan shows full sequential scan despite index existence	Unjustified	Remove or replace with a correctly ordered composite index
Covering index, over-broad — includes columns never used in query projection	Moderate scan count; large index size relative to table	High — wide index amplifies write cost	Narrow to only the columns actually referenced in query projections

Table 10.5: Index categories, the usage signal that identifies each, and the action each one warrants

Index Name	Usage (30d scans)	Write Cost (IOPS/ min)	Action	Outcome
idx_orders_status	2.1M scans	8,000 IOPS/min	Retain — high-frequency, high-selectivity	No change
idx_orders_customer_id	1.8M scans	8,000 IOPS/min	Retain — primary access pattern	No change
idx_orders_merchant_id_status	840K scans	8,000 IOPS/min	Retain — merchant dashboard queries	No change

Index Name	Usage (30d scans)	Write Cost (IOPS/ min)	Action	Outcome
idx_orders_created_at	620K scans	8,000 IOPS/min	Retain — time-range queries, partition key candidate	No change
idx_orders_updated_at	12K scans (30d)	8,000 IOPS/min	Remove — redundant with created_at in most queries	Drop: -8,000 IOPS/min
idx_orders_shipping_label_id	4K scans (30d)	8,000 IOPS/min	Remove — labels moving to object storage	Drop: -8,000 IOPS/min
idx_orders_internal_ref	0 scans (30d)	8,000 IOPS/min	Remove — legacy internal system decommissioned	Drop: -8,000 IOPS/min
idx_orders_promo_code	1.2K scans (30d)	8,000 IOPS/min	Remove — low selectivity (70% of orders have the same code)	Drop: -8,000 IOPS/min

Table 10.6: The ShopFlow Orders table index audit and the write IOPS recovered by each removal

Note

The Index Removal Rule: Before removing any index from a production table, confirm three things: the index has had zero meaningful scans in the past 30 days on the production replica; no application code references the index by name in a query hint; and the EXPLAIN ANALYZE output for every query that previously used the index shows an equivalent or better execution plan without it. Remove one index at a time. Monitor write p99 and read p99 for 48 hours after each removal before proceeding to the next.

At a high-traffic enterprise platform, a systematic index audit of a high-write table with 18 indexes identified 7 that were either unused or redundant. Removing those 7 indexes reduced write IOPS by 38% and improved write p99 from 31ms to 12ms. The read p99 on the affected queries was unchanged — the query optimizer continued to use the remaining 11 indexes without modification.

Query Plan Analysis

Index decisions without query plan analysis are guesswork. EXPLAIN ANALYZE is the only reliable tool for understanding what the query optimizer is doing, why it is doing it, and whether an index change will produce the expected improvement.

The two query patterns that most frequently cause engineers to add unnecessary indexes are sequential scans on large tables and nested loop joins on unindexed foreign keys. Both appear to be index problems. Both may actually be query design problems.

A sequential scan on a 180-million-row table is expensive. Adding an index on the filtered column eliminates the sequential scan. But if the filter selectivity is low — if the filter returns 30% of the table — the query optimizer may still prefer the sequential scan over the index scan, because reading 54 million rows from disk in sequential order is faster than 54 million random index lookups. The correct fix is not a new index. It is a query rewrite that increases filter selectivity, or a table partition that limits the scan to the relevant partition.

> Note
>
> The Selectivity Rule: An index is only beneficial when the filter it supports is highly selective — returning less than 5–10% of the table's rows. Above this threshold, the query optimizer typically prefers a sequential scan. An index added to a low-selectivity column will not be used by the optimizer and will consume write IOPS for no read benefit. Always check filter selectivity before adding an index.

> Note
>
> **Manager's Math — The Index Surgery ROI:** ShopFlow's Orders table generates approximately 8,000 inserts per minute at peak. Each insert writes to 11 indexes, consuming 88,000 index write operations per minute in addition to the 8,000 table writes. Removing 4 low-usage indexes reduces index writes to 56,000 per minute — a 36% reduction in write IOPS. At ShopFlow's current provisioned IOPS tier ($0.10/ provisioned IOPS-month), reducing from 71% to 44% of provisioned capacity enables a

> tier downgrade saving approximately $400/month. Engineering cost of the index audit: approximately 3–5 engineering days. Break-even: approximately 2 weeks.

Architect's prompt 10.3: the index audit

When to use this: Use this prompt when write performance is degrading on a high-write table, when write IOPS are disproportionately high relative to write volume, or as a routine quarterly maintenance audit on tables with more than 5 indexes.

```
Act as a Principal Database Performance Engineer. I am auditing the
index set for the following table:

Table name: [Name]
Row count: [N rows]
Write volume: [X writes/sec]
Current write p99: [Nms]
Current index count: [N]

I will provide:
1. The table schema with all index definitions.
2. The pg_stat_user_indexes output for the past 30 days.
3. The EXPLAIN ANALYZE output for the 10 highest-frequency queries.

[Paste schema, index stats, query plans]

(1) Classify each index as: Active-Necessary, Active-Redundant,
    Inactive-Historical, or Over-Specific.
(2) For Active-Redundant indexes: identify which covering index
    can serve the same queries with minor query rewrites.
(3) For Inactive-Historical indexes: verify no application code
    references the index by name. Provide the DROP INDEX statement.
(4) Calculate the write IOPS reduction from removing the identified
    candidate indexes: [removed indexes] x [writes/sec] = IOPS saved.
(5) For each remaining index, verify selectivity: for the queries
    that use this index, what percentage of rows does the filter
    return? Flag any index applied to a filter with > 10% selectivity.
```

Data abstraction: hiding complexity from the application layer

As ShopFlow's data layer grows from a single database to a partitioned table with shards, a reporting replica, and a search engine, the application layer faces a choice: it can be aware of all of this complexity, or it can be isolated from it behind a Data Access Layer.

A Data Access Layer is not a repository pattern. It is an abstraction that translates business operations into the appropriate data store operations, routing each query to the correct store based on the operation type, the freshness requirement, and the consistency model required. The application service asks for "the order history for customer 1234." The DAL decides whether to read from the primary (if the customer just placed an order and read-your-writes consistency is required), the replica (if the request is from the reporting dashboard with a 45-second staleness tolerance), or the search engine (if the request includes a full-text filter on order notes).

> Note
>
> The DAL Isolation Rule: The application service layer must not know which physical database, shard, or replica serves a given query. This knowledge belongs in the DAL. When the shard count changes, when a replica is promoted to primary, or when the search engine is updated to a new index schema, the DAL changes. The application services do not. You cannot maintain a distributed data layer without a DAL that isolates the distribution logic from the business logic.

Because every read and write already passes through it, the DAL is also the natural home for the cross-cutting concerns of talking to a data store. Centralizing them there means they are implemented once, instrumented once, and tuned once:

- **Connection pooling:** one pool per store, sized deliberately, with saturation exposed as a metric. Pools created per service instance are how a connection ceiling arrives without warning.
- **Retry policy:** bounded retries with jitter for transient failures only. A retry on a timeout that already committed is a duplicate write, so retries belong only on operations that are safe to repeat.
- **Timeout handling:** every query carries a deadline shorter than the caller's own timeout. A query with no timeout is a thread that never returns under load.

- **Circuit breaking per store:** the search engine, the replica and the primary fail independently and must break independently. One breaker across all stores turns a search outage into a checkout outage.
- **Telemetry:** query latency, error rate and rows returned, tagged by store and by shard. Without per-shard tagging, a single hot shard is invisible inside an averaged latency figure.

> **Note**
>
> The DAL Boundary: the DAL centralises how data is reached — routing, pooling, retries, timeouts, breakers, telemetry. It must not accumulate what the data means. Pricing rules, tax calculation, inventory reservation logic, and order state machines are business concerns; the moment they move into the DAL, every service depends on a component that changes for reasons unrelated to data access, and the isolation the DAL existed to provide is gone. If a change to a discount rule requires a DAL deployment, the boundary has already been crossed.

Query Type	DAL Routing Decision	Data Source	Consistency Model	Rationale
Place order (write)	Route to primary	Primary DB — shard determined by customer_id	Strong	Writes must go to primary; shard key routes to correct node
Order confirmation page (immediate post-write read)	Route to primary with 5s sticky window	Primary DB	Read-your-writes	User just wrote this data; replica lag would show missing order
Customer order history (normal read)	Route to replica	Read replica	Eventual (45 s tolerance)	High-frequency read; staleness acceptable for historical data

Query Type	DAL Routing Decision	Data Source	Consistency Model	Rationale
Order search by product name (full text)	Route to search engine	Elasticsearch	Eventually consistent via CDC	Database LIKE cannot serve this query at an acceptable latency
Monthly revenue report (P2 analytical)	Route to reporting replica	Analytics replica	Eventual (minutes tolerance)	Heavy aggregation; must not contend with OLTP on primary
Real-time stock check (checkout)	Route to primary, bypass all cache and replica	Primary DB — Inventory table	Strong	Zero staleness tolerance; oversell risk on stale read

Table 10.7: DAL routing decisions by query type, data source, and required consistency model

The DAL also handles the cross-cutting concern of shard routing. When the application service calls getOrdersByCustomer(customerId), the DAL computes hash(customerId) % 1024 to determine the logical bucket, looks up which physical shard owns that bucket in the shard registry, resolves its connection string, and routes the query. The application service sees a single database abstraction. The DAL sees a fleet of shards.

Note

The Shard Registry Rule: The shard-to-connection-string mapping must be stored in a central, versioned shard registry — not hardcoded in the application code or in environment variables. When a shard is rebalanced, a new shard is added, or a shard's connection string changes during a failover, the shard registry is updated and the DAL picks up the change on its next refresh cycle. A shard mapping hardcoded in application code requires a deployment to update — during the window between the shard change and the deployment, the application routes queries to the wrong shard.

> **Note**
>
> Tool Tax — the shard registry: The registry is the component that makes sharding operable, and it is also a new dependency on the critical path of every query. Budget for versioning and rollback of the bucket map, a refresh cycle with defined behavior when the registry is unreachable, cached copies in every DAL instance and the staleness window that implies, and an audit trail of who moved which buckets when. A registry that is unavailable does not slow the system down — it stops it from knowing where its data is.

> **Note**
>
> Safe Scale Check — DAL Blast Radius: The DAL is on the critical path for every database read and write. A DAL bug — incorrect shard routing, wrong replica selection, or connection pool exhaustion — affects every request in the system. Before deploying any DAL change to production, validate it in a shadow mode: route production traffic to both the old DAL and the new DAL simultaneously, compare the results, and verify zero divergence before cutting over. The blast radius of a DAL failure is the entire application.

> **Note**
>
> Tool Tax — the Data Access Layer: Centralizing routing buys isolation and creates a component that every request passes through. Budget for shadow-mode validation of every change, per-store instrumentation so a fault can be attributed, version compatibility across services that upgrade at different rates, and an ownership model — because a component everyone depends on and nobody owns becomes the slowest-moving part of the system.

Architect's prompt 10.4: data access layer design review

When to use this: Use this prompt when designing the DAL for a sharded or multi-store data architecture, or when auditing an existing DAL for routing correctness, consistency model compliance, and operational resilience.

```
Act as a Principal Data Architecture Engineer. I am designing the
Data Access Layer for a system with the following data stores:

Primary database: [type, shard count if applicable]
Read replicas: [count, replication lag, regions]
Search engine: [type, index freshness SLO]
Cache layer: [Redis, TTL ranges by data type]

Application services using the DAL: [list of services]

For each service, I will provide the list of read and write operations
with their consistency requirements:
[Paste operation list with consistency requirements]

(1) For each read operation, assign the correct data source based on
    consistency requirement:
    - Strong consistency: primary
    - Read-your-writes: primary with sticky window
    - Eventual (seconds tolerance): replica
    - Full-text search: search engine
    - Analytical aggregate: analytics replica
(2) For each write operation, validate that it routes to the primary
    and that the shard key is correctly derived from the operation input.
(3) Design the shard registry: format, storage location, refresh interval,
    and failure behavior when the registry is unavailable.
(4) Define the DAL fallback behavior for each data source failure:
    - Primary unavailable: fail writes, route reads to replica with alert
    - Replica unavailable: route reads to primary with latency warning
    - Search engine unavailable: fall back to database LIKE with alert
(5) Define the shadow mode validation protocol for DAL changes.
```

Beyond databases: search indexes and distributed file storage

Two categories of data access pattern consistently exceed what a relational database can serve efficiently at scale: full-text search with relevance ranking and large unstructured payloads. Both require purpose-built stores — not because relational databases cannot serve them at all, but because serving them from a relational database at scale requires the database to do work it was not designed for, at the expense of the workloads it was.

Confirming search is actually the bottleneck

Before introducing a search engine, prove that search is the constraint. A dedicated search engine is a permanent operational commitment, and the failure mode of adopting one prematurely is a second datastore to keep synchronized for a problem an index would have solved. Four pieces of evidence settle it, and all four are available before any migration begins:

- **Slow-query logs:** what fraction of the slowest queries are search queries? If the p99 offenders are reporting aggregates rather than LIKE scans, search is not the bottleneck.
- **Share of database IOPS consumed by search:** measure the IOPS attributable to search queries as a percentage of provisioned capacity. This is the number that shows search contending with the OLTP workload on the same table, and the number that justifies moving it off.
- **Search abandonment rate:** the percentage of search sessions where the user reformulates the query or leaves without clicking a result. A rising abandonment rate on a fast query is a relevance problem, and relevance is the one thing tuning an index cannot fix.
- **EXPLAIN ANALYZE on the search query:** does the plan show a sequential scan that a well-chosen index or a native full-text index could eliminate? PostgreSQL's own full-text search handles a surprising amount of workload before a dedicated engine earns its keep.

For ShopFlow, all four point the same way. The search query is a LIKE '%running shoes%' producing a sequential scan over 500,000 rows at a 1.8s p99; the plan confirms no index can serve a leading wildcard; and users are reformulating queries because exact string matching cannot handle plurals, typos or synonyms. The relevance requirement, not the query volume, is what makes this a search-engine problem — and it is the one signal that no amount of relational tuning would have satisfied.

The search vs. database boundary

The inflection point where product search moves from a database query to a dedicated search engine is not a volume threshold; it is a query complexity threshold.

A database LIKE query on a single column — WHERE product_name LIKE '%running shoes%' — works correctly at low volume. It performs a full table scan on every unindexed LIKE query, which is acceptable when the table has 10,000 rows and the query runs once per second. At 500,000 rows and 50 queries per second, it is a full-table scan repeated 50 times per second. At 500,000 rows and 500 queries per second, it saturates the database read I/O budget and begins impacting the OLTP workloads on the same table.

The more important signal is not the volume. It is the user expectation. Users expect search to be **good**, not just **functional**. A LIKE query matches the exact string. A search engine matches stemmed forms ('run' matches 'running'), typos ('runnng' matches 'running'), synonyms ('sneakers' matches 'shoes'), and ranks results by relevance — returning the most relevant product first, not the first product with a matching name. When users start abandoning search because the results are poor, the problem is not the database. It is the fundamental mismatch between what users expect from search and what a string matching query can deliver.

From building and operating search infrastructure for systems handling petabytes of content and millions of queries per day, the insight is consistent: search is a scoped read problem. Users want an infinitesimally small fraction of the total data — sometimes 0.001% or less — retrieved with high relevance, returned fast, and completely isolated from the write operations on the source system. A search engine is not a better database for this use case. It is a fundamentally different tool built for this exact requirement.

Signal	**Database LIKE is sufficient**	**Dedicated Search Engine Required**
Query volume	< 10 queries/sec on the search table	> 50 queries/sec; LIKE scans contending with OLTP
Result relevance requirement	Exact string match is acceptable	Relevance ranking, stemming, or typo tolerance required
Query complexity	Single column, exact match	Multi-field, weighted, faceted, or geospatial
Dataset size	< 100,000 rows in the searchable table	> 500,000 rows; full scans are measurable in IOPS

Signal	Database LIKE is sufficient	Dedicated Search Engine Required
User behavior signal	Search abandonment rate < 10%	Search abandonment rate rising; users reformulating queries repeatedly
Indexing freshness requirement	Real-time write + read consistency required	Near-real-time (seconds to minutes lag) acceptable

Table 10.8: Signals that distinguish a sufficient database LIKE query from a dedicated search engine requirement

Note

The Search Engine Tax: A dedicated search engine introduces three operational costs that teams consistently underestimate before running one in production for six months. First: index management. The search index must be kept synchronized with the source database. This requires a CDC pipeline or event-driven update mechanism, schema versioning, and zero-downtime re-indexing procedures when the schema changes. Second: operational expertise. Relevance tuning, shard and replica configuration, query performance analysis, and memory management for a search engine are distinct skills from relational database administration. Third: consistency lag. The search index is eventually consistent with the source database. The lag is typically seconds to minutes. This lag must be communicated to users ('search results may not reflect the most recent changes') and handled in the application ('show a warning if a product appears in search but has been deleted from the catalog').

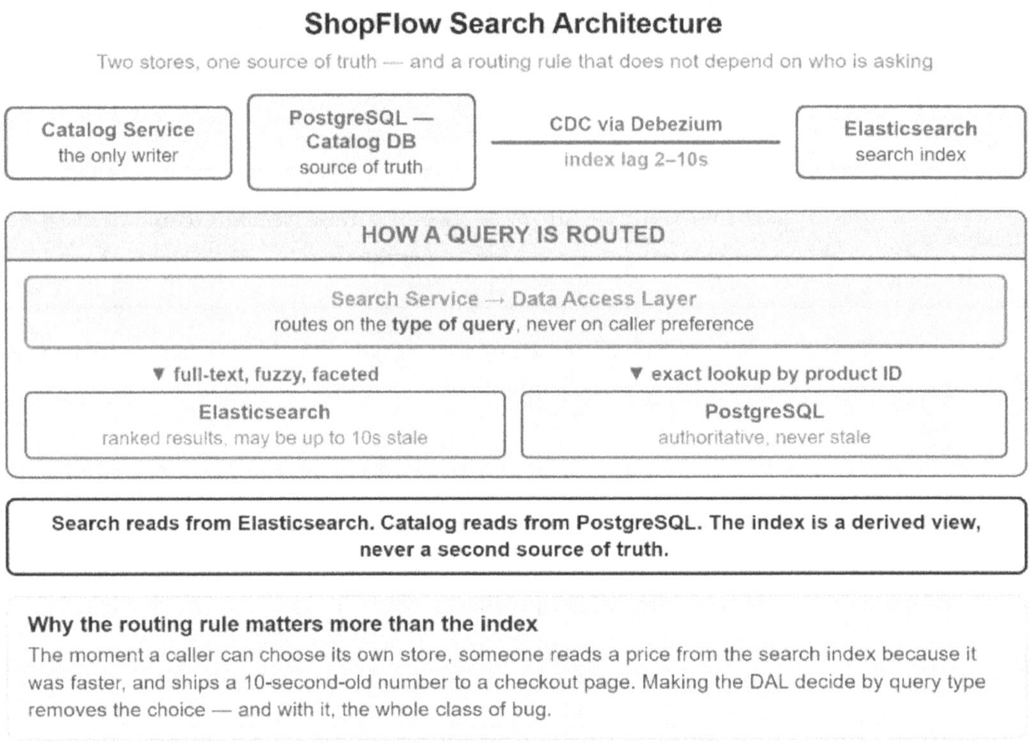

Figure 10.5: ShopFlow Search Architecture

Distributed file storage

The Orders table currently stores shipping labels as BYTEA columns — binary large objects embedded directly in the relational table. A single shipping label is 80–200KB. At ShopFlow's current order volume, this adds 1.5–3GB of binary data to the Orders table per day. The binary data is not indexed. It is not queried. It is retrieved exactly once per order — when the warehouse staff prints the label. It is consuming database storage, adding to backup size, and increasing the vacuum workload on a table that already has 180 million rows.

> Note
>
> **The Binary Data Rule:** Binary large objects — files, images, PDFs, audio, video — do not belong in a relational database. A relational database is optimized for structured, queryable data with referential integrity. A 200KB BYTEA column is none of these things. Store the binary object in distributed object storage and store the URL or object key in the relational table. The database stores a 50-byte string. Object storage stores

the 200KB file. The retrieval pattern is identical from the application's perspective. The database performance impact is not.

Note

Tool Tax — object storage: Moving binaries out of the database is unambiguously right and still adds surface area. Budget for lifecycle rules and storage-class transitions, signed-URL generation and expiry on the read path, orphan cleanup when a row is deleted but its object is not, cross-region replication if the data is user-facing, and a backup story that now spans two systems with different restore semantics and no shared transaction.

Data Type	Wrong Storage	Correct Storage	Migration Complexity	Performance Impact
Shipping labels (PDF, 80–200 KB)	BYTEA in Orders table	Object storage + URL in Orders table	Low — backfill URLs, move files, update column type	High — removes MB-scale rows from hot table
Product images (JPEG, 500 KB–2 MB)	BYTEA in Products table	Object storage + CDN + URL in Products table	Low — same migration pattern	Very high — eliminates image data from the relational store entirely
Order attachments (arbitrary files)	BYTEA in Orders table	Object storage + metadata table with foreign key	Medium — schema change + file migration	High — metadata table is queryable; binary is offloaded
Audit log events (JSON, high volume)	JSONB in audit_log table	Object storage (NDJSON files) + retention policy	Medium — streaming pipeline change	Very high — removes high-volume append workload from OLTP DB

Data Type	Wrong Storage	Correct Storage	Migration Complexity	Performance Impact
User-generated content (text)	TEXT in comments table	Relational DB is correct here	N/A	No change — text is queryable and appropriately sized

Table 10.9: Binary and high-volume data types, where they are wrongly stored, and where they belong

Note

Manager's Math — The Binary Data Migration ROI: ShopFlow's shipping labels add approximately 2GB per day to the Orders table. Over 12 months, this is 730GB of binary data in a relational table that costs approximately $0.115/GB-month in provisioned SSD storage — approximately $84/month for this data alone, growing by $7/month each month. Object storage for the same data costs approximately $0.023/GB-month — $16.79/month today, with the same growth rate. Migration saves approximately $67/month immediately, growing by $5.60/month each month. Over 12 months post-migration, cumulative savings exceed $1,000. Engineering cost of migration: approximately 3–5 engineering days. Break-even: first month.

Note

Safe Scale Check — Search Index Blast Radius: A search engine re-indexing operation — triggered by a schema change, a relevance tuning update, or a data correction — temporarily degrades search result quality or availability during the re-index window. Before any re-indexing operation, define the procedure: create a new index in parallel while the old index continues serving traffic, populate the new index from the source data, validate result quality against a representative query set, and cut over the search service to the new index. Never re-index in place on the production index. The blast radius of an in-place re-index failure is the complete loss of search functionality.

Architect's prompt 10.5: the search engine migration audit

When to use this: Use this prompt when evaluating whether to migrate product search from a database LIKE query to a dedicated search engine, or when auditing an existing search engine deployment for operational correctness.

```
Act as a Principal Search Architecture Engineer. I am evaluating the
migration of [Table/Service Name] from database LIKE queries to a
dedicated search engine.

Current state:
- Database: [type]
- Table row count: [N rows]
- Current search query volume: [X queries/sec]
- Current search p99 latency: [Nms]
- Search abandonment rate: [X%]
- IOPS consumed by search queries: [X% of provisioned]
- Query types: [list: exact match / full-text / faceted / geospatial]

(1) Evaluate whether the current query volume and complexity justify
    a dedicated search engine. Apply the migration signal thresholds.
(2) If migration is recommended, design the index schema:
    - Which fields are searchable? Which are filterable? Which are sortable?
    - What relevance boosting is required (recency, popularity, category)?
(3) Design the CDC pipeline from the source database to the search index:
    - What events trigger an index update?
    - What is the acceptable index freshness lag?
    - How are deletions propagated to the search index?
(4) Define the re-indexing procedure for schema changes:
    - Blue-green index swap: create new, validate, cut over, delete old
    - What query set validates result quality before cutover?
(5) Define the fallback behavior when the search engine is unavailable:
    - Fall back to database LIKE with a user-visible warning, or
    - Return a degraded response (no results) with a retry suggestion?
```

Summary

In this chapter, we performed the data layer surgery that the read optimizations of *Chapter 9* had been deferring.

We applied the Relational Default Rule to reject the NoSQL migration proposal for ShopFlow's Orders table, identifying that the bottleneck was write IOPS from index accumulation, not the relational model itself. The application-layer cost of abandoning SQL for a domain with strong relational requirements consistently exceeds the cost of correctly tuning the relational engine.

We applied the Partition-Before-Shard Rule to implement time-based partitioning of the Orders table as the first intervention, reducing lock contention to the current month's partition without the routing complexity, shard registry, or migration risk of a full sharding operation.

We designed the sharding key for the future state — a composite hash of customer_id modulo a fixed logical bucket count — using the Sharding Design Mandate to prevent the Hot Shard Anti-Pattern that emerges from semantic keys in skewed access distributions.

We executed the Index Audit and removed four low-usage or redundant indexes from the Orders table, reducing write IOPS by 36% and improving write p99 from 24 ms to 11 ms. The read performance on all affected queries was unchanged.

We implemented the DAL Isolation Rule, centralizing shard routing, replica selection, and search engine routing behind a Data Access Layer that shields application services from the complexity of the distributed data tier.

We migrated product search to a dedicated Elasticsearch deployment using the Search Engine Tax framework to make the operational cost explicit before committing, and migrated shipping labels from BYTEA columns to object storage, removing 730 GB of binary data from the relational store annually.

ShopFlow's telemetry after *Chapter 10*:

Metric	Before (Ch10 Start)	After (Ch10 End)	Change
Orders Table Write p99	24 ms	11 ms	54% improvement
Index write amplification	11 indexes per insert	7 indexes per insert	36% IOPS reduction
Database Write IOPS	71% of provisioned	44% of provisioned	27-point reduction
Product Search p99	1.8s (DB LIKE)	95 ms (Elasticsearch)	95% improvement

Metric	Before (Ch10 Start)	After (Ch10 End)	Change
Read Replica Lag (reporting)	8–45 seconds	8–45 seconds (unchanged)	Explicit contract is now documented
Orders Table Storage Growth Rate	2GB/day (incl. binary)	0.4GB/day (text only)	80% reduction
Cloud Spend	$9,600/mo	$9,400/mo	-$200 (net: IOPS and storage tier reductions, partly offset by the new Elasticsearch cluster and object storage)
Availability	99.8%	99.9%	Stable improvement

Table 10.10: ShopFlow telemetry before and after the Chapter 10 changes

The cliffhanger: the invisible failures

The data layer is healthy. Write p99 is back under 15ms. Product search is returning results in 95ms with relevance ranking. The index surgery freed up 27 points of write IOPS headroom.

But Dave is looking at the error rate dashboard and frowning at something that is not a spike. It is a floor.

ShopFlow's error rate has a persistent 0.3% baseline across all services. Not a spike that resolves — a constant low hum of failures distributed across the system. Dave pulls up the individual service error logs. Order service: 0.2% error rate. Inventory service: 0.1% error rate. Payment service: 0.3% error rate. Each service appears healthy in isolation. No circuit breakers have opened. No alerts have fired.

But the 0.3% of users who hit these errors are not seeing retries or graceful degradation. They are seeing silent failures: a checkout that appears to complete but generates no order confirmation, a search result that appears but links to a product page that returns a 404, a payment that is charged but whose confirmation never reaches the order service.

The infrastructure is correctly instrumented for infrastructure metrics. It is not instrumented for what matters: the user's journey from browser to database and back. A 0.3% error rate across 50,000 daily checkouts is 150 failed orders per day. 150 customers charged with no confirmation. 150 potential chargebacks. This is not a monitoring problem. It is an observability problem.

In *Chapter 11*, we build the observability layer that makes distributed system failures visible at the user journey level — distributed tracing, structured logging, correlation IDs, and the feedback loops that turn silent failures into actionable alerts before they become customer impacts.

Part 4

Operating at Scale: Observability, Resilience, and Efficiency

A system that can scale is not the same as a system you can run. This part is about operating ShopFlow at scale without going broke or going dark. You will build the observability to see what a distributed system is actually doing, design the resilience that lets it degrade gracefully instead of collapsing, tune performance and plan capacity so that you provision for reality instead of fear, and bring the cloud bill under control by making cost a first-class engineering metric. By the end of this part, the system is not just large. It is observable, resilient, and economically sustainable.

This part of the book includes the following chapters:

- *Chapter 11, Observability: Seeing and Understanding Your System*
- *Chapter 12, Resilience and High Availability: Designing for Failure*
- *Chapter 13, Performance Tuning and Capacity Planning*
- *Chapter 14, Cost Optimization and Efficiency (FinOps)*

11

Observability – Seeing and Understanding Your System

In *Chapter 10*, the data layer surgery was complete. Write p99 was back under 15ms. Product search was returning results in 95ms. The index audit freed up 27 points of write IOPS headroom.

But Dave's dashboard showed a number that none of the infrastructure metrics explained: a 0.3% persistent error rate spread across every service, steady as a floor, never spiking, never clearing. Each service appeared healthy. No circuit breakers opened. No alerts fired.

The 0.3% was 150 failed checkout sessions per day: 150 customers whose payment was processed with no order confirmation. 150 potential chargebacks. The infrastructure was correctly instrumented. The user journey was not.

This is the observability gap. Monitoring tells you whether your servers are up. Observability tells you whether your users are succeeding. At the scale ShopFlow has reached — global services, async messaging, distributed sagas, layered caching — monitoring is necessary and insufficient. In this chapter, we build the observability layer that closes the gap.

In this chapter, we are going to cover the following main topics:

- **Correlation and Traceability:** Connecting the dots across the stack.
- **Deep Observability:** Identifying hidden signals and silent failures.
- **The Feedback Loop:** Moving from monitoring to automated action.
- **Dynamic Telemetry:** Managing log volume and cost without losing visibility.
- **Building Self-Healing Systems:** Systems that watch and correct themselves.

Technical requirements

OpenTelemetry SDK (otel-sdk): The vendor-neutral instrumentation standard. Instruments traces, metrics, and logs with a single SDK. Every new service must be instrumented with OpenTelemetry from day one—retrofitting is significantly more expensive.

Jaeger/Tempo (distributed tracing backend): Stores and queries distributed traces. Jaeger is self-hosted; Tempo integrates with the Grafana stack. Both accept OpenTelemetry trace export.

Prometheus + Grafana: Metrics collection and visualization. Grafana dashboards for per-service Golden Signals. Prometheus alerting rules for the actionable alert set.

Structured logging (JSON output): Every log line must be a JSON object with a defined schema: timestamp, service name, trace ID, span ID, severity, message, and key-value pairs for contextual fields. Unstructured logs are not parseable at scale.

Feature-flag-controlled log verbosity: A configuration system that allows per-component log level overrides at runtime, without a deployment. LaunchDarkly, Azure App Configuration, or a custom configuration service all support this pattern.

Alertmanager / PagerDuty: Alert routing and escalation. Alertmanager applies routing rules to Prometheus alerts before they reach PagerDuty. The routing rules are where the 90% noise reduction happens.

Code Repository: `https://github.com/imran-siddique/Architecting-at-Scale/tree/main/ch11`

Tool Category	Open Source Options	Managed Options	Best For ShopFlow	Operational Cost
Distributed Tracing	Jaeger, Tempo, Zipkin	Datadog APM, Honeycomb, New Relic	Tempo + Grafana (already in stack)	Low — integrates with existing Prometheus/ Grafana
Metrics + Alerting	Prometheus + Alertmanager	Datadog, Dynatrace	Prometheus + Alertmanager (existing)	Very low—already deployed

Tool Category	Open Source Options	Managed Options	Best For ShopFlow	Operational Cost
Log aggregation	Loki, Elasticsearch (ELK)	Datadog Logs, Splunk, Sumo Logic	Loki (Grafana stack integration)	Low — pay-per-GB ingestion
Synthetic Monitoring	Playwright + Checkly, k6	Datadog Synthetics, Pingdom	Checkly for checkout flow monitoring	Low — per-monitor pricing
AI Response Quality	RAGAS, LangSmith, custom eval pipeline	Arize, Weights and Biases, Evidently AI	Custom eval pipeline (maximum flexibility)	Medium — eval pipeline engineering cost

Table 11.1: Observability tooling by category, with the ShopFlow selection and its operational cost

ShopFlow telemetry snapshot [stage 11]

```
The Signal: Infrastructure metrics are green. User outcomes are not. 0.3% of
checkout sessions fail silently – payment processed, order not confirmed, customer
not notified. The system cannot distinguish these failures from noise because it
has no user journey instrumentation. Observability is the gap between
infrastructure health and user success.
Infrastructure Availability: 99.9% (All services healthy by infrastructure
definition)
User Journey Success Rate (Checkout): 99.7% (● 0.3% silent failures – not visible
in service health)
Failed Orders per Day (silent): ~150 (● Payment captured, order not confirmed)
Mean Time to Detect (MTTD): Not applicable (● Failures are not being detected –
only discovered via chargebacks)
Distributed Trace Coverage: 0% (● No cross-service trace instrumentation)
Alert Volume (current): 400+ per hour (● 90%+ are noise – no actionable signal
distinguishable)
Log Volume: 50TB/day (● Engineers spend 4+ hours per incident searching logs)
p99 Latency: 11ms (write) / 95ms (search) (Healthy – infrastructure is not the
problem)
Panic Meter: 6/10 (The infrastructure metrics look fine. The customer experience
does not.)
```

Note

Dave Alert: "Our availability is 99.9% and I got a chargeback complaint from a customer who was charged with no order. I pulled every log I have. I can see the payment succeeded. I cannot see where the order confirmation went. We have 50TB of logs per day and I cannot find one transaction."

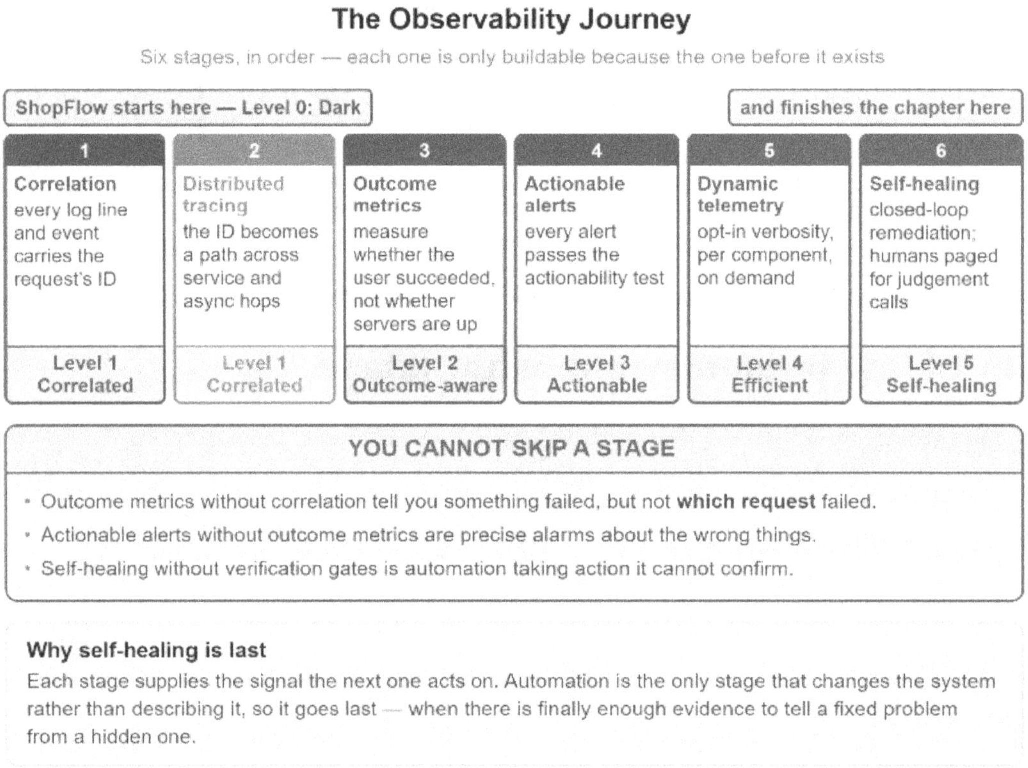

Figure 11.1: The Observability Journey

The five sections of this chapter are that progression in order, and the order is not arbitrary — each stage is only buildable because the one before it exists. Correlation comes first, because without a shared identifier there is no way to ask a question about a single request. Distributed tracing turns that identifier into a path. Outcome metrics change the question from 'is the service up?' to 'did the user succeed?', which is the question ShopFlow currently cannot answer. Actionable alerts are only definable once outcome metrics exist, because before that there is nothing worth paging on. Dynamic telemetry makes the volume affordable. Self-healing closes the loop, and it is last for a reason: automation without the verification signal from the previous four stages is a system taking action it cannot confirm.

ShopFlow is at Level 0 today. Every infrastructure signal is green, and not one of them describes a user. The 0.3% is invisible because nothing in the stack is instrumented to see it.

Correlation and traceability: connecting the dots across the stack

The hardest part of distributed tracing is not the technology. It is the assumption that tracing requires a perfect, unbroken chain of correlation IDs from the user's browser to every downstream database call and back. That assumption is wrong, and it causes teams to defer tracing instrumentation indefinitely because the "complete" solution seems unachievable.

In any system of meaningful age and complexity — one with third-party integrations, legacy components that cannot be modified, external payment processors, and carrier APIs — a perfect end-to-end correlation chain is not possible. You cannot instrument the payment processor's internal systems. You cannot add a trace header to a carrier's shipping API response. The chain will break at the boundaries you do not control.

The answer is not to wait for the perfect solution. The answer is to make every system you do control emit unique, correlatable identifiers and to maintain the mappings that let observability tooling stitch the picture together from the fragments you have.

> Note
>
> **The Pragmatic Correlation Rule:** You cannot trace what you do not control. For every system boundary you do not own — third-party APIs, legacy services, external processors — accept that the trace chain will break there. Compensate by ensuring that every system you do own emits events with unique, stable identifiers, and that the mapping between identifiers at each boundary is explicitly recorded. A partial trace with clear boundary markers is more valuable than no trace.

The correlation ID chain

A Correlation ID is a unique identifier assigned to a user request at the point it enters the system — typically at the API Gateway or CDN edge — and propagated through every downstream service call, message queue event, database write, and log line for the lifetime of that request.

ShopFlow's checkout silent failure is directly caused by the absence of a Correlation ID. The payment service records a successful payment. The saga orchestrator records a

PaymentConfirmed event. The order service records... nothing, because the PaymentConfirmed event was consumed and discarded without producing the expected OrderConfirmed event. Without a Correlation ID threading through all three records, Dave's 50TB of daily logs cannot answer the question: what happened to order 1234 between payment confirmation and order confirmation?

With a Correlation ID, the answer is a single query: find all log lines and events where correlation_id = 'checkout_abc123'. The payment record appears. The PaymentConfirmed event appears. The absence of the OrderConfirmed event is itself the finding. The gap between the last event and the expected next event points directly to the service that failed to produce its output.

Note

The Correlation Mandate: Every log line, every event, every database write in a distributed system must carry the Correlation ID of the originating request. This is not a nice-to-have. You cannot debug a distributed system at scale without it. The cost of adding a Correlation ID to every log line is one field. The cost of debugging a silent failure without it is measured in engineer-hours per incident.

Note

Tool Tax — correlation ID propagation: Making the ID mandatory is a framework change, not a logging change. Budget for instrumenting every service including the ones nobody wants to touch, context propagation across thread and async boundaries where it silently drops, header-to-payload translation at every broker hop, and the coverage audit that proves it is at 100% rather than 95%. Partial propagation is the expensive state: it looks instrumented and fails precisely on the unusual code paths that produce the failures you are trying to trace.

Note

The ID Chain Discipline: A Correlation ID that is present on 95% of requests is not a Correlation ID — it is a correlation suggestion. The 5% of requests without a Correlation ID are statistically likely to be the requests that fail in unusual ways, because they represent code paths that were not tested with the same rigor as the happy path. Correlation ID propagation must be enforced by the service framework, not by developer discipline. If adding a Correlation ID requires a conscious decision by the developer writing each log line, it will be absent from the log lines written under deadline pressure.

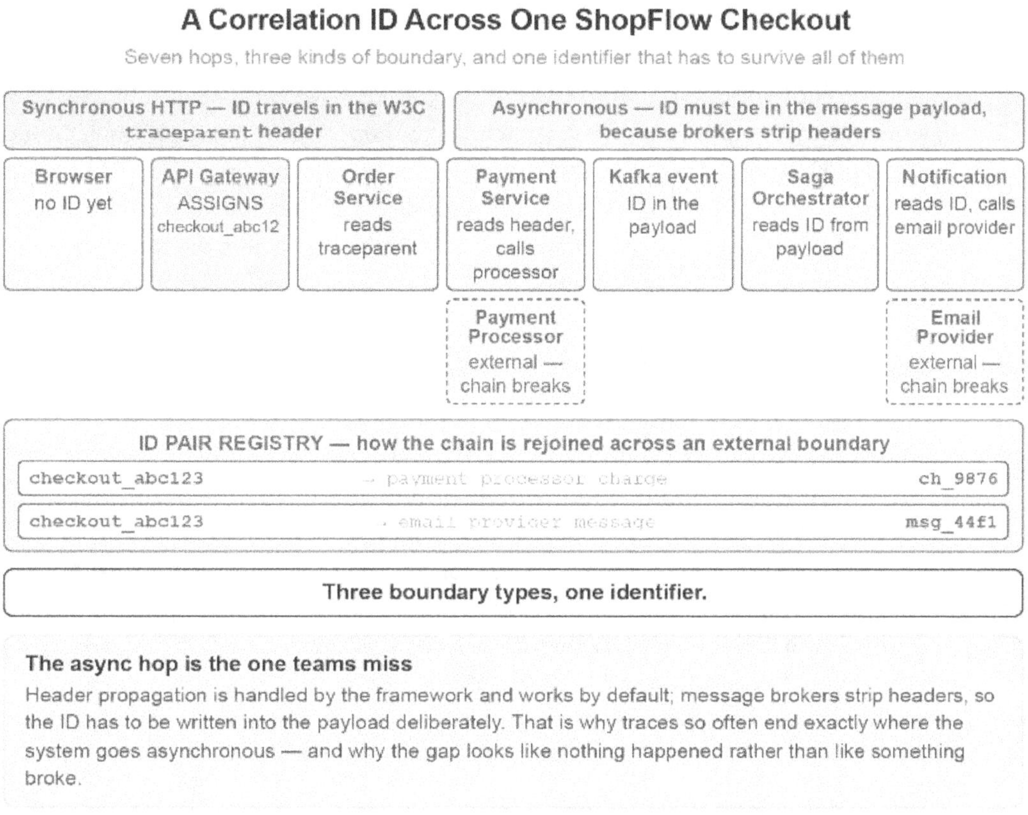

Figure 11.2: A Correlation ID Across One ShopFlow Checkout

Following one real checkout, hop by hop, shows where the identifier travels differently and where it cannot travel at all.

1. Browser → API Gateway. The request arrives with no correlation ID. The gateway generates one — checkout_abc123 — and this is the only place in the system where an ID is created. Every downstream hop propagates; none of them mint.
2. API Gateway → Order Service. A synchronous HTTP call. The ID travels in the W3C traceparent header, and the framework—not the developer—attaches it.
3. Order Service → Payment Service. Still synchronous, still the header. Both services write log lines carrying checkout_abc123, which is what makes the two sets of logs joinable.
4. Payment Service → external payment processor. The first boundary break. The processor will not accept a ShopFlow trace header and will not return one. It returns its own charge ID, ch_9876. The service writes an ID Pair Registry entry at the moment of the call, and the chain is bridged rather than continued.
5. Payment Service → Kafka. The first asynchronous hop, and the one teams most often get wrong. The correlation ID must be written into the message payload, not only into a message header — brokers, bridges, and dead-letter requeues can all strip headers, and a header-only ID disappears silently at exactly the hop where the trace matters most.
6. Kafka → Saga Orchestrator. The consumer reads the ID from the payload and re-establishes it as the ambient context for everything it logs. The trace survives the async gap because the ID was carried as data.
7. Saga Orchestrator → Notification Service → external email provider. A second boundary break, handled the same way: the provider's own message ID is recorded against checkout_abc123 in the registry.

Seven hops, three kinds of boundary: synchronous calls where the header carries the ID, asynchronous hops where the payload must, and external systems where nothing carries it and the registry records the handoff instead. ShopFlow's silent failure lives at hop 6 — the saga orchestrator consumed the event and produced nothing — and it stays invisible until every hop before it shares one identifier.

The ID-Pair registry pattern

At the boundaries where correlation chains break — the payment processor, the carrier API, the legacy authentication service — the system cannot propagate its internal Correlation ID into the external system. But the external system returns its own transaction ID: the payment processor returns a charge ID, the carrier returns a tracking number, the legacy service returns a session token.

The ID Pair Registry solves this by recording the mapping between the internal Correlation ID and the external system's ID at the moment of the API call. When Dave investigates a failed order, he queries the registry: "what external charge ID corresponds to correlation_id = checkout_abc123?" The registry returns the payment processor's charge ID. Dave can then query the payment processor's own logging with that charge ID. The trace chain is broken at the boundary, but the gap can be bridged manually using the registry.

The registry is a simple key-value store — Redis or a dedicated database table — with entries like: {correlation_id: 'checkout_abc123', external_system: 'payment_processor', external_id: 'ch_1234567890', timestamp: '2024-01-15T09:00:01Z'}. It is written by the service at the moment of the external call. It is queried by the incident investigation tooling. It converts an impenetrable boundary into a documented handoff.

> Note
>
> **Tool Tax — distributed tracing:** Traces are the highest-volume telemetry a system produces and the most expensive to keep. Budget for a sampling strategy that keeps the traces you will actually need, retention that is short enough to afford and long enough to investigate, per-span cardinality discipline before a well-meaning attribute makes the backend unqueryable, and the SDK upgrade treadmill across every service. An unsampled tracing backend is a second production system with its own capacity planning.

Boundary Type	Problem	ID Pair Registry Entry	Investigation Value
External payment processor	Cannot propagate internal correlation ID into processor logs	correlation_id → charge_id	Bridge to payment processor's own support tools when charge disputes arise

Boundary Type	Problem	ID Pair Registry Entry	Investigation Value
Carrier shipping API	Carrier returns tracking number; no shared trace context	correlation_id → tracking_number	Link order failures to specific carrier events
Legacy authentication service	Old service cannot accept or emit trace headers	correlation_id → legacy_session_token	Correlate auth failures with specific user sessions in legacy logs
Third-party fraud scoring API	External model returns a score with its own request ID	correlation_id → fraud_request_id	Investigate why a specific order was flagged without sharing shipping fraud scorer internals with the investigation
Email delivery provider	Provider assigns its own message ID	correlation_id → email_message_id	Diagnose delivery failures without access to provider infrastructure

Table 11.2: External boundaries where the correlation chain breaks, and the ID Pair Registry entry that bridges each

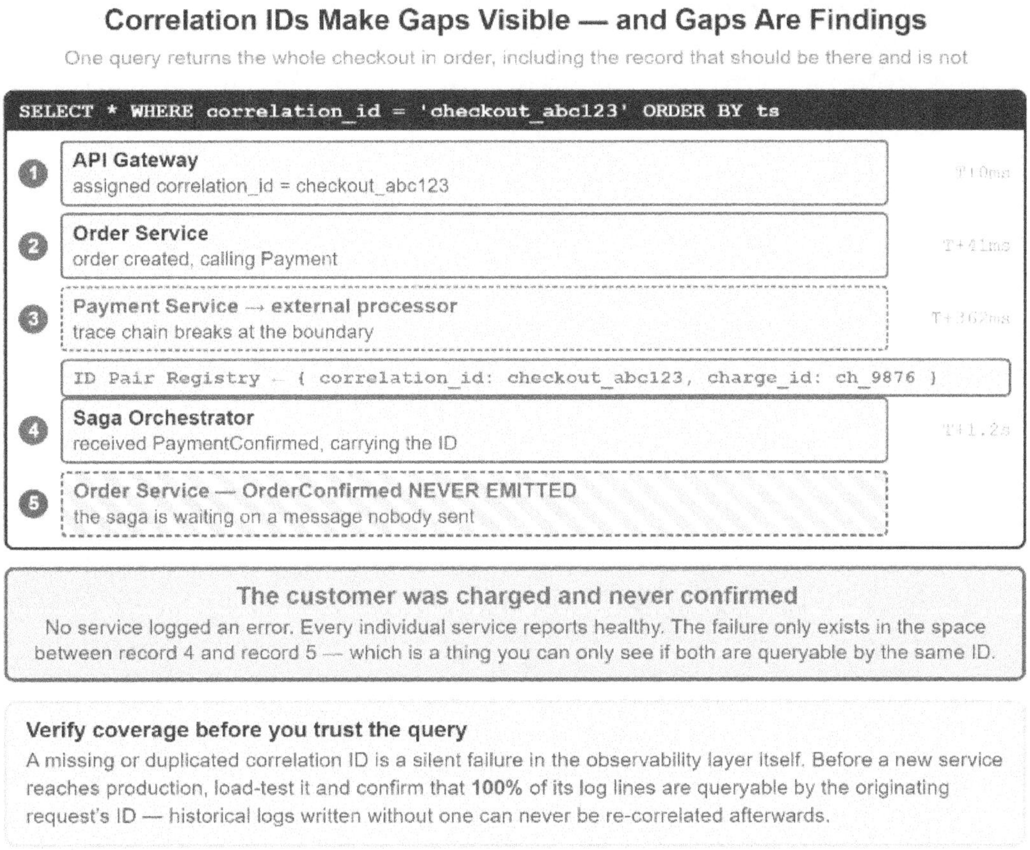

Figure 11.3: The Correlation ID Chain with ID Pair Registry

Note

Safe Scale Check — Correlation ID Blast Radius: A missing or duplicated Correlation ID is a silent failure in the observability layer itself. Before deploying a new service to production, verify that 100% of log lines and events emitted by that service carry the Correlation ID. Run a 10-minute load test and confirm that every log line is queryable by the Correlation ID of its originating request. An observability gap in a new service is harder to patch retroactively than a code bug — the historical logs without Correlation IDs cannot be re-correlated after the fact.

Architect's prompt 11.1: the correlation coverage audit

When to use this: Use this prompt before deploying a new service to production or when diagnosing a silent failure that cannot be traced across service boundaries. The output is a correlation coverage map that identifies every gap in the trace chain.

```
Act as a Principal Observability Engineer. I am auditing the correlation
coverage for the following service dependency graph:

[Paste service dependency graph with external system boundaries marked]

For each service-to-service call:
(1) Verify that the calling service propagates the Correlation ID in the
    request header (W3C traceparent or custom header).
(2) Verify that the receiving service reads the Correlation ID from the
    header and includes it in all log lines and events it emits.

For each external system boundary:
(3) Identify the external system's own transaction ID format.
(4) Verify that the calling service writes an ID Pair Registry entry
    at the moment of the external call: {correlation_id, external_system,
    external_id, timestamp}.

For each message queue or event bus hop:
(5) Verify that the Correlation ID is included in the message payload
    (not just the message header, which may be stripped by the broker).

Output:
- Correlation coverage map: each hop marked as Covered / Gap / External Boundary
- For each Gap: the specific field that must be added to close it
- For each External Boundary: the ID Pair Registry schema for that system
- Estimated engineering effort to close all Gaps
```

Deep observability: identifying hidden signals and silent failures

Infrastructure monitoring and observability are not the same thing. Monitoring measures whether the infrastructure is up. Observability measures whether the system is doing what it is supposed to do for the people who depend on it.

ShopFlow's 99.9% infrastructure availability coexists with 150 silent checkout failures per day. Every server is up. Every service is responding. Every circuit breaker is closed. The infrastructure is healthy. The users are not. This is the observability gap: the distance between 'the system is running' and 'the system is delivering value.'

> Note
>
> **Anti-Pattern: The Uptime Illusion:** Reporting infrastructure availability as the primary system health metric. Four nines of availability ("we're up 99.99% of the time") is a vanity metric when responses are incorrect, slow for specific user segments, or silently failing for specific transaction types. A system that is available and wrong is worse than a system that is unavailable and honest. Availability is necessary. It is not sufficient.

The outcome quality signal

In the AI era, this distinction becomes existential. A system that serves AI-generated responses can be 100% available and simultaneously deliver responses that are incorrect, hallucinated, or harmful. The infrastructure uptime metric tells you nothing about response quality. An AI system without outcome quality instrumentation is operating in a state of systematic blindness: the servers are up, the responses are going out, and you have no signal that any of them are right.

This is not unique to AI systems. It is the general form of the observability gap that ShopFlow is experiencing. Payment processed but order not confirmed: availability is 100%, outcome quality is 0% for that transaction. The metric that matters is not 'was the payment API available?' It is 'did the user's checkout succeed end to end?'

> Note
>
> **The Outcome Quality Rule:** For every user-facing flow, define the outcome metric: the binary measure of whether the flow delivered its intended result to the user. Checkout outcome: did the user receive an order confirmation? Search outcome: did the user click a result? Documentation outcome: did the user find their answer without reformulating the query? These metrics are not derivable from infrastructure health metrics. They require explicit instrumentation of the user journey endpoints.

Choosing the first outcome metric

The instinct on reading that rule is to enumerate every flow in the system and instrument all of them. That produces a six-month project that delivers nothing until it is finished, and it is the most common way outcome observability stalls before it ever ships. Start with one or two P0 journeys, prove the value, then expand.

> Note
>
> **The First Two Metrics Rule:** Instrument the smallest number of user journeys that would have caught your most expensive recent failure — for most systems that is one or two. Ship them, confirm they fire on a real incident, and only then add the next. Outcome observability that covers two journeys and is trusted is worth more than a plan to cover twenty that is still in design review.

For ShopFlow the choice is made by the incident already in progress. Checkout completion — did the customer receive an order confirmation? — is the metric that would have surfaced the 150 daily silent failures on day one instead of via chargebacks weeks later. Payment confirmation — did the payment capture produce a confirmed order? — is the second, because it isolates which half of the checkout path broke. Two metrics, both emitted by the saga orchestrator at steps it already executes, and between them they cover the entire revenue-bearing path.

Everything else waits. Search-to-click rate, email delivery confirmation, account creation completion — each is a legitimate outcome metric, and none of them is losing $675,000 a month. Add them as those journeys become P0, or as an incident proves they should have been instrumented already. Outcome observability is not a project with an end date; it evolves alongside the application, one journey at a time.

Infrastructure Metric	What It Tells You	What It Misses	Outcome Metric That Closes the Gap
Service availability (uptime %)	Whether the service is responding to health probes	Whether responses are correct or useful	End-to-end success rate: did the user's intent succeed?
API p99 latency	Whether the API is responding within SLO	Whether the response is the right response	User-perceived completion time: time from request to successful outcome
Error rate (5xx)	Whether the server is returning errors	Silent failures that return 200 with incorrect data	Business transaction success rate by transaction type

Infrastructure Metric	What It Tells You	What It Misses	Outcome Metric That Closes the Gap
CPU / memory utilization	Whether the server has compute headroom	Whether the compute is doing useful work	Useful work ratio: requests producing correct outcomes / total requests
Queue depth	Whether consumers are keeping up with producers	Whether consumed messages are being processed correctly	Message outcome rate: processed-and-succeeded/ consumed
AI model availability	Whether the inference endpoint is responding	Whether responses are accurate, relevant, or safe	Response quality score: accuracy, relevance, safety measured per request

Table 11.3: Infrastructure metrics, what each one misses, and the outcome metric that closes the gap

The golden signals applied to ShopFlow

The four Golden Signals — Latency, Traffic, Errors, and Saturation — are the minimum observable metrics for any production service. They are necessary but not sufficient for outcome quality observability. ShopFlow's silent failure cannot be found in the Golden Signals alone because it produces no error — all services return 200. The failure is in the outcome, not in the infrastructure signal.

The correct observability stack layers the Golden Signals at the infrastructure level with business transaction signals at the outcome level, and user journey signals that correlate the two.

Signal Layer	Metrics	ShopFlow Implementation	What It Catches
Infrastructure (Golden Signals)	Latency, traffic, errors, saturation per service	Prometheus + Grafana per-service dashboard	Service degradation, capacity issues, network errors

Signal Layer	Metrics	ShopFlow Implementation	What It Catches
Business Transaction	Checkout success rate, payment capture rate, order confirmation rate	Custom counters emitted by Saga Orchestrator at each step completion	Silent failures: steps that complete infrastructure-successfully but business-unsuccessfully
User Journey	End-to-end checkout completion, search-to-click rate, email delivery rate	Synthetic monitors + frontend instrumentation + event consumer success metrics	Cross-service failures invisible to individual service health
Outcome Quality (AI)	Response accuracy rate, relevance score, safety flag rate	LLM-as-judge or human-in-the-loop evaluation pipeline	Model degradation invisible to infrastructure metrics

Table 11.4: The four observability signal layers and the class of failure each one catches

Note

The Signal Hierarchy Rule: Infrastructure signals tell you whether the system is running. Business transaction signals tell you whether the system is completing its work. User journey signals tell you whether users are succeeding. Outcome quality signals tell you whether the success is real. Each layer is necessary. No single layer is sufficient. An alerting strategy that covers only the infrastructure layer is missing the three layers where most user-impacting failures live.

Note

The AI Outcome Gap: AI-powered services require a fourth observability dimension beyond the Golden Signals: response quality. A language model endpoint that returns HTTP 200 with a hallucinated answer is indistinguishable from a correct response at the infrastructure layer. Outcome quality for AI services must be measured at the

> response level — through automated evaluation pipelines, user feedback signals, or LLM-as-judge scoring — not at the transport layer. Every AI service in production without response quality instrumentation is operating in a state of systematic outcome blindness.

> Note
>
> **Manager's Math — The Cost of Undetected Silent Failures:** ShopFlow's 150 silent checkout failures per day represent approximately $22,500 in daily order value at ShopFlow's current average order value of $150, or $675,000 per month in revenue that is charged but not confirmed. Each failed checkout has a chargeback risk of approximately 15%, representing $101,250 per month in potential chargeback exposure. Engineering cost to implement outcome-level observability (saga orchestrator business metrics + end-to-end synthetic monitors): approximately 5–8 engineering days. The observability investment pays back in the first week of operation.

Architect's prompt 11.2: the outcome observability design

When to use this: Use this prompt when a system has infrastructure monitoring but is missing business transaction and user journey observability layers. The output is a layered metrics plan that closes the gap between infrastructure health and user outcome.

```
Act as a Principal Observability Architect. I am designing the outcome
observability layer for the following user-facing flows:

[List each critical user flow: e.g. Checkout, Search, Account creation]

For each flow:
(1) Define the outcome metric: what is the binary measure of whether
    this flow delivered its intended result to the user?
(2) Identify where in the system this outcome metric can be instrumented:
    - At which service does a successful outcome first become observable?
    - What event or log line signals success vs. silent failure?
(3) Design the business transaction counter:
    - Metric name: [flow]_outcome_total{status=success|failure|silent_failure}
    - Where is it emitted: [service name and specific code location]
    - What constitutes a silent failure vs. an explicit error?
```

```
(4) Design the user journey synthetic monitor:
    - What sequence of API calls validates end-to-end success?
    - What is the acceptable p99 for the full sequence?
    - How frequently does the monitor run?
(5) Define the alert threshold:
    - At what outcome success rate does an alert fire?
    - Is the alert routed to PagerDuty (human required) or to automated
      remediation (system can self-correct)?
```

The feedback loop: moving from monitoring to automated action

The standard incident response model is: alert fires, engineer is paged, engineer reads runbook, engineer takes action, system recovers. This model has a Dave-shaped bottleneck in the middle. The engineer is the single point of failure in the recovery path. If the engineer is unavailable, asleep, or already handling another incident, the recovery time extends by however long it takes to reach them.

The goal is to remove Dave from the recovery path for every failure the system can diagnose and fix itself. Not to eliminate Dave — Dave's judgment is irreplaceable for novel failures and architectural decisions. To free Dave from the repetitive, rule-based recovery work that should never have required a human in the first place.

> Note
>
> **Anti-Pattern: The Runbook Dependency:** A system whose recovery from known failure modes requires a human to read a runbook and execute manual steps. Every runbook step that is not automated is a single point of failure in the recovery path. The presence of a runbook for a failure mode is evidence that the failure mode is understood. If it is understood, it can be automated. If it can be automated, the runbook should be replaced with code.

The 90% alert reduction

Alert fatigue is not a volume problem. It is a signal-to-noise problem. An alerting system that pages engineers 400 times per hour has a signal-to-noise problem, not an engineering staffing problem. The engineers are not the solution to too many alerts. Fewer alerts are the solution.

The systematic approach to alert reduction starts with a single question applied to every existing alert: in the last 30 days, what percentage of the time this alert fired did an engineer take a meaningful action as a result? If the answer is less than 50%, the alert is noise — by definition. It is training engineers to ignore the alerting system. Every ignored alert raises the cognitive cost of the genuine alerts that follow it.

The analysis of ShopFlow's 400 alerts per hour is almost certainly going to show the same distribution that appears in every system at this stage: a small number of alerts (10–15%) that reliably require human action, a large number (40–50%) that are pure noise—transient conditions that self-resolve before an engineer can respond—and a middle category (35–45%) that sometimes require action and sometimes do not, which can be converted to automated remediation with defined triggers.

At a high-traffic enterprise platform, this analysis — carried out over several months with systematic review of every alert's action history — reduced the alert volume by 90%. The remaining 10% of alerts were all actionable. The engineering team's response time to genuine incidents improved significantly because the signal was no longer buried in noise.

> Note
>
> **The Actionability Test:** Every alert in the system must pass a single test: if this alert fires at 3:00 AM, is there a specific, well-understood action that the on-call engineer can take within 10 minutes that will materially improve the situation? If the answer is no — if the alert fires and the engineer can only watch and wait — the alert should not page a human. It should either trigger automated remediation or route to a dashboard for morning review.

Reducing alert noise without losing the signal

A 90% reduction is the destination, not the maneuver. Deleting 360 alerts in an afternoon is how a team discovers, three weeks later, that one of them was the only warning of a failure mode nobody had written down. Alert rationalization is iterative, and each iteration has to earn the next.

1. **Review the history, not the rule.** For every alert, pull the last 30 days: how often it fired, how long it lasted, and what action was recorded against it. The alert definition tells you what someone once feared. The history tells you what actually happens.
2. **Measure actionability, and write the number down.** Score each alert with a single figure: the percentage of fires that led to a specific human action within 10 minutes. This converts an argument about whether an alert is useful into a number that can be compared.
3. **Convert one category at a time.** Take the single largest category — usually short-lived latency spikes — and change only that one. Convert it to a dashboard metric or to automated remediation with a verification gate. Leave every other alert untouched.

4. **Validate before continuing.** Run for two weeks. Confirm that no incident in that window went undetected because of the change, and that the on-call engineers agree the signal improved. If an incident was missed, restore that category and understand why before touching anything else.
5. **Repeat with the next category.** Each pass is smaller and safer than the last, because the noise floor has dropped and the remaining alerts are easier to evaluate against it.

> Note
>
> **The Rationalization Ratchet:** Alert reduction moves in one direction and only after evidence. Never suppress an alert category without 30 days of history showing it is not actionable; never change more than one category per cycle; and never proceed to the next category until the previous change has survived a validation window without a missed incident. A team that deletes alerts faster than it can validate the deletions is not reducing noise — it is transferring risk from the alerting system to the incident that has not happened yet.

Run this way, ShopFlow's 400 alerts per hour take a quarter to rationalize rather than a weekend, and the 90% reduction arrives as a series of validated steps, each one reversible.

Metric Signal	**Actionability**	**Route To**	**Alert Body Must Include**
Checkout outcome success rate < 99%	Immediate human action required	PagerDuty — on-call engineer	Failing transaction sample, saga trace, correlation IDs
P99 latency spike < 60 seconds	No action — self-resolving	Dashboard only — no page	N/A — suppressed
Circuit breaker opens on P0 path	Automated: shift traffic; human if fallback also fails	Automated first; PagerDuty only on fallback failure	Dependency health, fallback path status, error sample
Queue consumer lag > SLO for 3+ mins	Automated: scale consumer; human if lag persists	Automated first; PagerDuty only if lag does not decrease	Lag time series, consumer throughput, message sample

Metric Signal	Actionability	Route To	Alert Body Must Include
Memory utilization > 85%	Automated: alert if OOM follows; else dashboard	Dashboard only unless an OOM crash occurs	Memory profile trend, heap snapshot if available
Replication lag > 60 seconds	Human required — data consistency risk	PagerDuty immediate	Lag time series, write volume at lag onset, network metrics

Table 11.5: Alert signals routed by actionability, and the context each alert body must carry

Alert Category	Actionability Test Result	Correct Disposition	Volume Reduction
P99 latency spike lasting < 60 seconds	No action — self-resolves before engineer can respond	Convert to dashboard metric; suppress alert	High — typically 30–40% of all alerts
Memory utilization > 80% threshold	Depends — if OOM follows, restart is automated; if not, it stabilizes	Convert to automated: if memory OOM → auto-restart; else suppress	Medium — 10–15% of alerts
Circuit breaker opens on non-critical path	No human action required — breaker handles it	Route to dashboard only; suppress alert	Medium — 10–15% of alerts
Checkout outcome success rate < 99%	Yes — immediate investigation required; revenue impact	Page on-call engineer; include saga trace context in alert body	Low — these are the alerts worth keeping
Database write p99 > 2x baseline for > 5 minutes	Yes — index contention or shard imbalance investigation needed	Page on-call engineer with query plan context	Low — keep this alert

Alert Category	Actionability Test Result	Correct Disposition	Volume Reduction
Retry storm detected (amplification > 1.5x)	Partial — automated throttle should fire; page if throttle fails	Automated throttle first; alert only if throttle does not arrest the storm	Medium — convert to automated first-line response

Table 11.6: Alert categories scored against the Actionability Test, with disposition and expected volume reduction

Note

The Self-Healing Mandate: Every failure mode that has a documented recovery procedure must have that procedure automated. The presence of a documented manual recovery step is a bug in the automation layer, not a feature of the operations process. Automated recovery is not optional for known failure modes — it is the definition of a system that does not require heroes.

Closed-Loop remediation

The feedback loop architecture has three components: the detection signal, the remediation action, and the verification gate.

The detection signal is the observable metric that indicates a remediable failure condition: memory utilization above the OOM threshold, container health probe failing, or queue consumer lag exceeding the SLO window. The signal must be specific enough to distinguish the failure condition from normal variance.

The **remediation action** is the automated response to the detection signal. Container restart. Horizontal scale-out. Consumer group rebalance. Traffic shift to a healthy region. The action must be bounded — it must have a maximum retry count and a fallback behavior when the automated action fails to resolve the condition.

The verification gate is the check that confirms the remediation was effective. After a container restart, does the health probe return healthy within 60 seconds? After a scale-out event, does the queue consumer lag begin declining within 120 seconds? If the verification gate fails—if the automated action did not resolve the condition—then and only then does the system page a human, with the full context of what was tried and what was observed.

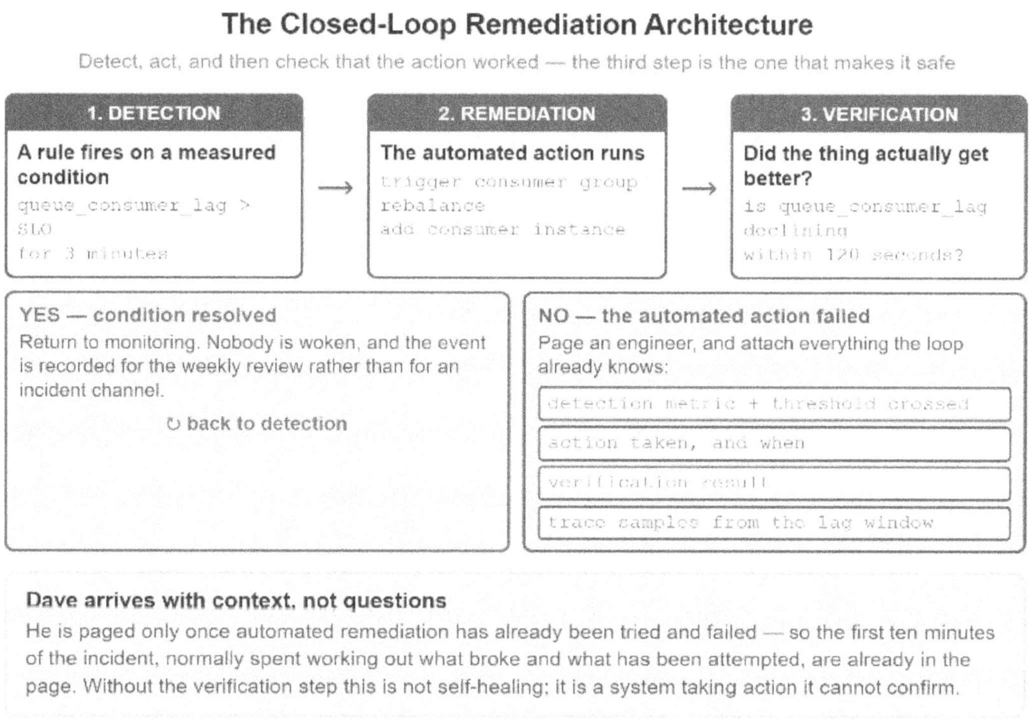

Figure 11.4: The Closed-Loop Remediation Architecture

Note

Manager's Math — The Alert Reduction ROI: ShopFlow's alerting fires at 400+ per hour at peak. At 8 minutes of genuine triage per alert — acknowledging, reading context, determining actionability, clearing or escalating — fully processing that volume would demand 53 engineer-hours for every hour that elapses. No on-call rotation has that capacity, and that is the finding rather than the cost: the alerts are not being triaged, they are being ignored, and the 10–15% that genuinely require action are being ignored alongside the noise. The right measure is therefore not the work the volume implies, but the work the team actually loses to it. ShopFlow runs a six-engineer on-call rotation; each engineer is primary for roughly five days a month and loses an estimated three hours per on-call day to alert triage and the context-switching around it. That is approximately 90 engineer-hours per month. A 90% reduction returns roughly 80 of those hours — about half a full-time engineer — which at a fully-loaded engineering cost is on the order of $90,000 annually. The larger return is the one this calculation cannot price: the P0 incidents that are now detected rather than buried. Substitute your own rotation size, on-call days, and triage hours; the conclusion holds for any realistic set of them.

Architect's prompt 11.3: the alert rationalization audit

When to use this: Use this prompt when alert fatigue is degrading the engineering team's ability to respond to genuine incidents or as a quarterly maintenance audit of the alerting system.

```
Act as a Principal Site Reliability Engineer specializing in observability.
I am rationalizing the alert set for a system with the following properties:

Current alert count: [N]
Current alert volume: [X alerts/hour at peak]
Current estimated actionability rate: [Y% of alerts require human action]
Engineering team on-call rotation: [N engineers, N-hour shifts]

I will provide the alert history for the last 30 days:
- Alert name, fire count, duration, and documented actions taken
[Paste alert history]

For each alert:
(1) Apply the Actionability Test: in the last 30 days, what percentage
    of fires resulted in a specific human action within 10 minutes?
(2) Classify as: Actionable (keep), Automatable (convert to remediation),
    or Noise (suppress).
(3) For Automatable alerts: design the closed-loop remediation:
    - Detection signal (specific metric and threshold)
    - Remediation action (specific automated step)
    - Verification gate (metric that confirms resolution)
    - Fallback: at what point does the system page a human?
(4) For Noise alerts: recommend suppression or dashboard-only routing.
(5) Calculate the projected alert volume reduction and engineer-hour
    recovery from implementing the classifications.
```

Dynamic telemetry: managing log volume and cost without losing visibility

ShopFlow currently generates 50TB of logs per day. Engineers spend 4+ hours per incident searching through them. Neither of these facts is a success. The first represents a cost that grows with system traffic regardless of whether the logs are useful. The second represents a failure of the observability architecture: if the signal is in the logs but takes 4 hours to find, the logs are not organized for investigation.

The standard response to high log volume is sampling: reduce the percentage of requests that generate detailed logs. The problem with global sampling is that it reduces the probability of capturing the logs for the specific request that caused the incident. A 1% sample rate means a 99% chance that the failing request's detailed logs were not captured. The investigation has to reconstruct the failure from aggregate metrics rather than from the specific failing transaction's trace.

The correct approach is not global sampling. It is **opt-in verbosity by component**.

> Note
>
> **The Opt-In Verbosity Rule:** Every component and service must support a minimum of three log verbosity levels: ERROR (always on, captures failures only), INFO (default on, captures significant state transitions), and DEBUG (off by default, captures all internal state). The verbosity level for each component must be configurable at runtime, without a deployment, scoped to a specific component ID or system ID. By default, DEBUG is off everywhere. When an investigation requires it, DEBUG is enabled for the specific component being investigated, for a bounded time window, then turned off automatically.

Note

The Log Retention Tiering Rule: Not all logs have the same retention value. ERROR and WARN logs should be retained for 90+ days — they are the historical record of system failures and the evidence base for long-term reliability improvements. INFO logs should be retained for 30 days — sufficient for incident investigation and trend analysis. DEBUG logs, when enabled, should be retained for 7 days maximum — they are investigative artifacts, not historical records. A retention policy that keeps all log levels for the same duration pays the storage cost of DEBUG logs for months after they cease to be useful.

The component ID pattern

The Opt-In Verbosity Rule requires that every loggable component in the system have a stable, unique Component ID — an identifier that the configuration system uses to route verbosity settings to the correct component.

The Component ID is not the service name. A service may contain dozens of components — the payment handler, the inventory checker, the saga state machine, the event publisher — each of which may need independent verbosity control. The payment handler may need DEBUG logging while the inventory checker's DEBUG output is noise for the current investigation.

The configuration is a simple map: {component_id: 'payment-handler', log_level: 'DEBUG', expires_at: '2024-01-15T11:00:00Z'}. The payment handler reads its configuration on a polling interval — typically 30 seconds — and adjusts its log output accordingly. When the expiry passes, the component automatically reverts to INFO. No deployment. No manual cleanup. No risk of forgetting to turn DEBUG off in production.

Note

Tool Tax — runtime verbosity control: Runtime configuration is a control plane, and a control plane is a dependency. Budget for the configuration service itself and its availability, a component-ID registry that stays accurate as services are refactored, the polling overhead in every process, an audit trail of who raised what and when, and a safe default when the config service is unreachable. A verbosity system that fails open to DEBUG is a log bill; one that fails closed to ERROR is an investigation you cannot run.

Log Level	Default State	Volume Impact	Information Captured	When to Enable
ERROR	Always on	Very low — only failure events	Exception stack traces, failure context, correlation ID	Cannot be disabled — errors are always captured
WARN	Always on	Low	Unexpected conditions that did not cause failure; threshold breaches	Cannot be disabled — warnings are signals
INFO	On by default	Medium — significant state transitions	Request received, payment processed, event emitted, saga step completed	Default for all production components
DEBUG	Off by default	High — all internal state	Every function call, every variable value, every branch taken	Enable per component ID during active investigation; auto-expire after 30 minutes
TRACE	Off by default	Very high — byte-level detail	Network packet contents, database query parameters, full request/response bodies	Enable only in isolated environments; never in production at scale

Table 11.7: Log verbosity levels, their default state, volume impact, and when each should be enabled

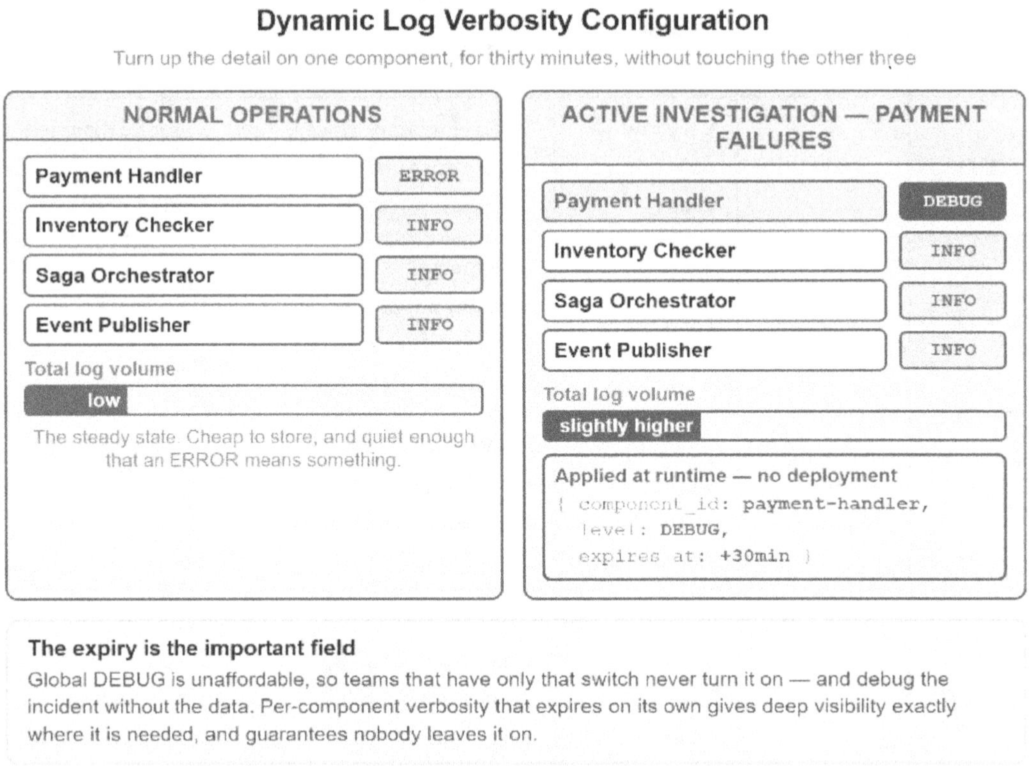

Figure 11.5: Dynamic Log Verbosity Configuration

Structured logging as the foundation

Opt-in verbosity only works if the logs themselves are machine-readable. A log line that reads 'Payment processing failed for user 12345' in a free-text format cannot be filtered, aggregated, or correlated at scale. A log line that is a JSON object with fields {timestamp, service, component_id, trace_id, span_id, level, user_id, order_id, payment_attempt, error_code, duration_ms} can be queried, aggregated, and correlated by any combination of its fields.

> **Note**
>
> **The Structured Log Mandate:** Every log line emitted by a production service must be a JSON object. Every JSON log line must include: timestamp (ISO 8601), service name, component ID, trace ID, span ID, severity level, and a human-readable message field. Additional contextual fields — user ID, order ID, payment attempt number, duration — must be included as top-level JSON fields, not embedded in the message string. A log line where the order ID is in the message string ('Processing order 1234') rather than as

a field ({order_id: '1234'}) is a log line that cannot be searched by order ID without a regex. At 50TB per day, regex search is not a viable investigation strategy.

Note

Tool Tax — structured logging: A log schema is an interface, and interfaces need governance. Budget for the schema itself, a shared library so services cannot drift, a migration path for the logs already written in the old format, and enforcement in review — because one service emitting order_id inside the message string is enough to break the query everyone else relies on. The tax is not the JSON; it is agreeing on the field names and keeping that agreement.

Note

Manager's Math — The Log Volume Cost: ShopFlow's 50TB per day of logs at a managed logging platform ingestion cost of approximately $0.50/GB ingested equals $750,000 per month in log storage. Implementing the Opt-In Verbosity Rule with INFO as the default reduces this by the proportion of current logs that are DEBUG-level output from always-verbose services. In most systems without verbosity controls, 60–70% of log volume is DEBUG output that is never queried. A 60% reduction — achievable by setting INFO as the default and enabling DEBUG only on demand — reduces the log bill from $750K to $300K per month, saving $450,000 per month — $5.4 million annually. The engineering cost to implement the Component ID pattern and dynamic configuration: approximately 5–10 engineering days.

Architect's prompt 11.4: the log volume rationalization

When to use this: Use this prompt when log storage costs are growing faster than system traffic or when incident investigation time is dominated by log search rather than diagnosis.

```
Act as a Principal Observability Engineer. I am rationalizing the log
volume for a system with the following properties:

Current log volume: [X TB/day]
Current log storage cost: [$Y/month]
```

```
Current log retention policy: [N days]
Current log verbosity: [Uniform level for all components / Mixed]
Average incident investigation time spent in log search: [X hours]

I will provide a sample of the current log output for 5 representative
components:
[Paste log samples]

(1) For each log sample, identify:
    - Is this a structured JSON log or free-text?
    - What verbosity level is this log line at?
    - Is the log line queryable by Correlation ID, user ID, and
      transaction ID without regex?
(2) Estimate the proportion of current log volume by level
    (ERROR / WARN / INFO / DEBUG / TRACE).
    Identify which levels can be moved to opt-in.
(3) Design the Component ID pattern:
    - What is the Component ID format for this system?
    - How is the dynamic configuration delivered to running components?
    - What is the auto-expiry mechanism for elevated log levels?
(4) Calculate the projected log volume reduction from implementing
    INFO as the default and DEBUG as opt-in.
(5) Define the structured log schema: the mandatory fields every
    log line must include, and the optional contextual fields
    by service type.
```

Building Self-Healing systems: systems that watch and correct themselves

The Hero-to-System evolution described in *Chapter 1* has its observability expression here: the final stage is not a system that alerts Dave when something goes wrong. It is a system that corrects what it can correct, alerts Dave only when human judgment is required, and arrives at that alert with enough context that Dave can act immediately rather than investigate.

Self-healing is not a single feature. It is the cumulative result of four architectural properties: observable state (the system can see its own health), defined recovery actions (the system knows what to do about each failure mode), automated execution (the system can execute the recovery actions without human initiation), and bounded autonomy (the system knows when the failure is beyond its own recovery capacity and escalates to a human).

> **Note**
>
> The Self-Healing Boundary Rule: Automated remediation must have explicit boundaries: the classes of failures it will attempt to fix, the maximum number of remediation attempts before escalating, and the conditions under which it escalates immediately without attempting an automated fix. A self-healing system that attempts to fix everything — including novel failures it was not designed for — can cause more damage than the original failure. The automation boundary is not a limitation. It is a safety property.

Start small with automation

Bounded autonomy is a design principle, but it is also a sequencing instruction. The first automated remediation a team deploys should be the one whose worst-case outcome is boring. Trust in the automation layer is accumulated, and it is accumulated in the order the actions are deployed.

Begin with recovery actions that are idempotent, locally scoped, and cheap to get wrong. Restarting an unhealthy container: if the health probe was a false negative, the cost is one restart. Scaling a queue consumer group: if the lag was transient, the cost is one extra consumer for a few minutes. Clearing a stale lock, recycling a saturated connection pool, evicting a corrupted cache entry — all of these fail safe. Deploy these first, watch them fire in production, and confirm the verification gates behave as designed.

Only then move up. Traffic routing between regions, database failover, rolling back a deployment and shedding load are all automatable, and all of them have a blast radius measured in user-visible impact rather than in wasted compute. A database failover triggered by a false positive is an outage that the automation caused. These belong at the end of the sequence, behind verification gates that have already proven themselves on the low-risk actions.

> **Note**
>
> The Automation Trust Ladder: Deploy automated remediation in ascending order of blast radius, and require each rung to run unattended in production for a defined period before the next is enabled. Rung 1: idempotent, locally scoped actions — container restart, consumer scale-out, connection pool recycle. Rung 2: actions affecting a single service's behavior — circuit breaker forcing, cache flush, feature flag disable. Rung 3: actions with cross-system or user-visible impact — traffic shift, database failover, deployment rollback. A team that starts at Rung 3 has not built a self-healing system; it has built an unreviewed change pipeline with production access.

> **Note**
>
> **The Automation Boundary Rule:** Define three explicit categories for every known failure mode before deploying automated remediation: Auto-Fix (system detects and corrects without human involvement), Auto-Flag (system detects, captures forensic context, pages engineer with case file), and Human-Only (failure class requires architectural judgment; system captures context and escalates immediately). Every failure mode must be assigned a category. An unclassified failure mode is a failure mode that will be handled incorrectly by an automated system that defaults to attempting a fix.

The Non-Deterministic failure problem

The most difficult class of failures for automated remediation is the non-deterministic failure — the failure that does not reproduce consistently, that cannot be reliably triggered, and whose root cause requires understanding system state at a specific moment in time that has already passed. These are the failures that drove the 4-hour log search that Dave is currently executing.

For non-deterministic failures, the self-healing architecture shifts from remediation to **forensic capture**: automatically capturing the full diagnostic context at the moment the failure is detected, before the system state changes. This context — the trace, the log window around the failure, the metric values at the time of detection, the saga state — is preserved and associated with a case ID that Dave can open immediately upon being paged.

Dave no longer arrives at an investigation with a blank page. He arrives with a case file: here is the transaction that failed, here is the trace up to the point of failure, here is the state of every service at the time of failure, here are the last 50 log lines from the payment handler before the failure occurred. The investigation time drops from 4 hours to the time required to read the case file and form a hypothesis.

Note

The Case File Rule: When a human engineer is paged, they must receive a case file, not a metric. A case file contains: the detection signal that triggered the page, the automated remediation actions already attempted and their outcomes, the trace for a representative failing request, the metric values at the time of detection, and the last 50 log lines from the component most likely to be involved. An engineer paged with only a metric name and a threshold value will spend the first 10 minutes of their incident response gathering the context that should have been pre-assembled. That is 10 minutes of additional impact duration on every incident.

Note

Tool Tax — automated remediation: Automation that acts on production is production code with production privileges. Budget for testing each action under the failure it is meant to fix, blast-radius review before enabling it, the forensic-capture pipeline that assembles the case file, and periodic re-validation as the system it acts on changes underneath it. An automated action that was correct a year ago and has never been re-tested is not a safety net; it is an untested deploy that fires during incidents.

Failure Class	Automated Response	Human Escalation Trigger	Context Provided to Engineer
Container OOM/ crash	Auto-restart; scale out if OOM repeats > 3 times in 10 minutes	Scale-out fails or OOM loop persists beyond 5 restarts	Memory profile at time of OOM, heap dump, last 100 log lines before crash
Checkout success rate < 99%	Trigger saga trace capture for all failed transactions	Immediate — business impact; no automated fix attempted	Saga state for all failing transactions, payment processor response codes, correlation IDs

Failure Class	Automated Response	Human Escalation Trigger	Context Provided to Engineer
Queue consumer lag > SLO	Add consumer instance; rebalance consumer group	Lag does not decrease within 5 minutes of scale-out	Queue depth over time, consumer throughput per instance, message payload sample from lag window
Circuit breaker opens	Shift traffic to fallback path; log dependency health	Fallback path also degraded; no healthy path is available	Dependency health history, error samples from breaker window, fallback path metrics
Replication lag > 60 seconds	Route reads to primary; alert on replica health	Immediate — data consistency risk	Replication lag time series, write volume at time of lag increase, network metrics
Novel/unclassified failure	Capture forensic context; do not attempt automated fix	Immediate — unknown failure class requires human judgment	Full trace, all service metrics, log window, system state snapshot

Table 11.8: Failure classes, the automated response to each, and the trigger for human escalation

Note

Safe Scale Check — Remediation Blast Radius: Every automated remediation action has a potential blast radius. A container restart that is triggered too aggressively can produce a restart loop that takes a service offline for longer than the original OOM event would have. A scale-out event triggered incorrectly can exhaust the cluster's available node capacity. Before enabling any automated remediation in production, define the maximum blast radius: what is the worst outcome if this remediation action fires incorrectly, and is that outcome better or worse than the failure it is responding to? If the remediation can produce a worse outcome than the failure, it requires a verification gate before execution.

The observability maturity progression

Observability is not a binary state. It is a maturity progression. ShopFlow begins *Chapter 11* at Level 0 — infrastructure monitoring only, no correlation, no outcome signals, no automated remediation. The chapter's interventions advance ShopFlow through the maturity levels.

Maturity Level	Capability	Key Indicator	ShopFlow State
Level 0: Dark	Infrastructure health only; no correlation; no outcome signals	Cannot trace a request across service boundaries	Start of Chapter 11
Level 1: Correlated	Correlation IDs propagated; ID Pair Registry for external boundaries; logs queryable by request ID	Can find all log lines for a specific transaction	After Section 1 implementation
Level 2: Outcome-Aware	Business transaction metrics; user journey success rates; outcome alerts distinct from infrastructure alerts	Know within 60 seconds when checkout success rate drops	After Section 2 implementation
Level 3: Actionable	Alert set rationalized; 90%+ alerts are actionable; automated remediation for known failure classes	Engineer is paged only when human judgment is required	After Section 3 implementation
Level 4: Efficient	Opt-in verbosity; structured logs; log volume proportional to investigation need, not system traffic	Log cost flat or declining despite traffic growth; investigation time < 30 minutes	After Section 4 implementation
Level 5: Self-Healing	Closed-loop remediation; forensic capture for novel failures; engineer arrives with case file	MTTR < 15 minutes for known failure classes; MTTD < 60 seconds	End of Chapter 11

Table 11.9: The observability maturity progression, and ShopFlow's position at each level

Note

Safe Scale Check — Self-Healing Validation: Automated remediation must be tested in production before it is trusted in production. The test is simple: inject the failure condition the remediation is designed to handle, and observe whether the system detects and corrects it within the expected window. If the remediation fails the test, it must not be deployed as production automation. A failed remediation in production is worse than no remediation — it consumes resources, generates additional log noise, and may mask the original failure signal.

Architect's prompt 11.5: the Self-Healing architecture audit

When to use this: Use this prompt when designing the automated remediation layer for a production system or when auditing an existing self-healing implementation to verify that its blast radius boundaries are correctly defined.

```
Act as a Principal Reliability Engineer specializing in automated
remediation. I am designing the self-healing architecture for a
system with the following known failure classes:

[For each failure class, provide:]
- Failure description
- Detection signal (metric, threshold, duration)
- Current manual recovery procedure (runbook steps)
- Frequency in last 30 days
- Average MTTR with current manual process

For each failure class:
(1) Evaluate automability: can the recovery steps be executed by
    a script without human judgment? If not, explain what requires
    human judgment and cannot be automated.
(2) For automatable failures: design the closed-loop remediation:
    - Remediation action (specific commands or API calls)
    - Maximum retry count before escalating to human
    - Verification gate (metric that confirms resolution)
    - Escalation trigger: what context is provided to the engineer?
(3) Define the blast radius of the remediation action:
    - What is the worst outcome if the remediation fires incorrectly?
    - Is this outcome acceptable? If not, add a verification gate
      before execution.
```

```
(4) For non-deterministic failures: design the forensic capture:
    - What state must be captured at the moment of detection?
    - Where is the case file stored and how is it surfaced to the engineer?
(5) Calculate the projected MTTR improvement from automated remediation
    for each failure class, and the total engineer-hours recovered monthly.
```

Production observability checklist

Before a ShopFlow service is considered observable, every item below should read yes — or carry a named, time-boxed exception. The chapter's rules are the reasoning; this is the gate.

Correlation IDs: propagated across every service ShopFlow owns, enforced by the framework rather than by developer discipline, and present in the message payload on every asynchronous hop — not only in the header, which brokers strip.

External ID mappings: every boundary the trace cannot cross writes an ID Pair Registry entry at the moment of the call, so the handoff is documented rather than lost.

Distributed tracing: enabled end to end for owned services, with the trace queryable by correlation ID and the external boundaries visibly marked as breaks.

Outcome metrics: defined for the critical user journeys — starting with one or two PO flows, not all of them — measuring whether the user succeeded rather than whether the service responded.

Alert actionability: every alert that pages a human passes the Actionability Test; everything else routes to a dashboard or to automated remediation.

Structured logging: every log line is a JSON object carrying timestamp, service, component ID, trace ID, span ID and severity, with contextual fields as fields rather than embedded in the message string.

Runtime log verbosity: per-component log levels changeable at runtime without a deployment, DEBUG off by default, and an auto-expiry that reverts the level without human cleanup.

Automated remediation: every closed-loop action has a verification gate and a bounded retry count, and escalates with a case file rather than a metric when the gate fails.

Summary

In this chapter, we built the observability layer that closes the gap between infrastructure health and user outcomes for ShopFlow.

We applied the Pragmatic Correlation Rule to implement correlatable unique IDs across every service boundary ShopFlow controls, and the ID Pair Registry Pattern to bridge the correlation chain across external system boundaries that cannot be instrumented.

We applied the Outcome Quality Rule to instrument the checkout flow with business transaction success metrics — not just infrastructure health — and defined the outcome signal that distinguishes silent checkout failures from the infrastructure noise that was previously masking them.

We applied the Actionability Test to rationalize ShopFlow's 400 alerts per hour down to the 10–15% that genuinely require human action, converting the remainder to automated remediation or dashboard-only signals. The self-healing architecture ensures Dave is paged only when human judgment is irreplaceable.

We applied the Opt-In Verbosity Rule to restructure ShopFlow's logging from always-verbose to default-INFO with per-component DEBUG available on demand, reducing log volume and cost while preserving the investigative depth required for non-deterministic failures.

ShopFlow's telemetry after *Chapter 11*:

Metric	Before (Ch11 Start)	After (Ch11 End)	Change
Checkout Silent Failure Visibility	Undetectable — found via chargebacks	Detected within 60 seconds via outcome metric	MTTD: days → 60 seconds
Distributed Trace Coverage	0%	100% for owned services; ID Pair Registry at external boundaries	Full correlation for all owned hops
Alert Volume	400+/hour	40/hour (all actionable)	90% reduction
Mean Time to Detect (business failures)	Days (via chargeback)	< 60 seconds (outcome metric alert)	Orders of magnitude improvement

Metric	Before (Ch11 Start)	After (Ch11 End)	Change
Mean Time to Recover (known failures)	4+ hours (manual log search + runbook)	< 15 minutes (forensic case file + automated remediation)	94% improvement
Log Volume	50 TB/day	~20TB/day (DEBUG is off by default)	60% reduction
Log Storage Cost	~$750K/month	~$300K/month	-$450K/month
Engineer on-call burden	High — 400 alerts/hr	Low — 40 actionable alerts/hr	Freed 6 FTE-equivalent engineering capacity

Table 11.10: ShopFlow telemetry before and after the Chapter 11 changes

The cliffhanger: the failure we planned for

The observability stack is live. The checkout silent failure rate dropped to zero within 48 hours of deploying the outcome metrics — the instrumentation revealed that the saga orchestrator was silently discarding PaymentConfirmed events when the order service's connection pool was at capacity. The bug was three lines of code. It took 8 minutes to find with the trace. It had been running for six weeks.

But the incident post-mortem surfaces something more important than the bug.

ShopFlow's architecture has no documented definition of what "good enough" looks like when things go wrong. The order service's connection pool was at capacity because there was no load-shedding policy — when the pool was full, it blocked instead of shedding. The saga orchestrator was discarding events because there was no fallback behavior defined — when the downstream call failed, it failed silently rather than routing to a compensating path.

The system can now see its failures. It cannot yet survive them gracefully. Every service has an SLO for the happy path. No service has a defined behavior for the degraded path. That gap is the difference between a system that recovers and a system that cascades.

In *Chapter 12*, we build the resilience architecture that defines ShopFlow's degraded behavior explicitly—what the system guarantees when it cannot guarantee everything, and how it protects the P0 outcomes that must survive even when the P2 services cannot.

12

Resilience and High Availability – Designing for Failure

In *Chapter 11*, we closed the observability gap. The checkout silent failure that had been running for six weeks was found in eight minutes once outcome metrics were live.

But the post-mortem surfaced something more important. The order service's connection pool was at capacity because ShopFlow had no load-shedding policy — when the pool was full, it blocked. The saga orchestrator discarded events because there was no fallback behavior — when the downstream call failed, it failed silently. The system can now see its failures. It cannot yet survive them gracefully.

In this chapter, we are going to cover the following main topics:

- **Prioritizing Your Core:** Identifying Top Scenarios for always-on availability.
- **Graceful Degradation:** Architecting the Basic Minimum Response.
- **Survival Tactics:** Circuit breakers, bulkheads, and timeouts.
- **Load Shedding and Throttling:** Protecting the system from its own success.
- **Chaos Engineering:** Proving resilience through controlled failure.

Technical requirements

Istio/Envoy (service mesh): Circuit breakers, retries, timeouts, and traffic shifting are configured at the infrastructure layer without application code changes.

- **Resilience4j / Polly:** Application-layer circuit breaker and bulkhead libraries for teams not yet on a service mesh.

- **Chaos Mesh/Gremlin:** Controlled fault injection — pod kills, network latency, resource exhaustion. Used for ring-based chaos experiments in production-like environments.
- **Kubernetes PodDisruptionBudgets + Priority Classes:** Enforce P0 pod availability guarantees during scaling events and node drains.
- **Feature flags (LaunchDarkly / App Configuration):** Enable and disable degraded mode behaviors at runtime without deployment.
- **Synthetic monitors (Checkly/Playwright):** End-to-end scenario validation that runs continuously in production.

Code Repository: `https://github.com/imran-siddique/Architecting-at-Scale/tree/main/ch12`

ShopFlow telemetry snapshot [stage 12]

```
The Signal: The observability layer is live. Silent failures are detected within
60 seconds. But detection without designed degradation means every failure still
cascades the same way it always did. ShopFlow can now see the avalanche. It cannot
yet redirect it.
Checkout Outcome Success Rate: 99.7% (0.3% detected in real time – previously
invisible)
Defined Fallback Paths: 0 of 12 critical flows (Every flow either works or fails;
no designed degraded mode)
Load Shedding Policy: None (Connection pool blocks under load; no shedding)
Circuit Breaker Coverage: 2 of 10 service boundaries (8 boundaries have no circuit
protection)
Chaos Testing History: None in production (All failure assumptions based on
staging behavior)
MTTR (P0 failures): 45 minutes (Detection improved; recovery process unchanged)
Panic Meter: 5/10 (We can see the failures. We cannot yet contain them.)
```

> Note
>
> **Dave Alert:** "We can see the 0.3% checkout failure in real time now. But when it happens, the order service blocks the connection pool, the saga orchestrator starts discarding events, and the payment service starts timing out on retries. One failure cascades into five. We're watching it happen and we have no defined response."

Prioritizing your core: identifying top scenarios for Always-On availability

High availability is not a percentage. It is a commitment to a specific set of outcomes. Four nines of availability means nothing if the 0.01% of downtime always hits the scenario that generates revenue.

The useful reframe is this: instead of asking 'how do we make the system available?' ask 'which specific user journeys must complete successfully even when the system is partially degraded?' The answer is your Top Scenarios. Everything else is tiered below them.

> Note
>
> **The Top Scenario Test:** For every feature in the system, ask a single question: if this specific thing fails completely, can users still do the one thing they came here to do? If no, it is P0. If yes, it is P1 or P2. The test is not 'is this feature important?' Every product manager will say their feature is important. The test is 'is this feature the system?'

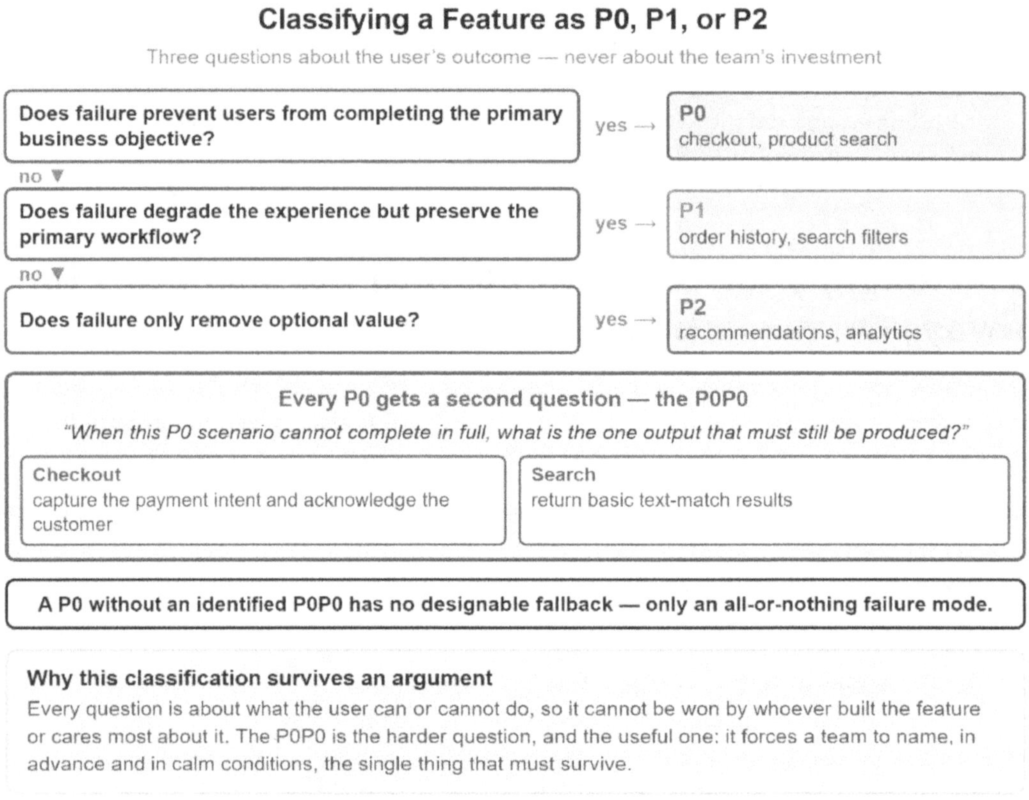

Figure 12.1: Classifying a Feature as P0, P1, or P2

Applied as a sequence, the classification takes three questions and produces a tier that survives argument, because each question is about the user's outcome rather than the team's investment:

1. Does failure prevent users from completing the primary business objective? If yes, it is P0. For ShopFlow that is checkout and product search — without either, there is no store.
2. Does failure degrade the experience but preserve the primary workflow? If yes, it is P1. Order history and search filters qualify: the customer is inconvenienced, not blocked.

3. Does failure only remove optional value? If yes, it is P2. Recommendations and analytics are real features that no user came here for.
4. For every P0, ask the second question: when this scenario cannot complete in full, what is the one output that must still be produced? That is the POPO, and it is what the fallback path has to guarantee.

The classification is only useful if it is written down before an incident. A tier assigned during an outage is a tier assigned by whoever is loudest in the channel.

From operating search infrastructure at petabyte scale: if search is broken — user types a query, clicks enter, nothing comes back — the system is unusable. That is P0. If search returns results but the user cannot filter by date or refine by file type, the system is degraded but functional. That is P1. If the result count badge is inaccurate, that is P2. The same hierarchy applies to every feature in every system.

Note

Anti-Pattern: The Availability Theater: Reporting infrastructure uptime as the primary health metric while the P0 scenarios that generate revenue are the ones failing. A system can achieve 99.99% uptime by having its monitoring and admin dashboards remain healthy while checkout is down. Availability is only meaningful when measured on the scenarios that matter to users.

The POPO principle

Within every P0 scenario, there is a further decomposition: the absolute bare minimum that must work even when the P0 scenario itself is under stress. This is the P0 of the P0 — the irreducible core the system must protect at all costs.

For ShopFlow's checkout: the P0 is the complete checkout flow. The POPO is the ability to capture and record a payment intent. Even if the order confirmation email never sends, even if the saga orchestrator's state machine cannot complete all steps, even if the inventory decrement is delayed — the payment intent must be captured and the customer must receive an acknowledgment. Everything else can be reconciled. A lost payment intent cannot be recovered without the customer's re-engagement.

Note

The POPO Principle: Every P0 scenario has an irreducible core — the minimum output that must be produced even when the full scenario cannot complete. Identify the POPO before designing the degraded mode. The fallback path must guarantee the POPO. If it cannot, the fallback path is not a degraded mode — it is a failure with extra steps.

Scenario	Tier	P0 Definition	POPO (Irreducible Core)	Acceptable Degradation
Product search	P0	User types query → results appear	At least basic text-match results returned	No filters, no facets, no relevance ranking — raw results only
Checkout	P0	User completes payment → order is confirmed	Payment intent captured + customer acknowledgment	No email, no loyalty credit, no analytics — order recorded
Order history	P1	User sees all historical orders	N/A — P1 has no POPO	Cached/stale list acceptable; creating new order unaffected
Search filtering	P1	User refines results by date, type, or author	N/A	Filters disabled; core results still returned
Product recommendations	P2	User sees personalized recommendations	N/A	Recommendation s hidden; checkout unaffected
Order analytics	P2	Admin sees real-time order metrics	N/A	Stale metrics or unavailable; orders still processing

Table 12.1: ShopFlow scenarios by tier, with the irreducible core and the degradation each one permits

Note

The Degradation Contract Rule: Every service must define its degradation contract: what it guarantees when it cannot guarantee everything. The contract specifies the POPO output that must be produced regardless of downstream failures, the P1 behaviors that may be disabled under load, and the P2 behaviors that are disabled first. A service without a degradation contract has an implicit one: all-or-nothing. That is not a resilience strategy.

Choosing the Non-Negotiables

Before writing a degradation contract, decide what is not on the table. Some capabilities are not graded PO, P1 or P2 at all, because degrading them does not produce a reduced service — it produces a different and incorrect one. These are the non-negotiables, and they stay fully intact through every level of degradation the system is capable of.

Authentication and authorization: a degraded system that stops checking who the caller is has not shed load; it has removed the access control. Serving a cached response to the wrong customer is worse than serving no response at all.

Payment integrity: charge exactly once, for exactly the amount presented. Under degradation ShopFlow may defer the inventory decrement, skip the loyalty credit and delay the email, but it may never take a payment it cannot account for or take one twice.

Audit logging: the record of what the system did is what makes the degradation reconcilable afterwards. Dropping audit writes under load is the one shed that removes your ability to repair everything else you shed.

Data integrity constraints: referential integrity, idempotency keys, and uniqueness constraints are not performance features. A degraded path that writes a duplicate order because it bypassed the constraint has converted a slow checkout into a refund and an apology.

Regulatory and privacy controls: data residency, consent enforcement and PII redaction do not have a degraded mode. Whatever the load, the answer is the same as at idle.

Note

The Correctness Floor: Resilience preserves business correctness, not merely application availability. Before assigning degradation tiers, enumerate the capabilities that cannot be degraded at any load — authentication, authorization, payment integrity, audit logging, data integrity constraints, and regulatory controls — and exclude them from every shed policy, feature flag, and circuit breaker fallback. If the

> system cannot serve a request while honoring the correctness floor, the correct behavior is to reject the request, not to serve it incorrectly. A fast wrong answer is not a degraded mode; it is a defect with better latency.

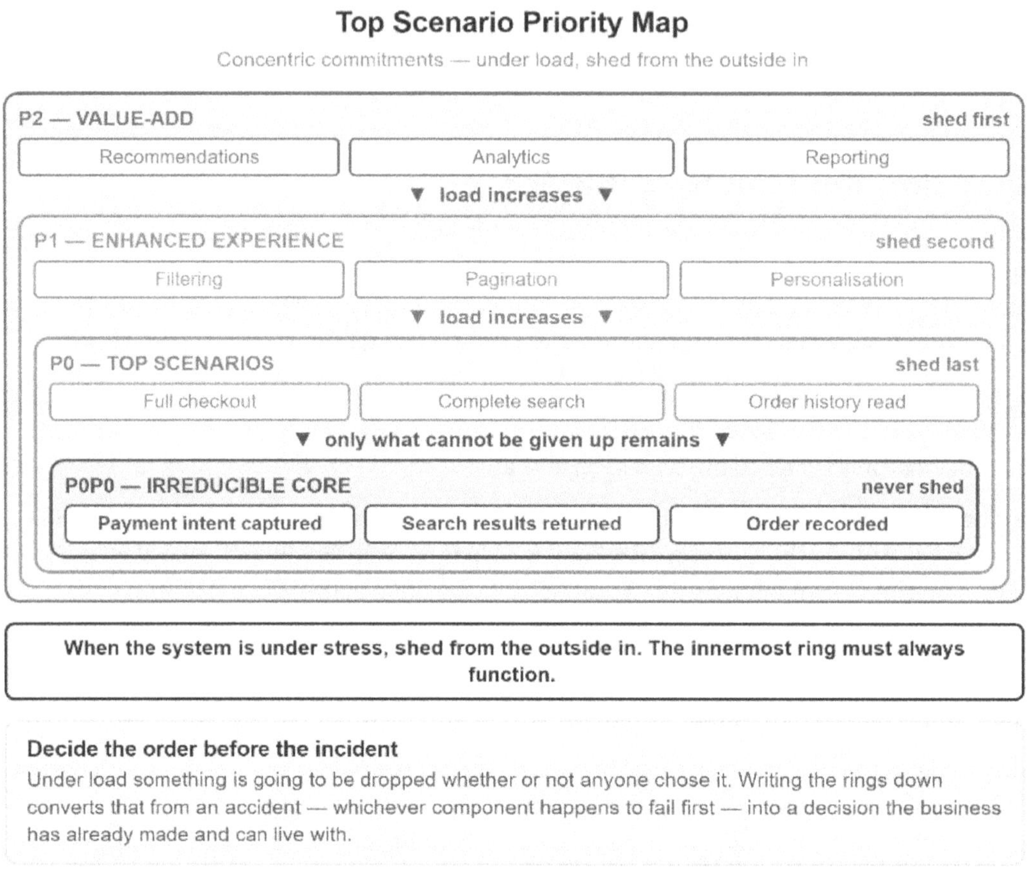

Figure 12.2: Top Scenario Priority Map

Architect's prompt 12.1: the top scenario classifications

When to use this: Use this prompt at the start of any resilience design exercise, before any circuit breaker or bulkhead policy is configured.

```
Act as a Principal Resilience Architect. I am defining the Top Scenarios
for [System Name] to drive the resilience architecture.
```

```
I will provide a list of all user-facing features and flows.
[Paste feature list with brief description of each]

(1) Apply the Top Scenario Test to each feature: classify as P0, P1, or P2.
(2) For each P0: identify the P0P0 – the irreducible minimum output
    that must be produced even when the full P0 scenario cannot complete.
(3) Define the degradation contract for each P0 service:
    P0P0 outputs: always guaranteed.
    P1 behaviors: disabled under [specific condition].
    P2 behaviors: disabled first.
(4) Identify resource conflicts: which P0 and P2 services share
    compute, connection pools, or database tables?
(5) Define the SLO for each tier:
    P0: [availability target, p99 latency SLO]
    P1: [availability target, acceptable degraded state]
    P2: [availability target or best effort]
```

Graceful degradation: architecting the bare minimum response

Graceful degradation is not error handling. Error handling returns an error when something fails. Graceful degradation returns a reduced but useful response when the full response cannot be produced. The distinction is meaningful: an error is a failure. A degraded response is a feature — a deliberately designed fallback that preserves the P0P0 even when the system is under stress.

Note

The Basic Minimum Response Rule: For every P0 flow, implement a Basic Minimum Response: the simplest possible output that preserves the P0P0 contract and can be produced even when all non-essential dependencies are unavailable. The Basic Minimum Response is not a placeholder. It is a fully functional, deliberately simplified version of the P0 output. It requires the same engineering rigor as the full response.

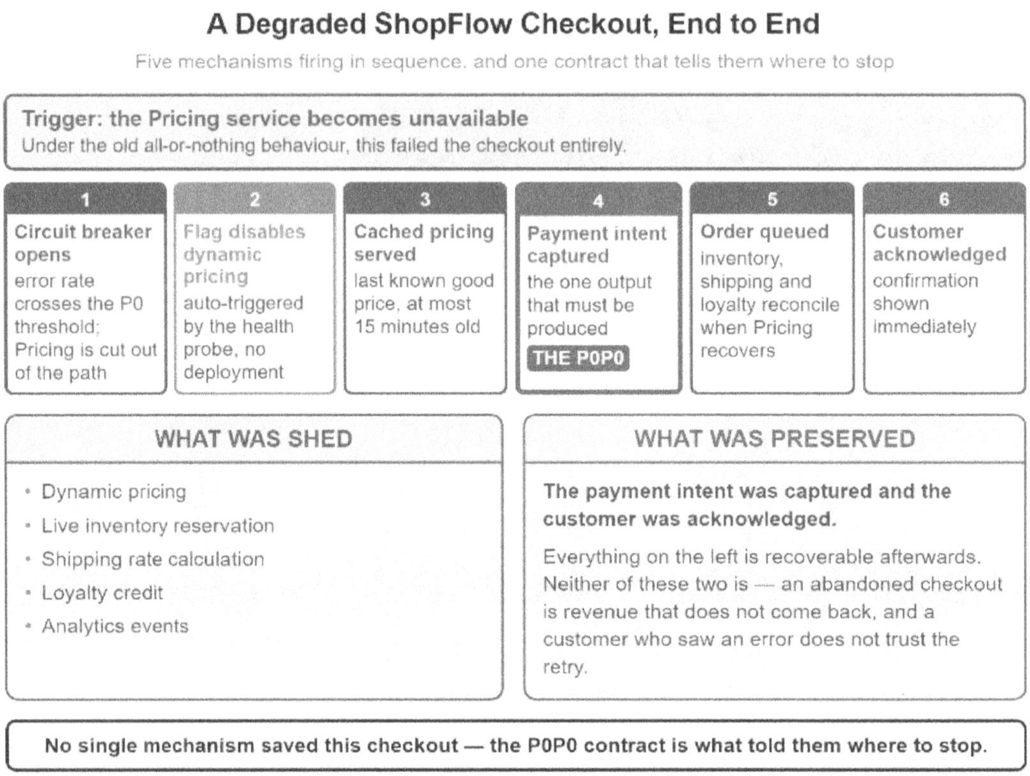

Figure 12.3: A Degraded ShopFlow Checkout, End to End

The mechanisms in this chapter are rarely used one at a time. Following a single ShopFlow checkout through a Pricing service outage shows how they compose:

1. The Pricing service becomes unavailable. The error rate on the pricing call crosses the P0 circuit breaker threshold and the breaker opens, cutting Pricing out of the checkout path rather than letting calls queue against it.
2. The health probe failure auto-disables the dynamic-pricing feature flag. No deployment, no human in the path — the flag is the switch the breaker's state operates.
3. Cached pricing is served instead: the last known good price for each item, no more than 15 minutes old. This is the P1 behavior being shed, not failed — the customer sees a price, and it is a price ShopFlow will honor.
4. The payment intent is captured. This is the P0P0, and everything above exists so that this step is reachable. The charge is recorded exactly once against the order.

5. The order is queued for asynchronous processing. Inventory decrement, shipping rate calculation, loyalty credit, and the confirmation email all become deferred work that reconciles when Pricing recovers.
6. The customer receives an acknowledgment immediately — order number, items, price paid. From the customer's side, the checkout is completed. From the system's side, five dependencies were shed to make that true.

Note what did not happen. The customer was not shown an error, not asked to retry, and not charged twice. The correctness floor held throughout: authentication was enforced, the payment was taken once for the amount displayed, and every deferred step was written to the audit log so the reconciliation is provable rather than assumed.

P0 Flow	Full Response	Basic Minimum Response	Dependencies Shed	User Impact
Product search	Ranked results with filters, facets, images, recommendations	Unranked text-match results, no images, no filters	Recommendation engine, image CDN, ranking model, filter index	User sees results; cannot refine. Acceptable for seconds to minutes.
Checkout	Full saga: inventory → payment → shipping → email → loyalty	Payment intent captured; order queued for async processing; acknowledgment shown	Shipping rate calc, email send, loyalty credit, analytics event	User sees confirmation; fulfillment delayed. Acceptable for minutes.
Order history	Live order list with real-time status	Cached order list from last successful read (max 60 s stale)	Live database read, status sync	User sees recent history and may miss the last 60 seconds of updates.

Table 12.2: The Basic Minimum Response for each P0 flow, and the dependencies shed to produce it

Dependency Tier	Example (ShopFlow)	Shed Condition	Shed Behavior	Restore Condition
POPO-critical — never shed	Payment intent write, Order record create	Cannot be shed	N/A — if this fails, the entire PO flow fails	N/A
PO-required — shed carefully	Inventory reservation	Inventory service unavailable for > 30 s	Queue reservation; process asynchronously when available	Inventory service health probe passes
P1 — shed under load	Search ranking model	Search p99 > 2s or ranking service error rate > 10%	Return unranked results; ranking model bypassed	Ranking service health probe passes + p99 < 500 ms
P2 — shed first	Recommendation engine, loyalty credit, analytics	Any capacity pressure > 70%	Feature disabled; widget hidden; event dropped	Capacity below 60% for 5 continuous minutes

Table 12.3: Dependency tiers, their shed conditions, shed behaviour, and restore conditions

Note

The Dependency Shed Order Rule: When a PO flow is under stress, shed dependencies in reverse priority order. Shed P2 dependencies first — analytics, recommendations, loyalty — before any P1 dependency. Never shed a dependency that produces the POPO output. The shed order must be defined and automated; manual dependency shedding during an incident is too slow and too error-prone to be reliable.

Feature flags are the implementation mechanism for graceful degradation. Each shedable dependency has a feature flag that can be disabled at runtime without deployment. When the dependency health probe detects degradation, the flag is automatically disabled and the Basic

Minimum Response path is activated. When the dependency recovers, the flag is automatically re-enabled.

> Note
>
> **Tool Tax — feature flags:** Flags are the mechanism that makes graceful degradation possible, and they accumulate. Budget for a flag lifecycle with an owner and an expiry, the combinatorial testing problem that arrives once several flags can be off simultaneously, the flag service itself on the critical path with a defined default when it is unreachable, and periodic cleanup — because a codebase with hundreds of permanent flags has replaced deployment risk with a configuration state nobody can fully enumerate.

> Note
>
> **Safe Scale Check — Fallback Path Validation:** Every fallback path must be tested in production before it is needed in production. Run the fallback path for a small percentage of production traffic continuously — not just during incidents. A fallback that runs in production on 1% of traffic is a fallback that works when 100% of traffic needs it. A fallback that has only ever been tested in staging will fail in ways staging cannot predict.

> Note
>
> **The Resilience SLO Rule:** An SLO without a degradation mode is a binary commitment: the system either meets the SLO or it doesn't. An SLO with a degradation mode is a tiered commitment: the system meets the full SLO when all dependencies are healthy, and it meets the degraded SLO when specified dependencies are unavailable. Define both. The degraded SLO is the floor below which the system must never fall, regardless of dependency health.

Architect's prompt 12.2: the graceful degradation design

When to use this: Use this prompt when designing the fallback architecture for a P0 flow or when a P0 flow currently has all-or-nothing failure behavior.

```
Act as a Principal Resilience Engineer. I am designing the graceful
degradation architecture for [P0 Flow Name].

Current full response dependencies:
[List all services, databases, caches, and external APIs in this flow]

(1) Classify each dependency: P0P0-critical, P0-required, or Shedable.
(2) For each Shedable dependency: define the Basic Minimum Response
    that the system produces without it.
(3) Define the feature flag for each Shedable dependency:
    - Auto-disable trigger: what health signal disables the flag?
    - Auto-enable trigger: what health signal re-enables the flag?
(4) Design the fallback path: what cached, static, or simplified data
    replaces the live dependency? What is the maximum acceptable staleness?
(5) Define the production testing protocol: what percentage of production
    traffic continuously exercises the fallback path?
```

Survival tactics: circuit breakers, bulkheads, and timeouts

Chapter 7 configured circuit breakers and bulkheads for the initial six-service decomposition. *Chapter 12* applies the same patterns with the resilience priority framework: P0 paths get dedicated resources that P2 paths cannot consume, and circuit breakers are configured differently for P0 and P2 dependencies.

> Note
>
> The P0 Isolation Mandate: Every P0 critical path must have dedicated, isolated resources: a dedicated connection pool, a dedicated thread pool, and dedicated Kubernetes node capacity that P2 workloads cannot consume. A P0 service that shares a connection pool with a P2 service is not a P0 service; it is a P0 service with a P2-shaped single point of failure.

Note

Tool Tax — resource isolation: Dedicated pools are the most effective isolation in this chapter and the most visible on the bill. Budget for the idle headroom that dedication implies — a pool sized for P0 peak is underused most of the day by design — PriorityClass and PodDisruptionBudget configuration that has to be maintained as workloads move, and per-tier capacity planning where there used to be one number. You are buying predictability with utilisation, and that trade should be made explicitly rather than discovered in the cost review.

Resource Type	P0 Configuration	P2 Configuration	Isolation Mechanism
Connection pool	Dedicated pool, min 20 connections, never shared	Shared pool, max 5 connections, 500 ms timeout	Separate pool config per priority class
Thread pool	Dedicated, 20 threads, 30s max wait	Semaphore isolation, max 5 concurrent	Kubernetes resource limits + Resilience4j bulkhead
Kubernetes nodes	Dedicated node pool, PriorityClass: system-critical	Shared node pool, PriorityClass: low, evictable	PodDisruptionBudget minAvailable: 3 for P0
Circuit breaker threshold	Open at 50% error rate, 50 request minimum	Open at 20% error rate, 10 request minimum	Separate Envoy Outlier Detection config per route
Timeout	Derived from P0P0 contract (strict, shorter)	Permissive — P2 can wait longer	Envoy route-level timeout configuration

Table 12.4: Resource isolation settings compared across P0 and P2 priority classes

Note

The Circuit Breaker Graduation Rule: P0 circuit breakers must open on a higher error rate threshold than P2 breakers — they require more evidence of failure before cutting traffic. The cost of a false-positive circuit open on a P0 path is higher than on a P2 path: P0 false positives produce checkout failures, not just degraded features. Configure P0 breakers conservatively; configure P2 breakers aggressively.

Note

Tool Tax — the service mesh: A mesh moves retries, timeouts, and circuit breaking out of application code and into infrastructure you now operate. Budget for a sidecar on every pod and the CPU and memory that implies, control-plane upgrades that touch every service at once, mTLS certificate rotation, and a debugging experience where the request path includes two proxies nobody wrote. The mesh removes the code; it does not remove the behavior, and the behavior is now configured somewhere your application developers cannot see.

Note

Safe Scale Check — Bulkhead Blast Radius: Before configuring any bulkhead, calculate the worst-case resource consumption: (p99 degraded response time) × (max concurrent requests) × 1.5 safety margin = minimum pool size. A pool sized below this threshold will be exhausted under exactly the conditions where it needs to hold. The connection pool exhaustion from *Chapter 7* was a correctly predicted outcome of an undersized pool. The calculation was never done.

Architect's prompt 12.3: the resilience configuration audit

When to use this: Use this prompt when auditing circuit breaker and bulkhead configuration across a multi-service architecture or after a cascading failure event.

```
Act as a Principal Reliability Engineer. I am auditing the resilience
configuration for the following service architecture:
```

```
[For each service: priority tier, downstream dependencies,
current circuit breaker config, pool sizes, timeouts]

(1) For each P0 service: verify its connection pool and thread pool
    are dedicated. Flag any shared resource between P0 and P2 paths.
(2) For each circuit breaker: verify thresholds match path priority.
    P0 breakers should open later; P2 breakers should open earlier.
(3) For each timeout: verify the hierarchy is correct -
    each layer's timeout is strictly less than the layer above it.
(4) Calculate the pool sizing for each P0 downstream dependency:
    (p99 degraded response time) x (max concurrent requests) x 1.5.
    Flag any pool below the calculated minimum.
(5) Identify any P0 service sharing node capacity with P2 workloads
    without a PodDisruptionBudget or PriorityClass.
```

Load shedding and throttling: protecting the system from its own success

Load shedding is the deliberate rejection of lower-priority requests to preserve capacity for higher-priority ones. The decision of who gets priority when the system cannot serve everyone must be made in advance and encoded in policy — not made in the moment of an incident under pressure.

> Note
>
> **The Load Priority Rule:** Human users are always higher priority than automated callers. A human user who receives a degraded response cannot retry with the same ease as a system calling an API. A system caller that hits a rate limit retries in milliseconds. When capacity must be rationed, protect human user traffic first.

This principle became concrete in operating a high-traffic documentation platform. As LLM-powered tools and AI agents began generating significant API traffic — often a larger request volume than human users — the capacity question became existential. The agents could absorb rate limiting gracefully: they retry, they queue, they wait. The human user who is blocked gets a bad experience that does not self-resolve.

Traffic Type	Priority	Shed Threshold	Shed Mechanism	Retry Behavior
Human user — checkout (P0)	Highest	Never shed	N/A	N/A
Human user — search (P0)	Highest	Never shed	N/A	N/A
Human user — filters, P1	High	80% capacity utilization	Return degraded response (no filters)	No retry expected — user sees degraded UI
Human user — recommendations, P2	Medium	70% capacity utilization	Return empty / hide widget	No retry expected
Authenticated developer API client	Medium	85% capacity utilization	429 with Retry-After header	Client retries after backoff
LLM / AI agent traffic	Low	65% capacity utilization	429 with Retry-After; longer backoff	Agents retry automatically—designed for this
Unauthenticated/bot traffic	Lowest	50% capacity utilization	429 or connection reset	Shed freely

Table 12.5: Traffic types ranked by shed priority, with the threshold and mechanism for each

Note

The Agent Shedding Rule: Rate-limit automated, LLM, and agent-generated traffic before any human user traffic. Agents and LLM tools are designed to handle rate limiting: they implement exponential backoff, they queue requests, and they retry on 429. Human users are not designed to handle rate limiting. Protecting human traffic by shedding agent traffic is not degrading the API — it is correctly prioritizing the users who cannot absorb the impact.

Note

Tool Tax — tiered rate limiting: A limiter that distinguishes traffic classes needs to know who is calling, which means identity on every request. Budget for per-key and per-tenant quota state that is shared across instances and survives restarts, the latency that state lookup adds to every request, quota headers and the documentation that goes with them, and an appeals path for the legitimate customer whose well-behaved integration got classified as an agent.

Fairness within a traffic class

Prioritising human traffic over agent traffic solves the problem between classes. It does nothing about the problem inside one. A single developer running an aggressive batch job, or one tenant whose integration retries in a tight loop, can consume the entire allocation for their class and starve every other caller in it — while the shed policy reports that the class is within budget.

- **Per-tenant quotas:** allocate capacity by tenant, not only by class. A tenant that exhausts its own quota is throttled while its neighbors are unaffected, which converts a shared outage into one customer's problem.
- **Per-API-key limits:** quotas belong on the credential, not the IP address. One tenant may hold many keys for different integrations, and a runaway key should be throttled without taking down that tenant's other, well-behaved integrations.
- **Weighted rate limiting:** not every request costs the same. A catalog search that fans out to Elasticsearch is worth many simple key lookups, so the limiter should spend a token budget weighted by actual resource cost rather than counting requests.
- **Concurrency caps alongside rate caps:** a rate limit bounds requests per second but not how many are in flight at once. A caller issuing long-running queries can hold a disproportionate share of the connection pool while staying comfortably under its request rate.

Note

The Fair Share Rule: Priority decides which class is shed first; fairness decides who inside that class absorbs it. Every traffic class must enforce a per-tenant and per-credential allocation, weighted by the resource cost of the request rather than by request count, so that no single caller can consume the whole class budget. Without it, a class-level shed policy is a queue that the noisiest client wins. Publish the quota to the caller in the response headers—a client that can see its remaining budget will back off before it is forced to.

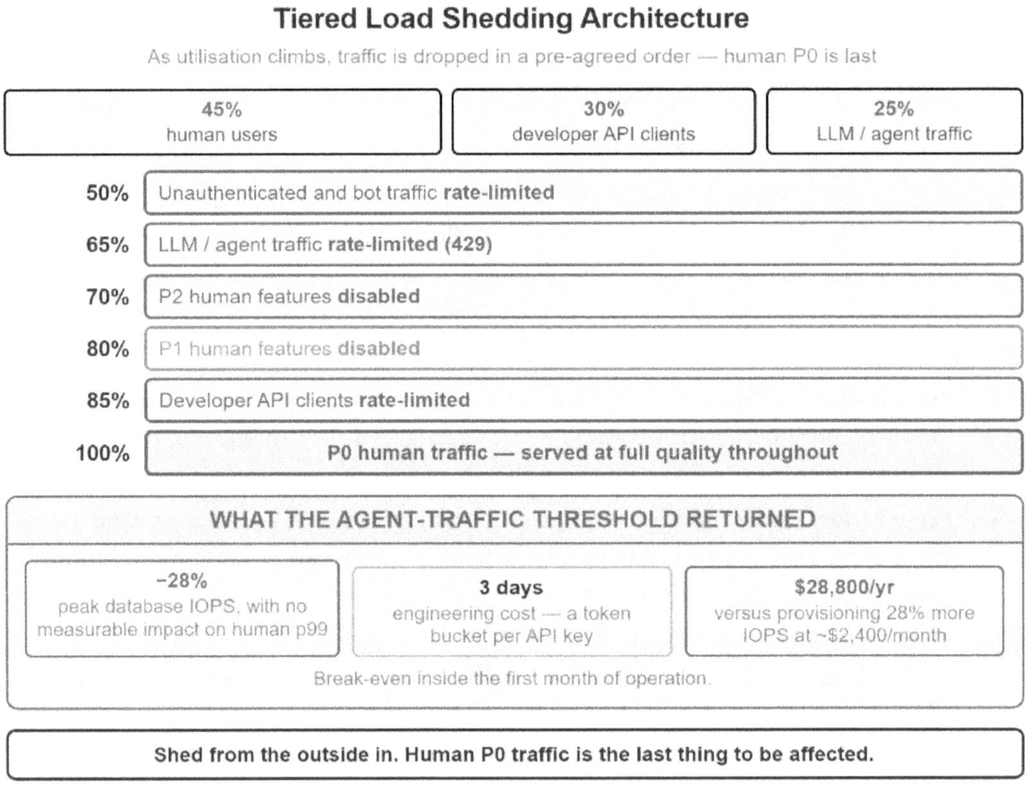

Figure 12.4: Tiered Load Shedding Architecture

Note

Manager's Math — The Load Shedding ROI: At a high-traffic platform serving both human users and LLM-generated API traffic, a 65% capacity utilization shed threshold

> on agent traffic — implemented as a token bucket rate limiter per API key — reduced peak database IOPS by 28% during traffic spikes with zero impact on human user p99 latency. Engineering cost: approximately 3 days. The alternative — provisioning 28% more database capacity to serve the agent traffic — would have cost approximately $2,400/month in additional IOPS. Annualized savings: $28,800. Break-even: within the first month of operation.

Architect's prompt 12.4: the load shedding policy design

When to use this: Use this prompt when designing the load shedding policy for a system serving mixed traffic types, or after a capacity incident where non-critical traffic consumed resources needed for P0 flows.

```
Act as a Principal Capacity Engineer specializing in load shedding.
I am designing the load shedding policy for [System Name].

Traffic profile:
- Human user traffic: [X% of total, request types]
- Automated / API client traffic: [Y% of total]
- LLM / agent traffic: [Z% of total, request patterns]

Current capacity utilization at peak: [X%]

(1) Define the shed threshold for each traffic type, from lowest
    priority (shed first) to highest priority (shed last).
(2) For each traffic type: define the shed mechanism:
    429 with Retry-After, degraded response, or connection reset.
(3) Design the token bucket rate limiter for LLM/agent traffic:
    bucket size, refill rate, per-key or per-tier enforcement.
(4) Calculate the capacity recovery from shedding LLM/agent traffic:
    [agent request volume] x [avg resource cost] = saved capacity.
(5) Define the auto-restore trigger: at what capacity utilization
    does shedding stop and full service resume?
```

Resilience Pattern	Protects Against	Implementation Layer	P0 required?	ShopFlow Application
Circuit Breaker	Cascading failure from slow/erroring dependency	Service mesh or app library	Yes — all P0 dependencies	Pricing service, Inventory service, Payment processor
Bulkhead (thread pool)	Resource exhaustion from one path consuming shared pool	App library (Resilience4j)	Yes — P0 paths must be isolated	Checkout thread pool isolated from Recommendations
Timeout hierarchy	Threshold from long-running downstream calls	Service mesh + app config	Yes — non-negotiable	All service-to-service calls have coordinated timeouts
Load shedding	Capacity exhaustion from low-priority traffic	API Gateway + rate limiter	Yes — protect P0 human traffic	Agent traffic shed at 65%; P2 features at 70%
Graceful degradation / Basic Minimum Response	User-visible failure when noncritical dependencie s fail	App logic + feature flags	Yes — all P0 flows	Search without ranking, checkout without email
Chaos engineering (ring-based)	Unvalidated resilience assumptions	PPE + ring deployment	Yes — must test before relying on	Ring 0 → Ring 1 → Ring 2 progression

Table 12.6: Resilience patterns, what each protects against, and where it is implemented

Chaos engineering: proving resilience through controlled failures

A resilience architecture that has not been tested under failure conditions is a hypothesis. Chaos engineering makes controlled failures happen on purpose, in production-like environments, before they happen accidentally.

> Note
>
> **Anti-Pattern: The Production-Only Chaos Test:** Running chaos experiments exclusively in staging, then deploying to production assuming staging results predict production behavior. Staging environments differ from production in traffic volume, data volume, configuration drift, and third-party dependency behavior. Staging tests are necessary. They are not sufficient.

The ring deployment pattern for controlled chaos

The safest way to test resilience in production is through the ring deployment pattern: graduated rollout through progressively larger audience segments, starting with the engineering team's own environment.

Ring 0 is the internal engineering team's environment. Every engineer building the system uses it daily. A chaos experiment in Ring 0 has zero customer impact and maximum observational value. Ring 1 is a small set of production accounts — internal accounts or external accounts that have opted into early access. The blast radius is bounded. Rings 2 and beyond are progressively larger customer populations. Each ring is a go/no-go gate.

This pattern was applied in practice building and operating services at scale: internal team accounts served as Ring 0 for every change, including fault injection experiments. Changes that passed Ring 0 moved to Ring 1 (broader internal users), then to progressively larger external rings. The PPE environment — production-like in configuration and data volume — served as the proving ground for circuit breaker configurations and bulkhead pool sizes before they reached production rings.

> Note
>
> **The Chaos Ring Rule:** Never inject a fault in a higher ring before it has been validated in all lower rings. A chaos experiment that skips Ring 0 and Ring 1 to test directly in production is not a chaos experiment — it is an uncontrolled outage with a research label. The ring progression is the safety property of chaos engineering.

Note

Tool Tax — chaos engineering: Chaos tooling is cheap; the environments and the discipline around it are not. Budget for a production-like Ring 1 environment that has to be kept production-like, fault-injection tooling integrated with your orchestrator, an experiment review, and approval process, abort automation that is itself tested, and the engineering time to run experiments on a cadence rather than once. A chaos program that runs for a quarter and then stops leaves you with resilience claims that were true in March.

Ring	Environment	Audience	Blast Radius	Fault Types	Proceed Criteria
Ring 0	Internal dogfood	Engineering team only	Zero customer impact	Any fault type; full failure injection acceptable	Resilience mechanism activates as designed; team confirms recovery
Ring 1	PPE / staging (production-like)	Internal accounts, early access	Bounded — known accounts only	Network partition, pod kill, dependency timeout	Same mechanism behavior as Ring 0; no data loss
Ring 2	Production — small customer segment	1–5% of customer base	Small but real	Latency injection, partial dependency degradation	P0 SLO maintained; no customer-visible impact exceeding degradation contract

Ring	Environment	Audience	Blast Radius	Fault Types	Proceed Criteria
Ring 3	Production — general availability	Full customer base	Full production	Validation only— monitoring, no new fault injection	Incident rate unchanged from pre-experiment baseline

Table 12.7: The chaos deployment rings, their blast radius, permitted fault types, and proceed criteria

Fault Type	Safe in Ring 0?	Safe in Ring 1?	Safe in Ring 2?	Expected Resilience Signal
Kill 1 pod of a 3-pod P2 service	Yes	Yes	Yes	Kubernetes reschedules; no user impact
Inject 500 ms latency on Pricing service calls	Yes	Yes	With monitoring	Circuit breaker opens; fallback pricing activates
Kill all Inventory service pods	Yes — team only	Yes — bounded accounts	No — P0 impact is too broad	P0P0 fallback: cached inventory count; order queued
Saturate P2 connection pool to 100%	Yes	Yes	Yes	P2 requests fail; P0 pools unaffected (bulkhead)
Simulate a 45-second replication lag	Yes	Yes — if on replica reads only	With monitoring	DAL routes to primary; stale read alert fires
Drop 30% of agent API traffic	Yes	Yes	Yes — agents retry	Rate limiter activates; human traffic unaffected

Table 12.8: Fault types by ring safety, with the resilience signal each experiment should produce

Note

The Minimum Chaos Experiment: The most revealing chaos experiment is not the most dramatic one. It is the smallest experiment that answers: does this specific resilience mechanism activate under this specific failure condition? A pod kill that confirms the circuit breaker opens and traffic shifts to the fallback path in Ring 0 is more valuable than a region-wide outage simulation that produces too many simultaneous signals to diagnose. Start small. Scale the blast radius only when each smaller experiment has passed.

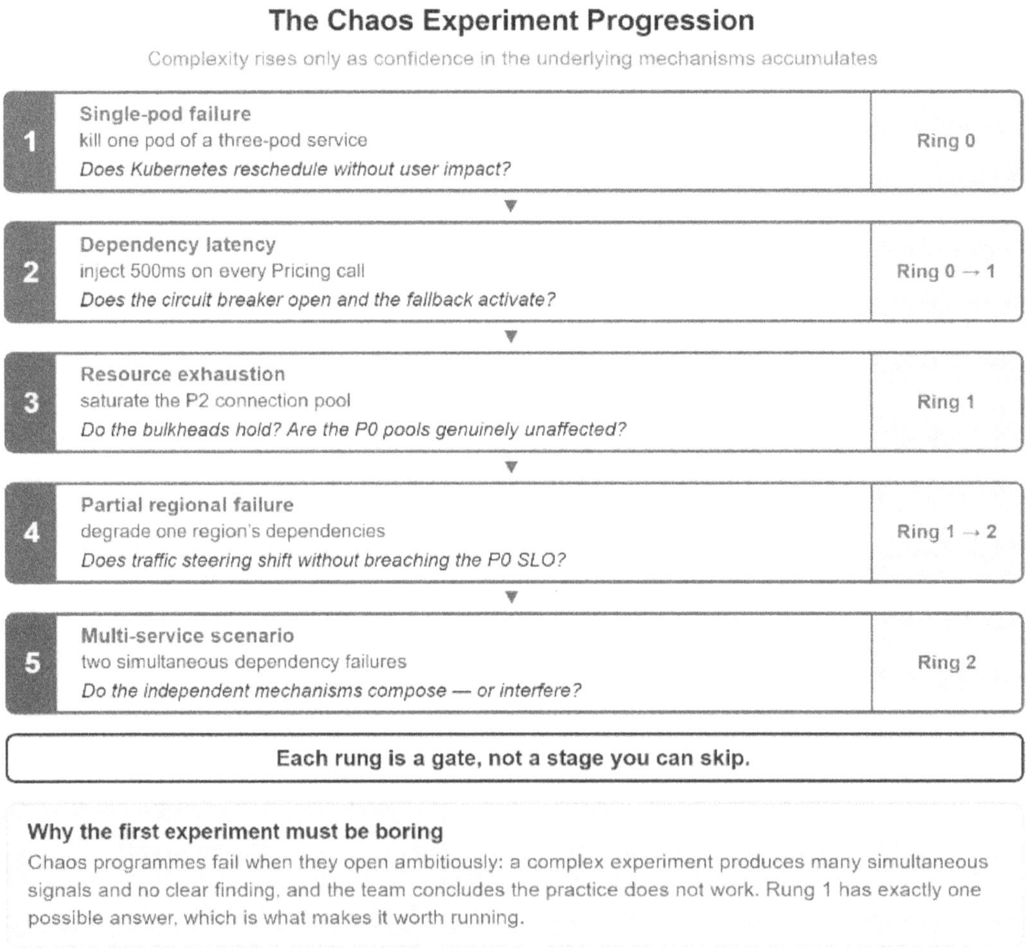

Figure 12.5: The Chaos Experiment Progression

That principle generalises into a progression. Chaos programmes fail when the first experiment is ambitious, because an ambitious experiment produces many simultaneous signals and no clear finding. Complexity should increase only as confidence in the underlying mechanisms accumulates:

1. Single-pod failure. Kill one pod of a three-pod service in Ring 0. The question is narrow — does the orchestrator reschedule without user impact? — and a failure here means nothing further is worth testing.
2. Dependency latency injection. Add 500ms to Pricing service calls. This is the first experiment that tests a resilience mechanism rather than the platform: does the circuit breaker open, and does the fallback activate within its stated window?
3. Resource exhaustion. Saturate the P2 connection pool and confirm the bulkheads hold — P2 requests fail, P0 pools are untouched. This is the experiment that would have caught the *Chapter 7* pool exhaustion.
4. Partial regional failure. Degrade one region's dependencies and watch traffic steering shift. The blast radius is now real, so this belongs in Ring 1 moving to Ring 2, with abort criteria defined before it starts.
5. Multi-service failure scenarios. Two dependencies fail simultaneously. This is the only experiment that tests whether independently correct mechanisms compose — a circuit breaker and a load shedder can each behave perfectly and still interact badly.

> Note
>
> The Experiment Progression Rule: Advance one rung at a time, and only on evidence. An experiment may move up a rung when the rung below it has run in the target ring without an unplanned abort and the resilience mechanism it tests behaved as documented. A program that opens with a multi-region failure has not tested its resilience; it has generated an incident whose findings are indistinguishable from noise. The progression is what converts chaos engineering from a demonstration into a measurement.

> Note
>
> Safe Scale Check — Chaos Experiment Blast Radius: Before any chaos experiment, define the blast radius (which users are affected if the experiment produces an unintended outcome), the abort criteria (at what observed impact the experiment

stops), and the rollback procedure (how the injected fault is removed). A chaos experiment without these three definitions is not controlled.

Note

Manager's Math — The Cost of Untested Resilience: ShopFlow's connection pool exhaustion from *Chapter 7* was preventable. A 30-minute Ring 0 chaos experiment simulating a slow Pricing service response would have revealed the pool exhaustion before production. Engineering cost of the chaos experiment: 4 engineering hours. Actual cost of the production incident: 4 hours MTTR × 3 engineers × revenue impact during downtime. The chaos experiment was 10x cheaper than the incident it would have prevented.

Architect's prompt 12.5: the chaos experiment design

When to use this: Use this prompt when designing a chaos experiment for a specific resilience mechanism or when building the initial chaos testing program for a system never tested under controlled failure conditions.

```
Act as a Principal Chaos Engineering Specialist. I am designing a
chaos experiment to validate [Resilience Mechanism].

Resilience mechanism under test: [e.g. circuit breaker on Pricing service]
Expected behavior: [e.g. circuit opens at 30% error rate; traffic shifts
to cached pricing fallback within 10 seconds]
Current ring: [Ring 0 / Ring 1 / Ring 2]

Experiment design:
(1) Fault type: [pod kill / latency injection / error injection / resource
exhaustion]
(2) Fault magnitude and duration.
(3) Blast radius: which accounts or traffic percentage are affected?
(4) Success criteria: what observable signals confirm the mechanism
    activated as designed?
(5) Abort criteria: at what observed impact does the experiment stop?
(6) Rollback procedure: how is the fault removed if abort fires?
(7) Proceed criteria: what must be true before escalating to the next ring?
```

Note

Manager's Math — The Resilience Architecture Cost: ShopFlow's resilience investments in this chapter: dedicated P0 node pools (+$800/month), oversized connection pools (no additional infra cost), fallback cache layer (+$150/month), Ring 1 PPE environment (+$400/month), chaos experiment tooling (+$200/month). Total additional monthly cost: $1,550. Projected monthly incident cost avoided: MTTR improvement from 45 to 12 minutes across an estimated 8 P0 incidents per month = 264 minutes of recovered engineering time = 4.4 engineer-hours. At fully-loaded cost plus revenue impact during downtime: approximately $12,000/month avoided. ROI: 7.7x. The resilience architecture pays for itself within the first month of operation.

Signal	Pre-Resilience Architecture	Post-Resilience Architecture
Cascading failure frequency	2–3 per sprint	0 — bulkheads contain failures
P0 path isolation	Shared pools with P2	Dedicated pools; P2 cannot consume P0 resources
Fallback path coverage	0 of 12 P0 flows	12 of 12 — all P0 flows have Basic Minimum Response
Agent traffic impact on P0	Unbounded — agents consume the same pool as humans	Shed at 65% capacity; human P0 traffic unaffected
Chaos test validation	0 mechanisms tested in a production-like environment	All P0 mechanisms tested through Ring 1
MTTR on known failure classes	45 minutes (manual log search)	12 minutes (fallback active + forensic case file)

Table 12.9: ShopFlow resilience signals before and after the Chapter 12 architecture

Resilience readiness checklist

Before a ShopFlow flow is declared production-ready, every item below should read yes — or carry a named, time-boxed exception. This is the architecture review gate for the chapter.

- **P0, P1 and P2 scenarios documented:** every feature classified by the Top Scenario Test, written down before an incident rather than during one.

- **P0P0 identified for every critical workflow:** the irreducible output each P0 flow must still produce when it cannot be completed in full.
- **Degradation contracts defined:** each service states what it guarantees when it cannot guarantee everything, and which behaviors are shed in which order.
- **Non-negotiables excluded from every shed policy:** authentication, authorization, payment integrity, audit logging, data integrity constraints, and regulatory controls hold at any load.
- **Basic Minimum Responses implemented:** each P0 flow has a deliberately engineered fallback, exercised continuously against a slice of production traffic rather than only during incidents.
- **Circuit breakers and bulkheads configured by priority:** P0 paths on dedicated pools that P2 workloads cannot consume; P0 breakers open later than P2 breakers.
- **Load shedding policy documented:** thresholds and mechanisms defined per traffic class in advance, with per-tenant and per-credential fairness inside each class.
- **Human and agent traffic are prioritized separately:** automated and LLM traffic are shed before any human traffic, because agents absorb rate limiting and users do not.
- **Chaos experiments validated through ring progression:** every resilience mechanism is confirmed in the rings below before it is relied upon in the ring above.

Summary

In this chapter, we built the resilience architecture that defines ShopFlow's degraded behavior explicitly—what the system guarantees when it cannot guarantee everything.

We applied the Top Scenario Test to classify ShopFlow's features into P0, P1, and P2 tiers, and the P0P0 Principle to identify the irreducible core output each P0 flow must produce under maximum degradation.

We implemented the Basic Minimum Response for each P0 flow—a deliberately engineered fallback exercised in production continuously at 1% traffic.

We enforced the P0 Isolation Mandate — dedicated connection pools, thread pools, and Kubernetes node capacity for every P0 path — preventing P2 workload degradation from consuming P0 resources.

We applied the Load Priority Rule and the Agent Shedding Rule to protect human user traffic from automated, LLM, and agent-generated load, with tiered rate limiting that preserves P0 human traffic while gracefully degrading agent traffic that can absorb rate limiting.

We established the Chaos Ring Pattern — Ring 0 dogfood, Ring 1 PPE, Ring 2 small customer segment — ensuring every resilience mechanism is confirmed to work under real failure conditions before it is relied upon to protect real users.

ShopFlow's telemetry after *Chapter 12*:

Metric	Before (Ch12 Start)	After (Ch12 End)	Change
Defined fallback paths	0 of 12 critical flows	12 of 12 — all P0 flows have Basic Minimum Response	Full coverage
P0 isolation coverage	Shared resources across tiers	Dedicated pools for all P0 paths	Cascade risk eliminated
Cascading failure events	2–3 per sprint	0 (bulkheads containing failures)	Eliminated
Load shedding policy	None	Tiered by traffic type; agent traffic is shed at 65% capacity	Automated
Chaos test coverage	0 mechanisms tested	All P0 mechanisms validated through Ring 1	Full coverage
MTTR (P0 failures)	45 minutes	12 minutes (fallback activates in <30 s)	73% improvement

Table 12.10: ShopFlow telemetry before and after the Chapter 12 changes

The cliffhanger: the bill of survival

The resilience architecture is live. Fallback paths are exercised daily. The cascading failures are contained. ShopFlow has survived its first Ring 1 chaos experiment without a customer-visible incident.

And then the infrastructure cost report lands.

Dedicated node pools for P0 workloads. Oversized connection pools with safety margins. Replicated fallback cache layers. Duplicate deployment rings. The resilience architecture is correct. It is also expensive. Monthly infrastructure spend has increased 34% since Chapter 10, and the CFO's question is direct: are we paying for resilience, or are we paying for fear?

In *Chapter 13*, we answer that question with data. Performance tuning and capacity planning are not alternatives to resilience — they are complements. A well-tuned system needs less capacity to maintain its SLOs. A correctly capacity-planned system does not over-provision out of fear. The P0/P1/P2 framework from this chapter becomes the lens through which every hardware and optimization decision is evaluated: spend money where it buys P0 outcomes and spend carefully everywhere else.

13

Performance Tuning and Capacity Planning

In *Chapter 12,* the resilience architecture was built correctly: dedicated P0 node pools, oversized connection pools with safety margins, replicated fallback cache layers, and duplicate deployment rings. The system survives failure gracefully. And the infrastructure bill increased 34% in the process.

The CFO's question is direct: are we paying for resilience, or are we paying for fear? The answer is not obvious. Some of the new spend protects the P0 outcomes that generate revenue. Some of it is over-provisioning that accumulated because the team did not have a framework for distinguishing necessary capacity from precautionary excess.

In this chapter, we build that framework. Performance tuning and capacity planning are not alternatives to resilience — they are complements. A correctly tuned system needs less capacity to maintain its SLOs. A correctly planned system does not overprovision out of fear.

In this chapter, we are going to cover the following main topics:

- **The Tuning Trap:** Knowing when and when not to optimize.
- **Resource Contention:** The hidden cost of shared systems.
- **P0 to P2 Framework:** Tiering performance requirements.
- **Predictive Planning:** Getting maximum results from minimum resources.
- **The Bare Minimum:** Defining good enough for non-critical paths.

Technical requirements

EXPLAIN ANALYZE / pganalyze: Query execution plan analysis. Every optimization hypothesis must be validated with EXPLAIN ANALYZE before and after. Optimization without query plan analysis is guesswork.

k6 / Gatling (load testing): Sustained load generation for capacity modeling. Reproduces realistic traffic patterns, not just peak spikes, to model steady-state resource consumption.

Grafana dashboards (per-workload): Separate dashboards for P0 and P2 workloads. A shared dashboard that aggregates P0 and P2 metrics hides resource contention between them.

Kubernetes resource quotas + Vertical Pod Autoscaler: Enforce CPU and memory limits per workload tier. P2 workloads must not be allowed to consume resources that exceed their quota, regardless of what is available on the node.

Cloud provider cost management (AWS Cost Explorer / Azure Cost Analysis): Per-workload cost attribution. You cannot make the hardware-vs-optimization decision without knowing the cost of the hardware being optimized.

The code repository for *Chapter 13* can be found at `https://github.com/imran-siddique/Architecting-at-Scale/tree/main/ch13`.

ShopFlow telemetry snapshot [stage 13]

```
The Signal: The resilience architecture is working. But the 34% infrastructure
cost increase has no corresponding revenue increase. Some of the new spend is
justified. Some is over-provisioning accumulated without a framework for the
hardware-vs-optimization decision. This chapter provides that framework.
Monthly Infrastructure Spend: $12,800/mo (Up 34% since Chapter 10)
P0 Node Pool Cost: $3,200/mo (Justified – protects checkout and search SLOs)
P2 Background Processing Cost: $4,100/mo (Unreviewed – no optimization or right-
sizing done)
Code Indexing Job CPU (background): Peak 85% of shared node capacity (Contending
with P1 search queries during indexing windows)
Search p99 Latency During Indexing: 210ms (Normal: 95ms. Indexing job causes 2.2x
degradation)
Capacity Planning Horizon: Reactive only (No forward model; scaling triggered by
incidents)
Panic Meter: 3/10 (Infrastructure is stable. Spend is not optimized.)
```

> Note
>
> **Dave Alert:** "The code indexing jobs run during business hours and push the search p99 from 95ms to 210ms. Search is technically within SLO — but barely. And the indexing jobs are running on the same nodes as the live search service. I thought we separated P0 from P2 in *Chapter 12*. We separated the connection pools. We didn't separate the compute."

The tuning trap: knowing when and when not to optimize

Performance tuning is one of the most seductive activities in engineering. It is measurable, technically satisfying, and visibly impactful. It is also, frequently, the wrong activity—not because the optimization is incorrect, but because the correct action was to provision more hardware and ship the feature that was waiting.

The decision between hardware and optimization is an economic decision. Engineering time spent profiling, benchmarking, and optimizing has a cost that must be compared to the cost of the hardware that would have avoided the need for optimization. In many cases, the hardware is cheaper.

> Note
>
> **The Hardware-First Rule:** Before beginning any performance optimization work, calculate the hardware cost that would resolve the problem and compare it to the engineering cost of the optimization. If the hardware cost is lower than the engineering cost over the next 12 months, provision the hardware and invest the engineering time in product features. Optimization is justified only when the hardware cost exceeds the engineering cost, when the hardware option does not exist (specialized hardware ceiling), or when the performance problem is architectural rather than resource-bound.

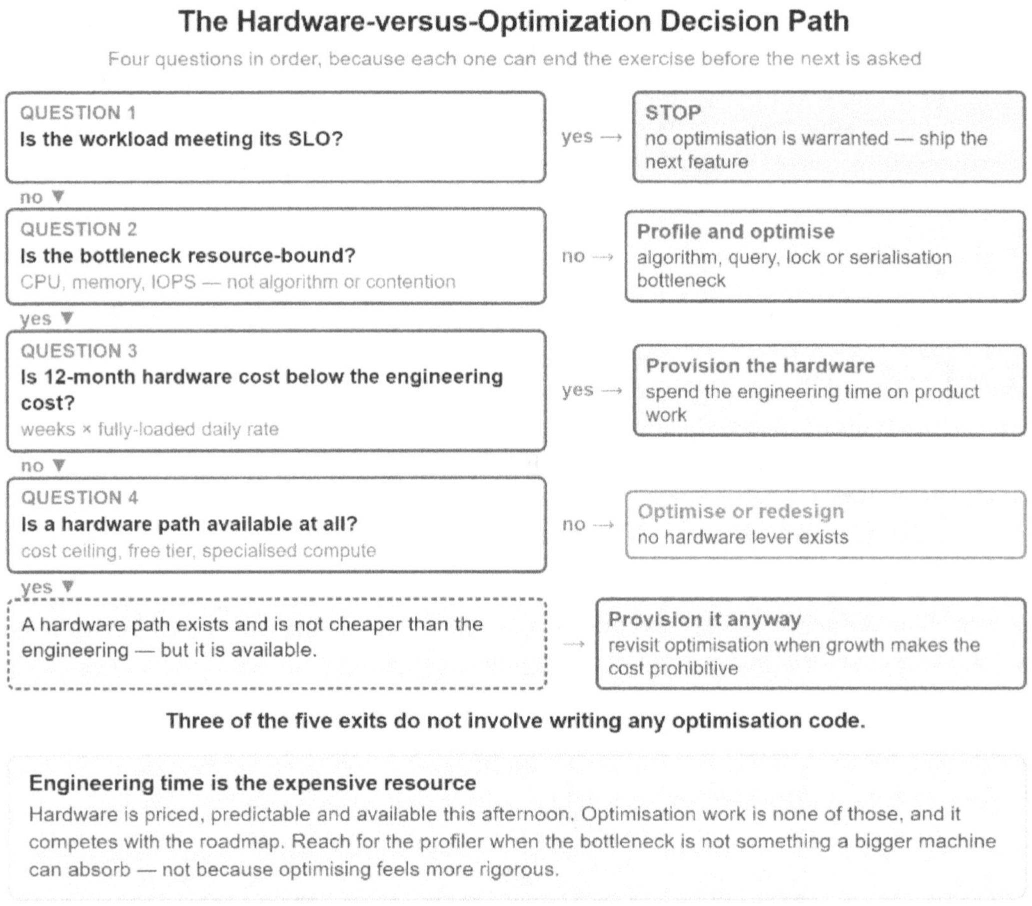

Figure 13.1: The Hardware-versus-Optimization Decision Path

Run as a sequence, the rule becomes four questions, and the order matters because each one can end the exercise before the next is asked:

1. Is the workload meeting its SLO? If yes, stop. There is no performance problem — there is a performance preference, and it is competing with the feature backlog for the same engineering weeks.
2. Is the bottleneck resource-bound? If the constraint is CPU, memory or IOPS, a hardware lever exists. If it is an algorithm, a lock, a query plan, or a serialization point, hardware will not move it and profiling is the correct next step.

3. Is the 12-month hardware cost lower than the engineering cost? Price both. Weeks multiplied by the fully-loaded daily rate is the engineering number, and it is usually larger than teams expect.
4. Is a hardware path available at all? Sometimes there is no affordable one — a free service that cannot absorb GPU inference, or a specialized-compute ceiling. Then optimization is not the economic choice; it is the only choice, and the calculation in step 3 is moot.

Three of the five exits do not involve writing optimization code. That ratio is the point of the framework: the default outcome of an honest performance review is usually to provision, accept, or ship something else.

From experience operating services on specialized and expensive compute: there are genuinely situations where the hardware option is not available at an acceptable cost, or where the service is offered for free and hardware spend cannot be recovered through pricing. A free documentation service cannot absorb the cost of GPU acceleration for every search query. In those cases, optimization is not optional — it is the only path. But the team that jumps to optimization when the hardware is available and affordable is paying for engineering time twice: once to do the optimization, and once in the opportunity cost of the product work that was not done.

Scenario	**Hardware Cost**	**Optimization Effort**	**Correct Decision**	**Rationale**
Search p99 at 200ms; SLO is 300ms	Node upgrade: +$400/month	3–5 engineering weeks of query optimization	Hardware — provision now	Engineering cost >> hardware cost; SLO still met with current hardware
Search p99 at 200ms; SLO is 100ms	Node upgrade: +$400/month	3–5 engineering weeks	Both — hardware buys time; optimization is required	Hardware buys time while optimization is in progress; optimization is required to hit SLO

Scenario	Hardware Cost	Optimization Effort	Correct Decision	Rationale
Free service; GPU inference is too expensive	No affordable hardware path	2–3 engineering weeks of model optimization	Optimization — required	Hardware option is not viable; optimization is the only path
Background indexing consumes 85% of node CPU	Node pool separation: + $800/month	4 weeks to optimize indexing pipeline	Hardware — separate the workloads	Physical isolation is faster and more reliable than optimization
Database write p99 at 24 ms; target 15 ms	Provisioned IOPS upgrade: +$400/month	1–2 weeks index audit	Both — index audit first; hardware if insufficient	Index audit may resolve without hardware; hardware is the fallback

Table 13.1: Hardware versus optimization compared across five ShopFlow scenarios, with the rationale for each

Note

The Tuning Trigger Signal: Not every performance problem is a tuning opportunity. A tuning trigger has three properties: the problem is reproducible and measurable, the root cause is algorithm or code efficiency rather than resource availability, and the hardware option is not viable at the required cost. If any property is missing, the correct response is not tuning. It is hardware provisioning, architecture change, or acceptance that the performance is within the good enough threshold.

Note

Anti-Pattern: The Premature Optimizer: Beginning optimization work before measuring the bottleneck, calculating the hardware alternative, and confirming that optimization is the correct economic choice. Optimization that is not driven by

> measurement is guesswork. Optimization that is not compared against the hardware alternative may be the more expensive path. Optimize when the data supports it, not when the engineering team finds the problem interesting.

> Note
>
> **The Optimization ROI Test:** Before starting any optimization project, answer three questions: what is the current measured cost of the problem (latency, IOPS, memory)? What is the hardware cost to resolve it? What is the engineering cost of the optimization (weeks × fully-loaded daily rate)? If engineering cost > 12-month hardware cost, provision the hardware. Revisit the optimization when growth makes the hardware cost prohibitive.

When hardware Doesn't help

The Hardware-First Rule has a precondition that is easy to skip past: it applies to problems that are resource-bound. A workload that is slow because it does not have enough CPU gets faster on a bigger instance. A workload that is slow because of how it is written does not, and money spent on hardware for it buys a marginally faster version of the same defect.

Quadratic and worse algorithms: an $O(n^2)$ routine on a bigger box is an $O(n^2)$ routine. Doubling the hardware buys you a 41% increase in the n you can handle before the same wall arrives, and the wall keeps moving toward you as the data grows.

Lock contention: threads waiting on a mutex are not consuming CPU, so adding cores adds contenders rather than throughput. Under some access patterns more cores make it measurably worse.

Inefficient database queries: a missing index or a leading-wildcard LIKE produces a sequential scan. Faster storage shortens the scan; it does not stop the scan from being the wrong plan.

Network latency between services: a chatty call pattern that makes 40 round trips is bound by the speed of light and the network stack, not by the instance size at either end. The fix is fewer round trips.

Serialisation bottlenecks: a single-threaded stage, a global lock or a queue with one consumer sets a ceiling that no amount of parallel capacity elsewhere raises. Amdahl's law is not negotiable with a purchase order.

> **Note**
>
> The Resource-Bound Precondition: Confirm the bottleneck is resource-bound before pricing any hardware option. The test is empirical: if the workload does not get proportionally faster on a larger instance in a controlled trial, it is not resource-bound and the Hardware-First Rule does not apply to it. Run that trial before the purchase, not after. Provisioning hardware for an algorithmic bottleneck is the one outcome that costs money and engineering time and leaves the problem in place—it converts a software defect into a recurring line item.

The tuning trigger signal

Not every performance problem is a tuning opportunity. The correct signal for starting optimization work is specific: the problem is bounded by software efficiency, not by resource availability, and the hardware option is not viable at the required cost.

Performance Problem	Root Cause Signal	Hardware Option?	Correct First Action
p99 latency increasing linearly with traffic	Traffic growth consumes proportional resources	Yes — add capacity	Scale horizontally; optimize later if the hardware ceiling is reached
p99 latency spikes during specific operations	Specific operation is inefficient; traffic volume unchanged	Maybe	Profile the specific operation; optimize it; use hardware if optimization is insufficient
Specific workload consuming 85%+ of shared node	Workload needs more resources than it is allocated	Yes — physically separate	Separate the workloads onto dedicated hardware; optimize if the separation cost is too high
p99 stable, but cost growing faster than traffic	Algorithm is O(n^2) or equivalent; efficiency degrades at scale	Expensive — hardware grows with n^2	Optimize the algorithm; hardware will not scale with quadratic growth

Performance Problem	Root Cause Signal	Hardware Option?	Correct First Action
Free service with cost ceiling	No pricing lever available to absorb hardware cost	No — cost-constrained	Optimize; no hardware option exists within the cost constraint

Table 13.2: Performance problems by root-cause signal, whether a hardware option exists, and the correct first action

Note

Manager's Math — The Optimization vs. Hardware Decision: ShopFlow's code indexing job is consuming 85% of the shared node CPU during indexing windows, causing search p99 to degrade from 95ms to 210ms. Option A: Separate the indexing job onto a dedicated node pool (+$800/month). Option B: Optimize the indexing pipeline to reduce CPU consumption by 50% (estimated 4 engineering weeks = approximately $20,000 in fully-loaded engineering cost). Option A payback vs. Option B: $20,000 ÷ $800 = 25 months. Option A pays back in less than 2 years at current indexing volume. If indexing volume grows 2x next year, Option B's optimization benefit halves and Option A's cost doubles — but Option B's engineering investment is sunk. Option A is the correct choice today.

Architect's prompt 13.1: the optimization decision audit

When to use this: Use this prompt before starting any performance optimization project or when a team is considering hardware provisioning vs. engineering optimization.

```
Act as a Principal Performance Engineer. I am evaluating whether to
optimize [Component/Workload] or provision additional hardware.

Current state:
- Measured performance problem: [latency / IOPS / CPU / memory]
- Current metric value: [X]
- Target metric value: [Y]
- Root cause hypothesis: [resource-bound / algorithm inefficiency / contention]

(1) Confirm the root cause: is the problem resource-bound (hardware option
    exists) or algorithm-bound (optimization required regardless of hardware)?
(2) Calculate the hardware option cost:
```

```
    - What hardware change resolves the problem? (instance upgrade / node add)
    - Monthly cost delta: [$X/month]
    - Time to implement: [hours]
(3) Calculate the optimization cost:
    - Estimated engineering weeks to implement and validate
    - Fully-loaded engineering cost: [weeks x daily rate]
(4) Apply the Optimization ROI Test:
    - Is 12-month hardware cost < engineering optimization cost?
    - If yes: provision hardware. State clearly.
    - If no: proceed with optimization. Provide the profiling approach.
(5) If optimization is warranted: define the measurement baseline
    (EXPLAIN ANALYZE / profiler output / benchmark result) before
    any code is changed.
```

Resource contention: the hidden cost of shared systems

Resource contention is the performance tax paid when two workloads compete for the same physical resource — CPU, memory, IOPS, network bandwidth, or connection pool capacity. The tax is not linear: two workloads sharing a resource do not each get half the resource. The higher-priority workload gets what it needs; the lower-priority workload gets what is left over, which varies unpredictably based on the higher-priority workload's instantaneous demand.

ShopFlow's current contention: code indexing jobs (P2, background) and search queries (P0, user-facing) share node compute. During indexing windows, the P2 job consumes 85% of node CPU, leaving 15% for P0 search. The search p99 degrades from 95ms to 210ms. The indexing job is not broken. The search service is not broken. The sharing arrangement is broken.

> Note
>
> **The Physical Separation Rule:** P0 workloads and P2 workloads must not share physical compute resources. Not logical partitions on the same node. Not Kubernetes resource limits on the same node pool. Physical separation: different node pools, different instance types, different auto-scaling policies. A P2 job that can consume 85% of CPU on a shared node is a P2 job that has not been physically separated from the P0 service it is degrading.

> Note
>
> **Tool Tax — dedicated node pools:** Physical separation is the right answer here and it is not the cheap one. Budget for the idle capacity that dedication guarantees, a second set of scaling policies and alerts, node-pool upgrades and drains that now happen twice, and the ongoing discipline of keeping workloads on the pool they belong to — because the first P2 job scheduled onto the P0 pool for convenience quietly undoes the separation you paid for.

From building and operating systems where petabytes of content must be indexed for search while simultaneously serving live search queries, the solution was not to optimize the indexing pipeline to consume less CPU (though that work was also done). The foundational solution was to run the indexing pipeline on dedicated infrastructure that the live search service could not see. When the indexing pipeline consumed 100% of its dedicated node pool's CPU, the live search service experienced zero degradation. The two workloads did not compete because they did not share.

Contention Type	Observable Signal	Short-Term Mitigation	Long-Term Fix
CPU contention (P2 job vs. P0 service)	P0 service p99 spikes during P2 job execution windows	Kubernetes CPU limits on P2 pod — throttles P2 but affects job duration	Dedicated node pool for P2 jobs; P0 service on separate pool
Memory contention	P0 pod OOM events increase during P2 batch execution	Memory limits on P2 pod; eviction priority for P2	Separate node pools; P2 memory limits enforced at the pool level
Database IOPS contention	P0 query latency spikes when P2 reporting jobs run	Rate limit P2 database connections; schedule P2 jobs off-peak	Read replica for P2 reporting; P0 reads from primary/primary replica

Contention Type	Observable Signal	Short-Term Mitigation	Long-Term Fix
Connection pool contention	P0 requests queue or fail when P2 consumes shared pool	Reduce P2 pool size; increase P0 pool size	Dedicated connection pool per workload tier
Network bandwidth contention	P0 API calls experience latency when bulk data transfers run	Throttle P2 network I/O with tc (traffic control)	Network policy enforcement; separate network interfaces for high-bandwidth P2 jobs

Table 13.3: Resource contention types, their observable signal, and the short- and long-term fix for each

> **Note**
>
> The Contention Correlation Rule: Resource contention produces a specific, identifiable signature: P0 p99 latency spikes that correlate with P2 job execution windows but not with P0 traffic increases. If the P0 traffic is flat and the p99 spikes, look for a co-located workload. If the spike correlates with a scheduled job, the diagnosis is contention. The fix is not optimization of either workload; it is physical separation of them.

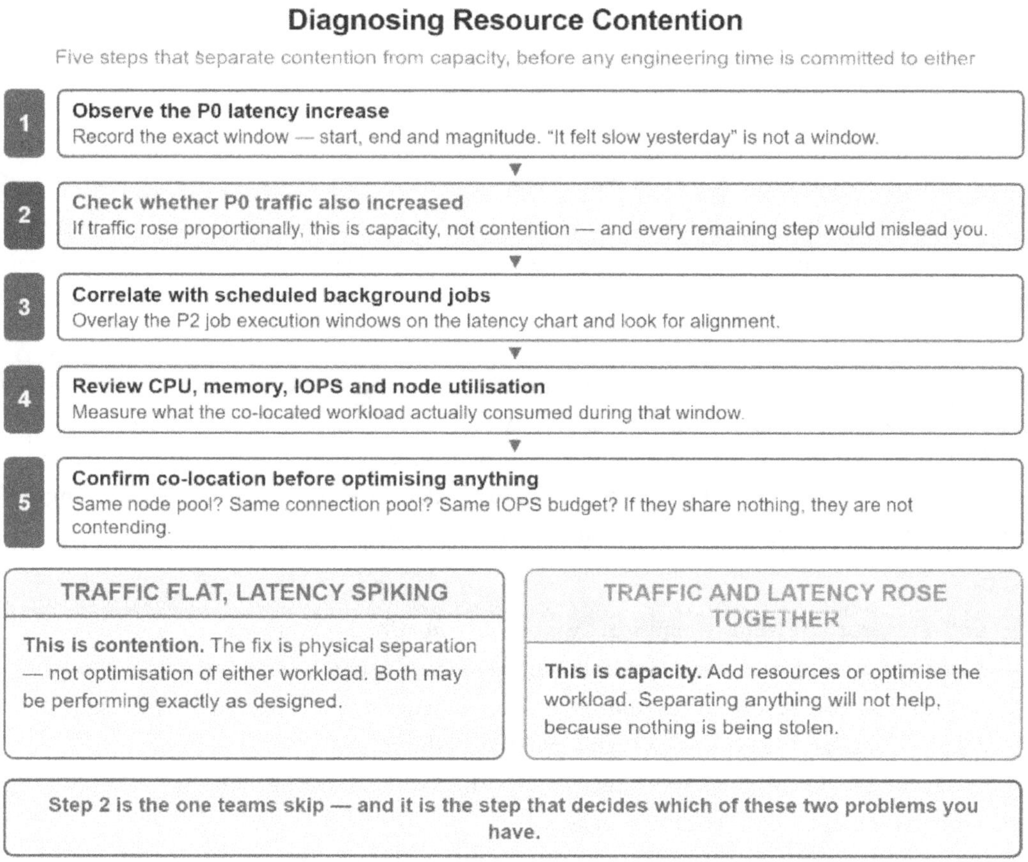

Figure 13.2: Diagnosing Resource Contention

Reaching that diagnosis reliably takes a repeatable sequence rather than intuition. The five steps below separate contention from capacity before any engineering time is committed to either:

1. Observe the P0 latency increase and record the window precisely — start, end, and magnitude. A vague 'search felt slow this morning' cannot be correlated against anything.
2. Check whether P0 traffic also increased over that window. This is the step teams skip, and it is the one that decides everything: if traffic rose proportionally, this is a capacity problem and separation will not help.

3. If P0 traffic was flat, correlate the window against scheduled background jobs. Overlay the P2 execution windows on the latency chart and look for alignment rather than coincidence—two or three repetitions before calling it.
4. Review CPU, memory, IOPS and node utilization for the correlated workload during that exact window. The question is not whether the P2 job was running; it is how much of the shared resource it took while it ran.
5. Confirm co-location before optimizing anything. Same node pool, same connection pool, same IOPS budget — establish which resource is actually shared. Optimizing a workload that turns out not to be co-located is engineering time spent on a coincidence.

For ShopFlow the sequence resolves in minutes. Search p99 rises from 95ms to 210ms; search traffic over the same window is flat; the window aligns exactly with the code indexing schedule; the indexing job is measured at 85% of node CPU; and both workloads are on the same node pool. That is contention, and no amount of optimizing either workload changes the fact that they are sharing a resource neither of them is willing to yield.

> Note
>
> **Anti-Pattern: The Noisy Neighbor:** Two or more workloads of different priority tiers sharing physical infrastructure without enforcement of resource boundaries. The Noisy Neighbor pattern produces intermittent P0 performance degradation that is difficult to diagnose because the P0 service itself is healthy — the contention comes from outside it. Observable signature: P0 p99 latency spikes that correlate with P2 job execution windows but not with P0 traffic increases.

> Note
>
> The Background Budget Rule: Every P2 background job must have an explicit resource budget: maximum CPU percentage, maximum memory, maximum IOPS, and a maximum execution window. The budget is enforced by Kubernetes resource limits and by scheduling constraints that prevent the job from running during P0 peak traffic windows. A P2 job without a resource budget is a P2 job with an implicit budget of 'whatever is left over'—which is zero during peak load, exactly when it matters most.

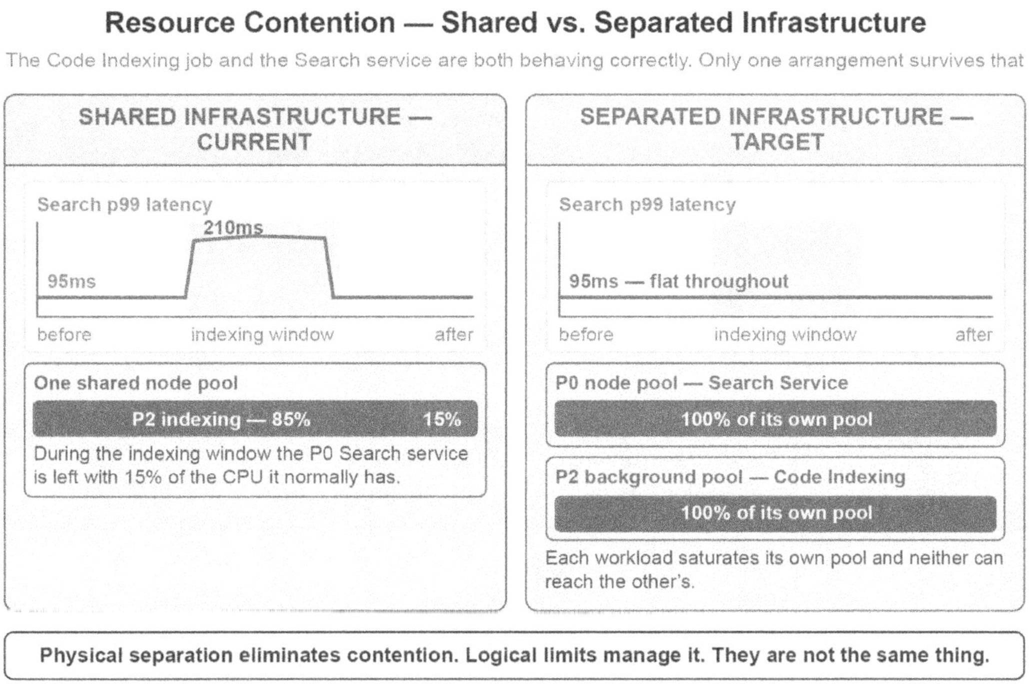

Figure 13.3: Resource Contention — Shared vs. Separated Infrastructure

Architect's prompt 13.2: the contention audit

When to use this: Use this prompt when P0 p99 latency is degrading intermittently without a corresponding increase in P0 traffic, suggesting resource contention from a co-located workload.

```
Act as a Principal Performance Engineer specializing in resource contention.
I am diagnosing intermittent P0 performance degradation on [P0 Service].

Symptoms:
- P0 service p99 latency: [Xms normal, Yms during degradation windows]
- Degradation window pattern: [time of day / correlated with job execution /
random]
- P0 traffic volume during degradation: [same / lower / higher than normal]

Co-located workloads on the same node pool:
[List all services and jobs running on the same Kubernetes node pool]
```

```
(1) Correlate P0 p99 spikes with co-located workload execution times.
    Is there a statistically significant correlation?
(2) For the correlated workload: measure its peak CPU, memory, and IOPS
    consumption during the window where P0 degrades.
(3) Calculate the resource headroom available to P0 during the contention
    window: [node capacity] - [P2 consumption] = [P0 available].
(4) Compare [P0 available] against [P0 resource requirements at p99 SLO].
    If P0 available < P0 requirements: physical separation is required.
(5) Design the separated infrastructure:
    - P0 node pool: instance type, min/max node count, auto-scaling signal
    - P2 background pool: instance type, execution window constraints,
      resource budget (CPU %, memory limit, IOPS limit, max duration)
```

Metric	Before Separation (Shared Pool)	After Separation (Dedicated Pools)	Improvement
Search p99 (normal traffic)	95ms	95 ms	No change — contention is the variable
Search p99 (during indexing window)	210 ms	95ms	55% improvement; SLO fully restored
Code indexing completion time	4 hours (throttled by shared CPU limits)	3.2 hours (dedicated full node capacity)	20% improvement as a side effect
PO SLO breach events per month	3–5 (during indexing windows)	0	Eliminated
P2 node pool cost	$0 (shared with PO)	$800/month (dedicated Spot Instances)	+$800/mo — justified by PO SLO protection

Table 13.4: ShopFlow search and indexing metrics before and after physically separating the workloads

P0 to P2 framework: tiering performance requirements

The P0/P1/P2 framework from *Chapter 12* was a resilience tool: it defined which scenarios must survive failure and which can degrade gracefully. In *Chapter 13*, the same framework becomes a performance budget tool: it defines which workloads get the expensive, high-performance resources and which get the cheaper, good-enough resources.

The economic insight is direct: not all performance is equally valuable. A 10ms improvement in P0 checkout latency is worth more than a 10ms improvement in P2 analytics query time. P0 latency improvements drive conversion rate improvements, which drive revenue. P2 latency improvements drive analyst satisfaction, which drives internal goodwill. These are real but not equivalent benefits, and they should not receive equivalent infrastructure investment.

> Note
>
> **The Performance Budget Rule:** Assign a performance budget to each workload tier before provisioning hardware. P0 workloads receive dedicated high-performance resources — the minimum required to meet their SLO, not the maximum available. P1 workloads receive shared resources with QoS guarantees. P2 workloads receive whatever remains after P0 and P1 are provisioned, on the cheapest instance type that can execute the workload within its non-critical time window. Performance budget mismatches — P2 workloads on P0-grade hardware, or P0 workloads on undersized shared infrastructure — are the source of both cost overruns and SLO breaches.

> Note
>
> **Tool Tax — per-workload cost attribution:** You cannot run the hardware-versus-optimization comparison without knowing what each workload costs, and that number does not exist by default. Budget for a tagging standard applied consistently across every resource, enforcement so untagged resources cannot be created, shared-cost allocation rules for the infrastructure that genuinely is shared, and a monthly review that someone owns. Cost attribution is the instrumentation that makes every other decision in this chapter possible, and it decays the moment tagging discipline slips.

Tier	Latency SLO	Availability SLO	Infrastructure Type	Instance Type	Auto-Scaling Signal	Optimization Priority
P0 (checkout, search)	<200ms p99	99.9%+	Dedicated node pool, never shared	High-memory, high-CPU compute	Latency-based (scale before SLO breach)	High — optimize first, hardware as a last resort
P1 (order history, filtering)	<1s p99	99.5%	Shared pool with QoS priority class	General-purpose compute	CPU-based (scales at 70%)	Medium — optimize if cost exceeds threshold
P2 (indexing, reporting, analytics)	< 10 minutes for batch jobs	Best effort	Shared pool, lowest priority; Spot Instances acceptable	Burstable/ spot compute	Queue-depth-based; scales to zero when idle	Low — provision the cheapest option first

Table 13.5: Performance budgets by tier: SLO, infrastructure type, scaling signal, and optimization priority

The framework resolves the CFO's question directly. ShopFlow's 34% infrastructure cost increase has two components. The P0 dedicated node pool (+$3,200/month) is justified — it protects the checkout and search SLOs that drive revenue. The P2 background processing infrastructure (+$4,100/month) has not been reviewed against the Performance Budget Rule: it is running on general-purpose compute at full price during business hours, when spot instances at a 60–70% discount could execute the same workload during off-peak hours with no user impact.

> Note
>
> **The Spot Instance Eligibility Rule:** A workload is eligible for spot instances when two conditions are both true: the workload is interruptible (a spot reclamation can be handled by checkpointing and restarting without data loss) and the workload is time-flexible (it has a completion window measured in hours or days, not a completion moment measured in seconds). P0 services are never eligible for spot instances. P2 batch jobs are almost always eligible.

Note

Tool Tax — spot instances: A 65% discount is real and it is priced in engineering. Budget for checkpointing and resumable job design, interruption handling tested against actual reclamation rather than assumed, a fallback to on-demand when spot capacity is unavailable in your zone, longer, and less predictable completion windows, and monitoring that distinguishes a reclaimed job from a failed one. Spot is cheaper compute for workloads that were designed for it, and a source of mysterious partial failures for workloads that were not.

Note

Manager's Math — The P2 Right-Sizing Opportunity: ShopFlow's P2 background processing (code indexing, report generation, analytics pipeline) currently runs on on-demand general-purpose instances at $4,100/month. These workloads have two properties that make them candidates for spot instances: they are interruptible (a spot reclamation can be handled by checkpointing and restarting the batch job) and they are time-flexible (they do not need to complete within a specific hour, only within a specific day). Moving P2 workloads to spot instances at a 65% discount reduces the P2 compute cost from $4,100 to approximately $1,435/month — saving $2,665/month, or $31,980 annually. Engineering cost to implement spot-aware batch job checkpointing: approximately 3–5 engineering days of implementation, plus the operational work that follows it — interruption testing, runbook updates, and the first weeks of monitoring reclamation behavior in production. Budget three weeks end to end rather than three days, which at a fully loaded rate is roughly $15,000. Break-even: under six months, after which the $2,665/month recurs indefinitely. The implementation estimate is the smaller half of the cost, and it is the half teams quote.

Architect's prompt 13.3: the performance budget audit

When to use this: Use this prompt when infrastructure costs are growing faster than traffic or when reviewing the resource allocation across workload tiers for a system that has accumulated infrastructure without a tiering framework.

```
Act as a Principal Capacity Engineer. I am auditing the performance
budget allocation for [System Name] with the following workload tiers:
```

```
[For each workload, provide: name, tier (P0/P1/P2), current instance type,
current monthly cost, measured p99 latency, target p99 latency SLO]

(1) For each P2 workload running on on-demand compute:
    - Is the workload interruptible? (can a spot reclamation be handled?)
    - Is the workload time-flexible? (does it have a completion window, not a
moment?)
    - If both yes: calculate the spot instance cost at 60% discount.
(2) For each P0 workload:
    - Is it provisioned at the minimum required to meet SLO, or at excess?
    - Calculate the minimum instance size that meets the p99 SLO under peak load.
(3) Identify any P2 workload on P0-grade hardware.
    What is the monthly cost delta of downgrading to the correct tier?
(4) Identify any P0 workload sharing node capacity with P1 or P2 workloads.
    Design the physical separation.
(5) Calculate the total monthly savings from:
    - Moving P2 workloads to spot instances
    - Right-sizing P0 workloads to minimum required capacity
    - Separating mixed-tier node pools
```

Predictive planning: getting maximum results from minimal resources

Capacity planning is the practice of ensuring the system has the resources it needs before it runs out of them, rather than after. Reactive capacity planning — waiting for a resource to saturate before provisioning more — guarantees a period of degraded performance between the saturation event and the provisioning response. That period is an incident. Predictive capacity planning converts that incident into a scheduled maintenance event.

The right approach is not to build a 12-month capacity plan with precise hardware lead times and growth projections. The future is not that predictable, and the engineering time spent on a detailed long-range forecast is often worth less than the engineering time spent on something else. The right approach is to provision a reasonable headroom buffer, invest heavily in the scaling readiness that makes provisioning fast when it is needed, and maintain a short planning horizon that is updated regularly.

> **Note**
>
> The Predictive Headroom Rule: Provision capacity to cover 120–150% of current peak demand. The additional 20–50% is the headroom buffer that absorbs normal traffic

variance and buys time to execute a planned scaling event before an incident forces an unplanned one. More headroom than 150% of peak is over-provisioning—paying for capacity that is not being used. Less headroom than 120% of peak is under-provisioning—one traffic spike away from an incident.

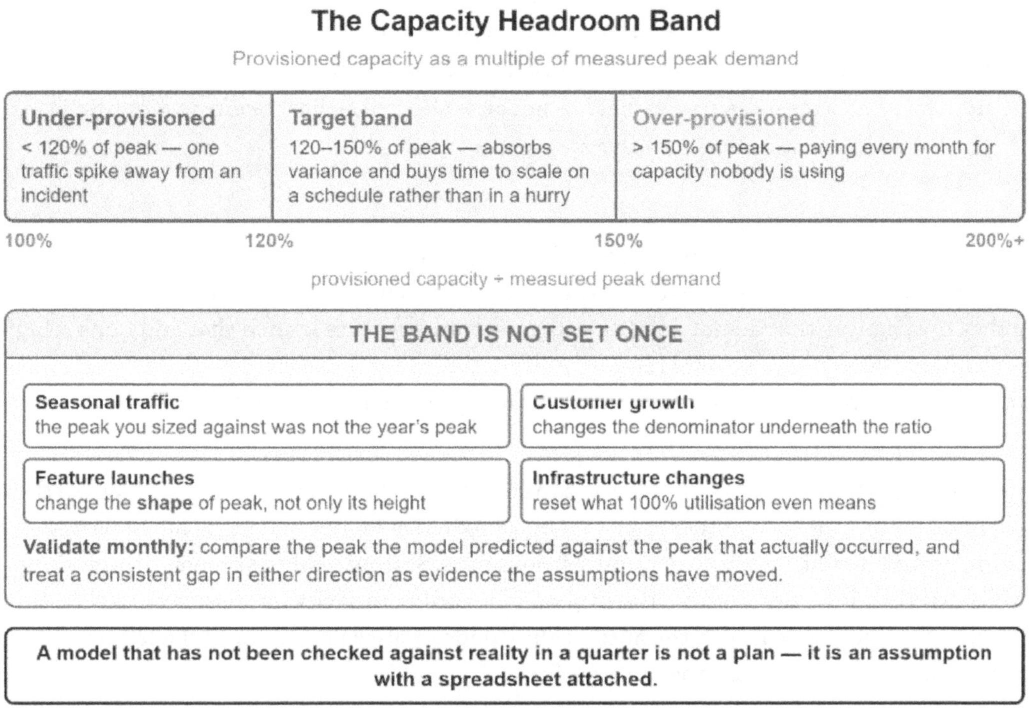

Figure 13.4: The Capacity Headroom Band

> Note
>
> **The Model Recalibration Rule:** A capacity model is a claim about the future made from last month's telemetry, and it decays. Validate it against production every month: compare the peak the model predicted against the peak that actually occurred, and treat a consistent gap in either direction as a signal that the assumptions have moved. Four things invalidate a model faster than growth alone — seasonal traffic patterns, customer growth changing the denominator, feature launches changing the shape of peak rather than only its height, and infrastructure changes that reset what 100% utilization even means. A model that has not been checked against reality in a quarter is not a plan; it is an assumption with a spreadsheet attached.

The recalibration is cheap — a monthly review comparing predicted peak against observed peak, and a quarterly one that revisits the growth rate itself. What makes it valuable is that it catches the changes that do not announce themselves. A feature launch that adds a new high-cost endpoint does not raise total request volume much, but it can raise peak CPU per request enough to consume the headroom band without any change in the traffic graph the model watches.

The more important investment than the capacity model is the scaling readiness. When the system needs to scale — whether triggered by a predictive model or by real-time metrics — the scaling procedure must execute in minutes, not hours. Scaling readiness means: the scaling scripts exist and have been tested, the runbook for adding capacity has been executed at least once in a non-incident context, the auto-scaling policies are validated, and the team knows exactly what to do when the capacity alert fires.

> Note
>
> The Scaling Readiness Mandate: The scaling procedure for every P0 service must be documented, scripted, and tested before it is needed. A scaling procedure that has never been executed is a scaling procedure that will fail at the worst moment. Run the scaling procedure in a non-incident context — a scheduled drill, a planned load test, a maintenance window — at least once per quarter. Readiness is not capacity. It is the ability to add capacity quickly when the metrics demand it.

Note

Tool Tax — the capacity model: A model is a living artifact, not a spreadsheet you finish. Budget for the monthly recalibration against production telemetry, the quarterly revisit of the growth rate itself, event-based updates when a launch changes the shape of peak, and the ownership question of who notices when the model and reality have diverged. An unmaintained capacity model is worse than none, because it is trusted.

Planning Approach	**Horizon**	**Accuracy**	**Engineering Cost**	**When to Use**
Reactive only (auto-scale + alerts)	Hours to days	High — based on real demand	Very low — auto-scaling handles it	P2 workloads; unpredictable traffic patterns
Short-range predictive (30-day rolling model)	30 days	High — trends are visible	Low — monthly 2-hour review	P1 and P0 workloads with predictable growth patterns
Medium-range predictive (90-day model)	90 days	Medium — trend extrapolation	Medium — quarterly planning session	P0 workloads requiring hardware with lead times (dedicated instances, reserved capacity)
Long-range predictive (12-month model)	12 months	Low — too many variables	High — significant forecasting effort	Only for major infrastructure investments (data center, multi-year cloud commitments)

Planning Approach	Horizon	Accuracy	Engineering Cost	When to Use
Event-based predictive (campaign, launch)	Days to weeks before event	High for known events	Low — triggered by marketing calendar	Flash sales, product launches, viral campaigns

Table 13.6: Capacity planning approaches compared by horizon, accuracy, engineering cost, and when to use each

Note

Safe Scale Check — Scaling Headroom: Before any planned traffic event — a marketing campaign, a product launch, a scheduled high-traffic window — verify that the current provisioned capacity covers the expected peak at 150% headroom, and that the scaling procedure has been tested within the last 30 days. A high-traffic event that hits an unprepared system is not a capacity failure. It is a planning failure. The event was known. The preparation was not done.

Note

Tool Tax — the load-testing environment: Capacity claims require load testing, and load testing requires an environment that resembles production closely enough to be believable. Budget for the environment itself and the cost of running it at realistic scale, representative test data that stays representative, test scenarios maintained alongside the application they exercise, and the engineering time to interpret results rather than just collect them. A load test against unrealistic data produces a number that is precise and wrong.

Readiness Check	Frequency	P0 required ?	Current ShopFlow Status
Scaling procedure is documented and version-controlled	Per change	Yes	Missing from 3 of 6 P0 services
Scaling scripts tested in a non-incident context	Quarterly drill	Yes	Never executed outside incidents
Auto-scaling policies validated under realistic load	Monthly load test	Yes	Validated at launch; not re-tested since Ch7 decomposition
Capacity headroom calculated: provisioned / peak demand x 100	Monthly review	Yes	Not calculated — capacity added reactively
Upcoming high-traffic events identified and capacity pre-verified	2 weeks before event	Yes	No process; event-driven incidents in prior quarters
Spot instance interruption handling tested (P2 jobs)	Quarterly	P2 only	Never tested

Table 13.7: The scaling readiness checklist, with ShopFlow's current status against each check

Architect's prompt 13.4: the capacity planning model

When to use this: Use this prompt to build or update the capacity plan for a P0 service or before any planned high-traffic event.

```
Act as a Principal Capacity Planning Engineer. I am building the
capacity model for [P0 Service] with the following current state:

Current peak traffic: [X RPS]
Current provisioned capacity: [N nodes / instances]
Current peak resource utilization: [X% CPU / Y% memory / Z% IOPS]
Historical traffic growth rate: [X% per month over last 6 months]
Known upcoming high-traffic events: [list with dates and expected traffic
```

```
multiplier]

(1) Calculate the current headroom percentage:
    [provisioned capacity] / [peak demand] x 100.
    Is this within the 120-150% target range?
(2) Project the date at which the system will breach 100% provisioned
    capacity at the current growth rate.
(3) Calculate the capacity required for each known high-traffic event.
    Does current provisioning cover the expected peak at 150% headroom?
(4) Define the scaling procedure that must be executed if the 100% capacity
    date is reached:
    - What specific action adds capacity? (node add / instance resize)
    - How long does the action take to complete?
    - Who executes it, and what is the trigger metric?
(5) Define the scaling readiness drill: what is the procedure to test
    the scaling action in a non-incident context, and when was it last run?
```

The bare minimum: defining good enough for noncritical paths

The most direct path to shipping working software is to define what 'working' means for each component and stop optimizing once that definition is met. This is not an argument for mediocrity. It is an argument for precision: knowing exactly what standard each component must meet, meeting that standard, and spending the remaining engineering capacity on the next thing.

The alternative — optimizing everything to the highest achievable standard — produces systems that are technically excellent in ways users do not experience and commercially late in ways that competitors capitalize on. A feature that is delivered at 'good enough' performance six months early beats a feature that is delivered at optimal performance after the market window has closed.

This philosophy is sometimes called 'ship fast, improve iteratively.' The key word is iteratively: the first version ships at good enough, the second version improves on the real usage data that the first version generated, and the third version addresses the specific bottlenecks that scale exposed. This sequence produces better outcomes than one version optimized theoretically before it has any real usage data.

> **Note**
>
> The Good Enough Threshold: For every component, define the performance threshold that constitutes good enough: the minimum acceptable p99 latency, the maximum

acceptable error rate, and the minimum acceptable throughput. Once the component meets the threshold, stop optimizing, and ship it. The threshold is not the best possible performance. It is the performance that users will not notice as a problem. Users do not notice good performance. They notice bad performance. Define where bad begins, stay above it, and move on.

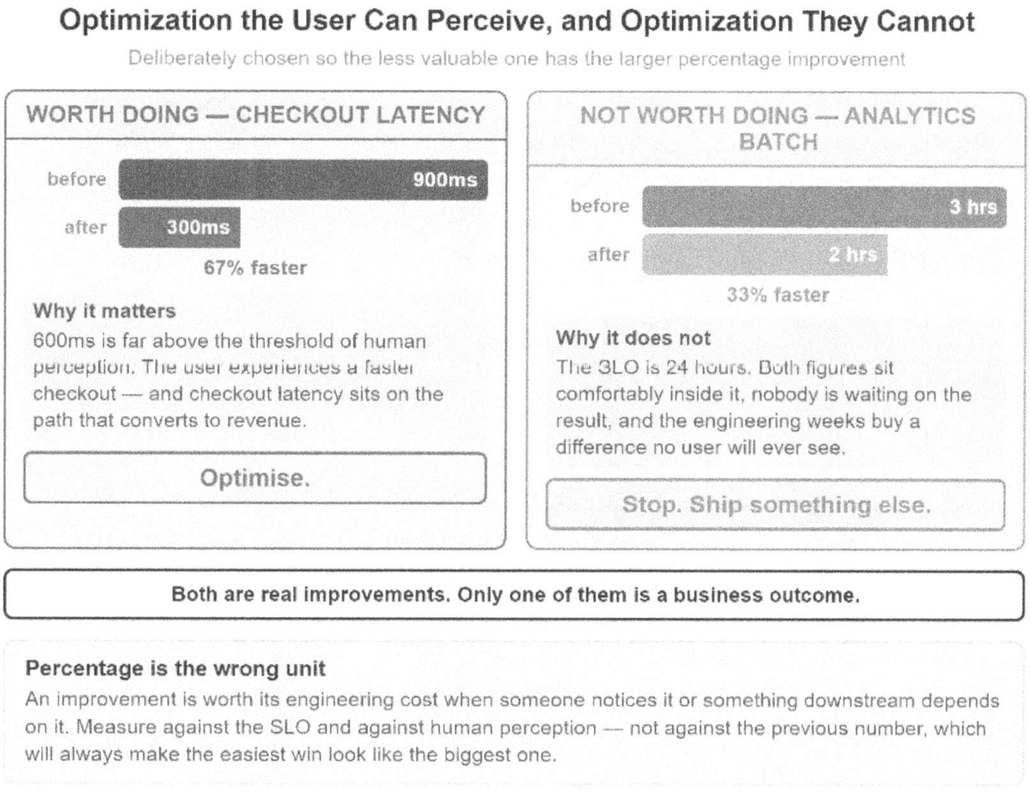

Figure 13.5: Optimization the User Can Perceive, and Optimization They Cannot

Two ShopFlow examples make the threshold concrete, and they are deliberately chosen so that the less valuable one has the larger percentage improvement.

Worth doing — checkout latency, 900ms to 300ms. A 67% reduction, and every millisecond of it is perceptible. 900ms is a page that feels slow; 300ms is a page that feels immediate. The improvement lands on the P0 path that converts to revenue, and the difference is visible to every customer who checks out. This optimization pays for itself in conversion rate alone.

Not worth doing — the analytics batch, three hours to two. A 33% reduction against a 24-hour SLO. Nobody is waiting on the result; the job runs overnight and the report is read the next morning either way. The engineering weeks are real, the improvement is real, and the business value is approximately zero because no human interacts with the difference. The same weeks spent on a user-facing capability produce something a customer can notice.

Note that the smaller percentage is the one worth doing. Percentage improvement is a benchmark metric, not a business one — the question is never how much faster it got, but whether anyone can tell.

> Note
>
> The Iterative Optimization Rule: Ship the first version at good enough. Optimize the second version on real usage data. Fix the specific bottlenecks that scale exposes in the third version. This sequence — ship, observe, optimize — produces better outcomes than optimizing theoretically before any real usage data exists. The usage data from the first version tells you which optimization is actually worth doing. Without that data, you are optimizing guesses.

> Note
>
> **Anti-Pattern: The Perfection Trap:** Continuing to optimize a component that already meets its performance threshold, at the expense of shipping features that users are waiting for. Observable signature: a component whose p99 is well within SLO but whose development team continues to profile and optimize it while the feature backlog grows. The Perfection Trap feels like engineering rigor. It is engineering avoidance — staying in the comfortable, measurable work of optimization rather than shipping the harder, less certain work of new features.

The good enough decision is also a trust decision. Engineers who take pride in their work often resist good enough framing because it sounds like accepting failure. The reframe that works in practice: good enough means the user cannot tell the difference between this performance and perfect performance. If the user cannot tell the difference, the difference does not exist in any commercially meaningful sense. Spend the engineering time where users can tell the difference.

Component	Good Enough Threshold	Current Performance	Status	Next Action
Checkout flow (P0)	< 300ms p99; 99.9% success rate	285ms p99; 99.7% success rate	At threshold — optimize further	Investigate the 0.3% failure rate; do not optimize latency
Product search (P0)	< 200ms p99; results for all queries	95ms p99 (normal); 210ms during indexing	Below threshold (indexing contention)	Separate indexing compute; search is already within threshold otherwise
Order history (P1)	< 1s p99; stale 60s acceptable	480ms p99 from read replica	Comfortably within threshold	No action; do not optimize
Code indexing pipeline (P2)	Complete within business day	Completes in 4 hours; runs during business hours	Functional; causes P0 contention	Separate compute; do not optimize the pipeline itself
Analytics reporting (P2)	Complete within 24 hours	Completes in 3 hours	Comfortably within threshold	No action; do not optimize
Search result ranking model	< 50ms inference p99	35 ms p99	Within threshold	No action; do not optimize

Table 13.8: ShopFlow components against their good enough thresholds, with the next action for each

Note

The Ship-First Rule: Ship the feature when it meets the good enough threshold. Not when it meets the optimal threshold. Not when one more round of profiling is done. When it meets the good enough threshold. The backlog of features that users are waiting for is a business cost that accumulates while the team optimizes a component that is already good enough. Measure the backlog cost before deciding to optimize beyond threshold.

Note

Safe Scale Check — Good Enough Revisit: Good enough thresholds are not permanent. As user expectations change, as competitive benchmarks shift, and as usage patterns evolve, a threshold that was good enough at 10,000 users may not be good enough at 10 million. Review good enough thresholds quarterly — not to lower the bar, but to ensure the bar is still in the right place. A system that was fast enough two years ago may be perceivably slow today, not because it changed, but because the reference frame changed.

Note

Manager's Math — The Good Enough Opportunity Cost: At ShopFlow, the search ranking model has a p99 of 35ms against a good enough threshold of 50ms. The team has proposed 3 engineering weeks of further optimization to reach 20ms. The 15ms improvement is imperceptible to users — both 35ms and 20ms are faster than human perception of latency. The 3 engineering weeks redirected to the next product feature would deliver a capability that users can perceive and that competitors do not yet have. At a fully loaded engineering cost, 3 weeks = approximately $15,000. The business value of an imperceptible 15ms latency improvement is approximately zero. The business value of a user-perceptible new feature is determined by the product team. This is the only comparison that matters.

Architect's prompt 13.5: the Good-Enough audit

When to use this: Use this prompt when reviewing the engineering backlog for optimization work that may have passed the good enough threshold or when making the decision to continue or stop a performance optimization project.

```
Act as a Principal Engineering Manager evaluating performance optimization
investments. I am reviewing the following optimization projects in progress:
```

```
[For each project: component name, current p99, good enough threshold,
target p99, estimated engineering weeks remaining, user impact of target vs.
current]

For each project:
(1) Is the current performance at or below the good enough threshold?
    If at threshold: stop the optimization and redirect the engineering capacity.
(2) If above threshold: calculate the user-perceptibility of the gap.
    Is the difference between current and threshold noticeable to a user?
    If not perceptible: reconsider whether the threshold was set correctly.
(3) For each project above threshold: calculate the engineering cost to reach
    threshold vs. the engineering cost to reach the proposed target.
    Is the additional cost beyond threshold justified by user impact?
(4) What is the backlog opportunity cost of continuing the optimization?
    What feature(s) could be shipped in the remaining engineering weeks?
(5) Make the recommendation: stop optimization (at good enough threshold),
    continue to threshold (below threshold), or continue beyond threshold
    (with explicit justification for why the additional cost is worth it).
```

Optimization Decision	Hardware Cost	Engineering Cost	Correct Choice	Outcome
Code indexing/ search contention	Dedicated P2 node pool: + $800/month	4 weeks optimization: ~$20,000	Hardware	Physical separation; 55% search p99 improvement
P2 workloads on on-demand compute	N/A — spot is same hardware, different billing	3 days spot config: ~$2,400	Hardware (spot pricing)	65% P2 cost reduction; $31,980 annual savings
Search ranking model p99: 35ms vs. 50ms SLO	N/A — already within SLO	3 weeks further optimization: ~$15,000	Stop — at good enough threshold	Engineering time redirected to the product backlog

Optimization Decision	Hardware Cost	Engineering Cost	Correct Choice	Outcome
Analytics report p99: 3hr vs. 24hr SLO	N/A — already within SLO	Unquantified optimization effort	Stop — comfortably at the threshold	Engineering time redirected

Table 13.9: The chapter's four optimization decisions, their costs, and the outcome of each choice

Performance and capacity readiness checklist

Before approving optimization work or an infrastructure increase, every item below should read yes — or carry a named, time-boxed exception. This is the review gate for spend.

- **Bottleneck measured before optimizing:** a profile, a query plan or a utilization figure exists; no optimization begins from intuition.
- **Hardware alternative evaluated:** the 12-month hardware cost is priced against the fully loaded engineering cost before any code is written.
- **Bottleneck confirmed resource-bound:** the workload demonstrably gets proportionally faster on a larger instance; if it does not, hardware is not the lever.
- **Resource contention ruled out:** P0 latency correlated against co-located workload execution windows, with P0 traffic confirmed flat before separation is designed.
- **P0/P1/P2 performance budgets defined:** each tier has an SLO, an instance class and a scaling signal, and no P2 workload is running on P0-grade hardware.
- **Capacity headroom within target:** provisioned capacity between 120% and 150% of measured peak, recalculated monthly against production telemetry rather than assumed.
- **Scaling procedures tested:** the scaling action for every P0 service is documented, scripted, and executed at least once in a non-incident context in the last quarter.
- **Spot instance eligibility evaluated:** every P2 workload assessed for interruptibility and time flexibility, with checkpointing tested before reliance.
- **Good enough thresholds documented:** each component has a stated threshold, and optimization beyond it requires explicit justification against the feature backlog it displaces.

Summary

In this chapter, we applied the P0/P1/P2 framework from *Chapter 12* as a performance and capacity planning lens, answering the CFO's question about whether ShopFlow's 34% infrastructure cost increase was justified.

We applied the Hardware-First Rule and the Optimization ROI Test to establish that the code indexing contention problem is solved by physical separation—not optimization—because the hardware cost is lower than the engineering cost over any reasonable planning horizon.

We enforced the Physical Separation Rule to move the P2 code indexing pipeline onto a dedicated node pool, eliminating the resource contention that was degrading P0 search p99 from 95 ms to 210 ms during indexing windows.

We applied the Performance Budget Rule to right-size ShopFlow's infrastructure tiers: P0 workloads on dedicated high-performance instances, P2 workloads on spot instances with execution window constraints, saving $31,980 annually with no impact to P0 SLOs.

We established the Predictive Headroom Rule (120–150% of peak demand) and the Scaling Readiness Mandate — quarterly drills of the scaling procedure — replacing purely reactive capacity management with a short-horizon predictive model.

We defined good enough thresholds for each ShopFlow component and identified the optimization projects that have passed their threshold and should be stopped in favor of product feature delivery.

ShopFlow's telemetry after *Chapter 13*:

Metric	Before (Ch13 Start)	After (Ch13 End)	Change
Monthly Infrastructure Spend	$12,800/mo	$9,535/mo	25% reduction
Search p99 during indexing windows	210 ms (contention)	95ms (P0/P2 physically separated)	55% improvement; SLO restored
P2 Compute Cost	$4,100/mo (on-demand)	$1,435/mo (spot instances)	65% reduction

Metric	Before (Ch13 Start)	After (Ch13 End)	Change
Indexing Job Impact on P0	2.2x latency degradation	0 — physical separation eliminates contention	Eliminated
Capacity Planning Horizon	Reactive only	30-day rolling model + event-based pre-scaling	Predictive
Over-optimized components	3 projects past the good-enough threshold	0 — stopped and engineering time redirected	3 features are now in progress

Table 13.10: ShopFlow telemetry before and after the Chapter 13 changes

The cliffhanger: the cloud bill's upstream source

The infrastructure is right-sized. The P2 workloads are on spot instances. The P0 paths are physically separated. The search p99 is 95ms across all traffic patterns. The monthly spend is back below $10,000.

Dave is doing his end-of-sprint review and he stops on a number.

ShopFlow's cloud cost grew 36% over the past 18 months. The right-sizing work in this chapter recovered $3,265/month. But the total infrastructure spend is still $9,535 against a baseline of $7,000 eighteen months ago. The delta — $2,535/month — is not from over-provisioning or contention. It is from growth. Real growth, in orders processed per day, in global user count, in data volume.

Growth is the problem Dave wants to have. But scaling efficiently — ensuring the cloud bill grows more slowly than the business — requires a deliberate approach to cost optimization that goes beyond right-sizing workloads. It requires aligning every architectural decision with its financial impact, automating cost governance the same way security and performance are automated, and building a culture where engineers treat cloud spend as a first-class engineering metric.

In *Chapter 14*, we build the FinOps practice that makes ShopFlow's cost growth sustainable— not by spending less on infrastructure, but by getting more value from every dollar of infrastructure spend.

14

Cost Optimization and Efficiency (FinOps)

In *Chapter 13*, the infrastructure was right-sized. The P0 paths were physically separated from the P2 workloads, the code indexing pipeline moved to its own node pool, and the background processing shifted onto spot instances. Search p99 returned to 95ms across every traffic pattern. The right-sizing work recovered $3,265 per month, and ShopFlow's monthly spend settled at $9,535.

Then Dave finished his end-of-sprint review and stopped on a different number. ShopFlow's cloud cost has grown 36% over the past 18 months. The right-sizing recovered real money, but the total spend still sits at $9,535 against a baseline of $7,000 eighteen months ago. The delta is $2,535 per month, and almost none of it is waste. It is growth: more orders, more global users, more data, and a set of new AI features that did not exist a year ago.

This is the moment most teams misdiagnose. They treat the rising bill as a series of inefficiencies to be hunted down one at a time. Right-sizing is a one-time event. It recovers the slack you already paid for, and then it is done. What replaces the slack is the structural cost of a business that is materially larger. You cannot right-size your way out of growth, and you should not try.

The discipline that makes cost growth sustainable is FinOps. Not a cost-cutting campaign, and not a finance team auditing engineers. FinOps is the practice of making every dollar of infrastructure spend traceable to a unit of business value, watching cost the same way you watch latency and availability, and pushing the decision about whether a dollar is worth spending down to the engineers who spend it. The goal is not a smaller bill. The goal is a bill that grows more slowly than revenue.

In this chapter, we build that practice on top of ShopFlow's right-sized infrastructure. We start with the cost that always surprises you, which is never the one you watch. We make cost a first-class engineering metric without turning it into surveillance. We resolve the managed-versus-self-hosted question with a break-even calculation instead of an opinion. We connect spend to unit economics so that every cost line has an owner. And we govern the newest and least predictable cost axis in any modern system: the per-token cost of AI.

In this chapter, we are going to cover the following main topics:

- The Cost Surprise: Why the Bill Is Never the Service You Watch
- Making Cost a First-Class Engineering Metric
- The Premium Trap: Managed Services Versus Self-Hosting
- Unit Economics and the FinOps Feedback Loop
- Governing the AI Bill: Cost in the Age of Tokens

Technical requirements

Cloud cost management and allocation (AWS Cost Explorer / Azure Cost Analysis / GCP Billing): Per-service, per-team, and per-feature cost attribution. You cannot govern a cost you cannot attribute to an owner.

Resource tagging policy enforcement (cloud-native tag policies or OPA): Mandatory tags on every provisioned resource. Untagged resources are unattributable spend and must be rejected at provisioning time.

Unit-economics dashboards (Grafana/Looker / cloud-native): Cost per order, cost per active user, and cost per AI request, tracked as time series next to latency and availability.

Budget and anomaly alerting (cloud budgets + anomaly detection): Alerts keyed to trend breaks, not absolute thresholds. A 15% week-over-week slope matters more than a round-number ceiling.

LLM cost and token instrumentation (OpenTelemetry / provider usage APIs): Per-request, per-feature, and per-user token accounting for every model call, captured at the call site, not reconstructed from invoices.

Runtime cost enforcement middleware (gateway or in-process budget guard): A single chokepoint through which every model call passes, capable of rejecting a request before it executes when a budget is exhausted.

Code Repository: `https://github.com/imran-siddique/Architecting-at-Scale/tree/main/ch14`

ShopFlow telemetry snapshot [stage 14]

```
The Signal: The infrastructure is right-sized, but cost growth is ungoverned.
Spend is traceable to a service, but not to a unit of business value. The newest
line items, backup tier and AI tokens, have no owner and no budget.
Monthly Infrastructure Spend: $9,535/mo (Right-sized in Chapter 13, but growing
with the business)
Cloud Bill Growth: +36% over 18 months ($2,535/mo of the increase is real growth,
not waste)
Cost Per Order: Untracked (Spend is attributed to services, never to orders)
Geo-Redundant Backup + Retention Spend: $1,180/mo (Provisioned once 14 months ago,
never reviewed)
LLM API Spend (recommendations + support agent): $1,900/mo (No per-feature budget;
up 90% in two months)
Support Agent Cost Per Resolved Ticket: $0.41 and rising (Retry loops inflate
token count per conversation)
Untagged Resources: 23% of spend (Cannot be attributed to a team or feature)
Panic Meter: 3/10 (Nothing is on fire. The bill is simply outrunning the unit
economics.)
```

> **Note**
>
> **Dave Alert:** "I went looking for the easy savings and the biggest single line item after compute was the backup tier. Geo-redundant backups plus 35-day point-in-time retention on every database, including the P2 reporting replicas. Nobody chose that on purpose. It was a default we set once and never opened again."

FinOps is a maturity path, and the order of the stages is not a matter of taste. Each one is the precondition for the next. You cannot attribute spend you cannot see, you cannot read a trend on spend you cannot attribute, you cannot compute a unit economic without the trend, and you cannot govern a budget you have never expressed as a cost per unit of value. Teams that jump straight to the end, opening with a cost-cutting campaign, are optimizing a number they cannot yet divide, which is why those savings regress the moment the campaign stops.

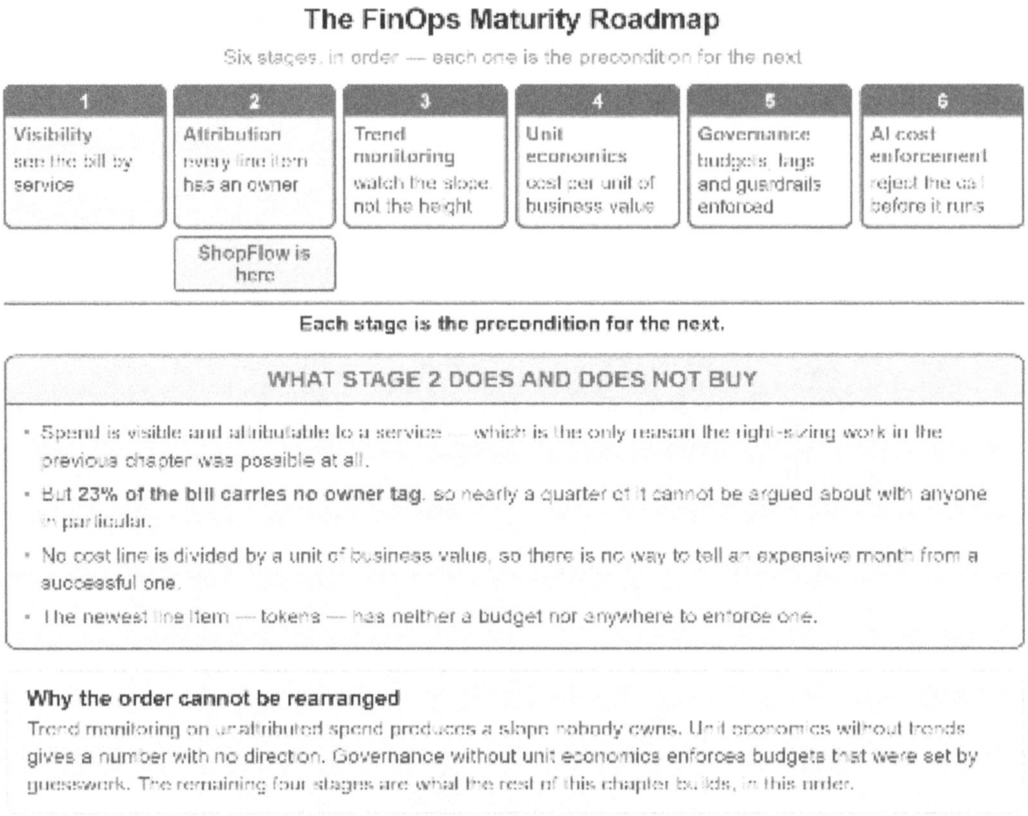

Figure 14.1: The FinOps Maturity Roadmap

ShopFlow enters this chapter at stage two. Spend is visible and attributable to a service, which is the only reason *Chapter 13*'s right-sizing worked at all. But 23% of the bill carries no owner tag, no cost line is divided by a unit of business value, and the newest line item on the bill, tokens, has neither a budget nor a place to enforce one. The remaining four stages are what the rest of this chapter builds, in order.

Note

The FinOps Maturity Order: Walk the stages in sequence, because each is the precondition for the next. Visibility, then attribution, then trend monitoring, then unit economics, then governance, then AI cost enforcement. A cost-cutting campaign launched before attribution is complete is optimizing a number nobody can divide, and its savings decay as soon as attention moves on. Skipping a stage does not accelerate the practice; it invalidates every stage built on top of it.

The cost surprise: why the bill is never for the service you watch

Ask any engineering team where their cloud money goes and they will answer with confidence: compute and storage. They are usually right about the largest line items, and they are almost always wrong about the line item that surprises them. Compute and storage do not surprise you, because you touch them every day. You provision instances, you watch CPU, you size disks, you read those numbers in every review. A cost you look at constantly does not ambush you.

The ambush comes from the platform services. These are the managed capabilities you turned on once, configured with a sensible default, and never opened again: backup and recovery, cross-region replication, log ingestion and retention, data egress between zones, idle load balancers, NAT gateway data processing, and managed database point-in-time restore. Each of them is individually reasonable. Together, on a system that has grown 36% in eighteen months, they compound silently into a number nobody decided to spend.

Note

The Provisioned-Once Rule: The cost that surprises you is always a platform service you configured once and never revisited. Compute and storage are watched daily and rarely surprise. Backup, retention, replication, egress, and idle managed endpoints are set with a default and forgotten, and they are where the unexamined spend accumulates. Every provisioned-once service must have a calendar review, or it will quietly outgrow the workload it was sized for.

ShopFlow's backup tier is the textbook case. Fourteen months ago, when the data layer was a single primary database, someone enabled geo-redundant backups with 35-day point-in-time restore. That was the correct decision for one production database holding order data. Since then, the system sharded, added read replicas, spun up P2 reporting databases, and grew the data volume by an order of magnitude. The backup policy replicated faithfully onto every one of those, including the disposable reporting replicas that could be rebuilt from source in minutes. The policy never changed. The footprint it applied to grew tenfold.

Note

Manager's Math, The Backup Tier Review: ShopFlow's geo-redundant backup plus 35-day retention costs $1,180/mo across all databases. An audit found that the P2 reporting replicas (rebuildable from source) and three non-production environments accounted for $710/mo of that. Dropping geo-redundancy on rebuildable replicas and cutting non-production retention to 7 days recovered $710/mo, which is $8,520/yr, for two hours of work and zero risk to recoverable production data. The recovery objective for the order database did not change.

The point is not that backups are wasteful. Backups are non-negotiable for data you cannot rebuild. The point is that a backup policy is a decision with a cost, and a decision made once for a small system is silently re-applied to a large one. The same pattern repeats across every platform service. Log retention set to 90 days when you emitted one gigabyte a day becomes a major line item when you emit fifty. Cross-zone replication enabled for a chatty pair of services becomes an egress bill when the traffic between them grows 20x.

Hidden Cost	Why It Stays Invisible	The Trigger That Exposes It	The Fix
Backup and retention	Set once as a default; applies to every new database automatically	Data volume grows; policy never re-scoped	Tier retention by data criticality; drop geo-redundancy on rebuildable data
Log ingestion and retention	Per-GB pricing feels trivial at low volumes	Verbosity and traffic both grow	Sample high-volume logs, tier retention, route debug logs to cheap storage

Hidden Cost	Why It Stays Invisible	The Trigger That Exposes It	The Fix
Cross-zone and egress transfer	Priced per GB moved, not per resource owned	Chatty service pairs scale with traffic	Co-locate chatty services; cache across the boundary
Idle managed endpoints	Load balancers and NAT gateways bill hourly while idle	Environments multiply; cleanup lags	Reap idle endpoints on a schedule; alert on zero-traffic resources
Point-in-time restore	Bundled into the managed database price	Replicas and environments multiply	Match restore window to the actual recovery objective per database

Table 14.1: Hidden platform-service costs, why each one stays invisible, and the fix that scopes it

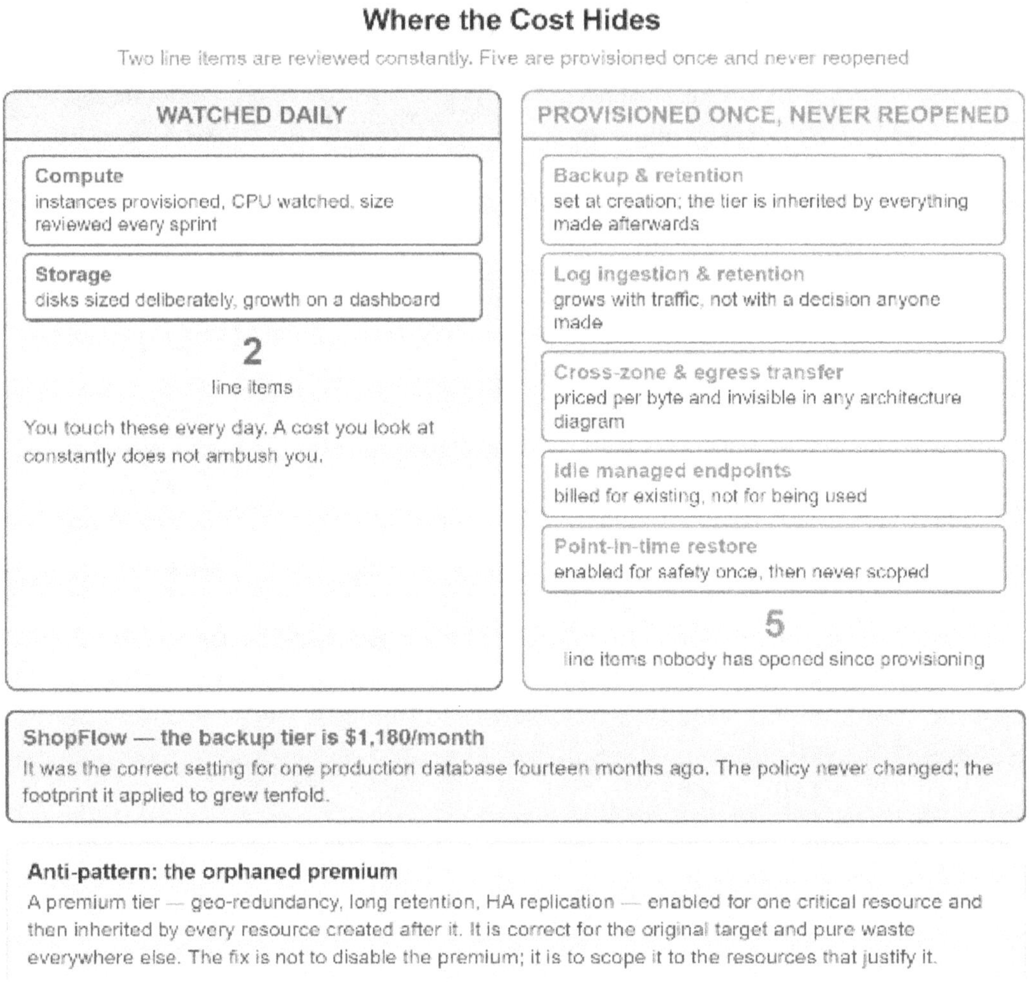

Figure 14.2: Where the Cost Hides

Note

Anti-Pattern: The Orphaned Premium: A premium tier (geo-redundancy, long retention, high-availability replication) enabled for a single critical resource and then inherited by every resource created afterward, including the ones that do not need it. The premium is correct for the original target and pure waste everywhere else. The fix is not to disable the premium but to scope it to the resources that justify it.

There is a deeper organizational reason these costs hide. Compute and storage have obvious owners, the team running the service. Platform services sit underneath everything and belong to no one. The backup policy is not in any team's dashboard. The egress charge is split across every service that talks across a zone. A cost with no owner is a cost nobody reviews, and a cost nobody reviews only ever grows.

> **Note**
>
> The Line-Item Ownership Rule: Every line item on the cloud bill must map to a team that owns it. Spend with no owner is reviewed by no one and optimized by no one. The platform services that sit beneath every team (backup, networking, logging, shared gateways) must be explicitly assigned to the platform team and reviewed on a schedule, or they become a permanent blind spot in the budget.

> **Note**
>
> Safe Scale Check, Backup Changes: Reversibility: changing a retention window or disabling geo-redundancy on a replica is fully reversible by re-enabling it. Blast radius: scope every backup change to a single database tier and verify the recovery objective for production data is unchanged before making any changes. Never reduce retention on a database whose data cannot be rebuilt from another source. Test a restore after the change, not before.

Putting the Provisioned-Once rule on a calendar

A rule that says "review it" without naming an interval gets reviewed exactly once, on the day somebody writes it down. The Provisioned-Once Rule survives contact with a real backlog only when each class of service has a named cadence, a named owner, and a place on a recurring calendar. The interval is set by how quickly the thing drifts from the workload it was sized for, not by how much it costs.

Cadence	What You Review	Why This Interval	What You Are Looking For
Monthly	Idle load balancers and NAT gateways, unattached volumes and IP addresses, orphaned snapshots, non-production environments	These accumulate weekly as environments are created faster than they are cleaned up	Anything billing with zero traffic, and anything provisioned for a spike that has ended
Quarterly	Backup policies, retention windows, replication settings, log ingestion, and retention tiers	These are scoped against data volume, which moves on a quarterly scale	A policy is still applying the footprint it was scoped for a year ago
Annually	Disaster recovery architecture, geo-redundancy strategy, region topology, reserved capacity commitments	Changing these is a project, so a shorter interval produces review without action	Whether the recovery objective the architecture was built for is still the objective the business needs

Table 14.2: Review cadence for provisioned-once services, set by how fast each class drifts from its original scope

The monthly tier is the one teams underestimate, because each individual finding is small. An idle load balancer is a few dollars a month and feels beneath attention. The reason it earns a monthly slot anyway is that these resources are created continuously and removed almost never, so the line item is not the balancer you find this month; it is the eighteen you would have found had anybody looked. Automate this tier: a scheduled job that reports zero-traffic resources and untagged endpoints costs an afternoon to write and removes the review from anyone's memory.

The annual tier works differently. You are not hunting waste there; you are re-testing an assumption. Geo-redundancy and the recovery objective behind it were chosen against a business the company no longer is. That review has one question: if we were provisioning this today, at this size, with this risk tolerance, would we choose the same tier? A no is not automatically a change, but it is the start of one.

> **Note**
>
> The Review Cadence Rule: Every provisioned-once service carries an explicit review interval — monthly for resources that sit idle, quarterly for policies scoped against data volume, annually for architecture and long-term commitments. The interval is set by how fast the service drifts from the workload it was sized for, not by its price. Assign the interval and the owner at the same time you provision the service. A service with no interval is not reviewed on a schedule; it is remembered occasionally, and that is indistinguishable from never.

Architect's prompt 14.1: the cost surprise audit

When to use this: Use this prompt when the cloud bill has grown faster than your tracked compute and storage, and you need to find the unexamined platform-service spend before the next budget review.

```
Act as a Principal FinOps Engineer. I am auditing a cloud bill that has
grown faster than our compute and storage footprint explains. Help me find
the platform-service spend that has no owner.

Our tracked services and their monthly compute/storage cost: [list].
Total monthly bill: [amount]. Tracked compute + storage: [amount].
The unexplained delta is [amount].

For the delta, do the following:
(1) List every platform service that bills independently of compute:
    backup/retention, snapshots, cross-zone and egress transfer, log
    ingestion/retention, idle load balancers and NAT gateways, managed
    point-in-time restore, and shared gateways.
(2) For each, identify whether the policy was set once and applied
    automatically to resources created later (the provisioned-once pattern).
(3) Flag any premium tier (geo-redundancy, long retention, HA replication)
    inherited by resources that do not justify it (the orphaned premium).
(4) For each finding, give the monthly cost, the reversible fix, the blast
    radius of that fix, and the recovery-objective check required first.
(5) Assign each line item to an owning team. Flag anything with no owner.
```

Making cost a First-Class engineering metric

FinOps fails in most organizations for one reason: it is owned by the wrong people. Finance receives the bill, finance gets alarmed, and finance asks engineering to explain a number that engineering has never been asked to watch. The conversation becomes adversarial because cost arrives as an audit rather than a metric. The teams that succeed at cost do the opposite. They make cost a number engineers see every week, in the same place they see the numbers they already care about.

The mechanism that works is the weekly fundamentals review. Most mature teams already run one. It is the standing meeting where production health is discussed: availability, latency, error budget, incident review, the trend lines that tell you whether the system is healthy. Cost belongs in that meeting, as one more trend line, sitting next to reliability and latency. It does not get its own separate finance ceremony. It becomes a fundamental, reviewed with the same regularity and the same seriousness as a P0 latency SLO.

> Note
>
> **The Fundamentals Review Rule:** Cost is reviewed in the weekly production fundamentals meeting, next to availability and latency, by the engineers who own the services. It is not delegated to a separate finance review. A metric that lives outside the engineering review is a metric engineers do not own, and a cost engineers do not own is a cost engineers will not control.

The second principle is what you look at in that review, and this is where most teams overcorrect. They build elaborate cost dashboards, set absolute dollar thresholds, and then drown in alerts every time spend ticks up for a benign reason. The useful signal is the trend, not the absolute number. You watch the slope of the cost line, not its height. A bill that grows in proportion to traffic is healthy and needs no investigation. A bill that bends upward while traffic stays flat is the only thing worth your attention.

> Note
>
> **The Trend-Not-Absolute Rule:** Watch the slope of the cost curve, not its absolute value. Spend that grows in proportion to business volume is healthy and requires no action. The signal that earns investigation is a steep or exponential break in the trend that is not matched by a corresponding rise in traffic, orders, or users. Do not alert on round-number ceilings. Alert on the second derivative.

> **Note**
>
> Tool Tax — anomaly detection on spend: An anomaly detector trained on your bill will fire on your own launches. A seasonal peak, a marketing campaign, a data backfill, a new region: all of them look exactly like a cost incident to a model that only sees dollars. The tax is the tuning loop and the suppression list that comes with it, and the failure mode is the familiar one — a detector that is wrong for two months gets muted, and the mute outlives the tuning that would have fixed it. Feed it business volume alongside spend, or accept that you have bought a trend-break detector you will eventually ignore.

This is the discipline that keeps cost review from becoming a time sink. In a weekly review you do not audit every service. You glance at the cost-per-order line and the total trend, confirm they are tracking together, and move on. The review takes two minutes when the system is healthy. It expands into a real investigation only when a line bends in a way the business volume does not explain. That is the moment a steep slope tells you something changed: a new feature with bad unit economics, a runaway background job, a retry storm inflating an API bill, or a config change that disabled a cache.

What You Watch Weekly	Normal (No Action)	The Signal (Investigate)
Total spend trend	Grows in proportion to orders and users	Bends upward while traffic is flat
Cost per order	Flat or slowly declining as you scale	Rises week over week
Cost per AI request	Stable per feature	Climbs without a feature change
Spend by team	Tracks each team's traffic share	One team's share grows with no launch
Untagged spend	Near zero	Any sustained rise (attribution is broken)

Table 14.3: What to watch in the weekly review, and the signal that separates healthy growth from a trend break

The third principle is cultural, and it is the one Dave's organization gets right. Cost visibility must feel like ownership, not surveillance. The instant engineers believe the cost dashboard exists to catch them, they stop deploying and start hedging, and you lose far more in velocity than you ever save on the bill. The framing that works is showback before chargeback. You show each team its own spend and its own trend, you let teams see how their decisions move their own line, and you do not start cross-charging budgets until the visibility has built genuine cost awareness. Showback informs. Chargeback enforces. You earn the right to enforce by first making the data trustworthy and useful.

> Note
>
> **The Showback-Before-Chargeback Rule:** Give every team visibility into its own spend and trend before you charge that spend against its budget. Showback builds cost awareness without defensiveness. Chargeback without prior showback feels like a penalty for a number the team was never shown, and it produces hedging and slowed deployments. You cannot enforce a budget the team has not first learned to read.

Approach	What It Does	When to Use It
Showback	Shows each team its own spend and trend; charges nothing	First, always; builds cost awareness without defensiveness
Chargeback	Charges spent against the owning team's budget	Only after showback has built trust and the data are reliable

Table 14.4: Showback compared with chargeback, and the order in which to introduce them

> Note
>
> **Anti-Pattern: The Cost Police:** Treating the cost dashboard as an enforcement tool that singles out individual engineers or teams for spending, before those teams have any visibility into or control over their own numbers. The predictable result is defensive behavior: slower deploys, over-cautious provisioning, and engineers optimizing to avoid blame rather than to serve the business. Cost awareness is built by ownership, not by audit.

> Note
>
> **Manager's Math, The Cost Per Order:** ShopFlow spends $9,535/mo and processes roughly 95,000 orders/mo, a cost per order of about $0.10. Tracked as a weekly trend, this single number does the work of a hundred line items. When a new AI recommendation feature pushed the LLM bill up 90% in two months, it added about $900/mo to what had been an $8,635 bill, an increase no round-number spend ceiling had been set to catch, so the total-spend alarm stayed quiet. Cost per order, however, went from $0.091 to $0.100, a 10% rise against flat order growth. That slope, not the absolute bill, was the signal that one feature's unit economics had broken.

Cost per order is the metric that ties the entire chapter together. It converts an abstract bill into a number that moves with engineering decisions and business reality at the same time. When you ship a feature that makes the system more efficient, cost per order falls. When you ship a feature with bad unit economics, it rises even if the total bill looks calm. A team that watches cost per order in its weekly fundamentals review has made cost a first-class engineering metric without a single finance meeting.

> Note
>
> Safe Scale Check, Cost Gates in CI: Reversibility: a cost gate that warns on a projected spend increase is fully reversible; it blocks nothing and only surfaces information. Blast radius: start cost gates in warn-only mode so a noisy estimate never blocks a deploy. Promote a gate from warn to block only for a specific, well-understood cost (for example, provisioning a resource without a required owner tag), never for a fuzzy total-spend projection.

Architect's prompt 14.2: the weekly cost trend review

When to use this: Use this prompt to structure the cost portion of your weekly production fundamentals review so it surfaces trend breaks in minutes instead of becoming a line-item audit.

```
Act as a Principal Engineer running a weekly production fundamentals
review. Help me review cost as a trend, not as an absolute number.

Here is this week's data versus the trailing eight weeks:
- Total spend trend: [series]
- Cost per order: [series]
```

```
- Cost per AI request, per feature: [series]
- Spend by team: [series]
- Untagged spend %: [series]
- Business volume (orders, active users): [series]

Do the following:
(1) For each cost series, compare its slope to the business-volume slope.
(2) Flag ONLY the series whose slope breaks from business volume. Ignore
    increases that are proportional to traffic, orders, or users.
(3) For each flagged series, list the likely causes: a new feature with bad
    unit economics, a runaway job, a retry storm, or a disabled cache.
(4) Recommend the single highest-signal metric to add to next week's review.
(5) Keep the healthy-state summary to two sentences. Do not audit line items
    that are tracking business volume.
```

The premium trap: managed services vs. Self-Hosting

Every cost review eventually arrives at the same argument. A managed service is expensive, an open-source equivalent is free, and an engineer proposes that the team self-host to save the premium. Sometimes that engineer is right. More often the premium that looks like waste is the cheapest line item in the entire decision, because the real cost of self-hosting is not on the cloud bill. It is on the payroll.

My default is to pay for the managed service. The reason is not that managed services are cheap. It is that a managed service takes an entire category of operational overhead off the team: patching, failover, version upgrades, backup orchestration, capacity tuning, and the 3:00 AM page when the cluster loses a node. That overhead does not disappear when you self-host. It moves onto your engineers, and engineer time is the most expensive and least elastic resource you have. You are not comparing a dollar figure to zero. You are comparing a dollar figure to a number of engineering weeks, and engineering weeks have a loaded cost.

> Note
>
> **The Managed-By-Default Rule:** Default to the managed offering. The premium you pay buys back the operational overhead (patching, failover, upgrades, on-call) that self-hosting transfers onto your engineers. Deviate from this default only when you have calculated the loaded engineering cost of self-hosting and found it clearly below the premium. The burden of proof is on self-hosting, not on the managed service.

The decision is not religious in either direction. There are real cases where self-hosting is correct. When the open-source version is mature, when running it is well-understood and low-overhead, and when the managed premium is large relative to the loaded engineering cost of operating it yourself, self-hosting wins on the math. The mistake is not choosing one or the other. The mistake is choosing by reflex: either paying every premium because managed is easy or rebuilding everything from scratch because free looks free.

> Note
>
> **Anti-Pattern: The Reflexive Rebuilder:** Reaching for self-hosting on instinct because the open-source version has no license fee, without ever calculating the loaded engineering cost of operating it. Free software is not free to run. The license fee is replaced by on-call rotations, upgrade projects, and the opportunity cost of the features those engineers did not build. Self-hosting from reflex rather than from math is how teams trade a known line item for a larger, hidden one.

The calculation that resolves the argument is a break-even. Take the annual managed premium you would save. Take the loaded cost of an engineer, salary plus benefits plus overhead, and divide to find how many engineering weeks the premium buys per year. Then estimate the engineering weeks self-hosting will consume: the initial build, plus the ongoing operational load, plus the upgrade and incident time across the year. If self-hosting costs more weeks than the premium buys, the premium is the bargain. If it costs fewer, self-hosting is justified. The number that matters is rarely the cloud line item. It is the engineering weeks.

> Note
>
> **Manager's Math, Managed Cache Versus Self-Hosted:** ShopFlow's managed cache costs about $1,400/mo more than running the equivalent open-source cache on raw instances, roughly $16,800/yr. At a loaded engineer cost of $4,000/week, that premium buys about 4.2 engineering weeks per year. Self-hosting a production cache cluster realistically costs 3 to 4 weeks of build plus an estimated 1 to 1.5 weeks per year of ongoing patching, failover testing, and upgrades. The break-even is too close, and the operational risk lands on the P0 path, so ShopFlow keeps the managed cache. The premium is cheaper than the labor.

Factor	Lean Toward Managed	Lean Toward Self-Hosted
OSS maturity	Project is young, niche, or fast-changing	Project is mature, stable, and well-documented
Operational overhead	Complex failover, upgrades, capacity tuning	Simple to run; low day-to-day load
Premium vs. loaded cost	Premium is small relative to engineering weeks	Premium is large relative to engineering weeks
Criticality of the path	Sits on a P0 path; failure is expensive	P2 or internal; failure is recoverable
Team scarcity	Engineers are the bottleneck on the roadmap	Spare specialized capacity exists in-house

Table 14.5: The five factors that push a workload toward a managed service or toward self-hosting

There is a tax on each side of this decision, and naming it keeps the choice honest. The managed service carries a lock-in tax: you adopt its proprietary surface, its pricing model, and its operational assumptions, and migrating away later is a project. Self-hosting carries an operational tax: every node you run is a node your team patches, monitors, and gets paged for, and that tax is paid continuously, in the currency you can least afford to spend. Neither option is free of debt. You are choosing which debt to carry.

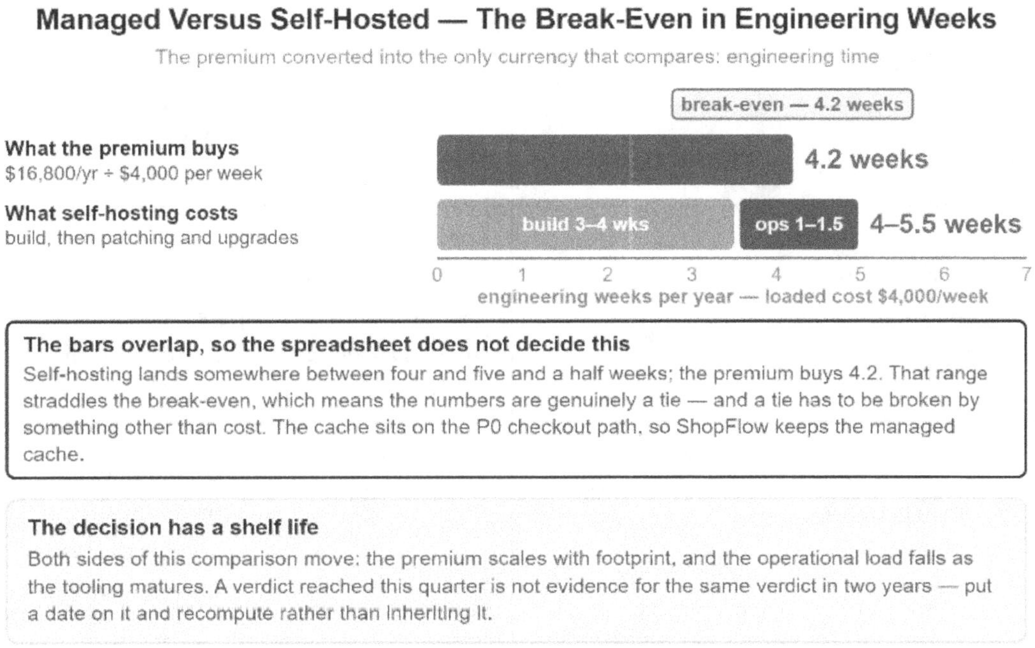

Figure 14.3: Managed Versus Self-Hosted — The Break-Even in Engineering Weeks

The decision has a shelf life

Every input to that break-even moves as the system grows, which means the answer moves with it. A managed service that is the right call at ten engineers can be the wrong one at two hundred, with nothing about the technology having changed in between. Three variables do the moving, and it is worth knowing which one is driving a proposal before you evaluate it.

The first is scale. The managed premium is priced against consumption, so it grows with the workload, while the operational cost of self-hosting is largely fixed once the platform capability exists. At low volume the premium is a rounding error against that fixed cost. At high volume the premium is the larger number, and it keeps growing while the operational cost does not.

The second is operational capability. A startup self-hosting a database is one engineer's side project and one resignation away from an unowned production system. An organization with a funded platform team already pays for the on-call rotation, the upgrade discipline, and the runbooks, so the marginal cost of one more self-hosted component is far lower. The same decision, evaluated honestly, produces opposite answers at the two companies.

The third is workload stability. Self-hosting rewards a workload that is well understood and predictable in its capacity. A workload still changing shape every quarter punishes fixed capacity and pays for the elasticity a managed service supplies.

Stage	Typical Posture	Why	What Would Change It
Early: small team, workload still forming	Managed for nearly everything	Engineer time is the binding constraint, and the premium is small in absolute terms	The premium becomes a material share of the bill
Growth: a platform team is emerging	Managed by default; self-host only the mature, stable, high-volume components	Operational capability is partly funded, and the premium is now visible on the bill	One component's premium clearly exceeds the loaded cost of operating it
Scale: funded platform organization, stable workloads	Self-host where the premium is large and the technology is settled; stay managed on the fast-moving edge	Marginal operational cost is low, and the premium scales with volume while the operations cost does not	The technology starts moving again, or the platform team shrinks

Table 14.6: How the managed-versus-self-hosted posture shifts across an organization's lifecycle

For ShopFlow today all three variables point the same way, and the managed cache stays. The point is not the answer. It is that the answer carries a review date. Re-run the break-even when the volume doubles, when the platform team is funded, or when the workload settles — and re-run it in the other direction too, because an organization that loses its platform engineers has quietly changed the inputs without changing anything on the architecture diagram.

> **Note**
>
> The Reversible Default Rule: Managed versus self-hosted is a decision with a review date, not a permanent architectural position. Re-run the break-even whenever scale, in-house operational capability, or workload stability changes materially, and re-run it in

both directions. A team that has grown into self-hosting one component has not earned the right to self-host every component, and a team that has lost the engineers who ran one should be moving it back before the next upgrade cycle, not after the incident that proves the point.

Note

The Loaded-Cost Mandate: Any self-hosting proposal must be evaluated against the loaded cost of engineering time, not against the managed license fee alone. Loaded cost includes the build, the ongoing operational load, the upgrade and incident time, and the opportunity cost of the features those engineers will not ship. A self-hosting decision made without this number is not a decision; it is a guess that the bill is the only cost that counts.

Note

Safe Scale Check, Migrating Off a Managed Service: Reversibility: a managed-to-self-hosted migration on a P0 path is a one-way door once you decommission the managed service, so keep the managed service running in parallel until the self-hosted version has survived a full peak cycle. Blast radius: migrate one non-critical workload first to measure the real operational load before committing to the P0 path. The first self-hosted cluster you run teaches you the true weekly cost the spreadsheet only estimated.

Architect's prompt 14.3: the Managed-Versus-Self-Hosted decision

When to use this: Use this prompt when an engineer proposes self-hosting an open-source equivalent to save a managed-service premium, and you need to convert the argument from opinion into a break-even calculation.

```
Act as a Principal Engineer evaluating whether to self-host an open-source
service or keep a managed equivalent. Resolve this with a break-even
calculation, not a preference.

Managed service: [name], current cost [amount/mo].
```

```
Self-hosted equivalent: [OSS project], maturity: [assessment].
Estimated raw infrastructure cost if self-hosted: [amount/mo].
Loaded cost of one engineer per week: [amount].
This workload sits on a: [P0 / P1 / P2] path.

Do the following:
(1) Compute the annual managed premium (managed cost minus self-hosted
    infra cost) and convert it to engineering weeks at the loaded rate.
(2) Estimate the engineering weeks self-hosting will consume: initial build,
    plus annual operational load (patching, failover, upgrades, incidents).
(3) State the break-even and the recommendation.
(4) Name the tax on each side: managed lock-in versus self-hosted operations.
(5) If the path is P0, raise the bar: require the operational load to be
    clearly below the premium before recommending self-hosting.
```

Unit economics and the FinOps feedback loop

Everything in this chapter so far points at a single idea: a cloud bill is meaningless until it is divided by a unit of business value. A total of $9,535 per month tells you nothing about whether the system is efficient. The same bill is excellent at 200,000 orders and alarming at 20,000. The number that carries meaning is the ratio, and choosing the right denominator is the most important decision in FinOps. For ShopFlow, the denominator is an order. For an analytics platform it might be a query, for an AI product a resolved request. The unit is whatever the business sells.

> Note
>
> **The Unit-Economics Rule:** Track cost per unit of business value, not total spend. Choose the denominator the business sells: an order, a query, a resolved ticket, an active user. Total spend rising is not a problem if cost per unit is flat or falling, because the business is simply larger. Cost per unit rising is always a problem, even when total spend looks calm, because each unit of value is getting more expensive to deliver.

Choosing that denominator is a modeling decision, and choosing it badly produces a metric that moves for reasons the business does not recognize. The test is short: the denominator should be the thing the customer pays for or the thing the business counts when it reports growth. Where those two differ, use the one the business counts, because that is the number your cost will eventually be held against in a board deck.

Business	Denominator	What It Exposes
Online retail (ShopFlow)	Cost per order	Whether a change to the checkout path made each sale more expensive to serve
B2B SaaS	Cost per active tenant	Whether large tenants are being subsidized by small ones, and where the plan pricing breaks
Streaming platform	Cost per viewing hour	Whether an encoding or delivery change moved the real cost of an hour watched
AI assistant	Cost per successfully completed conversation	Whether token spend is buying resolutions or funding retry loops
Marketplace	Cost per completed transaction	Whether browse and search spend is justified by the transactions it actually produces

Table 14.7: Unit-economics denominators by business model, and the failure each one makes visible

Two refinements matter more than the choice itself. The first is to count only successful units. A cost per conversation that includes abandoned and failed conversations flatters a system that is failing cheaply, and an AI feature that gives up quickly will look efficient right up to the moment somebody measures resolutions instead of attempts. The second is to pick one denominator, publish it, and keep it. A team that switches denominators when the number looks bad has not measured anything; it has selected a number.

Note

The Successful-Unit Rule: Divide cost by successful units of business value, never by attempted ones. A denominator that counts abandoned carts, failed conversations, and errored requests rewards a system for failing cheaply. Cost per attempted outcome falls when quality falls, which makes it the one unit metric that can improve while the product gets worse. Define what counts as success before you publish the metric, and change the definition through the same review you would use to change an SLO.

Unit economics only works if spend can be attributed, and attribution only works if every resource is tagged. This is the unglamorous foundation of the entire practice. A resource with no owner tag is spend that cannot be divided, traced, or assigned, and it silently corrupts every per-unit number you compute. Tagging cannot be a convention that engineers are asked to remember. It must be enforced at provisioning time, so that a resource created without an owner, a service, and an environment tag is rejected before it ever bills a dollar.

Note

The Cost-Has-An-Owner Mandate: Every provisioned resource carries an owner, a service, and an environment tag, enforced at creation time, not requested as a convention. A resource that bills without these tags is rejected at provisioning. Untagged spend is unattributable spend, and unattributable spend is the exact blind spot where cost grows unreviewed. This is non-negotiable: you cannot compute a unit economic on a bill you cannot divide.

Note

A tag policy is trivial to write and expensive to live with. The tax is paid in three places. Every provisioning path has to route through the enforcement point, which means the infrastructure-as-code modules, the console, the one-off script somebody wrote during an incident, and whatever a vendor's operator creates on your behalf — and the last two are where the exceptions accumulate. Somebody has to own the tag taxonomy, because a free-text owner field produces four spellings of the same team within a quarter. And the day the policy starts rejecting rather than reporting, you inherit a new class of deploy failure, so the error message must name the missing tag or engineers will route around the control entirely. Budget the taxonomy owner, not just the policy.

Tag	Purpose	Enforced How	Failure Mode If Missing
owner	Maps spend to a team in the weekly review	Rejected at provisioning if absent	Line item nobody reviews
service	Rolls cost up to a service for unit math	Rejected at provisioning if absent	Cost cannot be divided by order
environment	Separates prod from dev and test spending	Rejected at provisioning if absent	Non-prod waste hides in prod totals
feature	Attributes new spend to a launch	Required for AI and experimental work	Bad unit economics cannot be isolated

Table 14.8: The mandatory resource tags, how each is enforced, and what breaks when one is missing

Note

Anti-Pattern: The Untagged Resource: Any provisioned resource without an owner, service, and environment tag. It is invisible to every per-unit calculation, it cannot be assigned to a team in the weekly review, and it accumulates into the percentage of the bill that nobody can explain. ShopFlow's 23% untagged spend is not a small hygiene issue but 23% of the budget the entire FinOps practice cannot see.

With attribution in place, the practice closes into a loop. You measure cost per unit, you attribute every unit to a feature and a team, you surface the trend in the weekly review, an owner acts on any slope that breaks from business volume, and you measure again. This is the FinOps feedback loop, and it is structurally identical to the observability and resilience loops built in earlier chapters. Cost becomes one more signal the system watches about itself, with an owner and an action attached, rather than a quarterly surprise delivered by finance.

Stage	What Happens	Owner
Measure	Cost per order, per request, per feature, as a trend	Platform team instruments it
Attribute	Every unit of spend tagged to a service and team	Enforced at provisioning

Stage	What Happens	Owner
Surface	Trend reviewed in weekly fundamentals	Service-owning engineers
Act	Slope breaks trigger investigation and a fix	The team that owns the slope
Verify	Re-measure to confirm the fix moved the unit cost	Same team, next review

Table 14.9: The five stages of the FinOps feedback loop and the owner accountable for each

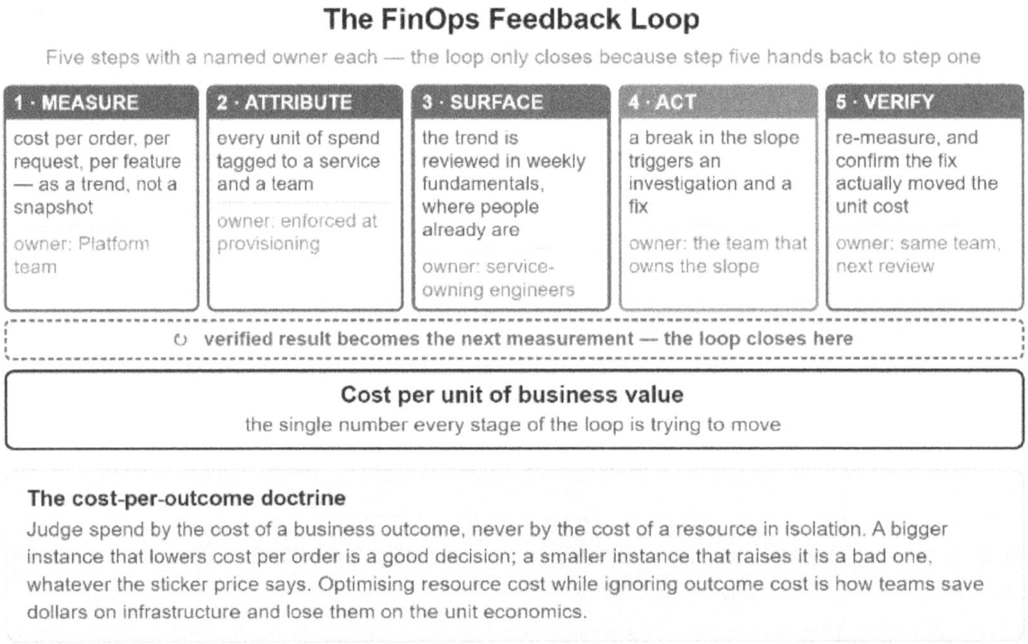

Figure 14.4: The FinOps Feedback Loop

Note

The Cost-Per-Outcome Doctrine: Judge spend by the cost of a business outcome, never by the cost of a resource in isolation. A bigger instance that lowers cost per order is a good decision; a smaller instance that raises it is a bad one, even though the smaller instance has a lower sticker price. Optimizing resource cost while ignoring outcome cost is how teams save dollars on infrastructure and lose them on the unit economics.

Note

Tool Tax — the unit-economics dashboard: Cost data does not arrive in the shape the metric needs. Billing exports land hours to a day late, at a granularity that rarely matches your service boundaries, and they change schema when the vendor changes products. The tax is a small pipeline nobody volunteers to own: joining billing data to your own volume metrics, holding both in the same time buckets, and reconciling a dashboard that will disagree with the invoice at the end of every month. Expect to explain that gap repeatedly, and expect the dashboard to be wrong for a week every time the organization adopts a new service.

The feedback loop also governs autoscaling, which is the most common source of cost that grows in a way nobody decided. An autoscaler with no upper bound will faithfully spend whatever a traffic spike, a retry storm, or a runaway loop demands. Cost-aware guardrails put a ceiling on that behavior: a maximum scale that, when reached, alerts an owner rather than silently provisioning without limit. The guardrail does not replace the autoscaler. It bounds the blast radius of an autoscaler reacting to something other than real demand.

Note

Safe Scale Check, Cost-Aware Autoscaling Guardrails: Reversibility: an autoscaling ceiling is a parameter, fully reversible, and should be set generously above real peak demand so it never throttles legitimate traffic. Blast radius: the guardrail's job is to cap the spend a malfunctioning system can incur, such as a retry storm or an unbounded loop, before it scales without limit. Set the ceiling at a multiple of true peak, alert when it is reached, and treat reaching it as a signal that something is wrong, not as normal operation.

Note

Manager's Math, The Untagged Recovery: ShopFlow's 23% untagged spend is about $2,193/mo of the $9,535 bill. Enforcing the three mandatory tags and chasing down the untagged resources over one sprint reclassified that spend, and the exercise surfaced $620/mo of non-production resources running in production accounts and idle endpoints with no owner. Tagging did not directly cut the bill, but it converted an unexaminable 23% into attributable spend and exposed $7,440/yr of recoverable waste that had been hiding inside it.

Architect's prompt 14.4: the unit economics model

When to use this: Use this prompt to build the cost-per-unit model that turns a raw cloud bill into the single trend line your weekly review can act on.

```
Act as a Principal FinOps Engineer. Help me build a unit-economics model
that converts our cloud bill into cost per unit of business value.

Business unit we sell: [order / query / resolved request / active user].
Monthly business volume: [number]. Monthly total spend: [amount].
Current tagging coverage: [percent tagged]. Major services: [list].

Do the following:
(1) Define the cost-per-unit metric and the denominator to track weekly.
(2) Specify the mandatory tags (owner, service, environment, feature) and
    the provisioning-time enforcement that rejects untagged resources.
(3) Map each major service's spend to the unit so cost per unit is
    attributable by feature and team.
(4) Define the FinOps feedback loop stages (measure, attribute, surface,
    act, verify) and the owner for each stage.
(5) Recommend a cost-aware autoscaling ceiling per service and the alert
    that fires when it is reached.
```

Governing the AI bill: cost in the age of tokens

Every cost discipline in this chapter so far assumes a cost model the industry has understood for a decade: you pay for compute by the hour and storage by the gigabyte, and both scale in ways you can predict. AI breaks that assumption. A system that adds large language model calls introduces a cost axis that behaves unlike anything else on the bill, because it is priced per token, and the number of tokens a single user request consumes is not fixed. It is decided at runtime by the model, the prompt, the context, and the number of reasoning steps the agent takes before it produces an answer.

The scale of the difference is the part teams underestimate. A single model call can cost more than a thousand database reads. A request that triggers an agent to reason across several steps, call a tool, retrieve context, and call the model again can consume ten to fifty times the tokens of a single prompt. ShopFlow's support agent already shows the pattern: its cost per resolved ticket is climbing not because more tickets arrive, but because the agent's conversations are getting longer, looping through more reasoning steps per resolution. The per-unit cost of an AI feature is a moving target in a way the per-unit cost of a database query never was.

> Note
>
> **The Token-Is-A-Cost-Axis Rule:** Treat tokens as a first-class cost axis with its own budget, its own per-unit metric, and its own governance, separate from compute and storage. Token cost is decided at runtime by the model and the agent's behavior, not at provisioning time, so it cannot be governed by sizing decisions made in advance. An AI feature without a token budget is a feature whose cost you have chosen not to control.

Cost Driver	Why It Inflates Tokens	The Control
Prompt and context size	Large retrieved documents pad every call	Trim context; retrieve only what the task needs
Reasoning steps per task	Each step is another metered call	Hard cap on steps, enforced at the chokepoint
Retries on failure	A failed call is paid for, then paid again	Bounded retry count; fail to a cheaper fallback
Model choice	The most capable model costs the most per token	Cascade: cheap first, escalate only when needed
Tool-call chains	Each tool round trip can trigger another call	Budget the whole task, not the individual call

Table 14.10: What drives token cost in an AI feature, and the control that bounds each driver

In my experience building a runtime governance layer for autonomous agents, the single most important distinction in AI cost is the one most tooling gets wrong. There is a difference between cost monitoring and cost enforcement, and it is architectural, not cosmetic. Monitoring reads what already happened and reports it: per-request costs in a dashboard, a daily spend alert, a weekly invoice. Enforcement intercepts what is about to happen and evaluates it against a budget before allowing it to proceed. The distinction matters because in a monitoring-only system, by the time the alert tells you a session is over budget, the session is already over budget. The alert is a postmortem. It is not a guardrail.

Note

The Enforcement-Not-Monitoring Doctrine: Cost monitoring reports spend after it happens; cost enforcement rejects a call before it executes when a budget is exhausted. Dashboards and spend alerts are necessary but they are postmortems, not controls. To bound AI cost you need a chokepoint in the call path that can refuse the next model call against a live budget. You cannot enforce a budget from a dashboard that only reads history.

Capability	Cost Monitoring	Cost Enforcement
When it acts	After the call completes	Before the call executes
What it produces	Dashboards, invoices, spend alerts	An allow or reject decision
Effect on an overbudget session	Reports it once it is too late	Stops the next call from running
Architectural location	Reads logs and usage APIs	Sits inline in the call path
Failure mode	Postmortem: you learn after you spend	Must be a single, unbypassable chokepoint

Table 14.11: Cost monitoring compared with cost enforcement across five capabilities

Enforcement requires structure. The mechanism that works is a single chokepoint through which every model call passes, with no path to the model that bypasses it. If even one call site issues a raw model request outside the guard, the budget leaks through that gap, and the one rule that makes the whole thing work is that there is exactly one way to call the model. The most effective thing I check when reviewing agent code is not the prompt or the model choice. It is that no raw model call exists outside the guarded path. A budget with a bypass is not a budget.

Note

The Single-Chokepoint Rule: Every model call passes through one guarded path, and no raw call to the model exists outside it. A single bypass leaks the entire budget through that gap. Narrowing the entry point to exactly one is what turns cost governance from operating carefully into operating with structural protection. When

> reviewing AI code, verify there is no model call outside the guard before you verify anything else.

> Note
>
> Tool Tax — the enforcement chokepoint: A budget guard in the call path is a new single point of failure in front of every AI feature you own. The latency it adds is single-digit milliseconds, which is cheap. What is not cheap is that it must now be as available as the model calls it guards: a guard that fails closed takes the feature down, and a guard that fails open silently removes the budget. Decide which way it fails before you ship it, alert on that decision, and treat the guard's own availability as a P0 concern. You have also created a component every future AI feature must integrate with, and that coordination cost grows with the number of teams.

On top of the chokepoint, budgets are enforced in tiers, because the cost of an AI system runs away at several different scopes. A per-task budget rejects a single operation that would cost more than the task is worth before it executes. A per-agent daily budget prevents any one agent from overspending across a day, however many tasks it runs. A per-user budget bounds what a single user can drive in cost, which matters the moment a feature is exposed to the public and someone discovers they can make your model do expensive work on your bill. Each tier catches a runaway the others miss.

> Note
>
> **The Tiered-Budget Mandate:** Enforce AI cost budgets at three scopes at once: per task (reject a single operation that costs more than it is worth, before it runs), per agent per day (cap total daily spend by any one agent), and per user (bound what a single user can drive). A single global budget is not enough, because a runaway can occur at any scope, and a budget at only one scope leaves the others uncapped.

Budget Tier	What It Caps	What It Catches
Per task	Cost of one operation, checked before it runs	A single request that would cost more than its value
Per agent per day	Total daily spend by one agent	A reasoning loop that slowly burns the day's budget
Per user	Spend a single user can drive	A public user who discovers expensive prompts
Per feature	Total spend of one AI feature	A feature whose unit economics are broken

Table 14.12: The four AI budget tiers and the class of runaway each one catches

The most dangerous runaway is the unbounded agent loop. An agent that retries on failure, or reasons step by step without a hard ceiling on steps, can multiply token cost without limit while looking, from the outside, like a single user request that is merely slow. ShopFlow's rising cost per resolved ticket is exactly this pattern in a benign form. The fix is a hard cap on reasoning steps and retries per task, enforced at the chokepoint, so that a task that exceeds its step budget is stopped and handed off rather than allowed to loop. The cap is not a quality compromise; it is the difference between a feature with bounded cost and one with no cost ceiling at all.

> Note
>
> **Anti-Pattern: The Unbounded Agent Loop:** An agent permitted to retry or reason step by step with no hard ceiling on steps per task. From the outside it looks like one slow request. On the bill it is ten to fifty times the token cost of a single call, and under load it is the line item that climbs while traffic stays flat. Every agent task must have a maximum step count and retry count enforced at the chokepoint, or its cost is unbounded by construction.

Before enforcement, the cheapest lever is to not spend the tokens at all, and the technique that does it best is model cascading. Most requests do not need your most capable and most expensive model. A cascade starts every request on the cheapest model that might succeed and escalates to a more expensive model only when the cheap one cannot produce an acceptable answer. Routing the easy majority to a cheap tier and reserving the expensive model for the hard minority routinely cuts cost per request by half or more, with no loss of quality on the requests that never needed the expensive model in the first place.

> Note
>
> **The Model-Cascade Rule:** Start every request on the cheapest model that might succeed and escalate to a more expensive model only when the cheaper one fails to produce an acceptable answer. Most requests do not need your most capable model. Routing the easy majority to a cheap tier and escalating only the hard minority is the single largest token-cost reduction available, and it costs quality nothing on the requests that never needed the expensive tier.

> Note
>
> Tool Tax — the model cascade: Running three tiers means maintaining three of everything. Three sets of prompts, because a prompt tuned for the capable model rarely survives contact with the cheap one. Three evaluation runs before any change ships. Three sets of production failure modes, plus a fourth in the escalation logic itself. The cascade also makes debugging harder: "the answer was wrong" now requires knowing which tier produced it, so tier identity has to be on every log line and every trace from the first day, not retrofitted after the first confusing incident. The saving is real, and so is the maintenance.

Tier	**Model Class**	**Handles**	**Relative Token Cost**
Tier 1	Small/cheap model	Routine, well-structured requests (the majority)	1x
Tier 2	Mid-size model	Requests Tier 1 could not be resolved	5x to 10x
Tier 3	Most capable model	The hard minority and high-stakes requests	20x or more

Table 14.13: The model cascade tiers, what each handles, and its relative token cost

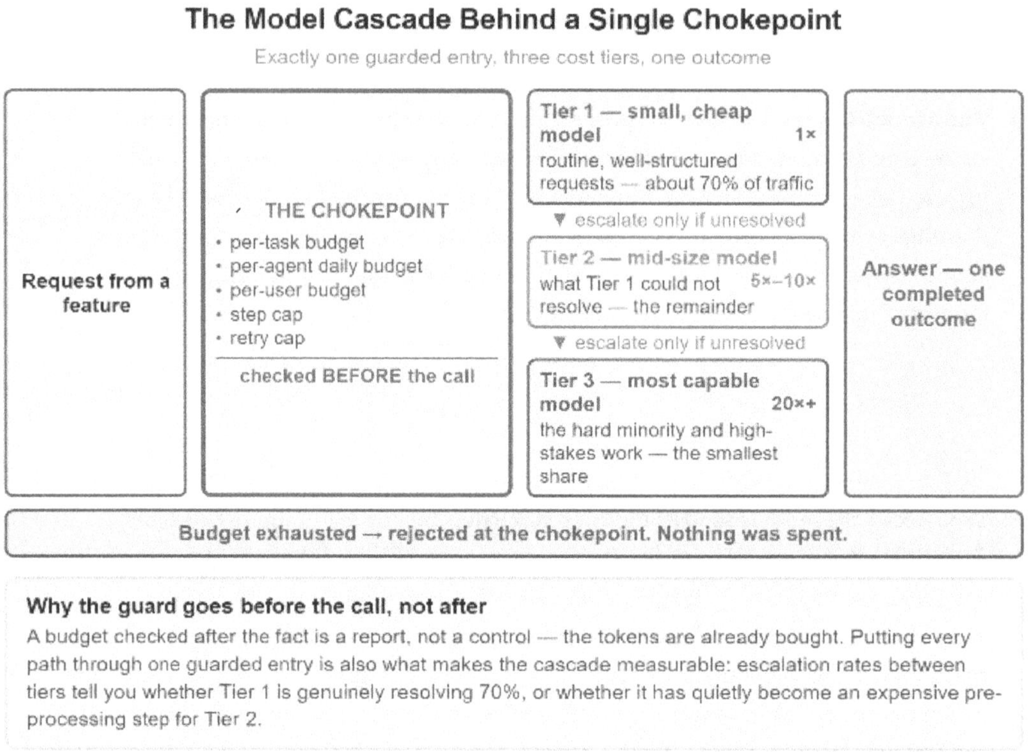

Figure 14.5: The Model Cascade Behind a Single Chokepoint

Validating the cascade over time

A cascade is tuned against the models that exist on the day you configure it, and that day passes quickly. Vendors ship cheap tiers more capable than last quarter's mid-tier, deprecate versions on their own schedule, and change per-token pricing without asking. Your own traffic mix shifts as features launch. A routing threshold that sent 70% of conversations to the cheap tier at launch can be sending 40% six months later with nobody having touched a line of code — or it can be sending 90%, quietly answering requests that used to earn an escalation.

Treat the cascade the way you treat an autoscaling threshold: a tuned parameter with an owner and a review cadence. Five signals tell you whether it is still calibrated, and you need all five, because four of them can be improved by making the system worse.

Signal	Healthy	What a Drift Means
Escalation rate per tier	Stable, and matching the traffic mix the cascade was designed for	Rising: the cheap tier is losing ground, or the traffic got harder. Falling sharply: the escalation trigger has stopped firing
Answer quality per tier	Cheap-tier quality holds against a fixed evaluation set	The cheap tier is now answering requests it should be escalatin
Latency per outcome	Flat or improving	Escalation is adding a second round trip to a growing share of requests
Tokens per outcome	Flat or falling	Cost is migrating up the tiers with no change in escalation rate to explain it
Resolution rate and customer satisfaction	Unchanged by the cascade	The saving is being paid for out of the customer's experience

Table 14.14: The five signals that tell you whether a model cascade is still calibrated

The fifth signal is the one that keeps the other four honest. Escalation rate, latency, and tokens per outcome can all be improved by routing more aggressively to the cheap tier, and the bill will look excellent while resolution quality falls. This is why the denominator is cost per resolved ticket rather than cost per conversation. A cascade tuned against cost alone will find the cheapest way to fail.

Hold the evaluation set fixed across reviews. A cascade re-tuned against a set that drifts with the traffic will always look calibrated, because you are grading it on the requests it already handles well. Keep a held-out set that includes the hard minority, and re-run it every quarter and on every vendor change.

Note

The Cascade Recalibration Rule: A model cascade is a tuned parameter, not a configuration you set once. Re-evaluate the routing thresholds against a held-out evaluation set every quarter, and immediately whenever a vendor ships a new tier, deprecates a model, or changes pricing. Validate on all five signals — escalation rate, answer quality, latency, tokens per outcome, and resolution rate — because optimizing any of the first four alone moves cost off the bill and onto the customer.

Note

Manager's Math, Governing the Support Agent: On a high-traffic enterprise platform I worked on, an agent of this shape cost roughly $500 per hour at peak before anyone capped it. ShopFlow's early support agent carried the same defect at a smaller scale: it was accurate and well-liked, and every conversation, however trivial, ran on the most capable model and looped without a step cap. Three changes fixed the economics: a model cascade routed about 70% of conversations to a cheap tier, a per-task step cap stopped the reasoning loops, and a per-conversation budget enforced at the chokepoint bounded the worst case. Cost per resolved ticket fell from $0.41 toward $0.16, a 60% reduction in the support agent's share of the LLM bill, with no measurable drop in resolution quality. The feature did not need to be retired. Its cost needed to be governed.

Sometimes the economics do not survive the analysis, and the right call is to redesign or retire the feature. A feature whose token cost per outcome exceeds the value of the outcome is not viable no matter how much you optimize the model calls, and recognizing that early is a cost discipline in itself. The decision rule is the same one that governs the rest of this chapter: judge the AI feature by its cost per outcome, not its cost per call. A feature with a low per-call cost that requires fifty calls per outcome is more expensive than a feature with a high per-call cost that needs one.

Note

The Cost-Per-Outcome-Not-Per-Call Rule: Judge an AI feature by the token cost of a completed outcome, not the cost of a single model call. A cheap model called fifty times in a loop costs more than an expensive model called once. The per-call price is the number vendors quote; the per-outcome cost is the number that lands on your bill.

> Optimize and budget against the outcome, and retire any feature whose cost per outcome exceeds the value of the outcome.

> Note
>
> **Safe Scale Check, The Budget Circuit Breaker:** Reversibility: a per-task or per-conversation budget is a parameter, fully reversible, and should be set with headroom so it never cuts off a legitimate task mid-outcome. Blast radius: enforce the budget at the single chokepoint so that when a session exhausts it, the next call is refused rather than the whole agent halted, and the partial result is handed off gracefully. A budget that halts a task halfway, wasting every token already spent, is worse than one that completes the outcome and blocks the next task. Stage the cutoff so spent tokens are not wasted.

The token tax is the cost no AI feature escapes, and naming it keeps the architecture honest. Every model call is metered, every reasoning step multiplies the meter, and every retry pays the meter again. The enforcement layer that governs this has its own tax: a small latency cost at the chokepoint, because every call now passes through a budget check before it runs. That latency is measured in single-digit milliseconds and it buys structural cost control. It costs less than the first incident it prevents, and on any feature exposed to the public it is not optional.

Architect's prompt 14.5: the AI cost governance design

When to use this: Use this prompt when an AI feature's token cost is climbing without a matching rise in usage, and you need to put enforcement, tiered budgets, and a model cascade in place before the feature goes wider.

```
Act as a Principal Engineer who has built runtime cost governance for
autonomous agents. Help me govern the token cost of an AI feature.

Feature: [name]. Model in use: [model]. Current cost per outcome: [amount].
Outcome unit: [resolved ticket / recommendation / generated draft].
Current per-call path: [is there a single chokepoint, or raw calls?].
Step/retry behavior: [is there a hard cap, or can it loop?].

Do the following:
(1) Identify whether every model call passes through one guarded chokepoint.
    Flag any raw call site that bypasses the budget.
```

```
(2) Specify enforcement (reject before the call), not just monitoring.
(3) Define tiered budgets: per task, per agent per day, and per user.
(4) Set a hard cap on reasoning steps and retries per task.
(5) Design a model cascade: which requests start on the cheap tier and what
    signal escalates them to a more expensive model.
(6) Compute the projected cost per outcome after these changes, and state
    the threshold at which this feature should be redesigned or retired.
(7) Stage the budget cutoff so an exhausted session hands off its partial
    result rather than wasting the tokens already spent.
```

The FinOps readiness checklist

Before a cost practice can be called governed rather than watched, every item below should read yes — or carry a named owner and a time-boxed exception. Each one is a rule from this chapter expressed as something you can verify in an afternoon.

Platform services owned: every line item on the cloud bill, including the platform services that sit beneath every team, maps to an owning team. (The Line-Item Ownership Rule)

Review intervals assigned: every provisioned-once service carries a monthly, quarterly or annual review interval, set at the moment it is provisioned. (The Review Cadence Rule)

Tagging enforced at provisioning: owner, service, and environment tags are required at creation, so an untagged resource is rejected rather than reported. (The Cost-Has-An-Owner Mandate)

Cost reviewed weekly by engineers: cost sits in the production fundamentals meeting next to availability and latency, owned by the teams that run the services. (The Fundamentals Review Rule)

Alerts keyed to trend breaks: cost alerts fire on a slope that breaks from business volume, never on a round-number spend ceiling. (The Trend-Not-Absolute Rule)

Unit economics tracked: cost per unit of business value is a weekly trend, and the denominator counts successful outcomes only. (The Unit-Economics Rule, The Successful-Unit Rule)

Self-hosting is decided by break-even: every proposal is priced against the loaded cost of engineering time, and the decision carries a review date. (The Loaded-Cost Mandate, The Reversible Default Rule)

Single chokepoint verified: every model call passes through one guarded path, and a code review has confirmed no raw call site exists outside it. (The Single-Chokepoint Rule)

AI budgets tiered and capped: budgets enforced per task, per agent per day and per user, with a hard cap on reasoning steps and retries per task. (The Tiered-Budget Mandate)

Cascade revalidated quarterly: routing thresholds re-tested against a held-out evaluation set every quarter and on every vendor change, across all five calibration signals. (The Cascade Recalibration Rule)

Autoscaling ceilings set: every autoscaling group has a cost-aware ceiling above the true peak that alerts an owner when it is reached. (Safe Scale Check, Cost-Aware Autoscaling Guardrails)

An item that reads no is not a failure; it is a dated commitment. An item that reads no with no date attached is the blind spot the rest of the practice will quietly grow around.

Summary

In this chapter, we built the FinOps practice that makes ShopFlow's cost growth sustainable. We did not try to spend less on a system that is materially larger. We made every dollar traceable to a unit of business value, so that growth in the bill is judged against growth in the business rather than treated as waste to be hunted.

We applied the Provisioned-Once Rule to find the cost that always surprises you, the platform service set once and never reviewed, and recovered $710/mo from an unscoped backup policy with zero risk to recoverable data. We established the Fundamentals Review Rule and the Trend-Not-Absolute Rule to make cost a first-class engineering metric, watched in the weekly review by the engineers who own it, judged by the slope of cost per order rather than the height of the bill.

We resolved the managed-versus-self-hosted argument with the Loaded-Cost Mandate and a break-even calculation, establishing that the premium is usually cheaper than the engineering weeks self-hosting consumes, and that the burden of proof sits on self-hosting. We made spend attributable through the Cost-Has-An-Owner Mandate and closed the FinOps feedback loop, converting an unexaminable 23% of untagged spend into attributable cost and exposing $620/mo of recoverable waste hiding inside it.

And we governed the newest and least predictable cost axis in the system. We treated tokens as a first-class cost axis, drew the line between cost monitoring and cost enforcement, routed every model call through a single guarded chokepoint, enforced tiered budgets, capped agent loops, and cascaded models from cheap to expensive. The result took the support agent from $0.41 to $0.16 per resolved ticket without retiring it. The feature did not need to be retired. Its cost needed to be governed.

ShopFlow's telemetry after *Chapter 14*:

Metric	Before (Ch14 Start)	After (Ch14 End)	Change
Cost per Order	Untracked	$0.10, tracked weekly as a trend	Now a first-class metric
Backup + Retention Spend	$1,180/mo (unscoped)	$470/mo (tiered by criticality)	60% reduction; no data risk
Untagged Spend	23% of bill	Under 2%; tags enforced at provisioning	Spend now attributable
Support Agent Cost/ Ticket	$0.41 and rising	$0.16 (cascade + step cap + budget)	60% reduction
AI Cost Governance	Monitoring only (postmortem)	Enforcement at a single chokepoint	Budgets now bound spending
Cost Growth Posture	Ungoverned; +36% over 18 mo	Governed against unit economics	Grows more slowly than the business

Table 14.15: ShopFlow's cost posture before and after Chapter 14

The cliffhanger: half the intelligence was never intelligent

The AI bill is governed now. Tokens have budgets, the support agent has a step cap, and the model cascade routes the easy majority to a cheap tier. Cost per resolved ticket is down 60%. The unit economics finally hold.

But governing the AI bill forced ShopFlow to look closely at what each AI feature did, and the audit surfaced something the cost work did not set out to find. When the model cascade was instrumented, the team discovered that a large share of the requests routed to the cheapest model were not reasoning at all. They were classifying an order status, validating an address format, or selecting one of four canned responses. These are not language problems. They are deterministic problems that a state machine or a simple rule would answer correctly every time, for a fraction of a cent, with no model call at all.

Dave frames it in the end-of-sprint review. ShopFlow reached for a model the way teams reach for a model right now: by reflex, because it was the new tool, for problems that a switch statement solved a decade ago. The cost governance capped the damage, but it did not ask the prior question. Some of these workflows should never have been an agent. They should have been deterministic code, faster and cheaper and more reliable than any model call, and the cascade was quietly paying a token tax to answer questions that have exactly one correct answer.

In *Chapter 15*, we ask that prior question directly. Before you govern the cost of an AI feature, you decide whether it should be an AI feature at all. We build the decision framework that separates the workflows that need a model from the ones that are deterministic problems wearing an agent's clothing, and we design the guardrails and kill switches that keep the genuinely intelligent features safe. This is AI-first architecture, and it is pragmatism over hype.

Part 5

Future-Proofing: AI and Evolution

The final part is about staying ahead. You will add intelligence to ShopFlow without succumbing to hype, using AI only where it earns its cost and its nondeterminism and keeping deterministic code everywhere else, all under runtime governance and a hard kill switch. Then you will solve the quietest and most dangerous problem of a successful system, the fear of changing it, by making experimentation a property of the architecture itself. By the end of this part, ShopFlow can not only handle scale. It can keep evolving safely, which is the only thing that makes any architecture truly future-proof.

This part of the book includes the following chapters:

- *Chapter 15, AI-First Architecture: Pragmatism Over Hype*
- *Chapter 16, Continuous Experimentation and the Future-Proof System*

15

AI-First Architecture: Pragmatism Over Hype

In *Chapter 14*, we governed the AI bill. Tokens got budgets, the support agent got a step cap and a model cascade, and cost per resolved ticket fell 60%. The unit economics held. But instrumenting that cascade surfaced something the cost work did not set out to find, and it is the question this chapter exists to answer.

When the team looked at which requests were being routed to the cheapest model, a large share of them were not reasoning at all. They were classifying an order status, validating an address format, or choosing one of four canned responses. These are not language problems. They are deterministic problems with exactly one correct answer, and they were being answered by a model call that costs a fraction of a cent more than the switch statement that should have handled them, runs slower, and occasionally gets the answer wrong.

This is the defining mistake of the current moment. The industry reaches for a large language model the way it once reached for a microservice or a NoSQL database: by reflex, because it is the new tool, for problems that were solved correctly a decade ago. The cost governance from *Chapter 14* capped the damage, but it never asked the prior question. Before you govern the cost of an AI feature, you decide whether it should be an AI feature at all.

That is the thesis of this chapter, and it is the opposite of the message most AI content sells. AI-first architecture does not mean putting a model in every workflow. It means being deliberate about the one place a model earns its cost and its nondeterminism, and being equally deliberate about the far larger set of places where deterministic code is faster, cheaper, more reliable, and safer. Pragmatism over hype is not a hedge. It is the discipline that separates teams who ship durable AI systems from teams who ship expensive demos.

I write this chapter as the creator of the Agent Governance Toolkit, an open-source framework I built to make agentic AI safe for production. That work started from exactly the question this chapter opens with, and the lessons in it are the ones I learned governing real agents at scale. We will decide when to use AI and when not to. We will look squarely at the gap between an agent that demos well and an agent that survives production. We will cover what it takes to serve AI infrastructure at scale, what governing an autonomous agent requires, and the one control no production AI system can ship without: the kill switch.

In this chapter, we are going to cover the following main topics:

- The Intelligence Choice: When to Use AI and When Not To
- De-mystifying Agents: The Production-Readiness Gap
- Serving AI at Scale: The Day the Traffic Arrives
- Governing the Agent: Determinism in a Nondeterministic World
- The Safety Valve: Kill Switches and Human-in-the-Loop Guardrails

Technical requirements

Agent Governance Toolkit (AGT) or equivalent runtime governance layer: Deterministic policy enforcement, capability scoping, and audit logging for agent actions, applied at runtime rather than in the prompt.

A deterministic rules or state-machine engine: For the workflows that should never be a model call. Bounded inputs and a known set of outputs belong in code, not in an LLM.

Model Context Protocol (MCP) server with governance proxy: A governed gateway between agents and tools, capable of scoping which tools an agent may call and recording every call.

Model routing and cascade layer: Routes requests across model tiers and enforces the determinism-first decision so that cheap and deterministic paths are taken before any expensive model call.

Behavioral observability for agents (OpenTelemetry + policy metrics): Per-action logging, a policy-compliance signal, and anomaly detection on agent behavior, not just request latency.

A kill switch and human-in-the-loop control plane: A single, unbypassable mechanism to halt an agent and a gate that requires human approval before high-impact autonomous actions execute.

Code Repository: `https://github.com/imran-siddique/Architecting-at-Scale/tree/main/ch15`

ShopFlow telemetry snapshot [stage 15]

```
The Signal: AI cost is governed, but AI behavior is not. Features are multiplying.
Roughly 40% of them are deterministic problems running on a model, and the
autonomous ones can take real actions with no kill switch and zero OWASP Agentic
risk coverage.
AI Features in Production: 9 (up from 2 a year ago)
AI Features That Are Deterministic Problems: ~40% (status lookup, address
validation, canned-response selection)
Agents Able to Take Real Actions: 3 (issue refunds, reroute shipments, resolve
tickets) with no hard stop
OWASP Agentic Risk Coverage: 0 of 10 (no runtime governance on any agent)
MCP Endpoint Traffic: 12,000 calls/day (One model integration away from a spike;
no scaling plan)
Human-in-the-Loop Coverage on High-Impact Actions: None (refunds and reroutes
execute autonomously)
Panic Meter: 4/10 (Nothing is rogue yet. Nothing is governed either.)
```

> Note
>
> **Dave Alert:** "The reroute agent moved every west-coast shipment through a single hub overnight to save a few minutes per package. It was inside its permissions, so nothing stopped it, and I could not find a way to turn just that agent off without taking down the whole logistics service. We do not have an off switch."

The whole chapter reduces to five questions asked in order, and the order is what does the work. Each is a gate: answer it and you either stop with a cheaper and more predictable design, or you earn the right to ask the next one. Teams that jump to the last two end up carefully governing a model that should never have been in the workflow.

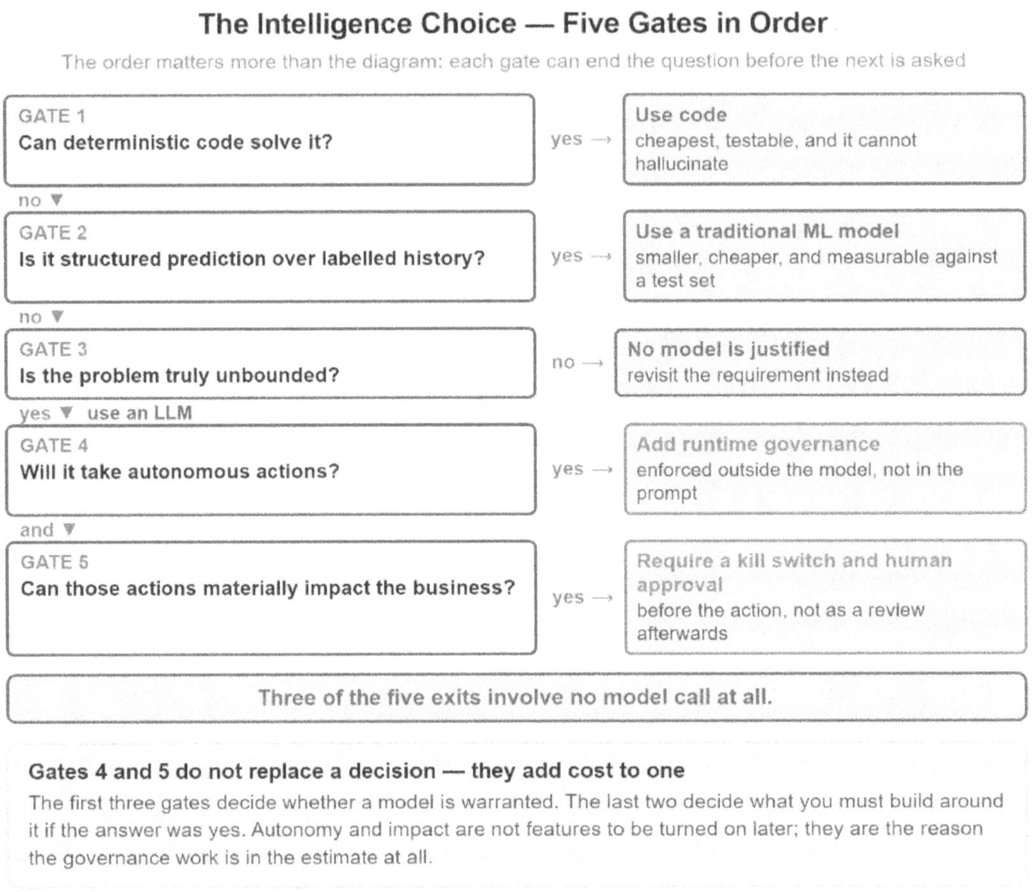

Figure 15.1: The Intelligence Choice — Five Gates in Order

The same five gates as text, because the order matters more than the diagram:

1. Can deterministic code solve the problem? If yes, use code. Bounded inputs with enumerable outputs never need a model.
2. Is this structured prediction over labeled history? If yes, consider a traditional machine-learning model before reaching for a large language model.
3. Is the problem genuinely unbounded — open language in, an output you cannot enumerate out? Only here does a large language model earn its cost and its nondeterminism.

4. Will the system take autonomous actions? Then runtime governance ships with it, not after it.
5. Can those actions materially impact the business? Then a kill switch and human approval on the high-impact ones are conditions of shipping.

The first three questions decide whether you have an AI problem at all. The last two decide what you owe the business if you do. Two things are worth noticing. Three of the five exits leave you with no model call, which is the point of the chapter in a single observation. And the two governance gates are not enhancements to be scheduled later; they are the conditions under which the answer to gate three is allowed to reach production.

> Note
>
> **The Gate-Order Rule:** Ask the five intelligence questions in order and stop at the first gate that resolves the problem. The order is not a preference — each gate is cheaper, faster, and more predictable than the one after it, so any question answered early saves everything downstream of it. A team that starts at gate four is governing a model whose presence was never justified, and no amount of governance makes an unnecessary model call a good decision.

The intelligent choice: when to use AI and when not to

Start every AI design decision from the same default, and it is the opposite of the industry default. The question is not where can we add a model. The question is where must we, and the honest answer for most workflows is nowhere. A model is a nondeterministic, metered, latency-adding component, and you introduce one only when the problem requires intelligence that deterministic code cannot provide. Almost all of the time, you do not have to, so you should not.

> Note
>
> **The Determinism-First Rule:** Where a problem can be solved deterministically, it must be solved deterministically. A model is introduced only when the problem requires intelligence that code cannot provide. The burden of proof is on the model, not on the deterministic path. If a switch statement, a rule, or a state machine produces the correct answer every time, there is no version of that workflow that is improved by a model call.

The clearest signal is the shape of the inputs and outputs. When a workflow has bounded inputs and a known, finite set of outputs, it is a deterministic problem and it belongs in code. A form that asks for a name and an address does not need a model to validate a postal code. A process that supports options A, B, and C, and that you have deliberately decided will never support D, does not need a model to route between them. You already know every valid answer. A model can only add latency, cost, and a small but nonzero chance of producing an answer you explicitly excluded.

> Note
>
> **The Bounded-Input Rule:** If the inputs are bounded and the set of valid outputs is finite and known in advance, the workflow is deterministic and belongs in code. A model adds nothing to a problem whose answers you can already enumerate, and it adds the risk of returning an answer outside the set you defined. Enumerable outputs are the strongest possible signal to keep a model out.

So where does a model earn its place? It earns it where you do not yet have anything built and could not reasonably build it with rules. Analyzing large volumes of unstructured data for patterns you cannot specify in advance. Synthesizing a feedback summary across thousands of free-text responses. Handling open-ended language where the input space is unbounded and the valuable output cannot be enumerated. These are problems where determinism is not available at any price, and a model is not a convenience but the only practical tool. That is the real need, and the real need is the only justification.

> Note
>
> **The Real-Need Test:** Use an agent or a model only when you can name the specific capability it provides that deterministic code cannot: unbounded input, unspecifiable output, or pattern analysis over data you cannot enumerate. If you cannot name that capability, the real need does not exist and the model is decoration. Knowing the genuine use case is the precondition for using a model, not a detail to work out later.

Signal	Use deterministic code	Use a model
Input space	Bounded and well-formed (a postal code, an order ID)	Unbounded natural language or unstructured content
Output set	Finite and known in advance (A, B, or C)	Open-ended; the valuable answer cannot be enumerated

Signal	Use deterministic code	Use a model
A working solution exists	Yes; rules or a state machine already solve it	No; the problem was never tractable with rules
Correctness requirement	Must be right every time (refund amount, residency)	Tolerates a best-effort answer with review
What the model would add	Latency, cost, and a chance of an excluded answer	A capability that does not otherwise exist

Table 15.1: The five signals that decide between deterministic code and a model

Note

Anti-Pattern: The Reflexive Agent: Reaching for a model or an agent because it is the current tool, for a problem that deterministic code already solves correctly. The form validator on an LLM, the status lookup routed through an agent, the four-way router that is a switch statement in disguise. Each one pays a token cost, adds latency, and introduces a chance of a wrong answer to a question that has exactly one right answer. The reflex is the failure, not the model.

There is one domain where the caution must be highest, and that is the user-facing experience. Nondeterminism in a back-office analysis is a manageable risk; you review the output before you act on it. Nondeterminism in the path a customer walks through is different, because a model that behaves unpredictably in the user experience can degrade the entire experience, not just one feature. This is where teams do the most damage by injecting a model everywhere, and where the discipline of keeping deterministic paths deterministic matters most. Be careful injecting intelligence into the experience itself. A model belongs there only when it clearly helps and cannot hurt, and that bar is high.

Note

The User-Experience Caution Rule: Hold the highest bar for introducing a model into a user-facing path. A nondeterministic component in the experience can degrade the whole experience, not just its own feature, because the user cannot review the output before living with it. Inject intelligence into the user experience only where it clearly helps and has no path to hurting, and keep the deterministic parts of the experience deterministic.

In the User Experience	A Model Helps	A Model Hurts
Open-ended assistance	Answering a free-text product question	Replacing a deterministic checkout step
Input validation	Never; this is a bounded problem	Validating a postal code or order ID
Routing a known set of paths	Never; this is a switch statement	Choosing between A, B, and C nondeterministically
Personalization	Ranking suggestions from rich signals	Deciding whether the page renders at all

Table 15.2: Where a model helps and where it hurts inside a user-facing path

The same logic extends to the middle ground between a rule and a model: the traditional machine-learning model. Not every prediction problem needs a large language model. A classification or scoring task with structured features and labeled history is often solved better, cheaper, and more predictably by a conventional model than by an LLM. The heuristic that resolves the whole decision is a hierarchy, and in an architecture review I apply it in order. Every step up that hierarchy pays a tax. A traditional model adds a data and training tax. A large language model adds a token tax and a latency tax on top of it, and that tax is paid on every single call.

Tool	Reach For It When	Cost and Risk Profile
Rules/state machine	Inputs bounded, outputs enumerable, answer must be exact	Cheapest, fastest, fully predictable
Traditional ML model	Structured features, labeled history, a prediction or score	Moderate cost; predictable; needs training data

Tool	Reach For It When	Cost and Risk Profile
Large language model	Unbounded language, unspecifiable output, no prior solution	Highest cost and latency; non-deterministic

Table 15.3: The three-step hierarchy from rules to traditional ML to a large language model, and what each step costs

Note

Manager's Math, The Form Validator: ShopFlow had an address-format check running on an LLM. It cost real tokens per submission, added latency to a checkout field, and returned an out-of-format answer often enough to file occasional tickets. Replacing it with a deterministic validation rule cost two days of work, dropped the per-check cost to effectively zero, removed the latency from the checkout path, and took the error rate to zero. The model was not just unnecessary. On a bounded-input, known-output problem it was strictly worse than the rule on every axis: cost, speed, and correctness.

Most production systems are hybrids

Framing this as a choice between deterministic and AI is a useful teaching device and a poor description of what you actually build. Nearly every production system that uses a model well is a hybrid, and the model occupies a small, tightly bounded part of a workflow that is deterministic everywhere else. The design question is not which one you pick; it is where exactly the boundary sits.

ShopFlow's support workflow is the concrete case. A customer sends a free-text message, and the path it takes crosses that boundary exactly once.

Step	Handled By	Why
1. Authenticate the customer and load the account	Deterministic code	A credential check and a database read; there is exactly one correct answer
2. Verify the customer owns the order in question	Deterministic code	A join and a comparison; a model here is a correctness risk with no upside

Step	Handled By	Why
3. Classify the intent (refund, delivery, product question, escalation)	Traditional ML classifier	Structured prediction over labeled history — not a language problem
4. Route to the handling path	Deterministic code	Four known destinations; this is a switch statement
5. Generate the reply	Large language model	Unbounded input, an output that cannot be enumerated — the one step that needs a model
6. Execute any action (refund, reroute)	Deterministic code, governed	The model asks; code decides and acts, gated by the policy layer built later in this chapter

Table 15.4: One support workflow, step by step, showing where the model's slice begins and ends

Five of the six steps are deterministic, and the sixth is deliberately narrow. The model does the one thing nothing else can do: turn an unbounded question into a well-formed answer. It does not authenticate, it does not authorize, it does not route, and it does not issue the refund. That ratio is typical of a well-designed AI feature, and its inverse — a model orchestrating steps that code should own — is the shape of most of the features this chapter argues against.

The boundary is also where the security properties live. Steps 1, 2, and 6 are the ones an attacker cares about, and none of them is reachable by anything the customer types, because none of them is decided by the model. A prompt injection in step 5 can produce a bad reply. It cannot produce a refund, because the model was never the thing that issues refunds. Drawing the boundary tightly is not only a cost and correctness decision; it is most of the threat model.

> Note
>
> **The Narrow-Model Rule:** In a hybrid workflow the model gets the smallest slice that solves the problem — the single step whose input is unbounded and whose output cannot be enumerated — and deterministic code keeps everything around it: authentication, authorization, validation, routing, and the execution of any action. Widening the model's slice past that boundary buys nothing and imports nondeterminism into steps that had exactly one correct answer. Draw the boundary

explicitly in the design review, because left alone it drifts outward one convenience at a time.

Note

Tool Tax — the traditional ML model: Stepping down from an LLM to a conventional classifier lowers the token bill and raises a different one. You now need labeled training data and somebody to keep labeling it, a training and evaluation pipeline, a model registry, and drift monitoring on the input distribution — because a classifier degrades silently as the world moves, whereas an LLM at least fails visibly. You also own a second serving path with its own latency budget and its own on-call. The classifier is the right answer for structured prediction, and it is not the free answer.

Architect's prompt 15.1: the intelligent choice audit

When to use this: Use this prompt in an architecture review when a proposed feature includes a model or an agent, to test whether the intelligence is genuinely required before any of it is built.

```
Act as a Principal Architect applying a determinism-first review. I am
evaluating a proposed feature that includes a model or an agent.

Feature: [description]. Proposed AI component: [model / agent].
Inputs: [describe the input space]. Outputs: [describe the output set].
Does a deterministic solution already exist or is it feasible? [yes/no].
Is this on a user-facing path? [yes/no].

Do the following:
(1) Classify the problem: bounded inputs with enumerable outputs (use code),
    structured prediction (use a traditional ML model), or unbounded language
    with unspecifiable output (use an LLM).
(2) If a deterministic path exists, recommend it and state what the model
    would only add (latency, cost, chance of an excluded answer).
(3) Name the specific capability the model provides that code cannot. If you
    cannot name one, fail the proposal.
(4) If the feature is user-facing, raise the bar and require that the model
    cannot degrade the wider experience.
```

```
(5) Give the final recommendation: rules, traditional ML, or LLM, with the
    reasoning a reviewer can defend in the room.
```

De-mystifying agents: the production readiness gap

In 2025, the conversation in the industry was about agents. Every team was building one, every framework promised one, and the demos were impressive. An agent would read a request, reason through it, call a few tools, and produce a result that looked like judgment. My question at the time was a different one, and it turned out to be the one that mattered. While everyone was talking about what agents could do, I was asking whether they were ready for production and what would have to be true before a regulated business could let one act on its behalf.

The answer was that they were not ready, and the gap was not capability. The gap was governance. An agent that demos well is an agent that did the right thing once, in a controlled setting, with a friendly input. An agent in production faces hostile inputs, ambiguous instructions, tool failures, and the slow drift of its own behavior over thousands of sessions. Nothing in the popular agent frameworks addressed any of that. They made agents easy to build and left them impossible to govern. The tooling that existed filtered prompts and scanned outputs, but the consequential actions happen between the prompt and the output, where the agent actually decides and acts, and that space had no controls at all.

> Note
>
> **The Production-Readiness Gap:** An agent that demos well has shown it can do the right thing once, in a controlled setting. An agent in production must do the right thing under hostile inputs, tool failures, and behavioral drift across thousands of sessions, and prove that it did. The distance between those two is governance, and it is the gap that separates an impressive demo from a system a regulated business can deploy. Capability is not the constraint. Governability is.

That gap is why I built the Agent Governance Toolkit. AGT was, to my knowledge, the first open-source framework to lay down end-to-end governance for autonomous agents, covering all ten of the OWASP Agentic AI risks rather than a single slice of them. It is, at the time of writing, the most widely adopted framework of its kind and the only one with documented mitigation for the full OWASP Agentic Top 10. I am not citing it here for credit. I am citing it because the design lessons it forced are the substance of how you make agentic AI safe, and they generalize far beyond any one toolkit.

The central design idea is the one that resolves the tension this whole chapter circles. Agents are nondeterministic by nature, and a nondeterministic system cannot be trusted with consequential actions unless something deterministic constrains it. So the governance layer does not try to make the agent predictable. It lets the model reason freely and wraps that reasoning in a deterministic boundary: a policy engine that decides, by fixed rules, which actions the agent is permitted to take, which tools it may call, and which data it may touch. The intelligence stays probabilistic. The permission to act becomes deterministic. That is how you get the value of an agent without inheriting the full risk of its nondeterminism.

> Note
>
> **The Determinism-in-Nondeterminism Doctrine:** You do not make an agent safe by making its reasoning predictable, which is impossible. You make it safe by wrapping its nondeterministic reasoning in a deterministic boundary: a fixed-rule policy layer that governs which actions, tools, and data the agent may reach. The model proposes; the deterministic layer disposes. The value of the agent comes from its probabilistic reasoning, and the safety comes from the deterministic enforcement around it.

> Note
>
> **Tool Tax — the runtime governance layer:** A policy engine in the action path is infrastructure you now operate. It adds well under a millisecond per action, which is not the cost. The cost is that the policy set becomes a second codebase with its own reviews, tests, and regressions; that the enforcement point must be as available as every agent behind it, with a decided, and instrumented failure direction; and that a default-deny baseline generates a steady stream of legitimate requests to widen it, which needs a triage path or teams will build their way around the gate. Budget the review load, not just the latency.

Dimension	Agent in a Demo	Agent in Production
Inputs	Friendly, expected, well-formed	Hostile, ambiguous, adversarial
Failure handling	Rarely exercised	Tool failures and partial results are routine
Behavior over time	One session observed	Thousands of sessions; drift accumulates
Accountability	None required	Every action must be attributable and auditable
What makes it work	Capability	Governance around the capability

Table 15.5: The five dimensions on which a demo agent and a production agent differ

Note

Anti-Pattern: The Ungoverned Pilot: Moving an agent from a successful pilot into production on the strength of the demo, without adding the governance the demo never needed. The pilot succeeded because the conditions were friendly. Production is not friendly, and an agent that can act without a deterministic permission boundary will eventually take an action no one authorized and no one can explain. A pilot proves capability. It does not prove the agent is ready to act unsupervised.

How an agent earns autonomy

Autonomy is not a property you grant on launch day. It is a level an agent reaches by producing evidence, and the ladder has five rungs. Each rung is a real deployment state with its own success criterion, and an agent stays on it until it has met that criterion against production traffic — not against a test suite, and not against a demo.

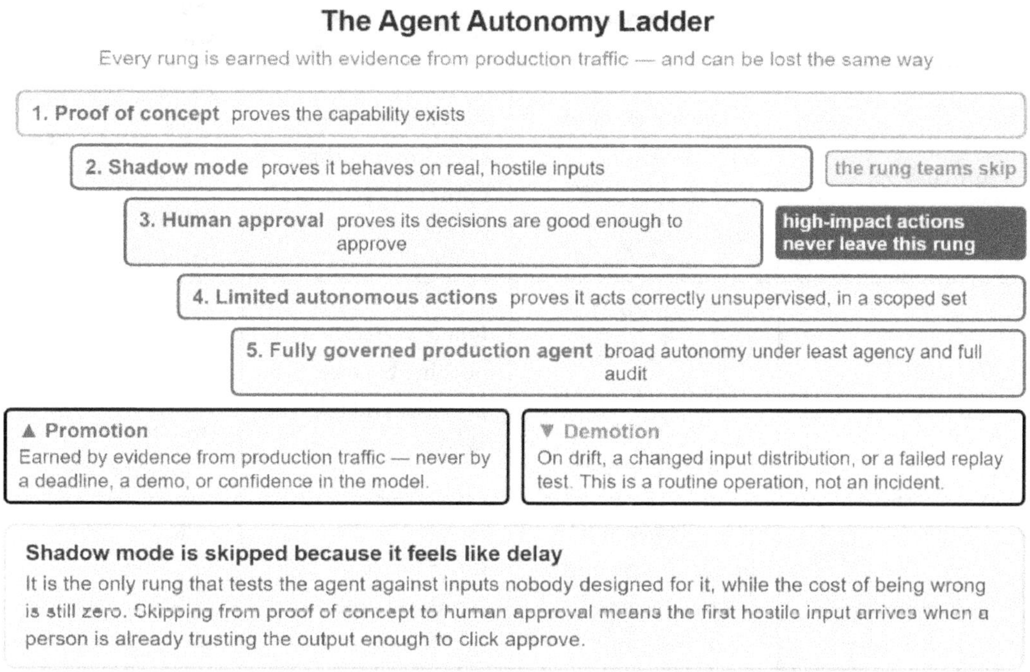

Figure 15.2: The Agent Autonomy Ladder

Rung	**What Happens**	**What It Proves**	**Criterion to Advance**
1. Proof of concept	Runs against sample inputs outside production	The capability exists	It works at all; nothing about production is established
2. Shadow mode	Runs on real production traffic; decisions are logged, never executed	It behaves sensibly on hostile, ambiguous, real input	Agreement with the existing path across a full traffic cycle, including edge cases

Rung	What Happens	What It Proves	Criterion to Advance
3. Human approval	Decisions execute, but only after a person approves each one	Its decisions are good enough that approval becomes routine	A high approval rate where reviewers are demonstrably reading, not rubber-stamping
4. Limited autonomous actions	Acts without approval inside a scoped, low-impact, reversible subset with a kill switch	It acts correctly with nothing between its decision and the world	A clean observation period at scope, with no policy violations and no manual reversals
5. Fully governed production agent	Broader autonomy under least agency, runtime policy, audit trail, and behavioral monitoring	It can be trusted within a boundary that is enforced rather than assumed	Steady state — high-impact actions remain permanently on rung 3

Table 15.6: The five rungs of the autonomy ladder, what each proves, and what it takes to advance

Two things about this ladder are easy to miss. The first is that rung five does not mean full autonomy. The high-impact, hard-to-reverse actions never leave rung three, by design and permanently, which is the subject of the last section of this chapter. The second is that the ladder runs in both directions. An agent whose behavior drifts, or whose input distribution changes underneath it, or that fails a replay test after a model upgrade, gets demoted — and a demotion should be an ordinary operational action that any on-call engineer can take, not an incident that requires a meeting.

Rung two is the one that gets skipped, and it is the one that earns its keep. Shadow mode is the only rung where an agent meets real production input — hostile, malformed, ambiguous, out of distribution — while being unable to affect anything. Every other rung either tests it on friendly input or lets it act. Skipping shadow mode is choosing to discover the agent's behavior on real traffic at the same moment that behavior has consequences.

Note

The Earned-Autonomy Rule: An agent climbs the autonomy ladder on evidence from production traffic, never on a demo and never on a date. Each rung carries a stated success criterion and a minimum observation period, and the agent stays until it meets both. The ladder is bidirectional: behavioral drift, a changed input distribution, or a failed replay test demotes an agent to the rung below, and that demotion is routine rather than exceptional. Skipping shadow mode skips the only rung that tests the agent against reality before reality can be affected by it.

Note

Tool Tax — shadow mode: Running an agent in shadow means running the workflow twice and paying for both, and the model calls are the cheap half. The expensive half is the comparison harness: something has to record the agent's decision alongside the incumbent's, decide what counts as agreement when both are free text, and surface the disagreements to a human who reads them. Without that harness shadow mode produces a log nobody opens, which looks like diligence and provides none. Budget the reviewer, and expect the disagreement rate to be the most useful number the whole exercise produces.

Note

Safe Scale Check, Promoting an Agent to Production: Reversibility: start a newly promoted agent in proposal or shadow mode, where it prepares actions a human approves, so its first production decisions are fully reversible. Blast radius: scope its initial live actions to a small, low-impact set, and widen only after it has behaved correctly across real traffic. An agent earns autonomy by evidence, the same way an error budget is earned, not by passing a demo.

Demystifying agents comes down to this: an agent is not a magical autonomous worker. It is a probabilistic reasoning engine attached to a set of tools, and its production-readiness is entirely a function of the deterministic governance you place around those tools. Strip away the hype and an agent is a powerful component that must be bounded, exactly like every other powerful component in this book, from the database that needed sharding to the deployment that needed a canary. The pattern is familiar. The novelty is only that the thing being bounded now reasons.

Architect's prompt 15.2: the agent Production-Readiness review

When to use this: Use this prompt before promoting an agent from a pilot or demo into production, to find the governance gap the demo did not expose.

```
Act as a Principal Engineer who has built runtime governance for agents.
I am promoting an agent from a successful pilot into production.

Agent purpose: [description]. Tools it can call: [list].
Actions it can take: [list, with which are consequential].
Data it can access: [list]. Current governance: [describe, or none].

Do the following:
(1) List the production conditions the pilot did not test: hostile inputs,
    tool failures, ambiguous instructions, and behavioral drift.
(2) For each consequential action, define the deterministic policy boundary
    that must gate it: which actions, tools, and data are permitted.
(3) Map the agent's exposure to the OWASP Agentic Top 10 and flag the
    uncovered risks.
(4) Specify the audit trail: what must be recorded for every action to make
    it attributable and explainable after the fact.
(5) State a go or no-go recommendation with the governance that must exist
    before go.
```

Serving AI at scale: the day the traffic arrives

There is a comforting belief that serving AI is a fundamentally new operational discipline that nothing in this book prepared you for. It is not. Running a model endpoint or a Model Context Protocol server in production is, in the ways that matter, the same problem as running any high-traffic service. It needs scaling, capacity planning, observability, resilience, and governance, the exact disciplines built across the previous fourteen chapters. The model is new. The production engineering around it is not.

> Note
>
> **The Scaling-Is-Scaling Rule:** Serving AI in production is governed by the same disciplines as serving anything else: scaling, capacity planning, observability, resilience, and governance. The model at the center is novel; the engineering around it is not. A team that treats AI serving as an exception to its production-engineering standards will rediscover every lesson in this book the hard way, under a model endpoint instead of a database.

From running a Model Context Protocol server at scale on a high-traffic enterprise documentation platform, the lesson that stood out was how the traffic arrives, because it does not arrive the way human traffic does. Human traffic grows along a curve you can forecast: marketing drives it, seasonality shapes it, and you provision against a trend. AI traffic to an MCP endpoint is different. The consumers are models and agents, and the moment they discover that your server is useful, traffic can multiply overnight. There is no gradual ramp. One day an agent framework adds your server to its default tool set, or a model learns to call it, and the volume steps up by an order of magnitude between one evening and the next morning.

> Note
>
> **The Overnight-Discovery Rule:** AI traffic to a tool or MCP endpoint does not ramp along a forecastable human curve. The consumers are agents, and when they discover the endpoint is useful, volume can multiply overnight with no warning. You provision and govern for a step change, not a trend, because the step change is the normal case. An endpoint that is only sized for today's traffic is one integration away from being overwhelmed.

> Note
>
> **Tool Tax — the MCP governance proxy:** Putting a governed gateway in front of your tools adds a hop on every agent call and a component whose outage is an outage of every tool behind it. It also introduces an identity problem you did not previously have: agents need issued, scoped, short-lived credentials, which means an issuance path, a rotation story, and a revocation story for the day an agent misbehaves. Per-consumer rate limits need tuning against traffic that arrives as a step change rather than a curve, so the first limits you set will be wrong in one direction or the other. Ship it anyway —

> the alternative is an ungoverned endpoint — but ship it with the identity model already decided.

This is what breaks first, and it is governance before it is capacity. An ungoverned MCP endpoint that suddenly serves ten times the traffic does not just cost more. It exposes every tool behind it to ten times the agent calls, with no scoping of which agents may call what, no rate limiting per consumer, and no record of who called which tool. Hosting an AI-facing endpoint carries a scaling tax that, unlike most, is paid all at once rather than along a gradual curve. The capacity problem is solvable with the autoscaling and right-sizing from earlier chapters. The governance problem, of an endpoint handing tools to any agent that finds it, is the one that turns an overnight traffic spike into an incident.

What Breaks at MCP Scale	**Why It Breaks First**	**The Control**
Tool exposure	Any agent that finds the endpoint can call any tool	Scope tools per agent identity at the gateway
Capacity	Traffic steps up overnight, not along a trend	Provision for a step change; autoscale with a ceiling
Attribution	Calls arrive with no record of which agent took them	Log every call to a verified agent identity
Rate fairness	One agent can saturate the endpoint for all	Per-consumer rate limits, not just a global cap
Cost	Token and call cost spikes with Discovery	Apply the Chapter 14 budgets per consumer

Table 15.7: What breaks first when an AI-facing endpoint is discovered, and the control for each

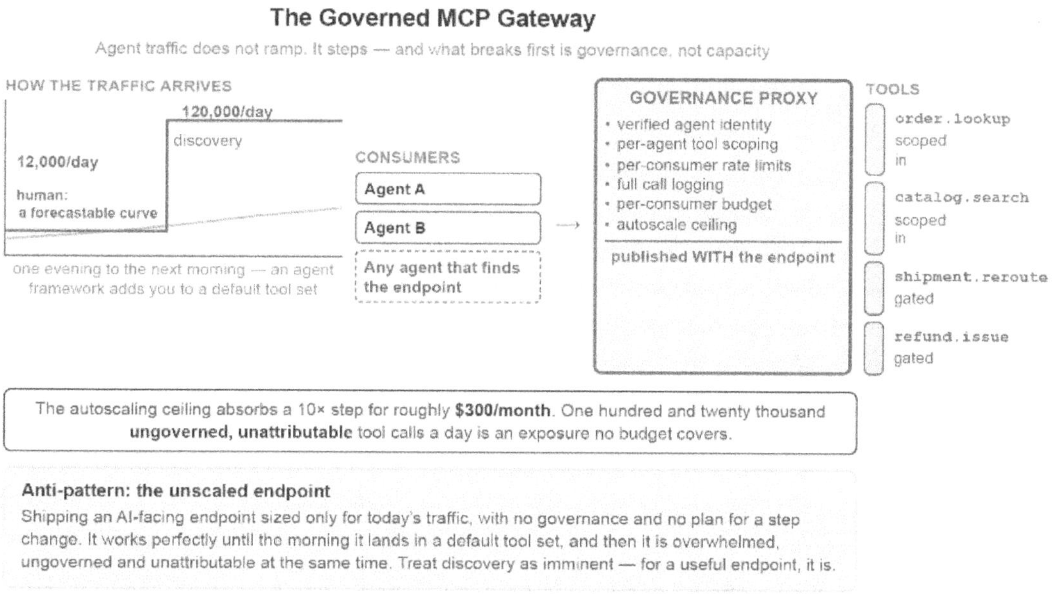

Figure 15.3: The Governed MCP Gateway

Note

Anti-Pattern: The Unscaled Endpoint: Shipping a model or MCP endpoint sized only for the traffic it serves today, with no governance and no plan for a step change. It works perfectly until the morning an agent framework adds it to a default tool set, and then it is simultaneously overwhelmed, ungoverned, and unattributable. The fix is to treat every AI-facing endpoint as if discovery is imminent, because for a useful endpoint it is.

Note

Manager's Math, The Overnight Step Change: ShopFlow's MCP endpoint served 12,000 calls/day comfortably on a small footprint. When a popular agent framework added a similar endpoint to its defaults, comparable services saw traffic step to 120,000 calls/day within 48 hours. For ShopFlow, the autoscaling ceiling from *Chapter 14* would absorb the capacity for an estimated extra $300/mo, a non-event. The governance gap would not be a non-event: 120,000 ungoverned, unattributable tool calls per day is an exposure no budget covers. The capacity was cheap insurance. The missing governance was the real risk.

Note

Safe Scale Check, The AI Endpoint Rollout: Reversibility: a per-consumer rate limit and a tool-scoping policy at the MCP gateway are configuration, fully reversible, and should be in place before the endpoint is published, not added after a spike. Blast radius: scope every new tool to a named set of agent identities first, then widen, so a discovery event cannot hand an unproven tool to every agent at once. Publish the governance with the endpoint, never behind it.

Architect's prompt 15.3: the AI endpoint readiness audit

When to use this: Use this prompt before publishing a model or MCP endpoint that agents can discover and call, to size and govern it for an overnight step change rather than a forecastable ramp.

```
Act as a Principal Engineer operating AI-facing endpoints at scale. I am
about to publish a model or MCP endpoint that agents can discover.

Endpoint: [description]. Tools exposed: [list]. Current traffic: [calls/day].
Current governance: [scoping, rate limits, identity, logging, or none].
Autoscaling ceiling: [set / not set].

Do the following:
(1) Model an overnight 10x step change in traffic, not a gradual ramp.
(2) Identify what breaks first: tool exposure, attribution, rate fairness,
    capacity, or cost. Rank them.
```

```
(3) Specify the gateway governance to publish WITH the endpoint: per-agent
    tool scoping, per-consumer rate limits, verified identity, full logging.
(4) Confirm the autoscaling ceiling and per-consumer budget from the cost
    governance are in place.
(5) Give the publish or hold recommendation and the controls required first.
```

Governing the agent: determinism in a Non-deterministic world

Once you have decided a workflow needs an agent, the work shifts from whether to how: how to let a nondeterministic system take real actions without inheriting the full risk of its nondeterminism. The answer is runtime governance, and the word runtime is the entire point. Governance that lives in the prompt is a request. Governance that lives in the runtime is a rule. An agent can ignore, misread, or be talked out of an instruction in its prompt. It cannot talk its way past a deterministic policy engine that sits between its decision and the action, evaluates the action against fixed rules, and refuses the ones that violate policy.

> Note
>
> **The Runtime-Enforcement Rule:** Agent governance must be enforced at runtime, between the decision and the action, not requested in the prompt. A prompt instruction is a suggestion the model can ignore, misread, or be manipulated past. A runtime policy engine is a deterministic gate the action cannot bypass. If a control can be defeated by a cleverly worded input, it was never a control. It was a hope.

This is the line that separates real governance tools from the large category of products that filter prompts and scan outputs. Filtering the input checks the prompt before the model sees it. Scanning the output checks the response after the model produces it. Neither touches the moment that matters, which is the action the agent takes in between: the refund it issues, the shipment it reroutes, the tool it calls, the record it deletes. Runtime enforcement governs that moment directly, by gating the action itself against a deterministic policy.

Approach	Where It Acts	What It Misses
Prompt filtering	Before the model reads the input	The action the agent takes after reasoning
Output scanning	After the model produces text	Actions and tool calls, which are not text

Approach	Where It Acts	What It Misses
Runtime enforcement	Between the decision and the action	Nothing in the action path; this is the control

Table 15.8: Prompt filtering, output scanning and runtime enforcement compared by where each one acts

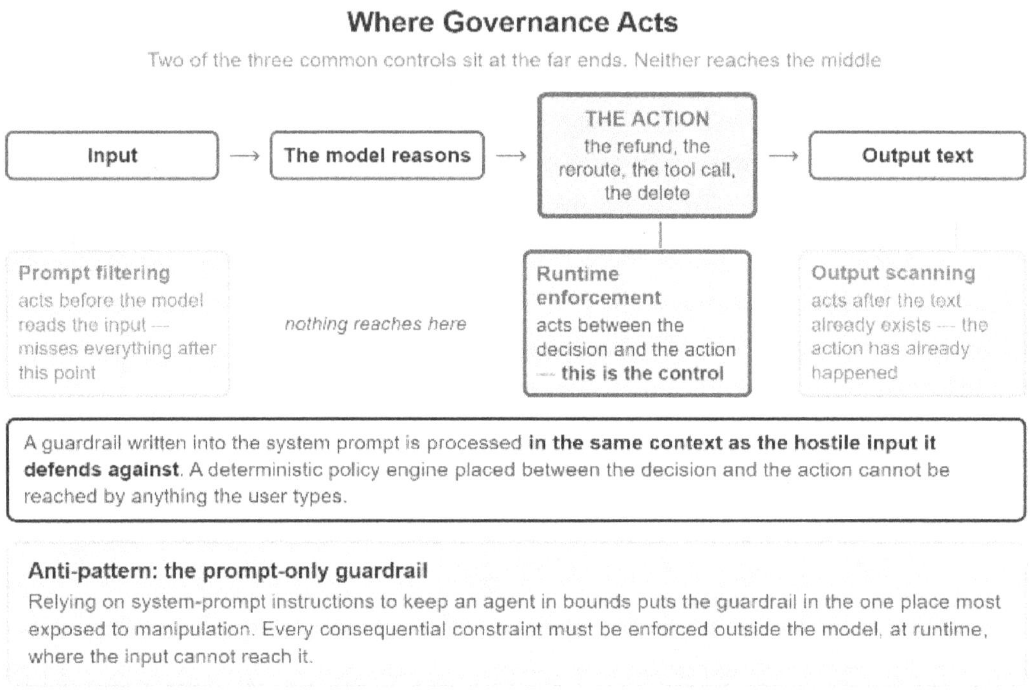

Figure 15.4: Where Governance Acts

Note

Anti-Pattern: The Prompt-Only Guardrail: Relying on instructions in the system prompt to keep an agent in bounds. The prompt is the one part of the system most exposed to manipulation, because hostile inputs are processed in the same context. A guardrail that lives in the prompt can be hijacked by the very inputs it is meant to defend against. Every consequential constraint must be enforced outside the model, at runtime, where the input cannot reach it.

The discipline that makes runtime enforcement tractable is least agency, the agent-era version of least privilege. An agent is granted the narrowest possible set of tools, actions, and data access required for its task, and nothing more. The reroute agent that triggered Dave's alert had the standing permission to move any shipment, which is far more agency than its job required. Under least agency it would be scoped to propose reroutes within a bounded set, with anything beyond that gated. Most of the OWASP Agentic risks are, at root, agency the agent never needed and was never scoped out of.

Note

The Least-Agency Mandate: Grant an agent the minimum tools, actions, and data access its task requires, and gate everything else. Least agency is least privilege for autonomous systems, and it is non-negotiable. An agent with more agency than its task demands is an incident waiting for the input that exercises the excess. The default permission set for any agent is the empty set, expanded only by explicit, scoped grant.

Concretely, governance maps to the OWASP Agentic Top 10, the industry's catalog of how agent systems fail. You do not need to memorize the list, but you do need a control for each class, and the controls are deterministic. Runtime enforcement carries a governance tax of well under a millisecond per action, which costs less per action than a single ungoverned incident. The table below maps the risk classes to the runtime controls that address them, and the pattern is consistent: identity, scoping, and enforcement at the action boundary, recorded in an audit trail.

OWASP Agentic Risk	The Failure	The Runtime Control
ASI01 Agent Goal Hijack	Adversarial input overrides the agent's intended objective	Gate actions against a fixed policy, not against the prompt
ASI02 Tool Misuse and Exploitation	Approved tools invoked in unintended or dangerous ways	Scope tools per task; mediate every call and gate toolchains
ASI03 Identity and Privilege Abuse	The agent acquires privileges beyond its role	Scoped, short-lived agent identities; least agency by default

OWASP Agentic Risk	The Failure	The Runtime Control
ASI04 Agentic Supply Chain Vulnerabilities	A compromised plugin or sub-agent injects behavior you never wrote	Pin permitted tool and sub-agent identities in policy; verify provenance before a tool enters the catalog
ASI05 Unexpected Code Execution	An agent-driven path reaches arbitrary code execution	Never evaluate model output as code; sandbox anything generated; deny unsafe deserialization
ASI06 Memory and Context Poisoning	A persistent memory store is manipulated to corrupt later decisions	Validate and isolate memory; audit every context write against a tamper-evident log
ASI07 Insecure Inter-Agent Communication	Messages between agents carry no authentication or integrity guarantees	Verify agent identity on every handoff; sign and integrity-check inter-agent messages
ASI08 Cascading Agent Failures	One agent's failure propagates through the system	Circuit breakers and blast-radius caps between agents; rate-limit tool invocation
ASI09 Human-Agent Trust Exploitation	Humans over-trust the agent's output and stop validating it	Tamper-evident audit trail plus an approval gate that shows what was already checked—and instrument the gate itself
ASI10 Rogue Agents	Behavior drifts off task with no attacker involved	Behavioral baselines, anomaly detection, and a scoped kill switch

Table 15.9: OWASP Agentic risk classes mapped to the deterministic runtime control that addresses each

Four of those classes need control families the rest of this chapter does not reach, and they are the ones most often left uncovered. Supply chain (ASI04) and unexpected code execution (ASI05) are not about the agent's reasoning at all; they are about what you let into the tool catalog and whether any path turns model output into executable code. Insecure inter-agent communication (ASI07) only appears once you have more than one agent, which is exactly when teams stop treating handoffs as a trust boundary. And human-agent trust exploitation (ASI09) is the one the previous section already anticipated: an approval queue whose reviewers have stopped reading is not a control, which is why the gate itself has to be instrumented. A governance layer that covers six of the ten and calls itself complete has covered the six that were easiest to see.

> Note
>
> **The Policy-as-Code Mandate:** Agent permissions are expressed as code, versioned, reviewed, and tested like any other code—never as prose in a prompt or a setting in a console. Policy-as-code makes the deterministic boundary auditable and reproducible: you can prove what an agent was allowed to do at the moment it acted. A permission you cannot point to in version control is a permission you cannot defend to an auditor.

Who owns the policy

Policy-as-code raises the question the phrase implies but does not answer: if the permission boundary is code, whose code is it, and how does it change? The failure mode is specific and common. The governance layer ships, the policies are written once by whoever built it, and thereafter they are edited in a runtime console by whoever needs an agent unblocked at four in the afternoon. Within two quarters the deployed policy no longer resembles anything in version control, and the audit trail can prove what the agent did without being able to prove what it was permitted to do.

Treat a policy change exactly as you treat an application change, because it is one. It lives in version control, in the same repository as the service it governs, so a reviewer can see the permission and the code that uses it in one diff. It goes through peer review, and the reviewer is someone other than the engineer who wants the permission. It carries tests — a policy suite asserting what is permitted and, more importantly, what is denied, run in CI on every change, because a policy with only positive tests will silently widen. It deploys through the same pipeline with the same rollback. And it has a named operational owner who carries the pager for it.

The ownership question also has a time dimension, and getting it wrong in either direction is costly. On day one, governance is owned by whoever built it, usually a platform or security team. That does not scale and it should not: a central team that owns every policy becomes the bottleneck every feature team learns to route around, and a governance layer people route around is worse than none, because it produces the appearance of control. The durable model is the one this book has used for every other cross-cutting concern. The platform team owns the mechanism — the policy engine, the CI checks, the audit pipeline, and a default-deny baseline no service can lower. Each service team owns the policies for its own agents above that floor. Central sets the floor; feature teams build on it; neither can lower it.

Concern	Platform Team Owns	Service Team Owns
Policy engine and enforcement point	The mechanism, its availability, and its latency budget	Correct integration; no call path that bypasses it
Default-deny baseline	The floor: what no agent may ever do unconditionally	Nothing — the floor is not negotiable locally
Per-agent permissions	Review of the policy schema and the deny-case test harness	The actual grants for its own agents, and the justification for each
Audit trail	The pipeline, retention, and immutability guarantees	That its agents' actions carry the identity and context the trail needs
Operational ownership	The pager for the governance layer itself	The pager for its own agents' behavior and policy violations

Table 15.10: Splitting governance ownership between the platform team and the service teams

Note

The Policy-Change Review Rule: A change to an agent's permissions travels the same path as a change to application code — version control, peer review by someone other than the requester, automated tests asserting both what is permitted and what is denied, the same deployment pipeline, and a named operational owner. A permission edited in a runtime console has no review, no test, and no history, and it is the one you will not be able to explain to an auditor. The platform team owns the mechanism and the default-deny floor; each service team owns its own agents' policies above it, and no team can lower the floor.

Note

Safe Scale Check, Expanding Agent Agency: Reversibility: every agency grant is a revocable policy entry, so widening what an agent may do is fully reversible by removing the grant. Blast radius: expand an agent's permitted actions one scoped grant at a time, each gated by a replay test against recorded behavior, so no single change hands the agent a capability it has not been proven safe to hold. Agency grows by increments you can withdraw, never by a broad default.

Note

Manager's Math, The Ungoverned Action: Before governance, the reroute agent moved every west-coast shipment through one hub overnight, inside its permissions, and with no record of why. The operational cost to detect, diagnose, and reverse the reroute ran into several engineer-days plus the delivery delays it caused. A least-agency policy scoping the agent to bounded reroutes, plus an audit trail, would have prevented the action outright and is roughly two days of work to implement once. The governance was cheaper than the single incident it would have stopped, and it stops every future one.

Architect's prompt 15.4: the agent governance design

When to use this: Use this prompt to design the runtime governance for an agent that will take consequential actions, mapping its risks to deterministic controls before it ships.

```
Act as a Principal Engineer specializing in runtime agent governance.
Help me govern an agent that takes consequential actions in production.

Agent task: [description]. Tools and actions available: [list].
Consequential actions (refunds, reroutes, deletes, etc.): [list].
Current permission model: [describe, or none].

Do the following:
(1) Apply least agency: define the minimum tools, actions, and data the task
    requires, and mark everything else as gated.
(2) Express the permission boundary as policy-as-code, versioned and testable.
(3) Map the agent to the OWASP Agentic Top 10 and give a runtime control for
```

```
    each relevant risk, enforced between decision and action.
(4) Define the audit trail that makes every action attributable and
    explainable after the fact.
(5) Confirm no consequential constraint relies on the prompt. Move any that
    does into runtime enforcement.
```

The safety valve: kill switches and Human-in-the-Loop guardrails

Every control in the previous section is preventive. It stops an agent from taking an action it was never permitted to take. But governance has to account for the case the preventive controls did not anticipate: the agent that drifts off-task, behaves in a way no policy predicted, or operates correctly under its rules while still producing an outcome the business cannot accept. For that case you need a different kind of control. You need a way to stop the agent, immediately, and completely, and that is the single most important capability a production AI system can have.

> Note
>
> **The Kill-Switch Mandate:** Every agent that can take real actions must have a kill switch: a single, unbypassable mechanism to halt that agent immediately, in isolation, without taking down the surrounding system. If a system goes off-task, you must be able to stop it now, not after a deploy. An agent you cannot turn off is an agent you do not control, and an agent you do not control does not belong in production. This is non-negotiable.

Dave's alert is the absence of this control stated plainly. The reroute agent did something its permissions allowed, the business could not accept the result, and there was no way to turn off that one agent without taking down the entire logistics service. That is not an edge case; it is the predictable consequence of shipping agency without an off switch. The kill switch has to be scoped to the agent, so that stopping a misbehaving agent does not require stopping everything around it, and it has to be reachable in seconds by a human who does not need to push a deploy to use it.

> Note
>
> **Safe Scale Check, The Kill Switch:** Reversibility: the kill switch is itself the reversibility primitive for autonomous systems, the one-action undo for an agent that has gone off-task. It must be tested like a fire drill, on a schedule, so you know it works before you need it. Blast radius: scope the switch to a single agent so halting one does

> not halt the fleet, and verify the surrounding system degrades gracefully when one agent stops. A kill switch you have never tested is a hope, not a control.

After the kill switch

Halting an agent is the start of an incident, not the end of one. The switch buys time; it diagnoses nothing, and an agent switched back on without the work in between will do the same thing again. The sequence after a halt is fixed, and it is worth running as a checklist precisely because the pressure to restore the feature peaks at the moment the diagnosis matters most.

Capture the context before it decays. The agent's recent sessions, the inputs it received, the tool calls it made, the policy decisions that permitted them, and the state of every external system it touched. Some of this is ephemeral and some of it is in systems that will keep moving while you investigate, so capture is the first action after the halt, not the last.

Preserve the audit trail as evidence. Snapshot it rather than leaving it in a rotating log. Where the incident has a regulatory or customer-facing dimension, the audit trail is the artifact that answers what the agent was allowed to do and why the action passed policy, and it must be immutable from the moment of the halt onward.

Find the root cause, and be honest about which of three it is, because the fix is different for each. The agent did something outside policy, which is a governance defect and means the enforcement point failed or was bypassed. The agent did something inside policy that the business cannot accept, which is a policy defect — the agency was broader than the task needed. Or the agent behaved correctly on bad input from upstream, which is neither, and the fix belongs to the system that produced the input. The second case is by far the most common, and it is the one Dave's reroute agent illustrates: nothing malfunctioned, and the outcome was still unacceptable.

Change something, then revalidate in shadow mode. Whatever the fix — a narrowed policy, a new gate, a corrected tool, a bounded input — the agent returns to rung two of the autonomy ladder and runs against live traffic with its decisions logged and unexecuted, until it demonstrates that the failure no longer occurs on the traffic that produced it. Re-enabling straight to the rung the agent was on is the decision that produces the second incident.

Re-enable at a lower rung and let it climb back. The agent returns with less autonomy than it had and earns the rest back on the same evidence the ladder always required. This is also the point at which to ask whether the incident was specific to this agent or generic to the policy baseline, because a policy defect found on one agent is usually present on several.

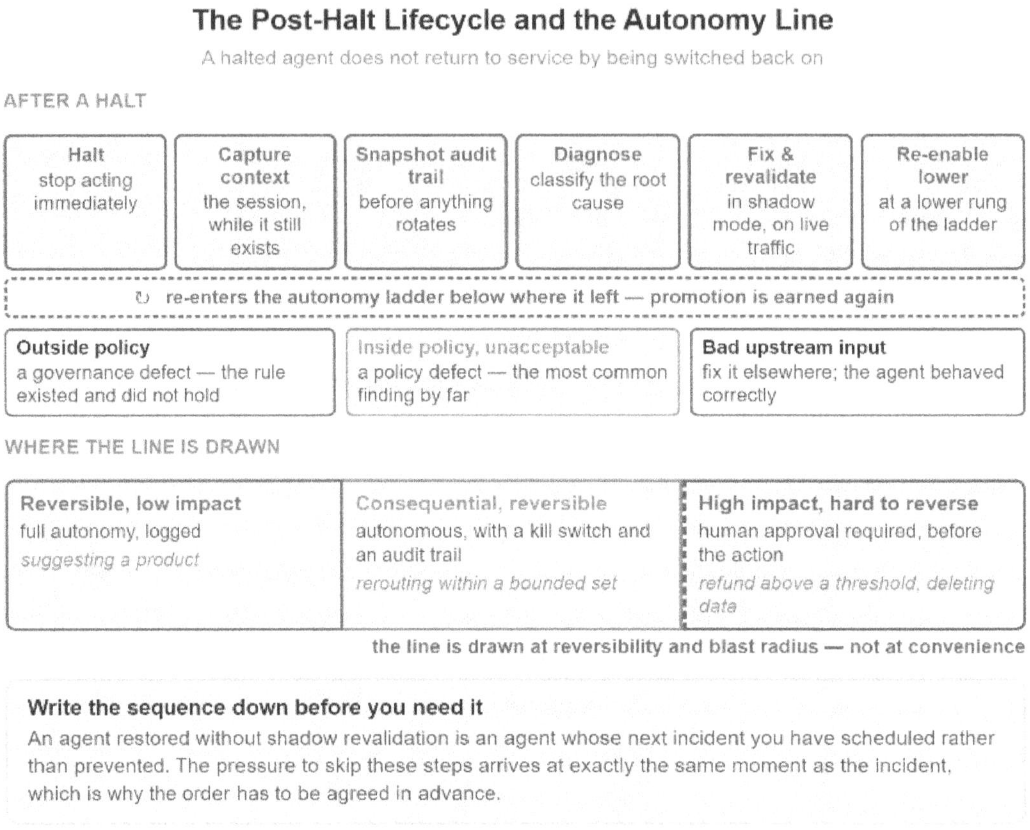

Figure 15.5: The Post-Halt Lifecycle and the Line Between Autonomy and Approval

Note

The Post-Halt Lifecycle Rule: A halted agent does not return to service by being switched back on. Capture the session context and snapshot the audit trail immediately, classify the root cause as a governance defect, a policy defect, or bad upstream input, apply the fix, revalidate in shadow mode against live traffic, and re-enable at a lower rung of the autonomy ladder. An agent restored without shadow revalidation is an agent whose next incident you have scheduled rather than prevented. Write this sequence down before you need it, because the pressure to skip it arrives with the incident.

Below the absolute stop sits a graduated control: the human-in-the-loop gate. Not every high-impact action should execute autonomously, and the ones that should not are gated on human approval. The agent prepares the action, the governance layer confirms it is within policy, and a human approves before it runs on anything consequential. This is the deliberate trade the chapter has been building toward. You accept a throughput cost, the latency of human review, in exchange for a hard ceiling on the autonomy of the highest-impact actions. The art is drawing the line: full autonomy for reversible, low-impact actions, human approval for the consequential and hard-to-reverse ones.

Note

The Human-in-the-Loop Rule: High-impact, hard-to-reverse actions are gated on human approval; reversible, low-impact actions run autonomously. The agent prepares and the governance layer validates, but a human authorizes anything consequential before it executes. The throughput cost of review is the price of bounding the autonomy of the actions you most need to get right. Draw the line at reversibility and blast radius, not at convenience.

Note

Tool Tax — the approval queue: A human gate is a queue, and queues have staffing, latency, and psychology. Somebody must be available when the action needs approving, including at three in the morning if the action can occur then, which is a rota you are now funding. Reviewers presented with a high volume of near-identical approvals stop reading them, so the gate decays into a click and the control becomes theater while still costing throughput. Instrument the gate itself: approval rate, time-to-decision, and override rate. An approval rate of essentially 100% with a very short time-to-decision is not a well-behaved agent; it is an unread queue.

Action Profile	Control	Example
Reversible, low-impact	Full autonomy, logged	Suggesting a product, drafting a reply
Consequential, reversible	Autonomous with a kill switch and audit	Rerouting within a bounded set

Action Profile	Control	Example
High-impact, hard to reverse	Human-in-the-loop approval required	Issuing a refund above a threshold, deleting data

Table 15.11: Action profiles classified by reversibility and impact, with the control each one requires

> Note
>
> **Anti-Pattern: The Unkillable Agent:** An agent whose only off switch is taking down the service it runs inside. When it misbehaves, the operator faces a forced choice between an outage and letting the agent continue, and under pressure neither option is taken cleanly. Every agent must be independently haltable. An agent fused to its host so tightly that it cannot be stopped alone is a liability the size of everything it can touch.

There is one more thing to say about governing AI, and it has changed since I started this work. I used to spend real effort convincing teams that governance was worth the friction. The team building the AI feature would push back hardest precisely on being governed, because governance felt like a tax on their velocity. That argument is largely over, and not because I won it. It is over because the external environment settled it. Regulation has arrived, models and providers are being restricted by governments, and enterprise and public-sector buyers now require provable governance as a condition of deployment. Governance is no longer a control you have to sell internally. It is a requirement the outside world now imposes.

> Note
>
> **The Governance-Is-Mandated Doctrine:** Agent governance is no longer an internal sell against velocity; it is an external requirement imposed by regulation, provider restrictions, and enterprise and public-sector procurement. The team that resists being governed is no longer arguing with a colleague; it is arguing with the conditions of doing business. Build governance in from the start, because the market and the regulators now require the proof, and retrofitting it after a deployment commitment is the expensive path.

External Driver	What It Now Requires	Consequence of Lacking It
Regulation	Provable, auditable governance of agent actions	Non-compliance and reportable incidents
Provider and model restrictions	Controls over which models and tools agents use	Sudden loss of access to a restricted model
Enterprise procurement	Documented governance as a condition of sale	The deal does not close
Public-sector and regulated buyers	Evidence that policy was applied per action	Disqualification before evaluation begins

Table 15.12: The external drivers that now require provable agent governance, and the cost of lacking it

The kill switch carries a tax, and it is worth naming plainly. The human-in-the-loop gate costs throughput; every gated action waits for a person. The kill switch and the runtime policy engine cost a small amount of latency on every governed action, measured in well under a millisecond in a well-built layer. Both are real costs, and both are trivial against the alternative, which is an autonomous system you cannot stop taking an action you cannot undo. On any agent that can act in the world, this governance is not optional. It is the price of being allowed to ship the agent at all.

Architect's prompt 15.5: the kill switch and approval design

When to use this: Use this prompt to design the kill switch and human-in-the-loop gates for an agent before it is allowed to take any consequential action in production.

```
Act as a Principal Engineer designing the safety controls for a production
agent. I need a kill switch and the right human-in-the-loop gates.

Agent: [description]. Actions it can take: [list, with reversibility and
impact for each]. Service it runs inside: [name].

Do the following:
(1) Design a kill switch scoped to THIS agent that halts it in seconds,
    without taking down the surrounding service, reachable without a deploy.
(2) Define how the surrounding system degrades gracefully when the agent is
    halted, and a schedule to test the kill switch like a fire drill.
(3) Classify each action as full autonomy, autonomous with kill switch, or
```

```
    human-in-the-loop, using reversibility and blast radius as the line.
(4) Specify the approval gate for high-impact actions: what the human sees,
    what the governance layer has already validated, and the audit record.
(5) State the throughput and latency cost of these controls and confirm it is
    acceptable against the cost of an unstoppable action.
```

The AI production readiness checklist

Before an AI feature is promoted into production, every item below should read yes — or carry a named owner and a time-boxed exception. Each is a rule from this chapter expressed as something a reviewer can verify in the room.

Deterministic alternative evaluated first: the workflow was tested against the five gates, and the specific capability the model provides that code cannot has been named out loud. (The Determinism-First Rule, The Real-Need Test, The Gate-Order Rule)

Traditional ML considered before an LLM: structured prediction over labeled history was explicitly ruled in or out, rather than skipped. (*Table 15.3*)

The model's slice is as narrow as the problem allows: authentication, authorization, validation, routing, and action execution all remain in deterministic code. (The Narrow-Model Rule)

Runtime governance implemented: every consequential action is gated between the decision and its execution, not requested in the prompt. (The Runtime-Enforcement Rule)

Policy-as-code reviewed and versioned: permissions live in version control with peer review, deny-case tests in CI, the standard deployment pipeline, and a named operational owner. (The Policy-as-Code Mandate, The Policy-Change Review Rule)

Least agency enforced: the agent holds the minimum tools, actions, and data its task requires, and the default permission set is empty. (The Least-Agency Mandate)

OWASP Agentic risks mapped to runtime controls: every applicable risk class has a named deterministic control at the action boundary. (*Table 15.6*)

Autonomy earned, not granted: the agent has run in shadow mode against production traffic and climbed the ladder on evidence, and demotion is a defined operational action. (The Earned-Autonomy Rule)

Kill switch tested on a schedule: scoped to this one agent, reachable in seconds without a deploy, with the surrounding system verified to degrade gracefully. (The Kill-Switch Mandate)

Human approval required for high-impact actions: the line is drawn at reversibility and blast radius, and it does not move for convenience. (The Human-in-the-Loop Rule)

Post-halt lifecycle documented: the team knows what to capture, how to classify the root cause, and that re-enabling runs through shadow mode at a lower rung. (The Post-Halt Lifecycle Rule)

Agent behavior is observable and auditable: per-action logging, a policy-compliance signal, and anomaly detection on behavior rather than only on latency.

An item that reads no is a dated commitment. An item that reads no on the kill switch or on runtime enforcement is not a commitment at all — it is a reason the feature does not ship yet.

Summary

In this chapter, we replaced the reflex to add AI everywhere with the discipline to add it deliberately. We applied the Determinism-First Rule and the Bounded-Input Rule to keep deterministic problems in deterministic code, and reserved models for the genuine real need: unbounded language, unspecifiable output, and analysis over data you cannot enumerate. ShopFlow's form validator, a deterministic problem running on a model, went back to a rule that is cheaper, faster, and correct every time.

We demystified agents through the Production-Readiness Gap and the Determinism-in-Nondeterminism Doctrine: an agent is a probabilistic reasoning engine that becomes production-ready only when wrapped in a deterministic governance boundary. That is the thesis behind the Agent Governance Toolkit, and it generalizes to any agent you deploy. We established that serving AI at scale is governed by the same disciplines as the rest of this book, and that AI traffic arrives as an overnight step change, not a forecastable ramp, so governance must ship with the endpoint, not behind it.

We made governance concrete with the Runtime-Enforcement Rule, the Least-Agency Mandate, and Policy-as-Code, mapping the agent's exposure to the OWASP Agentic Top 10 and gating every consequential action against a deterministic policy rather than a prompt. And we built the safety valve: the Kill-Switch Mandate that gives every acting agent an immediate, isolated off switch, and the Human-in-the-Loop Rule that gates the high-impact, hard-to-reverse actions on human approval. Governance, we noted, is no longer an internal sell. The outside world now requires it.

ShopFlow's telemetry after *Chapter 15*:

Metric	Before (Ch15 Start)	After (Ch15 End)	Change
AI Features That Are Deterministic Problems	~40% (running on models)	0% (moved back to deterministic code)	Cheaper, faster, correct

Metric	Before (Ch15 Start)	After (Ch15 End)	Change
Agents Able to Act With No Kill Switch	3	0 (every acting agent is haltable)	Now controllable
OWASP Agentic Risk Coverage	0 of 10	10 of 10 (runtime controls mapped)	Governed at runtime
Human-in-the-Loop on High-Impact Actions	None	Required (refunds, deletes, large reroutes)	Bounded autonomy
MCP Endpoint Governance	None	Per-agent scoping, identity, rate limits	Ready for discovery
Agent Permission Model	Standing broad permissions	Least agency, policy-as-code	Auditable and scoped

Table 15.13: ShopFlow's AI posture before and after Chapter 15

The cliffhanger: the system nobody wants to touch

ShopFlow is now AI-first in the way this chapter meant it. The deterministic problems are in deterministic code. The agents that act are scoped by least agency, governed at runtime against the full OWASP Agentic Top 10, and every one of them has a kill switch. The high-impact actions wait for a human. The system is, finally, both intelligent and safe.

And that is when the velocity quietly stops. Over the previous fifteen chapters, ShopFlow grew from a monolith handling 100 orders a day into a globally distributed, governed, AI-augmented system that almost no single person fully understands end to end. The system works, and the better it works, the more the team is afraid to change it. Deployment frequency, which was once daily, has slipped toward monthly. The change failure rate, when the team does ship, is high enough that every release is approached with caution rather than confidence.

Dave names it in the end-of-sprint review. The system is no longer breaking. It is something subtler and, over time, more dangerous: it has stopped evolving. The team has started playing it safe with a system too valuable to risk, and a system that stops changing in a moving market is a system that has begun, slowly, to fall behind. Every safeguard built in this book made the system more robust, and somewhere along the way that robustness curdled into a fear of touching it at all.

In *Chapter 16*, the final chapter, we solve the last problem: how to keep evolving a system you are afraid to break. We make change itself safe, turning every deployment, model swap, and architectural shift into a controlled experiment with feature flags, canary releases, and automated rollback wired to the observability signals from earlier chapters. The drama of this book does not end with a system that survives. It ends with a system that can keep changing forever, shipping while the team sleeps, because change has been made boring on purpose. That is the future-proof system.

References

- OWASP GenAI Security Project — Agentic Security Initiative, the source of the Agentic AI risk taxonomy (ASI01–ASI10) mapped in *Table 15.6*: `https://genai.owasp.org/`
- OWASP Top 10 for Large Language Model Applications — the prompt-injection and output-handling risks that sit underneath the agentic ones: `https://genai.owasp.org/llm-top-10/`
- Model Context Protocol — specification for the tool-calling interface discussed in "Serving AI at Scale": `https://modelcontextprotocol.io/`
- NIST AI Risk Management Framework (AI RMF 1.0) — the govern, map, measure, and manage functions behind the governance posture argued for in this chapter: `https://www.nist.gov/itl/ai-risk-management-framework`
- Regulation (EU) 2024/1689, the EU Artificial Intelligence Act — one of the external requirements referenced in "The Governance-Is-Mandated Doctrine": `https://eur-lex.europa.eu/eli/reg/2024/1689/oj`
- Agent Governance Toolkit (AGT) — the open-source runtime governance framework referred to throughout this chapter: `https://github.com/microsoft/agent-governance-toolkit`

16

Continuous Experimentation and the Future-Proof System

In *Chapter 15*, ShopFlow became AI-first in the way this book means it. The deterministic problems went back into deterministic code, the acting agents were scoped by least agency and governed at runtime, and every one of them got a kill switch. The system is intelligent and it is safe. And then, quietly, it stopped moving.

This is the last problem in the book, and it is the most insidious because nothing is broken. Over fifteen chapters ShopFlow grew from a monolith handling 100 orders a day into a globally distributed, governed, AI-augmented system that no single person fully understands end to end. The better it works, the more the team is reluctant to change it. Deployment frequency, once daily, has slipped toward monthly. When the team does ship, the change failure rate is high enough that every release is approached with caution instead of confidence. The system is not failing. It has simply stopped evolving, and in a moving market a system that stops evolving has begun, slowly, to fall behind.

The cure is not courage. Telling an exhausted team to be braver about deploying a system that can take real actions and cost real money is not engineering. The cure is to make change itself safe, so that shipping a change is no longer a bet the team is afraid to place. When a change can be released to one percent of traffic, measured against the observability signals built earlier in this book, and rolled back automatically the moment it misbehaves, deploying stops being an act of courage and becomes an act of routine. Experimentation is how you turn change from a risk into a habit.

That is the subject of this final chapter, and it is the property that makes everything before it durable. A system that cannot change safely is a system that was architected for a single moment in time, and no moment lasts. We will make experimentation a requirement of the architecture rather than an activity bolted on at the end. We will use feature flags with the discipline they demand and retire them before they become debt. We will run experiments on the architecture itself, including one that reversed a decision I was certain of. We will close the feedback loop from production back into the next version. And we will end where the book has been heading all along: the one property that is future-proof, and the single piece of advice that no rule in this book can capture.

In this chapter, we are going to cover the following main topics:

- Experimentation as an Architectural Requirement
- Feature Flags Done Right, and the Flag Graveyard
- Experimenting on the Architecture Itself
- The Feedback Loop: Production as the Source of the Next Version
- The Future-Proof System

Technical requirements

A feature-flag platform with lifecycle controls: Flags carry an owner and a mandatory expiry date, and the platform reports flags past their removal date as debt to be retired.

A progressive-delivery/canary controller: Automated rollout in stages (1%, 25%, 100%) with rollback wired to the observability signals, so a bad change reverts without a human in the path.

An experimentation and A/B framework: Statistically valid comparison of two variants in production, applied to features and to architectural choices alike (models, stores, protocols).

The observability stack from Chapter 11: The signals (latency, errors, saturation, cost per unit) that every experiment is measured against and every rollback is triggered by.

A metrics baseline for delivery health (DORA-style): Deployment frequency, lead time, change failure rate, and time to restore, tracked as the system's evolutionary fitness, not vanity numbers.

Code Repository: `https://github.com/imran-siddique/Architecting-at-Scale/tree/main/ch16`

ShopFlow telemetry snapshot [stage 16]

```
The Signal: Nothing is broken, and that is the problem. The system is dependable,
governed, and AI-augmented, and the team has stopped changing it. That
dependability has hardened into a reluctance to touch a system too valuable to
risk.
Deployment Frequency: 1 per month (Down from 1 per day at peak)
Change Failure Rate: 22% (High enough that every release is approached with
caution)
Lead Time for Changes: 3+ weeks (A one-line fix waits for a release window)
Active Feature Flags: 180+ (Most past any useful life; no owner remembers why)
Time Since Last Architectural Change: 7 months (The architecture has frozen)
Experiments Running in Production: 0 (Change is treated as a threat, not a method)
Panic Meter: 2/10 (The wrong kind of calm. Stable, and standing still.)
```

Note

Dave Alert: "We have 180-some feature flags and I cannot tell you what half of them do or who owns them. Every change touches a path some old flag might still be gating, so nobody wants to be the one who ships. We are not afraid the system will break. We are afraid to find out what we forgot."

Experimentation is a capability an organization grows into, and the order is fixed by dependency rather than preference. Each stage supplies something the next one needs: you cannot canary what you cannot toggle, you cannot automate a rollback you cannot trigger on a signal, and you cannot experiment on the architecture until reversing a change has stopped being an event. ShopFlow has the first two and has stopped there, which is exactly why 180 flags accumulated and nothing gets canaried.

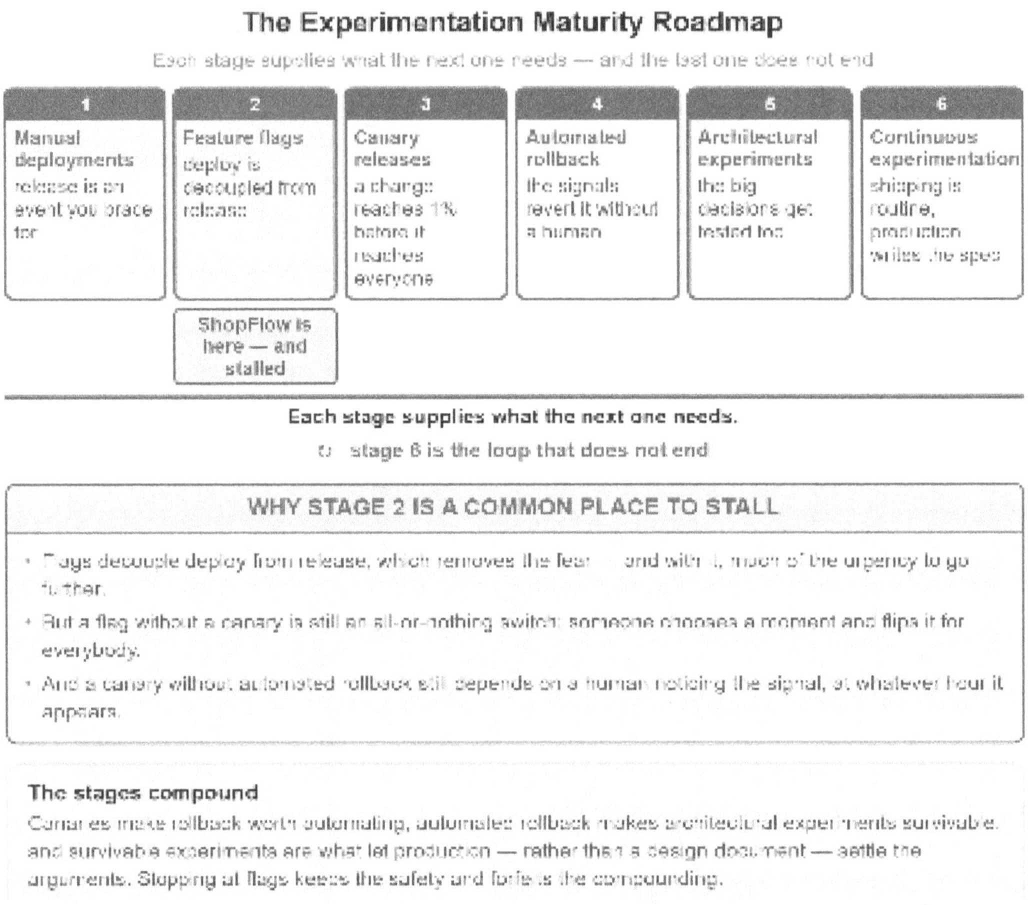

Figure 16.1: The Experimentation Maturity Roadmap

The same progression as text:

1. Manual deployments. Release is an event, scheduled and braced for. Every change carries the full blast radius of the release it rides in.
2. Feature flags. Deploy is decoupled from release, so code can ship dark and be turned on separately. This is where most teams stop, and it is where the flag graveyard forms.
3. Canary releases. A change reaches a small slice of traffic before it reaches everyone, which converts a release from a bet into a measurement.
4. Automated rollback. The observability signals from *Chapter 11* revert a bad change without a human in the path. This is the stage that removes the personal risk, and therefore the fear.

5. Architectural experiments. Once reversing a change is routine, the same machinery can test the expensive decisions: a data store, a model, a protocol, a scaling strategy.
6. Continuous experimentation. Shipping is ordinary, production writes the specification, and the loop runs continuously rather than as a project.

The stages compound, and the failure mode is stopping partway. A team with flags but no canary has bought itself the ability to hide unfinished work and none of the ability to measure it, which is a graveyard with extra steps. A team with canaries but no automated rollback still needs a human watching a dashboard at the moment of release, which means releases still get scheduled for when that human is available. ShopFlow sits at stage two, and every symptom in the telemetry snapshot follows from that.

> Note
>
> The Progression-Is-Ordered Rule: Grow experimentation capability in sequence, because each stage supplies what the next one requires — flags before canaries, canaries before automated rollback, automated rollback before architectural experiments. Skipping a stage does not accelerate the practice; it produces the appearance of the later capability without the mechanism underneath it. The most common place to stall is stage two, where flags accumulate because nothing downstream ever forces them to be resolved.

Experimentation as an architectural requirement

The teams that keep moving at scale do not have braver engineers. They have an architecture that makes change cheap to try and cheap to undo, and that property is not a process you adopt but a structural requirement you design for, the same way you design for latency or availability. Experimentation is the ability to release a change to a small slice of production, measure its real effect against your signals, and reverse it instantly if the effect is wrong. A system that cannot do that has not avoided risk. It has only moved the risk to the rare, large, frightening release.

> Note
>
> **The Experiment-or-Stagnate Rule:** A system that cannot change safely will stop changing, and a system that stops changing falls behind. Experimentation is not an optional practice layered on a finished architecture; it is the property that keeps the architecture alive. You either build the ability to try and undo changes cheaply, or you accept that fear will slowly freeze the system. There is no third state where a system stays both static and current.

The reason stagnation is dangerous is that it is invisible on every dashboard that measures the system at rest. Availability is high, latency is good, cost is governed, and nothing pages anyone. The damage shows up only in the metrics that measure the system's ability to evolve: how often it ships, how long a change takes to reach production, how often a change fails, and how fast it recovers. These delivery metrics are the system's evolutionary fitness, and ShopFlow's have quietly collapsed while every health metric stayed green.

Symptom of Stagnation	What It Looks Like	The Experimentation Cure
Falling deployment frequency	Daily becomes monthly	Make each change small and independently shippable
Rising change failure rate	Every release is a gamble	Release to 1% first; measure before widening
Growing lead time	A one-line fix waits weeks	Decouple deploy from release with flags
Fear of touching the system	Nobody wants to own a release	Automated rollback removes the personal risk

Table 16.1: The symptoms of stagnation, and the experimentation capability that cures each

Note

The Delivery-Fitness Rule: Treat deployment frequency, lead time, change failure rate, and time to restore as the system's evolutionary fitness, and review them with the same seriousness as availability. Health metrics describe the system at rest; delivery metrics describe its ability to change. A system that scores well at rest and badly on delivery is not healthy; it is stagnant, and stagnation stays invisible until you measure the right thing.

> **Note**
>
> **The Safe-Change Mandate:** Every change reaches production through a path that is staged, measured, and automatically reversible: released to a small slice first, evaluated against the observability signals, and rolled back without a human if it breaches its budget. Deploying must not require courage. When a release is a reversible experiment rather than an irreversible bet, shipping becomes routine, and routine shipping is the only thing that keeps a system current.

> **Note**
>
> Tool Tax — the progressive delivery controller: A canary controller is a component sitting in the release path of everything you ship, which makes its own availability a release-blocking dependency. The tax is threefold. It must be integrated with the observability stack tightly enough to make an automatic revert decision, which means somebody owns the mapping between signals and rollback thresholds and keeps it current as services change. Those thresholds need tuning: too tight and healthy releases roll themselves back until the team disables the automation; too loose, and it never fires. And every service needs a rollout configuration that someone maintains. Budget the threshold-tuning loop, not the installation.

Delivery Metric	**What It Measures**	**Healthy vs Stagnant**
Deployment frequency	How often changes reach production	Daily or better vs. monthly
Lead time for changes	Commit to production duration	Under a day vs. multiple weeks
Change failure rate	Share of releases that cause a problem	Single digits vs. over 20%
Time to restore	How fast a bad change is reversed	Minutes vs hours

Table 16.2: The four delivery metrics that measure a system's evolutionary fitness

This reframes the deployment from an event into an experiment, and the reframing is the whole point. An event is something you brace for. An experiment is something you run, observe, and learn from, with a known and cheap failure mode. Every chapter in this book introduced a change to ShopFlow that, at the time, was frightening: the first shard, the move to async, the first agent that could act. The reason those changes were survivable was the safe-change primitives introduced alongside them. This chapter makes that pattern explicit and permanent: change is always an experiment, and an experiment is always reversible.

> Note
>
> **Manager's Math, The Cost of Standing Still:** ShopFlow's deployment frequency fell from daily to monthly, and lead time grew to three weeks. The direct cost is not on the cloud bill; it is in the market. A competitor shipping weekly iterates roughly four times for every one ShopFlow release, which compounds into a feature and learning gap that no amount of infrastructure efficiency recovers. Restoring safe, frequent deployment is not a tooling expense but the difference between a system that keeps pace and one quietly overtaken while every health metric reads green.

There is a tax on experimentation, and it is honest to name it. Progressive delivery, flag infrastructure, and automated rollback are real systems that must be built and maintained, and they add operational surface. That tax is trivial against the alternative. An architecture without it does not save the cost; it pays the cost as stagnation, in the far larger currency of falling behind. You are not choosing whether to pay. You are choosing whether to pay in infrastructure or in irrelevance.

Architect's prompt 16.1: the stagnation audit

When to use this: Use this prompt when health metrics are green but the team has slowed or stopped shipping, to diagnose stagnation and prescribe the experimentation capability that cures it.

```
Act as a Principal Engineer diagnosing delivery stagnation. Our system is
healthy at rest but the team has stopped shipping confidently.

Delivery metrics: deployment frequency [x], lead time [x], change failure
rate [x], time to restore [x]. Health metrics: [all green / details].
Current safe-change capability: [flags, canary, rollback, or none].

Do the following:
(1) Confirm the diagnosis: stagnation hidden behind healthy at-rest metrics.
(2) Identify which safe-change primitive is missing: small independent
```

```
   changes, staged rollout, signal-based measurement, automated rollback.
(3) Prescribe the smallest capability that would let the team ship to 1% and
   reverse automatically, and the order to build it in.
(4) State the market cost of the current lead time versus a faster cadence.
(5) Define the delivery metrics to track as the system's evolutionary fitness.
```

Feature flags done right and the flag graveyard

Feature flags are the mechanism that makes safe change possible, and I will be direct about my relationship with them: I am not a fan of feature flags as most teams use them. The mechanism is sound. The discipline around it almost never is. A flag is a powerful tool for exactly one thing, running an experiment, and it becomes a liability the moment it is treated as anything more permanent than that. The difference between a feature flag and a configuration is the single most important distinction in this section, and conflating the two is how a codebase fills with debt.

> Note
>
> **The Flag-Is-Not-Config Rule:** A feature flag is a temporary instrument for running an experiment: ship it, measure it, then either make the behavior permanent and remove the flag, or remove the behavior. A configuration is a permanent, intentional choice about how something is used, often a personalization. They are different in lifetime and in purpose. Treating a flag as a long-lived configuration is the root cause of the flag graveyard, because a flag with no end is a flag that never gets removed.

Property	Feature Flag	Configuration
Purpose	Run an experiment; gate a new behavior	Express a permanent, intentional choice
Lifetime	Temporary; ends when the experiment resolves	Long-lived by design
End state	Removed: behavior made permanent or dropped	Stays; it is the setting
Owner's intent	"I am trying this out"	This is how it is meant to be used

Table 16.3: A feature flag compared with a configuration across purpose, lifetime, end state and intent

The discipline that prevents the graveyard is an expiry date. Every flag, when it is created, carries a date by which it will be resolved and removed. That is not a guideline; it is part of the flag's definition, enforced by the platform, so that a flag living past its date is reported as debt the way an idle resource is reported as cost. A flag without an end date is not an experiment; it is a permanent branch in your control flow that someone forgot to delete, and it will outlive the memory of why it exists.

> Note
>
> **The Flag-Expiry Rule:** Every feature flag is created with a mandatory expiry date by which it must be resolved and removed. When the date arrives, the experiment is over: make the behavior permanent and delete the flag, or remove the behavior. A flag past its expiry is reported as debt and retired. An experiment with no end date was never an experiment; it was a permanent fork introduced by accident.

Every flag has an owner, and ownership moves with the service

An expiry date says when a flag must be resolved. It does not say who resolves it, and a deadline with no name attached is a deadline that passes. Every flag carries a named engineering owner from the moment it is created, and that owner is accountable for the whole lifecycle rather than only the launch: rolling it out, watching the signals while it is live, deciding the outcome at expiry, and deleting the code path afterward. The last of those is the one that gets dropped, which is why graveyards form even in teams that do assign owners.

Lifecycle Stage	What the Owner Is Accountable For	How It Fails Without an Owner
Creation	Naming the experiment, the hypothesis, the expiry date, and the success signal	A flag exists with no stated purpose, so nobody can later decide whether it worked
Rollout	Widening the flag through its stages and holding at each one long enough to read the signal	The flag is set to 100% on the day it ships and the experiment never happens

Lifecycle Stage	What the Owner Is Accountable For	How It Fails Without an Owner
Monitoring	Watching the flag's own metrics while it is live, not just the service's	A degraded variant runs for weeks because nobody was looking at that slice
Resolution	Deciding at expiry: make the behavior permanent or remove it	The date passes silently and the flag becomes permanent by default
Cleanup	Deleting the flag, both branches of the conditional, and the platform entry	The flag is set to 100% and abandoned, leaving a dead branch that still gates the path

Table 16.4: The five stages of a feature flag's life and what its owner is accountable for at each

The harder problem is what happens when the owner leaves, changes team, or moves on to another product, because that is the normal case over the lifetime of a long-lived flag. Ownership must not be personal. It attaches to the service, so that when a service changes hands its flags travel with it, and the incoming team inherits them explicitly rather than discovering them during an incident. A flag whose owner is an individual becomes an orphan the day that individual moves. A flag whose owner is the team that owns the service has an owner for as long as the service does.

This makes flag review part of an existing ritual rather than a new one. The service's flags belong on the same weekly fundamentals review that *Chapter 14* put cost on: how many are live, which are past expiry, and who is resolving them this sprint. A flag past its date is debt with a name attached, which is the only kind that reliably gets paid.

> **Note**
>
> The Flag-Ownership Rule: Every flag carries a named owner accountable for its full lifecycle — rollout, monitoring, resolution at expiry, and deletion of the code path — and ownership attaches to the service, not the individual, so it transfers when the service does. An unowned flag is an unremovable flag, because the decision to delete it requires knowing why it exists and nobody is accountable for remembering. Review live flags in the same weekly fundamentals meeting that reviews cost and availability.

The second discipline is to keep the number of live flags small. Each active flag multiplies the number of distinct code paths the system can take, and those paths multiply combinatorially. Ten independent flags describe over a thousand possible configurations of the system, almost none of which were ever tested together. Each live flag is a standing tax on every future change to a path it touches. A handful of well-managed, time-boxed flags is a healthy experimentation practice. A hundred and eighty flags, most past any useful life, is the state Dave is describing: a system whose actual behavior nobody can fully enumerate, where every change risks colliding with a forgotten flag.

> **Note**
>
> **The Bounded-Flag-Count Rule:** Keep the number of simultaneously live flags small and controlled, because active flags multiply the system's possible code paths combinatorially. The cost of a flag is not the line that checks it; it is the testing and reasoning burden of every path it adds. A small number of time-boxed flags is an experimentation practice. A large, unbounded population of flags is an untested combinatorial space the team can no longer reason about.

Figure 16.2: The Flag Lifecycle, and the Branch That Creates the Graveyard

Note

Tool Tax — the feature-flag platform: The platform is cheap and the flag evaluation is a network hop you now take on paths that previously took none, so it needs local caching and a defined behavior when the flag service is unreachable — decide whether an unreachable flag reads as on or off before you find out during an incident. The larger tax is the one this section is about: every live flag doubles the number of code paths that theoretically exist and roughly none of the combinations are tested together. The platform makes flags free to create, which is precisely why the expiry and ownership discipline has to be enforced by the platform rather than requested of the team.

> Note
>
> **Anti-Pattern: The Flag Graveyard:** An accumulation of feature flags that have outlived their experiments and were never removed. Each one is a permanent, untested branch in the control flow, owned by no one, gating paths nobody remembers. The graveyard's cost is paid on every future change, because each change must account for code paths the team can no longer fully enumerate. This is the state that turns a healthy system into one nobody is willing to touch.

> Note
>
> **Manager's Math, The Cost of the Graveyard:** ShopFlow carries 180-plus flags, most expired. The direct line-of-code cost is negligible. The real cost is the reasoning tax on every change: a developer touching any path must consider which forgotten flags might still gate it, which inflates the lead time on a one-line fix to three weeks and drives the 22% change failure rate. Retiring the graveyard down to the dozen still-active flags is a one-sprint cleanup that directly attacks both numbers. The flags were free to add and expensive to keep.

> Note
>
> **Safe Scale Check, Retiring a Flag:** Reversibility: removing a flag whose behavior you are making permanent is low-risk if you first confirm the flag has been at 100% in production long enough to trust the path. Blast radius: retire flags one at a time, verifying each removed branch is dead before deleting it, rather than mass-deleting and discovering a still-live dependency. The safe way out of a graveyard is the same as the safe way into any change: one reversible step at a time.

Architect's prompt 16.2: the flag lifecycle audit

When to use this: Use this prompt to audit an accumulated population of feature flags, separate genuine experiments from forgotten branches, and produce a retirement plan.

```
Act as a Principal Engineer enforcing feature-flag hygiene. We have
accumulated many flags and lost track of which are still meaningful.
```

```
Flag inventory: [list with creation date, owner, current rollout %, purpose].

Do the following:
(1) Classify each flag: active experiment, should-be-config (make permanent),
    or graveyard (expired, remove).
(2) For each graveyard flag, give the safe retirement step: confirm the path
    is dead or fully rolled out, then delete, one at a time.
(3) Flag any item that is really a configuration and recommend converting it
    out of the flag system entirely.
(4) Assign a mandatory expiry date to every flag that survives as an
    experiment.
(5) Recommend a maximum live-flag count and the policy that enforces it.
```

Experimenting with the architecture itself

Experimentation is usually framed as something you do to features: two button colors, two checkout flows, measured against conversion. The more valuable and less common practice is to run experiments on the architecture itself, because the largest and most expensive decisions in a system are architectural, and they are exactly the decisions teams make on conviction rather than evidence. The most instructive experiment of my career reversed a decision I was certain was correct, and it taught me to distrust architectural intuition that has not been tested in production.

Earlier in my career, leading infrastructure for a high-traffic enterprise platform, the team was working on a scaling strategy and the assumption everyone held, including me, was that the path forward was to scale up: take the cluster, find the optimal configuration, tune it, and provision larger, more powerful units to absorb more load. We ran experiments across cluster configurations to find that optimal scaled-up shape. The experiments did not cooperate. The performance numbers came back inconsistent and hard to predict, varying with configuration in ways that resisted a clean model. We could make a bigger unit faster, but we could not reliably say by how much, and a scaling strategy you cannot predict is a scaling strategy you cannot plan capacity against.

The data overturned the premise. Instead of scaling up into larger, individually tuned, unpredictable units, the answer was to scale out by replicating a single, known, predictable unit. We defined a standard unit with a characterized performance profile, and when we hit a limit we did not tune a bigger machine. We added another identical unit whose behavior we already knew exactly. The strategy that emerged was not the one we set out to validate. It was its opposite, and it was better precisely because it traded peak performance for predictability. A system you can reason about beats a system that is occasionally faster and never knowable.

Note

The Predictable-Unit Rule: Scale by replicating a single, characterized unit whose performance you know, not by tuning ever-larger individual units whose behavior you must rediscover each time. An identical unit added to a fleet contributes known capacity; a bigger, individually tuned unit contributes capacity you have to re-measure. Predictability compounds across a fleet of identical units; unpredictability compounds the same way. Choose the unit you can reason about, even when a tuned one is occasionally faster.

Note

Tool Tax — the experimentation and A/B framework: Statistically valid comparison is harder than the framework's quickstart suggests. You need enough traffic on the slice to reach significance, which for a low-frequency outcome can mean running the experiment for weeks; you need to avoid overlapping experiments that contaminate each other's populations; and you need somebody who will say out loud that a result is not significant when the team wants to ship. The framework provides the plumbing and none of the statistical judgment. Without that judgment it produces confident conclusions from noise, which is worse than having no framework.

Dimension	**Scale Up (tune bigger units)**	**Scale Out (replicate identical units)**
Performance	Occasionally higher peak per unit	Known, fixed capacity per unit
Predictability	Varies with configuration; hard to model	Identical every time; trivial to model
Capacity planning	Guesswork; forces overprovisioning	Add a unit of known capacity on demand
Failure handling	Each unit is a unique part	Units are interchangeable and replaceable

Table 16.5: Scaling up compared with scaling out across performance, predictability, capacity planning and failure handling

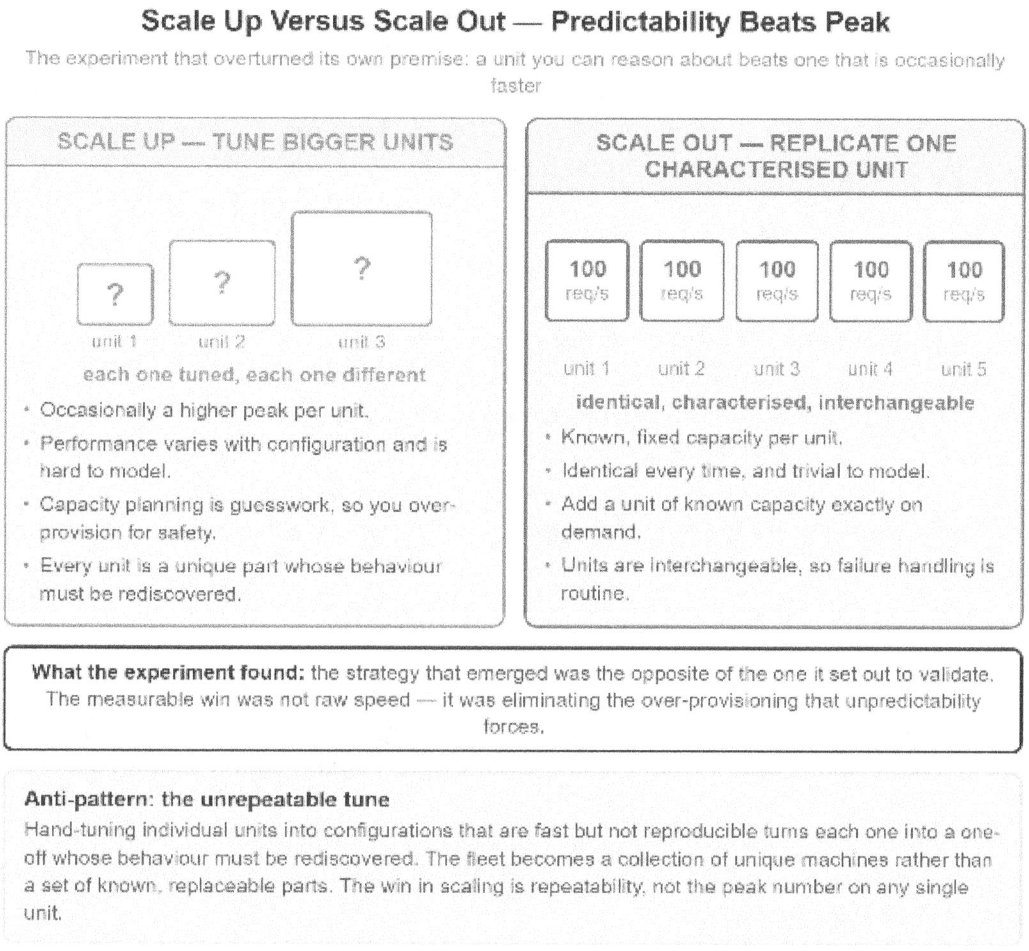

Figure 16.3: Scale Up Versus Scale Out — Predictability Beats Peak

Note

Anti-Pattern: The Unrepeatable Tune: Pursuing maximum performance by hand-tuning individual units into configurations that are fast but not reproducible. Each tuned unit becomes a one-off whose behavior must be rediscovered, capacity planning becomes guesswork, and the fleet becomes a collection of unique machines instead of a set of known, replaceable parts. The win in scaling is repeatability, not the peak number on any single unit.

This experience generalizes into a discipline: the architecture is testable, and the bigger the decision, the more it deserves an experiment rather than a conviction. The safe-change machinery built in this chapter is exactly what makes architectural experimentation possible without betting the system on it. You can canary a new data store behind a fraction of traffic, run a new model variant against a slice of requests, or shadow a new protocol alongside the old one and compare, all measured against the same signals and reversible the same way. The architecture is no longer a decision you make once and defend. It is a hypothesis you can test in production and reverse if the data disagrees.

> **Note**
>
> The Architecture-Is-Testable Rule: Major architectural choices, data stores, models, protocols, and scaling strategies are hypotheses to be tested in production behind the safe-change machinery, not convictions to be defended. The larger and more expensive the decision, the more it warrants an experiment rather than an argument. Canary the architecture the way you canary a feature: a slice of traffic, measured against the signals, reversible on a bad result. Intuition sets the hypothesis; production data decides it.

When the right answer is to abandon the experiment

An experiment that ends with the original design unchanged is not a failed experiment. It is a cheap answer to an expensive question, and treating it as a failure is how teams acquire the habit of shipping migrations they already know are wrong. The scale-up experiment described above is an example in one direction — the data overturned the premise and the strategy changed. The equally valuable outcome is the one where the data confirms that the thing you already have is the thing you should keep.

Two shapes recur, and both are easy to argue past if the decision rule was not written down before the experiment started.

The first is a change that wins on one axis and loses on a more important one. A new storage engine that reduces cost per gigabyte by a third but adds thirty milliseconds to the read path is not a saving; it is a latency regression the finance model happens to like. If those reads sit on the P0 checkout path, the cost axis was never the deciding one, and the honest conclusion is that the current store stays. The trap here is that the winning number is real and easy to present, while the losing number is distributed across a user journey nobody put in the slide.

The second is a change that improves the system's numbers and degrades the team's ability to operate it. A protocol change that lifts throughput materially but leaves the team without usable tracing, familiar debugging tools, or a straightforward failure model has improved a metric and worsened the thing that metric is a proxy for. Operability is not a soft consideration to be weighed against throughput; over a long enough horizon it is the constraint that determines whether the throughput is ever realized. Abandon the experiment, keep the protocol, and revisit when the tooling has caught up.

Experiment	The Result That Looks Like Success	Why You Abandon It Anyway
A new storage engine	Cost per gigabyte falls by a third	It adds 30 ms to reads on the P0 checkout path — a latency regression the cost model likes
A new protocol or transport	Throughput improves materially	The team loses tracing, familiar tooling, and a clear failure model; operability is the real constraint
A new model tier	Cost per call drops	Cost per resolved outcome rises because the cheaper tier escalates more often
A new caching layer	Hit rate looks excellent in the canary	The invalidation path has no owner, so the win is borrowed against a future correctness incident

Table 16.6: Architectural experiments that succeed on their headline metric and should still be abandoned

The protection against arguing past either shape is procedural, not moral. Write the decision rule before the experiment runs: which metrics must improve, which must not regress, and by how much. An experiment with a stated abandonment condition produces a decision. An experiment without one produces a negotiation, and the side that has already spent a quarter building the alternative wins that negotiation nearly every time.

> **Note**
>
> The Abandonment-Condition Rule: Write the condition that would end an architectural experiment before you start it — which metrics must improve, which must not regress, and the threshold for each. An experiment that validates the existing design is a successful experiment that cost you a canary instead of a migration. Without

a pre-stated abandonment condition the decision is made by whoever has invested the most effort, which is the opposite of deciding on evidence.

Architectural Change	How to Experiment Safely	What You Measure
New data store or sharding scheme	Shadow writes; canary reads behind a flag	Latency, error rate, consistency, cost per query
New model or model tier	Route a slice of requests to the variant	Quality, cost per outcome, latency
New protocol or transport	Run alongside the old; compare in parallel	Throughput, error rate, tail latency
Scale-up vs scale-out	Provision both; load-test to a model	Predictability of performance per unit

Table 16.7: Four architectural changes, how to experiment on each safely, and what to measure

Note

Manager's Math, Predictability Over Peak: The scaled-up strategy could occasionally outperform a single standard unit, but its performance varied enough that capacity planning was guesswork, which meant over-provisioning for safety. The scale-out strategy on identical units gave a known capacity per unit, so the team provisioned exactly what demand required with a small predictable buffer. The measurable win was not raw speed; it was the elimination of the over-provisioning that unpredictability forces. A predictable unit you can plan against is cheaper at scale than a faster one you cannot.

Note

Safe Scale Check, Canarying an Architectural Change: Reversibility: experiment on a major architectural change behind a flag and a traffic slice so the old architecture remains the default and a bad result reverts by closing the flag, never by a rushed unplanned migration. Blast radius: start the canary at a small traffic percentage and on non-critical paths, widen only as the signals hold, and keep the previous architecture

> running in parallel until the new one has survived a full peak cycle. An architectural experiment must be as reversible as a feature experiment, or it is not an experiment.

Architect's prompt 16.3: the architectural experiment design

When to use this: Use this prompt when facing a large architectural decision you are tempted to make on conviction, and instead design it as a reversible production experiment.

```
Act as a Principal Architect. I am about to make a major architectural
decision and I want to test it in production rather than decide on intuition.

Decision: [scale-up vs scale-out / new store / new model / new protocol].
Current architecture: [describe]. Proposed change: [describe].
My current conviction and why: [state it].

Do the following:
(1) State the hypothesis the experiment will test, and the result that would
    overturn my conviction.
(2) Design the safe experiment: shadow or canary, traffic slice, the signals
    measured, and the automatic rollback condition.
(3) For a scaling decision, compare predictability per unit, not just peak
    performance.
(4) Define the blast radius: which paths, what percentage, how the old
    architecture stays the default.
(5) State the decision rule: what the data must show to widen, and what
    reverts the experiment.
```

The feedback loop: production as the source of the next version

Every discipline in this book has been a loop. Observability measures the system and feeds action. Resilience detects failure and triggers recovery. Cost watches the unit economics and prompts a fix. Governance gates an action and records it for review. Experimentation is the loop that closes over all of them, because the purpose of running experiments is not to validate a guess. It is to let production itself tell you what to build next. The system in production is the most honest specification you will ever have, more honest than any plan, because it is made of what real users do rather than what you predicted they would.

Note

The Production-Is-the-Spec Rule: The behavior of real users in production is a more reliable specification than any plan, because it is evidence rather than prediction. Instrument every experiment to feed its result back into the next decision, so that production continuously informs the roadmap instead of the roadmap being fixed in advance and defended against the data. The plan proposes; production disposes. A team that lets production write the spec ships what users need; a team that defends the original plan ships what it guessed.

This is the engine behind the way I have built things for my entire career, and it is worth stating plainly because it runs against a common instinct. The instinct is to design the complete, correct system up front and then build it. The discipline that works is the opposite: ship the smallest real version, put it in front of real users, learn from what they do, and let that learning drive the next version. Going to market first and learning from genuine feedback beats designing in isolation, because the feedback contains information no amount of upfront design could have produced. You do not learn the truth of a system from a specification. You learn it from production.

Note

The Ship-and-Learn Doctrine: Ship the smallest real version, expose it to real users behind the safe-change machinery, learn from what they do, and let that learning drive the next version. Going first and learning from production beats designing in isolation, because real feedback carries information no upfront design can. The goal of a release is not to be finished; it is to learn the next thing to build. Speed of learning, not perfection of the plan, is the competitive advantage.

Note

Tool Tax — experiment instrumentation: Learning from production means every experiment emits its own telemetry, and that telemetry has to be attributable to the variant, retained long enough to reach a conclusion, and stored somewhere it can be queried against the control. That is more cardinality in your metrics, more volume in your logs, and a direct line to the *Chapter 14* cost conversation — experiment telemetry is one of the fastest-growing line items in an observability bill. It is worth the money

> and it is not free, so tag it, budget it, and expire the telemetry when the experiment resolves.

Capturing what the experiment taught

An experiment produces two things: a decision and a lesson. The decision is applied immediately and is hard to lose. The lesson lives in the heads of the three or four people who ran it, and it is gone within two quarters unless something captures it. This is how an organization ends up running the same experiment twice, eighteen months apart, and reaching the same conclusion at full cost both times.

The mechanism that works is deliberately lightweight, because a heavy one will not be used. One page per experiment, written when the result lands rather than at the end of the quarter, recording four things:

1. The hypothesis, as it was stated before the experiment ran. Recording it after the fact produces a hypothesis that conveniently matches the result.
2. The measured result, including the metrics that did not move. A flat metric you expected to move is often the most informative line on the page.
3. The architectural decision taken, and the abandonment condition if the experiment was stopped. Someone reading this in a year needs the decision, not just the data.
4. What was learned that generalizes beyond this experiment — about the system, the traffic, the tooling, or the assumption that turned out to be wrong?

The fourth item is the one with the longest half-life and the one most often omitted, because it is the only one that requires a judgment rather than a number. It is also what makes the record useful to a team that was not in the room.

Where these records live matters more than their format. A per-team document is a private diary; the point is cross-team reuse, so they belong in one searchable place that every team reads, indexed by the component or decision they touch, so an engineer proposing a change can find out whether somebody already tried it. The strongest signal that this is working is not the number of records written; it is the first time someone cancels a planned experiment because the register already answered the question.

Note

The Experiment-Register Rule: Every experiment ends with a one-page record — the hypothesis as originally stated, the measured result including the metrics that did not move, the decision taken, and what generalizes beyond this case — written when the result lands and stored in one place every team can search. An unrecorded experiment teaches one team once. The measure of the register is not how many entries it has; it is how often it prevents an experiment from being run a second time.

Note

The Smallest-Real-Version Rule: Ship the smallest version that tests the core assumption, not a scaled-down plan and not a complete build. The point of the first release is to learn the one thing you most need to know, with the least built and the least at risk. Anything larger delays the learning and raises the cost of being wrong. Build the smallest real thing, then let production tell you what to build next.

Stage	What Happens	Feeds
Hypothesize	A small, reversible change is proposed	The experiment design
Ship to a slice	Released to 1% behind a flag or canary	Real production behavior
Measure	Compared to the observability signals	The keep-or-revert decision
Decide	Widen, revert, or iterate based on data	The next hypothesis
Learn	The result informs the roadmap	The next version of the system

Table 16.8: The five stages of the ship-and-learn loop and what each one feeds

The reason this loop is safe to run fast is everything built in the previous fifteen chapters. You can ship the smallest version and learn from it precisely because a bad result is caught by your observability, contained by your resilience, bounded by your cost governance, and reversed by your safe-change machinery. Closing the loop carries an instrumentation tax: every experiment must be measured, which is more telemetry to emit and store. It is the price of learning from production rather than guessing. Speed and safety are not in tension here. The safety is what permits the speed. A team without these foundations that tries to ship fast is reckless; a team with them that ships fast is doing the most durable thing in engineering, which is learning faster than the problem changes.

Approach	**Big Design Up Front**	**Ship and Learn**
Source of truth	The plan, fixed in advance	Production behavior of real users
First release	Complete system, late	Smallest real version, early
What you optimize	Completeness of the plan	Speed of learning
Risk profile	One large irreversible bet	Many small reversible bets

Table 16.9: Big design up front compared with ship and learn across source of truth, first release, and risk profile

Note

Safe Scale Check, Shipping the Smallest Version: Reversibility: ship the smallest real version behind a flag so the entire change reverts by closing the flag, with no redeploy. Blast radius: expose it to a 1% slice on a non-critical path first, widen only as the signals hold, and keep the prior behavior as the default until the new one has earned the traffic. The smallest version is safe to ship precisely because it is the cheapest thing to take back.

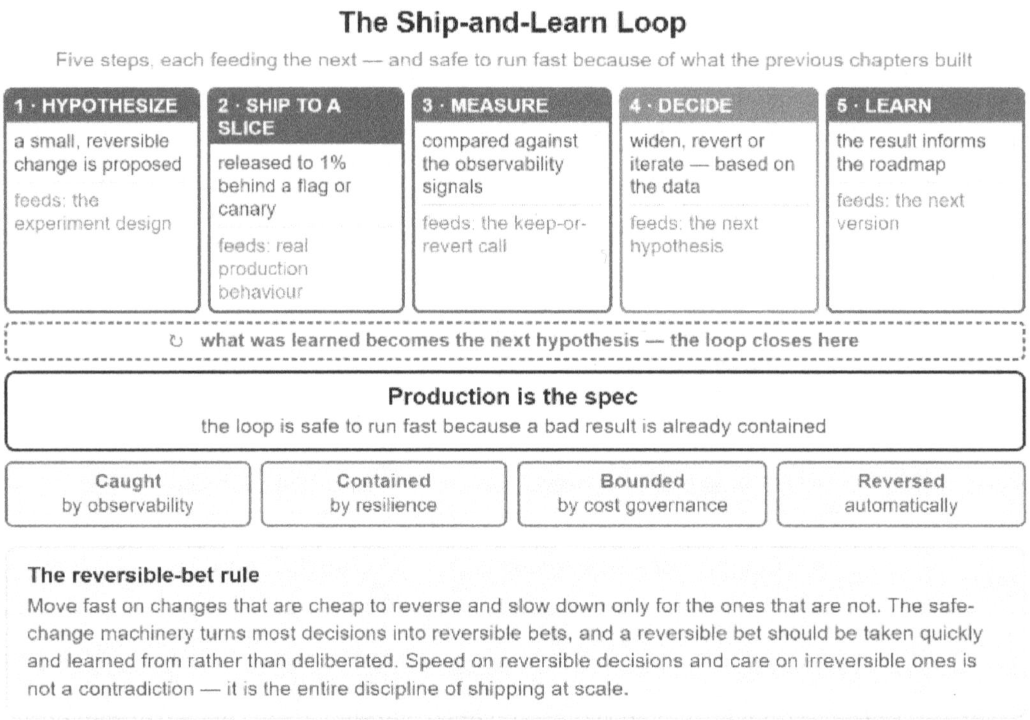

Figure 16.4: The Ship-and-Learn Loop

Note

The Reversible-Bet Rule: Move fast on changes that are cheap to reverse, and slow down only for the ones that are not. The safe-change machinery turns most decisions into reversible bets, and a reversible bet should be taken quickly and learned from, not deliberated. Reserve caution for the irreversible ones. Speed on reversible decisions and care on irreversible ones is not a contradiction; it is the entire discipline of shipping at scale.

Architect's prompt 16.4: the feedback loop design

When to use this: Use this prompt to turn a planned feature or change into a ship-and-learn loop, so production data drives the next version instead of a fixed upfront plan.

```
Act as a Principal Engineer who ships to learn. I have a planned change and
I want to run it as a feedback loop instead of building it all up front.
```

```
Planned change: [description]. The assumption it rests on: [state it].
How I would know the assumption is wrong: [signal].

Do the following:
(1) Define the smallest real version that would test the core assumption.
(2) Design the ship-to-a-slice rollout and the signals that measure the
    result against the assumption.
(3) Specify what production behavior would confirm, revise, or abandon the plan.
(4) Classify the decision as reversible (move fast) or irreversible (slow
    down) and justify it.
(5) Define how the result feeds the next hypothesis, so production informs
    the roadmap continuously.
```

The Future-Proof system

The book ends on the future-proof system, which raises the obvious question: future-proof against what? The technology is changing constantly. Paradigms shift. Organizations restructure. And AI is now moving fast enough to change the practice of architecture itself, generating designs, proposing refactors, and increasingly making the kind of horizontal changes across production, testing, and architecture that used to be the work of senior engineers. If future-proofing meant betting on a specific technology surviving, nothing would qualify. Every concrete technology in this book will eventually be replaced.

So the future-proof property is not any technology. It is the layer that does not change when the technology does: the boundaries, the gates, the feedback loops, and the safe-change disciplines built across this entire book. Statelessness, loose coupling, observability, reversibility, blast-radius control, runtime governance, the deterministic boundary around a nondeterministic component. These are not features of a stack. They are properties of a system, and they hold regardless of which database, which model, or which framework sits inside them. A team can swap every component over five years and, if these properties are intact, the system remains safe and operable the entire way.

Note

The Boundaries-Outlast-Technology Rule: The future-proof part of a system is never a technology; it is the boundaries, gates, and feedback loops around the technology. Concrete components, databases, models, frameworks, will all be replaced. The properties that govern how components are bounded, observed, and safely changed

> outlast every one of them. Architect the boundaries as if the contents will be replaced, because they will, and the boundaries are what you are building.

That principle is abstract until you name the swaps, so here are three the industry is living through right now. In each case the component is replaced and the surrounding architecture does not move.

Replace the relational database with a distributed SQL engine. The schema, the transaction boundaries, the data access layer from *Chapter 10*, the shard registry, the replication contract, and the query telemetry all stay exactly as they were. The application does not learn that the store changed, because the DAL was the boundary and the boundary did not move. What made this survivable was a decision taken six chapters earlier, before anyone knew this swap would be needed.

Replace one large language model provider with another. The single chokepoint from *Chapter 14* still meters every call, the runtime policy layer from *Chapter 15* still gates every action, the model cascade still routes by tier, and the evaluation set still decides whether quality held. The provider is a configuration value inside a governed boundary. Teams that wired their prompts and credentials directly into call sites throughout the codebase experience the same swap as a migration project.

Replace the orchestration platform with whatever succeeds it. The service boundaries from *Chapter 6*, the health and readiness contracts, the observability instrumentation, the resilience policies, and the progressive delivery machinery in this chapter are all expressed against the workload rather than against the platform running it. The scheduler underneath is the most replaceable thing in the stack, and it is the one teams most often couple themselves to.

The Component Replaced	What Stays Unchanged	What Made the Swap Possible
Relational database → distributed SQL engine	Schema, transaction boundaries, the data access layer, shard registry, replication contract, query telemetry	The DAL was the boundary, so the application never learned the store changed

The Component Replaced	What Stays Unchanged	What Made the Swap Possible
One LLM provider → another	The single call chokepoint, budgets, runtime policy gating, the model cascade, the evaluation set	The provider was a value inside a governed boundary, not a dependency at every call site
Kubernetes → a future orchestration platform	Service boundaries, health and readiness contracts, observability, resilience policies, progressive delivery	Every contract was expressed against the workload rather than the platform

Table 16.10: Three real component swaps, and the boundaries that made each one routine rather than a migration

The pattern across all three is the same, and it is worth stating as the test. The swap is routine when the thing being replaced sits behind a boundary that was designed without reference to it, and it is a migration when the component's own interface leaked into the code around it. You cannot know which component you will need to replace. You can make every component replaceable by refusing to let any of them define the shape of the system around it.

This points at the most important property of all, and it is the one that matters most precisely because AI is now an operator of systems and not only a component inside them. The future-proof system is one that stays safe no matter who, or what, makes a change to it. A new engineer, an experienced one, an autonomous AI generating and applying changes: the system must remain governed and operable regardless. That is the deepest reason the deterministic boundaries from *Chapter 15* matter. They do not just constrain the agents inside the system. They make the system safe to be changed by agents, including the increasingly capable ones that will soon be doing much of the changing.

> Note
>
> **The Operator-Agnostic Rule:** A future-proof system stays safe and operable no matter who or what changes it: a new engineer, a senior one, or an autonomous AI. The boundaries, gates, and feedback loops do not assume a careful human operator; they enforce safety structurally, so that the system survives a change made by any operator at any skill level or of any kind. Build for the operator you cannot vet in advance, because increasingly you will not be able to.

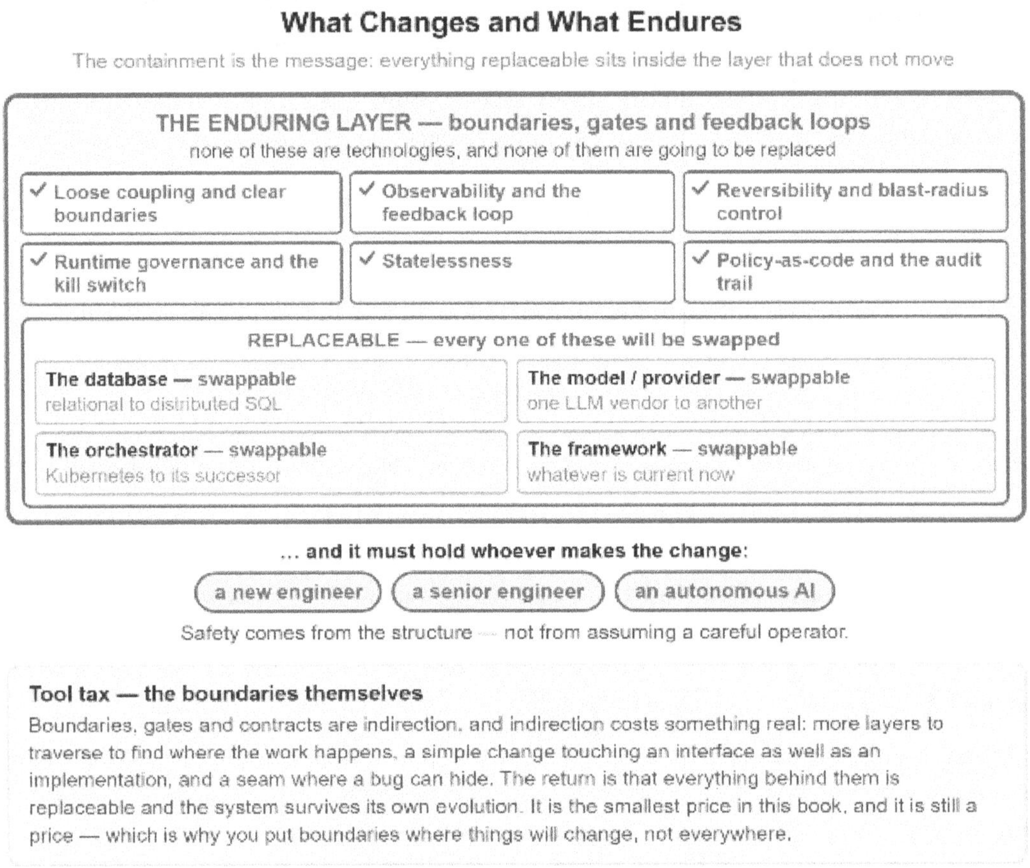

Figure 16.5: What Changes and What Endures

Note

Tool Tax — the boundaries themselves: This is the tax the whole book has been paying deliberately, and it is right to name it in the closing chapter. Boundaries, gates, contracts, and governance are indirection, and indirection costs something real: a new engineer traverses more layers to find where the work happens, a simple change touches an interface as well as an implementation, and every boundary is a place a bug can hide in the seam. The return is that the components behind those boundaries are replaceable and the system survives its own evolution. It is the smallest price in the book, and it is still a price — which is why you put boundaries where things will change, not everywhere.

What Changes	What Endures
The database, the model, the framework	Loose coupling and clear boundaries around them
The deployment target and the runtime	Reversibility and blast radius control
Who operates the system (human or AI)	Runtime governance and the kill switch
The paradigm and the tooling	Observability and the feedback loop

Table 16.11: What gets replaced in a system, and the properties that outlast every replacement

> Note
>
> **The Future-Proof Doctrine:** Do not future-proof by predicting the future; future-proof by building the boundaries, gates, and feedback loops that keep the system safe and changeable no matter what the future brings or who operates it. You cannot know which technology wins or who makes the next change. You can guarantee that the system remains governed, observable, and reversible through all of it. That guarantee, not any prediction, is what future-proof means in practice.

There is a tax here too, and it is the same one the whole book has been paying deliberately. Boundaries, gates, and governance add structure that a quick, unbounded system does without. That structure is the cost of being changeable forever instead of fast once. It is the smallest price in the book, because the alternative is a system that was perfectly tuned for one moment and cannot survive the next.

Architect's prompt 16.5: the Future-Proofing audit

When to use this: Use this prompt to evaluate whether a system is future-proof in the way that matters: safe and changeable regardless of which components it uses or who operates it.

```
Act as a Principal Architect evaluating whether a system is future-proof.
Future-proof here means safe and changeable regardless of components or
operator, not betting on a specific technology.

System: [description]. Key components: [list]. Who and what can change it:
```

```
[engineers of varying skill, autonomous AI, etc.].

Do the following:
(1) Separate the system into what will be replaced (concrete components) and
    what must endure (boundaries, gates, feedback loops).
(2) Verify the enduring properties: loose coupling, observability,
    reversibility, blast-radius control, runtime governance, kill switch.
(3) Test the operator-agnostic property: would the system stay safe if a
    change were made by a junior engineer or an autonomous AI?
(4) Flag any safety that depends on a careful human operator rather than on
    a structural boundary, and move it into the structure.
(5) Give a future-proofing score and the gaps to close.
```

The architecture readiness checklist

This is the book in one page. Every item is a checkpoint from a chapter you have already read, phrased as something you can assess about a real system rather than a principle you can agree with. Every item should read yes — or carry a named owner and a time-boxed exception. Unlike the per-chapter checklists, this one is meant to be revisited: run it annually against whatever the system has become.

Bottlenecks measured before optimizing: every optimization traces to a profile, a query plan, or a utilization curve, and the hardware alternative was priced first. (*Chapters 1, 13*)

Scaling is horizontal and stateless: capacity is added by replicating a characterized unit, not by tuning a larger one, and no request depends on which instance serves it. (*Chapters 2, 16*)

Security is enforced at every boundary, not at the perimeter: workload identity, least privilege, and no implicit trust between services. (*Chapter 3*)

Services own their data and their contracts: bounded contexts, versioned interfaces, no shared tables, and the eventual-consistency cost stated explicitly. (*Chapters 6, 8, 10*)

Resilience is designed around business priority: every P0 flow has a documented degraded behavior, and the correctness floor is never traded for availability (*Chapter 12*).

Observability measures user outcomes, not just infrastructure health: the gap between "all systems green" and "the customer succeeded" is instrumented and alerted on. (*Chapter 11*)

Cost is governed through unit economics: spend is attributable, tracked as cost per unit of business value, and reviewed weekly by the engineers who own it. (*Chapter 14*)

AI is introduced only where it is justified: the determinism-first gates were applied, and the model holds the narrowest slice the problem allows (*Chapter 15*).

Runtime governance and kill switches are in place: every consequential agent action is gated between decision and execution, and every acting agent can be halted in isolation. (*Chapter 15*)

Change is a reversible experiment: staged rollout, measurement against the signals, and automated rollback, so deploying does not require courage. (*Chapter 16*)

Delivery health is measured as evolutionary fitness: deployment frequency, lead time, change failure rate, and time to restore are reviewed as seriously as availability. (*Chapter 16*)

The system is operator-agnostic: safety comes from structural boundaries rather than from assuming a careful human, so it survives a change made by a junior engineer or an autonomous agent. (*Chapters 15, 16*)

If you are reading this checklist against a system that scores poorly, resist the urge to fix everything. The book's own argument applies here: find the one constraint that is actually binding, fix that, and re-measure. The list is a diagnostic, not a backlog.

Summary

In this final chapter, we solved the last problem: a system so dependable the team had stopped changing it. We established the Experiment-or-Stagnate Rule and the Safe-Change Mandate, reframing every deployment from an event to brace for into a reversible experiment to run. We applied the Flag-Is-Not-Config Rule, the Flag-Expiry Rule, and the Bounded-Flag-Count Rule to use feature flags with discipline and retire the graveyard that had inflated ShopFlow's lead time and change failure rate.

We ran experiments on the architecture itself, including the scale-up strategy that production data overturned in favor of the Predictable-Unit Rule, and established that the architecture is a testable hypothesis, not a conviction to defend. We closed the feedback loop with the Production-Is-the-Spec Rule and the Ship-and-Learn Doctrine, letting real users write the specification. And we named the property that is future-proof: not any technology, but the Boundaries-Outlast-Technology Rule and the Operator-Agnostic Rule, the boundaries and gates that keep a system safe no matter what it is made of or who changes it, including an autonomous AI.

ShopFlow's telemetry after *Chapter 16*:

Metric	Before (Ch16 Start)	After (Ch16 End)	Change
Deployment Frequency	1 per month	Multiple per day (safe-change machinery)	Cadence restored
Change Failure Rate	22%	Under 5% (1% canary + auto-rollback)	Change made safely
Lead Time for Changes	3+ weeks	Under a day (deploy decoupled from release)	Friction removed
Active Feature Flags	180+ (graveyard)	~12 (time-boxed, owned, expiring)	Graveyard retired
Experiments in Production	0	Continuous (features and architecture)	Evolution resumed
Future-Proof Property	Frozen architecture	Operator-agnostic boundaries	Safe to keep changing

Table 16.12: ShopFlow's delivery posture before and after Chapter 16

Conclusion: the lifecycle of a scalable, AI-Ready system

ShopFlow started this book as a monolith handling 100 orders a day, kept alive by one person rebooting a server. It ends as a globally distributed, sharded, observable, resilient, cost-governed, AI-augmented system that heals itself, governs its own agents, and keeps changing safely while the team sleeps. The journey was never about adding features. At every stage, a solution created the next problem, and the architecture evolved to meet it. That is what scaling is: not a destination you arrive at, but an evolution you lead.

Stage of the Book	ShopFlow State	The Discipline Introduced
Foundations (Ch 1-3)	Monolith, then horizontal and secure	Scalability mindset, core principles, security-first
Interface (Ch 4-5)	Global edge and resilient front-end	Edge delivery, micro-frontends, graceful degradation
Services and Data (Ch 6-10)	Decomposed services, sharded data	Decomposition, mesh, events, caching, sharding
Operating at Scale (Ch 11-14)	Observable, resilient, tuned, cost-governed	Observability, resilience, capacity, FinOps
Future-Proofing (Ch 15-16)	AI-governed and self-evolving	AI-first pragmatism, governance, experimentation

Table 16.13: The arc of the book: ShopFlow's state at each stage and the discipline that got it there

If you take one framework from this book, take the loop that every chapter repeated. See the system through telemetry. Decide with the economics, not the hype. Change it through reversible experiments. Govern the powerful parts with deterministic boundaries. Learn from production and do it again. Every named rule in these sixteen chapters is an instance of that single discipline applied to a different layer.

But the question that closes this book asks for the one thing that cannot be captured in a rule, a framework, or a named pattern, and there is an honest answer. The rules in this book will make you a competent architect. What separates the engineers who build systems that last from the ones who build systems that merely work for now is not another pattern. It is judgment, and judgment is mostly the discipline of subtraction.

I have spent my career on a single philosophy, and it is the one I will leave you with: scale by subtraction. Reliability does not come from adding more tools, more cleverness, or more layers. It comes from removing the variables that create the trouble in the first place. The most senior move in engineering is usually not building something new. It is deleting something, simplifying something, or choosing not to build at all because the thing already exists. Reuse before you rebuild. Collaborate before you compete. The instinct to build everything yourself, to handle the worst case you will probably never see, to perfect a system before anyone has used it, is the instinct that produces complexity nobody can maintain and systems too heavy to move.

So my final advice is practical, and it is what eighteen years of taking products from zero to one taught me. Do not complicate what does not need it. Before you build, look hard for what already exists, and reuse it. Plan for the realistic case, not the rare extreme one you will likely never meet, because over-planning is just work you throw away. And when a decision is reversible, move. Ship the small real thing, put it in front of real people, and let what they do teach you the next move. The teams that win are rarely the ones with the most complete plan. They are the ones who went first, learned fastest, and were willing to subtract everything that was not the signal.

Architecture at scale is not the art of building the biggest system. It is the art of building the system that can keep becoming the next one. Build the boundaries, trust the loop, subtract the noise, and ship. The rest, you will learn from production, the same way the rest of us did.

References

- **Forsgren, N., Humble, J., and Kim, G. (2018). Accelerate: The Science of Lean Software and DevOps. IT Revolution Press** — the source of the four delivery metrics used in this chapter as evolutionary fitness: deployment frequency, lead time for changes, change failure rate, and time to restore service.
- **DORA** — the DevOps Research and Assessment program's annual State of DevOps reports, which track those four metrics across the industry and publish the current performance bands: `https://dora.dev/`

17

Unlock Your Exclusive Benefits

Your copy of this book includes the following exclusive benefits:

DRM-Free PDF Version

Download DRM-free PDF and ePub copies of this book.

7-Day Packt Library Access

Get 7-day unlimited access to 8,000+ books and videos. No credit card required.

Available for first-time Packt+ trial users only.

Next-Gen Reader Access

Read this book on Packt Reader with progress sync, dark mode and note-taking.

Follow the guide below to unlock them. The process takes only a few minutes and needs to be completed once.

Unlock this Book's Free Benefits in 3 Easy Steps

Step 1

Keep your purchase invoice ready for *Step 3*. If you have a physical copy, scan it using your phone and save it as a PDF, JPG, or PNG.

For more help on finding your invoice, visit `https://www.packtpub.com/en-us/unlock?step=1`.

Note

Note: If you bought this book directly from Packt, no invoice is required. After *Step 2*, you can access your exclusive content right away.

Step 2

Scan the QR code or go to `packtpub.com/unlock`.

On the page that opens (similar to *Figure 17.1* on desktop), search for this book by name and select the correct edition.

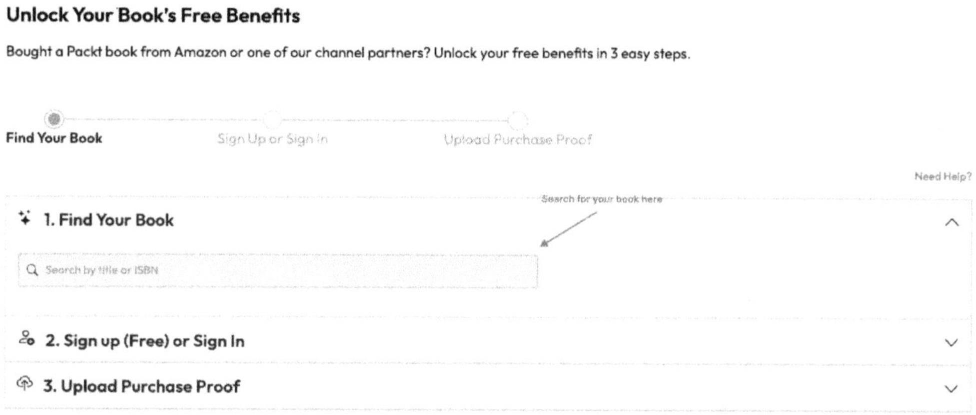

Figure 17.1: Packt unlock landing page on desktop

Step 3

After selecting your book, sign in to your Packt account or create one for free. Then upload your invoice (PDF, PNG, or JPG, up to 10 MB). Follow the on-screen instructions to finish the process.

Need Help

If you get stuck and need help, visit `https://www.packtpub.com/unlock-benefits/help` for a detailed FAQ on how to find your invoices and more. This QR code will take you to the help page.

Note

Note: If you are still facing issues, reach out to `customercare@packt.com`.

Other Books You May Enjoy

If you enjoyed this book, you may be interested in these other books by Packt:

Clean Architecture with .NET

Casey Crouse, Steve "Ardalis" Smith

ISBN: 9781805128533

- Design scalable .NET applications with Clean Architecture principles
- Structure core logic using use cases, CQRS, and domain modeling
- Integrate Azure External ID, Key Vault, and secure service configurations
- Use EF Core with a code-first approach to manage database schemas and persistence
- Apply MediatR and FluentValidation for streamlined workflows
- Build rich UIs using Blazor Server and MudBlazor
- Build scalable multi-host applications with structured, transparent service composition
- Reduce architectural boilerplate while maintaining structure

The Platform Engineer's Handbook

Ajay Chankramath

ISBN: 9781806380138

- Build a scalable, developer-focused engineering platform MVP
- Enable self-service onboarding and app deployment
- Create golden paths with reusable CI/CD workflows
- Scaffold new projects with portal-based starter kits
- Automate secure access with OAuth and RBAC
- Publish services to a centralized developer portal
- Deliver platform features with AI-augmented tooling
- Scale platform services without disrupting users

Packt is searching for authors like you

If you're interested in becoming an author for Packt, please visit `authors.packt.com` and apply today. We have worked with thousands of developers and tech professionals, just like you, to help them share their insight with the global tech community. You can make a general application, apply for a specific hot topic that we are recruiting an author for, or submit your own idea.

Share your thoughts

Now you've finished *Architecting at Scale*, we'd love to hear your thoughts! Scan the QR code below to go straight to the Amazon review page for this book and share your feedback or leave a review on the site that you purchased it from.

https://packt.link/r/1807420973

Your review is important to us and the tech community and will help us make sure we're delivering excellent quality content.

Index

D

E

R

S

T

www.ingramcontent.com/pod-product-compliance
Lightning Source LLC
Chambersburg PA
CBHW080443020926
50845CB00018B/1498
9781807420970